Application Development Using Visual Basic and .NET

ISBN 013093382-1

90000

9 780130 933829

The Integrated .NET Series from Object Innovations and Prentice Hall PTR

C#

- Introduction to C# Using .NET
  Oberg

- Application Development Using C# and .NET
  Stiefel/Oberg

VISUAL BASIC

- Introduction to Visual Basic Using .NET
  Wyatt/Oberg

- Application Development Using Visual Basic and .NET
  Oberg/Thorsteinson/Wyatt

VISUAL C++

- .NET Architecture and Programming Using Visual C++
  Thorsteinson/Oberg

WEB APPLICATIONS

- Fundamentals of Web Applications Using .NET and XML
  Bell/Feng/Soong/Zhang/Zhu

PERL

- Programming PERL in the .NET Environment
  Saltzman/Oberg

INTEGRATED .NET SERIES FROM OBJECT INNOVATIONS AND PRENTICE HALL PTR

Application Development Using Visual Basic and .NET

Robert J. Oberg

Peter Thorsteinson

Dana L. Wyatt

Prentice Hall PTR, Upper Saddle River, NJ 07458
www.phptr.com

Library of Congress Cataloging-in-Publication Data

A catalog record for this book can be obtained from the Library of Congress

Editorial/Production Supervision: *Nicholas Radhuber*
Acquisitions Editor: *Jill Harry*
Marketing Manager: *Dan DePasquale*
Manufacturing Buyer: *Maura Zaldivar*
Cover Design: *Anthony Gemmellaro*
Cover Design Direction: *Jerry Votta*
Interior Series Design: *Gail Cocker-Bogusz*

CONTENTS

PART TWO   VB.NET LANGUAGE   31

PART FIVE   ADVANCED UI PROGRAMMING USING VB.NET   443

PREFACE

For many years, Microsoft Visual Basic has been used as the ultimate rapid application development tool for Windows applications. Its ease of use revolutionized Windows programming, and successive generations of Visual Basic have progressively made it more powerful. VB6 can be used to implement complex multiple-tier applications using COM and COM+ components as well as traditional Windows desktop programs. But you could never quite do everything in Visual Basic that you could in a lower level language such as C++, and many projects would use a mixture of languages, with resulting complexity from interfacing between the diverse environments.

Microsoft's .NET brings a sea change to software development. The powerful Common Language Runtime and the vast .NET Framework class library provide a consistent software platform for *all* .NET programming languages. Visual Basic now enjoys virtually identical capabilities to other languages, including the new Visual C# and the ever-popular Visual C++, while preserving the basic ease of use and strong RAD features that have made Visual Basic so popular. The Common Language Specification and the Common Type System make interoperability between the different .NET languages almost seamless, while the power of each is such that for most projects you will probably never have to use a mixed language approach, unless other factors such as legacy code or programmer skill sets steer you in that direction.

There *is* substantial change to the Visual Basic language itself, and VB6 code will not run unmodified in the .NET environment. Also, the new version of the language, Visual Basic .NET, or just VB.NET, is now a fully object-oriented language with features such as interfaces, inheritance, and polymorphism. The result is that there is a definite learning curve when moving to VB.NET from VB6. And learning the new programming language is only part of the challenge. The much greater challenge is learning the .NET Framework and all its capabilities, including Windows Forms, ADO.NET, ASP.NET Web Forms, and Web services.

This book is written for the experienced programmer to help you quickly come up to speed on the VB.NET language and then go on to an in-depth study of the .NET Framework. It is a practical book for practicing professionals, and it has many examples and a realistic case study that continues through many of the chapters. The goal is to equip you to begin building significant applications using Visual Basic .NET and the .NET Framework.

The book is part of The Integrated .NET Series from Object Innovations and Prentice Hall PTR. Other books in the series provide a more a more basic introduction to VB.NET, discuss the issues of migrating to VB.NET, and cover other important .NET languages and topics in the Framework. See the front of this book for a list of titles in the series. This book, in substance and structure, is quite close to the companion titles *Application Development Using C# and .NET* and *.NET Architecture and Programming Using Visual C++*. A major difference between those books and this, besides using VB.NET as the language, is extensive coverage of GUI programming, including three chapters on Windows Forms and a chapter on GDI+.

Organization

The book is organized into six major parts and is structured to make it easy for you to navigate to what you need to learn. Part 1, consisting of the first two chapters, provides an overview that should be read by everyone. It answers the big question, *What is Microsoft .NET?* and outlines the programming model of the .NET Framework.

Part 2, consisting of Chapters 3 to 6, covers the VB.NET programming language. Even if you know classic Visual Basic, you should read this part, paying attention to the changes in data types (Chapter 3) and the new object-oriented features (Chapters 5). Chapter 6 covers important interactions between VB.NET and the .NET Framework. The Acme Travel Agency case study, which is elaborated throughout the entire book, is introduced in Chapter 5.

Part 3, consisting of Chapters 7 and 8, covers the fundamentals of Windows Forms. Windows Forms is a set of classes in the .NET Framework for writing graphical user interfaces. Programmers familiar with previous versions of Visual Basic will notice that this significantly changes the programming model, yet also introduces flexibility not previously available.

Part 4, consisting of Chapters 9 and 10, introduces important fundamental topics in the .NET Framework. Chapter 9 discusses assemblies and deployment, which constitute a major advance in the simplicity and robustness of deploying Windows applications, ending the notorious situation known as "DLL hell." Chapter 10 introduces important .NET Framework classes and covers the topics of metadata, serialization, threading, attributes, asynchronous programming, remoting, and memory management.

Part 5, consisting of Chapters 11 and 12, covers additional advanced topics in UI programming with VB.NET. Chapter 11 introduces GDI+, which provides a graphics programming model that is both more powerful and easier to use than the classic GDI model of traditional Windows. GDI+ is also completely accessible through Visual Basic. Chapter 12 introduces some important additional advanced topics, such as visual inheritance, MDI, and the use of ActiveX controls in .NET applications.

Part 6, consisting of Chapters 13 to 17, covers important parts of the .NET Framework that are useful in creating a variety of different applications. Chapter 13 covers ADO.NET, which provides a consistent set of classes for accessing both relational and XML data. Chapter 14 introduces the fundamentals of ASP.NET, including the use of Web Forms, for the development of Web sites. Chapter 15 covers SOAP and Web services, which provide an easy-to-use and robust mechanism for heterogeneous systems to interoperate. Chapter 16 covers the topic of security in detail, including Code Access Security and declarative security. Chapter 17 covers interoperability of .NET with legacy COM and Win32 applications.

Appendices introduce Visual Studio .NET and the debug and trace classes provided by .NET.

Sample Programs

The only way to really learn a major framework is to read and write many programs, including some of reasonable size. This book provides many small programs that illustrate pertinent features of .NET in isolation, which makes them easy to understand. The programs are clearly labeled in the text, and they can all be found in the software distribution that accompanies this book.

A major case study, the Acme Travel Agency, is progressively developed in a number of the chapters, beginning with Chapter 5. It illustrates many VB.NET and .NET Framework features working in combination, as they would in a practical application.

The sample programs are provided in a self-extracting file on the book's Web site. When expanded, a directory structure is created, whose default root is **c:\OI\NetVb**. The sample programs, which begin with the second chapter, are in directories **Chap02**, **Chap03**, and so on. All the samples for a given chapter are in individual folders within the chapter directories. The names of the folders are clearly identified in the text. An icon in the margin alerts you to a code example. Each chapter that contains a step of the case study has a folder called **CaseStudy**, containing that step. If necessary, there is a **readme.txt** file in each chapter directory to explain any instructions necessary for getting the examples to work.

Code
Example

As part of The Integrated .NET Series, the sample programs in this book are designed to integrate with sample programs from other books in the series. The sample programs for each book in the series are located in their own directories underneath **\OI**, so all the .NET examples from all books in the series will be located in a common area as you install them.

These programs are furnished solely for instructional purposes and should not be embedded in any software product. The software (including instructions for use) is provided "as is" without warranty of any kind.

Web Sites

The Web site for the book series is *www.objectinnovations.com/dotnet.htm.*

A link is provided at that Web site for downloading the sample programs for this book. Additional information about .NET technology is available at *www.mantasoft.com/dotnet.htm.*

The book sample programs are available at this Web site as well.

The Web site for the book also has a list of .NET learning resources that will be kept up to date.

Acknowledgments

We are indebted to Mike Meehan for helping to get this project off the ground, starting at a meeting at the PDC when Microsoft announced .NET. That conversation put into motion what has become a substantial series of books on .NET technology, in which this volume is the sixth. We would also like to thank Jill Harry from Prentice Hall for her ongoing support with this ambitious book project. Our editor, Nick Radhuber, has been very helpful, not only with this book but also in coordinating the whole series.

Several people at Microsoft helped in many ways with this book series: Steven Pratschner, Jim Hogg, Michael Pizzo, Michael Day, Krzysztof Cwalina, Keith Ballinger, and Eric Olsen. We thank them for taking time out from their very tight schedules to provide insight and clarification for a previous book in the series, contributing to a firm foundation for the current book. Any errors remaining, naturally, are the responsibility of the authors. Connie Sullivan and Stacey Giard coordinated technical sessions and helped assure our access to resources at Microsoft.

Michael Stiefel, an author of another book in our series, was a valuable resource for many of the chapters in this book. Michael was also instrumental in coordinating the previous technical reviews with people from Microsoft.

Robert would like to thank his wife, Marianne, for enormous support and encouragement of my extensive writing efforts, especially over the last 18 months. This book is almost the last for a while, and so you should be seeing more of me again real soon! I also want to thank my business associate, Ed Soong, for keeping things going at Object Innovations while I wrote. You will be seeing more of me in the business, too!"

Peter would like to thank his wife, Beth, and his daughter, Katie, for their pleasantness and charm. Peter would also like to thank Midas for being very patient about the issue of not being taken on enough walks lately.

Dana would like to thank Bob, a most patient co-author, for inviting her along on the roller coaster ride of book authorship. These VB.NET books have been a thrill. I'd like to thank Richard Reese for his insightful reviews of this manuscript. I'd like to thank my family, friends, and colleagues for allowing me to be distracted during this project. And, finally, I'd like to extend a special thanks to Brenda for her encouragement and belief that all things do come to an end!"

About this Series
Robert J. Oberg, Series Editor

Introduction

The Integrated .NET Book Series from Object Innovations and Prentice Hall PTR is a unique series of introductory and intermediate books on Microsoft's important .NET technology. These books are based on proven industrial-strength course development experience. The authors are expert practitioners, teachers, and writers who combine subject-matter expertise with years of experience in presenting complex programming technologies such as C++, MFC, OLE, and COM/COM+. These books *teach* in a systematic, step-by-step manner and are not merely summaries of the documentation. All the books come with a rich set of programming examples, and a thematic case study is woven through several of the books.

From the beginning, these books have been conceived as an *integrated whole*, and not as independent efforts by a diverse group of authors.. The initial set of books consists of three introductory books on .NET languages and four intermediate books on the .NET Framework. Each book in the series is targeted at a specific part of the important .NET technology, as illustrated by the diagram below.

		C# Learning Pathway	VB.NET Learning Pathway		
.NET Language Introductions	Programming PERL in the .NET Environment	Introduction to C# Using .NET	Introduction to Programming Visual Basic Using .NET		
Intermediate .NET Framework Titles		Application Development Using C# and .NET	**Application Development Using Visual Basic .NET**	.NET Architecture and Programming Using Visual C++	Fundamentals of Web Applications Using .NET and XML

Introductory .NET Language Books

The first set of books teaches several of the important .NET languages. These books cover their language from the ground up and have no prerequisite other than programming experience in some language. Unlike many .NET language books, which are a mixture of the language and topics in the .NET Framework, these books are focused on the languages, with attention to important interactions between the language and the framework. By concentrating on the languages, these books have much more detail and many more practical examples than similar books.

The languages selected are the new language C#, the greatly changed VB.NET, and Perl.NET, the open source language ported to the .NET environment. Visual C++ .NET is covered in a targeted, intermediate book, and JScript.NET is covered in the intermediate level .NET Web-programming book.

Introduction to C# Using .NET

This book provides thorough coverage of the C# language from the ground up. It is organized with a specific section covering the parts of C# common to other C-like languages. This section can be cleanly skipped by programmers with C experience or the equivalent, making for a good reading path for a diverse group of readers. The book gives thorough attention to the object-oriented aspects of C# and thus serves as an excellent book for programmers migrating to C# from Visual Basic or COBOL. Its gradual pace and many examples make the book an excellent candidate as a college textbook for adventurous professors looking to teach C# early in the language's life-cycle.

Introduction to Visual Basic Using .NET

Learn the VB.NET language from the ground up. Like the companion book on C#, this book gives thorough attention to the object-oriented aspects of VB.NET. Thus the book is excellent for VB programmers migrating to the more sophisticated VB.NET, as well as for programmers experienced in languages such as COBOL. This book would also be suitable as a college textbook.

.NET ARCHITECTURE OVERVIEW

.NET ARCHITECTURE OVERVIEW

Part 1, consisting of the first two chapters, provides an overview that should be read by everyone. It answers the big question, "What is Microsoft .NET?", and outlines the programming model of the .NET Framework. This information will equip you to understand the .NET environment as you study Visual Basic .NET and the .NET Framework in the rest of the book.

What Is Microsoft .NET?

*V*isual Basic .NET (or just VB.NET) represents the biggest change to the popular Visual Basic programming language since the original version 1.0. What is special about VB.NET is its tight integration into the .NET Framework. .NET is Microsoft's vision of applications in the Internet age. .NET provides enhanced interoperability features based upon open Internet standards. .NET improves the robustness of classic Windows applications. .NET offers developers a new programming platform and superb tools, with XML playing a fundamental role.

Microsoft .NET is a platform built on top of the operating system. Three years in the making before the public announcement, .NET represents a major investment by Microsoft. .NET has been influenced by other technological advances such as XML, Java, and COM.

Microsoft .NET provides

- The Common Language Runtime, a robust runtime platform.
- Multiple language development, with no language being preferred over any other.
- The .NET Framework, an extensible programming model, which provides a very large class library of reusable code available to any .NET language.
- Support for a networking infrastructure built on top of Internet standards that allows a high level of communication among applications.
- Support for the new industry standard of Web services. Web services represent a new mechanism of application delivery that extends the idea of component-based development to the Internet.
- ASP.NET, which allows you to use standard programming practices to develop Web applications.

5

- A Deployment model that allows for versioning and the end of "DLL Hell."
- A Security model that is easy for programmers to use in their programs.
- An interoperability mechanism that enables .NET programs to access legacy code, including COM components.
- Powerful development tools.

In this chapter we will look at the big picture of .NET and then see how VB.NET fits into it.

Microsoft and the Web

The World Wide Web has been a big catch-up challenge to Microsoft. Actually, the Web coexists quite well with Microsoft's traditional strength, the PC. Through a PC application, the browser, a user gains access to a whole world of information.

The Web relies on standards such as HTML, HTTP, and XML, which are essential for communication among diverse users on a wide variety of computer systems and devices.

While complex, the Windows PC is quite standardized. While the Web is based on standard protocols, there is a Tower of Babel of multiple languages, databases, development environments, and devices running on top of those protocols. This exploding complexity of technology exacerbates a growing shortage of knowledge workers who can build the needed systems using the new technologies. .NET provides the infrastructure so that programmers can concentrate on adding value in their applications without having to reinvent solutions to common programming problems.

Applications in the Internet Age

Originally, the Web was a vast information repository. Browsers would make requests for pages of existing information, and Web servers would deliver this information as static HTML pages. Even when interactive Web applications were introduced, HTML, which combines information with the details of how it is formatted for viewing, was still used.

XML provides a standard way of transmitting data independent of its formatting. XML can thus provide ways for companies to agree on standards for documents and information flows, such as purchase orders and invoices. E-commerce can then be automated among cooperating companies (B2B). XML, however, only describes the data; it does not supply the actions to be performed on that data. For that we need Web services.

Web Services

One of the most important aspects of .NET is the support for Web services. Based on the industry standard SOAP protocol, Web services allow you to expose your applications' functionality across the Internet. From the perspective of a .NET programmer, a Web Service is no different from any other kind of service implemented by a class in a .NET language. The programming model is the same for calling a function within an application, in a separate component on the same machine, or as a Web Service on a different machine.

This inherent simplicity will make it very easy for companies to create and host applications. If desired, a whole application could be completely outsourced, removing issues of development, deployment, and maintenance. Or you could use third-party Web services that did not exist when you designed your application.

ASP.NET

.NET includes a totally redone version of the popular Active Server Pages technology, known as ASP.NET. Whereas ASP relied on interpreted script code in languages with limited capabilities interspersed with page-formatting commands, ASP.NET code can be written in any NET language, including C#, VB.NET, JScript, and C++ with Managed Extensions. Since ASP.NET code is compiled, you can separate your interface code from your business logic in a separate "code behind" file. Although C#, VB.NET, and JScript may be left as embedded script within the Web page, managed C++ must be placed in a code behind file.

ASP.NET provides Web forms, which vastly simplifies creating Web user interfaces.

Drag-and-drop in Visual Studio .NET makes it very easy to lay out forms. You can add code to form events such as a button click.

ASP.NET will automatically detect browser capability. For high-end browsers, code can be executed on the client. For low-end browsers, the server does the processing and generates standard HTML. All this is done transparently to the developer by ASP.NET.

The combination of Web services and compiled full-blown languages such as C#, VB.NET, and managed C++, allows Web programming to follow an object-oriented programming model, which had not been possible with ASP scripting languages and COM components.

Open Standards and Interoperability

The modern computing environment contains a vast variety of hardware and software systems. Computers range from mainframes and high-end servers to workstations and PCs and to small mobile devices such as PDAs and cell phones. Operating systems include traditional mainframe systems, many flavors of UNIX, Linux, several versions of Windows, real-time systems, and special systems such as PalmOS for mobile devices. Many different languages, databases, application development tools, and middleware products are used.

In the modern environment, few applications are an island unto themselves. Even shrink-wrapped applications deployed on a single PC may use the Internet for registration and updates. The key to interoperability among applications is the use of standards. Since applications typically run over a network, a key standard is the communications protocol used.

Communications Protocols

TCP/IP sockets is highly standard and widely available. Too much detail, however, has to be mastered in order for programmers to be productive in writing robust distributed applications. Somewhat higher is the remote procedure call (RPC), but RPC is still very complex, and there are many flavors of RPC. Popular are higher level protocols, such as CORBA, RMI, and DCOM. These are still complex and require special environments at both ends. These protocols suffer other disadvantages, such as difficulty in going across firewalls.

One communication protocol has become ubiquitous: HTTP. For this reason, Microsoft, IBM, and other vendors have introduced a new protocol called SOAP (Simple Object Access Protocol). SOAP uses text-based XML to encode object method requests and the accompanying data. The great virtue of SOAP is its simplicity, leading to ease of implementation on multiple devices. While SOAP can run on top of any protocol, its ability to run on top of standard Internet protocols, such as HTTP, allows it to pass through firewalls without any connectivity problems.

Windows on the Desktop

Microsoft began with the desktop. The modern Windows environment has become ubiquitous. Countless applications are available, and most computer users are at least somewhat at home with Windows. While Microsoft has made much progress in modernizing Windows, there are still significant problems.

Problems with Windows

Maintaining a Windows PC is a chore, because applications are quite complex. They consist of many files, Registry entries, shortcuts, and so on. Different applications can share certain DLLs, and installing a new application can overwrite a DLL an existing application depends on, possibly breaking an old application (DLL Hell). Removing an application is a complex operation and is often imperfectly done.

A PC can gradually become less stable, sometimes requiring the drastic cure of reformatting the hard disk and starting from scratch. While there is tremendous economic benefit to using PCs, because standard applications are inexpensive and powerful and the hardware is cheap, the savings are reduced by the cost of maintenance.

Windows was originally developed when personal computers were not connected over a network and security was not an issue. While security was built into Windows NT and Windows 2000, the programming model is difficult to use.

The Glass House and Thin Clients

The old "glass house" model of a central computer that controls all applications has had an appeal, and there has been a desire to move toward "thin clients" of some sort. But the much heralded "network PC" never really caught on. There is too much of value in standard PC applications. Users like the idea of their "own" PC, with their data stored safely and conveniently on their local computer. Without broadband connectivity, a server-based application such as word processing would not perform very well. Security is also a very difficult issue to solve with thin clients. The personal computer is undoubtedly here to stay.

A Robust Windows

With all the hype about .NET and the Internet, it is important to realize that .NET has changed the programming model to allow the creation of much more robust Windows applications. Applications no longer rely on storing extensive configuration data in the fragile Windows Registry. .NET applications are self-describing, containing metadata within the program executable files themselves. Different versions of an application or component can be deployed side by side. Applications can share components through the Global Assembly Cache. Versioning is built into the deployment model. A straightforward security model is part of .NET. Windows Forms technology is a new paradigm for building Windows GUI applications.

A New Programming Platform

Let us look at what we have just discussed from the point of view of .NET as a new programming platform:

- Code can be validated to prevent unauthorized actions.
- It is much easier to program than the Win32 API or COM.
- All or parts of the platform can be implemented on many different kinds of computers (as has been done with Java).
- All the languages use one class library.
- Languages can interoperate with each other.

There are several important features to the .NET platform:

- .NET Framework
- Common Language Runtime
- Multiple language development
- Development tools

.NET Framework

Modern programming relies heavily on reusable code provided in libraries. Object-oriented languages facilitate the creation of class libraries, which are flexible, have a good degree of abstraction, and are extensible by adding new classes and basing new classes on existing ones, "inheriting" existing functionality.

The .NET Framework provides over 2,500 classes of reusable code, which can be called by all the .NET languages. The .NET Framework is extensible, and new classes can inherit from existing classes, even those implemented in a different language.

Examples of classes in the .NET Framework include Windows programming, Web programming, database programming, XML, and interoperability with COM and Win32. The .NET Framework is discussed in the next chapter and throughout the rest of the book.

Common Language Runtime

A *runtime* provides services to executing programs. Traditionally, there are different runtimes for different programming environments. Examples of runtimes include the standard C library, MFC, the Visual Basic runtime, and the Java Virtual Machine. The runtime environment provided by .NET is called the Common Language Runtime, or CLR.

MANAGED CODE AND DATA

The CLR provides a set of services to .NET code (including the .NET Framework, which sits on top of the CLR). In order to make use of these services, .NET code has to behave in a predictable fashion, and the CLR has to understand the .NET code. For example, to do runtime checking of array boundaries, all .NET arrays have identical layout. NET code can also be restricted by type safety requirements.

As we will discuss in the next chapter, the restrictions on .NET code are defined in the Common Type System (CTS) and its implementation in the Microsoft Intermediate Language (MSIL or IL). The CTS defines the types and operations that are allowed in code running under the CLR. For example, it is the CTS that restricts types to using single implementation inheritance. MSIL code is compiled into the native code of the platform.

.NET applications contain metadata, or descriptions of the code and data in the application. Metadata allows the CLR, for example, to automatically serialize data into a storage.

Code that can use the services of the CLR is called managed code.

Managed data is allocated and deallocated automatically. This automatic deallocation is called *garbage collection*. Garbage collection reduces memory leaks and similar problems.

Microsoft and ECMA

Microsoft has submitted specifications for the C# programming language and core parts of the .NET Framework to the European Computer Manufacturers Association (ECMA) for standardization. The ECMA specification defines the platform-independent Common Language Infrastructure (CLI). The CLR can be thought of as the CLI plus the Base Class Libraries (BCL). The BCL has support for the fundamental types of the CTS, such as file I/O, strings, and formatting. Since the CLR is platform-dependent, it makes use of the process and memory management models of the underlying operating system.

The ECMA specification defines the Common Intermediate Language (CIL). The ECMA specification allows for CIL to be compiled into native code or interpreted.

VERIFIABLE CODE

Managed code can be checked for type safety. Type-safe code cannot be subverted. For example, a buffer overwrite cannot corrupt other data structures or programs. You can only enter and leave methods at fixed points; you cannot calculate a memory address and start executing code at an arbitrary point. Security policy can be applied to type-safe code. For example, access to certain files or user interface features can be allowed or denied. You can prevent the execution of code from unknown sources.

Not all code that makes use of the facilities of the CLR is necessarily type safe. The classical example is managed C++. Managed C++ code can make use of CLR facilities such as garbage collection, but cannot be guaranteed to be type safe.

Multiple Language Development

As its name suggests, the CLR supports many programming languages. A "managed code" compiler must be implemented for each language. Microsoft itself has implemented compilers for managed C++, Visual Basic .NET, Jscript, and the new language C#. Well over a dozen other languages are being implemented by third parties, among them COBOL by Fujitsu and Perl by ActiveState. To accommodate the use or creation of .NET data types, however, new syntax often has to be introduced. Nonetheless, programmers do not need to be retrained in a completely new language in order to gain the benefits of .NET. Legacy code can be accessed through the interoperability mechanism.

Development Tools

A practical key to success in software development is a set of effective tools. Microsoft has long provided great tools, including Visual C++ and Visual Basic. With .NET they have combined their development tools into a single integrated environment called Visual Studio .NET.

- VS.NET provides a very high degree of functionality for creating applications in all the languages supported by .NET.
- You can do multiple language programming, debugging, and so on.
- VS.NET has many kinds of designers for forms, databases, and other software elements.

As with the languages themselves, third parties can provide extensions to Visual Studio .NET, creating a seamless development environment for their language that interoperates with the other .NET language. The tool set includes extensive support for building Web applications and Web services. There is also great support for database application development.

The Importance of Tools

The importance of tools should not be underestimated. Ada, a very powerful programming language, never achieved widespread use. While part of the initial vision was to create a standard Ada Programming Support Environment (APSE), most of the attention was paid to specifying the language, not the APSE. Consequently, Ada never did develop any development environment comparable to that of Visual Studio, Smalltalk, or some of the Java IDEs.

Visual Studio .NET will be highly tuned for productivity, and much training will be available. Microsoft has far more resources to throw at Visual Studio .NET than do smaller vendors in the highly fragmented tools market. Java is highly standardized in the language and API, but tools, which are required for productivity, are not standard.

The Role of XML

XML is ubiquitous in .NET and is highly important in Microsoft's overall vision. Some uses of XML in .NET include

- XML can be used to model data in coordination with ADO.NET datasets.
- XML is used in configuration files.
- XML documentation can be automatically generated by some .NET languages.
- XML is used for encoding requests and responses in Web services.
- XML is used to describe and transmit data in Web services.

Success Factors for Web Services

The ultimate success of Microsoft's Internet vision depends on two external factors: the infrastructure of the Internet and the success of the proposed Web services business model. The widespread use of Web services depends on having high bandwidth widely available. This capability will probably indeed materialize within the next several years. The prospect for the business model remains to be seen.

It is important to understand that the overall .NET technology includes far more than the widely hyped Internet part. The more robust Windows platform and the very powerful .NET Framework and tools will be enduring features.

VB.NET and the .NET Framework

What does all this mean for Visual Basic? Plenty. VB.NET has been implemented as a fully compliant .NET language, which means that it compiles to managed code that runs on the CLR. It can use all the features of the .NET Framework and is fully on par with the new language C#, which was designed explicitly for .NET. VB.NET now supports inheritance, the explicit definition of interfaces, structured exception handling, strong type checking, free threading, and a more general event model. Visual Basic now does not take a back seat to any language.

The basic syntax of VB.NET is the same as in previous versions, but there are some differences in details. On the whole, when you get used to it, the new features are more consistent to work with than the classical language. For example, there is now only one form of assignment, without a special **Set** statement for assigning object references.

What everyone knows is that VB.NET is *not* compatible with older versions of Visual Basic, and converting a large program is not a trivial task. Microsoft supplies tools to help, but it is not an automated procedure. Thus VB6 will be around for a long time for legacy applications.

Interoperating with legacy VB6 code is not the only interoperability scenario. Applications exist in many languages and many platforms. .NET has very strong support for interoperability. To go across platforms, you can make use of Web services and the SOAP protocol, a topic we discuss in Chapter 15. Within the Windows environment, you can make use of the Platform Invocation Services (PInvoke) and COM interoperability, a topic covered in Chapter 17. Because VB6 provides good support for COM, you can easily wrap VB6 code in COM objects and call them from VB.NET through the COM interop layer. You can also use ActiveX controls in VB.NET applications.

The bottom line is that with VB.NET you do not have to leave anything behind, and you have an extremely powerful language and platform for writing new code going forward. There is a learning curve for this new language and environment, and that is what this book is all about.

Summary

Microsoft .NET is a new platform built on top of the operating system. It provides many capabilities for building and deploying both standard applications and new Web-based ones. Web services allow applications to expose functionality across the Internet, typically using the SOAP protocol. SOAP supports a high degree of interoperability, since it is based on widely adopted standards such as HTTP and XML.

.NET uses managed code running on the Common Language Runtime that employs the Common Type System. The .NET Framework is a very large class library available consistently across many languages. XML plays a fundamental role in .NET. All this functionality can be used to build more robust Windows applications as well as Internet applications.

VB.NET is a completely modernized version of Visual Basic that works seamlessly with the .NET Framework. There is strong interoperability support in .NET that enables new applications created in VB.NET to work with legacy

VB6 applications and with applications written in other languages and on other platforms.

In the next chapter we will go deeper into .NET and begin exploring the .NET programming model.

.NET Fundamentals

What kind of problems is .NET designed to solve? .NET solves problems that have plagued programmers in the past. .NET helps programmers develop the applications of the future. This chapter is designed to present an overview of Microsoft .NET by looking at a simple program rather than talking in vague generalities. While we will start discussing Microsoft .NET in detail in Chapter 7, this chapter will enable you to get a feel for the big picture right away.

Problems of Windows Development

Imagine a symphony orchestra where the violins and the percussion sections had different versions of the score. It would require a heroic effort to play the simplest musical composition. This is the life of the Windows developer. Do I use MFC? Visual Basic or C++? ODBC or OLEDB? COM interface or C-style API? Even within COM: Do I use IDispatch, dual, or pure v-table interfaces? Where does the Internet fit into all of this? Either the design had to be contorted by the implementation technologies that the developers understood or the developers had to learn yet another technological approach that was bound to change in about two years.

Deployment of applications can be a chore. Critical entries have to be made in a Registry that is fragile and difficult to back up. There is no good versioning strategy for components. New releases can break existing programs, often with no information about what went wrong. Given the problems with the Registry, other technologies used other configuration stores, such as a metabase or SQL Server.

Security in Win32 is another problem. It is difficult to understand and difficult to use. Many developers ignored it. Developers who needed to apply security often did the best they could with a difficult programming model. The rise of Internet-based security threats transforms a bad situation into a potential nightmare.

Despite Microsoft's efforts to make development easier, problems remained. Many system services had to be written from scratch, essentially providing the plumbing code that had nothing to do with your business logic. MTS/COM+ was a giant step in the direction of providing higher level services, but it required yet another development paradigm. COM made real component programming possible. Nonetheless, you either did it simply, but inflexibly, in Visual Basic, or powerfully, but with great difficulty, in C++, because of all the repetitive plumbing code you had to write in C++.

Applications of the Future

Even if .NET fixed all the problems of the past, it would not be enough. One of the unchanging facts of programming life is that the boundaries of customer demand are always being expanded.

The growth of the Internet has made it imperative that applications work seamlessly across network connections. Components have to be able to expose their functionality to other machines. Programmers do not want to write the underlying plumbing code; they want to solve their customers' problems.

.NET Overview

The Magic of Metadata

To solve all these problems .NET must provide an underlying set of services that is available to all languages at all times. It also has to understand enough about an application to be able to provide these services.

Serialization provides a simple example. Every programmer at some time or another has to write code to save data. Why should every programmer have to reinvent the wheel of how to persist nested objects and complicated data structures? Why should every programmer have to figure out how to do this for a variety of data stores? .NET can do this for the programmer. Programmers can also decide to do it themselves if required.

To see how this is done, look at the **Serialize** sample associated with this chapter. For the moment, ignore the programming details of VB.NET, which will be covered in the next four chapters, and focus on the concepts.

```vb
' Serialize.vb

Imports System
Imports System.Collections
Imports System.IO
Imports System.Runtime.Serialization.Formatters.Soap

<Serializable()> Class Customer
    Public name As String
    Public id As Long
End Class

Module Test
    Sub Main()
        Dim list As New ArrayList()
        Dim cust As New Customer()
        cust.name = "Charles Darwin"
        cust.id = 10
        list.Add(cust)

        cust = New Customer()
        cust.name = "Isaac Newton"
        cust.id = 20
        list.Add(cust)

        Dim x As Customer
        For Each x In list
            Console.WriteLine(x.name & ": " & x.id)
        Next

        Console.WriteLine("Saving Customer List")
        Dim s As New FileStream("cust.txt", _
                     FileMode.Create)
        Dim f As New SoapFormatter()
        f.Serialize(s, list)
        s.Close()

        Console.WriteLine("Restoring to New List")
        s = New FileStream("cust.txt", FileMode.Open)
        f = New SoapFormatter()
        Dim list2 As ArrayList
        list2 = CType(f.Deserialize(s), ArrayList)
        s.Close()

        For Each x In list2
            Console.WriteLine(x.name & ": " & x.id)
```

```
      Next
      Console.WriteLine("Press enter to continue...")
      Console.ReadLine()
   End Sub

End Module
```

We have defined a **Customer** class with two fields: a **name** and an **id**. The program first creates an instance of a collection class that will be used to hold instances of the **Customer** class. We add two **Customer** objects to the collection and then print out the contents of the collection. The collection is then saved to disk. It is restored to a new collection instance and printed out. The results printed out will be identical to those printed out before the collection was saved.[1]

We wrote no code to indicate how the fields of the customer object are saved or restored. We did have to specify the format (SOAP) and create the medium to which the data was saved. The .NET Framework classes are partitioned so that where you load/save, the format you use to load/save, and how you load/save can be chosen independently. This kind of partitioning exists throughout the .NET Framework.

The **Customer** class was annotated with the **Serializable** attribute in the same way the **Public** attribute annotates the name field. If you do not want your objects to be serializable, do not apply the attribute to your class. If an attempt is then made to save your object, an exception will be thrown and the program will fail.[2]

Attribute-based programming is used extensively throughout .NET to describe how the Framework should treat code and data. With attributes, you do not have to write any code; the Framework takes the appropriate action based on the attribute. Security can be set through attributes. You can use attributes to have the Framework handle multithreading synchronization. Remoting of objects becomes straightforward through the use of attributes.

The compiler adds this **Serializable** attribute to the *metadata* of the **Customer** class to indicate that the Framework should save and restore the object. Metadata is additional information about the code and data within a .NET application. Metadata, a feature of the Common Language Runtime, provides such information about the code as

---

1. The sample installation should have provided an executable file Serialize.exe that you can run. If not, double-click on the Visual Studio .NET solution file that has the .sln suffix. When Visual Studio comes up, hit Control-F5 to build and run the sample.
2. Comment out the **Serializable** attribute in the program (you can use the Visual Basic comment ' syntax) and see what happens.

- Version and locale information.
- All the types.
- Details about each type, including name, visibility, and so on.
- Details about the members of each type, such as methods, the signatures of methods, and the like.
- Attributes.

Since metadata is stored in a programming-language-independent fashion with the code, not in a central store such as the Windows Registry, it makes .NET applications self-describing. The metadata can be queried at runtime to get information about the code (such as the presence or absence of the **Serializable** attribute). You can extend the metadata by providing your own custom attributes.

In our example, the Framework can query the metadata to discover the structure of the **Customer** object in order to be able to save and restore it.

Types

Types are at the heart of the programming model for the CLR. A type is analogous to a class in most object-oriented programming languages, providing an abstraction of data and behavior, grouped together. A type in the CLR contains

- Fields (data members)
- Methods
- Properties
- Events

There are also built-in primitive types, such as integer and floating-point numeric types, string, and so on. We will discuss types under the guise of classes and value types when we cover VB.NET.

.NET Framework Class Library

The **Formatter** and **FileStream** classes are just two of more than 2,500 classes in the .NET Framework that provide plumbing and system services for .NET applications. Some of the functionality provided by the .NET Framework includes

- Base class library (basic functionality such as strings, arrays, and formatting)
- Networking
- Security
- Remoting
- Diagnostics
- I/O
- Database
- XML

- Web services that allow us to expose component interfaces over the Internet
- Web programming
- Windows user interface

Interface-Based Programming

Suppose you want to encrypt your data and therefore do not want to rely on the Framework's serialization. Your class can inherit from the **ISerializable** interface and provide the appropriate implementation. (We will discuss how to do this in a later chapter.) The Framework will then use your methods to save and restore the data.

How does the Framework know that you implemented the **ISerializable** interface? It can query the metadata related to the class to see if it implements the interface! The Framework can then use either its own algorithm or the class's code to serialize or deserialize the object.

Interface-based programming is used in .NET to allow your objects to provide implementations to standard functionality that can be used by the Framework. Interfaces also allow you to program using methods on the interface rather than methods on the objects. You can program without having to know the exact type of the object. For example, the formatters (such as the SOAP formatter used here) implement the **IFormatter** interface. Programs can be written using the **IFormatter** interface and thus are independent of any particular current (binary, SOAP) or future formatter and still work properly.

Everything Is an Object

So if a type has metadata, the runtime can do all kinds of wonderful things. But does everything in .NET have metadata? Yes! Every type, whether it is user-defined (such as **Customer**) or part of the Framework (such as **FileStream**), is a .NET object. All .NET objects have the same base class, the system's **Object** class. Hence, everything that runs in .NET has a type and therefore has metadata.

In our example, the serialization code can walk through the **ArrayList** of customer objects and save each one as well as the array it belongs to, because the metadata allows it to understand the object's type and its logical structure.

Common Type System

The .NET Framework has to make some assumptions about the nature of the types that will be passed to it. These assumptions are the *Common Type System* (CTS). The CTS defines the rules for the types and operations that the

Common Language Runtime will support. It is the CTS that limits .NET classes to single implementation inheritance. Since the CTS is defined for a wide range of languages, not all languages need to support all features of the CTS.

The CTS makes it possible to guarantee type safety, which is critical for writing reliable and secure code. As we noted in the previous section, every object has a type, and therefore every reference to an object points to a defined memory layout. If arbitrary pointer operations are not allowed, the only way to access an object is through its public methods and fields. Hence, it is possible to verify an object's safety by analyzing only the object. There is no need to know or analyze all the users of a class.

How are the rules of the CTS enforced? The Microsoft Intermediate Language (MSIL or IL) defines an instruction set that is used by all .NET compilers. This intermediate language is platform-independent. The MSIL code can later be converted to a platform's native code. Verification for type safety can be done once based on the MSIL; it need not be done for every platform. Since everything is defined in terms of MSIL, we can be sure that the .NET Framework classes will work with all .NET languages. Design no longer dictates language choice; language choice no longer constrains design.

MSIL and the CTS make it possible for multiple languages to use the .NET Framework, since their compilers produce MSIL. This is one of the most visible differences between .NET and Java, which in fact share a great deal in philosophy.

ILDASM

The Microsoft Intermediate Language Disassembler (ILDASM) can display the metadata and MSIL instructions associated with .NET code. It is a very useful tool both for debugging and for increasing your understanding of the .NET infrastructure. You can use ILDASM to examine the .NET Framework code itself.[3] Figure 2–1 shows a fragment of the MSIL code from the **Serialize** example, where we create two new customer objects and add them to the list.[4]

---

3. ILDASM is installed on the Tools menu in Visual Studio .NET. It is also found in the Microsoft.NET\FrameworkSDK\Bin subdirectory. You can invoke it by double-clicking on its Explorer entry or from the command line. If you invoke it from the command line (or from VS.NET), you can use the /ADV switch to get some advanced options.
4. Open **Serialize.exe** and click on the plus (+) sign next to Test. Double-click on Main to bring up the MSIL for the Main routine.

```
Test::Main : void(string[])                                                    _□×
IL_0000: newobj    instance void [mscorlib]System.Collections.ArrayList::.ctor()
IL_0005: stloc.0
IL_0006: newobj    instance void Customer::.ctor()
IL_000b: stloc.1
IL_000c: ldloc.1
IL_000d: ldstr    "Charles Darwin"
IL_0012: stfld    string Customer::name
IL_0017: ldloc.1
IL_0018: ldc.i4.s  10
IL_001a: conv.i8
IL_001b: stfld    int64 Customer::id
IL_0020: ldloc.0
IL_0021: ldloc.1
IL_0022: callvirt  instance int32 [mscorlib]System.Collections.ArrayList::Add(object)
IL_0027: pop
IL_0028: newobj    instance void Customer::.ctor()
IL_002d: stloc.1
IL_002e: ldloc.1
IL_002f: ldstr    "Isaac Newton"
IL_0034: stfld    string Customer::name
IL_0039: ldloc.1
IL_003a: ldc.i4.s  20
IL_003c: conv.i8
IL_003d: stfld    int64 Customer::id
IL_0042: ldloc.0
IL_0043: ldloc.1
IL_0044: callvirt  instance int32 [mscorlib]System.Collections.ArrayList::Add(object)
IL_0049: pop
IL_004a: ldloc.0
```

FIGURE 2–1   Code fragment from Serialize example.

The **newobj** instruction creates a new object reference using the constructor parameter. **Stloc** stores the value in a local variable. **Ldloc** loads a local variable.[5]

Language Interoperability

Having all language compilers use a common intermediate language and common base class make it *possible* for languages to interoperate. But since all languages need not implement all parts of the CTS, it is certainly possible for one language to have a feature that another does not.

5. You can read about the MSIL instruction set and the CLR in the book *Compiling for the .NET Common Language Runtime (CLR)* by John Gough, Prentice Hall, 2002.

The *Common Language Specification* (CLS) defines a subset of the CTS representing the basic functionality that all .NET languages should implement if they are to interoperate with each other. This specification enables a class written in Visual Basic .NET to inherit from a class written in C++ with Managed Extensions or C#, or to make interlanguage debugging possible. An example of a CLS rule is that method calls need not support a variable number of arguments, even though such a construct can be expressed in MSIL.

CLS compliance applies only to publicly visible features. A class, for example, can have a private member that is non-CLS compliant and still be a base class for a class in another .NET language. For example, VB.NET code should not define public and protected class names that differ only by case sensitivity, since languages such as VB.NET are not case sensitive. Private fields could have case-sensitive names.

Microsoft itself is providing several CLS-compliant languages: C#, Visual Basic .NET, and C++ with Managed Extensions. Third parties are providing additional languages (there are over a dozen so far). ActiveState is implementing Perl and Python. Fujitsu is implementing COBOL.

Managed Code

In the serialization example, a second instance of the **Customer** object was assigned to the same variable (**cust**) as the first instance without freeing it. None of the allocated storage in the example was ever deallocated. .NET uses automatic garbage collection to reclaim memory. When memory allocated on the heap becomes orphaned, or passes out of scope, it is placed on a list of memory locations to be freed. Periodically, the system runs a garbage collection thread that returns the memory to the heap.

By having automatic memory management, the system has eliminated memory leakage, which is one of the most common programming errors. In most cases, memory allocation is much faster with garbage collection than with classic heap allocation schemes. Note that variables such as **cust** and **list** are object references, not the objects themselves. This makes the garbage collection possible.

Garbage collection is one of several services provided by the *Common Language Runtime* (CLR) to .NET programs. Data that is under the control of the CLR garbage collection process is called managed data. Managed code is code that can use the services of the CLR. .NET compilers that produce MSIL can produce managed code.

Code is typically verified for type safety before compilation. This step is optional and can be skipped for trusted code. One of the most significant differences between verified and unverified code is that verified code cannot use pointers. Code that uses pointers could subvert the CTS and access any memory location. You cannot program with pointers in VB.NET—that is one of the differences between VB.NET and C#.

Type-safe code cannot be subverted. A buffer overwrite is not able to corrupt other data structures or programs. Methods can only start and end at well-defined entry and exit points. Security policy can be applied to type-safe code. For example, access to certain files or user interface features can be allowed or denied. You can prevent the execution of code from unknown sources. You can prevent access to unmanaged code to prevent subversion of .NET security. Type safety also allows paths of execution of .NET code to be isolated from one another.

Assemblies

Another function of the CLR is to load and run .NET programs.

.NET programs are deployed as assemblies. An *assembly* is one or more EXEs or DLLs with associated metadata information. The metadata about the entire assembly is stored in the assembly's manifest. The manifest contains, for example, a list of the assemblies upon which this assembly is dependent.

In our **Serialize** example there is only file in the assembly, **Serialize.exe**. That file contains the metadata as well as the code. Since the manifest is stored in the assembly and not in a separate file (like a type library or registry), the manifest cannot get out of sync with the assembly. Figure 2–2 shows the metadata in the manifest for this example.[6] Note the **assembly extern** statements that indicate the dependencies on the Framework assemblies **mscorlib** and **System.Runtime.Formatters.SOAP**. These statements also indicate the version of those assemblies that **serialize.exe** depends on.

Assemblies can be versioned, and the version is part of the name for the assembly. To version an assembly it needs a unique name. Public/private encryption keys are used to generate a unique (or strong) name.

Assemblies can be deployed either privately or publicly. For private deployment, all the assemblies that an application needs are copied to the same directory as the application. If an assembly is to be publicly shared, an entry is made in the *Global Assembly Cache* (GAC) so that other assemblies can locate it. For assemblies put in the GAC, a strong name is required. Since the version is part of the assembly name, multiple versions can be deployed side by side on the same machine without interfering with each other. Whether you use public or private deployment, there is no more DLL Hell.

Assembly deployment with language interoperability makes component development almost effortless. We discuss issues of deployment in Chapter 9.

---

6. Open **Serialize.exe** in ILDASM and double-click on the MANIFEST item.

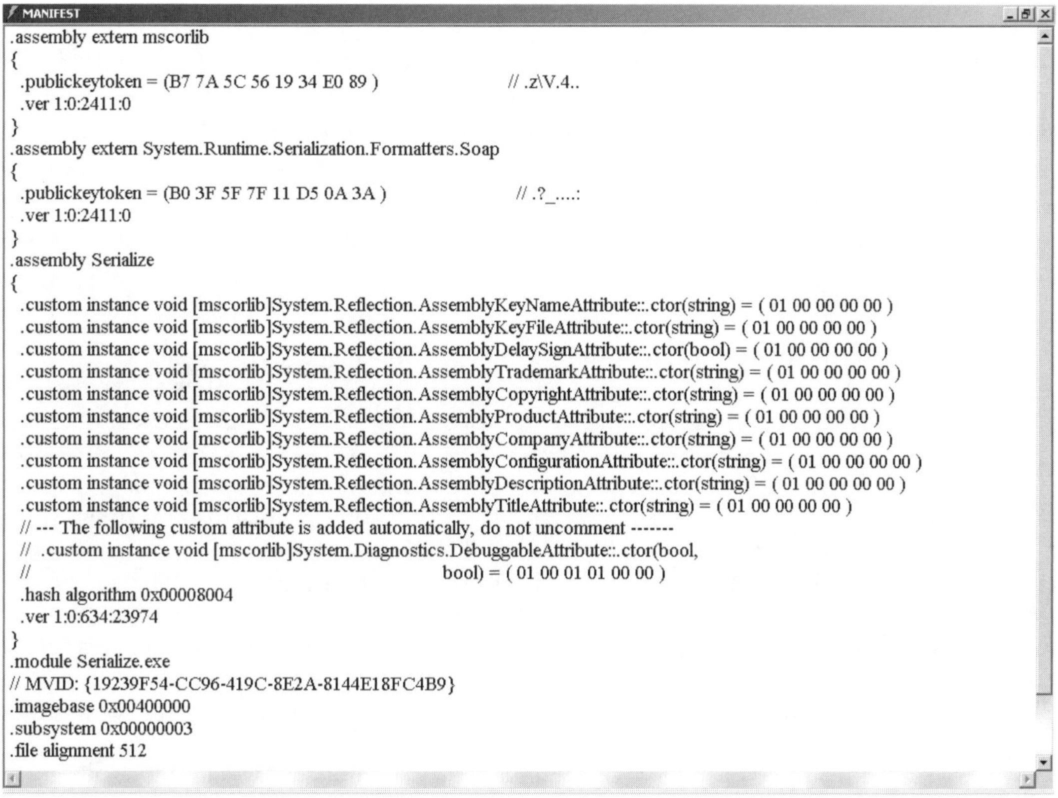

```
/ MANIFEST                                                                        _|&|x
.assembly extern mscorlib
{
  .publickeytoken = (B7 7A 5C 56 19 34 E0 89 )              // .z\V.4..
  .ver 1:0:2411:0
}
.assembly extern System.Runtime.Serialization.Formatters.Soap
{
  .publickeytoken = (B0 3F 5F 7F 11 D5 0A 3A )              // .?_....:
  .ver 1:0:2411:0
}
.assembly Serialize
{
  .custom instance void [mscorlib]System.Reflection.AssemblyKeyNameAttribute::.ctor(string) = ( 01 00 00 00 00 )
  .custom instance void [mscorlib]System.Reflection.AssemblyKeyFileAttribute::.ctor(string) = ( 01 00 00 00 00 )
  .custom instance void [mscorlib]System.Reflection.AssemblyDelaySignAttribute::.ctor(bool) = ( 01 00 00 00 00 )
  .custom instance void [mscorlib]System.Reflection.AssemblyTrademarkAttribute::.ctor(string) = ( 01 00 00 00 00 )
  .custom instance void [mscorlib]System.Reflection.AssemblyCopyrightAttribute::.ctor(string) = ( 01 00 00 00 00 )
  .custom instance void [mscorlib]System.Reflection.AssemblyProductAttribute::.ctor(string) = ( 01 00 00 00 00 )
  .custom instance void [mscorlib]System.Reflection.AssemblyCompanyAttribute::.ctor(string) = ( 01 00 00 00 00 )
  .custom instance void [mscorlib]System.Reflection.AssemblyConfigurationAttribute::.ctor(string) = ( 01 00 00 00 00 )
  .custom instance void [mscorlib]System.Reflection.AssemblyDescriptionAttribute::.ctor(string) = ( 01 00 00 00 00 )
  .custom instance void [mscorlib]System.Reflection.AssemblyTitleAttribute::.ctor(string) = ( 01 00 00 00 00 )
  // --- The following custom attribute is added automatically, do not uncomment ------
  // .custom instance void [mscorlib]System.Diagnostics.DebuggableAttribute::.ctor(bool,
  //                           bool) = ( 01 00 01 01 00 00 )
  .hash algorithm 0x00008004
  .ver 1:0:634:23974
}
.module Serialize.exe
// MVID: {19239F54-CC96-419C-8E2A-8144E18FC4B9}
.imagebase 0x00400000
.subsystem 0x00000003
.file alignment 512
```

FIGURE 2–2   *Manifest for the Serialize assembly.*

JIT Compilation

Before executing on the target machine, MSIL has to be translated into the machine's native code. This can be done either before the application is called or at runtime. At runtime, the translation is done by a just-in-time (JIT) compiler. The Native Image Generator (Ngen.exe) translates MSIL into native code ("pre-translation") so that it is already translated when the program is started.

The advantage of pre-translation is that optimizations can be performed. Optimizations are generally impractical with JIT because the time it takes to do the optimization can be longer than it takes to compile the code. Startup time is also faster with pre-translation because no translation has to be done when the application starts.

The advantage of JIT is that it knows what the execution environment is when the program is run and can make better assumptions, such as register assignments, when it generates the code. Only the code that is actually executed is translated; code that never gets executed is never translated.

In the first release of .NET, the Native Image Generator and the JIT compiler use the same compiler. No optimizations are done for Ngen; its only current advantage is faster startup. For this reason, we do not discuss Ngen in this book.

Performance

You may like the safety and ease-of-use features of managed code, but you might be concerned about performance. Early assembly language programmers had similar concerns when high-level languages came out.

The CLR is designed with high performance in mind. With JIT compilation, the first time a method is encountered, the CLR performs verifications and then compiles the method into native code (which will contain safety features, such as array bounds checking). The next time the method is encountered, the native code executes directly. Memory management is designed for high performance. Allocation is almost instantaneous, just taking the next available storage from the managed heap. Deallocation is done by the garbage collector, which has an efficient multiple-generation algorithm.

You do pay a penalty when security checks have to be made that require a stack walk, as we will explain in Chapter 16.

Web pages use compiled code, not interpreted code. As a result, ASP.NET is much faster than ASP.

For 98 percent of the code that programmers write, any small loss in performance is far outweighed by the gains in reliability and ease of development. High-performance server applications might have to use technologies such as ATL Server and C++.

Summary

.NET solves many of the problems that have plagued Windows development in the past. There is one development paradigm for all languages. Design and programming language choices are no longer in conflict. Deployment is more rational and includes a versioning strategy. While we will talk more about it in later chapters, metadata, attribute-based security, code verification, and type-safe assembly isolation make developing secure applications much easier. The plumbing code for fundamental system services is provided, yet you can extend or replace it if you must.

The Common Language Runtime provides a solid base for developing applications of the future. The CLR is the foundation whose elements include the Common Type System, metadata, and the Common Language Specification. As we shall see in future chapters, .NET makes it easier to develop Internet applications for both service providers and customer-based solutions. With the unified development platform .NET provides, it will be much easier than in the past for Microsoft or others to provide extensions.

All this is made possible by putting old technologies together in the CLR creatively: intermediate languages, type-safe verification, and of course metadata. As you will see, metadata is used in many features in .NET.

We shall expand on these topics in the course of the book. We next cover the VB.NET language. Depending on your knowledge of VB.NET, you might be able to skip Chapters 3 and 4 and skim Chapters 5 and 6. Chapter 5 introduces the Acme Travel Agency case study, which is used throughout the book. Chapter 6 covers important topics about the interaction of VB.NET and the .NET Framework.

VB.NET LANGUAGE

VB.NET LANGUAGE

Part 2 , consisting of Chapters 3–6, covers the VB.NET programming language. Even if you know classic Visual Basic, you should read this part, paying attention to the changes in data types (Chapter 3) and the new object-oriented features (Chapters 5). Chapter 6 covers important interactions between VB.NET and the .NET Framework. The Acme Travel Agency case study, which is elaborated throughout the entire book, is introduced in Chapter 5.

VB.NET Essentials, Part I

*I*n this chapter we begin coverage of the essentials of the VB.NET language, which has undergone radical improvements from previous versions of Visual Basic.

Traditionally, Visual Basic has been used as a visual development tool to create Windows programs. Later versions of Visual Basic have also made the language useful for creating COM components and other server programs without a visual interface. VB.NET brings full flexibility to Visual Basic, enabling you to use the language to create any kind of program in the .NET environment, including components, Web applications, and Web services. You can also create console programs that run locally and do not have a Windows user interface. Although normally you will use the powerful Visual Studio .NET development environment, it is also possible to build VB.NET applications using simple command-line tools. In the first part of the chapter we provide an overview of VB.NET as a visual development environment and also explain the new feature of using VB.NET to create console applications.

A "Hello, world" program introduces the basic structure of VB.NET programs. We then cover variables, operators, control structures, formatting, methods, and input/output. Classes are fundamental in VB.NET, and we examine them in some detail. Besides the standard features, VB.NET adds some convenience features, such as properties. We cover the essentials of data types in VB.NET, which correspond to types in the Common Type System (CTS) used in all .NET languages. We discuss the fundamental distinction between value and reference types and see how to convert between them using boxing and unboxing operations.

Although we start out slowly, orienting you to the environment and dissecting the basic structure of a VB.NET program, our pace in this chapter and in the rest of Part 2 is somewhat fast paced, as we want to quickly cover the essentials of the VB.NET language so that the rest of the book can focus on the .NET Framework classes and the different kinds of applications that can be created using these classes. For a more leisurely and complete treatment of VB.NET as a programming language, please refer to our book *Introduction to Visual Basic Using .NET.*

Visual Studio .NET and Console Applications

Visual Basic has traditionally been associated with visual development, as is suggested by its name. But now you can also build applications using command-line tools, and you can create console applications that do not have a Windows user interface. In this section we will first preview using Visual Studio .NET to create a Windows application, and then we look at the new feature of console applications.

Visual Studio .NET

The Visual Basic development environment is Visual Studio, which has also provided a visual tool for other languages, such as Visual C++ and Visual J++. With Visual Studio 6.0 there was a separate IDE for the different languages. All this changes with Visual Studio .NET. In keeping with the .NET Framework, in which different .NET languages share the Common Language Runtime (CLR) and the .NET Framework Class Library, Visual Studio .NET provides *one* IDE that can be used by all the .NET languages.

You can refer to Appendix A for help in coming up to speed on Visual Studio .NET. If you have used Visual Studio before, you should find the new version quite intuitive and easy to use. When you start Visual Studio .NET and create a new project (File | New | Project), you will see a window in which you can select different languages in the left panel, and you can choose from among many different project types in the right panel. See Figure 3–1.

If you would like to try a little experiment, create a new Visual Basic project using Windows Application (the default) as the template. Navigate to the **Demos** directory for this chapter, **C:\OI\NetVb\Chap03\Demos**, for the Location, and accept the suggested name **WindowsApplication1**. Click OK. You will now see this Visual Studio main window, which presents a rather elaborate user interface for the new project, as illustrated in Figure 3–2. There are various menus and toolbars. There is a palette of various controls, which you can drag onto a form. There is a property panel in which you can set properties for controls and for the form itself. You can easily add handlers for form events and control events, such as clicking a button. In short, the development paradigm is just like classic Visual Basic.

Beginning in Chapter 7 we will learn all about creating Windows applications, but right now, just build the project. You can use either Build | Build

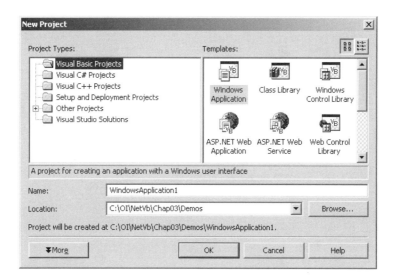

FIGURE 3–1   *You can create different kinds of projects in different languages using Visual Studio .NET.*

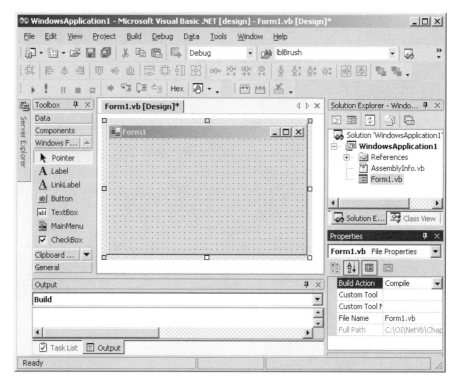

FIGURE 3–2   *Main window in Visual Studio for a new Windows Application project.*

Solution or Build | Build WindowsApplication1 from the menu. (These are the same in this case, because the solution has only one project.) You can also use corresponding toolbar buttons, which are shown visually on the menu. You can run the application from the menu Debug | Start or Debug | Start Without Debugging. Again, there are corresponding toolbar buttons. This "starter" application simply displays a blank form, as shown in Figure 3–3. There are the standard control buttons on the top of the form, and you can close the form in the usual way by clicking the "X" button at the top right of the form.

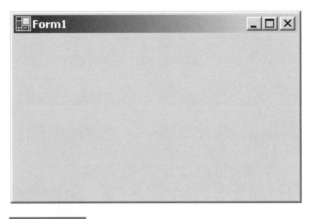

FIGURE 3–3 *Starter application is just a blank form.*

Console Applications

One of the new things about VB.NET is that you can now create console applications, which provide a simple command-line user interface in a DOS window. If you would like to try another simple experiment, create another new project in Visual Studio. In the Templates panel you will have to scroll to find the Console Application project type. Again, make the location the **Demos** directory for this chapter and accept the suggested name of **ConsoleApplication1** for your new application. For a console project, there is no form. Instead, Visual Studio shows a code window. Figure 3–4 shows the main window for the new project, where we have added just a single line of code, creating a simple "Hello, world" application. We will discuss this code in the next section.

For now, just build and run the application. If you run the program without debugging, a console window will be created and will stay open, and you will see the following output:

```
Hello, world
Press any key to continue
```

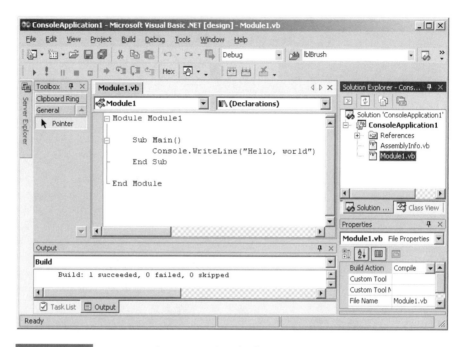

Main window in Visual Studio for a new Console Application.

If you run under the debugger, a console window will open briefly and then immediately close. You will need to do something in your program, such as prompt for input, to ensure that the console window stays open. We discuss this issue later in the chapter.

Console Applications Versus Windows Applications

Just what is the difference between a console application and a Windows application? Under .NET, there actually are four different kinds of executables that can be built, distinguished by a compiler option and a flag in the executable IL file. The four options are

- Windows Application
- Console Application
- Class Library
- Module

We will discuss class library and module in Chapter 9. Using Visual Studio, you can build a project as either a Windows Application, a Console Application, or a Class Library. As an example, let's see what happens if we build **WindowsApplication1** as a Console Application. In the Visual Studio Solution Explorer pane on the right side of the main window, right-click over

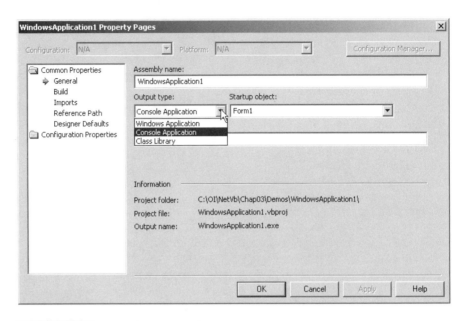

FIGURE 3–5   *Changing the output type to Console Application.*

the project **WindowsApplication1** and choose Properties from the context menu. A property page comes up. In the combo box for Output type choose Console Application, as illustrated in Figure 3–5.

What do you suppose will happen when you build and run the application using the modified setting? The project builds fine, and when you run it, the blank form appears as before. But now, a console window is also displayed, which will stay open as long as the application is running. If you run it under the debugger, the console window stays open after the application window is closed and displays the message

`Press any key to continue`

You could actually write to this console window in your program code, which is a technique that is sometimes useful in debugging Windows applications.

So the compiler setting is actually quite trivial. What really distinguishes a Windows application is the program code, which will involve using the Windows Forms classes, as discussed in Chapter 7.

In this chapter and in the rest of Part 2 we will create exclusively console applications, allowing us to focus on the VB.NET programming language without being distracted by learning about Windows Forms. Let's begin simply, with "Hello, world." We will also learn about compiling using the command line.

Hello World in VB.NET

Code Example

Whenever learning a new programming language, a good first step is to write and run a simple program that will display a single line of text. Such a program demonstrates the basic structure of the language, including output. Here is "Hello, world" in VB.NET (See the **Hello** directory for this chapter.)

```
' Hello.vb

Module Hello
   Public Sub Main()
      System.Console.WriteLine("Hello, world")
   End Sub
End Module
```

Compiling and Running (Command Line)

We already introduced the Microsoft Visual Studio .NET IDE (integrated development environment), and you can learn more in Appendix A. You can also use the command-line tools of the .NET Framework SDK. You will almost always use Visual Studio to build your programs rather than the command-line compiler. However, it is good to know about both techniques. And for a few things, you need to use the command-line tools. For example, you cannot build a Module from within Visual Studio (it is not listed as an available Output type, as illustrated in Figure 3–5).

Be sure to get the environment variables set up properly, as described in the sidebar. To compile this program at the command line, use the **vbc** command.

```
>vbc Hello.vb
```

An executable file **Hello.exe** will be generated. To execute your program, type at the command line

```
>Hello
```

The program will now execute, and you should see displayed the greeting

```
Hello, world
```

Setting Environment Variables

In order to run command-line tools such as the VB compiler using a simple program name such as **vbc** rather than a complete path, we must set certain environment variables. To do so, we can use a batch file, **corvars.bat**, which can be found in the **bin** directory of the Framework SDK.

If you have Visual Studio .NET installed, you can ensure that the environment variables are set up by starting your command prompt session from Start | Programs | Microsoft Visual Studio .NET | Visual Studio .NET Tools | Visual Studio .NET Command Prompt.

Program Structure

We will now dissect this simple "Hello" program as an illustration of the structure of VB.NET programs.

COMMENTS AND FILE EXTENSION

The program begins with a one-line comment (which is used to identify the name of the file, a convention we'll follow in many of our sample programs). A line beginning with a single quote is present only for documentation purposes and is ignored by the compiler. VB.NET files have the extension **.vb**.

```
' Hello.vb
...
```

MODULE

Every VB.NET program has at least one *module* or *class*. A class is the foundation of VB.NET's support of object-oriented programming. A class encapsulates data (represented by *variables*) and behavior (represented by *methods*). All of the code defining the class (its variables and methods) will be contained between the **Module** and **End Module** or **Class** and **End Class** code lines. A module is like a class, but unlike a class, it cannot be instantiated to create an object. We will discuss classes in detail later.

```
Module Hello
    ...
End Module
```

MAIN PROCEDURE

In every EXE program, there is a distinguished module or class, which has a subroutine procedure named **Main**, which is the starting point for the application. This **Main** procedure (also called a method) must be declared as a parameterless **Public Sub** (and in the case of a class, it must be declared as **Shared**).

```
Public Sub Main()
    System.Console.WriteLine("Hello,  world")
End Sub
```

Startup Object

Every program in a .NET language must have a **Main** method. This applies to Windows applications as well as to console applications. But if you examine the code in **Form1.vb** in the **WindowsApplication1** program we created, you won't find a **Main** method. What's going on?

If you look at the property page for the **WindowsApplication1**, you will see that **Form1** is designated as the Startup object. With this setting, the system will supply the appropriate **Main** method for you, which will call the **Run** method of the **Application** class.

STATEMENTS

Every method in VB.NET has zero or more *statements*. A statement is terminated by a carriage return.

```
System.Console.WriteLine("Hello, world")
```

A statement may be spread out over several lines using the line continuation character, which is the underscore. There must be at least one space at the end of the line before the underscore. We will use this underscore notation extensively in this book, because many statements will be too long to fit on one line (especially the short lines used in typesetting this book).

```
System.Console.WriteLine( _
    "Hello, world")
```

The **System.Console** class provides support for standard console input and output. For example, the method **System.Console.WriteLine** displays a character string followed by a new line.

Namespaces and Imports

Much standard functionality in VB.NET is provided through many classes in the .NET Framework. Related classes are grouped into *namespaces*. Many useful classes, such as **Console**, are in the **System** namespace. The fully qualified name of a class is specified by the namespace followed by a dot followed by a class name, such as **System.Console**.

An **Imports** statement allows a class to be referred to by its class name alone. For example, the **Imports** statement is used in the following to allow the short name **Console** to be used rather than the fully qualified name **System.Console**. The program **HelloWithImports** provides an alternate implementation of our "Hello" program.

Code Example

```
' HelloWithImports.vb

Imports System

Module Hello
    Public Sub Main()
        Console.WriteLine("Hello, world")
    End Sub
End Module
```

NAMESPACES IN VISUAL STUDIO PROJECTS

Code Example

If you look at the file **Module1.vb** in the **ConsoleApplication1** project, you will see the following code:

```
Module Module1

    Sub Main()
        Console.WriteLine("Hello, world")
    End Sub

End Module
```

This program is almost identical to our handcrafted "Hello" program. But if you look carefully, you will see the **Console** class is used without the **System** qualification, and there is no **Imports** statement. What is going on here?

Bring up Properties for the **ConsoleApplication1** project (right-click in Solution Explorer and select Properties from the context menu). Select Imports in the left panel, and you will see Project imports in the right panel, as shown in Figure 3–6.

As you can see, the **System** namespace is imported for you automatically, as well as several other namespaces that are commonly used in VB.NET applications.

You should be cautious in using project imports, because making an import apply to a whole project can diminish the usefulness of having the namespace available to avoid ambiguities. When you have an **Imports** statement explicitly in a particular file, it applies only to that file.

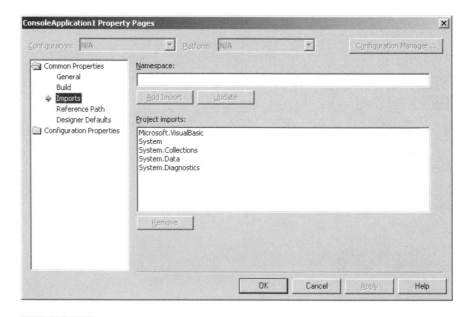

FIGURE 3–6   *Project imports for a Console Application.*

ROOT NAMESPACE

When you create a project in Visual Studio, it will be placed in a default namespace, called the root namespace, which is the same as the name of the project. If you want to access any classes in the executable built from this executable from outside the executable, you will need to qualify them using this namespace, or else use an **Imports** statement. You can change this namespace using the Properties of the project. Figure 3–7 illustrates the root namespace for the **ConsoleApplication1** example. We won't need to be concerned with the root namespace for a while, because all our applications will be creating a single assembly, all in the same namespace. But later, when we create class libraries in Chapter 9, the root namespace will become important.

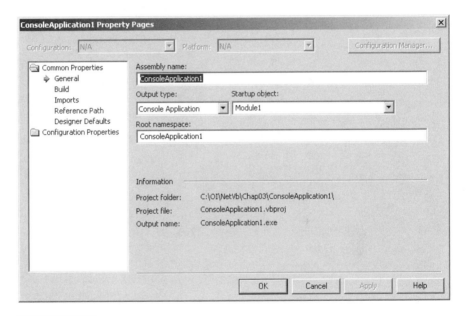

FIGURE 3–7   *Root namespace for a Console Application.*

STARTUP OBJECT IN A CONSOLE APPLICATION

The main source file name of our **ConsoleApplication1** example is **Module1.vb** and the module is named **Module1**. If we change those to more natural names, such as **Hello.vb** and **Hello**, we will get an error when we try to rebuild the project:

```
'Sub Main' was not found in 'ConsoleApplication1.Module1'.
```

The remedy is to change the startup object, which we can do by right-clicking over the project in Solution Explorer and choosing Properties from

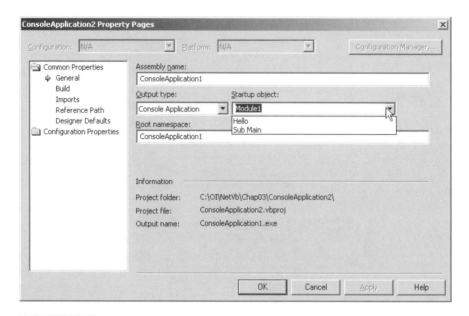

FIGURE 3–8   *Changing the startup object in a Console Application.*

the context menu. See Figure 3–8. Change the startup object to Hello. You can then rebuild and run the program. This version of the "Hello, world" application is illustrated in the folder **ConsoleApplication2**, where we have also changed the name of the assembly to **Hello**, and we have changed the solution and project names to **ConsoleApplication2**. We have blanked out the namespace.

Performing Calculations in VB.NET

Our "Hello, world" program illustrated the basic structure of a VB.NET program, but we will need a slightly more elaborate example to show the use of other basic programming constructs, such as variables, expressions, and control structures. The example illustrates a number of features, which we will explain later. Our next example is a simple calculator for an IRA account. We calculate the accumulation of deposits to an IRA of $2000.00 a year at 6% interest for 10 years, assuming that each deposit is made at the end of the year. Our calculation is performed in two ways:

● In a loop, year by year, accumulating a total as we go.
● Using a formula.

Code Example

The example program is in the folder **Ira\Step1**.

```
' Ira.vb - Step 1

Imports System

Module Ira
    Public Sub Main()
        Dim years As Integer = 10
        Dim rate As Decimal = 0.06D
        Dim amount As Decimal = 2000D
        Dim interest As Decimal
        Dim total As Decimal = 0D
        Console.WriteLine( _
            "{0,4} {1,12} {2,12} {3,12}", _
            "Year", "Amount", "Interest", "Total")
        Dim i As Integer = 1
        While i <= years
            interest = total * rate
            total += amount + interest
            Console.WriteLine( _
                "{0, -4} {1, 12:C} {2, 12:C} {3, 12:C}", _
                i, amount, interest, total)
            i += 1
        End While
        Console.WriteLine()
        Console.WriteLine( _
            "Total using formula = {0}", _
            IraTotal(years, rate, amount))
    End Sub
    Private Function IraTotal(ByVal years As Integer, _
     ByVal rate As Double, ByVal amount As Double) As Double
        Dim total As Double = _
            amount * (Math.Pow(1 + rate, years) - 1) / rate
        Dim total_in_cents As Long = Math.Round(total * 100)
        total = total_in_cents / 100
        Return total
    End Function
End Module
```

If you compile and run it, you will see this output:

Year	Amount	Interest	Total
1	$2,000.00	$0.00	$2,000.00
2	$2,000.00	$120.00	$4,120.00
3	$2,000.00	$247.20	$6,367.20
4	$2,000.00	$382.03	$8,749.23
5	$2,000.00	$524.95	$11,274.19
6	$2,000.00	$676.45	$13,950.64
7	$2,000.00	$837.04	$16,787.68
8	$2,000.00	$1,007.26	$19,794.94
9	$2,000.00	$1,187.70	$22,982.63
10	$2,000.00	$1,378.96	$26,361.59

```
Total using formula = 26361.59
```

Variables

In VB.NET variables are always of a specific data type. Some common types are **Integer** for integers and **Double** for floating-point numbers. VB.NET has the **Decimal** data type, which has a high degree of precision, suitable for financial calculations.

You must declare variables before you use them, and you may optionally initialize them.

```
Dim years As Integer = 10
Dim rate As Decimal = 0.06D
Dim amount As Decimal = 2000D
Dim interest As Decimal
Dim total As Decimal = 0D
```

If an initial value is not specified in the declaration, the variable is automatically initialized. For example, an uninitialized **Decimal** variable is set to zero. We will discuss initialization later in the chapter.

Variables must be either local within a method or members of a class. There are no global variables in VB.NET.

Literals

A *literal* is used when you explicitly write a value in a program rather than represent it with a variable name. An integer literal is represented by an ordinary base-10 integer, an octal integer, or a hexadecimal integer. An octal integer is indicated with the &O[1] prefix, such as &O77 (which is 63 in base 10). A hexadecimal literal is indicated with the &H prefix, such as &H7FFF (which is 32,767 in base 10). The suffixes **S**, **I**, and **L** are used to designate Short, Integer, and Long. A floating-point literal is represented by a number with a decimal point or by exponential notation. You may determine the type[2] that is used for storing a literal by a suffix. The suffix **F** indicates single precision (32-bit) floating point. The suffix **R** indicates double precision (64-bit) floating point. The **Single** and **Double** types are often suitable for scientific and engineering purposes. The suffix **D** indicates **Decimal**, which is usually more suitable for financial calculations, and it represents a high precision (128-bit) fixed-point number.

```
Dim rate As Decimal = 0.06D
Dim amount As Decimal = 2000D
```

---

1. That is the letter O, not the number 0.
2. We discuss VB.NET types, such as **Single**, **Double**, and **Decimal**, later in the chapter.

A character string literal is represented by a sequence of characters in double quotes.

```
Dim file1 As String = "c:\test2.txt"
Dim str As String = "Welcome to VB.NET"
```

VB.NET Operators and Expressions

You can combine variables and literals via operators to form expressions. The VB.NET operators are similar to those in other .NET languages.

One of the newest features of VB.NET is its new *compound assignment* operators that perform arithmetic operations as part of the assignment. Here are examples from the **Ira** program:

```
i += 1         ' this is equivalent to i = i + 1
total += amount + interest     ' this is equivalent to
               ' total = total + amount + interest
```

There are six new compound assignment operators available in VB.NET. They are demonstrated in the following example:

```
Dim x As Single = 4.6

x *= 2         ' multiply x by 2
x /= 2         ' divide x by 2
x += 2         ' add 2 to x
x -= 2         ' subtract 2 from x
x \= 2         ' divide (integer) x by 2
```

There is also a compound assignment operator for string concatenation. The following expression concatenates an exclamation point to the end of the string contained in the variable **buf:**

```
Dim buf As String = "Hello"
x &= "!"
```

New Operators in VB.NET

VB.NET introduces several operators that are new to VB6 programmers. **OrElse** and **AndAlso** provide shortcut evaluation of conditional expressions. And the assignment operators **^=**, ***=**, **/=**, **\=**, **+=**, **-=**, and **&=** provide shortcuts for common operations.

Precedence rules determine the order in which operators within expressions are evaluated. Operators are applied in the precedence order shown in Table 3–1. Operators within a row have equal precedence. For operators of equal precedence within the same expression, the order of evaluation is from left to right, as they appear in an expression. Order of evaluation can be explicitly controlled by using parentheses.

TABLE 3–1	Operator Precedence in VB.NET

Category	Operators
Primary	All non-operator expressions (literals, variables)
Exponentiation	^
Unary negation	+, -
Multiplicative	*, /
Integer division \	
Modulus	Mod
Additive	+, -
Concatenation	&
Relational	=, <>, <, >, <=, >=, Like, Is, TypeOf...Is
Conditional NOT	Not
Conditional AND	And, AndAlso
Conditional OR	Or, OrElse
Conditional XOR	Xor

Output and Formatting

The **Console** class in the **System** namespace supports two simple methods for performing output:

- **WriteLine** writes out a string followed by a new line.
- **Write** writes out just the string without the new line.

You can write out other data types by relying on the **ToString** method of **System.Object**, which will provide a string representation of any data type. **System.Object** is the base class from which all classes inherit. We will discuss this class in Chapter 6, where you will also see how to override **ToString** for your own custom data types. You can use the string concatenation operator **&** to build up an output string.

```
Dim x As Integer = 24
Dim y As Integer = 5
Dim z As Integer = x * y
Console.Write("Product of " & x.ToString() + _
    " and " & y.ToString())
Console.WriteLine(" is " & z.ToString())
```

The output is all on one line:

```
Product of 24 and 5 is 120
```

PLACEHOLDERS

A more convenient way to build up an output string is to use *placeholders* such as {0}, {1}, and so on. An equivalent way to do the output shown above is

```
Console.WriteLine("Product of {0} and {1} is {2}", x, y, z)
```

The program **OutputDemo** illustrates the output operations just discussed.

We will generally use placeholders for our output from now on. Placeholders can be combined with formatting characters to control output format.

FORMAT STRINGS

VB.NET has extensive formatting capabilities, which you can control through placeholders and format strings.

- Simple placeholders: {n}, where n is 0, 1, 2, … , indicating which variable to insert
- Control width: {n,w}, where w is width (positive for right justified and negative for left justified) of the inserted variable
- Format string: {n:S}, where S is a format string indicating how to display the variable
- Width and format string: {n,w:S}

A format string consists of a format character followed by an optional precision specifier. Table 3–2 shows the available format characters.

TABLE 3–2   *Format Characters*

Format Character	Meaning
C	Currency (locale specific)
D	Decimal integer
E	Exponential (scientific)
F	Fixed point
G	General (E or F)
N	Number with embedded commas
X	Hexadecimal

SAMPLE FORMATTING CODE

The sample program in **Ira\Step1** provides an example. The header uses width specifiers, and the output inside the loop uses width specifiers and the currency format character.

```
. . .
    Console.WriteLine( _
        "{0,4} {1,12} {2,12} {3,12}", _
        "Year", "Amount", "Interest", "Total")
    Dim i As Integer = 1
    While i <= years
        interest = total * rate
        total += amount + interest
        Console.WriteLine( _
            "{0, -4} {1, 12:C} {2, 12:C} {3, 12:C}", _
            i, amount, interest, total)
        i += 1
    End While
. . .
```

Control Structures

The preceding code fragment illustrates a **While ... End While** loop. VB.NET supports several control structures, including the **If** and **Select** decision statements as well as **For** and **While** loops.

- While ... End While
- Do While ... Loop
- Do Until ... Loop
- Do ... Loop While
- Do ... Loop Until
- For ... Next
- For Each ... Next
- If ... Then ... End If
- If ... Then ... Else ... End If
- If ... Then ... ElseIf ... Then ... End If
- Select ... Case ... End Select
- With ... End With
- GoTo
- Return
- SyncLock ... End SyncLock
- Throw
- Try ... Catch ... Finally

Most of these will be familiar to Visual Basic programmers. The **Throw** and **Try** statements are used in exception handling. We will discuss exceptions later in this chapter. The **SyncLock** statement can be used to enforce synchronization in multithreading situations. We will discuss multithreading in Chapter 10.

SELECT CASE STATEMENT

A **Select Case** statement is used to execute one of several groups of statements, depending on the value of a test expression. The test expression must be one of the following data types: **Boolean**, **Byte**, **Char**, **Date**, **Double**, **Decimal**, **Integer**, **Long**, **Object**, **Short**, **Single**, or **String**.

Code Example

After a particular case statement is executed, control automatically continues after the following **End Select**. The program **SelectDemo** illustrates use of the **Select Case** statement in VB.NET.

```
. . .
Select Case (scores(i))
    Case 1
        Console.WriteLine("Very Low")
    Case 2
        Console.WriteLine("Low")
    Case 3
        Console.WriteLine("Medium")
    Case 4 To 5
        Console.WriteLine("High")
    Case Else
        Console.WriteLine("Special Case")
End Select
. . .
```

Methods

Our **Ira\Step1** example program has a method **IraTotal** for computing the total IRA accumulation by use of a formula. In VB.NET, *every* function is a method of some class or module; there are no freestanding global functions. If a method does not refer to any instance variables of the class, the method can be declared as **Shared**. We will discuss instance data of a class later in this chapter. If a method is accessed only from within a single class, it may be designated as **Private**. Note the use of the **Private** keyword in the **Ira\Step1** example. The **Shared** keyword is not used however, since the example uses a module instead of a class. All methods in a module are shared by default.

Also in the **Ira\Step1** example, note the use of the **Pow** and **Round** methods of the **Math** class, which is another class in the **System** namespace. These methods are shared methods. To call a shared method from outside the class in which it is defined, place the name of the class followed by a period before the method name.

```
. . .
Private Function IraTotal(ByVal years As Integer, _
    ByVal rate As Double, ByVal amount As Double) As Double
    Dim total As Double = _
        amount * (Math.Pow(1 + rate, years) - 1) / rate
    Dim total_in_cents As Long = _
```

```
          Math.Round(total * 100)
      total = total_in_cents / 100
      Return total
   End Function
   . . .
```

Console Input in VB.NET

Our first **Ira** program is not too useful, because the data are hardcoded. To perform the calculation for different data, you would have to edit the source file and recompile. What we really want to do is allow the user of the program to enter the data at runtime.

Code Example

An easy, uniform way to do input for various data types is to read the data as a string and then convert it to the desired data type. Use the **ReadLine** method of the **System.Console** class to read in a string. Use the **ToXxxx** methods of the **System.Convert** class to convert the data to the type you need. This can be seen in the **Ira\Step2** example.

```
Console.Write("amount: ")
Dim data As String = Console.ReadLine()
amount = Convert.ToDecimal(data)
```

Using Console Input to Pause

We mentioned earlier in the chapter that if you run a Visual Studio console application under the debugger, the console window will close automatically when the program exits. If you want to keep the window open, you can place a **ReadLine** statement at the end of your **Main** procedure. The program **HelloWithPause** provides an illustration.

```
Sub Main()
    Console.WriteLine("Hello, world")
    Console.Write("Press Enter to exit")
    Dim str As String = Console.ReadLine()
End Sub
```

Code Example

Although console input in VB.NET is fairly simple, we can make it even easier using object-oriented programming. We can encapsulate the details of input in an easy-to-use wrapper class, **InputWrapper** (which is not part of VB.NET or the .NET Framework class library, and was created for this book).

USING THE INPUTWRAPPER CLASS

In VB.NET, you instantiate a class by using the **New** keyword.

```
Dim iw As InputWrapper = New InputWrapper()
```

This code creates the object instance **iw** of the **InputWrapper** class.

Code
Example

The **InputWrapper** class wraps interactive input for several basic data types. The supported data types are **int**, **double**, **decimal**, and **string**. Methods **getInt**, **getDouble**, **getDecimal**, and **getString** are provided to read those types from the command line. A prompt string is passed as an input parameter. The directory **InputWrapper** contains the files **InputWrapper.vb**, which implements the class, and **TestInputWrapper.vb**, which tests the class. (For convenience, we provide the file **InputWrapper.vb** in each project where we use it.)

You can use the **InputWrapper** class without knowing its implementation. With such encapsulation, complex functionality can be hidden by an easy-to-use interface. (A listing of the **InputWrapper** class is in the next section.)

Here is the code for **Ira\Step2**. We read in the deposit amount, the interest rate, and the number of years, and we compute the IRA accumulation year by year. The first input is done directly, and then we use the **Input-Wrapper** class. The bolded code illustrates how to use the **InputWrapper** class. Instantiate an **InputWrapper** object **iw** by using **new**. Prompt for and obtain input data by calling the appropriate **getXXX** method.

```
' Ira.vb - Step 2

Imports System

Module Ira
   Public Sub Main()
      Dim iw As InputWrapper = New InputWrapper()
      Dim amount As Decimal      ' annual deposit amount
      Dim rate As Decimal        ' interest rate
      Dim years As Integer       ' number of years
      Dim total As Decimal       ' total accumulation
      Dim interest As Decimal    ' interest in a year
      Console.Write("amount: ")
      Dim data As String = Console.ReadLine()
      amount = Convert.ToDecimal(data)
      rate = iw.getDecimal("rate: ")
      years = iw.getInt("years: ")
      total = 0D
      Console.WriteLine( _
         "{0,4} {1,12} {2,12} {3,12}", _
         "Year", "Amount", "Interest", "Total")
      Dim i As Integer = 1
      While i <= years
         interest = total * rate
         total += amount + interest
         Console.WriteLine( _
            "{0, -4} {1, 12:C} {2, 12:C} {3, 12:C}", _
            i, amount, interest, total)
         i += 1
```

```
      End While
      Console.WriteLine( _
         "   Total using formula = {0}", _
         IraTotal(years, rate, amount))
   End Sub
   Private Function IraTotal(ByVal years As Integer, _
    ByVal rate As Double, ByVal amount As Double) As Double
      Dim total As Double = _
         amount * (Math.Pow(1 + rate, years) - 1) / rate
      Dim total_in_cents As Long = _
         Math.Round(total * 100)
      total = total_in_cents / 100
      Return total
   End Function
End Module
```

INPUTWRAPPER CLASS IMPLEMENTATION

The **InputWrapper** class is implemented in the file **InputWrapper.vb**. You should find the code reasonably intuitive, given what you already know about classes.

```
' InputWrapper.vb
'
' Class to wrap simple stream input
' Datatype supported:
'      int
'      double
'      decimal
'      string

Imports System

class InputWrapper
    Public Function getInt(ByVal prompt As String) _
     As Integer
        Console.Write(prompt)
        Dim buf As String = Console.ReadLine()
        Return Convert.ToInt32(buf)
    End Function
    Public Function getDouble(ByVal prompt As String) _
     As Double
        Console.Write(prompt)
        Dim buf As String = Console.ReadLine()
        Return Convert.ToDouble(buf)
    End Function
    Public Function getDecimal(ByVal prompt As String) _
     As Decimal
        Console.Write(prompt)
        Dim buf As String = Console.ReadLine()
        Return Convert.ToDecimal(buf)
```

```
      End Function
      Public Function getString(ByVal prompt As String) _
       As String
          Console.Write(prompt)
          Dim buf As String = Console.ReadLine()
          Return buf
      End Function
End Class
```

Note that, unlike the method **IraTotal**, the methods of the **InputWrap-per** class are used outside of the class so they are marked as *public*.

If bad input data is presented, an *exception* will be thrown. Exceptions are discussed in Chapter 5.

Classes

In this section we carefully examine the VB.NET *class*, which is fundamental to programming in VB.NET. For illustration we introduce two classes, **Customer** and **Hotel**, which will be elaborated in a case study that is used throughout the book. We will introduce the case study itself in Chapter 5.

Classes as Structured Data

VB.NET defines primitive data types that are built into the language. Data types, such as **Integer** and **Decimal**, can be used to represent simple data. VB.NET provides the *class* mechanism to represent more complex forms of data. Through a class, you can build up structured data out of simpler elements, which are called data members, or *fields*. (See **TestCustomer\Step0**.)

```
' Customer.vb  - Step 0 (same as Step 1)

Public Class Customer
    Public CustomerId As Integer
    Public FirstName As String
    Public LastName As String
    Public EmailAddress As String
    Public Sub New( _
     ByVal first As String, _
     ByVal last As String, _
     ByVal email As String)
       FirstName = first
       LastName = last
       EmailAddress = email
    End Sub
End Class
```

Customer is now a new data type. A Customer class object has a **CustomerId**, a **FirstName**, a **LastName**, and an **EmailAddress**.

CLASSES AND OBJECTS

A class represents a "kind of," or type of, data. It is somewhat analogous to the built-in types like **Integer** and **Decimal**. A class can be thought of as a template from which individual instances can be created. An instance of a class is called an object. The fields, such as **CustomerId** and **FirstName** in our example, are sometimes also called *instance variables.*

REFERENCES

There is a fundamental distinction between the primitive data types, such as **Integer**, and the extended data types that can be created using classes. When you declare a variable of a primitive data, you are allocating memory and creating the actual instance. This is because the variable itself contains its own data value.

```
Dim x as Integer '4 bytes of memory have been allocated
```

When you declare a variable of a class type (an *object reference*), you are only obtaining memory for a *reference* to an object of the class type. No memory is allocated for the object itself, which may be quite large. This behavior is identical to what happens in Java.

```
'cust is a reference to a Customer object
Dim cust As Customer
' The object itself does not yet exist
```

CONSTRUCTORS

Through a constructor, you can initialize individual objects in any way you wish. Besides initializing instance data, you can perform other appropriate initializations (e.g., open a file).

A constructor is like a special method that is automatically called when an object is created via the **New** keyword. A constructor

- has no return type (i.e., a subroutine)
- has the name **New**
- should usually have **public** access
- may take parameters, which are passed when invoking **New**

You use the **New** keyword to instantiate object instances, and you pass desired values as parameters.

DEFAULT CONSTRUCTOR

If you do not define a constructor in your class, VB.NET will implicitly create one for you. It is called the *default constructor* and takes no arguments. The default constructor will assign instance data, using any assignments in the class definition. Fields without an initializer are assigned default values (0 for numerical data types, empty string for **String**, and so on.) The default constructor is called when an object instance is created with **New** and no parameters. If you provide code for any constructor in your class, you must explicitly define a default constructor with no arguments, if you want one.

INSTANTIATING AND USING AN OBJECT

You instantiate an object by the **New** operator, which will cause a constructor to be invoked.

```
cust = New Customer( _
    "Rocket", _
    "Squirrel", _
    "rocky@frosbitefalls.com")
' Customer object now exists and cust is a reference to it
```

Once an object exists, you work with it, including accessing its fields and methods. Our simple **Customer** class at this point has no methods, only four fields. You access fields and methods using a dot.

cust.CustomerId = 1 ' all fields have now been assigned

TestCustomer\Step0 provides a simple test program to exercise the **Customer** class. Note that an unassigned field of a class receives a default value, such as 0, when an object is instantiated.

ASSIGNING OBJECT REFERENCES

Code
Example

TestCustomer\Step1 provides a more complete test program to exercise the **Customer** class. Two object instances are created, an assignment is made of one object reference to another, and a field is assigned a value.

```
' TestCustomer.vb - Step1

Imports System

Module TestCustomer
    Public Sub Main()
        Dim cust1, cust2 As Customer
        cust1 = New Customer( _
            "Rocket", _
            "Squirrel", _
            "rocky@frosbitefalls.com")
        cust1.CustomerId = 1
        cust2 = New Customer( _
            "Bullwinkle", _
            "Moose", _
            "moose@wossamotta.edu")
```

```
        cust2.CustomerId = 2
        ShowCustomer("cust1", cust1)
        ShowCustomer("cust2", cust2)
        cust1 = cust2 ' cust1, cust2 refer to same object
        cust1.EmailAddress = "bob@podunk.edu"
        ShowCustomer("cust1", cust1)
        ShowCustomer("cust2", cust2)
    End Sub
    Private Sub ShowCustomer( _
      ByVal label As String, ByVal cust As Customer)
        Console.WriteLine("---- {0} ----", label)
        Console.WriteLine( _
            "CustomerId = {0}", cust.CustomerId)
        Console.WriteLine( _
            "FirstName = {0}", cust.FirstName)
        Console.WriteLine( _
            "LastName = {0}", cust.LastName)
        Console.WriteLine( _
            "EmailAddress = {0}", cust.EmailAddress)
    End Sub
End Module
```

Figure 3–9 shows the object references **cust1** and **cust2** and the data they refer to after the objects have been instantiated and the **CustomerId** field has been assigned.

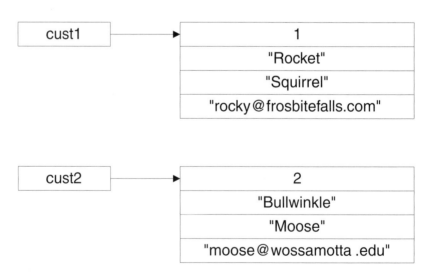

cust1 →	1
	"Rocket"
	"Squirrel"
	"rocky@frosbitefalls.com"

cust2 →	2
	"Bullwinkle"
	"Moose"
	"moose@wossamotta .edu"

FIGURE 3–9   *Two object references and the data they refer to.*

When you assign an object variable, you are assigning only the reference; *there is no copying of data.*[3] Figure 3–10 shows both object references and their data after the assignment:

```
cust1 = cust2 ' cust1, cust2 refer to same object
```

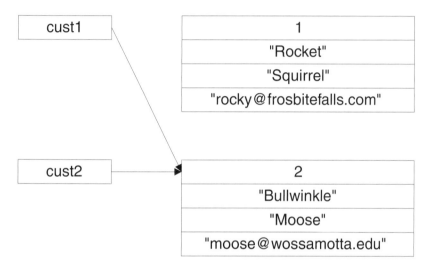

FIGURE 3–10 *Two references refer to the same data.*

Now consider what happens when you assign a new value to a field of one object,

```
cust1.EmailAddress = "bob@podunk.edu"
```

You will now see the same data through both object references, since they refer to the same object. Here is the output from running **TestCustomer\Step1**.

```
---- cust1 ----
CustomerId = 1
FirstName = Rocket
LastName = Squirrel
EmailAddress = rocky@frosbitefalls.com
---- cust2 ----
CustomerId = 2
FirstName = Bullwinkle
LastName = Moose
EmailAddress = moose@wossamotta.edu
```

3. C and C++ programmers will recognize assignment of references as similar to assignment of pointers.

```
---- cust1 ----
CustomerId = 2
FirstName = Bullwinkle
LastName = Moose
EmailAddress = bob@podunk.edu
---- cust2 ----
CustomerId = 2
FirstName = Bullwinkle
LastName = Moose
EmailAddress = bob@podunk.edu
```

GARBAGE COLLECTION

Through the assignment of a reference, an object may become orphaned. Objects may also be orphaned when they pass out of scope (i.e., when a local reference variable is lost as the method it is declared in returns). Such an orphan object (or "garbage") takes up memory in the computer, which can now never be referenced. In Figure 3–2 the customer with **CustomerId** of 1 is now garbage.

The CLR automatically reclaims the memory of unreferenced objects. This process is known as *garbage collection*. Garbage collection takes up some execution time, but it is a great convenience for programmers, helping to avoid a common program error known as a *memory leak*.[4] Garbage collection is discussed in more detail in Chapter 10.

Methods

Typically, a class will specify *behavior* as well as data. A class *encapsulates* data and behavior in a single entity. A method specifies the behavior and consists of either a **Function** or a **Sub** defined within the class, with the following characteristics:

- An optional access specifier, typically **Public** or **Private**
- A return type for a **Function**, (a **Sub** is used if no data is returned)
- A method name, which can be any legal VB.NET identifier
- A parameter list, enclosed by parentheses, which specifies data that is passed to the method (can be empty if no data is passed)
- A method body, enclosed by **Function** and **End Function** or **Sub** and **End Sub**, which contains the code that the method will execute

Here is an example of a method in the **Hotel** class taken from the **Hotel.vb** source file in the **TestHotel\Step1** example.

Code
Example

---

4. Memory leaks have always plagued C and C++ programmers, but languages such as VB.NET, previous versions of Visual Basic, and Java have been spared this nightmare.

```
Public Sub RaisePrice(ByVal amount As Decimal)
    rate += amount
End Sub
```

In this example there is no data returned, so it is implemented with a **Sub**. The method name is **RaisePrice**, the parameter list consists of a single parameter of type **Decimal**, and the body contains one line of code that increments the member variable **rate** by the value that is passed in as a parameter.

PUBLIC AND PRIVATE

Fields and methods of a VB.NET class can be specified as **Public** or **Private**. Normally, you declare fields as **Private**. A private field can be accessed only from within the methods defined in the same class, not from outside the class.

```
Public Class Hotel
    Private city As String
    Private name As String
    Private number As Integer = 50
    Private rate As Decimal
    . . .
```

Note that in VB.NET you can initialize fields where they are declared, as shown in the case of the field named **number**.

Methods may be declared as either **Public** or **Private**. Public methods can be called from outside of the class and are often used to perform calculations and to manipulate private field data. You may also provide public "accessor" methods to provide access to private fields.

```
    . . .
    Public Function GetRate() As Decimal
        Return rate
    End Function
    Public Sub SetRate(ByVal val As Decimal)
        rate = val
    End Sub
    . . .
```

You may also have private methods, which can be thought of as helper functions for use within the class. Rather than duplicating code in several places, you may create a private method, which will be called wherever it is needed internally. An example is the **ShowHotel** method in **TestHotel.vb**.

THE KEYWORD ME

Sometimes it is convenient within code for a method to be able to access the current object reference. VB.NET defines the keyword **Me** (similar to the keyword **this** in C++, Java, and C#), which is a special variable that always refers to the current object instance. With **Me** you can then refer to the instance variables, but usually, you can simply refer to them directly without using **Me** explicitly. The **Hotel** class has a constructor to initialize its instance data with values passed as parameters. We can make use of the same names for parameters and fields and remove ambiguity by using the **Me** variable explicitly. Here is the code for the **Hotel** constructor:

```
Public Sub New( _
 ByVal city As String, _
 ByVal name As String, _
 ByVal number As Integer, _
 ByVal rate As Decimal)
    Me.city = city
    Me.name = name
    Me.number = number
    Me.rate = rate
End Sub
```

SAMPLE PROGRAM

Code Example

The program **TestHotel\Step1** illustrates all the features we have discussed so far. Here is the class definition:

```
' Hotel.vb - Step 1

Public Class Hotel
    Private city As String
    Private name As String
    Private number As Integer = 50
    Private rate As Decimal
    Public Sub New( _
     ByVal city As String, _
     ByVal name As String, _
     ByVal number As Integer, _
     ByVal rate As Decimal)
        Me.city = city
        Me.name = name
        Me.number = number
        Me.rate = rate
    End Sub
    Public Sub New()
    End Sub
    Public Function GetCity() As String
        Return city
    End Function
    Public Function GetName() As String
        Return name
    End Function
    Public Function GetNumber() As Integer
        Return number
```

```
        End Function
    Public Sub SetNumber(ByVal val As Integer)
        number = val
    End Sub
    Public Function GetRate() As Decimal
        Return rate
    End Function
    Public Sub SetRate(ByVal val As Decimal)
        rate = val
    End Sub
    Public Sub RaisePrice(ByVal amount As Decimal)
        rate += amount
    End Sub
End Class
```

Here is the test program:

```
' TestHotel.vb - Step 1

Imports System

Module TestHotel
    Sub Main()
        Dim generic As Hotel = New Hotel()
        ShowHotel(generic)
        Dim ritz As Hotel = New Hotel( _
            "Atlanta", "Ritz", 100, 95D)
        ShowHotel(ritz)
        ritz.RaisePrice(50D)
        ritz.SetNumber(125)
        ShowHotel(ritz)
    End Sub
    Private Sub ShowHotel(ByVal hotel As Hotel)
        Console.WriteLine( _
            "{0} {1}: number = {2}, rate = {3:C}", _
            hotel.GetCity(), hotel.GetName(), _
            hotel.GetNumber(), hotel.GetRate())
    End Sub
End Module
```

Here is the output:

```
: number = 50, rate = $0.00
Atlanta Ritz: number = 100, rate = $95.00
Atlanta Ritz: number = 125, rate = $145.00
```

Properties

The encapsulation principle leads us to typically store data in private fields
and to provide access to this data through public accessor methods that allow

us to set and get values. For example, in the **Hotel** class we provide a method **GetCity** to access the private field **city**. You don't need any special syntax; you can simply provide methods and call these methods what you want, typically **GetXXX** and **SetXXX**.

VB.NET provides a special *property* syntax that simplifies client code. You can access a private field as if it were a public member. Here is an example of using the **Number** property of the **Hotel** class.

```
ritz.Number = 125
Console.WriteLine( _
    "There are now {0} rooms", ritz.Number)
```

Code
Example

As you can see, the syntax using the property is a little more concise. Properties were popularized in Visual Basic and are now part of .NET and available in selected other .NET languages, such as C# and managed C++. The program **TestHotel\Step2** illustrates implementing and using several properties, **City**, **Name**, **Number** and **Rate**. The first two properties are read-only (only **Get** defined), and the other properties are read/write (both **Get** and **Set**). It is also possible to have a write-only property (only **Set** defined). Here is the code for the properties **Name** (read-only) and **Number** (read-write) in the second version of the **Hotel** class. Notice the syntax and the VB.NET keyword **Value** to indicate the new value of the field. The private fields are now spelled with an "m_" prefix (short for member variable) to distinguish them from the corresponding property names, preventing a compiler error.

```
' Hotel.vb - Step 2

Public Class Hotel
    Private m_City As String
    Private m_Name As String
    Private m_Number As Integer
    Private m_Rate As Decimal
    ...
    Public ReadOnly Property Name() As String
       Get
           Name = m_Name
       End Get
    End Property
    Public Property Number() As Integer
       Get
           Number = m_Number
       End Get
       Set(ByVal Value As Integer)
          m_Number = Value
       End Set
    End Property
    ...
```

Shared Fields and Methods

In VB.NET, a field normally is defined on a *per-instance* basis, with a unique value for each object instance of the class. Sometimes it is useful to have a single value associated with the entire class as a whole. This type of field is called a **Shared** field, or a class variable as opposed to an instance variable. Like instance data members, shared data members can be either **Public** or **Private**. To access a public shared member, you use the dot notation, but in place of an object reference before the dot, you use the name of the class.

SHARED METHODS

A method may also be declared as **Shared**. A shared method can be called without instantiating the class. If you declare the **Main** method in a module, you do not declare it as shared, since all methods in a module are inherently shared; however, if you declare a **Main** method in a class, you must declare it as shared. This allows the runtime system to call **Main** without instantiating an object.

You call a shared method by using the dot notation, with the class name in front of the dot. You can call a shared method without an instance, and a shared method can only access shared data members and not instance data members.

Shared methods may be declared **Public** or **Private**. A private shared method, like other private methods, may be used as a helper function within a class, but not called from outside the class.

SAMPLE PROGRAM

Our previous **Customer** class relied on the user of the class to assign a **CustomerId** for the customer. A better approach is to encapsulate the assignment of this field within the class itself, so that a unique ID will be automatically generated every time a new **Customer** object is created. It is easy to implement such a scheme by using a shared field **nextCustId**, which is used to assign a new ID. Every time the ID is assigned, **nextCustId** is incremented. **TestCustomer\Step2** demonstrates this solution and also illustrates the use of a shared method. Here is the code defining the **Customer** class:

Code
Example

```
' Customer.vb - Step 2

Public Class Customer
    Public CustomerId As Integer
    Public FirstName As String
    Public LastName As String
    Public EmailAddress As String
    Private Shared nextCustId As Integer = 1
    Public Sub New( _
     ByVal first As String, _
```

```
    ByVal last As String, _
    ByVal email As String)
      CustomerId = nextCustId
      nextCustId += 1
      FirstName = first
      LastName = last
      EmailAddress = email
  End Sub
  Public Shared Function GetNextId() As Integer
      Return nextCustId
  End Function
End Class
```

Here is the test program:

```
' TestCustomer.vb - Step 2

Imports System

Module TestCustomer
    Sub Main()
        Console.WriteLine("next id = {0}", _
        Customer.GetNextId())
        Dim cust1, cust2 As Customer
        cust1 = new Customer("John", "Doe", _
            "john@rocky.com")
        cust2 = new Customer("Mary", "Smith", _
            "mary@moose.edu")
        ShowCustomer("cust1", cust1)
        ShowCustomer("cust2", cust2)
    End Sub
    Private Sub ShowCustomer( _
     ByVal label As String, ByVal cust As Customer)
     ...
```

Note that the shared method **GetNextId** is accessed through the *class* **Customer** and not through an object reference such as **cust1**. Note the fact that **Main** is an implicitly shared method, since it is a member of a module, and is invoked by the runtime without an instance of an object being created. Here is the output from the program:

```
next id = 1
---- cust1 ----
CustomerId = 1
FirstName = John
LastName = Doe
EmailAddress = john@rocky.com
---- cust2 ----
CustomerId = 2
FirstName = Mary
LastName = Smith
EmailAddress = mary@moose.edu
```

Shared Constructor

Besides having shared fields and shared methods, a class may also have a *shared constructor*. A shared constructor is called only once, before any object instances have been created. A shared constructor is defined by prefixing the constructor with **Shared**. A shared constructor must take no parameters and has no access modifier (such as **Public** or **Private**).

In some languages, such as C++, where there can be global variables not attached to any class, you may initialize a library through the constructor for a global object. In VB.NET there are no such freestanding global objects, but you can achieve similar initialization through use of a shared constructor. As a somewhat whimsical example of a shared constructor, consider the **SharedWorld** program, which provides an alternative implementation of "Hello, World." This program displays the text Hello, World, proving that the shared constructor automatically executes first, displaying the text Hello, . Then later, the call to the **World** method displays the word World.

Code
Example

```
' SharedWorld.vb

Public Class Hello
    Shared Sub New()
        System.Console.Write("Hello, ")
    End Sub
    Public Shared Sub World()
        System.Console.WriteLine("World")
    End Sub
End Class

Module Module1
    Sub Main()
        Hello.World()
    End Sub
End Module
```

Constant and Read Only Fields

If you want to make sure that a variable or field always has the same value, you can assign the value via an initializer and use the **Const** modifier. After its one-time initialization at runtime, the value cannot be changed. You can also define a field or property to be **ReadOnly**, with the same effect.

The program **ConstantHotel** illustrates the use of both **Const** and **ReadOnly**. In both cases, you will get a compiler error if you try to modify the value after it has been initialized.

```
' ConstantHotel.vb

Public Class Hotel
    Public Const rate As Decimal = 100D
```

```
    Public ReadOnly name As String
    Public Sub New(ByVal name As String)
        Me.name = name
    End Sub
End Class
```

Here is the test program:

```
' TestHotel.vb

Imports System

Module TestHotel
    Sub Main()
        Dim Hotel As Hotel = New Hotel("Ritz")
        Console.WriteLine("rate = {0:C}", Hotel.rate)
        ' Hotel.rate = 150D         // illegal
        Console.WriteLine("hotel name = {0}", Hotel.name)
        ' hotel.name = "Sheraton" // illegal
    End Sub
End Module
```

Here is the output:

```
rate = $100.00
hotel name = Ritz
```

VB.NET Type System

In VB.NET, there is a fundamental distinction between *value* types and *reference* types. Value types have storage allocated immediately on the stack when the variable is declared. Reference types have storage allocated on the heap when they are instantiated, not when they are just declared, and the variable is only a reference to the actual object containing the data.

We have been looking at classes in some detail. A class defines a reference type. In this section we survey the entire VB.NET type system, including simple types such as **Integer** and **Decimal**. In VB.NET, a **Structure** has many similarities to a **Class**, but it is a value type. This means that assigning from one structure variable to another causes the entire structure to be copied, rather than just a reference being copied. Another important kind of value type in VB.NET is an **Enum**, which defines a related set of constants (i.e., an enumeration).

We will examine several other important types, including string, array, interface, and delegate. We will discuss the default values that get assigned to variables when there is not an explicit initialization. We will see that all types in VB.NET are rooted in a fundamental base class called **Object**. In VB.NET, "everything is an object," and value types are transparently converted to object references as needed through a process known as *boxing*. The inverse process, *unboxing*, returns an object to the value type from which it came.

Overview of Types in VB.NET

In VB.NET there are two kinds of types:
- Value types
- Reference types

VALUE TYPES

Value types directly contain their data. Each variable of a value type has its own copy of the data. Value types typically are allocated on the stack and are automatically destroyed when the variable goes out of scope. Value types include the simple types like **Integer** and **Decimal**, as well as structures, and enumeration types.

REFERENCE TYPES

Reference types do not contain data directly but only refer to data. Variables of reference types store references to data, called objects. Two different variables can reference the same object. Reference types are allocated on the *managed heap* and eventually get destroyed through a process known as *garbage collection*.

Reference types include class types, array types, interfaces, and delegates.

Value Types

In this section we survey all the value types, including the simple types, structures, and enumerations.

SIMPLE TYPES

The simple data types (also known as the primitive data types) are general-purpose value data types, including numeric, character, boolean, and date types.

- The **SByte** data type is an 8-bit signed integer.
- The **Byte** data type is an 8-bit unsigned integer.
- The **Short** data type is a 16-bit signed integer.
- The **Integer** data type is a 32-bit signed integer.
- The **Long** data type is a 64-bit signed integer.
- The **Char** data type is a Unicode character (16 bits).
- The **Single** data type is a single-precision floating point.

- The **Double** data type is a double-precision floating point.
- The **Decimal** data type is a decimal type with 28 significant digits (typically used for financial calculations).
- The **Boolean** data type is a Boolean (**true** or **false**).
- The **Date** data type is a represents a date and time.

TYPES IN SYSTEM NAMESPACE

There is an exact correspondence between the simple VB.NET types and types in the **System** namespace. VB.NET reserved words are simply aliases for the corresponding types in the **System** namespace. Table 3–3 shows this correspondence.

TABLE 3–3   *Types in VB.NET and the System Namespace*

VB.NET Reserved Word	Type in System Namespace
SByte	System.SByte
Byte	System.Byte
Short	System.Int16
Integer	System.Int32
Long	System.Int64
Char	System.Char
Single	System.Single
Double	System.Double
Decimal	System.Decimal
Boolean	System.Boolean
Date	System.DateTime

STRUCTURES

A **Structure** is a value type, which can group heterogeneous types together. It can also have methods. The key difference between a class and a structure is that a class is a *reference* type and a structure a *value* type. A class must be instantiated explicitly using **New**. The new instance is created on the heap, and memory is managed by the system through a garbage-collection process. A new instance of a structure is created on the stack, and the instance will be deallocated when it goes out of scope.

There are different semantics for assignment, whether done explicitly or via call by value mechanism in a method call. For a class, you will get a second object reference, and both object references refer to the same data. For a structure, you will get a completely independent copy of the data in the structure.

A structure is a convenient data structure to use for moving data across a process or machine boundary, and we will use structures in our case study. For example, we will use a struct to represent customer data

```
Public Structure CustomerListItem
    Public CustomerId As Integer
    Public FirstName As String
    Public LastName As String
    Public EmailAddress As String
End Structure
```

ENUMERATION TYPES

Another kind of value type is an *enumeration* type. An enumeration type is a distinct type with named constants. Every enumeration type has an underlying type, which is one of the following.

- **Byte**
- **Short**
- **Integer**
- **Long**

An enumeration type is defined through an **Enum** declaration.

```
Public Enum BookingStatus As Byte
    HotelNotFound        ' 0 implicitly
    RoomsNotAvailable    ' 1 implicitly
    Ok = 5               ' explicit value
End Enum
```

If the type is not specified, **Integer** is used. By default, the first **Enum** member is assigned the value 0, the second member 1, and so on. Constant values can be explicitly assigned.

You can make use of an enumeration type by declaring a variable of the type indicated in the **Enum** declaration (e.g., **BookingStatus**). You can refer to the enumerated values by using the dot notation. Here is some illustrative code:

```
...
Dim status As BookingStatus
status = hotel.ReserveRoom(name, dateTime)
If status = BookingStatus.HotelNotFound Then
   Console.WriteLine("Hotel not found")
End If
...
```

Reference Types

A variable of a reference type does not directly contain its data but instead provides a *reference* to the data stored in the heap. In VB.NET, there are the following kinds of reference types:

- Classes (including **String** and **Object**)
- Arrays (even if the elements are a value type)
- Interfaces
- Delegates

Reference types can have the special value **Nothing**, which indicates the absence of an instance. VB.NET uses the **Nothing** keyword for this purpose, rather than the VB 6.0 keywords **Empty** and **Null**, which are no longer supported.

We have already examined classes in some detail, and we will look at arrays in Chapter 4. Interfaces and delegates will be covered in Chapter 6.

CLASS TYPES

A class type defines a data type that can have fields, methods, constants, and other kinds of members. Class types support *inheritance*. Through inheritance a derived class can extend or specialize a base class. We will discuss inheritance in Chapter 5.

Two classes in the .NET Framework class library are particularly important: **Object** and **String**.

OBJECT

The **Object** class type is the ultimate base type for all types in all .NET languages. Every VB.NET reference type derives directly or indirectly from **Object**. The fully qualified name is **System.Object**. It has methods such as **ToString**, **Equals**, and **Finalize**, which we will study later.

STRING

The **String** class encapsulates a Unicode character string. The string type is a **NotInheritable** class. (A **NotInheritable** class is one that cannot be used as the base class for any other classes.)

The **String** class inherits directly from the root **Object** class. String literals are defined using double quotes. There are useful built-in methods for **String**. For now, note that the **Equals** method can be used to test for equality of strings.

```
Dim a As String = "hello"
If a.Equals("hello") Then
   Console.WriteLine("equal")
Else
```

```
        Console.WriteLine("not equal")
     End If
```

There are also overloaded[5] operators for comparing strings:

```
If a = "hello" Then
    . . .
```

We will study **String** in detail later in Chapter 4.

Default Values

Several kinds of variables are automatically initialized to default values:

- Shared variables
- Instance variables of class and struct instances
- Local variables
- Array elements

The default value of a variable of reference type is **Nothing**. For simple types (primitive value types) the default field values correspond to a bit pattern of all zeros:

- For **Integer** types, the default value is 0.
- For **Char**, the default value is the Unicode value zero.
- For **Single**, the default value is 0.0F.
- For **Double**, the default value is 0.0R.
- For **Decimal**, the default value is 0.0D.
- For **Boolean**, the default value is **False**.

For an **Enum** type, the default value is 0. For a **Structure** type, the default value is obtained by setting all value type fields to their default values, as described above, and all reference type fields to **Nothing**.

Boxing and Unboxing

One of the strong features of .NET is that is has a unified type system. Every type, including the simple built-in types such as **Integer**, derives from **System.Object**. In .NET, "everything is an object."

A language such as Smalltalk also has such a feature but pays the price of inefficiency for simple types. Languages such as C++ and Java treat simple built-in types differently from objects, thus obtaining efficiency but at the cost of a non-unified type system.

.NET languages, such as VB.NET, enjoy the best of both worlds through a process known as *boxing*. Boxing converts a value type such as **Integer** or

---

5. An operator is overloaded if it applies to different kinds of data types. The = operator is used for numerical data types and also for the **String** data type.

a **Structure** to an object reference and this is done implicitly and automatically. *Unboxing* converts a boxed value type (stored on the heap) back to an unboxed simple value (stored on the stack). Unboxing is done through a type conversion known as a type cast. Specific type casts can be accomplished using the **CObj**, **CByte**, **CShort**, **CInt**, **CLng**, **CSng**, **CDbl**, **CDec**, **CChar**, **CBool**, **CDate**, and **CStr** keywords. In addition, **AscW** and **ChrW** can be used to convert between **Char** and **Integer** types. You can also use the general casting keyword **CType** to convert to an arbitrary type.

```
Dim x As Integer = 5
Dim o As Object = x ' boxing
x = CType(o, Integer) ' unboxing
```

Summary

In the first part of the chapter we provided an overview of VB.NET as a visual development environment and also explained the new feature of using VB.NET to create console applications. We then began a systematic but concise coverage of the essentials of the VB.NET language, which should equip you to start writing nontrivial programs. We surveyed variables, operators, control structures, formatting, methods, and input/output. We examined classes in detail, and we looked at some convenience features, such as properties. We covered the essentials of data types in VB.NET, which map to the Common Type System. We discussed the fundamental distinction between value and reference types, and saw how to convert between them using boxing and unboxing operations.

In the next chapter we will continue our study of VB.NET essentials by looking at strings, arrays, and at a number of utility functions.

VB.NET Essentials, Part II

*I*n this chapter we continue our coverage of VB.NET language essentials. VB.NET and the .NET Framework have the **String** class that represents immutable strings and the **StringBuilder** class that can be used for dynamically changing strings. We examine arrays in VB.NET and some operations provided by the **System.Array** class. We then cover some additional topics concerning methods, including parameter passing, variable-length parameter lists, method overloading, and operator overloading.

We next look at a number of utility functions provided in VB.NET. The **Microsoft.VisualBasic** namespace offers many of the functions that were previously built in to the language. Many other important utility functions are provided in the **System** namespace. A final brief section shows how to handle command-line arguments in VB.NET programs.

Strings

Characters and strings are very important data types in practical programming. VB.NET provides a **String** type in the **System** namespace. As a class, **String** is a reference type. The VB.NET compiler provides additional support to make working with strings more concise and intuitive. In this section we will first look at characters and then outline the main features of the **String** class. We will look at string input, at the additional support provided by VB.NET, and at the issues of string equality. The section that follows surveys some of the useful methods of the **String** class. The section after that discusses the **StringBuilder** class.

Characters

VB.NET provides the primitive data type **Char** to represent individual characters. A character literal is represented by a character enclosed in double quotes followed by the suffix C.

```
Dim ch1 As Char = "a"C
```

A VB.NET **Char** is represented internally as an unsigned two-byte integer. You can cast back and forth between **Char** and integer data types.

```
Dim ch1 As Char = "a"C ' ch1 is now 'a'
Dim n As Integer = AscW(ch1)
n += 1
ch1 = ChrW(n) ' ch1 is now 'b'
```

The relational operators **=**, **<**, **>**, and so on apply to **char**.

```
Dim ch1 As Char = "a"C
Dim ch2 As Char = "b"C
If ch1 < ch2 Then ' expression is True
    . . .
End If
If ch1 >= ch2 Then ' expression is False
    . . .
End If
```

ASCII AND UNICODE

Traditionally, a one-byte character code called ASCII has been used to represent characters. ASCII code is simple and compact. But ASCII cannot be employed to represent many different alphabets used throughout the world.

Modern computer systems usually use a two-byte character code called Unicode. Most modern (and several ancient) alphabets can be represented by Unicode characters. ASCII is a subset of Unicode, corresponding to the first 255 Unicode character codes. For more information on Unicode, you can visit the Web site *www.unicode.org*. VB.NET uses Unicode to represent characters and strings.

SPECIAL CHARACTERS

You can represent any Unicode character in a VB.NET program by using the **CChar** type conversion. You may use hexadecimal digits if it is convenient.

```
Dim ch1 As Char = ChrW(&H41) ' 41 (hex) is 65 (dec) or 'A'
```

A number of nonprinting characters can be handled, as well as characters like quotation marks that would be difficult to represent otherwise. A double-quote character can be represented as two double-quote characters within a literal string. For example, the code

```
Console.WriteLine("""Hello""")
```

will result in the output

```
"Hello"
```

Other difficult characters can be represented using their Unicode values. Table 4–1 shows the values for several such characters. For example, the following code will display the words "Hello" and "World" on separate output lines, since &HA represents the line feed character.

```
Dim str As String = "Hello" + ChrW(&HA) + "World"
Console.WriteLine(str)
```

There are also a number of Visual Basic constants of the form **vbXxxx** that you can use. For example, you can use **vbLf** as an alternative in the previous example.

```
Dim str As String = "Hello" + vbLf + "World"
```

These constants are in the **Microsoft.VisualBasic** namespace, which is discussed later in this chapter. This namespace is added by default to projects created in Visual Studio.

TABLE 4–1	*Some Character Code Values*	
Name	**Value**	**Visual Basic Constant**
Single quote	&H27	
Double quote	&H22	
Backslash	&H5C	
Null	&H0	vbNullChar
Alert	&H7	
Backspace	&H8	vbBack
Form feed	&HC	vbFormFeed
Line feed	&HA	vbLf
Carriage return	&HD	vbCr
New Line	&HD + &HA	VbLfCr or VbNewLine
Horizontal tab	&H9	vbTab
Vertical tab	&HB	vbVerticalTab

String Class

The **String** class inherits directly from **Object** and is a **NotInheritable** class, which means that you cannot further inherit from **String**. We will discuss inheritance and **NotInheritable** classes in Chapter 5. When a class is

NotInheritable, the compiler can perform certain optimizations to make methods in the class more efficient.

Instances of **String** are *immutable,* which means that once a string object is created, it cannot be changed during its lifetime. Operations that appear to modify a string actually return a new string object. If, for the sake of efficiency, you need to modify a string-like object directly, you can make use of the **StringBuilder** class, which we will discuss in a later section.

A string has a zero-based index accessed via its **Chars** indexed property, which can be used to access individual characters in a string. That means that the first character of the string **str** is **str.Chars(0)**, the second character is **str.Chars(1)**, and so on.

By default, comparison operations on strings are case-sensitive, although there is an overloaded version of the **Compare** method that permits case-insensitive comparisons.

The empty string (which is a string object containing no characters) is distinguished from a string reference set to **Nothing**. If a string has not been initialized, it will be **Nothing**. Any string, including the empty string, compares greater than a **Nothing** string reference. Two **Nothing** references compare equal to each other.

Language Support

The VB.NET language provides a number of features to make working with strings easier and more intuitive.

STRING LITERALS AND INITIALIZATION

Code
Example

You can define a **String** literal by enclosing a string of characters in double quotes. The proper way to initialize a string variable with a literal value is to supply the literal after an equals sign. You do not need to use **new** as you do with other data types. Here are some examples of string literals and initializing string variables. See the program **StringLiterals**.

```
Dim s1 As String = "bat"
Dim path As String = "c:\OI\NetVb\Chap04\Concat\"
Dim greeting As String = """Hello, world"""
Console.WriteLine(s1)
Console.WriteLine(path)
Console.WriteLine(greeting)
```

This produces the following output.

```
bat
c:\OI\NetVb\Chap04\Concat\
"Hello, world"
```

CONCATENATION

Code Example

The **String** class provides a method **Concat** for concatenating strings. In VB.NET, you can use the operators **&** and **&=** to perform concatenation. The program **Concat** illustrates string literals and concatenation.

```
' Concat.vb
'
' Demonstrates string literals and concatenation

Imports System

Module Concat
    Public Sub Main()
        Dim s1 As String = "bat"
        Console.WriteLine("s1 = {0}", s1)
        Dim s2 As String = "man"
        Console.WriteLine("s2 = {0}", s2)
        s1 &= s2
        Console.WriteLine(s1)
        Dim path1 As String = "c:\OI\NetVb\Chap04\Concat"
        Console.WriteLine("path1 = {0}", path1)
        Dim path As String = "c:\OI\NetVb\Chap04\Concat\"
        Dim file As String = "Concat.vb"
        path = path + file
        Console.WriteLine(path)
        Dim greeting As String = """Hello, world"""
        Console.WriteLine(greeting)
    End Sub
End Module
```

Here is the output:

```
s1 = bat
s2 = man
batman
path1 = c:\OI\ NetVb\Chap04\Concat
c:\OI\ NetVb\Chap04\Concat\Concat.vb
"Hello, world"
```

& and + for Concatenation

The proper string concatenation operator in VB.NET is &. Often, the + operator will work too, but not always. In some contexts when using + the compiler will attempt to convert the string to a numerical data type, and you will get an illegal cast exception. Always use & for string concatenation.

INDEX

You can extract an individual character from a string using the **Chars** indexed property and a zero-based index.

```
Dim s1 As String = "bat"
Dim ch As Char = s1.Chars(0) ' contains 'b'
```

RELATIONAL OPERATORS

In general, for reference types, the **=** operator checks if the *object references* are the same, not whether the contents of the memory locations referred to are the same. However, the **String** class overloads these operators so that the textual content of the strings is compared. The program **StringRelation** illustrates using these relational operators on strings.

Code
Example

```
' StringRelation.vb

Imports System

Module StringRelation
    Public Sub Main()
        Dim a1 As String = "hello"
        Dim a2 As String = "hello"
        Dim b As String = "HELLO"
        Dim c As String = "goodbye"
        Console.WriteLine("{0} = {1}: {2}", a1, a2, a1=a2)
        Console.WriteLine("{0} = {1}: {2}", a1, b, a1=b)
        Console.WriteLine("{0} <> {1}: {2}", a1, c, a1<>c)
        Console.WriteLine("{0} < {1}: {2}", a1, c, a1<c)
    End Sub
End Module
```

The output of this program follows.

```
hello = hello: True
hello = HELLO: False
hello <> goodbye: True
hello < goodbye: False
```

String Equality

To fully understand issues of string equality, you should be aware of how the compiler stores strings. When string literals are encountered, they are entered into an internal table of string identities. If a second literal is encountered with the same string data, an object reference will be returned to the existing string in the table; no second copy will be made. As a result of this compiler optimization, the two object references will be the same, as represented in Figure 4–1.

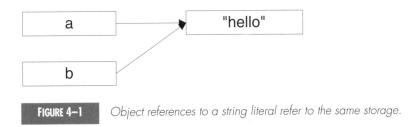

FIGURE 4–1 *Object references to a string literal refer to the same storage.*

You should not be misled by this fact to conclude that two object references to the same string data will always be coalesced into the same object. If the contents of the strings get determined at runtime, for example, by the user inputting the data, the compiler has no way of knowing that the second string should have an identical object reference. Hence you will have two distinct object references, which happen to refer to the same data, as illustrated in Figure 4–2.

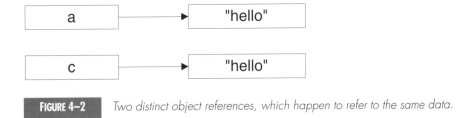

FIGURE 4–2 *Two distinct object references, which happen to refer to the same data.*

When strings are checked for equality, either through the relational operator **=** or through the **Equals** method, a comparison is made of the *contents* of the strings, not of the object references. So in both the previous cases the strings **a** and **b** will check out as equal if they contain the same data, even if they are distinct objects. You have to be more careful with other reference types, where reference equality is *not* the same as content equality.

String Comparison

The fundamental way to compare strings for equality is to use the **Equals** method of the **String** class. There are several overloaded versions of this function, including a shared version that takes two **String** parameters and a non-shared version that takes one **String** parameter that is compared with the current instance. These methods perform a case-sensitive comparison of the contents of the strings. A **Boolean** value of **True** or **False** is returned.

If you wish to perform a case-insensitive comparison, you may use the **Compare** method. This method has several overloaded versions, all of them

shared. Two strings, s1 and s2, are compared. An integer is returned express-
ing the lexical relationship between the two strings, as shown in Table 4–2.

TABLE 4–2	*Return Values of the Compare Method*
Relationship	**Return Value**
s1 less than s2	negative integer
s1 equal to s2	0
s1 greater than s2	positive integer

A third parameter allows you to control the case sensitivity of the comparison. If you use only two parameters, a case-sensitive comparison is performed. The optional third parameter is a **Boolean**. A value of **False** calls for
a case-sensitive comparison, and a value of **True** calls for ignoring case.

Code
Example

See the program **StringCompare** for an illustration of a number of
comparisons, using both the **Equal** and **Compare** methods.

```
' StringCompare.vb

Imports System

Module StringCompare
    Public Sub Main()
        Dim a1 As String = "hello"
        Dim a2 As String = "hello"
        Dim b As String = "HELLO"
        Dim c As String = "goodbye"
        Console.WriteLine("{0}.Equals({1}): {2}", _
            a1, a2, a1.Equals(a2))
        Console.WriteLine("String.Equals({0},{1}): {2}", _
            a1, a2, String.Equals(a1, a2))
        Console.WriteLine("Case sensitive...")
        Console.WriteLine("String.Compare({0},{1}): {2}", _
            a1, b, String.Compare(a1, b))
        Console.WriteLine("Case insensitive...")
        Console.WriteLine( _
            "String.Compare({0},{1},true): {2}", _
            a1, b, String.Compare(a1, b, True))
        Console.WriteLine("Order relation...")
        Console.WriteLine("String.Compare({0},{1}): {2}", _
            a1, c, String.Compare(a1, c))
        Console.WriteLine("String.Compare({0},{1}): {2}", _
            c, a1, String.Compare(c, a1))
    End Sub
End Module
```

Here is the output:

```
hello.Equals(hello): True
String.Equals(hello,hello): True
Case sensitive...
String.Compare(hello,HELLO): -1
Case insensitive...
String.Compare(hello,HELLO,true): 0
Order relation...
String.Compare(hello,goodbye): 1
String.Compare(goodbye,hello): -1
```

String Input

The **Console** class has methods for inputting characters and strings. The **Read** method reads in a single character (as an **Integer**). The **ReadLine** method reads in a line of input, terminated by a carriage return, line feed, or combination, and will return a **String**. In general, the **ReadLine** method is the easier to use and synchronizes nicely with **Write** and **WriteLine**. The program **ReadStrings** illustrates reading in a first name, middle initial, and a last name. All input is done via **ReadLine**. The middle initial as a character is determined by extracting the character at position 0.

```
Imports System

Module ReadStrings
    Public Sub Main()
        Console.Write("First name: ")
        Dim first As String = Console.ReadLine()
        .Console.Write("Initial: ")
        Dim initial As String = Console.ReadLine()
        Dim ch As Char = initial.Chars(0)
        Console.Write("Last name: ")
        Dim last As String = Console.ReadLine()
        Dim name As String = first + " " + ch + ". " + last
        Console.WriteLine("name = {0}", name)
    End Sub
End Module
```

Our **InputWrapper** class (introduced in Chapter 3) has a method **getString**, which provides a prompt and reads in a string.

String Methods and Properties

In this section we will survey a few useful methods and properties of the **String** class. Many of the methods have various overloaded versions. We show representative versions. Consult the online documentation for details on

Code Example

these and other methods. The program **StringMethods** demonstrates all the examples that follow.

String.Length

```
Public ReadOnly Property Length As Integer
```

This property returns the length of a string. Notice the convenient shorthand notation that is used for declaring a property.

```
Dim str As String = "hello"
Dim n As Integer = str.Length        ' 5
```

String.ToUpper

```
Overloads Public Function ToUpper() As String
```

This method returns a new string in which all characters of the original string have been converted to uppercase.

```
str = "goodbye"
str = str.ToUpper()        ' GOODBYE
```

String.ToLower

```
Overloads Public Function ToLower() As String
```

This method returns a new string in which all characters of the original string have been converted to lowercase.

```
str = str.ToLower()        ' goodbye
```

String.Substring

```
Overloads Public Function Substring( _
   ByVal startIndex As Integer, _
   ByVal length As Integer _
) As String
```

This method returns a substring that starts from a specified index position in the value and continues for a specified length. Remember that the index of the first character in a string is 0.

```
Dim substring As String = str.Substring(4, 3) ' bye
```

String.IndexOf

```
Overloads Public Function IndexOf( _
   ByVal value As String _
) As Integer
```

This method returns the index of the first occurrence of the specified string. If the string is not found, −1 is returned.

```
str = "goodbye"
Dim n1 As Integer = str.IndexOf("bye") ' 4
Dim n2 As Integer = str.IndexOf("boo") ' -1
```

StringBuilder Class

As we have discussed, instances of the **String** class are immutable. As a result, when you manipulate an instance of **String**, you are actually obtaining a new **String** instance. Depending on your applications, creating all these instances may be taxing on performance. The .NET library provides a special class **StringBuilder** (located in the **System.Text** namespace) in which you may directly manipulate the underlying string without creating a new instance. When you are done, you can create a **String** instance out of an instance of **StringBuilder** by using the **ToString** method.

A **StringBuilder** instance has a capacity and a maximum capacity. These capacities can be specified in a constructor when the instance is created. By default, an empty **StringBuilder** instance starts out with a capacity of 16. As the stored string expands, the capacity will be increased automatically. The program **StringBuilderDemo** provides a simple demonstration of using the **StringBuilder** class. It shows the starting capacity and the capacity after strings are appended. At the end, a **String** is returned.

```
' StringBuilderDemo.vb

Imports System
Imports System.Text

Module StringBuilderDemo
    Public Sub Main()
        Dim build As StringBuilder = New StringBuilder()
        Console.WriteLine("capacity = {0}", build.Capacity)
        build.Append("This is the first sentence." + vbLf)
        Console.WriteLine("capacity = {0}", build.Capacity)
        build.Append("This is the second sentence." + vbLf)
        Console.WriteLine("capacity = {0}", build.Capacity)
        build.Append("This is the last sentence." + vbLf)
        Console.WriteLine("capacity = {0}", build.Capacity)
        Dim str As String = build.ToString()
        Console.Write(str)
    End Sub
End Module
```

Here is the output:

```
capacity = 16
capacity = 34
capacity = 70
capacity = 142
```

```
This is the first sentence.
This is the second sentence.
This is the last sentence.
```

Arrays and Parameterized Properties

Arrays are another important data type in practical programming. In VB.NET, arrays are objects. They are a reference data type. They are based on the class **System.Array** and so inherit the properties and methods of this class. After examining one-dimensional arrays, we examine two higher dimensional varieties known as jagged and rectangular arrays. A jagged array is an array of arrays, and each row can have a different number of elements. In rectangular arrays, all rows have the same number of elements. Arrays are a special kind of collection, which means that the **For Each** loop can be used for iterating through array elements.

We conclude the section with a discussion of parameterized default properties, which provide a way to access encapsulated data in a class as a property with an array notation.

Arrays

An array is a collection of elements with the following characteristics.

- All array elements must be of the same type. The element type of an array can be any type, including an array type. An array of arrays is referred to as a *jagged* array.
- An array may have one or more dimensions. For example, a two-dimensional array can be visualized as a table of values. The number of dimensions is known as the array's *rank*.
- Array elements are accessed using one or more computed integer values, each known as an *index*. A one-dimensional array has one index.
- In VB.NET, an array index starts at 0, as in C, C++, C#, and Java.
- The elements of an array are created when the array object is created. The elements are automatically destroyed when there are no longer any references to the array object.

DEFINING AND USING ARRAYS

In VB.NET, an array variable is defined by including parenthesis after the variable name. The variable declared is a *reference* to an array object. You create the array elements and establish the upper bound(s) of the array using the **New** operator.

```
' defines a 1-dimensional array of integers
Dim a() as Integer
' create array elements
a = New Integer(9) {}
```

The new array elements start out with the appropriate default values for the type (0 for **Integer**). The upper bound of this array is 9, which means there are 10 elements, with an index ranging from 0 through 9.

You can indicate that you are done with the array elements by assigning the array reference to **Nothing**.

```
a = Nothing
```

The garbage collector is now ready to deallocate the array and its elements.

Upper Bounds of an Arrays Is Specified in VB.NET

It is important to note that the number in parenthesis on an array declaration is the upper bounds of the dimension. Thus, if the number in parenthesis is 9, there are actually 10 elements in that dimension!

Lower Bounds of an Array Always Begins at 0 in VB.NET

VB6 programmers should note that the lower bound of an array is always 0 in VB.NET. In VB6, both lower and upper array bounds could be specified when declaring the array.

You may declare and initialize the elements in an array with one statement, using the following syntax:

```
Dim primes () As Integer = {2, 3, 5, 7, 11}
```

In this example, **primes** references a one-dimensional array of five integers. If you want to initialize a two-dimensional array, you must define row 1, then row 2, and so on. For each row, you must define each element in the row. For example:

```
Dim matrix(,) As Integer = {{1, 2, 3}, {4, 5, 6}}
```

You may use the following code to print out the contents of the matrix. The **UBound** function is used to determine the upper bound of any specified dimension of an array.

```
For i = 0 To UBound(matrix, 1)
   For j = 0 To UBound(matrix, 2)
      Console.Write("{0,5}", matrix(i, j))
   Next
   Console.WriteLine()
Next
```

Output from the code above would be

```
1     2     3
4     5     6
```

System.Array

Code
Example

Arrays are objects. **System.Array** is the abstract base class for all array types. Accordingly, you can use the properties and methods of **System.Array** on any array. Here are some examples, shown in the **ArrayMethods** example.

- **Length** is a property that returns the number of elements currently in the array.
- **Sort** is a static method that will sort the elements of an array.
- **BinarySearch** is a static method that will search for an element in a sorted array, using a binary search algorithm.

```
Dim a() As Integer = {5, 2, 11, 7, 3}
Array.Sort(a)   ' sorts the array
Dim i As Integer
For i = 0 To a.Length - 1
   Console.Write("{0} ", a(i))
Next
Console.WriteLine()
Dim target As Integer = 5
Dim index As Integer = Array.BinarySearch(a, target)
If index < 0 Then
   Console.WriteLine("{0} not found", target)
Else
   Console.WriteLine("{0} found at {1}", target, index)
End If
```

Here is the output:

```
2 3 5 7 11
5 found at 2
```

Sample Program

Code
Example

The program **ArrayDemo** is an interactive test program for arrays. A small array is created initially, and you can create new arrays. You can populate an array either with a sequence of square numbers or with random numbers. You can sort the array, reverse the array, and perform a binary search (which assumes that the array is sorted in ascending order). You can destroy the array by assigning the array reference to **Nothing**.

Interfaces for System.Array

If you look at the documentation for methods of **System.Array**, you will see many references to various *interfaces,* such as **IComparable**. By using such interfaces, you can control the behavior of methods of **System.Array**. For example, if you want to sort an array of objects of a class that you define, you must implement the interface **IComparable** in your class so that the **Sort** method knows how to compare elements to carry out the sort. The .NET Framework provides an implementation of **IComparable** for all the primitive types. We will come back to this point after we discuss interfaces in Chapter 6.

Random-Number Generation

The **ArrayDemo** program contains the following code for populating an array with random integers between 0 and 100.

```
Dim rand As Random = New Random()
Dim i As Integer
For i = 0 To size - 1
   array(i) = rand.Next(100)
Next
```

The .NET Framework provides a useful class, **Random**, in the **System** namespace that can be used for generating pseudo-random numbers for simulations.

RANDOM CONSTRUCTORS

The **Random** class has two constructors. One constructor takes no parameters, which uses a default seed. The other constructor takes an **Integer** parameter named seed. The default seed is based on date and time, resulting in a different stream of random numbers each time. By specifying a seed, you can produce a deterministic stream.

RANDOM.NEXT METHODS

There are three overloaded **Next** methods that return a random **Integer**.

```
Overridable Overloads Public Function Next() As Integer
Overridable Overloads Public Function Next( _
  ByVal maxValue As Integer) As Integer
Overridable Overloads Public Function Next( _
  ByVal minValue As Integer, ByVal maxValue As Integer) _
  As Integer
```

The first **Next** method returns an integer greater than or equal to zero and less than **Int32.MaxValue**. The second method returns an integer greater than or equal to zero and less than **maxValue**. The third method returns an integer greater than or equal to **minValue** and less than or equal to **max-Value**.

RANDOM.NEXTDOUBLE METHOD

The **NextDouble** method produces a random double between 0.0 and 1.0.

```
Overridable Public Function NextDouble() As Double
```

Jagged Arrays

You can declare an array of arrays, also known as a jagged array. Each row can have a different number of elements. You can also create the array of rows, specifying how many rows there are (each row is itself an array).

```
Dim binomial()() As Integer = New Integer(rows - 1)() {}
```

Next, you create the individual rows.

```
binomial(i) = New Integer(i) {}
```

Finally, you can assign individual array elements.

```
binomial(0)(0) = 1
```

Code Example

The example program **Pascal** creates and prints Pascal's triangle using a two-dimensional jagged array. Higher dimensional jagged arrays can be created following the same principles.

Rectangular Arrays

VB.NET also permits you to define rectangular arrays, where all rows have the same number of elements. First you declare the array and create all the array elements, specifying the number of rows and columns.

```
Dim rows As Integer = 5
Dim columns As Integer = 5
Dim MultTable(,) As Integer = _
    New Integer(rows - 1, columns - 1) {}
```

Then you can assign individual array elements.

```
MultTable(i, j) = i * j
```

Code Example

The example program **RectangularArray** creates and prints out a multiplication table.

Higher dimensional rectangular arrays can be created following the same principles.

Arrays as Collections

The class **System.Array** supports the **IEnumerable** interface. Hence arrays can be treated as *collections*, a topic we will discuss in Chapter 6. This means that a **For Each** loop can be used to iterate through the elements of an array.

The **Pascal** example code mentioned above contains nested **For Each** loops to display the jagged array. The outer loop iterates through all the rows, and the inner loop iterates through all the elements within a row.

```
Dim binomial()() As Integer = New Integer(rows - 1)() {}
...
Console.WriteLine( _
   "Pascal triangle via nested For Each loop")
Dim row() As Integer
For Each row In binomial
   Dim x As Integer
   For Each x In row
      Console.Write("{0} ", x)
   Next
   Console.WriteLine()
Next
```

Indexing With Default Parameterized Properties

VB.NET provides various ways to help the user of a class access encapsulated data. Earlier in the chapter we saw how *properties* can provide access to a single piece of data associated with a class, making it appear like a public field. In this section we will see how *default parameterized properties* provide a similar capability for accessing a group of data items, using an array index notation. Such indexing can be provided when there is a private array or other collection.

Code Example

The program **TestHotel\Step3** provides an illustration. This version of the **Hotel** class adds the capability to make hotel reservations, and the private array **m_reservations** stores a list of reservations in the form of **ReservationListItem** structure instances. The **Hotel** class provides the read-only property **NumberReservations** for the number of reservations in this list, and it provides a default read-write property for access to the elements in this list based on an integer parameter used as an index.

```
' Hotel.vb - Step 3

Imports System

Public Structure ReservationListItem
   Public CustomerId As Integer
   Public ReservationId As Integer
   Public HotelName As String
   Public City As String
```

```
      Public ArrivalDate As DateTime
      Public DepartureDate As DateTime
      Public NumberDays As Integer
End Structure
...
Public Class Hotel
   Private m_city As String
   Private m_name As String
   Private m_number As Integer
   Private m_rate As Decimal
   Private Const MAXDAY As Integer = 366
   Private m_numGuests() As Integer
   Private m_nextReservation As Integer = 0
   Private m_nextReservationId As Integer = 1
   Private Const MAXRESERVATIONS As Integer = 100
   Private m_reservations() As ReservationListItem
    ...
   Public ReadOnly Property NumberReservations() _
    As Integer
      Get
         Return m_nextReservation
      End Get
   End Property

   Default Public Property reservations( _
    ByVal index As Integer) As ReservationListItem
      Get
         Return m_reservations(index)
      End Get
      Set(ByVal Value As ReservationListItem)
         m_reservations(index) = Value
      End Set
   End Property
    ...
```

The test program **TestHotel.vb** illustrates reading and writing individual array elements using the index notation.

```
' Change the CustomerId of first reservation
Dim item As ReservationListItem = ritz(0)
item.CustomerId = 99
ritz(0) = item
ShowReservations(ritz)
```

The **Default** keyword means that you can access the property using only the object reference, without having to use a fully qualified name that includes the name of the property.

```
ritz.reservations(0) = item     ' fully qualified
ritz(0) = item                  ' short-hand
```

Default Properties Must Take a Parameter in VB.NET

In VB6 simple properties without parameters could be default. For example, controls would have **Text** as a default property. You could then assign a string to the textbox **txtName** using the code **txtName = "John Smith"** in place of **txtName.Text = "John Smith"**.

Such default simple properties are not allowed in VB.NET, because there is no special notation for assigning object references (i.e., there is no **Set** keyword in VB.NET). This implies that the statement **txtName = ...** means you are assigning something to the object reference **txtName**, not to some property of it.

However, when there is a parameter to the property, ambiguity with assigning an object reference cannot arise, because there will always be the parameter on the left hand side and not just an object reference. Thus default properties with parameters are feasible.

More about Methods

In this section we look at several other topics pertaining to methods in VB.NET:

- Parameter passing
- Variable-length parameter lists
- Method overloading
- Optional parameters

Parameter Passing

Programming languages have different mechanisms for passing parameters. One mechanism is known as *call-by-value*. This means that the actual data values are copied and passed to the method being called. These copied values are pushed onto the stack, and the called function obtains independent copies of the values. Any changes made to these values will not be propagated back to the calling program. VB.NET supports this mechanism of parameter passing using the **ByVal** keyword, but VB.NET also supports *call-by-reference* parameters.

Some terminology will help us in the following discussion. Storage is allocated on the stack for method parameters. This storage area is known as the *activation record*. It is popped off when the method is no longer active. The *actual parameters* of a method are the parameters as seen within the method call (i.e., in the method client code). The *formal parameters* of a method are the expressions between commas in the parameter list of the called method.

Value Parameters

Parameter passing is the process of initializing the storage of the formal parameters by the actual parameters. Passing parameters with the **ByVal** keyword is known as *call-by-value,* in which the values of the actual parameters are copied into the storage of the formal parameters. Call-by-value is "safe," because the method never directly accesses the actual parameters, only its own local copies. But there are drawbacks to call-by-value:

- There is no direct way to modify the value of an argument. You may use the return type of the method, but that allows you to pass only one value back to the calling program.
- There is overhead in copying a large object.

The overhead in copying a large object is borne when you pass a struct instance. If you pass a class instance, or an instance of any other reference type, you are passing only a reference and not the actual data itself. This may sound like call-by-reference, but what you are actually doing is passing a reference by value.

Code Example

The **ValueMath** example shows how to pass parameters to a method using call-by-value.

```
' Function call with actual parameters
sum = ValueMath.Add(5, 7)
...
' Function implementation with formal parameters
Public Shared Function Add( _
 ByVal x As Integer, _
 ByVal y As Integer) _
   As Integer
   Return x + y
End Function
...
```

Reference Parameters

Consider a situation in which you want to pass more than one value back to the calling program. VB.NET provides a clean solution through *reference parameters*. You declare a reference parameter with the **ByRef** keyword, which is placed before the formal parameter. A reference parameter does not result in any copying of a value. Instead, the formal parameter and the actual parameter refer to the same storage location. Thus, changing the formal parameter will result in the actual parameter changing, as both are referring to exactly the same storage location.

Code Example

The program **ReferenceMath** illustrates using **ByRef** parameters. There is a single method, **Calculate**, which passes back two values as reference parameters.

```
' ReferenceMath.vb

Public Class ReferenceMath
   Public Shared Sub Calculate( _
    ByVal x As Integer, _
    ByVal y As Integer, _
    ByRef sum As Integer, _
    ByRef prod As Integer)
      sum = x + y
      prod = x * y
   End Sub
End Class
```

Notice the use of the **ByRef** keyword in front of the third and fourth formal parameters. Here is the corresponding test program:

```
' TestReferenceMath.vb

Public Module TestReferenceMath
   Public Sub Main()
      Dim sum As Integer = 0, product As Integer = 0
      ReferenceMath.Calculate(5, 7, sum, product)
      Console.WriteLine("sum = {0}", sum)
      Console.WriteLine("product = {0}", product)
   End Sub
End Module
```

We use the **ByRef** keyword only on the formal parameters, not on the actual parameters.

Method Overloading

In most traditional programming languages, you need to create unique names for all your methods. If methods do basically the same thing but apply only to different data types, it becomes tedious to create artificially unique names. For example, suppose you have a **FindMax** method that can find the maximum of two **Integer** or two **Long** or two **String** parameters. If we need to come up with a unique name for each method, we would have to create method names such as **FindMaxInteger**, **FindMaxLong**, and **FindMaxString**.

In VB.NET, as in other object-oriented languages such as C#, C++, and Java, you may *overload* method names. That is, different methods can have different names if they have different *signatures*. Two methods have the same signature if they have the same number of parameters, the parameters have the same data types, and the parameters are in the same order. The return type does not contribute to defining the signature of a method.

At runtime the compiler will resolve a given invocation of the method by trying to match up the actual parameters with formal parameters. A match occurs if the parameters match exactly or if they can match through an implicit conversion. For the exact matching rules, consult the *VB.NET Language Specification*.

The program **OverloadDemo** example illustrates method overloading. The method **FindMax** is overloaded to take either **Long** or **String** parameters. The method is invoked three times, for **Integer**, **Long**, and **String** parameters. There is an exact match for the case of **Long** and **String**. The call with **Integer** actual parameters can resolve to the **Long** version, because there is an implicit conversion of **Integer** into **Long**.

```
' OverloadDemo.vb

Imports System

Public Module OverloadDemo
   Public Sub Main()
      Dim x1 As Integer = 5, x2 = 7
      Dim y1 As Long = 5000000000L, y2 = 7000000000L
      Dim s1 As String = "fifteen", s2 As String = "seven"
      Console.WriteLine("max of {0}, {1} = {2}", _
         x1, x2, FindMax(x1, x2))
      Console.WriteLine("max of {0}, {1} = {2}", _
         y1, y2, FindMax(y1, y2))
      Console.WriteLine("max of {0}, {1} = {2}", _
         s1, s2, FindMax(s1, s2))
   End Sub

   Function FindMax(ByVal a As Long, ByVal b As Long) _
    As Long
      If a < b Then
         Return b
      Else
         Return a
      End If
   End Function

   Function FindMax(ByRef a As String, ByRef b As String) _
    As String
      If String.Compare(a, b) <= 0 Then
         Return b
      Else
         Return a
      End If
   End Function
End Module
```

Variable-Length Parameter Lists

Our **FindMax** methods in the **OverloadDemo** example are very specific with respect to the number of parameters—there are always exactly two parameters. Sometimes you may want to be able to work with a variable number of parameters—for example, to find the maximum of two, three, four, or more numbers. VB.NET provides the **ParamArray** keyword, which you can use to indicate that an array of parameters is provided. Sometimes you may want to provide both a general version of your method that takes a variable number of parameters and also one or more special versions that take an exact number of parameters. The special version will be called in preference, if there is an exact match. The special versions are more efficient. The program **VariableMax** illustrates a general **FindMax** method that takes a variable number of parameters. There is also a special version that takes two parameters. Each method prints out a line identifying itself, so you can see which method takes precedence. Here is the program:

Code Example

```
' VariableMax.vb

Imports System

Public Module VariableMax
   Public Sub Main()
      Console.WriteLine( _
         "max of {0}, {1} = {2}", _
         5, 7, FindMax(5, 7))
      Console.WriteLine( _
         "max of {0}, {1}, {2} = {3}", _
            500, 5, 7, FindMax(500, 5, 7))
      Console.WriteLine( _
         "max of {0}, {1}, {2}, {3} = {4}", _
         500, 5, 7, 80, FindMax(500, 5, 7, 80))
   End Sub

   Function FindMax( _
    ByVal a As Integer, _
    ByVal b As Integer) As Integer
      Console.WriteLine("FindMax with Two Parameters")
      If a < b Then
         Return b
      Else
         Return a
      End If
   End Function

   Function FindMax( _
    ByVal ParamArray args() As Integer) As Integer
      Console.WriteLine( _
         "FindMax with Variable Number of Parameters")
      Dim imax As Integer = Int32.MinValue
      Dim i As Integer
      For i = 0 To args.Length - 1
         If args(i) > imax Then
```

```
                    imax = args(i)
              End If
         Next
         Return imax
      End Function
End Module
```

Here is the output:

```
FindMax with Two Parameters
max of 5, 7 = 7
FindMax with Variable Number of Parameters
max of 500, 5, 7 = 500
FindMax with Variable Number of Parameters
max of 500, 5, 7, 80 = 500
```

Optional Parameters

VB.NET allows parameters to be defined as optional. That is, the calling statement may or may not pass a value for that parameter. If optional parameters are defined, a default value for them must be specified. When arguments are passed, the actual argument is used. When no argument is passed, the default value for the parameter is used.

To define a parameter as optional, the keyword **Optional** is used. The default value for the parameter is specified using the assignment operator and a value after the declaration. The example **OptionalParameters** illustrates the use of these parameters.

```
' Calculates shipping costs; assumes that the Rapid Express
' is the default shipper. Shipper codes are:
' 1=Rapid Express, 2=Quick Shippers, 3=SS Transport

Private Function CalcCost(ByVal weight As Integer, _
  Optional ByVal shipper As Integer = 1) As Decimal

   Select Case shipper
      Case 1
         ' calculate cost for Rapid Express
         Return 11.5 + (weight - 1) * 7.95
      Case 2
         ' calculate cost for Quick Shippers
         Return 19 + (weight - 1) * 4.25
      Case 3
         ' calculate cost for SS Transport
         Return 2.9 + (weight - 1) * 2.25
   End Select
   Return -1
```

```
End Function
```

This function can be called in any of the following ways:

```
Dim sc As Decimal
sc = CalcCost(4)      ' omit optional parameter

sc = CalcCost(4, 1) ' specify default for optional
                    ' parameter

sc = CalcCost(4, 3) ' specify any value for optional
```

Optional parameters are most useful when a procedure is typically called with a certain value for a procedure, but may occasionally be called with a different value.

Optional Parameters Must Specify a Default Value

VB6 programmers should be aware that VB.NET requires all optional parameters to specify a default value. In VB6, this was not the case. A VB6 programmer could use the function **IsMissing** to determine whether a parameter was passed. **IsMissing** is not supported in VB.NET.

VB.NET Utility Functions

Visual Basic has been a powerful and easy-to-use language for many years, in part because many common operations are intrinsic to the language. With VB.NET, these operations have become members of the **Microsoft.VisualBasic** namespace. This namespace provides many of the functions that were previously built in to the language. By making the functions part of the .NET Framework Class Library, they become available to other .NET languages, not just VB.NET. In addition, the .NET **System** namespace provides many other functions that VB programmers will find useful. This chapter outlines several types of utility functions available to VB.NET programmers, ranging from common mathematical operations to financial functions to character and string manipulation operations. For a detailed discussion of these functions and many example programs, please consult Chapter 8 of our book *Introduction to Visual Basic Using .NET.*

Overview

In this section we give an overview of the variety of useful functions that are available. On the book's software distribution we provide a set of example programs, which should help you get up and running. You can find detailed descriptions of the functions in the .NET Framework SDK documentation.

Table 4–3 provides a summary of the various groups of utility functions that are available. We show the namespace for the classes that implement the functions

TABLE 4–3	*VB.NET Utility Functions*
Function Group	**Namespace(s)**
Math	System.Math
Financial	Microsoft.VisualBasic.Financial
Informational	Microsoft.VisualBasic.Information
Conversion	Built-in (CInt, CStr, CType, etc.) System (Convert class) Microsoft.VisualBasic.Conversion
Control Characters	Microsoft.VisualBasic.ControlChars Microsoft.VisualBasic.Constants
Character Manipulation	System (Char structure)
String Manipulation	System (String, StringBuilder classes) Microsoft.VisualBasic.Strings
Date and Time	System (DateTime and TimeSpan structures) Microsoft.VisualBasic.DateTime
Format	System (String.Format method) Microsoft.VisualBasic.Strings
Environment	System.Environment

Math Functions

There are many mathematical functions available in the .NET Framework. These functions include algebraic functions such as **Log** and **Sqrt**, as well as trigonometric functions such as **Sin** and **Cos**. There are also constants **E** and **PI**.

In VB.NET most mathematical functions are provided by the **System.Math** class in .NET Framework class library. Many of these functions replace functions that were a part of the .VB6 language.

Code Example

The **MathFunctions** program illustrates the use of some of the mathematic functions available to Visual Basic .NET programmers as well as the use of the **System.Math** constants. You will notice that because the exponentiation (∧) and remainder (**Mod**) operators are part of the Visual Basic language, the .NET functions **Exp**, **Pow**, and **IEEERemainder** provide alternate ways of performing operations that are already part of the programming language.

Financial Functions

Code Example

There are many financial functions available for use by VB.NET programmers. The **Microsoft.VisualBasic.Financial** namespace is home to many functions that were found in previous versions of Visual Basic. Table 4–4 lists some of the more useful functions. Examples of the use of many of these functions can be found in the program **FinancialFunctions**.

TABLE 4–4   *Financial Functions available in VB.NET*

Microsoft.VisualBasic. Financials functions	Description
DDB	Uses the double-declining balance method to find the depreciation of an asset.
FV	Calculates the future value of an annuity.
IPmt	Finds the interest payment for a given period of an annuity based on periodic fixed payments and a fixed interest rate.
MIRR	Finds the modified internal rate of return for a series of periodic cash flows (payments and receipts).
NPer	Finds the number of periods for an annuity based on periodic fixed payments and a fixed interest rate.
NPV	Finds the net present value of an investment based on a series of periodic cash flows (payments and receipts) and a discount rate.
Pmt	Calculates the payment for annuity.
PPmt	Finds the principal payment for a given period of an annuity based on periodic fixed payments and a fixed interest rate.
PV	Calculates the present value of an annuity.
SLN	Uses the straight-line method to find the depreciation of an asset.
SYD	Uses the sum-of-years digits method to find the depreciation of an asset.

Informational Functions

There are functions in the **Micrsoft.VisualBasic.Information** namespace that can be used to make decisions about the type of contents of a variable. In general these functions would be used to preserve compatibility with existing VB code. For newer code, you should be able to accomplish the same task using native .NET functions.

Conversion Functions

The most basic type of conversion involves use of built-in functions such as **CInt**. The spirit of the use of these functions is the same as in earlier versions of VB, but details are different, because VB.NET has a different set of data types, and some data types have changed size (for example, **Integer** is 32 bits in VB.NET and was only 16 bits in earlier versions of VB). For more elaborate conversions in new code, you should use the **Convert** class of the **System** namespace. The **Microsoft.VisualBasic.Conversion** namespace is available to preserve compatibility with conversions in legacy VB code.

Control Characters

The **Microsoft.VisualBasic.ControlChars** namespace contains a collection of character constants that represent control characters. Here are some examples:

- **Back**
- **Cr**
- **Lf**
- **CrLf**
- and so forth

As we saw earlier in the chapter in Table 4–1, you can also use the classic VB constants of **vbBack**, **vbCr**, **vbLf**, **vbCrLf**, and so forth.

Character Manipulation Functions

The **Microsoft.VisualBasic.Strings** namespace contains several functions, such as **Asc**, **AscW**, **Chr**, and so on, that can be useful when working with characters. For new code, you should use methods of the **Char** structure.

String Manipulation Functions

For new code, you should use the .NET **String** and **StringBuilder** classes, which we discussed earlier in the chapter. For compatibility with older VB code, you can make use of functions in the **Microsoft.VisualBasic.Strings** namespace.

Date and Time

For compatibility with previous VB code, you can use functions in the **Microsoft.VisualBasic.DateTime** namespace. For new code, use the **DateTime** structure in the **System** namespace, which is identical to the built-in VB.NET **Date** type. Because of its importance in many applications, you should take time to familiarize yourself with the new .NET **DateTime** structure and its many useful properties and methods.

Basically, **DateTime** represents dates and times ranging from 12 midnight, January 1 of the year 1 A.D. to 11:59:59 of December 31 of the year 9999 A.D. Time values are measured in units of 100 nanoseconds, called *ticks*. A **TimeSpan** structure can be used to represent an interval of time. Table 4–5 shows some of the common properties and methods of **DateTime**.

TABLE 4–5	*Selected Methods and Properties of DateTime*	
Member	**Property or Method**	**Description**
Now	Shared Method	Current local date and time
ToString	Method (several overloads)	String representation, available in a variety of formats
DayOfYear	Property	Day of the year of this instance
DayOfWeek	Property	Day of the week of this instance
Hour	Property	Hour component of this instance
Minute	Property	Minute component of this instance
Ticks	Property	Number of 100 nanosecond ticks
Add	Method	Add a TimeSpan to a DateTime

Code
Example

The program **DateTimeDemo** illustrates these operations. The current date and time is found and displayed in various ways. The following are a few of the many formats available for displaying a **DateTime** using the **ToString** method:

- d or short date
- D or long date
- t or short time
- T or long time

A **TimeSpan** object is created using one of several overloaded constructors. The constructor in this program takes as parameters a day, hour, minute, and second. We want to find a time 30 days and 1 hour in the future. The date and time at this future moment are displayed. Here is the code:

```
Module DateTimeDemo

    Sub Main()
        Dim dt As DateTime = DateTime.Now
        Console.WriteLine("Current date and time")
        Console.WriteLine("DateTime = {0}", dt)
        Console.WriteLine("Date (short) = {0}", _
            dt.ToString("d"))
        Console.WriteLine("Date (long) = {0}", _
```

```
                        dt.ToString("D"))
            Console.WriteLine("Time (short) = {0}", _
                dt.ToString("t"))
            Console.WriteLine("Time (long) = {0}", _
                dt.ToString("T"))

            'Some other date and time metrics
            Console.WriteLine("DayOfYear = {0}", _
                dt.DayOfYear)
            Console.WriteLine("DayOfWeek = {0}", _
                dt.DayOfWeek)
            Console.WriteLine("Hour = {0}", _
                dt.Hour)
            Console.WriteLine("Minute = {0}", _
                dt.Minute)
            Console.WriteLine("Ticks = {0}", _
                dt.Ticks)

            'TimeSpan of 30 days and 1 hour
            Dim ts As New TimeSpan(30, 1, 0, 0)
            Console.WriteLine("30 days and 1 hour later")
            dt = dt.Add(ts)
            Console.WriteLine("DateTime = {0}", dt)
        End Sub

End Module
```

Here is the output:

```
Current date and time
DateTime = 2/11/2002 5:06:11 PM
Date (short) = 2/11/2002
Date (long) = Monday, February 11, 2002
Time (short) = 5:06 PM
Time (long) = 5:06:11 PM
DayOfYear = 42
DayOfWeek = Monday
Hour = 17
Minute = 6
Ticks = 631490439719857312
30 days and 1 hour later
DateTime = 3/13/2002 6:06:11 PM
```

Format Functions

Code
Example

The **String** data type has several methods to help you format information, including the methods **Format**, **PadLeft**, and **PadRight**. There are additional formatting functions in the **Microsoft.VisualBasic.Strings** namespace. The following code examples are taken from the program **FormatFunctions**.

The **Format** method is useful for formatting numbers. It uses the same syntax that is used in the **WriteLine** method. It returns a value representing the formatted string. For example:

```
Dim s As String
Dim n As Decimal = 123.45

s = String.Format("Amount = {0,10:C}", n)
Console.WriteLine(s)
```

The output of this example is:

```
Amount =      $123.45
```

If you only want to control the formatting of string values, that is, make them align the way you want, then use the **PadLeft** and **PadRight** methods. The methods require that you specify the total width of the string that you want returned, including the text before padding, and they create a return value padded to the desired width.

In the following code, a string is built by padding two column headings. The pad character is a space.

```
Dim heading1 As String = "Number"
Dim heading2 As String = "Power"

Dim heading As String = heading1.PadRight(12) & _
                        heading2.PadLeft(13)
Console.WriteLine(heading)

Dim i As Integer
Dim value As Long
For i = 0 To 31
   value = 2 ^ i
   Console.WriteLine("2^{0,-10}{1,13:N0}", i, value)
Next
```

The format for the variable **i** specifies a field width of 10, left justified. The format for the variable **value** indicates a field width of 13, right justified, numeric (N) with 0 digits after the decimal. The column heading for **i** was padded to a width of 12 to correspond to the output of the value **i** (width 10) combined with the two characters in the literal "2^". Output of this example is:

```
Number                 Power
2^0                        1
2^1                        2
2^2                        4
2^3                        8
2^4                       16
2^5                       32

.  .  .
2^28          268,435,456
```

```
2^29          536,870,912
2^30        1,073,741,824
2^31        2,147,483,648
```

The **PadLeft** and **PadRight** methods can also be used specify a padding character. In the following example, a decimal account is preceded by asterisks:

```
Dim s As String
Dim n As Decimal = 123.45

s = n.ToString()
s = s.PadLeft(9, "*"c)
Console.WriteLine(s)
```

The output is:

```
***123.45
```

Environment Functions

The **System.Environment** namespace contains a collection of properties and methods that can be used to gather information about the environment that an application is running in. Table 4–6 lists some of the more useful functions:

TABLE 4–6	*Environment Functions in VB.NET*
Function	**Description**
CurrentDirectory	Returns a string containing the name of the current working directory.
Exit	Terminates the process.
GetCommandLineArgs	Returns an array of strings representing the command line arguments that were used to launch the program.
GetEnvironmentVariables	Returns all environment variables and their values.
MachineName	Returns a string containing the NetBIOS name of the computer.
OSVersion	Returns an OperatingSystem object that can be queried to determine information about the current operating system.
TickCount	Returns the number of milliseconds that have elapsed since the system started. Useful for benchmarking the execution speed of code.
UserName	Returns a string containing the user name of the person who started the thread.

The program **EnvironmentFunctions** shown below illustrates the use of some of these methods. It uses **TickCount** to benchmark the performance of the application. You will notice from the output that it executes much more slowly from within the Visual Studio IDE. The program displays the name of the user and the name of the machine that the program runs on.

```vbnet
' Demonstrates the use of the Environment functions

Imports System
Imports Microsoft.VisualBasic.ControlChars

Module EnvironmentFunctions

    Sub Main()
        ' Get the tick when the application begins
        Dim startTick As Long
        startTick = Environment.TickCount

        ' Find the user and machine name
        Dim userName As String = Environment.UserName
        Dim machineName As String = Environment.MachineName

        Console.WriteLine( _
          "Current user on machine {0} is {1}", _
          machineName, userName)

        ' Get the tick at the end of the application
        Dim endTick As Long
        endTick = Environment.TickCount

        ' Write benchmarking times to the console
        Console.WriteLine( _
          "The code took {0} milliseconds to execute", _
          endTick - startTick)
    End Sub

End Module
```

Command-Line Arguments

Code
Example

Command-line arguments are provided as an array of **String** objects obtained via the **Environment.GetCommandLineArgs** method.[1] An integer exit code can be returned to the operating system via the **Environment.ExitCode** property to indicate the overall success or failure of the program upon termination. This is useful for controlling batch scripts or other programs that execute your VB.NET program. The **Environment** class provides access to other useful information, such as environment strings and the current directory. This example is provided in the **AccessEnvironmentInfo** directory.

```
Module AccessEnvironmentInfo

    Public Sub Main()
        Dim cmds() As String = _
            Environment.GetCommandLineArgs()
        Dim cmdArg As String
        For Each cmdArg In cmds
            Console.WriteLine(cmdArg)
        Next
        Environment.ExitCode = 0  '0 usually means success
    End Sub
End Module
```

Summary

In this chapter we examined some standard types, such as **String**, **String-Builder**, and **Array**. We covered some additional topics concerning methods, including parameter passing, variable-length parameter lists, and method overloading. We saw how to handle command-line arguments in VB.NET. We looked at a number of common utility functions in VB.NET, which are found in either the **System** namespace or the **Microsoft.VisualBasic** namespace.

A number of examples pertained to a hotel reservation system. In the next chapter, we will study object-oriented programming in VB.NET, and we will extend our hotel reservation example to a case study, which will be continued throughout the rest of the book. We will also look at exception handling in VB.NET.

1. To establish command-line arguments within Visual Studio, right-click on the project node (not the solution node) in Solution Explorer, choose Properties, and select the Debugging under Configuration Properties. Then enter the desired space-delimited command-line argument text into the command-line arguments text field. Then, when you run the program from within Visual Studio, these command-line arguments will be in effect.

Inheritance and Exceptions in VB.NET

Visual Basic has long supported the notion of class and an object-based programming model. VB.NET brings to Visual Basic the concept of *inheritance,* which has long been considered one of the cornerstones of object-oriented programming. Visual Basic has also provided an exception handling mechanism through the **OnError** construct. VB.NET provides *structured exception handling*, which is a more robust exception handling mechanism that is shared among all the .NET languages.

In this chapter we study in detail these important features of VB.NET. First we review the fundamentals of object-oriented programming. Next, the Acme Travel Agency case study is introduced. This case study is developed throughout the entire book as we explain more about .NET. We consider some abstractions that will enable us to implement a reservation system for a variety of resources, and we provide an implementation of a hotel reservation system. The abstract base classes we define provide reusable code that enables us to easily implement other kinds of reservation systems. The key is finding the right abstractions.

We will see how VB.NET language features facilitate object-oriented programming. Certain details of VB.NET, such as use of access control (**Public**, **Private**, and **Protected**) and properties can help express abstractions in a way that is safe and easy to use. We will then look at other object-oriented features of VB.NET, such as **Overridable**[1] methods, method hiding, and poly-

---

1. The VB.NET keyword **Overridable** makes a method virtual, which means that it is dynamically dispatched at runtime rather than being bound at compile time. Virtual methods support one of the pillars of object-oriented programming, known as polymorphism.

111

morphism. A problem in languages supporting inheritance is the fragile base class problem,[2] and we will see how VB.NET helps in avoiding this pitfall.

We discuss exception handling in VB.NET in some detail, including the use of user-defined exception classes (which rely on inheritance) and structured exception handling.

This chapter is very much driven by our case study. We introduce object-oriented features of VB.NET as we elaborate the case study. At the end of the chapter we cover additional concepts not illustrated by the case study.

Review of Object-Oriented Concepts

In this preliminary section we review the fundamentals of object-oriented programming. If you are an experienced C++ or Java programmer, you may skim through this section as a refresher and begin your careful reading with the next section, where we introduce the case study. If you are primarily a Visual Basic programmer, then reading this section is recommended.

Objects

Objects have both a real-world and a software meaning. The object model describes a relationship between them.

OBJECTS IN THE REAL WORLD

The term *object* has an intuitive real-world meaning. There are concrete, tangible objects, such as a ball, an automobile, and an airplane. There are also more abstract objects that have a definite conceptual meaning, such as a committee, a patent, or an insurance contract.

Objects have both attributes (or characteristics) and operations that can be performed upon them. A ball has a size, a weight, a color, and so on. Operations may be performed on the ball, such as throw, catch, and drop.

There can be various types of relationships among classes of objects. One, for example, is a specialization relationship, such as an automobile is a specific kind of vehicle. Another is a whole/part relationship, such as an automobile consists of an engine, a chassis, wheels, and other parts.

OBJECT MODELS

Objects can also be used in programs. Objects are useful in programming because you can set up a software model of a real-world system. Software

---

2. The fragile base class problem refers to breaking binary compatibility with existing client programs when a new version of a component with different class members is deployed. This is explained in greater detail later in this chapter.

objects abstract the parts of objects in the real world that are relevant to the problem being solved. The model can then be implemented as software using a programming language. A software system implemented in this way tends to be more faithful to the real system, and it can be changed more readily when the real system is changed.

There are formal languages for describing object models. The most popular language is UML (Unified Modeling Language), which is a synthesis of several earlier modeling languages. Formal modeling languages are beyond the scope of this book, but we will find that informal models are useful.

REUSABLE SOFTWARE COMPONENTS

Another advantage of objects in software is that they can facilitate reusable software components. Hardware has long enjoyed significant benefits from reusable hardware components. For example, computers can be created from power supplies, printed circuit boards, and other components. Printed circuit boards in turn can be created from chips. The same chip can be reused in many different computers, and new hardware designs do not have to be done from scratch.

With appropriate software technology, similar reuse is feasible in software systems. Objects provide the foundation for software reuse.

OBJECTS IN SOFTWARE

An *object* is a software entity containing data *(state)* and related functions *(behavior)* as a self-contained module. For example, a **HotelBroker** object may contain a list of hotels (the state) and provide operations to add a hotel and make a reservation (behavior).

ABSTRACTION

An *abstraction* captures the essential features of a real-world object, suppressing unnecessary details. All instances of an abstraction share these common features. Abstraction helps us deal with complexity. For example, consider the problem of booking a reservation. There are many different kinds of things you might want to reserve, such as a hotel, an airplane flight, or a conference room. Such "reservables" have many differences, but they have certain essentials in common, such as a capacity.

ENCAPSULATION

The implementation of an abstraction should be hidden from the rest of the system, or *encapsulated*. For example, the list of hotels may be contained in several different kinds of data structures, such as an array, a collection, or a database. The rest of the system should not need to know the details of the internal representation.

Classes

A *class* is a template for objects with common behavior and common structure. A class allows creation of new objects of the same type. An object is an instance of some class. We refer to the process of creating an individual object as *instantiation*.

Classes can be related in various ways, such as by *inheritance* and by *containment*.

INHERITANCE

Inheritance is a key feature of the object-oriented programming paradigm. You abstract out common features of your classes and put them in a high-level base class. You can add or change features in more specialized derived classes, which "inherit" the standard behavior from the base class. Inheritance facilitates code reuse and extensibility.

Consider **Reservable** as a base class, with derived classes **Hotel** and **Flight**. All reservables share some characteristics, such as a capacity. Different kinds of reservables differ in other respects. For example, a hotel has a city and a name, while a flight has an origin and a destination. Figure 5–1 illustrates the relationship among these different kinds of reservables.

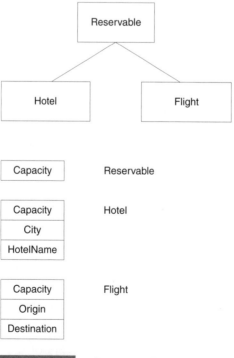

FIGURE 5–1   *Inheritance relationship among different reservable classes.*

ABSTRACT CLASSES

Sometimes a class is not meant to be instantiated, but only to provide a template for derived classes. The **Reservable** class is an example—it is too abstract to actually instantiate. Only specific kinds of reservable classes, such as **Hotel** and **Flight,** may be instantiated. We call a class such as **Reservable** that cannot be instantiated an *abstract* class. A class that can be instantiated is called a *concrete* class.

RELATIONSHIPS AMONG CLASSES

Classes may be related to each other in various ways.

- The inheritance (IS-A) relationship specifies how one class is a special case of another class. A **Hotel** (subclass or derived class) is a special kind of **Reservable** (superclass or base class).
- The composition (HAS-A) relationship specifies how one class (the whole) is made up of other classes (the parts). A **HotelBroker** (whole) has a list of **Hotel** objects.
- A weaker kind of relationship (USES-A) can be identified when one class merely makes use of some other class by calling on its methods to carry out work.

Polymorphism

Consider the problem of generating a payroll for various categories of employees. Different kinds of employees may have their pay calculated in a different manner. A salaried employee receives a fixed salary. A waged employee is paid according to the number of hours worked. A sales employee is paid according to the commissions earned on sales that were made.

A traditional approach is to maintain a type field in an employee structure and to perform processing in a **Select Case** statement, with a Case for each type of employee. Such use of **Select Case** statements is error prone and requires much maintenance when adding a new employee type.

An alternative is to localize the intelligence to calculate pay in each employee class, which will support its own specialized **GetPay** method. Generic payroll code can then be written that will handle different types of employees and will not have to be modified to support each additional employee type. Provide a **GetPay** method in the base class and an override of this method in each derived class. Call **GetPay** through an object reference to a general **Employee** object. Depending on the actual employee class referred to, the appropriate **GetPay** method will be called.

The ability for the same method call to result in different behavior depending on the object through which the method is invoked is referred to as *polymorphism*. Polymorphism can greatly simplify complex systems and is an important part of the object-oriented paradigm.

You should not try to coerce your design so that you can take advantage of polymorphism. We will see in our Acme Travel Agency case study that we have three different abstract base classes, but we do not need polymorphism to achieve quite general behavior. On the other hand, the .NET Framework classes use polymorphism heavily, as we shall see beginning in Chapter 6. Later in this chapter we will provide a small example of polymorphism using an employee class hierarchy, as outlined above.

Acme Travel Agency Case Study: Design

The Acme Travel Agency provides various services, including the booking of hotel, plane, and car rental reservations. We will use this simple theme of booking reservations to illustrate various features of .NET throughout the book. In this chapter we design the architecture of a general system for booking different kinds of reservations. We illustrate the reservation system with an implementation of a hotel broker system that supports the following basic features:

- Add a hotel to the list of hotels.
- Show all the hotels.
- Show all the hotels in a particular city.
- Reserve a hotel room for a range of dates.
- Show all the reservations.
- Show all the reservations for a particular customer.

The system also maintains a list of customers. Customers may register by giving their name and email address, and they will be assigned a customer ID. The following features are supported in the basic customer management subsystem:

- Register as a customer.
- Change the email address of a customer.
- Show a single customer or all the customers.

In this chapter various lists, such as hotels, reservations, and customers, will be maintained as arrays. In the next chapter we will use .NET collections in place of arrays, and we will implement more features, such as the ability to delete a hotel, cancel a reservation, and the like. In later chapters we will extend the case study in various ways, such as providing a graphical user interface, storing all data in a database, deploying as a Web application, and so on.

Code Example

The code for our case study is in the **CaseStudy** folder for this chapter.

Designing the Abstractions

Bearing in mind that eventually we want to implement not only a hotel reservation system, but also a system for other kinds of reservations, including plane and car rental, it behooves us at the beginning to look for appropriate abstractions. The more functionality we are able to put in base classes, the less work we will have to do in order to implement a particular kind of reservation system. On the other hand, having more functionality in the base classes can reduce the range of problems to which they are applicable. Good design is a balancing act.

Another attribute of well-designed abstractions is that they will survive major changes in implementation. As we shall see later in this book, our VB.NET abstractions of the hotel reservation system remain intact as we implement the system on an SQL Server database.

These abstractions will be represented in VB.NET by abstract classes (classes declared with the **MustInherit** keyword), defined in the file **Broker.vb** in the **CaseStudy** folder for this chapter.

RESERVABLE

Our first abstraction is the thing we are looking to reserve. We will denote this abstraction as simply **Reservable**. The basic issue in reservations is resource usage. There are a limited number of reservable resources. Hence the key attribute of a **Reservable** is **Capacity**. For example, a hotel may have 100 rooms. A flight may have 250 seats. We will also want a unique identifier for a **Reservable**, which we will denote by **m_unitid**. (The shorter name **m_unitid** is used in preference to the longer, more awkward name **m_reservableid**. Later we will see other use of the terminology "unit." For example, the method to add a reservable is called **AddUnit**.)

For our applications, we are going to introduce an additional attribute, **Cost**. There is a room rate for a hotel, a ticket cost for a flight, and so on. Note that this attribute may not be applicable to all things that are being reserved. For example, a conference room within a company may not have a cost assigned to it. However, our applications are for commercial customers, so we choose to include **Cost** in our model.

Simplifications

Because our case study is designed to illustrate concepts in VB.NET and the .NET Framework, we will choose many simplifications in our design so that we do not become bogged down in detailed design issues. For example, in real life a hotel has several different kinds of rooms, each having a different rate. Similarly, an airplane flight will have different classes of seats. Here the situation in real life is even more complicated, because the price of a seat may vary wildly depending on when the reservation is made, travel restrictions, and so on. To make life simple for us, we are assuming that each instance of a particular reservable will have the same cost.

In VB.NET we will represent a **Reservable** by an *abstract class* with the **MustInherit** keyword.

```
Public MustInherit Class Reservable
    Private Shared m_nextid As Integer = 0
    Protected m_unitid As Integer
    Protected Friend Capacity As Integer
    Protected Friend Cost As Decimal
    Public Sub New( _
     ByVal capacity As Integer, _
     ByVal cost As Decimal)
        Me.Capacity = capacity
        Me.Cost = cost
        m_unitid = m_nextid
        m_nextid += 1
    End Sub
End Class
```

A constructor allows us to specify the **capacity** and **cost** when the object is created. The **m_unitid** is initialized with a shared variable named **m_nextid** that is automatically incremented. This ID starts out at 0, because it is also going to be used in our implementation as an index into a two-dimensional array to track the number of customers having a reservation at a given reservable on a given date.

We will discuss the role of the **Private**, **Protected**, **Public**, and **Friend** access control specifiers later.

RESERVATION

When a customer books a reservation of a reservable, a record of the reservation will be made. The **Reservation** class holds the information that will be stored.

```
Public MustInherit Class Reservation
    Public ReservationId As Integer
    Public UnitId As Integer
    Public DateTime As DateTime
    Public NumberDays As Integer
    Private Shared m_nextReservationId As Integer = 1

    Public Sub New()
        ReservationId = m_nextReservationId
        m_nextReservationId += 1
    End Sub
End Class
```

The **ReservationId** is automatically generated by incrementing a shared member named **m_nextReservationId**, starting with the value 1. The **UnitId** member identifies the reservable that was booked. **DateTime** is the starting date of the reservation, and **NumberDays** specifies the number of days for which the reservation was made.

BROKER

Our third abstraction, **Broker**, models a broker of any kind of reservable and is also represented by an abstract class. It maintains a list of reservables, represented by the array **m_units**, and a list of reservations, represented by the array **m_reservations**. The two-dimensional array **m_numCust** keeps track of the number of customers having a reservation at a given reservable on a given day.

```
Public MustInherit Class Broker
    Private m_maxDay As Integer
    Private Const m_MAXRESERVATION As Integer = 10
    Private Shared m_nextReservation As Integer = 0
    Private Shared m_nextUnit As Integer = 0
    Private m_numCust(,) As Integer
    Protected m_reservations() As Reservation
    Protected m_units() As Reservable

    Public Sub New( _
     ByVal MaxDay As Integer, _
     ByVal MaxUnit As Integer)
        m_maxDay = MaxDay
        m_numCust = New Integer(MaxDay, MaxUnit) {}
        m_units = New Reservable(MaxUnit) {}
        m_reservations = _
            New Reservation(m_MAXRESERVATION) {}
    End Sub
    ...
```

RESERVATIONRESULT

A simple structure is used for returning the result from making a reservation.

```
Public Structure ReservationResult
    Public ReservationId As Integer
    Public ReservationCost As Decimal
    Public Rate As Decimal
    Public Comment As String
End Structure
```

The **Rate** is the cost for one day, and **ReservationCost** is the total cost, which is equal to the number of days multiplied by the cost for one day. The **ReservationId** is returned as –1 if there was a problem, and an explanation of the problem is provided in the **Comment** field. This structure is created so that result information can be passed in distributed scenarios, such as Web services, where you cannot throw exceptions.

Base Class Logic

The base class **Broker** not only represents the abstraction of a broker of any kind of reservable, it also contains general logic for booking reservations and maintaining a list of reservations. Our ability to capture this logic abstractly gives power to this base class and will make implementing reservations in a derived class relatively simple.

RESERVE

The core method of the **Broker** class is **Reserve**.

```
Protected Function Reserve( _
 ByRef res As Reservation) As ReservationResult
    Dim unitid As Integer = res.UnitId
    Dim dt As DateTime = res.DateTime
    Dim numDays As Integer = res.NumberDays
    Dim result As ReservationResult = _
         New ReservationResult()
    ' Check if dates are within supported range
    Dim day As Integer = dt.DayOfYear - 1
    If (day + numDays > m_maxDay) Then
       result.ReservationId = -1
       result.Comment = "Dates out of range"
       Return result
    End If
    ' Check if rooms are available for all dates
    Dim i As Integer
    For i = day To day + numDays - 1
       If m_numCust(i, unitid) >= _
        m_units(unitid).Capacity Then
          result.ReservationId = -1
          result.Comment = "Room not available"
          Return result
       End If
    Next
    ' Reserve a room for requested dates
    For i = day To day + numDays - 1
       m_numCust(i, unitid) += 1
    Next
    ' Add res to reservation list and return result
    AddReservation(res)
    result.ReservationId = res.ReservationId
    result.ReservationCost = _
       m_units(unitid).Cost * numDays
    result.Rate = m_units(unitid).Cost
    result.Comment = "OK"
    Return result
End Function
```

The **Reserve** method is designed to implement booking several different kinds of reservations. Thus the **Reservation** object, which will be stored in the list of reservations, is created in a more specialized class derived from **Broker** and is passed as a parameter to **Reserve**. For example, a **HotelBroker** will book a **HotelReservation**, and so on. The **UnitId**, **DateTime**, and **NumberDays** fields are extracted from the **Reservation** object, and a **ReservationResult** object is created that is returned.

```
Protected Function Reserve( _
 ByRef res As Reservation) As ReservationResult
   Dim unitid As Integer = res.UnitId
   Dim dt As DateTime = res.DateTime
   Dim numDays As Integer = res.NumberDays
   Dim result As ReservationResult = _
      New ReservationResult()
   . . .
```

Next we check that all the dates requested for the reservation are within the supported range (which for simplicity we are taking as a single year). We make use of the **DateTime** structure from the **System** namespace. We return an error if a date lies out of range.

```
' Check if dates are within supported range
Dim day As Integer = dt.DayOfYear - 1
If (day + numDays > m_maxDay) Then
   result.ReservationId = -1
   result.Comment = "Dates out of range"
   Return result
End If
 . . .
```

Now we check that space is available for each date, using the **m_numCust** array that tracks how many customers currently have reservations for each day and comparing against the capacity. The first dimension of this two-dimensional array indexes on days, and the second dimension indexes on the unit ID. (Note that for simplicity we have given our fields and methods names suitable for our initial application, a **HotelBroker**.)

```
' Check if rooms are available for all dates
Dim i As Integer
For i = day To day + numDays - 1
   If m_numCust(i, unitid) >= _
    m_units(unitid).Capacity Then
      result.ReservationId = -1
      result.Comment = "Room not available"
      Return result
   End If
Next
 . . .
```

Next, we actually reserve the unit for the requested days, which is implemented by incrementing the customer count in **m_numCust** for each day.

```
' Reserve a room for requested dates
For i = day To day + numDays - 1
   m_numCust(i, unitid) += 1
Next
...
```

Finally, we add the reservation to the list of reservations and return the result.

```
' Add res to reservation list and return result
AddReservation(res)
result.ReservationId = res.ReservationId
result.ReservationCost = _
   m_units(unitid).Cost * numDays
result.Rate = m_units(unitid).Cost
result.Comment = "OK"
Return result
End Function
```

LISTS OF RESERVATIONS AND RESERVABLES

The **Broker** class also maintains lists of **Reservation** and **Reservable** objects. For our simple array implementation, we only implement methods for adding elements. In a later version, we will provide logic to add and remove elements from lists.

```
Private Sub AddReservation(ByRef res As Reservation)
   m_reservations(m_nextReservation) = res
   m_nextReservation += 1
End Sub
Protected Sub AddUnit(ByRef unit As Reservable)
   m_units(m_nextUnit) = unit
   m_nextUnit += 1
End Sub
```

Designing the Encapsulation

In our current implementation of **Broker** all lists are represented by arrays. Since this implementation may not (and in fact will not) be preserved in later versions, we do not want to expose the arrays themselves or the subscripts that are used for manipulating the arrays. We provide public properties **NumberUnits** and **NumberReservations** to provide read-only access to the private variables **m_nextUnit** and **m_nextReservation**.

```
Public ReadOnly Property NumberUnits() As Integer
   Get
      Return m_nextUnit
   End Get
End Property
Public ReadOnly Property NumberReservations() _
 As Integer
   Get
      Return m_nextReservation
   End Get
End Property
```

In our **Reservation** class the simple fields **ReservationId**, **UnitId**, **DateTime**, and **NumberDays** are not likely to undergo a change in representation, so we do not encapsulate them. Later, if necessary, we could change some of these to properties without breaking client code. For now, and likely forever, we simply use public fields.

```
Public MustInherit Class Reservation
   Public ReservationId As Integer
   Public UnitId As Integer
   Public DateTime As DateTime
   Public NumberDays As Integer
   . . .
```

Inheritance in VB.NET

VB.NET supports a single inheritance model. Thus a class may derive from a single base class, and not from more than one. (In fact, as we saw in the previous chapter, every class in VB.NET ultimately derives from the root class **System.Object.**[3] This single inheritance model is simple and avoids the complexities and ambiguities associated with multiple inheritance, as in C++. Although a VB.NET class can inherit only from a single base *class*, it may inherit from several *interfaces*, a topic we will discuss in the next chapter.

In this section we discuss inheritance in connection with a further elaboration of our hotel reservation case study. In the following section we will cover additional features of inheritance in VB.NET, illustrated by an employee class hierarchy.

---

3. In previous versions of VB, the **Variant** type represented the universal data type. In VB.NET, the **Object** class is the universal data type. The **Variant** type is no longer supported in VB.NET. **Variant** is still a reserved word, but it has no actual syntactical use in VB.NET.

Inheritance Fundamentals

With inheritance, you factor the abstractions in your object model and put the more reusable abstractions in a high-level base class. You can add or change features in more specialized derived classes, which "inherit" the standard behavior from the base class. Inheritance facilitates code reuse, extensibility, and maintainability. A derived class can also provide a more appropriate interface to existing members of the base class.

Consider **Reservable** as a base class, with derived classes such as **Hotel**. All reservables share some characteristics, such as an ID, a capacity, and a cost. Different kinds of reservables differ in other respects. For example, a hotel has a **City** and a **HotelName**.

VB.NET INHERITANCE SYNTAX

You implement inheritance in VB.NET by specifying the derived class in the **Class** statement with the keyword **Inherits** followed by the base class. The file **HotelBroker.vb** in the **CaseStudy** folder illustrates deriving a new class **Hotel** from the class **Reservable**.

```
' HotelBroker.vb

Imports System

Namespace OI.NetVb.Acme⁴

    Public Class Hotel
        Inherits Reservable
        Public City As String
        Public HotelName As String

        Public Sub New( _
         ByRef city As String, _
         ByRef name As String, _
         ByVal number As Integer, _
         ByVal cost As Decimal)
           MyBase.New(number, cost)
           Me.City = city
           HotelName = name
        End Sub

        Public ReadOnly Property HotelId() As Integer
           Get
               Return m_unitid
           End Get
```

---

4. We discuss creating a namespace with the **Namespace** directive later in the chapter.

```
            End Property

    Public ReadOnly Property NumberRooms() As Integer
        Get
            Return Capacity
        End Get
    End Property

    Public ReadOnly Property Rate() As Decimal
        Get
            Return Cost
        End Get
    End Property
End Class
```

The class **Hotel** automatically has all the members of **Reservable**, and in addition has the fields **City** and **HotelName**.

CHANGING THE INTERFACE TO EXISTING MEMBERS

The base class **Reservable** has the Protected member **m_unitid**. Private and Protected members are intended for internal use and are not exposed as such to the outside world. A Protected member, while not accessible to the outside world, is accessible to derived classes. In the **Hotel** class, which inherits from **Reservable**, we provide the public property **HotelId** to give clients read-only access to the Protected member **m_unitid**. When we implement a property in this way, we can choose a name that is meaningful, such as **HotelId**, in place of a more abstract name, such as **m_unitid**, used in the base class. Also, the implementation details of such an encapsulated member may be changed without breaking existing code that accesses the public property.

INVOKING BASE CLASS CONSTRUCTORS

If your derived class has a constructor with parameters, you may wish to pass some of these parameters along to a base class constructor. In VB.NET you can conveniently invoke a base class constructor by calling **MyBase.New**, with the desired parameter list.

```
        Public Sub New( _
          ByRef city As String, _
          ByRef name As String, _
          ByVal number As Integer, _
          ByVal cost As Decimal)
            MyBase.New(number, cost)
            Me.City = city
            HotelName = name
        End Sub
```

Note that the syntax allows you to explicitly invoke a constructor only of an immediate base class. There is no notation that allows you to directly invoke a constructor higher up the inheritance hierarchy.

Access Control

VB.NET has two means for controlling accessibility of class members. Access can be controlled at both the class level and the member level.

Class Accessibility

An access modifier can be placed in front of the **Class** keyword to control which code can get at the class at all. Access can be further restricted by member accessibility, discussed in the next subsection.

PUBLIC

The most common access modifier of a class is **Public**, which makes the class available to all code in the program. Whenever we are implementing a class that all code can use, we want to make it **Public**.

FRIEND

The **Friend** modifier makes a class available within the current assembly, which can be thought of as a logical EXE or DLL. (Assemblies were introduced in Chapter 2 and will be discussed in more detail in Chapter 9.) All of our projects so far have built a single assembly, with both the client test program and the class(es) in this assembly. That means that if we had used **Friend** for the class modifier, the programs would have still worked. But later, if we put our classes into a DLL and tried to access them from a client program in a separate EXE, any **Friend** classes would not be accessible. So using **Public** for class accessibility is generally a good idea.

A common use of the **Friend** modifier is for helper classes that are intended to be used only within the current assembly, and not generally.

Member Accessibility

Access to individual class members is controlled by placing an access modifier such as **Public** or **Private** in front of the member. Member access can only further restrict access to a class, not widen it. Thus if you have a class with **Friend** accessibility, making a member **Public** will not make it accessible from outside the assembly.

PUBLIC

A **Public** member can be accessed from outside the class, even from other assemblies.

PRIVATE

A **Private** member can be accessed only from within the class (but not from derived classes).

PROTECTED

Inheritance introduces a third kind of accessibility, **Protected**. A protected member can be accessed from within the class and from within any derived classes.

FRIEND

A **Friend** member can be accessed from within classes in the same assembly but not from classes outside the assembly.

PROTECTED FRIEND

A **Protected Friend** member can be accessed by any class within the assembly and by any derived class from outside the assembly.

Access Control in the Case Study

The **Reservable** class in the file **broker.vb** illustrates the member access-control options that we have been discussing.

```
Public MustInherit Class Reservable
   Private Shared m_nextid As Integer = 0
   Protected m_unitid As Integer
   Protected Friend Capacity As Integer
   Protected Friend Cost As Decimal

   Public Sub New( _
    ByVal capacity As Integer, _
    ByVal cost As Decimal)
      Me.Capacity = capacity
      Me.Cost = cost
      m_unitid = m_nextid
      m_nextid += 1
   End Sub
End Class
```

The shared member **m_nextid** is strictly **Private**, because it is used for automatically generating an ID and has no use outside the class. The member

m_unitid is **Protected** because it is used in derived classes, such as **Hotel**, but not elsewhere. The members **Capacity** and **Cost** are used both in derived classes (such as **Hotel**) and in the class **Broker**, which is not a derived class but is in the same assembly. The **Protected Friend** access-control specification is ideal for this case. Note that if we had used just **Friend**, the program would have still compiled. But since later we may wish to implement derived classes in other assemblies, **Protected Friend** is more appropriate. Finally, the constructor is **Public**, so that it can be accessed from any code in the program.

Acme Travel Agency Case Study: Implementation

With the abstractions **Reservable**, **Reservation**, and **Broker** already in place, it now becomes very easy to implement a reservation system for a particular kind of reservable, such as a **Hotel**. Figure 5–2 illustrates our inheritance hierarchy. **Hotel** derives from **Reservable**, **HotelReservation** derives from **Reservation**, and **HotelBroker** derives from **Broker**.

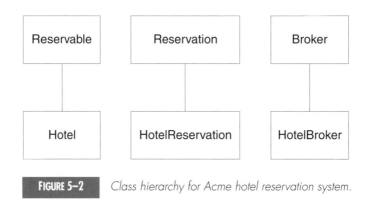

FIGURE 5–2   *Class hierarchy for Acme hotel reservation system.*

In this section we will examine key pieces of the implementation of the case study, which is in the **CaseStudy** folder for this chapter.

Running the Case Study

Code
Example

Before proceeding with our code walkthrough, it would be a good idea to build and run the case study. The program **TestBroker.exe** is a console application. By typing "help" at the command prompt, you can obtain a list of commands:

```
Enter command, quit to exit
H> help
The following commands are available:
```

```
hotels      shows all hotels in a city
all         shows all hotels
cities      shows all cities
add         adds a hotel
book        book a reservation
bookings    show all bookings
register    register a customer
email       change email address
show        show customers
quit        exit the program
H>
```

Experiment with this program until you have a clear understanding of its various features.

HotelReservation

HotelReservation is a simple class derived from **Reservation**. The code is in the file **hotelbroker.vb**. It adds some additional public fields and provides the property **ArrivalDate** as a more meaningful wrapper around the generic **DateTime** field of the base class.

```
Public Class HotelReservation
   Inherits Reservation

   Public CustomerId As Integer
   Public HotelName As String
   Public City As String
   Public DepartureDate As DateTime

   Public Property ArrivalDate() As DateTime
      Get
         ArrivalDate = DateTime
      End Get
      Set(ByVal Value As DateTime)
         DateTime = Value
      End Set
   End Property
End Class
```

HotelBroker

The heart of the implementation is the **HotelBroker** class, derived from **Broker**. The code is also in the file **hotelbroker.vb**.

```
Public Class HotelBroker
   Inherits Broker

   Private Const m_MAXDAY As Integer = 366
```

```
Private Const m_MAXUNIT As Integer = 10
Private Const m_MAXCITY As Integer = 5
Private Shared m_nextCity As Integer = 0
Private m_cities() As String

Public Sub New()
   MyBase.New(m_MAXDAY, m_MAXUNIT)
   m_cities = New String(m_MAXCITY) {}
   AddHotel("Atlanta", "Dixie", 100, 115D)
   AddHotel("Atlanta", "Marriot", 500, 70D)
   AddHotel("Boston", "Sheraton", 250, 95D)
End Sub
...
```

There are constants for various array definitions and a new array to hold the cities. The constructor passes some array definitions to the base class, initializes the **m_cities** array, and adds some starter hotels as test data.

The next part of the code defines a **NumberCity** property and provides a method to add a hotel.

```
Public ReadOnly Property NumberCity() As Integer
    Get
        Return m_nextCity
    End Get
End Property

Public Function AddHotel( _
 ByRef city As String, _
 ByRef name As String, _
 ByVal number As Integer, _
 ByVal cost As Decimal) As String
    If FindId(city, name) <> -1 Then
      Return "Hotel is already on the list"
    End If
    Dim hotel As Hotel = New Hotel( _
       city, name, number, cost)
    AddUnit(hotel)
    AddCity(city)
    Return "OK"
End Function
...
```

Private helper functions are provided to find the ID of a hotel and to add a city to the list of cities. A city can be added only if it is not already on the list; duplicates are not permitted.

```
Private Function FindId( _
 ByRef city As String, _
 ByRef name As String) As Integer
    Dim i As Integer
```

```
   For i = 0 To NumberUnits - 1
      Dim hotel As Hotel = m_units(i)
      If hotel.City = city And _
       hotel.HotelName = name Then
         Return hotel.HotelId
      End If
   Next
   Return -1
End Function

Private Sub AddCity(ByRef city As String)
   ' check if city already on list, add if not
   If (Not Contains(city)) Then
      m_cities(m_nextCity) = city
      m_nextCity += 1
   End If
End Sub

Private Function Contains(ByRef city As String) _
 As Boolean
   Dim i As Integer
   For i = 0 To NumberCity - 1
      If (m_cities(i) = city) Then
         Return True
      End If
   Next
   Return False
End Function
```

Methods are provided to show all the hotels, all the hotels in a given city, and to show the cities. You may wish to examine these methods in the solution provided, for a review of formatting in VB.NET. We do not show these methods here.

We finally come to the key method **Reserve**, which is used to book a hotel reservation.

```
Public Overloads Function Reserve( _
 ByVal customerId As Integer, _
 ByRef city As String, _
 ByRef name As String, _
 ByVal dt As DateTime, _
 ByVal numDays As Integer) As ReservationResult
   Dim id As Integer = FindId(city, name)
   If id = -1 Then
      Dim result As ReservationResult = _
         New ReservationResult()
      result.ReservationId = -1
      result.Comment = "Hotel not found"
      Return result
   End If
```

```
        Dim res As HotelReservation = _
            New HotelReservation()
        res.UnitId = id
        res.CustomerId = customerId
        res.HotelName = name
        res.City = city
        res.ArrivalDate = dt
        res.DepartureDate = dt.Add( _
            New TimeSpan(numDays, 0, 0, 0))
        res.NumberDays = numDays
        Return Reserve(res)
    End Function
```

The code in this class is very simple, because it relies upon logic in the base class **Broker**. An error is returned if the hotel cannot be found on the list of hotels. Then a **HotelReservation** object is created, which is passed to the **Reserve** method of the base class. (Note use of the **Overloads** keyword, and the fact that the base class **Reserve** has a different signature than the **Reserve** method in the derived class.) We create the reservation object in the derived class because we are interested in all the fields of the derived **HotelReservation** class, not just the fields of the base **Reservation** class. We have previously used the **DateTime** structure, and we now use the **TimeSpan** structure in calculating the departure date by adding the number of days of the stay to the arrival date. This calculation relies on the fact that the **Add** method is provided by the **DateTime** structure.

Customers

No reservation system can exist without modeling the customers that use it. The **Customers** class in the file **customer.vb** maintains a list of **Customer** objects. Again we use an array as our representation. This code has very similar structure to code dealing with hotels, and so we show it only in outline form, giving the data structures and the declarations of the public methods and properties.

```
' Customer.vb

Imports System

Namespace OI.NetVb.Acme

    Public Class Customer
        Public CustomerId As Integer
        Public FirstName As String
        Public LastName As String
        Public EmailAddress As String
        Private Shared m_nextCustId As Integer = 1
        Public Sub New( _
```

```vbnet
        ByRef first As String, _
        ByRef last As String, _
        ByRef email As String)
          CustomerId = m_nextCustId
          m_nextCustId += 1
          FirstName = first
          LastName = last
          EmailAddress = email
        End Sub
    End Class

  Public Class Customers
      Private m_customers As Customer()
      Private Shared m_nextCust As Integer = 0
      Public Sub New(ByVal MaxCust As Integer)
          m_customers = New Customer(MaxCust) {}
          RegisterCustomer( _
              "Rocket", _
              "Squirrel", _
              "rocky@frosbitefalls.com")
          RegisterCustomer( _
              "Bullwinkle", _
              "Moose", _
              "moose@wossamotta.edu")
      End Sub
      Public ReadOnly Property NumberCustomers(...
      ...
      Public Function RegisterCustomer(...
      ...
      Private Sub Add(ByRef cust As Customer)
      ...
      Public Sub ShowCustomers(...
      ...
      Private Function FindIndex(...
      ...
      Public Sub ChangeEmailAddress(...
      ...
    End Class
End Namespace
```

Namespace

All case study code is in the namespace **OI.NetVb.Acme**. All of the files defining classes begin with a **Namespace** directive. There is a corresponding **Imports** directive, which you will see in the file **TestHotel.vb**.[5]

---

5. If you look at the properties for the project, you will see that we have made the "Root namespace" blank. If we had not done so, the actual namespace would have been **TestHotel.OI.NetVb.Acme**.

```
' Customer.vb

Imports System

Namespace OI.NetVb.Acme
...
```

TestHotel

The **TestHotel** class in the file **TestHotel.vb** contains an interactive program to exercise the **Hotel** and **Customer** classes supporting the commands shown previously, where we suggested running the case study. There is a command loop to read in a command and then exercise it. There is a big **Try** block around all the commands with a **Catch** handler afterward. (We discuss exception handling with **Try...Catch** later in the chapter.) Note the **Imports** statements to gain access to the namespaces.

```
' TestHotel.vb

Imports System
Imports OI.NetVb.Acme

Module TestHotel
    Sub Main()
        Const MAXCUST As Integer = 10
        Dim hotelBroker As HotelBroker = New HotelBroker()
        Dim customers As Customers = New Customers(MAXCUST)
        Dim iw As InputWrapper = New InputWrapper()
        Dim cmd As String
        Console.WriteLine("Enter command, quit to exit")
        cmd = iw.getString("H> ")
        While Not cmd.Equals("quit")
            Try
                If (cmd.Equals("hotels")) Then
                    Dim city As String = _
                        iw.getString("city: ")
                    hotelBroker.ShowHotels(city)
                ElseIf (cmd.Equals("all")) Then
                    hotelBroker.ShowHotels()
                ElseIf (cmd.Equals("cities")) Then
                    ...
                Else
                    hotelhelp()
                End If
            Catch e As Exception
                Console.WriteLine( _
                    "Exception: {0}", e.Message)
            End Try
            cmd = iw.getString("H> ")
```

```
        End While
      End Sub
      Private Function hotelhelp()
        Console.WriteLine( _
          "The following commands are available:")
        ...
      End Function
End Module
```

More about Inheritance

Our case study has illustrated many important features of object-oriented programming, but there is more to the story. Methods in a derived class may *hide* the corresponding method in the base class, possibly making use of the base class method in their implementation. Alternatively, the base class may have *virtual methods,* which are not bound to an object at compile time but are bound dynamically at runtime. A derived class may *override* a virtual method. This dynamic binding behavior enables *polymorphic* code, which is general code that applies to classes in a hierarchy, and the specific class that determines the behavior is determined at runtime.

VB.NET provides keywords **Overridable** and **Overrides** that precisely specify in base and derived classes, respectively, that the programmer is prescribing dynamic binding. By providing a mechanism to specify polymorphic behavior in the language, VB.NET helps programs deal with an issue known as the *fragile base class problem,* which can result in unexpected behavior in a program when a base class in a library is modified but the program that uses the library is unchanged.

Employee Class Hierarchy

In this section we will use a much simpler class hierarchy to illustrate some important concepts. The base class is **Employee**, which has a public field **Name**. There are two derived classes. The **SalaryEmployee** class has a private **m_salary** field. The **WageEmployee** class has private fields for an hourly **m_rate** of pay and for the number of **m_hours** worked. Figure 5–3 illustrates this simple class hierarchy.

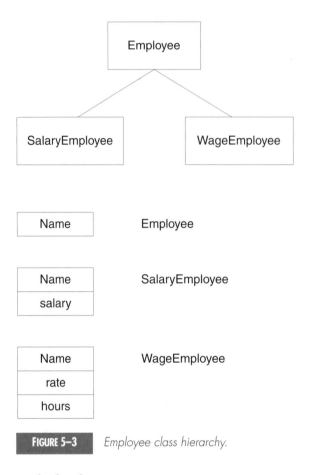

FIGURE 5-3   *Employee class hierarchy.*

Method Hiding

A derived class inherits the methods of its base class, and these inherited methods are automatically available "as is." Sometimes we may want the derived class to do something a little different for some of the methods of the base class. In this case we will put code for these changed methods in the derived class, and we say the derived class "hides" the corresponding methods in the base class. Note that hiding a method requires that the signatures match exactly, and the **Shadows** keyword is used. (As we discussed in Chapter 4, methods have the same signature if they have the same number of parameters, and these parameters have the same types and modifiers, such as **ByRef** or **ByVal**. The return type does not contribute to defining the signature of a method.)

In VB.NET, if you declare a method in a derived class that has the same signature as a method in the base class, you will get a compiler warning message. In such a circumstance, there are two things you may wish to do. The first is to *hide* the base class method, which is what we discuss in this section. The second is to *override* the base class method, which we will discuss in the next section.

To hide a base class method, place the keyword **Shadows** in front of the method in the derived class. When you hide a method of the base class, you may want to call the base class method within your implementation of the new method. You can do this by using the keyword **MyBase**, followed by a period, followed by the method name and parameters.

Code Example

The example program **HideEmployee** illustrates method hiding. This program has the **Employee** base class and the **SalaryEmployee** derived class. Each class has a **Show** method. The derived class's **Show** method hides the **Show** method of the base class. But the derived class can call the base class **Show** method through the **MyBase** keyword. Here is the code:

```
' Employee.vb

Imports System

Public Class Employee
    Public Name As String

    Public Sub New(ByRef name As String)
       Me.Name = name
    End Sub

    Public Sub Show()
       Console.WriteLine("name = {0}", Name)
    End Sub
End Class

Public Class SalaryEmployee
    Inherits Employee

    Private m_salary As Decimal

    Public Sub New( _
     ByVal name As String, ByVal salary As Decimal)
       MyBase.New(name)
       Me.m_salary = salary
    End Sub

    Public Shadows Sub Show()
       MyBase.Show()
       Console.WriteLine("salary = {0:C}", m_salary)
    End Sub
End Class
```

If you delete the **Shadows** keyword in the derived class **Show** method, you will get a compiler warning message:

```
warning BC40004: 'sub Show' conflicts with 'sub Show' on
the base class 'Employee' - they have the same name.  Use
the 'Shadows' keyword if you want to hide the name in the
base class.
```

Static Binding

In VB.NET the normal way methods are tied to classes is through *static binding*. That means that the object reference type is used at compile time to determine the class whose method is called. The **HideEmployee** program we just looked at illustrates static binding, using a simple **Employee** class and a derived **SalaryEmployee** class. Here is the test program:

```
' TestEmployee.vb

Imports System

Module TestEmployee
    Sub Main()
        Dim emp As Employee = New Employee("Ellen")
        Dim sal As SalaryEmployee = _
           New SalaryEmployee("Sally", 100D)
        emp.Show()
        sal.Show()
        'sal = emp
        emp = sal
        emp.Show()
    End Sub
End Module
```

In this program **emp** is an object reference of type **Employee**. Calling **Show** through this object reference will *always* result in **Employee.Show** being called, no matter what kind of object **emp** may actually be referring to. Here is the output. Notice that the second time we call **Show** through **emp** we are still getting the **Employee** version of **Show** (only the name is displayed).

```
name = Ellen
name = Sally
salary = $100.00
name = Sally
Press any key to continue
```

TYPE CONVERSIONS IN INHERITANCE

This program also illustrates another feature of inheritance, type conversions. After the objects **emp** and **sal** have been instantiated, the object references will be referring to different types of objects, one of type **Employee** and the other of type **SalaryEmployee**. Note that the **SalaryEmployee** object has an additional field, **m_salary**.

The test program tries two type conversions:

```
'sal = emp
emp = sal
```

The first assignment is illegal, as you can verify by uncommenting it, recompiling, and then trying to run the program. This will result in a **System.InvalidCastException** being thrown. Suppose the assignment were allowed. Then you would have an object reference of type **SalaryEmployee** referring to an **Employee** object. If the conversion "down the hierarchy" (from a base class to a derived class) were allowed, it would result in data corruption if the nonexistent member were written to.

```
emp = sal
```

This assignment is perfectly safe and legal. We are converting "up the hierarchy." This is okay because of the IS-A relationship of inheritance. A salary employee "is an" employee. It is a special kind of employee. Everything that applies to an employee also applies to a salary employee. There is no "extra field" in the **Employee** class that is not also present in the **SalaryEmployee** class.

Virtual Methods

In VB.NET you can specify that a method in VB.NET will be bound *dynamically*. Only at runtime will it be determined whether the base or derived class's method will be called. The program **VirtualEmployee** illustrates this behavior. The file **VirtualEmployee.vb** contains class definitions for a base class and a derived class, as before. But this time the **Show** method is declared as virtual in the base class with the **Overridable** keyword. In the derived class the **Show** method is declared the **Overrides** keyword (in place of **Shadow** that we used before with method hiding). Now the **Show** method in the derived class does not hide the base class method but rather *overrides* it.

Code Example

```
' VirtualEmployee.vb

Imports System

Public Class Employee
   Public Name As String

   Public Sub New(ByVal name As String)
```

```
        Me.Name = name
    End Sub

    Public Overridable Sub Show()
        Console.WriteLine("name = {0}", Name)
    End Sub
End Class

Public Class SalaryEmployee
    Inherits Employee

    Private m_salary As Decimal

    Public Sub New( _
     ByVal name As String, _
     ByVal salary As Decimal)
        MyBase.New(name)
        m_salary = salary
    End Sub

    Public Overrides Sub Show()
        MyBase.Show()
        Console.WriteLine("salary = {0:C}", m_salary)
    End Sub
End Class
```

We use the same test program as in the previous example. Here is the output. Now, the second time we call **Show** through **sal**, we will be getting the **SalaryEmployee.Show** method, showing the salary as well as the name, rather than the **Employee.Show** method of the base class. This is known as virtual method invocation, or dynamic binding, and it is polymorphism in action.

```
name = Ellen
name = Sally
salary = $100.00
name = Sally
salary = $100.00
Press any key to continue
```

VIRTUAL METHODS AND EFFICIENCY

Virtual method invocation (dynamic binding) is slightly less efficient than calling an ordinary nonvirtual method (static binding). With a virtual method call, there is some overhead at runtime associated with determining which class's method will be invoked. VB.NET allows you to specify in a base class whether you want the flexibility of a virtual method or the slightly greater efficiency of a nonvirtual method. You simply decide whether or not to use the keyword **Overridable**. (In some languages all methods are virtual, and you don't have this choice.)

METHOD OVERRIDING

The **Overrides** keyword in VB.NET is very useful for making programs clearer. In some languages, such as C++, there is no special notation for overriding a method in a derived class. You simply declare a method with the same signature, as a method in the base class, and overriding is implicit, or even accidental. If the base class method is a virtual method, the behavior is to override. If the base class method is not virtual, the behavior is to hide. In VB.NET this behavior is made explicitly clear in the derived class.

The Fragile Base Class Problem

One subtle pitfall in object-oriented programming is the fragile base class problem. Suppose the **Overrides** keyword syntax did not exist. Suppose further that you derive a class from a third-party class library, and you have a method in the derived class that does not hide or override any method in the base class.

Now a new version of the class library comes out, and the base class has a new virtual method whose signature happens to match one of the methods in your class. Now you can be in trouble! Classes that derive from your class may now behave in unexpected ways. Code that was "expected" to call the new method in the class library—or in code in a derived class that deliberately overrides this method—may now call your method that has nothing whatever to do with the method in the class library.

This situation is rare, but if it occurs, it can be extremely vicious. Fortunately, VB.NET helps you avoid such situations by requiring you to use the **Overrides** keyword if you are indeed going to perform an override. If you do not specify either **Overrides** or **Shadow** and a method in your derived class has the same signature as a method in a base class, you will get a compiler warning. Thus, if you build against a new version of the class library that introduces an accidental signature match with one of your methods, the compiler will warn you.

COM and the Fragile Base Class Problem

There is no implementation inheritance in Microsoft's Component Object Model (COM). Microsoft used the fragile base class problem as a rationale for not providing implementation inheritance in COM. The issue is much more important for binary components, such as COM objects, than for traditional class libraries distributed with source code, because if the problem arises and you have no source for the library, your options are limited. The real killer is for the problem not to reveal itself during development and testing, but to crop up in the field after the application has been deployed.

Microsoft .NET has aims similar to those COM had in providing binary components in multiple languages. The VB.NET Override concept uses a corresponding feature of .NET, so .NET is able to effectively utilize implementation inheritance with less risk than was the case with COM.

Polymorphism

Virtual functions make it easy to write polymorphic code in VB.NET. Our employee example illustrates the concept of polymorphic code. Imagine a large system with a great many different kinds of employees. How will you write and maintain code that deals with all these different employee types?

A traditional approach is to have a "type field" in an employee structure. Then code that manipulates an employee can key off of this type field to determine the correct processing to perform, perhaps using a **Select Case** statement. Although straightforward, this approach can be quite tedious and error prone. Introducing a new kind of employee can require substantial code maintenance, since all code that uses the structure must be upgraded.

Polymorphism can offer a cleaner solution. You organize the different kinds of employees in a class hierarchy, and you structure your program so that you write general-purpose methods that act upon an object reference whose type is that of the base class that does not change. Your code calls virtual methods of the base class. The call will be automatically dispatched to the appropriate derived class, depending on what kind of employee is actually being referenced. If you add new derived classes, the existing client code that only knows about the generalized base class will not have to be changed. This greatly reduces maintenance effort.

You trade off a slight degradation in runtime performance for more reliable code and less development effort.

Code Example

The program in **PolyEmployee\Step1** provides an illustration. The **GetPay** method is virtual, and methods in the derived class override it. Here is the code for the base class:

```
' Employee.vb

Public Class Employee
   Public Name As String

   Public Sub New(ByVal name As String)
      Me.Name = name
   End Sub

   Public Overridable Function GetPay() As Decimal
      Return 1D
   End Function
End Class
```

Methods in the derived classes override the virtual method in the base class. Here is the code for **SalaryEmployee**:

```
' SalaryEmployee.vb

Public Class SalaryEmployee
```

```
    Inherits Employee

    Private m_salary As Decimal
    ...
    Public Overrides Function GetPay() As Decimal
       Return m_salary
    End Function
End Class
```

The **WageEmployee** class provides its own override of **GetPay**, where pay is calculated differently.

```
' WageEmployee.vb

Imports System

Public Class WageEmployee
    Inherits Employee

    Private m_rate As Decimal
    Private m_hours As Double
    ...
    Public Overrides Function GetPay() As Decimal
       Return m_rate * Convert.ToDecimal(m_hours)
    End Function
End Class
```

The payoff comes in the client program, which can now call **GetPay** polymorphically. Here is the code for the test program:

```
' TestPoly.vb

Imports System

Module TestPoly
    Private m_employees() As Employee
    Private Const m_MAXEMPLOYEE As Integer = 10
    Private m_nextEmp As Integer = 0

    Public Sub Main()
       m_employees = New Employee(m_MAXEMPLOYEE) {}
       AddSalaryEmployee("Amy", 500D)
       AddWageEmployee("Bob", 15D, 40)
       AddSalaryEmployee("Charlie", 900D)
       PayReport()
    End Sub

    Private Sub AddSalaryEmployee( _
     ByVal name As String, ByVal salary As Decimal)
       m_employees(m_nextEmp) = _
         New SalaryEmployee(name, salary)
```

```
        m_nextEmp += 1
    End Sub

    Private Sub AddWageEmployee( _
     ByVal name As String, _
     ByVal rate As Decimal, _
     ByVal hours As Double)
       m_employees(m_nextEmp) = _
          New WageEmployee(name, rate, hours)
       m_nextEmp += 1
    End Sub

    Private Sub PayReport()
        Dim i As Integer
        For i = 0 To m_nextEmp - 1
           Dim emp As Employee = m_employees(i)
           Dim name As String = emp.Name.PadRight(10)
           Dim pay As String = _
              String.Format("{0:C}", emp.GetPay())
           Dim str As String = name + pay
           Console.WriteLine(str)
        Next
    End Sub
End Module
```

Here is the output:

```
Amy        $500.00
Bob        $600.00
Charlie    $900.00
```

Abstract Classes

Sometimes it does not make sense to instantiate a base class. Instead, the base class is used to define a standard template to be followed by the various derived classes. Such a base class is said to be *abstract,* and it cannot be instantiated. In VB.NET you can designate a base class as abstract by using the keyword **MustInherit**. The compiler will then flag an error if you try to instantiate the class.

An abstract class may have abstract methods, which are not implemented in the class but only in derived classes. The purpose of an abstract method is to provide a template for polymorphism. The method is called through an object reference to the abstract class, but at runtime the object reference will actually be referring to one of the concrete derived classes. The keyword **MustOverride** is used to declare abstract methods in an abstract class. An abstract method has no body, and it is not terminated with the regular **End Function** or **End Sub** keywords.

An abstract class can be used to provide a cleaner solution of our poly-morhphic payroll example. In the Step 1 solution we discussed previously, there was a virtual function **GetPay** in the base class that returned an arbitrary amount of $1.00, which is really quite silly and artificial. We know that this method will never actually be called, and it is going to be overridden. In fact, the **Employee** class will itself never be instantiated. Hence we make **Employee** an abstract class by marking it with the **MustInherit** keyword, and we make **GetPay** an abstract method by marking it with the **MustOverride** keyword. This solution is illustrated in **PolyEmployee\Step2**. Note that the **GetPay** method in the **Employee** class now does not have a silly, artificial implementation. In fact, it has no implementation at all!

Code Example

```
' Employee.vb

Imports System

Public MustInherit Class Employee
    Public Name As String
    Public Sub New(ByVal name As String)
        Me.Name = name
    End Sub
    Public MustOverride Function GetPay() As Decimal
End Class
```

Non-Inheritable Classes

At the opposite end of the spectrum from abstract classes are *non-inheritable* (also known as *sealed*) classes. While you *must* derive from an abstract class, you *cannot* derive from a non-inheritable class. A non-inheritable class pro-vides functionality that you can use as is, but you cannot derive from the class and hide or override any of its methods. An example in the .NET Framework class library of a non-inheritable class is **System.String**.

Marking a class as non-inheritable protects against unwarranted class derivations. It can also make the code a little more efficient, because any virtual functions inherited by the sealed class are automatically treated by the compiler as nonvirtual.

In VB.NET you use the **NotInheritable** keyword to mark a class as non-inheritable.

Heterogeneous Collections

A class hierarchy can be used to implement heterogeneous collections that can be treated polymorphically. For example, you can create an array whose element type is that of a base class. Then you can store within this array object references whose type is the base class, but which actually may refer to instances of various derived classes in the hierarchy. You may then iterate through the array and call on virtual methods. The appropriate method, as determined by late binding, will be called for each object in the array.

The program **PolyEmployee** example illustrates a heterogeneous array of three employees, which are a mixture of salary and wage employees.

Exceptions

An inevitable part of programming is dealing with error conditions of various sorts. This section introduces the exception-handling mechanism of VB.NET, beginning with a discussion of the fundamentals of error processing and various alternatives that are available. We then carefully go through the VB.NET exception mechanism, which includes a **Try** block, **Catch** handlers, and a **Finally** block. You can raise exceptions by means of a **Throw** statement. The .NET class library provides an **Exception** class, which you can use to pass information about an exception that occurred. To further specify your exception and to pass additional information, you can derive your own class from **Exception**. When handling an exception, you may want to throw a new exception. In such a case you can use the *inner exception* feature of the **Exception** class to pass the original exception on with your new exception.

Exception Fundamentals

The traditional way to deal with runtime errors is to have the functions you call return a status code. The status code may have a particular value for a good return and other values to denote various error conditions. The calling function should check this status code, and if an error was encountered, it performs appropriate error handling. This function in return may pass an error code to its calling function, and so on up the call stack.

Although straightforward, this mechanism has a number of drawbacks. The basic disadvantage is lack of robustness. The called function may have impeccable error-checking code and return appropriate error information, but all this information is useless if the calling function does not make use of it. The program may continue operation as if nothing were amiss and some time later crash for some mysterious reason. Also, status codes are nonstandard. A 0 may indicate success in one case but failure in another. And the caller and callee have to agree on return codes and their meaning.

Another disadvantage is that every function in the call stack must participate in the process, or the chain of error information will be broken. Also, undesirable flow control can leave certain code unexecuted, without performing all its cleanup work.

Furthermore, constructors cannot return a status code, and other methods may be better used for returning useful data rather than a status code.

.NET EXCEPTION HANDLING

VB.NET provides an *exception* mechanism that can be used for reporting and handling errors. An error is reported by "throwing" an exception. The error is handled by "catching" the exception. This mechanism is very similar in concept to that for exceptions in C#, C++, and Java.

Exceptions are implemented in .NET by the Common Language Runtime, so exceptions can be thrown in one .NET language and caught in another. The exception mechanism involves the following elements:

- Code that might encounter an exception should be enclosed in a **Try** block.
- Exceptions are caught in a **Catch** block.
- An exception object is passed as a parameter to a **Catch**. The data type of the exception object is **System.Exception** or a derived type.
- You may have multiple **Catch** blocks. A match is made based on the data type of the exception object.
- An optional **Finally** clause contains code that will be executed whether or not an exception is encountered.
- In the called method, an exception is raised through a **Throw** statement.

EXCEPTION FLOW OF CONTROL

The general structure of code that might encounter an exception is shown below:

```
Try
    ' code that might cause an exception to be thrown
Catch e As ExceptionClass1
    ' code to handle this type of exception
Catch e As ExceptionClass2
    ' code to handle this other type of exception
' possibly more catch handlers
Finally
    ' cleanup code that is executed whether or not
    ' an exception is caught or if catch handler itself
    ' throws an exception
End Try
```

Each catch handler has a parameter specifying the data type of the exception that it can handle. The exception data type can be **System.Exception** or a class ultimately derived from it. If an exception is thrown, the *first* catch handler that matches the exception data type is executed, and then control passes to the statement just after the catch block(s). If no handler is found, the exception is thrown to the next higher "context" (e.g., the function that called the current one). If no exception is thrown inside the try block, all the catch handlers are skipped.

CONTEXT AND STACK UNWINDING

As the flow of control of a program passes into nested blocks, local variables are pushed onto the stack and a new "context" is entered. Likewise, a new context is entered on a method call, which also pushes a return address onto the stack.

If an exception is not handled in the current context, it is passed to successively higher contexts until it is finally handled (or else is "uncaught" and is handled by a default system handler).

When the higher context is entered, VB.NET adjusts the stack properly, a process known as *stack unwinding*. In VB.NET exception handling, stack unwinding involves both setting the program counter and cleaning up variables (popping stack variables and marking heap variables as free so that the garbage collector can deallocate them).

SYSTEM.EXCEPTION

The **System.Exception** class provides a number of useful methods and properties for obtaining information about an exception.

- **Message** returns a text string providing information about the exception. This message is set when the exception object is constructed. If no message is specified, a generic message will be provided indicating the type of the exception. The **Message** property is read-only. (Hence, if you want to specify your own message, you must construct a new exception object, as done in the example above.)
- **StackTrace** returns a text string providing a stack trace at the place where the exception arose.
- **InnerException** holds a reference to another exception. When you throw a new exception, it is desirable not to lose the information about the original exception. The original exception can be passed as a parameter when constructing the new exception. The original exception object is then available through the **InnerException** property of the new exception. (We will provide an example of using inner exceptions later in this chapter.)

EXAMPLE PROGRAM

Now let's look at some code that illustrates the principles we have discussed so far. The program also illustrates using the **Exception** class to pass a string as a message when we throw an exception. We will use a simplified version of our **Hotel** class. This hotel accepts reservations for only a single date. There is a property **Capacity** and there are methods **MakeReservation** and **CancelReservation**. A reservation has an ID, a customer name, and the number of rooms requested. (In this example we have added a feature. Previously, a customer could reserve only a single room. We are now allowing multiple room requests. This is to simplify exercising our program to bump against the exception condition of exceeding the capacity of the hotel.) There is a property, **NumberReservations**, and an indexer to allow the calling program to access the reservation list.

There are several possible exceptions:

- User does not request a positive number of rooms.
- Room request exceeds the capacity of the hotel.
- Index out of range when attempting to store reservation in array of reservations.

The first two exceptions are thrown explicitly by our **Hotel** class, and the index out-of-range exception is thrown by the .NET library.

Our example program is in the directory **HotelException\Step1**.

Code Example

```
' HotelException.vb - Step 1

Imports System

Public Structure ReservationListItem
    Public ReservationId As Integer
    Public CustomerName As String
    Public NumberRooms As Integer
End Structure

Public Class Hotel
    Private m_capacity As Integer
    Private m_numGuests As Integer
    Private m_nextReservation As Integer = 0
    Private m_nextReservationId As Integer = 1
    Private Const MAXRESERVATIONS As Integer = 3
    Private m_reservations() As ReservationListItem

    Public Sub New(ByVal capacity As Integer)
        m_capacity = capacity
        m_reservations = _
            New ReservationListItem(MAXRESERVATIONS - 1) {}
    End Sub

    Public Function MakeReservation( _
      ByVal cust As String, _
      ByVal rooms As Integer) As Integer
        ' Requested number of rooms should be positive
        If rooms <= 0 Then
            Throw New Exception( _
                "Please request positive number of rooms")
        End If
        ' Check if rooms are available
        If (m_numGuests + rooms > Capacity) Then
            Throw New Exception("Rooms not available")
```

```
        End If
        ' Reserve the room for requested dates
        m_numGuests += rooms
        ' Fill in information for reservation
        Dim item As ReservationListItem
        item.ReservationId = m_nextReservationId
        m_nextReservationId += 1
        item.CustomerName = cust
        item.NumberRooms = rooms
        ' Add reservation to list, return reservation id
        reservations(m_nextReservation) = item
        m_nextReservation += 1
        Return item.ReservationId
    End Function
    ...
```

The next code fragment is the test program. Notice that we place the entire body of the command-processing loop inside a try block. The catch handler prints an error message that is passed within the exception object. Then, after either normal processing or displaying an error message, a new command is read in. This simple scheme provides reasonable error processing, as a bad command will not be acted upon, and the user will have an opportunity to enter a new command.

```
' Test.vb

Imports System

Module TestHotel
    Public Sub Main()
        Dim iw As InputWrapper = New InputWrapper()
        Dim hotel As Hotel = New Hotel(10)
        ShowHotel(hotel)
        Dim cmd As String
        Console.WriteLine("Enter command, quit to exit")
        cmd = iw.getString("H> ")
        While (Not cmd.Equals("quit"))
            Try
                If (cmd.Equals("new")) Then
                    Dim capacity As Integer = _
                        iw.getInt("capacity: ")
                    hotel = New Hotel(capacity)
                    ShowHotel(hotel)
                ElseIf (cmd.Equals("book")) Then
                    Dim customer As String = _
                        iw.getString("customer name: ")
                    Dim rooms As Integer = _
                        iw.getInt("number of rooms: ")
                    Dim id As Integer = _
                        hotel.MakeReservation( _
```

```
                customer, rooms)
            Console.WriteLine( _
                "Reservation has been booked")
            Console.WriteLine( _
                "ReservationId = {0}", id)
        ElseIf (cmd.Equals("cancel")) Then
            Dim id As Integer = _
                iw.getInt("reservation id: ")
            hotel.CancelReservation(id)
        ElseIf (cmd.Equals("show")) Then
            ShowReservations(hotel)
        Else
            hotelHelp()
        End If
    Catch e As Exception
        Console.WriteLine( _
            "Exception: {0}", e.Message)
    End Try
    cmd = iw.getString("H> ")
  End While
End Sub
...
```

Here is a transcript of a sample run. We try several kinds of errors.

```
The hotel has 10 rooms
Enter command, quit to exit
H> book
customer name: bob
number of rooms: xxx
Exception: Input string was not in a correct format.
H> book
customer name: bob
number of rooms: -5
Exception: Please request positive number of rooms
H> book
customer name: bob
number of rooms: 5
Reservation has been booked
ReservationId = 1
H> book
customer name: mary
number of rooms: 6
Exception: Rooms not available
H> book
customer name: mary
number of rooms: 3
Reservation has been booked
ReservationId = 2
H> book
customer name: david
```

```
number of rooms: 1
Reservation has been booked
ReservationId = 3
H> show
1       bob             5
2       mary            3
3       david           1
H> book
customer name: ellen
number of rooms: 1
Exception: Exception of type
System.IndexOutOfRangeException was thrown.
H>
```

Notice that we threw two of the exceptions ourselves. A third (entering "xxx" for the number of rooms) was caught by the .NET library inside our **InputWrapper** class. A fourth (index out of range) was also caught by .NET inside the **Hotel** class. Our catch handler deals with all these different exceptions in a simple, uniform manner.

User-Defined Exception Classes

You can do basic exception handling using only the base **Exception** class, as previously illustrated. In order to obtain finer-grained control over exceptions, it is frequently useful to define your own exception class, derived from **Exception**. You can then have a more specific catch handler that looks specifically for your exception type. You can also define other members in your derived exception class so that you can pass additional information to the catch handler.

We will illustrate by enhancing the **MakeReservation** method of our **Hotel** class. We want to distinguish between the two types of exceptions we throw. The one type is essentially bad input data (a nonpositive value). We will continue to handle this exception in the same manner as before (that is, bad input data gives rise to a format exception, thrown by .NET library code). We will define a new exception class **RoomException** to cover the case where the hotel does not have enough rooms to fulfill the request. In this case we want to allow the user an opportunity to submit another reservation request with fewer rooms. Our example program is **HotelException\Step2**. Here is the definition of our new exception class. This class is defined using inheritance, which we discussed earlier in this chapter.

Code
Example

```
Public Class RoomException
    Inherits Exception

    Private m_available As Integer

    Public Sub New( _
```

```
    ByVal message As String, _
    ByVal available As Integer)
        MyBase.New(message)
        m_available = available
    End Sub

    Public ReadOnly Property Available() As Integer
        Get
            Return m_available
        End Get
    End Property
End Class
```

Note that we define a property **Available** that can be used to retrieve the information about how many rooms are available. The constructor of our exception class takes two parameters. The first is an error message string, and the second is the number of rooms available. We pass the message string to the constructor of the base class by calling **MyBase.New**. We must also modify the code of the **Hotel** class to throw our new type of exception when too many rooms are requested.

```
' HotelException.vb - Step 2
...
Public Class Hotel
    ...
    Public Function MakeReservation( _
    ByVal cust As String, _
    ByVal rooms As Integer) As Integer
        ' Requested number of rooms should be positive
        If rooms <= 0 Then
            Throw New Exception( _
                "Please request positive number of rooms")
        End If
        ' Check if rooms are available
        Dim available As Integer = m_capacity - m_numGuests
        If rooms > available Then
            Throw New RoomException( _
                "Rooms not available", available)
        End If
        ...
```

Finally, we modify the code in our test program that processes the "book" command. We place the call to **MakeReservation** inside another **try** block, and we provide a catch handler for a **RoomException**. In this catch handler we allow the user an opportunity to request fewer rooms. Here is the code:

```
...
ElseIf (cmd.Equals("book")) Then
    Dim customer As String = iw.getString( _
```

```
        "customer name: ")
    Dim rooms As Integer = iw.getInt("number of rooms: ")
    Dim id As Integer
    Try
        id = hotel.MakeReservation(customer, rooms)
    Catch e As RoomException
        Console.WriteLine("Exception: {0}", e.Message)
        Console.WriteLine( _
           "{0} rooms are available", e.Available)
        ' try again
        rooms = iw.getInt("number of rooms: ")
        id = hotel.MakeReservation(customer, rooms)
    End Try
    Console.WriteLine("Reservation has been booked")
    Console.WriteLine("ReservationId = {0}", id)
    ...
```

Here is a transcript of a sample run of our program:

```
The hotel has 10 rooms
Enter command, quit to exit
H> book
customer name: bob
number of rooms: 11
Exception: Rooms not available
10 rooms are available
number of rooms: 5
Reservation has been booked
ReservationId = 1
```

Structured Exception Handling

One of the principles of structured programming is that a block of code should have a single entry point and a single exit point. The single exit point is convenient, because you can consolidate cleanup code in one place. The **GoTo** statement is usually bad, because it facilitates breaking this principle. But there are other ways to violate the principle of a single exit point, such as multiple **Return** statements from a method.

Multiple return statements may not be too bad, because these may be encountered during normal, anticipated flow of control. But exceptions can cause a particular difficulty, since they interrupt the normal flow of control. In a common scenario you can have at least *three* ways of exiting a method:

- No exception is encountered, and all catch handlers are skipped.
- An exception is caught, and control passes to a catch handler and then to the code after the catch handlers.
- An exception is caught, and the catch handler itself throws another exception. Then code after the catch handler will be bypassed.

The first two cases do not present a problem, as control passes to the code after the catch handlers. But the third case is a source of difficulty.

FINALLY BLOCK

The structured exception handling mechanism in VB.NET resolves this problem with a **Finally** block. The **Finally** block is optional, but if present, must appear immediately after the **Catch** handlers. It is guaranteed, in all three cases described above, that the code in the **Finally** block will *always* execute before the method is exited.

We illustrate use of **Finally** in the "cancel" command of our **Hotel** example. See the directory **HotelException\Step3**. There are several ways to exit this block of code, and the user might become confused about whether a cancellation was actually made or not. We insert a **Finally** block that will *always* display all the reservations. Here is the code:

```
ElseIf (cmd.Equals("cancel")) Then
   Dim id As Integer = _
      iw.getInt("reservation id: ")
      Try
         hotel.CancelReservation(id)
      Catch e As Exception
         Console.WriteLine( _
            "Exception: {0}", e.Message)
         id = iw.getInt("reservation id: ")
         hotel.CancelReservation(id)
      Finally
         ShowReservations(hotel)
      End Try
   . . .
```

It is instructive to compare the "book" and "cancel" commands. In the "book" command there is code after the catch handler. This code will be executed if the catch handler is skipped (no exception). The code will also be executed if the catch handler exits normally (user enters a small enough number of rooms). But if an exception is thrown inside the catch handler, this code will be skipped. In the case of "cancel," there is a **Finally** block. The code inside the **Finally** block will always be executed, even if the catch handler throws an exception (user enters an invalid ID a second time).

Inner Exceptions

In general it is wise to handle exceptions, at least at some level, near their source, because you have the most information available about the context in which the exception occurred. A common pattern is to create a new exception object that captures more detailed information and throw this onto the calling program. So that information is not lost about the original exception, you may pass the original exception as a parameter when constructing the new exception. Then the calling program can gain access to both exceptions through the **InnerException** property of the exception object.

The program **HotelException\Step3** also illustrates using inner exceptions. In the **MakeReservation** method we explicitly check for an **IndexOutOfRangeException**. We throw a new exception, which we construct by passing the original exception as a parameter.

```
' Add reservation to list and return reservation id
Try
    m_reservations(m_nextReservation) = item
    m_nextReservation += 1
Catch e As IndexOutOfRangeException
    Throw New Exception( _
        "Reservation table size exceeded", e)
End Try
```

In the test program we make use of the **InnerException** property.

```
Catch e As Exception
    Console.WriteLine("Exception: {0}", e.Message)
    If Not e.InnerException Is Nothing Then
        Console.WriteLine( _
            "InnerException: {0}", _
            e.InnerException.Message)
    End If
End Try
```

Multiple Catch Handlers

You may have several catch handlers for the same try block. Each catches a different type of exception. The first catch handler that matches the exception object will be executed.

The program **HotelException\Step3** also illustrates using multiple catch handlers. In the test program we have handlers for both **FormatException** and **Exception**.

```
Catch e As FormatException
    Console.WriteLine( _
        "Please enter your data in correct format")
Catch e As Exception
    Console.WriteLine("Exception: {0}", e.Message)
    If Not e.InnerException Is Nothing Then
        Console.WriteLine( _
            "InnerException: {0}", _
            e.InnerException.Message)
    End If
End Try
```

Here is a sample run of the program. When we use an incorrect format, the first catch handler is invoked. When we use the correct format, but an illegal negative value for the number of rooms, we don't get a match for the first catch handler, but we do get a match for the second, since we are using the base **Exception** class.

```
The hotel has 10 rooms
Enter command, quit to exit
H> book
customer name: bob
number of rooms: xxx
Please enter your data in correct format
H> book
customer name: bob
number of rooms: -1
Exception: Please request a positive number of rooms
H>
```

Summary

In this chapter we studied, in detail, the object-oriented aspects of VB.NET, with an emphasis on inheritance. After a review of the fundamentals of object-oriented programming, we introduced the Acme Travel Agency case study, which runs as a strand throughout the entire book. We examined the suitable abstractions that enable us to implement a reservation system for a variety of resources that may be reserved, and we provided an implementation of a hotel reservation system. The abstract base classes we defined provide reusable code that can enable us to easily implement other kinds of reservation systems. The key to good design is to find the right abstractions.

We saw how VB.NET language features facilitate object-oriented programming. Certain details of VB.NET, such as use of access control (**Public**, **Private**, **Protected**, and **Friend**) and properties, can help express abstractions in a way that is safe and easy to use.

We then looked at other object-oriented features of VB.NET, such as virtual methods, method hiding, method overriding, and polymorphism. A pitfall in languages supporting inheritance is the fragile base class problem, and we have seen how VB.NET helps in avoiding this pitfall.

Finally, we discussed exception handling in VB.NET.

VB.NET in the .NET Framework

VB.NET as a language has become much more elegant and powerful than previous versions of Visual Basic. To fully use its capabilities, you need to understand how it works within the .NET Framework. We begin with the root class **Object**. Collections are examined next, including the methods of the **Object** class that should be overridden to tap into the functionality provided by the .NET Framework. We then introduce interfaces, which allow you to rigorously define a contract for a class or structure to implement. In VB.NET a class can implement multiple interfaces, even though it can inherit implementation from only one class. Interfaces allow for dynamic programming. You can even query a class at runtime to see whether it supports a particular interface.

The interfaces supporting collections are examined in detail. We investigate issues involved in copying objects, such as shallow copy and deep copy. To support the copying of objects in VB.NET, you implement the **ICloneable** interface. We explore generic interfaces in the .NET Framework programming model and compare the .NET and COM component models. A further illustration of generic interfaces is provided by sorting in different orders with the **IComparable** interface. The examples offer insight into the workings of frameworks, which are more than class libraries. In a framework, you call the framework, and the framework calls you. Your code can be viewed as the middle layer of a sandwich. This key insight can help you grasp what makes .NET programming "tick." VB.NET uses this concept in delegates and events. Two simple and intuitive examples are presented: a stock market simulation and an online chat room. The chapter concludes with a discussion of attributes, which are pervasive in the .NET Framework.

System.Object

As we have already seen, every type in VB.NET, whether it is a value type or a reference type, ultimately inherits from the root class **System.Object**. The class **ValueType** inherits directly from **Object. ValueType** is the root for all value types, such as structures and simple types like **Integer** and **Decimal**.

Public Instance Methods of Object

There are four public instance methods of **Object**, three of which are virtual and frequently overridden by classes.

EQUALS

```
Overridable Overloads Public Function Equals( _
 ByVal obj As Object) As Boolean
```

This method compares an object with the object passed as a parameter and returns **True** if they are equal. **Object** implements this method to test for reference equality. **ValueType** overrides the method to test for content equality. Many classes override the method to make equality behave appropriately for the particular class.

TOSTRING

```
Overridable Public Function ToString() As String
```

This method returns a human-readable string representation of the object. The default implementation returns the type name. Derived classes frequently override this method to return a meaningful string representation of the particular object.

GETHASHCODE

```
Overridable Public Function GetHashCode() As Integer
```

This method returns a hash value for an object, suitable for use in hashing algorithms and hashtables. You should normally override this method if you override **ToString**.

GETTYPE

```
Public Function GetType() As Type
```

This method returns type information for the object. This type information can be used to get the associated metadata through *reflection*, a topic we discuss in Chapter 10.

Protected Instance Methods

There are two protected instance methods, which can be used only within derived classes.

MEMBERWISECLONE

```
Protected Function MemberwiseClone() As Object
```

This method creates a shallow copy of the object. To perform a deep copy, you should implement the **ICloneable** interface. We will discuss shallow and deep copy later in this chapter.

FINALIZE

```
Overrides Protected Sub Finalize()
```

This method allows an object to free its resources and perform other cleanup operations before the object is reclaimed by garbage collection. The Finalize method is invoked automatically by the garbage collector, but in a nondeterministic manner. Once an object is no longer needed, the Finalize method will be called at a time determined by the garbage collector, but the program itself cannot predict exactly when this will happen. We discuss finalization in Chapter 10.

Generic Interfaces and Standard Behavior

If you are used to a language like Smalltalk, the set of behaviors specified in **Object** may seem quite limited. Smalltalk, which introduced the concept of a class hierarchy rooted in a common base class, has a very rich set of methods defined in its **Object** class. I counted 38 methods![1] These additional methods support features such as comparing objects and copying objects. The .NET Framework class library has similar methods, and many more. But rather than putting them all in a common root class, .NET defines a number of standard *interfaces*, which classes can optionally support. This kind of organization, which is also present in Microsoft's Component Object Model (COM) and in Java, is very flexible. We will study interfaces later in this chapter, and we will discuss some of the generic interfaces of the .NET Framework.

---

1. The methods of Smalltalk's **Object** class are described in Chapters 6 and 14 of *Smalltalk-80: The Language and its Implementation*, by Adele Goldberg and David Robson.

Using Object Methods in the Customer Class

As a simple illustration of **Object** methods, let's look at our **Customer** class before and after overriding the **Equals**, **ToString**, and **GetHashCode** methods.

DEFAULT METHODS OF OBJECT

Code
Example

If our class does not provide any overrides of the virtual instance methods of **Object**, our class will inherit the standard behavior. This behavior is demonstrated in **CustomerObject\Step1**.

```
' Customer.vb

Public Class Customer
    Public CustomerId As Integer
    Public FirstName As String
    Public LastName As String
    Public EmailAddress As String
    Public Sub New( _
     ByVal id As Integer, _
     ByVal first As String, _
     ByVal last As String, ByVal email As String)
        CustomerId = id
        FirstName = first
        LastName = last
        EmailAddress = email
    End Sub
End Class
```

Here is the test program:

```
' TestCustomer.vb

Imports System

Module TestCustomer
    Sub Main()
        Dim cust1 As Customer
        Dim cust2 As Customer
        cust1 = New Customer( _
            99, "John", "Doe", "john@rocky.com")
        cust2 = New Customer( _
            99, "John", "Doe", "john@rocky.com")
        ShowCustomerObject("cust1", cust1)
        ShowCustomerObject("cust2", cust2)
        CompareCustomerObjects(cust1, cust2)
    End Sub

    Private Sub ShowCustomerObject( _
```

```
     ByVal label As String, ByVal cust As Customer)
       Console.WriteLine("---- {0} ----", label)
       Console.WriteLine( _
          "ToString() = {0}", cust.ToString())
       Console.WriteLine( _
          "GetHashCode() = {0}", cust.GetHashCode())
       Console.WriteLine( _
          "GetType() = {0}", cust.GetType())
     End Sub

     Sub CompareCustomerObjects( _
      ByVal cust1 As Customer, _
      ByVal cust2 As Customer)
       Console.WriteLine( _
          "Equals() = {0}", cust1.Equals(cust2))
     End Sub
End Module
```

Run the test program and you will see this output:

```
 ---- cust1 ----
ToString() = CustomerObject.Customer
GetHashCode() = 4
GetType() = CustomerObject.Customer
---- cust2 ----
ToString() = CustomerObject.Customer
GetHashCode() = 6
GetType() = CustomerObject.Customer
Equals() = False
```

The default implementation is not at all what we want for our **Customer** object. **ToString** returns the name of the class, not information about a particular customer. **Equals** checks for reference equality, not equality of contents. In our example, we have two different references to **Customer** objects with the same content, and **Equals** return **False**.

OVERRIDING METHODS OF OBJECT

The version of the project in **CustomerObject\Step2** demonstrates overriding these virtual methods. Our override of **Equals** tests for content equality.

```
 ' Customer.vb

Public Class Customer
   Public CustomerId As Integer
   Public FirstName As String
   Public LastName As String
   Public EmailAddress As String
   Public Sub New( _
    ByVal id As Integer, _
```

```
     ByVal first As String, _
     ByVal last As String, ByVal email As String)
        CustomerId = id
        FirstName = first
        LastName = last
        EmailAddress = email
     End Sub

     Public Overloads Overrides Function Equals( _
      ByVal obj As Object) As Boolean
        Dim cust As Customer = obj
        Return (cust.CustomerId = CustomerId)
     End Function

     Public Overrides Function GetHashCode() As Integer
        Return CustomerId
     End Function

     Public Overrides Function ToString() As String
        Return FirstName & " " & LastName
     End Function
End Class
```

The test program is identical. Here is the new output:

```
---- cust1 ----
ToString() = John Doe
GetHashCode() = 99
GetType() = CustomerObject.Customer
---- cust2 ----
ToString() = John Doe
GetHashCode() = 99
GetType() = CustomerObject.Customer
Equals() = True
```

Collections

The .NET Framework class library provides an extensive set of classes for working with collections of objects. These classes are all in the **System.Collections** namespace and implement a number of different kinds of collections, including lists, queues, stacks, arrays, and hashtables. The collections contain **Object** instance references. Since all types derive ultimately from **Object**, any built-in or user-defined type may be stored in a collection.

In this section we will look at a representative class in this namespace, **ArrayList**, and see how to use array lists in our programs.

ArrayList Example

To get our bearings, let's begin with a simple example of using the **ArrayList** class. An array list, as the name suggests, is a list of items stored like an array. An array list can be dynamically sized and will grow as necessary to accommodate new elements being added.

Collection classes are made up of instances of type **Object**. We will create and manipulate a collection of **Customer** objects. We could just as easily create a collection of any other built-in or user-defined type. If our type were a value type, such as **Integer**, the instance would be boxed before being stored in the collection. When the object is extracted from the collection, it will be unboxed back to **Integer**.

Code Example

Our example program is **CustomerCollection**. It initializes a list of customers and then lets the user show the customers, register a new customer, unregister a customer, and change an email address. A simple "help" method displays the commands that are available:

```
Enter command, quit to exit
H> help
The following commands are available:
   register    register a customer
   unregister  unregister a customer
   email       change email address
   show        show customers
   quit        exit the program
```

Before examining the code, it would be a good idea to run the program to register a new customer, show the customers, change an email address, unregister a customer, and show the customers again. Here is a sample run of the program:

```
H> show
id (-1 for all): -1
   1   Rocket      Squirrel    rocky@frosbitefalls.com
   2   Bullwinkle  Moose       moose@wossamotta.edu
H> register
first name: Bob
last name: Oberg
email address: oberg@objectinnovations.com
id = 3
H> email
customer id: 1
email address: rocky@objectinnovations.com
H> unregister
id: 2
H> show
id (-1 for all): -1
   1   Rocket      Squirrel    rocky@objectinnovations.com
   3   Bob         Oberg       oberg@objectinnovations.com
```

CUSTOMERS CLASS

All the code for this project is in the folder **CustomerCollection**. The file **customer.vb** has code for the **Customer** and **Customers** classes. The code for **Customer** is almost identical to what we looked at previously. The only addition is a special constructor that instantiates a **Customer** object with a specified ID. We use this constructor in the **Customers** class when we remove an element and when we check if an element is present in the collection.

```
Public Class Customer
   ...
   Public Sub New(ByVal id As Integer)
      CustomerId = id
      FirstName = ""
      LastName = ""
      EmailAddress = ""
   End Sub
   ...
End Class
```

The **Customers** class contains a list of customers, represented by an **ArrayList**.

```
Public Class Customers
   Private m_customers As ArrayList
   Public Sub New()
      m_customers = New ArrayList()
      RegisterCustomer( _
         "Rocket", _
         "Squirrel", _
         "rocky@frosbitefalls.com")
      RegisterCustomer( _
         "Bullwinkle", _
         "Moose", _
         "moose@wossamotta.edu")
   End Sub

   Public Function RegisterCustomer( _
    ByVal firstName As String, _
    ByVal lastName As String, _
    ByVal emailAddress As String) As Integer
      Dim cust As Customer = New Customer( _
         firstName, lastName, emailAddress)
      m_customers.Add(cust)
      Return cust.CustomerId
   End Function

   Public Function UnregisterCustomer( _
    ByVal id As Integer)
      Dim cust As Customer = New Customer(id)
      m_customers.Remove(cust)
```

```
    End Function

    Public Sub ChangeEmailAddress( _
     ByVal id As Integer, _
     ByVal emailAddress As String)
        Dim cust As Customer
        For Each cust In m_customers
            If cust.CustomerId = id Then
                cust.EmailAddress = emailAddress
                Return
            End If
        Next
        Throw New Exception("id " & id & " not found")
    End Sub

    Public Sub ShowCustomers(ByVal id As Integer)
        If Not CheckId(id) And id <> -1 Then
            Return
        End If
        Dim cust As Customer
        For Each cust In m_customers
            If (id = -1 Or id = cust.CustomerId) Then
                Dim sid As String = _
                    cust.CustomerId.ToString().PadLeft(4)
                Dim first As String = _
                    cust.FirstName.PadRight(12)
                Dim last As String = _
                    cust.LastName.PadRight(12)
                Dim email As String = _
                    cust.EmailAddress.PadRight(20)
                Dim str As String = _
                sid & "    " & first & "    " & _
                        last & "    " & email
                Console.WriteLine(str)
            End If
        Next
    End Sub

    Private Function CheckId(ByVal id As Integer) _
     As Boolean
        Dim cust As Customer = New Customer(id)
        Return m_customers.Contains(cust)
    End Function
End Class
```

The bold lines in the listing show the places where we are using collection class features. In Chapter 4 we have already used **For Each** with arrays. The reason **For Each** can be used with arrays is that the **Array** class, like **ArrayList**, implements the **IEnumerable** interface that provides the foundation for the **For Each** syntax. We will discuss **IEnumerable** and the other collection interfaces later in this chapter.

The **Add** and **Remove** methods, as their names suggest, are used for adding and removing elements from a collection. The **Remove** method searches for an object in the collection that **Equals** the object passed as a parameter. Our special constructor creates an object having the id of the element we want to remove. Since we provided an override of the **Equals** method that bases equality on **CustomerId**, the proper element will be removed.

Similarly, the **Contains** method used in our **CheckId** helper method also relies on the override of the **Equals** method.

Compare the code in this program with the use of arrays in the code in the previous chapter's case study. The collection code is much simpler. Using collections makes it easy to remove elements as well as add them. Using arrays, you would have to write special code to move array elements to fill in the space where an element was deleted. Also, collections are not declared to have a specific size, but can grow as required.

Interfaces

Interface is a very fundamental concept in computer programming. A large system is inevitably decomposed into parts, and it is critical to precisely specify the interfaces between these parts. Interfaces should be quite stable, as changing an interface affects multiple parts of the system. In VB.NET, **Interface** is a keyword and has a very precise meaning. An interface is a reference type, similar to an abstract class, which *specifies* behavior as a set of methods, properties, and events.[2] An interface is a contract. When a class or structure implements an interface, it must adhere to that contract.

Interfaces are a useful way to partition functionality. You should first specify interfaces and then design appropriate classes to implement the interfaces. While a class in VB.NET can inherit implementation from only one other class, it can implement multiple interfaces.

Interfaces facilitate dynamic programs—you can query a class at runtime to see whether it supports a particular interface, and take action accordingly. Interfaces in VB.NET and .NET are conceptually very similar to interfaces in Microsoft's COM, but as we will see, they are *much* easier to work with.

In this section we will study the fundamentals of interfaces and provide illustrations using some small sample programs. Then we will restructure our

---

2. We discuss events later in this chapter.

Acme case study to take advantage of interfaces and explore their use in detail. After that we will examine several important generic interfaces in the .NET library, which will help us gain an understanding of how VB.NET and the .NET library support each other to help us develop powerful and useful programs.

Interface Fundamentals

Object-oriented programming is a useful paradigm for helping to design and implement large systems. Using classes helps us to achieve abstraction and encapsulation. Classes are a natural decomposition of a large system into manageable parts. Inheritance adds another tool for structuring our system, enabling us to factor out common parts into base classes, helping us to accomplish greater code reuse.

The main purpose of an interface is to specify a *contract* independently of implementation. It is important to understand that conceptually the *interfaces come first*.

INTERFACES IN VB.NET

In VB.NET **Interface** is a keyword, and you define an interface in a manner similar to defining a class. Like classes, interfaces are reference types. The big difference is that there is no implementation code in an interface; it is pure specification. Also note that an interface can have properties as well as methods (it could also have other members, such as events). As a naming convention, interface names usually begin with a capital I.

The **IAccount** interface specifies operations to be performed by classes that implement the **IAccount** interface.

```
Interface IAccount
    Sub Deposit(ByVal amount As Decimal)
    Sub Withdraw(ByVal amount As Decimal)
    ReadOnly Property Balance() As Decimal
    Sub Show()
End Interface
```

This interface illustrates the syntax for declaring the read-only **Balance** property—you specify the fact that it is a read-only property, followed by the property name and data type. This interface also specifies methods to be furnished by classes that implement this interface.

IMPLEMENTING AN INTERFACE

In VB.NET you specify that a class or structure implements an interface, such as **IAccount**, by using the **Implements** keyword as shown in the following **AccountC** class. A class can inherit from a class and implement one or more interfaces. In this case the base class should appear first in the derivation list.

```
Public Class AccountC
   Inherits Account
   Implements IAccount
   ...
End Class
```

In our example the classes **AccountC** and **AccountW** implement the interface **IAccount** that specifies methods to be implemented, and also inherit from the class **Account** that provides implementations for those methods. This is accomplished by simply calling the inherited version via the **MyBase** keyword. The result is that **AccountC** and **AccountW** indirectly implement the interface via inheritance.

We will examine a full-blown example of interfaces with the reservation-broker inheritance hierarchy later in the chapter, when we implement the next step of the case study.

Code
Example

As a small example, consider the program **InterfaceDemo**. The interface **IAccount** is defined, and two different classes, **AccountC** and **AccountW**, implement the interface. These implementations differ only in the **Show** method. The **AccountC** implementation performs console output to display the account balance, and **AccountW** uses a Windows message box.[3] The **Deposit** and **Withdraw** methods and the **Balance** property are all implemented in the **Account** base class, which is inherited by **AccountC** and **AccountW**, and accessed via the **MyBase** keyword.

```
' Account.vb

Imports System
Imports System.Windows.Forms

Interface IAccount
    Sub Deposit(ByVal amount As Decimal)
    Sub Withdraw(ByVal amount As Decimal)
    ReadOnly Property Balance() As Decimal
    Sub Show()
End Interface

Public Class Account
    Private m_balance As Decimal
    Public Sub New()
        m_balance = 100
    End Sub
```

---

3. We will discuss Windows programming in Chapter 7. The example program has all needed references to libraries, and all you need to do to display a message box is call the **Show** method of the **MessageBox** class.

```
   Public Overridable Sub Deposit(ByVal amount As Decimal)
      m_balance += amount
   End Sub

   Public Overridable Sub Withdraw(ByVal amount As Decimal)
      m_balance -= amount
   End Sub

   Public Overridable ReadOnly Property Balance() _
    As Decimal
      Get
         Return m_balance
      End Get
   End Property
End Class

Public Class AccountC
   Inherits Account
   Implements IAccount

   Public Overrides Sub Deposit(ByVal amount As Decimal) _
    Implements IAccount.Deposit
      MyBase.Deposit(amount)
   End Sub

   Public Overrides Sub Withdraw(ByVal amount As Decimal) _
    Implements IAccount.Withdraw
      MyBase.Withdraw(amount)
   End Sub

   Public Overrides ReadOnly Property Balance() _
    As Decimal Implements IAccount.Balance
      Get
         Return MyBase.Balance()
      End Get
   End Property

   Public Sub Show() Implements IAccount.Show
      Console.WriteLine("balance = {0}", Balance)
   End Sub
End Class

Public Class AccountW
   ...
End Class
```

USING AN INTERFACE

You may call methods of an interface through an object reference to the class,
or you may obtain an interface reference and call the methods through this

interface reference.[4] The test program in the file **InterfaceDemo.vb** demonstrates both. We obtain the interface reference **iacc** by an implicit cast when
we do the assignment to the object reference **acc** or **accw**. Note the polymorphic behavior of the call to **Show**, using console or Windows output depending on which object is being used.

```
' InterfaceDemo.vb

Imports System

Module InterfaceDemo
    Sub Main()
        ' Use an object reference
        Dim acc As AccountC = New AccountC()
        acc.Deposit(25)
        acc.Show()
        ' Use an interface reference
        Dim iacc As IAccount = acc
        iacc.Withdraw(50)
        iacc.Show()
        ' Use interface reference for another class
        ' that implements IAccount
        Dim accw As AccountW = New AccountW()
        iacc = accw
        iacc.Show()
    End Sub
End Module
```

Multiple Interfaces

Our first example illustrated two classes providing different implementations
of the same interface. Another common scenario is for a class to implement
multiple interfaces, and in VB.NET it is easy to test at runtime which interfaces
are implemented by a class.

Code
Example

Our example program is **MultipleInterfaces**, which also illustrates
interface inheritance. The interfaces **IBasicAccount**, **IDisplay**, and **IAccount**
are defined in the file **AccountDefs.vb**.

```
' AccountDefs.vb

Interface IBasicAccount
    Sub Deposit(ByVal amount As Decimal)
    Sub Withdraw(ByVal amount As Decimal)
```

---

4. As we will see later in the chapter when we discuss explicit interface implementation, you can force a client program to use an interface reference and not a
   class reference.

```
   ReadOnly Property Balance() As Decimal
End Interface

Interface IDisplay
   Sub Show()
End Interface

Interface IAccount
   Inherits IBasicAccount, IDisplay
End Interface
```

INTERFACE INHERITANCE

Interfaces can inherit from other interfaces. Unlike classes in VB.NET, for which there is only single inheritance, there can be multiple inheritance of interfaces. In the following code snippet, the interface **IBasicAccountDisplay** is declared by inheriting from the two smaller interfaces, **IBasicAccount** and **IDisplay**. The advantage of factoring an interface into two smaller interfaces is an increase in flexibility. For example, a class implementing **IBasicAccount** may run on a server, where it would not be appropriate to implement **IDisplay**.

When declaring a new interface using interface inheritance, you can also introduce additional methods, as illustrated for a hypothetical interface **IBasicAccountDisplay**.

```
Interface IBasicAccountDisplay
   Inherits IBasicAccount, IDisplay
   Sub NewMethod()
End Interface
```

IMPLEMENTING MULTIPLE INTERFACES

A class implements multiple interfaces by specifying each interface in its inheritance list and by providing code for the methods of each interface. A method may be implemented through inheritance from a base class. The file **Account.vb** in the **MultipleInterfaces** project illustrates two classes. **BasicAccount** implements only the interface **IBasicAccount**, but **Account** actually implements two interfaces. It explicitly implements **IDisplay**, and it implicitly implements **IBasicAccount**, via inheritance from **BasicAccount**.

```
 ' Account.vb

Imports System

Public Class BasicAccount
   Implements IBasicAccount

   Private m_balance As Decimal
```

```
Public Sub New()
   m_balance = 100
End Sub

Public Sub Deposit(ByVal amount As Decimal) _
 Implements IBasicAccount.Deposit
   m_balance += amount
End Sub

Public Sub Withdraw(ByVal amount As Decimal) _
 Implements IBasicAccount.Withdraw
   m_balance -= amount
End Sub

Public ReadOnly Property Balance() As Decimal _
 Implements IBasicAccount.Balance
   Get
      Return m_balance
   End Get
End Property
End Class

Public Class Account
   Inherits BasicAccount
   Implements IDisplay

   Public Sub Show() Implements IDisplay.Show
      Console.WriteLine("balance = {0}", Balance)
   End Sub
End Class
```

USING MULTIPLE INTERFACES

The test program **MultipleInterfaces.vb** illustrates using (or trying to use) the two interfaces with an **Account** object and a **BasicAccount** object. Both interfaces can be used with **Account**, but we cannot use the **IDisplay** interface with **BasicAccount**. In our code we perform a conversion from **BasicAccount** to **IDisplay** within a **try** block. The code compiles,[5] but we get a runtime **InvalidCastException**, which we catch. The program also illustrates that we can sometimes take a reasonable, alternative course of action if the desired interface is not available. In our case, we are able to perform the output ourselves, making use of the **Balance** property of the **IBasicAccount** interface.

---

5. The compiler would flag an error message here if you had set the strict build option. To do this, go into Project | Properties, and in Build properties, set the Option Strict to On.

```vb
' MultipleInterfaces.vb

Imports System

Module MultipleInterfaces
    Sub Main()
        Dim iacc As IBasicAccount
        Dim idisp As IDisplay
        ' Use an Account object, which has full
        ' functionality
        Dim acc As Account = New Account()
        iacc = acc
        idisp = acc
        iacc.Deposit(25)
        idisp.Show()
        ' Use BasicAccount object, with reduced
        ' functionality
        Dim bacc As BasicAccount = New BasicAccount()
        iacc = bacc
        iacc.Withdraw(50)
        Try
            idisp = bacc
            idisp.Show()
        Catch e As InvalidCastException
            Console.WriteLine("IDisplay is not supported")
            Console.WriteLine(e.Message)
            ' Display the balance another way
            Console.WriteLine("balance = {0}", iacc.Balance)
        End Try
    End Sub
End Module
```

Here is the output from running the program:

```
balance = 125
IDisplay is not supported
Exception of type System.InvalidCastException was thrown.
balance = 50
```

Dynamic Use of Interfaces

A powerful feature of interfaces is their use in dynamic scenarios, allowing us to write general code that can test whether an interface is supported by a class. If the interface is supported, our code can take advantage of it; otherwise our program can ignore the interface. We could in fact implement such dynamic behavior through exception handling, as illustrated previously. Although entirely feasible, this approach is very cumbersome and would lead to programs that are hard to read. VB.NET provides the **TypeOf ... Is** operator to facilitate working with interfaces at runtime.

Code
Example

As an example, consider the program **DynamicInterfaces**, which uses the interface definitions and class implementations from our previous example. The test program illustrates using the VB.NET **TypeOf...Is** keyword to check whether the **IDisplay** interface is supported.

```
' DynamicInterfaces.vb

Imports System

Module DynamicInterfaces
    Public Sub Main()
        Dim iacc As IBasicAccount
        Dim idisp As IDisplay
        Dim bacc As BasicAccount = New BasicAccount()
        iacc = bacc
        iacc.Withdraw(50)
        ' Check if idisp is IDisplay using TypeOf ... Is
        If TypeOf bacc Is IDisplay Then
            idisp = bacc
            idisp.Show()
        Else
            Console.WriteLine("IDisplay is not supported")
            ' Display the balance another way
            Console.WriteLine("balance = {0}", iacc.Balance)
        End If
    End Sub
End Module
```

Here is the output from running the test program:

```
IDisplay is not supported
balance = 50
```

THE TYPEOF ... IS OPERATOR

The **TypeOf ... Is**[6] operator dynamically checks if the runtime type of an object is compatible with a given type. The result is a Boolean value. The **TypeOf ... Is** operator can be used to check if an object refers to a class supporting a given interface, as illustrated in our **DynamicInterfaces** program.

```
        If TypeOf bacc Is IDisplay Then
            idisp = bacc
            idisp.Show()
        Else
```

---

6. The VB.NET **is** operator is similar to **type_id** in C++ and the **is** operator in C#.

The **TypeOf ... Is** operator is useful if you want to check whether an interface is supported but you don't need to directly call a method of the interface. Later in the chapter we will see an example of this situation, when we discuss the **IComparable** interface. If the elements of a collection support **IComparable**, you will be able to call a **Sort** method on the collection. The **Sort** method calls the **CompareTo** method of **IComparable**, although your own code does not.

Interfaces in VB.NET and COM

There are many similarities between .NET and COM. In both, the concept of interface plays a fundamental role. Interfaces are useful for specifying contracts. Interfaces support a very dynamic style of programming.

In COM you must yourself provide a very elaborate infrastructure in order to implement a COM component. You typically implement a class factory for the creation of COM objects. You must implement the **QueryInterface** method of **IUnknown** for the dynamic checking of interfaces. You must also implement **AddRef** and **Release** for proper memory management.

With VB.NET (and other .NET languages) the Common Language Runtime does all this for you automatically. You create an object via **New**. You check for an interface via **TypeOf ... Is** and obtain the interface by a type conversion assignment. The garbage collector takes care of memory management for you.

Resolving Ambiguity in Interfaces

When working with interfaces, an ambiguity can arise if a class implements two interfaces and each has a method with the same name and signature. As an example, consider the following versions of the interfaces **IAccount** and **IStatement**. Each interface contains the method **Show**.

```
Interface IAccount
    Sub Deposit(ByVal amount As Decimal)
    Sub Withdraw(ByVal amount As Decimal)
    ReadOnly Property Balance() As Decimal
    Sub Show()
End Interface

Interface IStatement
    ReadOnly Property Transactions() As Integer
    Sub Show()
End Interface
```

How can a class that implements both of these interfaces specify implementations for both of the **Show** methods that have the same name? The

Code Example

answer is to use an alias for each of the method implementations in the derived class. You can use the interface name to qualify the method, as illustrated in the program **Ambiguous**.[7] In the **Ambiguous** example, the **IAccount** version of **Show** is named **IAccount_Show**, and the **IStatement** version of **Show** is named **IStatement_Show**. These method names are typically not used explicitly by client code. Rather, the client code usually calls on the name of the method as it is defined in the interfaces. **IAccount_Show** implements **IAccount.Show** and displays only the balance. **IStatement_Show** implements **IStatement.Show** and displays both the number of transactions and the balance.

```
// Account.vb (project "Ambiguous")
...
Public Class Account
   Implements IAccount, IStatement

   Private m_balance As Decimal
   Private m_numXact As Integer = 0

   Public Sub New(ByVal balance As Decimal)
      m_balance = balance
   End Sub

   Public Sub Deposit(ByVal amount As Decimal) _
    Implements IAccount.Deposit
      m_balance += amount
      m_numXact += 1
   End Sub

   Public Sub Withdraw(ByVal amount As Decimal) _
    Implements IAccount.Withdraw
      m_balance -= amount
      m_numXact += 1
   End Sub

   Public ReadOnly Property Balance() As Decimal _
    Implements IAccount.Balance
      Get
         Return m_balance
      End Get
   End Property

   Public Sub IAccount_Show() Implements IAccount.Show
      Console.WriteLine("balance = {0}", Balance)
```

---

7. Actually, any distinct names will do, but using the interface name as part of the method name helps make it more recognizable and meaningful.

```
      End Sub

      Public ReadOnly Property Transactions() As Integer _
        Implements IStatement.Transactions
          Get
              Return m_numXact
          End Get
      End Property

      Public Sub IStatement_Show() Implements IStatement.Show
          Console.WriteLine( _
              "{0} transactions, balance = {1}", _
              m_numXact, Balance)
      End Sub
End Class
```

Here is the client code that exercises the **IAccount** and **IStatement** interfaces. For comparison, we show making the call through both an interface reference and an object reference.

```
' Ambiguous.vb

Imports System

Module Ambiguous
  Sub Main()
      Dim acc As Account = New Account(100)
      Dim iacc As IAccount = acc
      Dim istat As IStatement = acc
      iacc.Show()          'calls IAccountShow
      istat.Show()         'calls IStatementShow
      acc.IAccount_Show()
      acc.IStatement_Show()
  End Sub
End Module
```

Acme Travel Agency Case Study: Step 2

We will now apply our knowledge of interfaces to a little restructuring of the Acme case study. A major benefit of using interfaces is that they raise the level of abstraction somewhat, helping you to understand the system by way of the interface contracts, without worrying about how the system is implemented.

As usual, our case study code is in the **CaseStudy** directory for this chapter.

The Contracts

There are two main sets of contracts in the Acme Travel Agency Case Study. The first specifies operations on customers, and the second, operations involving hotels.

CUSTOMER CONTRACT

The **ICustomer** interface shown below specifies the methods to be used by clients in the Acme Travel Agency system.

```
Public Interface ICustomer
   Function RegisterCustomer( _
     ByVal firstName As String, _
     ByVal lastName As String, _
     ByVal emailAddress As String) As Integer
   Sub UnregisterCustomer(ByVal id As Integer)
   Function GetCustomer( _
     ByVal id As Integer) As ArrayList
   Sub ChangeEmailAddress( _
     ByVal id As Integer, _
     ByVal emailAddress As String)
End Interface
```

The **RegisterCustomer**, **UnregisterCustomer**, and **ChangeEmailAddress** method definitions are exactly the same as the methods we implemented in the **Customers** class. The **GetCustomer** method is new. Previously, we had a **ShowCustomers** method, which displayed a list of customers to the console. This method was strictly temporary. For general use we want to return data and let the client decide what to do with it. The **GetCustomer** method returns information about one or all customers in an array list. If –1 is passed for the ID, the list will contain all the registered customers. Otherwise, the list will contain the customer information for the customer with the given ID. If no customer has that ID, the list will be empty.

HOTEL CONTRACTS

We next look at the functionality of the class **HotelBroker**. The methods divide fairly naturally into three groups.

- Hotel information, such as the cities where hotels are available and the hotels within a city
- Hotel administration, such as adding or deleting a hotel or changing the number of rooms and rate of a hotel
- Hotel reservations, such as booking or canceling a reservation or obtaining a list of reservations

Accordingly, we create three interfaces for the **HotelBroker**. These interfaces are defined in **AcmeDefinitions.vb**.

```
Public Interface IHotelInfo
    Function GetCities() As ArrayList
    Function GetHotels() As ArrayList
    Function GetHotels( _
        ByVal city As String) As ArrayList
End Interface

Public Interface IHotelAdmin
    Function AddHotel( _
        ByVal city As String, _
        ByVal name As String, _
        ByVal numberRooms As Integer, _
        ByVal rate As Decimal) As String
    Function DeleteHotel( _
        ByVal city As String, _
        ByVal name As String) As String
    Function ChangeRooms( _
        ByVal city As String, _
        ByVal name As String, _
        ByVal numberRooms As Integer, _
        ByVal rate As Decimal) As String
End Interface

Public Interface IHotelReservation
    Function MakeReservation( _
        ByVal customerId As Integer, _
        ByVal city As String, _
        ByVal hotel As String, _
        ByVal checkinDate As DateTime, _
        ByVal numberDays As Integer) _
        As ReservationResult
    Sub CancelReservation(ByVal id As Integer)
    Function FindReservationsForCustomer( _
        ByVal customerId As Integer) As ArrayList
End Interface
```

The Implementation

We examined the Step 1 implementation of the hotel brokerage system in detail in Chapter 5. The Step 2 implementation uses collections in place of arrays, and it passes information to the client rather than display information directly.

STRUCTURES

One detail of our implementation concerns the data structures used to pass lists to the client. We use the **ArrayList** class. But what do we store in each array list? We could use **Customer** objects and **Hotel** objects. The problem here is that these classes have implementation-specific data in them that the client code does not need, as well as the information fields that the client code does care about. To obtain implementation-neutral representations, we introduce several structures.

In **Customers.vb** we define the **CustomerListItem** structure for passing customer information.

```
Public Structure CustomerListItem
    Public CustomerId As Integer
    Public FirstName As String
    Public LastName As String
    Public EmailAddress As String
End Structure
```

In **AcmeDefinitions.vb** we define structures for hotels, reservations, and reservation results.

```
Public Structure HotelListItem
    Public City As String
    Public HotelName As String
    Public NumberRooms As Integer
    Public Rate As Decimal
End Structure

Public Structure ReservationListItem
    Public CustomerId As Integer
    Public ReservationId As Integer
    Public HotelName As String
    Public City As String
    Public ArrivalDate As DateTime
    Public DepartureDate As DateTime
    Public NumberDays As Integer
End Structure

Public Structure ReservationResult
    Public ReservationId As Integer
    Public ReservationCost As Decimal
    Public Rate As Decimal
    Public Comment As String
End Structure
```

The **ReservationResult** returns a **ReservationId** of −1 if there is a problem, along with an explanation of the problem in the **Comment** field. Otherwise, "OK" is returned in the **Comment** field.

We invite you to examine the code in the **CaseStudy** folder and to build and run the program.

Generic Interfaces in .NET

The .NET Framework exposes much standard functionality through generic interfaces, which are implemented in various combinations by classes in the Framework itself, and which can also be implemented by your own classes in order to tap into standard functionality defined by the Framework. In this section we will look at several categories of operations that are supported by these standard, generic interfaces.

- Collections
- Copying objects
- Comparing objects

Our survey of generic interfaces is by no means exhaustive, but our sampling should give you a good understanding of how generic interfaces work in the .NET Framework.

Collection Interfaces

Now that we understand the concept of interfaces, we are equipped to take a closer look at collections, and in particular at the **ArrayList** class that we have used so heavily in the case study. If we look at the definition of **ArrayList**, we see that it implements four standard interfaces.

```
Public Class ArrayList
    Implements IList, ICollection, IEnumerable, ICloneable
```

The first three interfaces form a simple interface hierarchy, as shown in Figure 6–1. As you go down the hierarchy, additional methods are added until **IList** specifies a fully featured list.

The fourth interface, **ICloneable**, is independent and is used to support deep copying. As a simple illustration of the collection interfaces, we provide the program **StringList**. Here is the **Main** method. We'll look at the individual helper methods as we examine the various collection interfaces.

```
' StringList.vb

Imports System
Imports System.Collections

Module StringList
    Private m_list As ArrayList
    Sub Main()
        ' Initialize strings and show starting state
        m_list = New ArrayList(4)
        ShowCount()
        AddString("Amy")
        AddString("Bob")
```

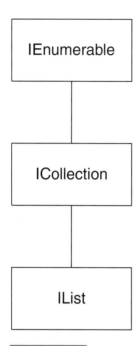

FIGURE 6-1   *Interface hierarchy for lists.*

```
        AddString("Charlie")
        ShowEnum(m_list)   ' enumerator
        ShowCount()
        ' Add two more string and show state again
        AddString("David")
        AddString("Ellen")
        ShowList(m_list) ' for each
        ShowCount()
        ' Remove two strings from list and show state
        RemoveString("David")
        RemoveAt(0)
        ShowArray(m_list) ' index notation
        ShowCount()
        ' Try to remove two strings not in list
        RemoveString("Amy")
        RemoveAt(3)
    End Sub
    ...
```

Here is the output:

```
list.Count = 0
list.Capacity = 4
Amy
```

```
Bob
Charlie
list.Count = 3
list.Capacity = 4
Amy
Bob
Charlie
David
Ellen
list.Count = 5
list.Capacity = 8
array[0] = Bob
array[1] = Charlie
array[2] = Ellen
list.Count = 3
list.Capacity = 8
List does not contain Amy
No element at index 3
```

INTERFACE DOCUMENTATION

Predefined interfaces are documented in the online .NET Framework SDK documentation. Figure 6–2 illustrates the documentation of the **IEnumerable** interface. The right-hand pane has a language filter button ▼, which we have used to show only VB.NET versions. If you are using the interface in one of the .NET Framework classes that implement the interface, you do not need to implement any of the methods yourself, since they are implemented for you. If you are creating your own class that supports an interface, you must provide implementations of all the methods of the interface. In either case, the documentation describes the interface methods for you.

IENUMERABLE AND IENUMERATOR

The basic interface that must be supported by collection classes is **IEnumerable**, which has a single method, **GetEnumerator**.

```
Public Interface IEnumerable
    Function GetEnumerator() As IEnumerator
End Interface
```

GetEnumerator returns an interface reference to **IEnumerator**, which is the interface used for iterating through a collection. This interface has the read-only property **Current** and the methods **MoveNext** and **Reset**.

```
Public Interface IEnumerator
    ReadOnly Property Current As Object
    Function MoveNext() As Boolean
    Sub Reset()
End Interface
```

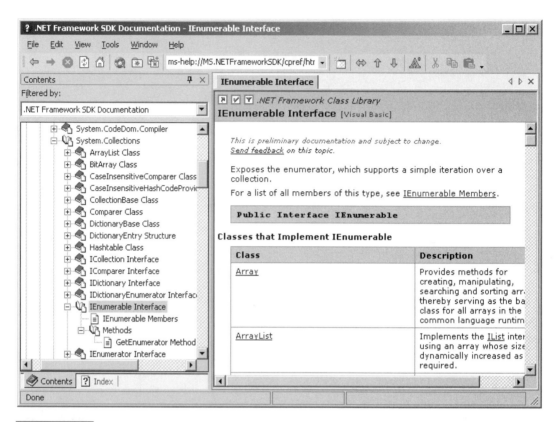

FIGURE 6–2 *.NET Framework SDK documentation for IEnumerable interface.*

The enumerator is initially positioned *before* the first element in the collection, and it must be advanced before it is used. The **ShowEnum** method (in the **StringList** example) illustrates using an enumerator to iterate through a list.

```
Private Sub ShowEnum(ByVal array As ArrayList)
    Dim iter As IEnumerator = Array.GetEnumerator()
    Dim more As Boolean = iter.MoveNext()
    While (more)
        Dim str As String = iter.Current
        Console.WriteLine(str)
        more = iter.MoveNext()
    End While
End Sub
```

This pattern of using an enumerator to iterate through a list is so common that VB.NET provides a special kind of loop, known as **For Each**, that can be used for iterating through the elements of *any* collection. Here is the comparable code using **For Each**.

```
Private Sub ShowList(ByVal array As ArrayList)
   Dim str As String
   For Each str In array
      Console.WriteLine(str)
   Next
End Sub
```

ICOLLECTION

The **ICollection** interface is derived from **IEnumerable** and adds a **Count** property and a **CopyTo** method as well as **IsSynchronized** and **SyncRoot** properties.

```
Public Interface ICollection
   Inherits IEnumerable

   ReadOnly Property Count As Integer
   ReadOnly Property IsSynchronized As Boolean
   ReadOnly Property SyncRoot As Object
   Sub CopyTo(ByVal array As Array, ByVal index As Integer)
End Interface
```

The synchronization properties **IsSynchronized** and **SyncRoot** can help you deal with thread safety issues. "Is it thread safe?" is a question frequently asked about library code. The short answer to this question for the .NET Framework class library is no. This does not mean that the designers of the Framework did not think about thread safety issues. On the contrary, there are many mechanisms to help you write thread-safe code when you need to. The reason that collections are not automatically thread safe is that your code should not have to pay the performance penalty to enforce synchronization when it is not running in a multithreading scenario. If you do need thread safety, you may use the thread-safety properties as required. We discuss the .NET mechanisms for thread synchronization in Chapter 10.

Our **StringList** program illustrates use of the **Count** property of **ICollection**. The **Capacity** property is not defined in any interface, but is rather exposed by the **ArrayList** class itself.

```
Private Sub ShowCount()
   Console.WriteLine("list.Count = {0}", m_list.Count)
   Console.WriteLine( _
      "list.Capacity = {0}", m_list.Capacity)
End Sub
```

ILIST

The **IList** interface is derived from **ICollection** and provides methods for adding an item to a list, removing an item, and so on. A default parameterized property (**Item**) is provided that enables array notation to be used. (We discussed parameterized properties in Chapter 4.)

```
Public Interface IList
   Inherits ICollection, IEnumerable

   ReadOnly Property IsFixedSize As Boolean
   ReadOnly Property IsReadOnly As Boolean
   Default Property Item(ByVal index As Integer) As Object
   Function Add(ByVal value As Object) As Integer
   Sub Clear()
   Function Contains(ByVal value As Object) As Boolean
   Function IndexOf(ByVal value As Object) As Integer
   Sub Insert(ByVal index As Integer, ByVal value _
     As Object)
   Sub Remove(ByVal value As Object)
   Sub RemoveAt(ByVal index As Integer)
End Interface
```

Our **StringList** sample code illustrates using the indexer and the **Add**, **Contains**, **Remove**, and **RemoveAt** methods.

```
Private Sub ShowArray(ByVal array As ArrayList)
   Dim i As Integer = 0
   While i < array.Count
      Console.WriteLine("array[{0}] = {1}", i, array(i))
      i += 1
   End While
End Sub
...
Private Sub AddString(ByVal str As String)
   If m_list.Contains(str) Then
      Throw New Exception("list contains " & str)
   End If
   m_list.Add(str)
End Sub

Private Sub RemoveString(ByVal str As String)
   If m_list.Contains(str) Then
      m_list.Remove(str)
   Else
      Console.WriteLine("List does not contain {0}", str)
   End If
End Sub

Private Sub RemoveAt(ByVal index As Integer)
   Try
```

```
        m_list.RemoveAt(index)
    Catch e As ArgumentOutOfRangeException
        Console.WriteLine("No element at index {0}", index)
    End Try
End Sub
```

Copy Semantics and ICloneable

Sometimes you have to make a copy of an object. When you copy objects that contain objects and object references, you have to be aware of the nuances of copy semantics. We will compare reference copy, shallow memberwise copy, and deep copy. We will see that by implementing the **ICloneable** interface in your class, you can perform a deep copy.

Recall that VB.NET has value types and reference types. A value type contains all its own data, while a reference type refers to data stored somewhere else. If a reference variable gets copied to another reference variable, both will refer to the same object. If the object referenced by the second variable is changed, the first variable will also reflect the new value. Sometimes you want this behavior, but sometimes you do not.

SHALLOW COPY AND DEEP COPY

A structure in VB.NET automatically implements a *memberwise* copy, sometimes known as a *shallow copy*. The **Object** root class has a protected method, **MemberwiseClone**, which will perform a memberwise copy of members of a class.

If one or more members of a class are of a reference type, this memberwise copy may not be good enough. The result will be two data member references to the same data, not two independent copies of the data. To actually copy the data itself and not merely the data member references, you will need to perform a *deep copy*. Deep copy can be provided at either the language level or the library level. In C++ deep copy is provided at the language level through a *copy constructor*. In VB.NET deep copy is provided by the .NET Framework through a special interface, **ICloneable**, which you can implement in your classes in order to enable them to perform deep copy.

EXAMPLE PROGRAM

Code Example

We will illustrate all these ideas in the program **CopyDemo**. This program makes a copy of a **Course** instance. The **Course** class consists of a title and a collection of students.

```
' Course.vb

Imports System
Imports System.Collections
```

```
Public Class Course
   Implements ICloneable

   Public Title As String
   Public Roster As ArrayList

   Public Sub New(ByVal titleText As String)
      Title = titleText
      Roster = New ArrayList()
   End Sub

   Public Sub AddStudent(ByVal name As String)
      Roster.Add(name)
   End Sub

   Public Sub Show(ByVal caption As String)
      Console.WriteLine("-----{0}-----", caption)
      Console.WriteLine( _
         "Course : {0} with {1} students", _
         Title, Roster.Count)
      Dim name As String
      For Each name In Roster
         Console.WriteLine(name)
      Next
   End Sub

   Public Function ShallowCopy() As Course
      Return Me.MemberwiseClone()
   End Function

   Public Function Clone() As Object _
     Implements ICloneable.Clone

     Dim course As Course = New Course(Title)
     course.Roster = Roster.Clone()
     Return course
   End Function
End Class
```

The test program constructs a **Course** instance **c1** and then makes a copy **c2** using reference copy, shallow copy, and deep copy, as described in the next three sections.

REFERENCE COPY BY ASSIGNMENT

The first way the copy is performed is by the straight assignment **c2 = c1**. Now we get two references to the same object, and if we make any change through the first reference, we will see the same change through the second reference. The first part of the test program illustrates such an assignment.

```vb
' CopyDemo.vb

Imports System
Imports System.Collections

Module CopyDemo
    Private c1 As Course
    Private c2 As Course

    Sub Main()
        Console.WriteLine("Copy is done via c2 = c1")
        InitializeCourse()
        c1.Show("original")
        c2 = c1
        c2.Show("copy")
        c2.Title = ".NET Programming"
        c2.AddStudent("Charlie")
        c2.Show("copy with changed title and new student")
        c1.Show("original")
        ...
    End Sub

    Private Sub InitializeCourse()
        c1 = New Course("Intro to VB")
        c1.AddStudent("John")
        c1.AddStudent("Mary")
    End Sub
End Module
```

We initialize with the title "Intro to VB.NET" and two students. We make the assignment **c2 = c1** and then change the title and add another student for **c2**. We then show both **c1** and **c2**, and we see that both reflect the changes, meaning that the reference **c1** has been copied to **c2**, and **c2** no longer references the object that it originally did. Here is the output from this first part of the program:

```
Copy is done via c2 = c1
-----original-----
Course : Intro to VB.NET with 2 students
John
Mary
-----copy-----
Course : Intro to VB.NET with 2 students
John
Mary
-----copy with changed title and new student-----
Course : .NET Programming with 3 students
John
Mary
Charlie
```

```
-----original-----
Course : .NET Programming with 3 students
John
Mary
Charlie
```

MEMBERWISE CLONE

Next we will illustrate doing a memberwise copy, which can be accomplished using the **MemberwiseClone** method of **Object**. Since this method is Protected, we cannot call it directly from outside the **Course** class. Instead, in **Course** we define a method, **ShallowCopy**, which is implemented using **MemberwiseClone**.

```
' Course.vb

Imports System
Imports System.Collections

Public Class Course
   Implements ICloneable
   ...
   Public Function ShallowCopy() As Course
      Return Me.MemberwiseClone()
   End Function
   ...
End Class
```

Here is the second part of the test program, which calls the **Shallow-Copy** method. Again, we change the title and a student in the second copy.

```
' CopyDemo.vb

Imports System
Imports System.Collections

Module CopyDemo
   ...
   Sub Main()
      ...
      Console.WriteLine()
      Console.WriteLine( _
         "Copy is done via c2 = c1.ShallowCopy()")
      InitializeCourse()
      c2 = c1.ShallowCopy()
      c2.Title = ".NET Programming"
      c2.AddStudent("Charlie")
      c2.Show("copy with changed title and new student")
      c1.Show("original")
      ...
   End Sub
EndModule
```

Here is the output of this second part of the program. Now the **Title** field has its own independent copy, but the **Roster** collection is just copied by reference, so each copy refers to the same collection of students.

```
Copy is done via c2 = c1.ShallowCopy()
-----copy with changed title and new student-----
Course : .NET Programming with 3 students
John
Mary
Charlie
-----original-----
Course : Intro to VB.NET with 3 students
John
Mary
Charlie
```

USING ICLONEABLE

The final version of copy relies on the fact that our **Course** class supports the **ICloneable** interface and implements the **Clone** method. To clone the **Roster** collection, we use the fact that **ArrayList** also implements the **ICloneable** interface, as discussed earlier in the chapter.

```
' Course.vb

Imports System
Imports System.Collections

Public Class Course
   Implements ICloneable
   . . .
   Public Function Clone() As Object _
    Implements ICloneable.Clone

      Dim course As Course = New Course(Title)
      course.Roster = Roster.Clone()
      Return course
   End Function
   . . .
End Class
```

Here is the third part of the test program, which calls the **Clone** method. Again, we change the title and a student in the second copy.

```
' CopyDemo.vb

Imports System
Imports System.Collections

Module CopyDemo
   . . .
```

```
Sub Main()
   ...
   Console.WriteLine()
   Console.WriteLine( _
      "    Copy is done via c2 = c1.Clone()")
   InitializeCourse()
   c2 = c1.Clone()
   c2.Title = ".NET Programming"
   c2.AddStudent("Charlie")
   c2.Show("copy with changed title and new student")
   c1.Show("original")
   ...
End Sub
EndModule
```

Here is the output from the third part of the program. Now we have completely independent instances of **Course**. Each has its own title and set of students.

```
Copy is done via c2 = c1.Clone()
-----copy with changed title and new student-----
Course : .NET Programming with 3 students
John
Mary
Charlie
-----original-----
Course : Intro to VB.NET with 2 students
John
Mary
```

Comparing Objects

We have quite exhaustively studied *copying* objects. We now examine *comparing* objects. To compare objects, the .NET Framework uses the interface **IComparable**. In this section we use the interface **IComparable** to sort an array.

SORTING AN ARRAY

Code Example

The **System.Array** class provides a static method, **Sort**, that can be used for sorting an array. The program **ArrayName** illustrates applying this **Sort** method to an array of **Name** objects, where the **Name** class simply encapsulates a **String** through a read-only property **Text**. Here is the main program.

```
' ArrayName.vb

...

Module ArrayName
   Sub Main()
      Dim array() As Name = New Name(10) {}
```

```
        array(0) = New Name("Michael")
        array(1) = New Name("Charlie")
        array(2) = New Name("Peter")
        array(3) = New Name("Dana")
        array(4) = New Name("Bob")
        If TypeOf array(0) Is IComparable Then
            array.Sort(array)
        Else
            Console.WriteLine( _
                "Name does not implement IComparable")
        End If
        Dim name As Name
        For Each name In array
            If Not name Is Nothing Then
                Console.WriteLine(name)
            End If
        Next
    End Sub
End Module
```

IMPLEMENTING ICOMPARABLE

In order for the **Sort** method to function, there must be a way of comparing the objects that are being sorted. This comparison is achieved through the **CompareTo** method of the interface **IComparable**. Thus, to sort an array of a type you define, you must implement **IComparable** for your type.

```
Public Interface IComparable
    Function CompareTo(ByVal obj As Object) As Integer
End Interface
```

Here is the implementation of the **Name** class, with its implementation of **IComparable**.

```
Public Class Name
    Implements IComparable

    Private m_text As String

    Public Sub New(ByVal text As String)
        Me.m_text = text
    End Sub

    Public ReadOnly Property Text() As String
        Get
            Return m_text
        End Get
    End Property

    Public Function CompareTo(ByVal obj As Object) _
     As Integer Implements IComparable.CompareTo
```

```
      Dim s1 As String = Me.m_text
      Dim s2 As String = obj.Text
      Return String.Compare(s1, s2)
   End Function

   Public Overrides Function ToString() As String
      Return Text
   End Function
End Class
```

Understanding Frameworks

Our example offers some insight into the workings of frameworks. A framework is *more* than just a library. In a typical library, you are only concerned with your code calling library functions. In a framework, you call into the framework *and the framework may call back into your class methods*. Your program can be viewed as the middle layer of a sandwich.

- Your code calls the bottom layer.
- The top layer calls your code.

The .NET Framework is an excellent example of such an architecture. There is rich functionality that you can call directly. There are many interfaces, which you can optionally implement to make your program behave appropriately when called by the framework, often on behalf of other objects.

Delegates

Interfaces facilitate writing code so that your program can be **called into** by some other code. This style of programming has been available for a long time, under the guise of "callback" functions. In this section we examine **delegates** in VB.NET, which can be thought of as type-safe and object-oriented callback functions. Delegates are the foundation for a design pattern, known as **events**, which we'll look at in the next section.

A *callback function* is one which your program specifies and "registers" in some way, and which then gets called by other code. In C and C++ callback functions are implemented using function pointers.

In VB.NET you can encapsulate a reference to a method as a delegate object. A delegate can refer to either a static method or an instance method. When a delegate refers to an instance method, it stores both an object instance and an entry point to the instance method. The instance method can then be called through this object instance. When a delegate object refers to a static method, it stores just the entry point of this static method.

You can pass this delegate object to other code, which can then call your method. The code that calls your delegate method does not have to know at compile time which method is going to be called at runtime.

In VB.NET a delegate is considered a reference type that is similar to a class type. A new delegate instance is created just like any other class instance, using the **New** operator. In fact, VB.NET delegates are implemented by the .NET Framework class library as a class, derived ultimately from **System.Delegate**.

Delegates are object oriented and type safe, and they enjoy the safety of the managed code execution environment.

Declaring a Delegate

You declare a delegate in VB.NET using a special notation with the keyword **Delegate** and the signature of the encapsulated method. A naming convention suggests that your name should end with "Callback."

Code
Example

We illustrate delegates in the sample program **DelegateAccount.** Here is an example of a delegate declaration from the file **DelegateAccount.vb**. The name **NotifyCallback** is arbitrary, but note that it follows the convention of ending with "Callback."

```
Public Delegate Sub NotifyCallback( _
 ByVal balance As Decimal)
```

Defining a Method

When you instantiate a delegate, you will need to specify a method, which must match the signature in the delegate declaration. The method may be either a static method or an instance method. Here are some examples of methods that can be hooked to the **NotifyCallback** delegate:

```
Private Shared Sub NotifyCustomer(ByVal balance As Decimal)
   Console.WriteLine("Dear customer,")
   Console.WriteLine( _
      "    Account overdrawn, balance = {0}", balance)
End Sub

Private Shared Sub NotifyBank(ByVal balance As Decimal)
   Console.WriteLine("Dear bank,")
   Console.WriteLine( _
      "    Account overdrawn, balance = {0}", balance)
End Sub

Private Sub NotifyInstance(ByVal balance As Decimal)
   Console.WriteLine("Dear instance,")
   Console.WriteLine( _
      "    Account overdrawn, balance = {0}", balance)
End Sub
```

Creating a Delegate Object

You instantiate a delegate object with the **New** operator, just as you would with any other class. The following code illustrates creating two delegate objects. The first delegate variable, named **custDlg**, is associated with a static method named **NotifyCustomer**. The second one, named **instDlg**, is associated with an instance method named **NotifyInstance**. The second delegate object internally will store both a method entry point and an object instance that is used for invoking the method.

```
Dim custDlg As NotifyCallback = _
   New NotifyCallback(AddressOf NotifyCustomer)
...
Dim da As DelegateAccount = New DelegateAccount()
Dim instDlg As NotifyCallback = _
   New NotifyCallback(AddressOf da.NotifyInstance)
```

Calling a Delegate

You "call" a delegate just as you would a method. The delegate object is not a method, but it has an encapsulated method. The delegate object "delegates" the call to this encapsulated method, hence the name "delegate." In the following code the delegate object **m_notifyDlg** is called whenever a negative balance occurs on a withdrawal. In this example the **m_notifyDlg** delegate object is initialized in the method **SetDelegate**.

```
Private m_notifyDlg As NotifyCallback
...
Public Sub SetDelegate(ByVal dlg As NotifyCallback)
   m_notifyDlg = dlg
End Sub
...
Public Sub Withdraw(ByVal amount As Decimal)
   m_balance -= amount
   If m_balance < 0 Then
      m_notifyDlg(Balance) 'call the delegate
   End If
End Sub
```

Combining Delegate Objects

A powerful feature of delegates is that you can combine them. Delegates are "multicast," in which they have an invocation list of methods. When such a delegate is called, all the methods on the invocation list will be called in the order they appear in the invocation list. The **Combine** method of the **Delegate** class can be used to combine the invocation methods of two delegate objects. The **Remove** method of the **Delegate** class can be used to remove methods from the invocation list.

```
Dim custDlg As NotifyCallback = _
   New NotifyCallback(AddressOf NotifyCustomer)
Dim bankDlg As NotifyCallback = _
   New NotifyCallback(AddressOf NotifyBank)
Dim currDlg As NotifyCallback = _
   NotifyCallback.Combine(custDlg, bankDlg)
...
currDlg = NotifyCallback.Remove(currDlg, bankDlg)
```

In this example we construct two delegate objects, each with an associated method. We then create a new delegate object whose invocation list will consist of both the methods **NotifyCustomer** and **NotifyBank**. When **currDlg** is called, these two methods will be invoked. Later on in the code we remove the **bankDlg** delegate. Once this is done, the **NotifyBank** method is no longer in the delegate's invocation list, and the next time **currDlg** is called, only **NotifyCustomer** will be invoked.

Complete Example

Code Example

The program **DelegateAccount** illustrates using delegates in our bank account scenario. The file **DelegateAccount.vb** declares the delegate **NotifyCallback**. The class **DelegateAccount** contains methods matching the signature of the delegate. The **Main** method instantiates delegate objects and combines them in various ways. The delegate objects are passed to the **Account** class, which uses its encapsulated delegate object to invoke suitable notifications when the account is overdrawn.

Observe how this structure is dynamic and loosely coupled. The **Account** class does not know or care which notification methods will be invoked in the case of an overdraft. It simply calls the delegate, which in turn calls all the methods on its invocation list. These methods can be adjusted at runtime.

Here is the code for the **Account** class:

```
' Account.vb

Public Class Account
   Private m_balance As Decimal
   Private m_notifyDlg As NotifyCallback

   Public Sub New( _
    ByVal balance As Decimal, _
    ByVal dlg As NotifyCallback)
      m_balance = balance
      m_notifyDlg = dlg
   End Sub
```

```
Public Sub SetDelegate(ByVal dlg As NotifyCallback)
   m_notifyDlg = dlg
End Sub

Public Sub Deposit(ByVal amount As Decimal)
   m_balance += amount
End Sub

Public Sub Withdraw(ByVal amount As Decimal)
   m_balance -= amount
   If m_balance < 0 Then
      m_notifyDlg(Balance) 'call the delegate
   End If
End Sub

Public ReadOnly Property Balance() As Decimal
   Get
      Return m_balance
   End Get
End Property
End Class
```

Here is the code declaring and testing the delegate:

```
' DelegateAccount.vb

Imports System

Public Delegate Sub NotifyCallback( _
 ByVal balance As Decimal)

Class DelegateAccount 'Note: This is a Class, not a Module
   Shared Sub Main()
      Dim custDlg As NotifyCallback = _
         New NotifyCallback(AddressOf NotifyCustomer)
      Dim bankDlg As NotifyCallback = _
         New NotifyCallback(AddressOf NotifyBank)
      Dim currDlg As NotifyCallback = _
         NotifyCallback.Combine(custDlg, bankDlg)
      Dim acc As Account = New Account(100, currDlg)
      Console.WriteLine("balance = {0}", acc.Balance)
      acc.Withdraw(125)
      Console.WriteLine("balance = {0}", acc.Balance)
      acc.Deposit(200)
      acc.Withdraw(125)
      Console.WriteLine("balance = {0}", acc.Balance)
      currDlg = NotifyCallback.Remove(currDlg, bankDlg)
      acc.SetDelegate(currDlg)
      acc.Withdraw(125)
      Dim da As DelegateAccount = New DelegateAccount()
      Dim instDlg As NotifyCallback = _
```

```
        New NotifyCallback(AddressOf da.NotifyInstance)
      currDlg = NotifyCallback.Combine(currDlg, instDlg)
      acc.SetDelegate(currDlg)
      acc.Withdraw(125)
  End Sub

  Private Shared Sub NotifyCustomer( _
   ByVal balance As Decimal)
      Console.WriteLine("Dear customer,")
      Console.WriteLine( _
          "    Account overdrawn, balance = {0}", balance)
  End Sub

  Private Shared Sub NotifyBank( _
   ByVal balance As Decimal)
      Console.WriteLine("Dear bank,")
      Console.WriteLine( _
          "    Account overdrawn, balance = {0}", balance)
  End Sub

  Private Sub NotifyInstance( _
   ByVal balance As Decimal)
      Console.WriteLine("Dear instance,")
      Console.WriteLine( _
          "    Account overdrawn, balance = {0}", balance)
  End Sub
End Class
```

Here is the output from running the program. Notice which notification methods get invoked, depending upon the operations that have been performed on the current delegate object.

```
balance = 100
Dear customer,
   Account overdrawn, balance = -25
Dear bank,
   Account overdrawn, balance = -25
balance = -25
balance = 50
Dear customer,
   Account overdrawn, balance = -75
Dear customer,
   Account overdrawn, balance = -200
Dear instance,
   Account overdrawn, balance = -200
```

Stock Market Simulation

Code
Example

As a further illustration of the use of delegates, consider the simple stock-market simulation, implemented in the directory **StockMarket**. The simulation consists of two modules:

● The **Admin** module provides a user interface for configuring and running the simulation. It also implements operations called by the simulation engine.
● The **Engine** module is the simulation engine. It maintains an internal clock and invokes randomly generated operations, based on the configuration parameters passed to it.

Figure 6–3 shows the high-level architecture of the simulation.

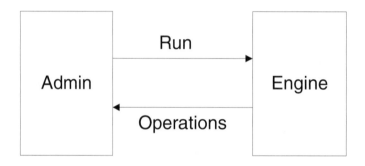

| **FIGURE 6–3** | *Architecture of stock-market simulation.* |

The following operations are available:

● PrintTick: shows each clock tick.
● PrintTrade: shows each trade.

The following configuration parameters can be specified:

● Ticks on/off
● Trades on/off
● Count of how many ticks to run the simulation

RUNNING THE SIMULATION

Build and run the example program in **StockMarket**. Start with the default configuration: Ticks are OFF, Trades are ON, Run count is 100. (Note that the results are random and will be different each time you run the program.) If you enter the command *run,* then the output shows columns of data for clock tick, stock, price, and volume.

```
Ticks are OFF
Trades are ON
```

```
Run count = 100
Enter command, quit to exit
: run
    2  ACME     23    600
   27  MSFT     63    400
   27  IBM     114    600
   38  MSFT     69    400
   53  MSFT     75    900
   62  INTC     27    800
   64  MSFT     82    200
   68  MSFT     90    300
   81  MSFT     81    600
   83  INTC     30    800
   91  MSFT     73    700
   99  IBM     119    400
:
```

The available commands are listed when you type *help* at the colon prompt. The commands are

```
count     set run count
ticks     toggle ticks
trades    toggle trades
config    show configuration
run       run the simulation
quit      exit the program
```

DELEGATE CODE

Two delegates are declared in the **Admin.vb** file.

```
Public Delegate Sub TickCallback(ByVal ticks As Integer)
Public Delegate Sub TradeCallback( _
 ByVal ticks As Integer, _
 ByVal stock As String, _
 ByVal price As Integer, _
 ByVal volume As Integer)
```

As we saw in the previous section, a delegate is similar to a class, and a delegate object is instantiated by **New**.

```
Dim tickDlg As TickCallback = _
   New TickCallback(AddressOf PrintTick)
Dim tradeDlg As TradeCallback = _
   New TradeCallback(AddressOf PrintTrade)
```

A method is passed as the parameter to the delegate constructor. The method signature must match that of the delegate.

```
Public Sub PrintTick(ByVal ticks As Integer)
   Console.Write("{0} ", ticks)
   If (++printcount = LINECOUNT) Then
```

```
        Console.WriteLine()
        printcount = 0
      End If
    End Sub
```

PASSING THE DELEGATES TO THE ENGINE

The **Admin** class passes the delegates to the **Engine** class in the constructor of the **Engine** class.

```
Dim engine As Engine = New Engine(tickDlg, tradeDlg)
```

RANDOM-NUMBER GENERATION

The heart of the simulation is the **Run** method of the **Engine** class. At the core of the **Run** method is assigning simulated data based on random numbers. We use the **System.Random** class, which we discussed in Chapter 4 in connection with the **ArrayDemo** program.

```
While (i < stocks.Length)
   Dim r As Double - rangen.NextDouble()
   If (r < tradeProb(i)) Then
      Dim delta As Integer = _
         price(i) * volatility(i)
      If (rangen.NextDouble() < 0.5) Then
         delta = -delta
      End If
      price(i) += delta
      Dim volume As Integer = _
         rangen.Next(minVolume, maxVolume) * 100
      tradeOp( _
         tick, stocks(i), _
         price(i), volume)
   End If
   i += 1
End While
```

USING THE DELEGATES

In the **Engine** class, delegate references are declared:

```
Dim tickOp As TickCallback
Dim tradeOp As TradeCallback
```

The delegate references are initialized in the **Engine** constructor:

```
 Public Sub New( _
  ByVal tickOp As TickCallback, _
  ByVal tradeOp As TradeCallback)
   Me.tickOp = tickOp
   Me.tradeOp = tradeOp
End Sub
```

The method that is wrapped by the delegate object can then be called through the delegate reference:

```
If showTicks Then
     tickOp(tick)
```

Events

Delegates are the foundation for a design pattern known as *events*. Conceptually, servers implement *incoming* interfaces, which are called by clients. In a diagram, such an interface may be shown with a small bubble (a notation used in COM). Sometimes a client may wish to receive notifications from a server when certain "events" occur. In such a case the server will specify an *outgoing* interface. The server defines the interface and the client implements it. In a diagram, such an interface may be shown with an arrow (again, a notation used in COM). Figure 6–4 illustrates a server with one incoming and one outgoing interface. In the case of the outgoing interface, the client will implement an incoming interface, which the server will call.

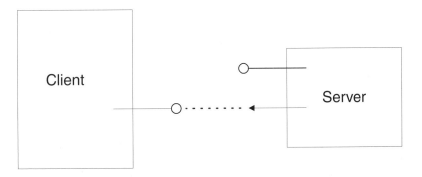

FIGURE 6–4   *A server with an incoming interface and an outgoing interface.*

A good example of a programming situation with events is a graphical user interface. An event is some external action, typically triggered by the user, to which the program must respond. Events include user actions such as clicking a mouse button or pressing a key on the keyboard. A GUI program must contain *event handlers* to respond to or "handle" these events. We will see many examples of GUI event handling in Chapter 7, where we discuss Windows Forms, and we'll look at a simple Windows Forms example in the next section.

Events in Visual Basic and VB.NET

From the very beginning, Visual Basic has provided an easy-to-use mechanism for dealing with events. Consider the following VB6 program **MouseEventVb6**, which displays a blank form and puts up a message box whenever the user clicks the mouse.

```
Private Sub Form_Click()
   MsgBox ("Mouse was clicked!")
End Sub
```

This code is simple but somewhat inflexible, based on a naming convention. The **Click** event is tied to the **Form** base class by the name **Form_Click**.

By contrast, consider the comparable VB.NET program **MouseEventVb-Net**.

```
Public Class Form1
   Inherits System.Windows.Forms.Form

#Region " Windows Form Designer generated code "
...
   Private Sub Form1_Click(ByVal sender As Object, _
     ByVal e As EventArgs) Handles MyBase.Click
      MessageBox.Show("Mouse was clicked!")
   End Sub
End Class
```

The VB.NET code uses the **Handles** keyword to identify the event. Any name can be used for the handler function. In fact, you can have several functions handling the same event, reflecting the fact that VB.NET events use multicast delegates under the hood.

The example code we have just examined illustrates *static event handling,* which is easy to use and follows a syntax that is a natural extension of VB6 event handling. VB.NET also supports *dynamic event handling*, where event handlers can be added or removed at runtime. We will look at dynamic event handling first, because it is tied closely to the underlying delegate mechanism that we have studied. We will then discuss static event handling.

Dynamic Event Handling

The .NET Framework provides an easy-to-use implementation of the event paradigm built on delegates. VB.NET simplifies working with .NET events by providing the keyword **Event** and the **AddHandler** and **RemoveHandler** keywords to hook up event handlers to events and to remove them. The Framework also defines a base class **EventArgs** to be used for passing arguments to event handlers. There are a number of derived classes defined by the Framework for specific types of events, such as **MouseEventArgs**, **ListChangedEventArgs**, and so forth. These derived classes define data members to hold appropriate argument information.

An event handler is a delegate with a specific signature,

```
Public Delegate Sub EventHandler( _
  ByVal sender As Object, ByVal e As EventArgs)
```

The name **EventHandler** is arbitrary. The first argument represents the source of the event, and the second argument contains data associated with the event.

We will examine this dynamic event architecture in the example program **EventDemo\Step1**, which implements a simple chat room.

SERVER-SIDE EVENT CODE

We begin with server-side code, in **ChatServer.vb**. The .NET event architecture uses delegates of a specific signature. Two delegates are declared in this example.

```
Public Delegate Sub JoinHandler( _
  ByVal sender As Object, ByVal e As ChatEventArg)
Public Delegate Sub QuitHandler( _
  ByVal sender As Object, ByVal e As ChatEventArg)
```

The first parameter specifies the object that sent the event notification. The second parameter is used to pass data along with the notification. Typically, you will derive a class from **EventArg** to hold your event specific data.

```
Public Class ChatEventArg
   Inherits EventArgs
   Public m_name As String
   Public Sub New(ByVal name As String)
     m_name = name
   End Sub
End Class
```

Two delegate object references are declared using the keyword **Event**.

```
Public Class ChatServer
   ...
   Public Event Join As JoinHandler
   Public Event Quit As QuitHandler
End Class
```

Helper methods are typically provided to facilitate calling the delegate object(s) that have been hooked up to the event. The **RaiseEvent** keyword is used to actually call the delegate via the event.

```
Protected Sub OnJoin(ByVal e As ChatEventArg)
   RaiseEvent Join(Me, e)
```

```
End Sub

Protected Sub OnQuit(ByVal e As ChatEventArg)
    RaiseEvent Quit(Me, e)
End Sub
```

Typically, access is specified as **Protected** so that a derived class has access to this helper method, whereas external code has no business calling it. You can then "fire" the event by calling the helper method at any point in any method of your event source class. The **EventDemo\Version 1** example happens to do this in methods named **JoinChat** and **QuitChat**.

```
Public Sub JoinChat(ByVal name As String)
    m_members.Add(name)
    OnJoin(New ChatEventArg(name)) 'fire the Join event
End Sub

Public Sub QuitChat(ByVal name As String)
    m_members.Remove(name)
    OnQuit(New ChatEventArg(name)) 'fire the Quit event
End Sub
```

CLIENT-SIDE EVENT CODE

The client provides event handler functions. These are the callback functions called by the server.

```
Public Sub OnJoinChat( _
 ByVal sender As Object, _
 ByVal e As ChatEventArg)
    Console.WriteLine( _
        "sender = {0}, {1} has joined the chat", _
        sender, _
        e.m_name)
End Sub

Public Sub OnQuitChat( _
 ByVal sender As Object, _
 ByVal e As ChatEventArg)
    Console.WriteLine( _
        "sender = {0}, {1} has quit the chat", _
        sender, e.m_name)
End Sub
```

The client hooks the handlers to the events, using the **AddHandler** keyword. Once the handlers are established, the client may choose to join or quit the chat server at will.

```
Sub Main()
    Dim chat As ChatServer = _
        New ChatServer("OI Chat Room")
```

```
' Register to receive event notifications
AddHandler chat.Join, AddressOf OnJoinChat
AddHandler chat.Quit, AddressOf OnQuitChat
' Call methods on the server
chat.JoinChat("Michael")
chat.JoinChat("Bob")
chat.JoinChat("Sam")
chat.ShowMembers("After 3 have joined")
chat.QuitChat("Bob")
chat.ShowMembers("After 1 has quit")
End Sub
```

All of the registered handlers will get invoked when the event delegate is called. You may unregister a handler at any time with the **RemoveHandler** keyword.

Chat Room Complete Example (Step 1)

Code Example

The chat room example in **EventDemo\Step1** illustrates the complete architecture on both the server and client sides. The server provides the following methods:

- JoinChat
- QuitChat
- ShowMembers

Whenever a new member joins or quits, the server sends a notification to the client. The event handlers print out an appropriate message. Here is the output from running the program:

```
sender = OI Chat Room, Michael has joined the chat
sender = OI Chat Room, Bob has joined the chat
sender = OI Chat Room, Sam has joined the chat
--- After 3 have joined---
Michael
Bob
Sam
sender = OI Chat Room, Bob has quit the chat
--- After 1 has quit---
Michael
Sam
```

CLIENT CODE

The client program provides event handlers. It instantiates a server object and then hooks up its event handlers to the events. The client then calls methods on the server. These calls will trigger the server, firing events back to the client, which get handled by the event handlers.

```
' ChatClient.vb

Imports System

Module ChatClient
    Public Sub OnJoinChat( _
     ByVal sender As Object, _
     ByVal e As ChatEventArg)
        Console.WriteLine( _
            "sender = {0}, {1} has joined the chat", _
            sender, _
            e.m_name)
    End Sub

    Public Sub OnQuitChat( _
     ByVal sender As Object, _
     ByVal e As ChatEventArg)
        Console.WriteLine( _
            "sender = {0}, {1} has quit the chat", _
            sender, e.m_name)
    End Sub

    Sub Main()
        Dim chat As ChatServer = _
            New ChatServer("OI Chat Room")
        ' Register to receive event notifications
        AddHandler chat.Join, AddressOf OnJoinChat
        AddHandler chat.Quit, AddressOf OnQuitChat
        ' Call methods on the server
        chat.JoinChat("Michael")
        chat.JoinChat("Bob")
        chat.JoinChat("Sam")
        chat.ShowMembers("After 3 have joined")
        chat.QuitChat("Bob")
        chat.ShowMembers("After 1 has quit")
    End Sub
End Module
```

SERVER CODE

The server provides code to store in a collection the names of people who have joined the chat. When a person quits the chat, the name is removed from the collection. Joining and quitting the chat triggers firing an event back to the client. The server also contains the "plumbing" code for setting up the events, including declaration of the delegates, the events, and the event arguments. There are also helper methods for firing the events.

```
' ChatServer.vb

Imports System
```

```
Imports System.Collections

Public Class ChatEventArg
    Inherits EventArgs
    Public m_name As String
    Public Sub New(ByVal name As String)
        m_name = name
    End Sub
End Class

Public Delegate Sub JoinHandler( _
 ByVal sender As Object, ByVal e As ChatEventArg)
Public Delegate Sub QuitHandler( _
 ByVal sender As Object, ByVal e As ChatEventArg)

Public Class ChatServer
    Private m_members As ArrayList = New ArrayList()
    Private m_chatName As String
    Public Event Join As JoinHandler
    Public Event Quit As QuitHandler

    Public Sub New(ByVal chatName As String)
        Me.m_chatName = chatName
    End Sub

    Public Overrides Function ToString() As String
        Return m_chatName
    End Function

    Protected Sub OnJoin(ByVal e As ChatEventArg)
        RaiseEvent Join(Me, e)
    End Sub

    Protected Sub OnQuit(ByVal e As ChatEventArg)
        RaiseEvent Quit(Me, e)
    End Sub

    Public Sub JoinChat(ByVal name As String)
        m_members.Add(name)
        OnJoin(New ChatEventArg(name)) 'fire the Join event
    End Sub

    Public Sub QuitChat(ByVal name As String)
        m_members.Remove(name)
        OnQuit(New ChatEventArg(name)) 'fire the Quit event
    End Sub

    Public Sub ShowMembers(ByVal msg As String)
        Console.WriteLine("--- " & msg & "---")
        Dim member As String
```

```
      For Each member In m_members
           Console.WriteLine(member)
      Next
   End Sub
End Class
```

It may appear that there is a fair amount of such plumbing code, but it is *much* simpler than the previous connection-point mechanism used by COM for events. Also, most of the plumbing is on the server side, not the client side. It is quite easy to write programs that handle events. Static event handling makes the job even easier.

Static Event Handling

Static event handling in VB.NET is simpler but less flexible. If a class implements events, you may declare an object reference to that class using the **WithEvents** keyword. The VB.NET compiler will then look for matching procedures with the **Handles** keyword and, under the hood, instantiate delegates and add handlers.

Code Example

As an example, consider **EventDemo\Step2**. The server program is unchanged. The client program now uses static event handling.

```
' ChatClient.vb
' Step 2 - Static Event Handling

Imports System

Module ChatClient
    Dim WithEvents chat As ChatServer

    Public Sub OnJoinChat( _
     ByVal sender As Object, _
     ByVal e As ChatEventArg) Handles chat.Join
        Console.WriteLine( _
          "sender = {0}, {1} has joined the chat", _
          sender, e.m_name)
    End Sub

    Public Sub OnQuitChat( _
     ByVal sender As Object, _
     ByVal e As ChatEventArg) Handles chat.Quit
        Console.WriteLine( _
          "sender = {0}, {1} has quit the chat", _
          sender, e.m_name)
    End Sub

    Sub Main()
        Dim chat As ChatServer = _
          New ChatServer("OI Chat Room")
```

```
      ' Don't need these AddHandler calls
      ' AddHandler chat.Join, AddressOf OnJoinChat
      ' AddHandler chat.Quit, AddressOf OnQuitChat
      ' Call methods on the server
      chat.JoinChat("Michael")
      chat.JoinChat("Bob")
      chat.JoinChat("Sam")
      chat.ShowMembers("After 3 have joined")
      chat.QuitChat("Bob")
      chat.ShowMembers("After 1 has quit")
   End Sub
End Module
```

Attributes

A modern approach to implementing complex code is to let the system do it for you. There must be a way for the programmer to inform the system of what is desired. In the .NET Framework such cues can be given to the system by means of *attributes*.

Microsoft introduced attribute-based programming in Microsoft Transaction Server (MTS). The concept was that MTS, not the programmer, would implement complex tasks such as distributed transactions. The programmer would "declare" the transaction requirements for a COM class, and MTS would implement it. This use of attributes was greatly extended in the next generation of MTS, known as COM+. In MTS and COM+ attributes are stored in a separate repository, distinct from the program itself.

Attributes are also used in Interface Definition Language (IDL), which gives a precise specification of COM interfaces, including method signatures and parameter marshaling. Part of the function of IDL is to make it possible for a tool to generate proxies and stubs for remoting a method call across a process boundary or even across a network. When parameters are passed remotely, it is necessary to give more information than when they are passed within the same process. For example, within a process, you can simply pass a reference to an array. But in passing an array across a process boundary, you must inform the tool of the size of the array. This information is communicated in IDL by means of attributes, which are specified using a square-bracket notation. Here is an example of IDL that shows the use of attributes.

```
[
   object,
   uuid(AAA19CDE-C091-47BF-8C96-C80A00989796),
   dual,
   pointer_default(unique)
]
```

```
interface IAccount : IDispatch
{
    [id(1)] HRESULT Deposit([in] long id, [in] long amount);
    [id(2)] HRESULT Withdraw([in] long id, [in] long
amount);
    [id(3)] HRESULT GetBalance([in] long id,
               [out] long *pBal);
    [id(4)] HRESULT GetAllBalances([in, out] long* pCount,
               [out, size_is(*pCount)] long balances[]);
};
```

If you are experienced with COM, such IDL will be familiar to you. If not, just notice the general structure of how attributes are used. Attributes such as **object** and **uuid** are applied to the interface, the **id** attribute is applied to methods, and the attributes **in**, **out**, and **size_is** are applied to parameters.

A problem with attributes in both MTS/COM+ and IDL is that they are separate from the program source code. When the source code is modified, the attribute information may get out of sync with the code.

Attributes in .NET

In .NET, attributes are declared with angle brackets, unlike IDL. Also unlike IDL, the attributes are part of the program source code. When compiled into intermediate language, the attributes become part of the metadata. There are some predefined attributes in VB.NET, there are many attributes associated with various .NET classes, and there is a mechanism to create custom attributes for your own classes. In this section we look at the general characteristics of how attributes are used, beginning with a simple example of using one of the predefined attributes in VB.NET. In later chapters attributes associated with specific .NET classes will be used extensively, and in Chapter 10, after we've discussed Reflection, we will see how to create and use custom attributes.

The **AttributeDemo** program provides a simple example of using the predefined VB.NET attribute **Conditional**, which is used to mark a method to be executed only if a preprocessor symbol is defined.

```
' AttributeDemo.vb

#Const LINUX = True
'#Const UNIX = True

Imports System
Imports System.Diagnostics

Module AttributeDemo
    Sub Main()
```

```
      Notice()
      MultiNotice()
      Console.WriteLine("Goodbye")
   End Sub

   <Conditional("UNIX")> _
   Private Sub Notice()
      Console.WriteLine("Notice: Unix version")
   End Sub

   <Conditional("UNIX"), Conditional("LINUX")> _
   Private Sub MultiNotice()
      Console.WriteLine("Notice: Some version of Unix")
   End Sub
End Module
```

Conditional is one of three predefined attributes in VB.NET.[8] Its full name is **ConditionalAttribute**, but VB.NET has the convenience feature that when an attribute's name ends with the **Attribute** suffix, you may drop the suffix. **Conditional** is used to mark a method with a symbol. If that symbol is defined by the preprocessor, calls to the method will be included; otherwise, calls will be omitted. The **Conditional** attribute is multiuse, which means that it may be used several times in front of a method. For example, in the code above the **MultiNotice** method is conditioned on either UNIX or LINUX, and calls to this method will be included if either symbol is defined. The preprocessor **#Const** directive[9] defines the symbol LINUX. The UNIX symbol is commented out, so it is not defined (unless done via a compiler option, which we'll look at shortly). The **Conditional** attribute requires the namespace **System.Diagnostics**. (We will discuss .NET diagnostic support in detail in Appendix B.)

Running the program produces the following output:

```
Notice: Some version of Unix
Goodbye
```

The call to **Notice** is omitted, but the call to **MultiNotice** is included. You may experiment with this program by defining the symbol UNIX (you can just uncomment it), or define no symbols, and so on. Then run the program again and to see which what code executes.

---

8. The other two predefined attributes in VB.NET are **Obsolete** and **Attribute-Usage**. **Obsolete** is used to mark a program entity that should not be used, causing the compiler to issue a warning or error message if it is used. We will discuss **AttributeUsage** in Chapter 10 in connection with custom attributes.
9. VB.NET (unlike C, C++, and C#) does not allow the use of the **#define** preprocessor directives to define macros.

PREPROCESSOR SYMBOLS USING COMPILER OPTION

Besides using a **#Const** preprocessor directive in your source code, you can also define preprocessor symbols using the **/define** command-line option of the VB.NET compiler. For example, you can define the symbol UNIX using the following command:

```
vbc /define:UNIX=True AttributeDemo.vb
```

You can also specify preprocessor directives in Visual Studio. In Solution Explorer right-click on the project node. From the context menu choose Properties. Select Build from Configuration Properties, and enter your desired string (such as UNIX=True) in the Custom constants text field, as illustrated in Figure 6–5.

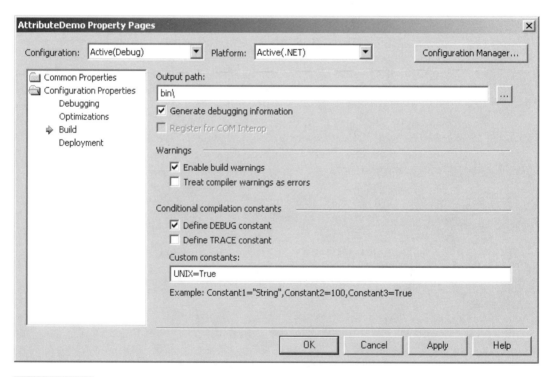

Specifying a preprocessor symbol in Visual Studio.

USING ATTRIBUTES

The **AttributeDemo** example demonstrated an attribute with a single **String** parameter. Attributes can take multiple parameters, and there can also be named parameters. Named parameters are useful when there are many different parameters, and in a particular case you might use only some of them. Named parameters can appear in any order.

As an example, the **DllImport** attribute takes a single positional parameter (the name of the DLL) and several named parameters. Here is an example[10] of using the **DllImport** attribute, with named parameters **CharSet** and **CallingConvention**:

```
<DllImport("KERNEL32.DLL", CharSet:=CharSet.Unicode,
CallingConvention:=CallingConvention.StdCall)>
```

We will see examples of the use of **DllImport** in Chapter 17, when we discuss the Platform Invocation Service (or PInvoke), which enables you to call unmanaged code through functions implemented in a DLL.

ATTRIBUTE TARGETS

An attribute may be applicable to different kinds of entities. In the COM IDL example we saw examples of attributes for interfaces, methods, and parameters. In .NET attributes may be applied to many different kinds of entities, including

- assembly
- module
- class
- struct
- interface
- method
- parameter

There are many more. The specification of legal entities to which an attribute may be applied is part of the definition of an attribute, and you will get a compiler error message if you attempt to use an attribute on the wrong kind of entity. When we discuss custom attributes in Chapter 10, we will see how to specify the legal attribute targets for our own attributes.

Summary

This chapter explored several important interactions between VB.NET and the .NET Framework, beginning with the root class **Object**. We examined collections, including the methods of the **Object** class that should be overridden to tap into the functionality provided by the .NET Framework. We introduced

---

10. This is not in any example code provided for this chapter; however, see Chapter 17.

interfaces, which allow you to rigorously define a contract for a class to implement. While a class in VB.NET can inherit from only one other class, it can implement multiple interfaces. Another benefit of interfaces is that they facilitate very dynamic programs. VB.NET provides convenient facilities to query a class at runtime to see whether it supports a particular interface.

The interfaces supporting collections were examined in detail, and copy semantics were explored. While C++ relies on its copy constructor language feature, in VB.NET you provide the capability by implementing a special interface, **ICloneable**. This led to an exploration of the role of generic interfaces in the .NET Framework programming model and to a comparison of the .NET and COM component models. A further illustration of programming with generic interfaces was provided by sorting in different orders with the **IComparable** interface. The examples offered insight into the workings of frameworks, which are more than just class libraries. In a framework, you call the framework, and the framework calls you. Your code can be viewed as the middle layer of a sandwich. This key insight can help you grasp what makes .NET programming tick.

This behavior of being called into has been around for a long time in the form of callback functions. The chapter included a careful examination of delegates and events. Delegates are the underlying mechanism used in events. VB.NET allows you to program for events using both dynamic event handling and static event handling. Two simple and intuitive examples were presented: a stock market simulation and a chat room.

Finally, we covered attributes, which can be used to modify the behavior of entities of our program according to our specifications.

This chapter concludes our exploration of the VB.NET programming language. In the next chapter we begin our detailed examination of the .NET Framework with a study of user interface programming using Windows Forms.

FUNDAMENTALS OF WINDOWS FORMS

FUNDAMENTALS OF
WINDOWS FORMS

Part 3, consisting of Chapters 7 and 8, covers the fundamentals of Windows Forms. Windows Forms is a set of classes in the .NET Framework for writing Graphical User Interfaces. Programmers familiar with previous versions of Visual Basic will notice that this significantly changes the programming model, yet also introduces flexibility not previously available.

Windows Forms

*M*ost users in today's world interact with computer applications using a graphical user interface or GUI. In this chapter, we learn how to implement a GUI using the Windows Forms classes of the .NET Framework. Windows programming typically involves the extensive use of tools and wizards to simplify the process. However, all this automation can obscure the fundamentals of what is going on. Therefore, we begin our discussion of Windows programming by illustrating the use of the .NET Framework SDK to create simple Windows applications from scratch, without use of any special tools. We examine the fundamentals of forms and controls in Windows Forms, as well as the principles of event handling.

At this point, we switch over to using Visual Studio .NET, which makes it easy to create a starter project, draw controls using the Forms Designer, add event handlers, and perform other tasks. This chapter covers some of the most common controls, such as labels, text boxes, buttons, check boxes, radio buttons, list boxes, and combo boxes. It also discusses the use of menus, tool bars, and status bars. Upcoming chapters will examine additional controls, the use of GDI+ and a GUI for our Acme Travel Agency case study.

Windows Forms Hierarchy

Windows Forms is that part of the .NET Framework that supports building traditional GUI applications on the Windows platform. It provides a large set of classes that make it easy to create sophisticated user interfaces. These classes are available to all .NET languages.

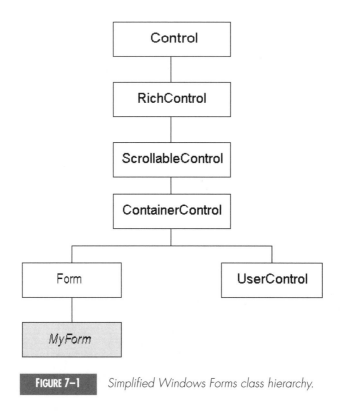

FIGURE 7-1 *Simplified Windows Forms class hierarchy.*

A VB.NET windows application will typically have a main window implemented by deriving from the **Form** class. Figure 7–1 illustrates how your class derives from the Windows Forms hierarchy.

Windows Applications Using the .NET SDK

To gain insight into how Windows Forms works, it will be helpful to build a simple application using only the .NET Framework SDK. See the program **ByHand** and its progressive steps. None of these steps use Visual Studio. The file **build.bat** is a simple batch file that you should run at the command prompt to build the executable.

Step 1: A Simple Form

Code Example

The following code illustrates a bare-bones Windows application. It is Step 1 of the example **ByHand**.

```
Imports System.Windows.Forms

Class MainWindow
   Inherits System.Windows.Forms.Form

   Public Shared Sub Main()
      Application.Run(new MainWindow())
   End Sub

End Class
```

Our **MainWindow** class inherits from **System.Windows.Forms.Form**. The key to Windows Forms programming is the **Form** base class. This class contains a great deal of functionality, which is inherited by form classes that we design.

The class **System.Application** has shared methods, such as **Run** and **Exit**, to control an application. Our form's **Main** method instantiates a new form and runs it as the main window using the **Application** class.

You can build this application at the command line using the batch file **build.bat**. To run the batch file, open up a DOS window and navigate to the **ByHand\Step1** directory and type **build**. Remember that you must have the environment variables set up properly. (If you bring up a DOS window by running the Visual Studio .NET Command Prompt, you can be sure that your environment variables are set properly.) The **build.bat** file contains:

```
vbc /t:winexe /r:System.dll,System.Windows.Forms.dll
   BasicWindow.vb
```

The /t flag specifies the target is a Windows executable. The /r flag specifies there are references to the required .NET libraries, **System.dll** and **System.Windows.Forms.dll**.

After you have built the application using the batch file, you can run it by typing **BasicWindow** at the command line. You can also double-click on the file **BasicWindow.exe** in Windows Explorer. Figure 7–2 shows this simple application. Although trivial, it already has a great deal of functionality, which it inherited from the **Form** base class. You can drag the window around, resize it, minimize it, maximize it, open the system menu (click in top left of the window), and so forth.

Step 2: Customizing the Form

The form can be customized by manipulating the various properties and methods that were inherited from **Windows.Forms.Form.Form**. In Step 2 of **ByHand,** we have added a caption to the window and changed the size of the form.

```
Imports System.Windows.Forms

Class MainWindow
   Inherits System.Windows.Forms.Form
```

FIGURE 7–2 *A bare-bones Windows Forms application (Step 1).*

```
Public Sub New()
   MyBase.New()
   Me.Text = "First Program"
   Me.Height = 175
End Sub

Public Shared Sub Main()
   Application.Run(new MainWindow())
End Sub

End Class
```

The constructor of the form does initializations. The **Text** property specifies the caption that is to be shown in the title bar of the form. The **Height** property sets or retrieves the height of the new form in pixels. There are many other properties of controls that can be set or retrieved. We review many of the common properties via examples in this book, but the .NET Framework documentation should be your source for a complete listing. Figure 7–3 shows this new version of the application.

FIGURE 7–3 *A Windows Forms application with custom caption and size (Step 2).*

Windows Messages

Visual Studio .NET supplies a tool called Spy++, which can be used to "spy" on windows, gaining some understanding of things taking place under the hood. Spy++ can be started from the Visual Studio Tools menu. With the Step 2 version of **BasicWindow.exe** running, start Spy++. Bring up the Find Window dialog from the menu Spy | Find Window. Click on the Messages radio button. See Figure 7–4.

FIGURE 7–4   *The Finder Tool lets you select a window to spy upon.*

Using the left mouse button, drag the Finder Tool over the window of the **BasicWindow** application and release the button. Now, as you interact with the **BasicWindow** window, you will see *windows messages* displayed in a window of Spy++, as illustrated in Figure 7–5.

The Windows operating system sends messages to applications in response to user actions such as clicking a mouse button, typing at the keyboard, and selecting a menu. A Windows application is designed to respond to these messages.

The nice thing about Windows programming using the .NET Framework classes is that we do not have to concern ourselves with the structure of these messages or the mechanics of how they are processed. We simply identify the messages that are of interest to us and build procedures that handle the events. We have already seen how simple it is to build a basic Windows application. In

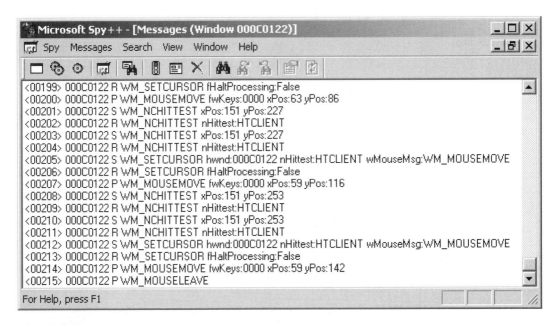

FIGURE 7–5   *Spy++ can display Windows Messages.*

the next few sections, we will progressively implement some basic features of Windows Forms programming, including adding controls and trapping events.

Controls

The **System.Windows.Forms.Control** class implements the basic functionality required by classes that display to the user. It also handles user input through the mouse and keyboard. At last check, there were well over twenty controls in the .NET Framework SDK that were derived from the **Control** class, including **Button**, **Label** and **TextBox**.

The **Control** class defines a set of properties and methods common to all controls. You will find yourself using many of these for each control you add to a window. Properties include:

- **Name**, which represents the name of the control.
- **Left** and **Top**, which represent the x and y coordinates, in pixels, of the top left edge of the control on the parent window (these values are also accessible by referencing the **Location** property).
- **Width** and **Height**, which represent the width and height, in pixels, of the control (these values are also accessible by referencing the **Size** property).
- **Text**, which represents the text (often the caption) associated with the control.

- **BackColor**, which will contain a value from the **System.Drawing.Color**.

You can find all the properties and methods associated with a class in the .NET Framework Documentation. The screenshot in Figure 7–6 shows the overview of the **Control** class help. The "Control Members" link on the page can be used to learn about the various properties and methods.

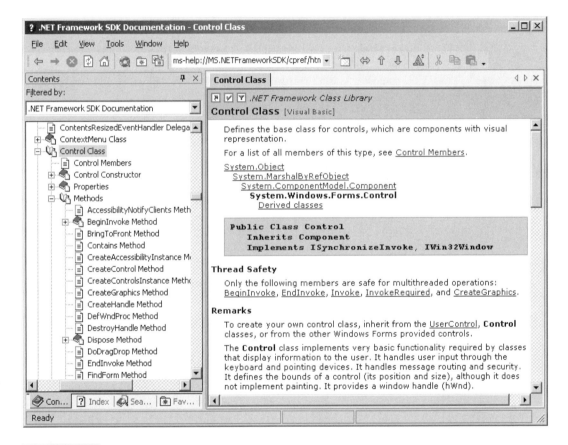

FIGURE 7–6 *Documentation of properties and methods in the Control class.*

Windows Forms Event Handling

GUI applications are event-driven, that is, the application executes code in response to user events, such as clicking the mouse, choosing a menu item, and so on. Each form or control has a predefined set of events. For example, every form has a **MouseDown** event and every control has a **Click** event.

Windows Forms employs the .NET event model,[1] which uses delegates to bind events to the methods that handle them. The Windows Forms classes use multicast delegates. A multicast delegate maintains a list of the methods it is bound to. When an event occurs in an application, the control raises the event by calling the delegate for that event. The delegate then calls all the methods it is bound to. However, VB.NET hides most of this from the programmer.

To handle the **Click** event of a **Button** object, the following code would be required:

```
Dim WithEvents btnCalc As Button = New Button()
...
Public Sub btnCalc_Click(ByVal sender As System.Object, _
  ByVal e as System.EventArgs) Handles btnCalc.Click

End Sub
```

The event handler uses the **Handles** keyword to indicate what event from which object that it responds to. The handler for the **Click** event receives parameters representing the sending object and corresponding event arguments.

To design a handler procedure that can handle events for more than one control, you must identify each event using **Handles**. Then, you must use the **sender** parameter to determine which control generated the event.

```
Dim WithEvents btnCalc As Button = New Button()
Dim WithEvents btnClear As Button = New Button()
...
' In the constructor, you would assign each control a name
btnCalc.Name = "btnCalc"
btnClear.Name = "btnClear"
...

Public Sub ClearOrCalc(ByVal sender As System.Object, _
  ByVal e as System.EventArgs) Handles btnClear.Click, _
  btnCalc.Click

    If CType(sender, Button).Name = "btnClear" Then
```

---

1. You may wish to review the discussion of delegates and events in Chapter 6.

```
        ' logic for btnClear
    ElseIf CType(sender, Button).Name = "btnCalc" Then
        ' logic for btnCalc
    End If
```

End Sub

You can find all the events associated with a class in the .NET Framework documentation. The screen shot in Figure 7–7 shows the predefined events associated with the **Control** class.

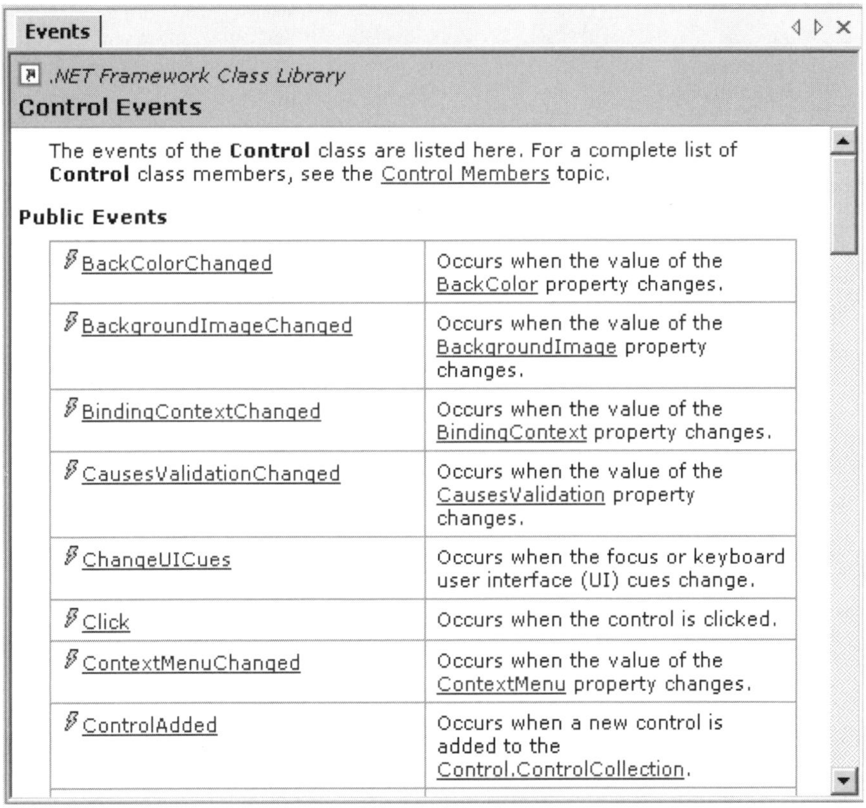

Events		◁ ▷ ✕
⊡ *.NET Framework Class Library*		
Control Events		
The events of the **Control** class are listed here. For a complete list of **Control** class members, see the Control Members topic.		
Public Events		
⫤ BackColorChanged	Occurs when the value of the BackColor property changes.	
⫤ BackgroundImageChanged	Occurs when the value of the BackgroundImage property changes.	
⫤ BindingContextChanged	Occurs when the value of the BindingContext property changes.	
⫤ CausesValidationChanged	Occurs when the value of the CausesValidation property changes.	
⫤ ChangeUICues	Occurs when the focus or keyboard user interface (UI) cues change.	
⫤ Click	Occurs when the control is clicked.	
⫤ ContextMenuChanged	Occurs when the value of the ContextMenu property changes.	
⫤ ControlAdded	Occurs when a new control is added to the Control.ControlCollection.	

FIGURE 7–7   *Documentation of events in the Control class.*

Step 3: Adding a Button to the Form

In Step 3 of our **ByHand** example, we will add a button to the form. It's caption will be "Click Me." When clicked, it will display a message box containing the greeting "Hello World." Figure 7–8 shows a run of the application.

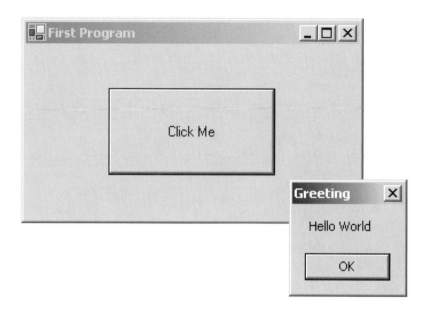

FIGURE 7–8   *Using a button and displaying a message box with a form (Step 3).*

Here is the code for Step 3.

```
Imports System.Windows.Forms

Class MainWindow
   Inherits System.Windows.Forms.Form

   Private WithEvents btnClickMe As Button

   Public Sub New()
      MyBase.New()
      Me.Text = "First Program"
      Me.Height = 175

      InitializeComponent()
   End Sub

   Private Sub InitializeComponent()
      btnClickMe = New Button()
```

```
        btnClickMe.Name = "btnClickMe"
        btnClickMe.Text = "Click Me"
        btnClickMe.Size = _
           New System.Drawing.Size(Me.ClientSize.Width/2, _
                                   Me.ClientSize.Height/2)
        btnClickMe.Location = _
           New System.Drawing.Point(Me.ClientSize.Width/4, _
                                    Me.ClientSize.Height/4)

        Me.Controls.Add(btnClickMe)
    End Sub

    Public Sub btnClickMe_Click(ByVal sender As _
      System.Object, ByVal e as System.EventArgs) _
      Handles btnClickMe.Click

        MessageBox.Show("Hello World", "Greeting")

    End Sub

    Public Shared Sub Main()
        Application.Run(new MainWindow())
    End Sub

End Class
```

The class contains the variable **btnClickMe** that represents the instance of the button. It was declared using **WithEvents** so that we could handle the events that it generates.

The constructor has been designed to call **InitializeComponent** to instantiate the button, then set the **Name** and **Text** properties. Our algorithm for the button **Size** and **Location** properties indicates that the button consumes half of the width and half of the height of the client area of the form, and is centered within the form. The **Size** and **Point** classes, which are used for the button's **Size** and **Location** properties, are in the **System.Drawing** namespace. The button is then added to the form's **Controls** collection.

Finally, the **btnClickMe_Click** procedure was defined to handle the **Click** event of **btnClickMe**. It uses the **MessageBox** class to display a simple message box with a caption of "Greeting" and containing the message "Hello World."

You can build the application at the command line using the batch file **build.bat**. We have had to add an additional reference. **System.Drawing.dll** is required because the **Point** and **Size** types we referenced are defined in this library. Our **build.bat** file now resembles:

```
vbc /t:winexe /r:System.dll,System.Drawing.dll,
   System.Windows.Forms.dll BasicWindow.vb
```

Step 4: Using Label and TextBox Controls

Code
Example

Step 4 of our **ByHand** application illustrates the use of a **Label** and a **Text-Box** control to collect the user's name. The name is then used in the greeting that is displayed when the "Click Me" button is clicked. The **TextBox** control allows you to insert characters wherever you wish in the control, cut and paste (Ctrl+X and Ctrl+V), and so forth. Figure 7–9 illustrates the application after a name has been entered and the "Click Me" button clicked.

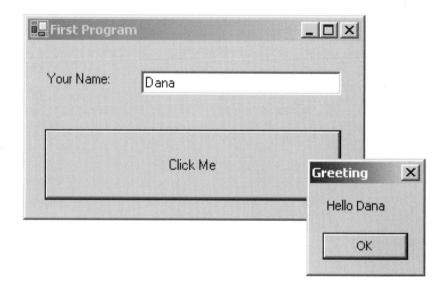

FIGURE 7–9   *Using a label and text box on a form (Step 4).*

Here is the final version of Step 4. We had to run it many times with different values for the **Location** and **Size** properties of each control until we found values that made our form look the way we wanted it to.

```
Imports System.Windows.Forms

Class MainWindow
   Inherits System.Windows.Forms.Form

   Private WithEvents lblName As Label
   Private WithEvents txtName As TextBox
   Private WithEvents btnClickMe As Button

   Public Sub New()
      MyBase.New()
      Me.Text = "First Program"
```

```
      Me.Height = 175

      InitializeComponent()
  End Sub

  Private Sub InitializeComponent()
      lblName = New Label()
      lblName.Name = "lblName"
      lblName.Text = "Your Name:"
      lblName.Size = New System.Drawing.Size(75, 30)
      lblName.Location = New System.Drawing.Point(15,25)
      Me.Controls.Add(lblName)

      txtName = New TextBox()
      txtName.Name = "txtName"
      txtName.Text = ""
      txtName.Size = New System.Drawing.Size(175, 30)
      txtName.Location = New System.Drawing.Point(100,25)
      Me.Controls.Add(txtName)

      btnClickMe = New Button()
      btnClickMe.Name = "btnClickMe"
      btnClickMe.Text = "Click Me"
      btnClickMe.Size = _
          New System.Drawing.Size(260, 60)
      btnClickMe.Location = _
          New System.Drawing.Point(15, 75)
      Me.Controls.Add(btnClickMe)
  End Sub

  Public Sub btnClickMe_Click(ByVal sender As _
    System.Object, ByVal e as System.EventArgs) _
    Handles btnClickMe.Click

      MessageBox.Show("Hello " & txtName.Text, "Greeting")

  End Sub

  Public Shared Sub Main()
      Application.Run(new MainWindow())
  End Sub

End Class
```

As you can see, using the **Label** and **TextBox** controls is very easy. We instantiate them and assign initial values to their **Location**, **Size**, and **Text** properties. We can reference the text displayed by the label or entered by the user in the text box by referencing the control's **Text** property.

Visual Studio .NET and Forms

Although it is perfectly feasible to create Windows Forms applications using only the command-line tools of the .NET Framework SDK, in practice it is much easier to use Visual Studio .NET. You can get started by creating a Windows Application project, which provides starter code and sets up references to the required .NET libraries. You can then use the Forms Designer to drag and drop controls from a toolbox onto your forms. The Forms Designer inserts all the needed boilerplate code to make your controls work within your forms. There is a Properties window which makes it easy to set properties of your controls at design time. You can also set properties via code at runtime.

The same Forms Designer can be used in all .NET languages. A similar designer is available for visually drawing Web Forms, which we will discuss in Chapter 14 on ASP.NET.

Windows Forms Demonstration

To become acquainted with using Visual Studio .NET to create Windows applications, we will recreate the **ByHand** example shown previously. Because this process is interactive, it is outlined below in numbered steps:

Code Example

1. Using Visual Studio .NET, create a VB.NET project named **Greeting** that is a Windows Application in the **Demos** folder. See Figure 7–10. (The completed solution is found in the **Greeting** folder.).

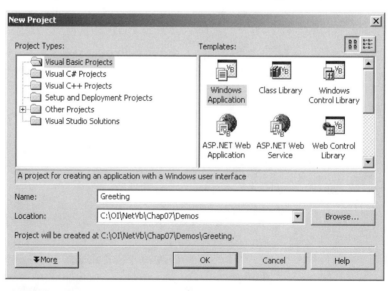

FIGURE 7–10   *Creating a new Windows Application project.*

2. Open the Toolbox by dragging the mouse over the vertical Toolbox tab on the left side of the main Visual Studio window. If the Toolbox tab does not show, you can open it using the menu View | Toolbox. You can make the Toolbox stay open by pushing the "push-pin" next to the X on the title bar of the Toolbox. (The little yellow box will say "Auto Hide" when you pause the mouse over the push-pin.) See Figure 7–11.

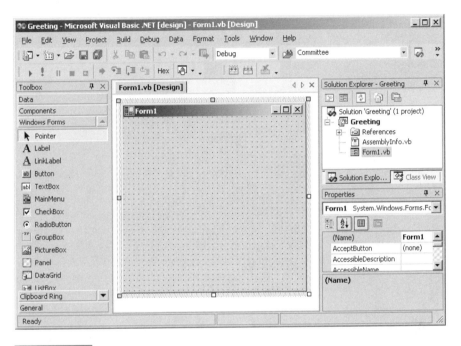

FIGURE 7–11   *The Toolbox and an empty form.*

3. From the Toolbox, drag a button, a label, and a text box to the form. See Figure 7–12.

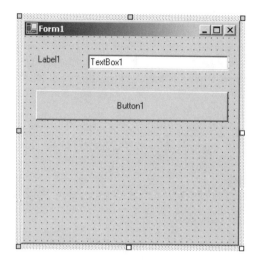

Placing controls from the Toolbox onto a form.

4. Click on **Label1** in the Forms Designer. This will select that control. The Properties window, just beneath the Solution Explorer, can be used to make changes to properties of controls. Change the **Name** property to **lblName** and the **Text** property to "Your Name:". After you type the desired value, hit the carriage return. Figure 7–13 shows the Properties window after you have changed the properties of the first label.

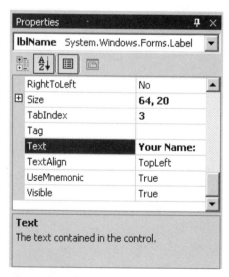

Changing property values in the Properties window.

5. Enter property values for the remaining controls and the form as shown in Table 7–1.

TABLE 7–1	*Property values for the Greeting form*	
Control Type	**Name**	**Text**
Textbox	txtName	(blank)
Button	btnClickMe	**Click Me**
Form	MainWindow	**Second Program**

6. Change the file name that will be used for the form by right-clicking on the form in the Solutions Explorer window and choose Rename from the menu. Name the file **MainWindow.vb**.

7. Resize the form to the size desired by dragging the sizing handles on the middle of each side. (If they don't appear, select the form by clicking on it first.)

8. Reposition the controls on the form as desired by dragging them with the mouse. You can manually resize the controls and try to align them, or you can use the Format menu. To use the Format menu:

    a. Select two or more controls using the mouse. Hold down the control key as you click on each control.

    b. The *last* control you select will have darker handles indicating it has focus and will be the "dominant" control regarding formatting.

    c. You can use the Format | Make Same Size | Height menu to make all selected controls have the same height as the dominant control.

    d. You can use the Format | Align | Top menu to align all selected controls along the same top position as the dominant control.

    e. There are many other options under the Format menu that you should investigate in order to produce professional-quality window designs. There is also a Layout toolbar you can use to gain access to control layout and formatting features.

9. Set the tab order of the controls by using the View | Tab Order menu. Click on each control in the order that you want to tab through the controls. (Always put labels just before the control they label in the tab order.) See Figure 7–14.

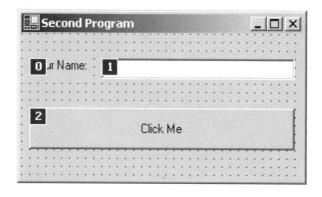

FIGURE 7–14   *Setting the tab order of controls on a form.*

10. When you are satisfied with the appearance of your form, save the project. Your form should now look similar to Figure 7–15.

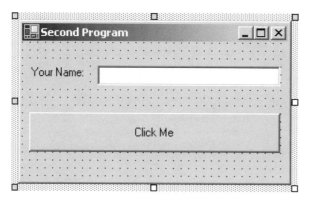

FIGURE 7–15   *A form for the Greeting application.*

11. Add an event handler for your Click Me button by double-clicking on the button.

12. In the handler procedure that was generated, add the following code:

```
Private Sub btnClickMe_Click(ByVal sender As _
  System.Object, ByVal e As System.EventArgs) _
  Handles btnClickMe.Click

  MessageBox.Show("Hello " & txtName.Text, "Greeting")

End Sub
```

13. Build the application. You will get the following error because you have changed the name of the default form that was generated for you. You must change the startup form to **MainWindow**. To do this right-click on the project in the Solution Explorer window and select Properties. See Figure 7–16.

```
Startup code 'Sub Main' was specified in 'Greeting.Form1',
but 'Greeting.Form1' was not found.
```

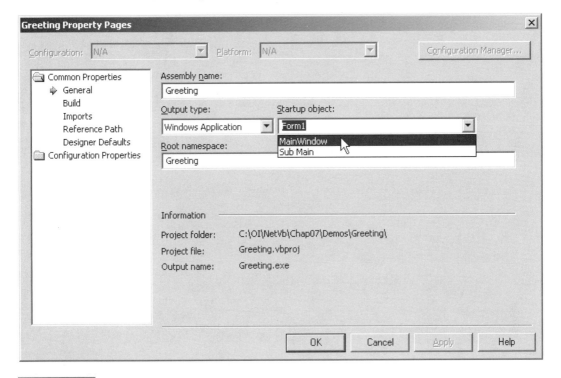

Setting a project's Startup form.

14. Build and run the application. It should behave like the **ByHand** program seen in the previous section.

Design Window and Code Window

To be effective using Windows Forms projects in Visual Studio, you should understand how to easily switch between the Design window, where you work with controls on a form, and the Code window, where you work with source code. To bring up the Code window, click on the View Code ▤ toolbar button in the Solution Explorer. You may also go back to the Design window by clicking on the View Designer ▦ toolbar button.

Visual Studio .NET indicates the windows that are open using horizontal tabs at the top of the principal window area. You can use these tabs to select among the open windows. Figure 7–18 in the next section shows the open Code window and a tab along the top indicating the Design window for that form is also open.

Adding Event Handlers Using Visual Studio

There are two main ways you can add event handlers in Visual Studio. The simplest is to double-click on a control, which will add the handler for the "primary" event associated with a control. For example, the primary event of a button is **Click** and the primary event of a form is **Load**. But a control may have many different events. You can use two dropdown lists at the top of the Code window to add other event handlers. In the left-side dropdown you can select the control, and in the right-side dropdown you can select the event. For adding event handlers for the form itself you can choose (Base Class Events) in the left-side dropdown. Figure 7–17 illustrates adding a handler for the **Closing** event.

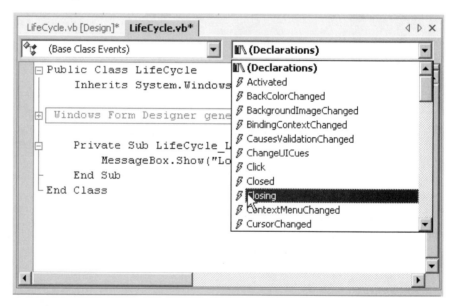

FIGURE 7–17   *Adding a handler for the Closing event.*

Life Cycle of a Windows Form

Sometimes you need to add initialization code to run when a form is first displayed and cleanup code to run at the time the form is closed. You could add initialization code to the constructor of the form. For a Visual Studio .NET Windows application you could also add the code to the **InitializeComponent** method (discussed in the next section). Both of these approaches involve tweaking code generated by Visual Studio that is normally hidden. A third option for initialization, and the most common, is the handler of the **Load** event.

There are two events associated with closing a form. The first is **Closing**. At this point you can still block the closing of the form. For example, you may want to prompt the user to save open files. The second event is **Close**. At this point the form is about to close and there is nothing you can do to stop it. The program **LifeCycle\Version 1** illustrates handling the **Load**, **Closing**, and **Close** events. The event handlers simply display a message box.

Code
Example

```
Public Class LifeCycle
    Inherits System.Windows.Forms.Form
    ...

    Private Sub LifeCycle_Load( _
     ByVal sender As System.Object, _
     ByVal e As System.EventArgs) Handles MyBase.Load
        MessageBox.Show("Loading")
    End Sub

    Private Sub LifeCycle_Closing(ByVal sender As Object, _
     ByVal e As System.ComponentModel.CancelEventArgs)_
     Handles MyBase.Closing
        MessageBox.Show("Closing")
    End Sub

    Private Sub LifeCycle_Closed(ByVal sender As Object, _
     ByVal e As System.EventArgs) Handles MyBase.Closed
        MessageBox.Show("Closed")
    End Sub

End Class
```

Overriding Virtual Methods of a Form

The **Form** class has a number of protected overridable methods OnXxxxx, whose base class implementation raises the Xxxxx event. Thus the **OnLoad** method raises the **Load** event, and so forth. This means that you could also perform initialization in **OnLoad** as well as in a handler for the **Load** event.

Which approach is better? In some documentation you will see that Microsoft recommends overriding the virtual method. This approach is indeed slightly more efficient. But if you do override the virtual method, you *must* call the base class method, or else the corresponding event will not get raised, which may introduce bugs into your program. You may find it less error-prone to simply handle the event.

You can add overrides in Visual Studio in a manner similar to adding event handlers. In the left-side dropdown in the Code window choose (Overrides), and in the right-side dropdown select the method you want to override.

The program **LifeCycle\Version 2** illustrates overriding the **OnLoad**, **OnClosing**, and **OnClose** methods and also handling the corresponding events. An interesting feature of this program is that it is built as a console application. The only difference between a console application and a Windows application is that the former will provide a console into which you can write with methods such as **System.Console.WriteLine**. If the proper Windows Forms code is present, the console application will display a window. Here is the code for this sample application. In place of using a message box to display output, we make calls to **Console.WriteLine**. Also note that we are careful to call the base class method in all our override methods.

```
Public Class LifeCycle
    Inherits System.Windows.Forms.Form

#Region " Windows Form Designer generated code "
...

    Private Sub LifeCycle_Load( _
     ByVal sender As System.Object, _
     ByVal e As System.EventArgs) Handles MyBase.Load
        Console.WriteLine("Loading")
    End Sub

    Private Sub LifeCycle_Closing(ByVal sender As Object, _
     ByVal e As System.ComponentModel.CancelEventArgs) _
     Handles MyBase.Closing
        Console.WriteLine("Closing")
    End Sub

    Private Sub LifeCycle_Closed(ByVal sender As Object, _
     ByVal e As System.EventArgs) Handles MyBase.Closed
        Console.WriteLine("Closed")
    End Sub

    Protected Overrides Sub OnClosed( _
     ByVal e As System.EventArgs)
        Console.WriteLine("OnClosed")
        MyBase.OnClosed(e)
    End Sub

    Protected Overrides Sub OnClosing( _
     ByVal e As System.ComponentModel.CancelEventArgs)
        Console.WriteLine("OnClosing")
        MyBase.OnClosing(e)
    End Sub
```

Code Example

```
Protected Overrides Sub OnLoad( _
  ByVal e As System.EventArgs)
    Console.WriteLine("OnLoad")
    MyBase.OnLoad(e)
  End Sub
End Class
```

Here is the console output:

```
OnLoad
Loading
OnClosing
Closing
OnClosed
Closed
```

As an experiment, you may wish to comment out the calls to the base class methods and run the program again.

Under the Hood of a VS.NET Windows Application

When you create a Windows Application project, it provides starter code for the main form and sets up references to the required .NET libraries. The Windows Forms Designer interface can then be used to design the forms.

Code Generated by Windows Form Designer

As you can see from Figure 7–18, the Code window hides the code that was generated by the Forms Designer. It uses a **Region** directive to place a + (plus) next to a code segment. When collapsed, the **Region** directive displays a comment. When the + is clicked, the Code window expands the code.

The code generated by the Forms Designer defines a class that was derived from **System.Windows.Forms.Form**.

```
Public Class MainWindow
  Inherits System.Windows.Forms.Form
```

The constructor calls **InitializeComponent** to build and initialize all controls that are on the form. You can then provide initialization for any variables.

```
Public Sub New()
  MyBase.New()

  'This call is required by the Windows Form Designer.
  InitializeComponent()

  'Add any initialization after the
  'InitializeComponent() call
End Sub
```

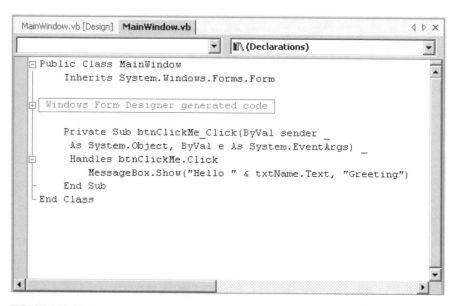

MainWindow.vb [Design] **MainWindow.vb**   ◁ ▷ ✕

┌─────────────────────────────────┐ ┌─────────────────────────────┐
│   ▼│ │▐▌\ **(Declarations)**   ▼│
└─────────────────────────────────┘ └─────────────────────────────┘

```vb
Public Class MainWindow
    Inherits System.Windows.Forms.Form

    Windows Form Designer generated code

    Private Sub btnClickMe_Click(ByVal sender _
     As System.Object, ByVal e As System.EventArgs) _
     Handles btnClickMe.Click
        MessageBox.Show("Hello " & txtName.Text, "Greeting")
    End Sub
End Class
```

FIGURE 7–18   *The Code window hides generated code.*

The class also defines the **Dispose** method, which is used to clean up the form's contents before the form is destroyed. We discuss the Dispose design pattern and garbage collection in Chapter 10.

```vb
'Form overrides dispose to clean up the component list.
Protected Overloads Overrides Sub Dispose(ByVal _
 disposing As Boolean)

   If disposing Then
      If Not (components Is Nothing) Then
         components.Dispose()
      End If
   End If
   MyBase.Dispose(disposing)
End Sub
```

It defines variables that reference the control objects that were placed on the form:

```vb
Friend WithEvents lblName As System.Windows.Forms.Label
Friend WithEvents btnClickMe As System.Windows.Forms.Button
Friend WithEvents txtName As System.Windows.Forms.TextBox
```

Finally, we see the **InitializeComponent** method that was called in the constructor. It instantiates each control and initializes each property that has a non-default value. It also adds each control to the form's **Controls** collection via the **AddRange** method. By calling the form's **SuspendLayout** before the properties are set, and calling **ResumeLayout** at the end, the form waits until all controls have been specified before triggering any **Layout** events. As the comment states, the code in this method should not be modified because it is updated by the Form Designer.

```
'NOTE: The following procedure is required by the Windows
'      Form Designer
'It can be modified using the Windows Form Designer.
'Do not modify it using the code editor.
<System.Diagnostics.DebuggerStepThrough()> _
Private Sub InitializeComponent()
   Me.lblName = New System.Windows.Forms.Label()
   Me.txtName = New System.Windows.Forms.TextBox()
   Me.btnClickMe = New System.Windows.Forms.Button()
   Me.SuspendLayout()
   '
   'lblName
   '
   Me.lblName.Location = New System.Drawing.Point(8, 24)
   Me.lblName.Name = "lblName"
   Me.lblName.Size = New System.Drawing.Size(64, 20)
   Me.lblName.TabIndex = 0
   Me.lblName.Text = "Your Name:"
   '
   'txtName
   '
   Me.txtName.Location = New System.Drawing.Point(80, 24)
   Me.txtName.Name = "txtName"
   Me.txtName.Size = New System.Drawing.Size(192, 20)
   Me.txtName.TabIndex = 1
   Me.txtName.Text = ""
   '
   'btnClickMe
   '
   Me.btnClickMe.Location = New System.Drawing.Point(8, 72)
   Me.btnClickMe.Name = "btnClickMe"
   Me.btnClickMe.Size = New System.Drawing.Size(264, 40)
   Me.btnClickMe.TabIndex = 2
   Me.btnClickMe.Text = "Click Me"
   '
   'MainWindow
   '
   Me.AutoScaleBaseSize = New System.Drawing.Size(5, 13)
   Me.ClientSize = New System.Drawing.Size(280, 141)
   Me.Controls.AddRange _
      (New System.Windows.Forms.Control() _
      {Me.txtName, Me.btnClickMe, Me.lblName})
   Me.Name = "MainWindow"
   Me.Text = "Second Program"
   Me.ResumeLayout(False)
End Sub
```

The class definition terminates with any event handlers and other code you wrote.

As you can see, using Visual Studio .NET to generate a Windows application is much easier!

Dialog Boxes

Dialog boxes provide an easy way for a user to interact with a Windows application. A dialog box provides a number of controls to facilitate data input and/or data output.

Dialog boxes are types of forms that have special characteristics. For example, they typically do not have a system menu, they have no minimize or maximize buttons, and they have a border that does not permit them to be resized. These can be set using the form's **ControlBox**, **MinimizeBox**, **MaximizeBox**, and **FormBorderStyle** properties.

A dialog box can be a *modal* dialog or a *modeless* dialog. When a modal dialog is displayed, the user cannot work elsewhere in the application until the dialog is closed. If the user tries to do something else on the main form while the dialog is open, he or she hears a beep. When a modeless dialog is displayed, the user can work elsewhere in the application while the dialog is open. This chapter discusses modal dialogs. Modeless dialogs are discussed in Chapter 12.

A modal simple dialog that you have already used is the .NET **MessageBox** class. It can be used to display an informational message or allow a user to answer a yes or no question.

.NET Dialog Documentation

Dialogs are explained clearly in the Documentation in the .NET Framework. Look in "Dialog Boxes in Windows Forms" under "Creating Windows Forms Applications." It is noteworthy that the principles of dialog boxes are the same in all .NET languages. This is in sharp contrast to the days before .NET, when, for example, dialogs in Visual Basic and in Visual C++ were totally different. Figure 7–19 shows the entry point to this documentation.

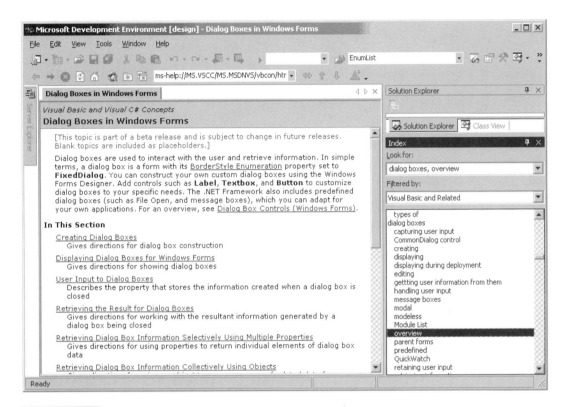

FIGURE 7-19 *Documentation on dialog boxes using the .NET Framework.*

MessageBox

The .NET **MessageBox** class is the simplest form of a dialog. It contains text, buttons, and symbols that provide and/or gather information. To display a message box, you must call the shared method **Show**, which has several parameters that define:

- The message text.
- The title of the message box window.
- The buttons that are displayed (a value from the **MessageBoxButtons** enumeration which include **OK, OkCancel, YesNo, YesNoCancel** and others).
- The icon that is displayed (a value from the **MessageBoxIcon** enumeration which include **None, Question, Information, Exclamation,** and **Error**).
- The identity of the default button displayed (a value from the **MessageBoxDefaultButton** enumeration which includes **Button1, Button2,** and **Button3**).

To display a message that indicates the user has failed to complete all required fields on an input dialog, you can write the following code. See Figure 7–20.

```
MessageBox.Show( _
    "Please enter a reservation id", _
    "Hotel Reservations", _
    MessageBoxButtons.OK, _
    MessageBoxIcon.Exclamation)
```

| FIGURE 7-20 | *Using a message box.* |

Custom Dialogs

Custom dialogs can be created and used by performing the following actions:

- Add a second form to an existing project, and configure various properties on the new dialog to control its appearance.
- Add properties to the dialog to access data in the dialog's controls.
- Configure the OK and Cancel button's **DialogResult** property so that you can determine which button was pressed.
- Write code to display the dialog.
- Write code to respond to the dialog result.

Code Example

To demonstrate modal dialogs, we work on a simple GUI version of our Acme Travel Agency. Starter code has been provided in **Demos\HotelAdmin**, backed up in **HotelAdmin\Version 0**. Solution code for this demo is provided in **HotelAdmin\Version 1**. Figure 7–21 illustrates the design of our main window (which leaves some empty areas on the form for additional features).

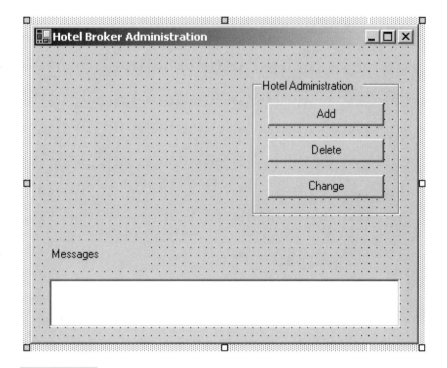

FIGURE 7–21 *The main window design for Hotel Administration.*

Step 1: Creating a New Dialog

- To create a new dialog, we begin by using the Project | Add Windows Form menu. It prompts us for a form name, and we choose **NewHotelDialog**. (See Figure 7–22).

This new form is inserted in our project and is now shown in the Solutions Explorer window. We can begin placing controls on it from the Toolbox and configuring the properties as needed. For this example, we have designed our form using four labels, four textboxes and four buttons as shown in Figure 7–23.

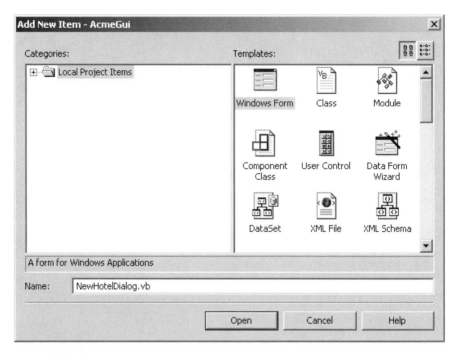

FIGURE 7–22 *Adding a new form.*

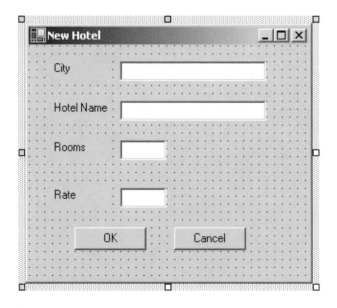

FIGURE 7–23 *Designing a new dialog.*

We must now set the properties for the controls and form as shown in Table 7–2.

TABLE 7–2	Property values for the NewHotelDialog form

Control Type	Name	Text	Other Properties
Label	lblCity	City	
Textbox	txtCity	(blank)	
Label	lblHotelName	Hotel	
Textbox	txtHotelName	(blank)	
Label	lblNumberRooms	Rooms	
Textbox	txtNumberRooms	(blank)	
Label	lblRate	Rate	
Textbox	txtRate	(blank)	
Button	cmdOK	OK	DialogResult: OK
Button	cmdCancel	Cancel	DialogResult: Cancel
Form	NewHotelDialog	New Hotel	AcceptButton: cmdOK CancelButton: cmdCancel FormBorderStyle: FixedDialog MaximizeBox: False MinimizeBox: False

The **DialogResult** property provides predetermined behavior for buttons. It can be set to any of several values, including **OK, Cancel, Yes,** and **No.** For each of the values (except **None**), the button automatically closes the dialog and assigns the button's **DialogResult** property to the form's **DialogResult** property. The form's **DialogResult** property is returned from the form's **ShowDialog** method and can be used to determine which button was pressed to close the form.

You should now add properties to **NewHotelDialog** that can be used to access the values in the controls. Add the following code to your dialog:

```
Public Property City() As String
   Get
      Return txtCity.Text
   End Get
   Set(ByVal Value As String)
      txtCity.Text = Value
   End Set
End Property

Public Property HotelName() As String
   Get
      Return txtHotelName.Text
```

```
      End Get
      Set(ByVal Value As String)
         txtHotelName.Text = value
      End Set
End Property

Public Property NumberRooms() As Integer
   Get
      Return Convert.ToInt32(txtNumberRooms.Text)
   End Get
   Set(ByVal Value As Integer)
      txtNumberRooms.Text = Value.ToString()
   End Set
End Property

Public Property Rate() As Decimal
   Get
      Return Convert.ToDecimal(txtRate.Text)
   End Get
   Set(ByVal Value As Decimal)
      txtRate.Text = Value.ToString()
   End Set
End Property
```

It is a good idea to set your dialog's properties to respond like other Windows dialogs. Set the form's **AcceptButton** property to the control used for your OK button and it will interpret an **Enter** key as a click on the OK button. Set the form's **CancelButton** property to the control used for your Cancel button, it will interpret the **Escape** key as a click on the Cancel button.

Step 2: Displaying a Dialog

- To display a dialog, we must create an instance of the form class. The form's **ShowDialog** method can then be used to display the dialog as a modal dialog. It returns the value of the **DialogResult** property.

In Step 1 of the **HotelAdmin** project, we have already added the following code to reference the **HotelBroker** and **HotelListItems**.

```
Public Class MainAdminForm
   Inherits System.Windows.Forms.Form

   Private hotelBroker As HotelBroker
   Private currHotel As HotelListItem

   ...
   Public Sub New()
      MyBase.New()
      InitializeComponent()
```

```
      hotelBroker = New HotelBroker()
   End Sub
   ...
End Class
```

To display the **NewHotelDialog** form, trap **Click** event on **cmdAdd** and add the following code:

```
Private Sub cmdAdd_Click(ByVal sender As System.Object, _
  ByVal e As System.EventArgs) Handles cmdAdd.Click

   Dim dlg As NewHotelDialog = New NewHotelDialog()
   If currHotel.HotelName <> "" Then
      dlg.City = currHotel.City
      dlg.HotelName = currHotel.HotelName
      dlg.NumberRooms = currHotel.NumberRooms
      dlg.Rate = currHotel.Rate
   Else
      dlg.City = ""
      dlg.HotelName = ""
      dlg.NumberRooms = 0
      dlg.Rate = 0
   End If

   Dim status As DialogResult = dlg.ShowDialog()

   If status = DialogResult.OK Then
      Dim comment As String = hotelBroker.AddHotel( _
        dlg.City, dlg.HotelName, dlg.NumberRooms, dlg.Rate)
      If comment = "OK" Then
         txtMessages.Text = "Hotel " & dlg.HotelName _
           & " has been added"
      Else
         txtMessages.Text = comment
      End If
   End If

End Sub
```

When you run the program, you should now be able to press the Add button and enter new hotels. The hotel is added to the **HotelBroker**. A confirmation message is placed in the **txtMessages** textbox. In a future step, we will add the ability to display all hotels that have been added in a list box.

Step 3: Validating a Dialog's Data

Many dialogs do not blindly accept all data. Instead, they enforce rules relating to the content, format, and range of data before allowing the user to successfully choose an OK button.

We are going to enforce the rule that a user must enter a non-blank city and hotel, and the rooms and rate boxes must be non-negative numeric values. We will also enforce the rule that the user may not edit an item in a list box so that it becomes blank.

To begin, add the new .NET **ErrorProvider** control to your form and name it **errHotel**. It does not appear on the form, but rather in a special section below the form. (See Figure 7–24.) We use it to display an error icon and error messages next to invalid data.

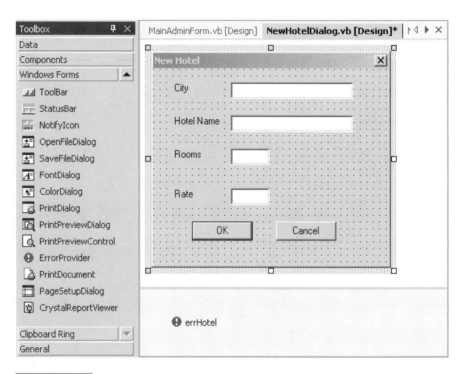

FIGURE 7–24   *Placing an ErrorProvider control on a form.*

To implement these data validation requirements, we will write the following code in the **Click** event of **cmdOK.** If the data is invalid, we will call the **SetError** method on the **ErrorProvider** control to indicate the error message and the control it is associated with. We then prohibit the closing of the dialog by assigning the form's **DialogResult** property the value **None**.

```
Private Sub cmdOK_Click(ByVal sender As System.Object, _
  ByVal e As System.EventArgs) Handles cmdOK.Click

    Dim dataOK As Boolean = True
```

```
   ' Remove any earlier error messages
   errHotel.SetError(txtCity, "")
   errHotel.SetError(txtHotelName, "")
   errHotel.SetError(txtNumberRooms, "")
   errHotel.SetError(txtRate, "")

   If Trim(txtCity.Text) = "" Then
      dataOK = False
      errHotel.SetError(txtCity, "City must be non-blank")
   End If
   If Trim(txtHotelName.Text) = "" Then
      dataOK = False
      errHotel.SetError(txtHotelName,
                        "Hotel must be non-blank")
   End If
   If Not (IsNumeric(txtNumberRooms.Text) AndAlso _
         Convert.ToInt32(txtNumberRooms.Text) >= 0) Then
      dataOK = False
      errHotel.SetError(txtNumberRooms, _
                        "Number of rooms must be " & _
                        "non-negative, numeric value")
   End If
   If Not (IsNumeric(txtRate.Text) AndAlso _
         Convert.ToInt32(txtRate.Text) >= 0) Then
      dataOK = False
      errHotel.SetError(txtRate, _
                        "Rate must be non-negative, " & _
                        "numeric value")
   End If
   If Not dataOK Then
      Me.DialogResult = DialogResult.None
   End If
End Sub
```

Figure 7–25 shows the New Hotel dialog with invalid data. The error message is displayed as a tool tip over the error icon.

Step 4: Adding ToolTips for Controls

A user-friendly feature to add to your user interface is tooltips. They display help strings when the mouse hovers over a control (as we saw with the **ErrorProvider** control in the previous section.).

To begin, add the new .NET **ToolTip** control to your form and name it **tipsHotel**. It appears alongside of the **ErrorProvider** control. After the **ToolTip** control is added, the Properties window for most visible controls on the form now list a **ToolTips** property. (See Figure 7–26).

To finish out Step 1 of the **HotelAdmin** demonstration, set the **ToolTips** property of each control to the value shown in Table 7–3.

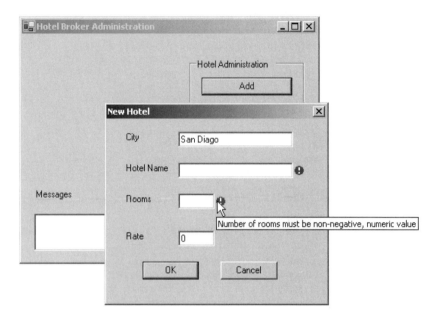

FIGURE 7–25 *Using the ErrorProvider to display error messages.*

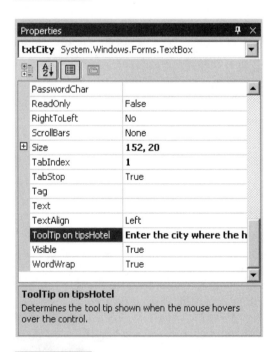

FIGURE 7–26 *Placing a ToolTip control on a form.*

TABLE 7–3	ToolTip Property Values for the NewHotelDialog Form	
Control Type	**Name**	**ToolTip**
Textbox	txtCity	Enter the city where the hotel is located
Textbox	txtHotelName	Enter the hotel name
Textbox	txtNumberRooms	Enter the number of rooms available
Textbox	txtRate	Enter the rate per night

Figure 7–27 illustrates how tool tips are displayed at run time.

| FIGURE 7–27 | Using the ToolTip control to display help strings. |

Controls

To be able to develop sophisticated Windows applications, you must become familiar with the capabilities of a variety of controls and support classes available in .NET. We begin by examining some of the properties that are common to all controls. We will continue this discussion in Chapters 8 and 12. But your investigation shouldn't end after you read these chapters. You should spend time reading the .NET Framework documentation Help that is provided with VB.NET.

Common Properties

The **Control** class defines many properties that are common to all controls:

- The **Enabled** property indicates whether the control is enabled.

- The **Font** property indicates the font used by the control.
- The **Location** property indicates the location of the control on the form.
- The **Size** property indicates the size of the control.
- The **TabIndex** property indicates the position of the control in the form's tab order.
- The **TabStop** property indicates the whether control has a tab stop.
- The **Text** property indicates the text displayed by the control.
- The **Visible** property indicates whether the control is visible.

Each specific control defines additional properties and methods unique to that control. We have already discussed the **Label**, **TextBox**, **Button**, **ErrorProvider** and **ToolTip** controls. In this section, will discuss some of the other controls that are commonly used in Windows applications.

Using a Radio Button with a Group Box

The **RadioButton** control is used to allow users to select an option from a set of mutually exclusive options. When the user selects one radio button within a group, the other radio buttons clear automatically. All radio button controls within a given container constitute a group. Usually, a programmer will use a **GroupBox** control to group the radio buttons that work together.

In the program **StylesOfGreetings\Step 1**, we use radio buttons to select the style of the greeting that will be displayed. Figure 7–28 illustrates the result of running this program.

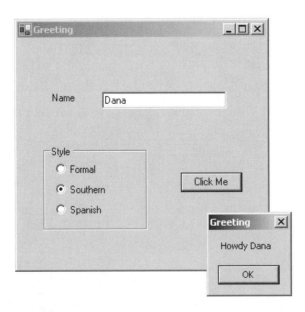

FIGURE 7–28   *Using the RadioButton control to provide options.*

Step 1: Drawing the Radio Button Group

To design this form, you must place the radio buttons in a logical grouping. The **GroupBox** is typically used for this purpose. The **GroupBox** control must be drawn first, then each radio button can be drawn and moved into the area within the group box. If you have two group boxes that each contain several radio buttons, both groups of buttons would be mutually exclusive.

In this application, the properties were set as shown in Table 7–4.

Code
Example

TABLE 7–4	*Property Values for the StylesOfGreetings Application (Step 1)*		
Control Type	**Name**	**Text**	**Other Properties**
Label	lblName	Name	
Textbox	txtName	(blank)	
GroupBox	txtCity	Style	
RadioButton	rdoFormal	Formal	Checked: True
RadioButton	rdoSouthern	Southern	
RadioButton	rdoSpanish	Spanish	
Button	btnClickMe	Click Me	
Form	MainWindow	Greeting	AcceptButton: btnClickMe

Step 2: Determining Which Radio Button is Selected

Next, we added code in the **btnClickMe's Click** event. In this handler, you can use the radio button's **Checked** property to determine if it selected. The code is shown below:

```
Private Sub btnClickMe_Click(ByVal sender As Object, _
 ByVal e As System.EventArgs) Handles btnClickMe.Click

    Dim s As String

    If rdoFormal.Checked = True Then
        s = "Hello "
    ElseIf rdoSouthern.Checked = True Then
        s = "Howdy "
    Else
        s = "Hola "
    End If

    s = s & txtName.Text
    MessageBox.Show(s, "Greeting")

End Sub
```

Using a CheckBox

A checkbox is used to allow the user to choose an option using a true/false or yes/no type of box. The **CheckBox** control is similar to the **RadioButton** control, except that each checkbox can be checked or unchecked individually without affecting another checkbox.

In the program **StylesOfGreetings\Step 2,** we will display a standard greeting unless the user checks the personalize button and enters a name. To do this, we made some small changes to the form's appearance. Figure 7–29 illustrates the form's new design-time appearance.

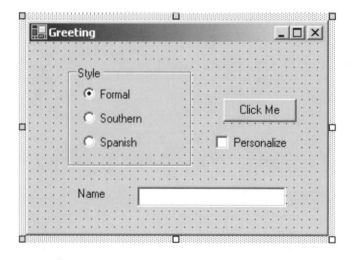

FIGURE 7–29 *Using the CheckBox control to provide options.*

Additional properties that were set in this application are shown in Table 7–5.

TABLE 7–5 *Property Values for the StylesOfGreetings Application (Step 2)*

Control Type	Name	Text	Other Properties
Label	lblName	Name	Visible: False
Textbox	txtName	(blank)	Visible: False
CheckBox	chkPersonalize	Personalize	Checked: False

When **chkPersonalize** is checked, and **txtName** is visible, the Click Me button uses the name in the greeting. When **chkPersonalize** is unchecked, **lblName** and **txtName** are invisible and the Click Me button uses a standard greeting in the language specified.

To achieve this, we added the line of code indicated below in the **btnClickMe's Click** event. We also added code to the **CheckedChanged** event handler for **chkPersonalize**. The two event handlers for this form are shown below:

```
Private Sub btnClickMe_Click(ByVal sender As Object, _
 ByVal e As System.EventArgs) Handles btnClickMe.Click

   Dim s As String

   If rdoFormal.Checked = True Then
      s = "Hello "
   ElseIf rdoSouthern.Checked = True Then
      s = "Howdy "
   Else
      s = "Hola "
   End If

   s = s & txtName.Text
   MessageBox.Show(s, "Greeting")
   txtName.Text = ""

End Sub

Private Sub chkPersonalize_CheckedChanged(ByVal sender _
 As System.Object, ByVal e As System.EventArgs) _
 Handles chkPersonalize.CheckedChanged

   lblName.Visible = Not lblName.Visible
   txtName.Visible = Not txtName.Visible

End Sub
```

Figures 7–30 illustrates the messages that can be displayed both with and without the checkbox checked.

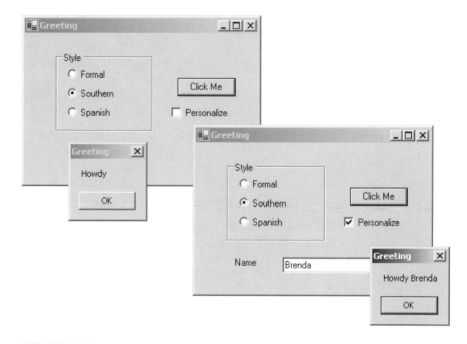

FIGURE 7–30   *Output from CheckBox example.*

Using List Controls (ListBox and ComboBox)

The **ListBox** and **ComboBox** controls are two of the most common list controls used in Windows applications. They can be used to allow the user to enter data by selecting an item from a list. The **ListBox** allows both single-selection and multiple-selection, while the **ComboBox** allows you to type text if you don't find the selection you desire in the list.

The **ComboBox** control also has a **DropDownStyle** property that allows the control to be used in one of three modes:

- **DropDown** (the default) displays a textbox-like control with an arrow next to it that can be used to drop down the list. An item can be selected from the list or typed into the textbox-like control.
- **Simple** displays a textbox-like control with a list just below it that is always visible. An item can be selected from the list or typed into the textbox-like control.
- **DropDownList** displays a non-textbox-like control with an arrow next to it that can be used to drop down the list. An item must be selected from the list.

Items can be added to a list box or combo box either statically (at design time) or dynamically (at runtime). These controls manage the list using the **Items** property. The **Items** property represents the *collection* of items in the list and can be used to access properties such as **Count** and **Item**, and methods such as **Add**, **AddRange**, **Clear**, **Insert**, **Remove**, and **RemoveAt**. Other properties that apply to the control itself, such as **Enabled**, **SelectedIndex**, **Sorted**, and **Visible**, belong to the **ListBox** or **ComboBox** class.

In this section, we will add a list box to our Acme Travel Agency case study that displays all the hotels that have been added. We will also let the user select a hotel from the list box to edit or delete. If you want to follow along on the computer, you may continue in the **Demos\HotelAdmin** folder, or copy the code in **HotelAdmin\Version 1** to a new folder. We will create Version 2 of this program.

You should begin by adding a few additional controls to your **MainAdminForm**. They are shown in Figure 7–31 and summarized in Table 7–6.

Code
Example

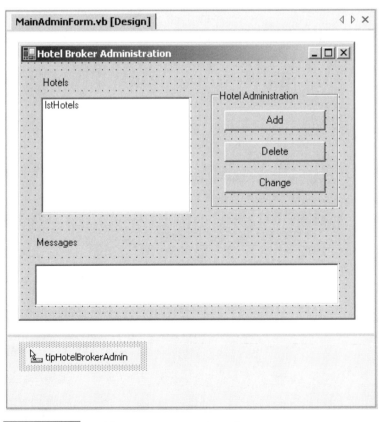

FIGURE 7–31   *Adding a ListBox control to a form.*

TABLE 7–6	Property Values for New Controls in HotelAdmin Main Form		
Control Type	**Name**	**Text**	**Other Properties**
Label	Label1	Hotels	
ToolTip	tipHotelAdmin		
ListBox	lstHotel	n/a	ToolTip:
			Lists city, hotel, # of rooms and rate

Step 1: Adding Data to a ListBox

To add items dynamically at runtime, you must use the **Items.Add** method or the **Items.Insert** method. **Add** inserts at the end of the list (unless the **Sorted** property is true), whereas **Insert** allows you to specify the insertion position.

```
List1.Items.Add("Mary")
List1.Items.Insert(3,"Mark")
```

If you have a large number of items to add to the list, you can turn off repainting of the control until all items have been added using the **BeginUpdate** and **EndUpdate** methods.

```
List1.BeginUpdate()
For I = 1 To 100
   List1.Add("Item " & I)
Next
List1.EndUpdate()
```

For **HotelAdmin\Version 2**, we will write code to take the data that is in **HotelBroker** and display it in a list box. You must add the following helper procedure to your **MainAdminForm** class. It uses the **Items.Add** method to add to the list box.

```
Private Sub ShowHotelList(ByRef array As ArrayList)
   lstHotels.Items.Clear()
   If array Is Nothing Then
      Return
   End If
   Dim hotel As HotelListItem
   For Each hotel In array
      Dim city As String = hotel.City.Trim()
      Dim name As String = hotel.HotelName.Trim()
      Dim rooms As String = hotel.NumberRooms.ToString()
      Dim rate As String = hotel.Rate.ToString()
      Dim str As String = city & "," & name & "," & rooms _
                          & "," & rate
      lstHotels.Items.Add(str)
   Next
End Sub
```

You must then modify both the **Load** event handler and the **Click** event handler for the Add button to call **ShowHotelList** as needed. Add the bolded code shown below to the specified procedures.

```
Private Sub MainForm_Load(ByVal sender As System.Object, _
 ByVal e As System.EventArgs) Handles MyBase.Load
    hotelBroker = New hotelBroker()
    ShowHotelList(hotelBroker.GetHotels())
End Sub

Private Sub cmdAdd_Click(ByVal sender As System.Object, _
 ByVal e As System.EventArgs) Handles cmdAdd.Click

    ...
    Dim status As DialogResult = dlg.ShowDialog()
    If status = DialogResult.OK Then
       Dim comment As String = hotelBroker.AddHotel( _
          dlg.City, dlg.HotelName, dlg.NumberRooms, _
          dlg.Rate)
       If comment = "OK" Then
          ShowHotelList(hotelBroker.GetHotels())
          txtMessages.Text = "Hotel " & dlg.HotelName & _
                           " has been added"
       Else
          txtMessages.Text = comment
       End If
    End If
End Sub
```

You can now run the application, and you should see some test data provided in the **HotelBroker** class displayed in the list box, as illustrated in Figure 7–32.

Step 2: Selecting an Item in a ListBox

An item in a list is selected by clicking on the item. This action generates a **SelectedIndexChanged** event. The properties **SelectedIndex** and **SelectedItem** are set by the user's clicking action. When no item is selected, **SelectedIndex** is −1.

If the item is a multiple-selection listbox, the code is more complicated. The **SelectedItems** property maintains the collection of selected items. Its property **Count** identifies the number of items selected. These may then be accessed through the subscriptable property **Item**. For example:

```
Dim s As String
Dim index As Integer
s = List1.SelectedItems.Item(0)
For index = 1 To List1.SelectedItems.Count - 1
   s &= ", " & List1.SelectedItems.Item(index)
Next
```

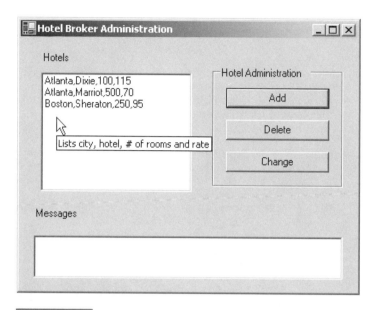

FIGURE 7–32 *ListBox displays information about hotels.*

For **HotelAdmin\Version 2**, we will write code to maintain a variable with information about the hotel that is currently selected in the list box. Recall that we already added the variable **currHotel** to the form:

```
Public Class MainAdminForm
    Inherits System.Windows.Forms.Form

    Private hotelBroker As HotelBroker
    Private currHotel As HotelListItem

    . . .
```

We can then trap the **SelectedIndexChanged** event of **lstHotels**. In this handler procedure, we will use the **SelectedItem** property to extract the current hotel selection. We must parse the hotel information from the comma-delimited that **SelectedItem** returns. The **Split** method from the **String** class returns us a list of the individual strings that were separated by a specified delimiter. Add the following code to your demo:

```
Private Sub lstHotels_SelectedIndexChanged(ByVal sender _
  As System.Object, ByVal e As System.EventArgs) _
  Handles lstHotels.SelectedIndexChanged
    If lstHotels.SelectedIndex <> -1 Then
       Dim selected As String = lstHotels.SelectedItem
       Dim sep As Char() = New Char() {","c}
       Dim fields() As String
```

```
      fields = selected.Split(sep)
      currHotel = New HotelListItem()
      currHotel.City = fields(0)
      currHotel.HotelName = fields(1)
      currHotel.NumberRooms = Convert.ToInt32(fields(2))
      currHotel.Rate = Convert.ToDecimal(fields(3))
   Else
      currHotel.HotelName = ""
   End If
End Sub
```

Step 3: Removing Data from a ListBox

To remove items from a list, the **Remove** method is used to remove the first occurrence of a specified string. The **RemoveAt** method is used to remove the occurrence at a specified index.   For example:

```
List1.Items.Remove("Mary")
List1.Items.RemoveAt(2)
```

The **Items.Clear** method can be used to remove all items from the list box.

For **HotelAdmin\Version 2**, we will use the currently selected hotel in the implementation of our delete button. However, rather than remove an item from the list box, we will remove it from our **HotelBroker** object and then repopulate the list box.

You must add the following code for the **Click** event of cmdDelete. It will remove the selected hotel and redisplay the list. If you re-examine the **Show-AllHotels** method, you will see that the first line of code clears the list box.

```
Private Sub cmdDelete_Click(ByVal sender As _
  System.Object, ByVal e As System.EventArgs) _
  Handles cmdDelete.Click
   Dim comment As String = _
      hotelBroker.DeleteHotel(currHotel.City, _
                              currHotel.HotelName)
   If comment = "OK" Then
      ShowHotelList(hotelBroker.GetHotels())
      txtMessages.Text = "Hotel " & currHotel.HotelName & _
                         " has been deleted"
   Else
      txtMessages.Text = comment
   End If
End Sub
```

Step 4: Changing Hotel Data

As a final step in our **HotelAdmin** example program, we implement the Change button, which allows the user to change the number of rooms and the rate of a selected hotel. Clicking the Change button brings up the dialog illustrated in Figure 7–33.

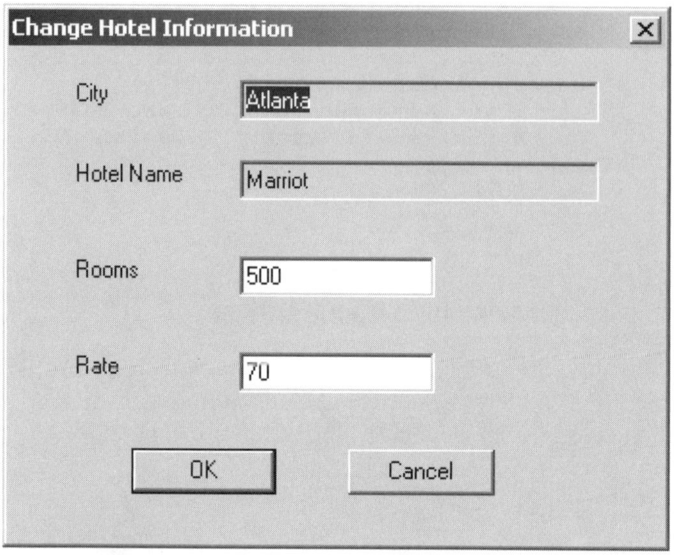

FIGURE 7-33   *Dialog for changing information about hotels.*

There are no new concepts illustrated by this feature, so we do not show the code here. You may examine it in the example code. The project at this point is stored in **HotelAdmin\Version 2**.

Acme Travel Agency Case Study (Step 3)

The Acme Travel Agency case study was introduced in Chapter 5, where we used arrays as our data structures for storing lists of hotels, customers, and reservations. In Chapter 6, we changed the implementation to use collections in place of arrays. We provided a command-line user interface. In the **Case-Study** folder of the present chapter, we provide a graphical user interface for the application that is implemented by using Windows Forms.

We have already developed much of the basic hotel management functionality in this chapter via the **HotelAdmin** demos. The **CaseStudy** version uses a similar GUI with additional options. The Customers button on the **MainAdminForm** brings up a Customer Management dialog, which shows a list of currently registered customers. You may select a customer by clicking in the list box.

The Reservation button on the **MainAdminForm** brings up a Hotel Reservations dialog. It allows you to:

- Make a reservation. Simply enter the customer's Id, check-in date, and the number of days they plan to stay. Specify the city and hotel by selecting from a listbox. Then click the Make Reservation button.

- Show all the reservations. Enter a particular customer Id,[2] and click Show Reservations.
- Clear reservations. You may clear the reservations list box by clicking the Clear Reservations button.
- Cancel a reservation. Simply enter a particular Reservation Id, which may either be typed in or selected by clicking in the Reservations list box. Then click the Cancel Reservations button.

The Acme Travel Agency case study is used extensively in the following chapters, so you may wish to experiment with it at this point. The graphical user interface makes exercising the case study much easier than our previous command-line interface. On the other hand, the command-line interface and a simple global **try** block around the whole command loop made it easy to check for all exceptions. Such an approach is not feasible for a GUI program. In an industrial-strength application you should check for exceptions wherever they may occur. Our case study is simplified for instructional purposes, and we have not attempted to be thorough in catching exceptions. Another simplification we made is not checking that a Customer Id used in making a reservation corresponds to a real, registered customer. The database implementation in Chapter 13 does provide such a check.

Summary

In this chapter, we learned how to implement a GUI using the Windows Forms classes of the .NET Framework. We began by using the .NET Framework SDK to create simple Windows applications from scratch. Controls can be instantiated, placed and sized on a form without the use of any special tools. The .NET event mechanism is used to handle user interaction such as button clicks.

Visual Studio .NET greatly simplifies Windows programming. The Forms Designer lets you drag controls from the Toolbox onto your forms, and you can set properties of the controls at design time. You can also easily add event handlers. Dialog boxes are a special kind of form, and you can pass information between a parent form and a dialog through the use of properties in the dialog. These forms can contain a number of different types of controls, and we examined several basic ones, such as buttons, textboxes and list boxes. Finally, we introduced a graphical version of the Acme Travel Agency case study.

---

2. A Customer Id of –1 will show the reservations for all customers.

Using Controls

Visual Basic .NET supports a variety of features that can be used to build sophisticated, yet easy-to-use, graphical user interfaces with Windows Forms. In this chapter, we will explore how menus, toolbars, and status bars can be added to an application. We will also examine several different types of controls, including calendar controls, range controls and list controls. By selecting the proper type of control to communicate with the user, the user's interaction with the application can be made more pleasant. In addition, validation and verification of the user's input by the application can be enhanced. For example, when a user must enter a department name, allowing them to select the name from a list rather than having them type the department name (and possibly misspelling it) reduces errors.

Menus

Menus are one of the primary ways that users interact with many applications. Each window can display its own menu, although it is more common to find a menu only on the main window. Each window can also display a context menu, if the programmer so chooses. A context menu is one that is displayed when the user right-clicks with the mouse to display a popup menu.

MainMenu Control

The **MainMenu** control can be used to design, display, and manage a menu that is attached to the top of the client area of the window. We demonstrate the use of menus by building a new version of the **HotelAdmin** program we

Code Example

saw in the previous chapter. In this example, named **HotelAdmin2**, we have the following main menu structure:

```
File            Hotels         Help
    Exit            Add            About...
                    Edit
                    Delete
```

The underscore underneath a letter of the menu caption identifies the letter as a menu shortcut. You can press the ALT key and the letter to select the menu containing that shortcut. If a menu is already displayed, an item can be selected using only its shortcut key. For example, the key sequence ALT+T+E generates the same event as if you select the Hotels | Edit menu using the mouse. To define a menu shortcut key, you must place an ampersand (&) in the caption before the letter that is the shortcut key. For example, "E&xit" would underline the letter *x* on the menu and associate it as the shortcut key.

Menu items may also have an accelerator key attached to them. For example, F4 might be the equivalent of Add, or CTRL+D might be the equivalent of Exit. Whereas a shortcut must use a letter from the caption as the shortcut key, an accelerator is free to use a combination of CTRL, ALT, SHIFT, and keys from the keyboard. The accelerator key is assigned by setting the **Shortcut** property of a menu item.

Step 1: Using the MainMenu Control

The **MainMenu** control is used to design menus. As you can see in Figure 8–1, we have modified the startup form for the application by removing the command buttons and placing a **MainMenu** control on the form. It has been named it **mnuHotelBroker**. When it is drawn on the form, an icon appears in a separate window where other special controls such as the **ErrorProvider** and **ToolTip** controls are placed. It has also attached a menu to the form that we can now modify.

Each item on the menu has a set of properties associated with it that can be manipulated using the Properties window. The properties unique to the **MainMenu** control include:

- **Checked** indicates whether a check mark is next to menu caption.
- **RadioChecked** indicates whether a round check mark is next to the menu caption.
- **Shortcut** indicates the accelerator key (Ctrl-X, etc.) that should be assigned to the menu item.
- **ShortcutVisible** indicates whether the accelerator identity is displayed next to the menu caption.

Table 8–1 shows the property values used to define the menu shown at the beginning of this section. To set these properties, click on the menu that is attached to the form. Enter the **Text** property value in the area displayed. You can then use the Properties window to set the remaining properties.

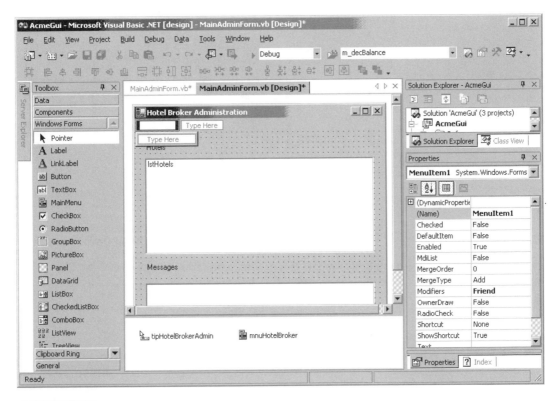

FIGURE 8–1 *Using the MainMenu control.*

TABLE 8–1	*Property Values for the MainMenu Control in the HotelBroker2 Startup Form*	
Text	**Name**	**Shortcut**
&File	mnuFile	
E&xit	mnuExit	CtrlD
Ho&tel	mnuHotels	
&Add	mnuAdd	
&Edit	mnuEdit	
&Delete	mnuDelete	
&Help	mnuHelp	
&About...	mnuAbout	

Step 2: Responding to Menu Events

Each menu item has a **Click** event associated with it. It must be handled in order to provide a response to the user's selection of that menu item. For example, the **Click** event handlers for the **HotelAdmin2's** Exit and About menus are shown below. The handler for Exit closes **MainForm**. The handler for About displays a message box.

```
Private Sub mnuExit_Click(ByVal sender As System.Object, _
  ByVal e As System.EventArgs) Handles mnuExit.Click

    Me.Close()

End Sub

Private Sub mnuAbout_Click(ByVal sender As System.Object, _
  ByVal e As System.EventArgs) Handles mnuAbout.Click

    MessageBox.Show("Hotel Broker Administration v1.1", _
       "About HotelAdmin", MessageBoxButtons.OK, _
       MessageBoxIcon.Information)

End Sub
```

In the event handlers for each of the three items on the Hotels menu, we have added code to display the appropriate dialog. (We simply moved the code in the **Click** event of the buttons from last chapter's **HotelAdmin** example into the **Click** event of the respective menu.) Figure 8–2 shows the new GUI for our **HotelAdmin2** application.

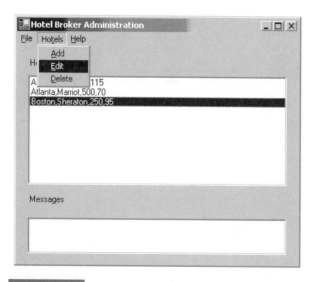

FIGURE 8–2   *HotelAdmin2's startup form.*

Step 3: Controlling Menu Appearance

Menu items have properties such as **Checked**, **Enabled** and **Visible** that can be used to control their appearance on the menu. In our **HotelAdmin2** application, we do not want the users to be able to select Edit or Delete if they do not have any hotel in the listbox selected, so we must enable or disable those items programmatically.

We will handle the **Popup** event of **mnuHotels**. This event is generated when the user selects Hotels but before the associated dropdown menu appears. In it, we will enable or disable the appropriate items under **mnuHotels** before they are displayed.

```
Private Sub mnuHotels_Popup(ByVal sender As Object, _
  ByVal e As System.EventArgs) Handles mnuHotels.Popup

   If lstHotels.SelectedIndex <> -1 Then
      mnuEdit.Enabled = True
      mnuDelete.Enabled = True
   Else
      mnuEdit.Enabled = False
      mnuDelete.Enabled = False
   End If

End Sub
```

Figure 8–3 shows the Hotels dropdown when there is no selected hotel. As you can see, the Edit and Delete menu items are disabled.

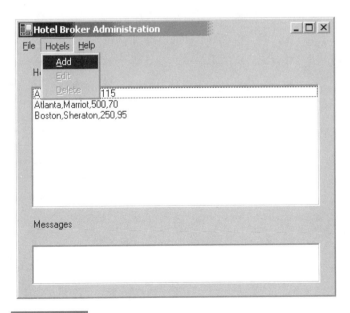

FIGURE 8–3   *Controlling menu appearance.*

ContextMenu Control

The **ContextMenu** control can be used to display a floating popup menu that is displayed when the user right-clicks on a control or other area of the form. Typically, context menus provide shortcuts to commonly used items on the main menu. In the **HotelAdmin2** program, we will provide a context menu with the three Hotel menu options (Add, Edit and Delete). To add a context menu for a form, we must perform the following actions:

- Add the **ContextMenu** control to the form and set its **Name** property to **mnuContext**.
- Set the **ContextMenu** property of the form to **mnuContext**. (See Figure 8–4.)
- Add menu items to the context menu and associate them with an event handler. We do this programmatically. If the menu item's **Click** event cannot be associated with an existing handler, we must also write the handler function(s).

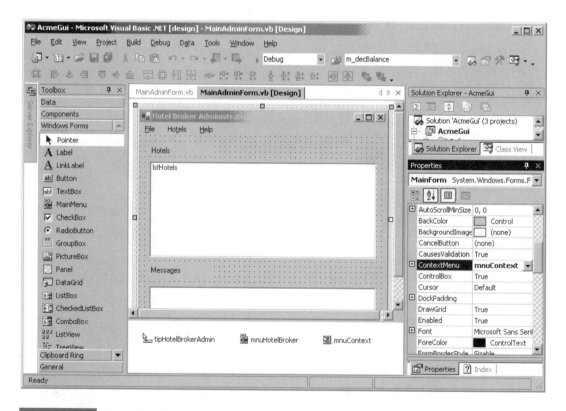

FIGURE 8–4   *Using the ContextMenu control.*

We will initialize our context menu when the form loads because the items on the menu are always the same, regardless of where the user right-clicks or what data is on the form.

All menu controls have a **MenuItems** property that represents the *collection* of items on the menu. Using this property, you can access methods such as **Add** and **Remove** to manipulate the items on the menu. The code for our form's **Load** event handler is shown below. It adds three items to the context menu and associates a **Click** event handler function with each.

```
Private Sub MainForm_Load(ByVal sender As Object, _
 ByVal e As System.EventArgs) Handles MyBase.Load

    mnuContext.MenuItems.Add("Add Hotel", _
       New EventHandler(AddressOf mnuAdd_Click))
    mnuContext.MenuItems.Add("Edit Selected Hotel", _
       New EventHandler(AddressOf mnuEdit_Click))
    mnuContext.MenuItems.Add("Delete Selected Gotel", _
       New EventHandler(AddressOf mnuDelete_Click))

End Sub
```

Because the main menu already had event handlers that responded to Add, Edit and Delete selections from the menu, we used those handlers for the corresponding context menu item handlers. If we did not have existing handler functions that could have been associated with the context menu's **Click** event, we would have built a standard **Click** event handler and associated it as the handler procedure. In this version of the form's **Load** event handler, we associated the **ClickedOnContextMenu** procedure as the event handler for all menu items on the context menu.

```
Private Sub MainForm_Load(ByVal sender As Object, _
 ByVal e As System.EventArgs) Handles MyBase.Load

    mnuContext.MenuItems.Add("Add Hotel", _
       New EventHandler(AddressOf ClickedOnContextMenu))
    mnuContext.MenuItems.Add("Edit Selected Hotel", _
       New EventHandler(AddressOf ClickedOnContextMenu))
    mnuContext.MenuItems.Add("Delete Selected Hotel", _
       New EventHandler(AddressOf ClickedOnContextMenu))

End Sub
```

The selection of any item on the context menu will send us to the **ClickedOnContextMenu** functions shown below. To determine which menu selection caused the **Click** handler to be invoked we could have referenced the handler's **System.Object** parameter. All **Click** event handlers are passed a **System.Object** parameter and a **System.EventArgs** parameter. The **System.Object** parameter, named **sender** by the wizard that writes

handler functions, identifies the control that caused the event. In the
ClickedOnContectMenu handler we would write because of the last version of our **Load** event handler, we would convert the **sender** parameter to
a **MenuItem** parameter using **CType**. We would then extract the **Text** property of the menu item to determine which item from the context menu was
selected.

```
Private Sub ClickedOnContextMenu(ByVal sender As _
  System.Object, ByVal e As System.EventArgs)

    Dim mnuSelected As MenuItem = CType(sender, MenuItem)

    If mnuSelected.Text = "Add Hotel" Then
        ' Code to handle Add goes here
    ElseIf mnuSelected.Text = "Edit Selected Hotel" Then
        ' Code to handle Edit goes here
    ElseIf mnuSelected.Text = "Delete Selected Hotel" Then
        ' Code to handle Delete goes here
    End If

End Sub
```

If we want to know when the context menu is being displayed so that
we may set check marks or disable menu items, we must handle the content
menu's **PopUp** event. Inside this handler, we can determine the state of the
application and modify the menu's appearance as needed. Items on the context menu can be accessed via the subscriptable **MenuItems** property.

To complete our **HotelAdmin2** program, we will disable the Edit and
Delete menus when they are displayed on the context menu. See Figure 8–5.

```
Private Sub mnuContext_Popup(ByVal sender As _
  System.Object, ByVal e As System.EventArgs) _
  Handles mnuContext.Popup

    If lstHotels.SelectedIndex <> -1 Then
        ' Enable Edit and Delete
        mnuContext.MenuItems(1).Enabled = True
        mnuContext.MenuItems(2).Enabled = True
    Else
        ' Disable Edit and Delete
        mnuContext.MenuItems(1).Enabled = False
        mnuContext.MenuItems(2).Enabled = False
    End If

End Sub
```

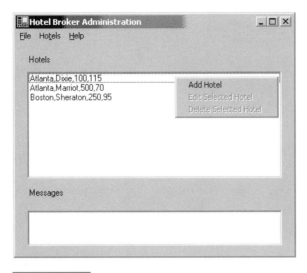

FIGURE 8-5   *Controlling ContextMenu appearance.*

Toolbars

The **ToolBar** control is used on forms to display a row of buttons that invoke commands (similar to clicking a menu item). VB.NET toolbars generally use an **ImageList** control to maintain the images displayed by the toolbar. Each button on the toolbar is associated with an image from the image list.

The **ToolBar** class has a **Buttons** collection that represents the buttons on the toolbar. Properties such as **Appearance**, **Autosize**, and **Wrapable** control the appearance of the toolbar.

The **ToolBarButton** class has properties that configure the individual buttons on the toolbar. This class has many interesting properties, including:

- **ImageIndex** indicates the image number from the **ImageList** control of the image associated with this button.
- **Text** indicates the text that may optionally be displayed on a button.
- **ToolTipText** indicates the tool tip text displayed for the button.

Code
Example

In the following two sections, we will examine the simple **Calculator** program and see how toolbars and status bars may be added to the program. **Calculator** allows the user to enter two numbers and select toolbar buttons to indicate add, subtract, multiply or divide. The result is displayed in a label. A status bar shows the type of the last operation as well as the current time. A main menu has options for File | Exit and Help | About. Figure 8–6 illustrates the completed program's appearance.

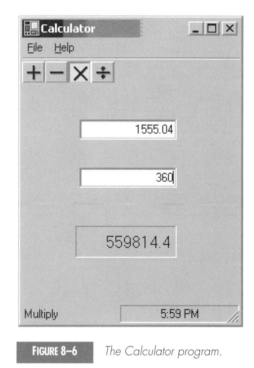

FIGURE 8–6   *The Calculator program.*

Step 1: Setting up the ImageList Control

To manage the images on the toolbar, we added an **ImageList** control to the form and named it **imgList**. Its **Images** collection is used to manage the images in the list. To assign manage the Images collection, you must click on the **Images** property in the Properties window. The Image Collection Editor is displayed. You can press the Add button to load various images. As you can see in Figure 8–7, we loaded mathematical icons into the list from the **..\Microsoft Visual Studio.NET\Common7\Graphics\Icons\Misc** directory. The toolbar that we want to design will use icons for add, subtract, multiply, and divide (MISC18.ICO through MISC21.ICO). These were loaded into the **ImageList** in positions 0, 1, 2, and 3, respectively.

Step 2: Configuring the Toolbar Control

To configure the toolbar control for our calculator, we must set its **ImageList** property to **imgList**. We then add buttons to the toolbar by selecting the toolbar's **Buttons** property from the Properties window. The ToolBarButton Collection Editor shown in Figure 8–8 can be used to add our four buttons.

Table 8–2 summarizes the properties we set for our four buttons.

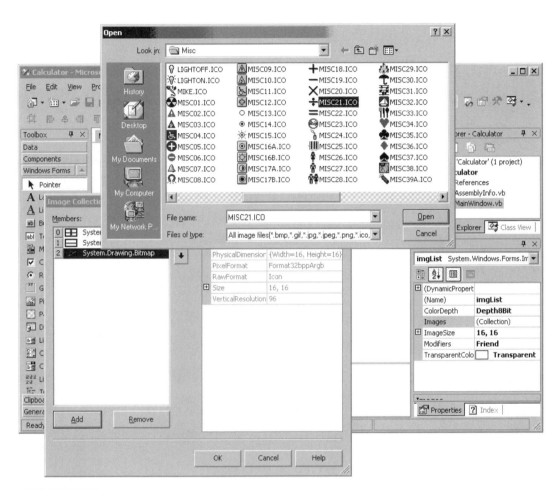

FIGURE 8–7   *Using the Image Collection Editor.*

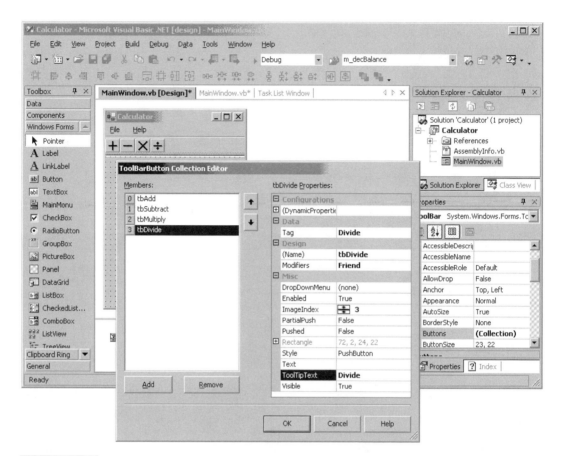

FIGURE 8–8   *The ToolBarButton Collection Editor.*

TABLE 8–2   *Property Values for the Calculator Toolbar Buttons*

Button	Name	Other Properties
0	tbAdd	ImageIndex: 0 Tag: Add ToolTipText: Add
1	tbSubtract	ImageIndex:1 Tag: Subtract ToolTipText: Subtract
2	tbMultiply	ImageIndex: 2 Tag: Multiply ToolTipText: Multiply
3	tbDivide	ImageIndex: 3 Tag: Divide ToolTipText: Divide

The **ToolTipText** property displays tool tips when the user hovers the mouse over the toolbar button. The **Tag** property, which is a property available in all .NET controls, is unused by .NET. This makes it a convenient placeholder for application data. In our case, we are using it to "tag," or identify, our toolbar button. It will be referenced in the handler that responds to a click on a toolbar button.

A toolbar button also has a **Text** property. When it its set, the text appears below the icon on the toolbar button.

Step 3: Responding to Toolbar Events

The **ToolBar** control generates a **ButtonClick** event any time any of the buttons on the toolbar is selected. The handler for this event is passed a **ToolBarButtonClickEventArgs** parameter that has a property that references the button was selected. The button is identified through its **ImageIndex, Text** or **Tag** property.

In the previous step, we placed a descriptive string of the button's purpose in the **Tag** property of each button. Therefore, we will code the toolbar's **ButtonClick** event as follows:

```
Private Sub toolBar_ButtonClick(ByVal sender As _
 System.Object, ByVal e As _
 System.Windows.Forms.ToolBarButtonClickEventArgs) _
 Handles toolBar.ButtonClick

   Dim n1 As Double = Val(txtNum1.Text)
   Dim n2 As Double = Val(txtNum2.Text)

   ' This call is described in the next section
   SetGUIChecks(toolBar.Buttons(e.Button.ImageIndex))

   Select Case e.Button.Tag
      Case "Add"
         lblResult.Text = n1 + n2
      Case "Subtract"
         lblResult.Text = n1 - n2
      Case "Multiply"
         lblResult.Text = n1 * n2
      Case "Divide"
         lblResult.Text = n1 / n2
   End Select

End Sub
```

We used the function **Val** instead of **CDbl** or **Convert.ToDouble** in this handler to convert data from the text boxes because **Val** returns zero if the string is blank.

Step 4: Controlling Toolbar Button Appearance

The **ToolBarButton** class has several properties that control the appearance of individual buttons, including:

- **Enabled** indicates whether the button is enabled.
- **Pushed** indicates whether the button is pushed.
- **Visible** indicates whether the button is visible.

In our calculator, we will implement behavior that will give the last toolbar button that was clicked a "pushed" look. (Note: Typically, buttons stay pushed only when they indicate that an application's data is in a particular *state*. We will push the last button used so that we can tell which operation was used to calculate the answer displayed.)

The toolbar's **Click** event, discussed in Step 3, calls **SetGUIChecks** and passes it the **ToolBarButton** that was clicked. This procedure sets the appearance of our toolbar buttons and is coded as shown below:

```
Private Sub SetGUIChecks(ByVal btn As ToolBarButton)
    ' Unselect all buttons
    Dim i As Integer
    For i = 0 To 3
        toolBar.Buttons(i).Pushed = False
    Next

    ' Update toolbar appearance
    btn.Pushed = True
End Sub
```

At this point, the **Calculator** program should be functional. We will now add a status bar to display additional information to the user.

Status Bars

The **StatusBar** control can be used to display a status bar on a form. The **StatusBar** control has a **Panels** property that can be accessed at runtime. It represents a collection of individual **StatusBarPanel** objects. The **StatusBarPanel** class defines several properties that can be used to manipulate the panels, including the following:

- **Alignment** controls whether text in a panel is left, center, or right aligned.
- **Autosize** controls whether the panel automatically sizes itself to occupy the remaining area on the status bar. Choices include **None** and **Spring**.
- **BorderStyle** controls the type of border used for the panel.

- **Text** controls the contents of the panel.
- **Width** and **MinWidth** control the width (in pixels) of the panel.

Step 1: Adding the StatusBar Control

To add a status bar to a program, use the **StatusBar** control. The **StatusBar** control is a visible control that positions itself as an empty window aligned with the bottom of the form. To configure the individual panels on the status bar, you must modify the **Panels** collection. The StatusBarPanel Collection Editor can be launched by selecting the **Panels** collection using the Properties window (see Figure 8–9.)

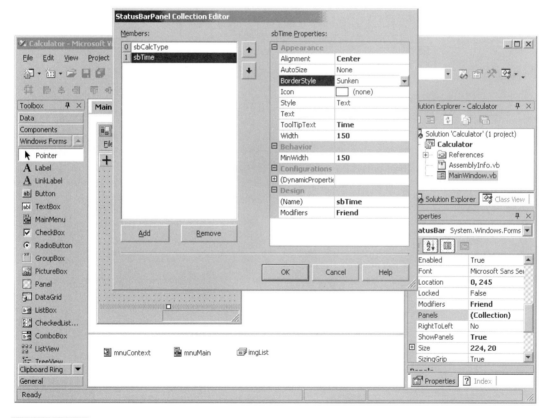

FIGURE 8–9   *The StatusBarPanel Collections editor.*

Table 8–3 summarizes the properties we set for our two panels.

TABLE 8–3	*Property Values for the Calculator Status Bar Panels*	
Panel	**Name**	**Other Properties**
0	sbCalcType	Autosize: Spring BorderStyle: None Style: Text ToolTipText: Last operation Width: 100 MinWidth: 10
1	sbTime	Alignment: Center BorderStyle: Sunken Style: Text ToolTipText: Current Time Width: 150 MinWidth: 150

Step 2: Displaying Information in the Status Bar

To display information in a status bar panel that has a **Style** property of **Text**, we must modify that panel's **Text** property. For **Calculator**, we will modify the **SetGUIChecks** procedure to write the calculation type to the first panel. Each toolbar button's **Tag** property contains text that we can use when displaying the operation type to the status bar panel.

```
Private Sub SetGUIChecks(ByVal mnu As MenuItem, _
 ByVal btn As ToolBarButton)

   ' Unselect all buttons
   Dim i As Integer
   For i = 0 To 3
      toolBar.Buttons(i).Pushed = False
   Next

   ' Update toolbar and statusbar
   btn.Pushed = True
   statusBar.Panels(0).Text = btn.Tag

End Sub
```

Step 3: Using the Timer Control to Display Time

The **Timer** control is an invisible VB.NET control that causes an event to be generated at regular intervals. In our case, we will use it to assist us in keeping the clock on the status bar accurate.

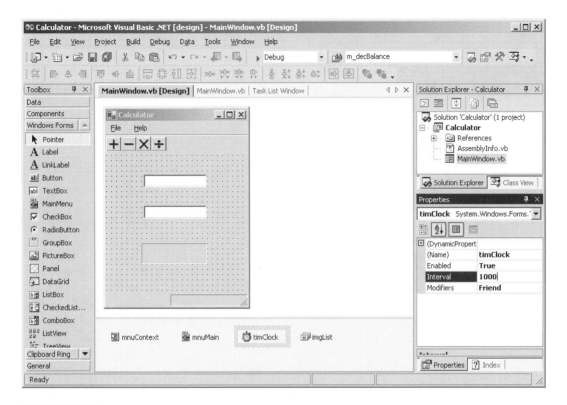

FIGURE 8–10   *Using the Timer control.*

The **Timer** control is fairly simple. It has two properties of interest: **Enabled** and **Interval**. When the timer is enabled, it generates a **Tick** event every *n* milliseconds, where *n* is the **Interval** value. Figure 8–10 shows the **Timer** control on our **MainForm** and its associated properties. We selected an interval of 1000 so that the **Tick** event will happen once every second.

In the **Tick** event handler, we have placed the following code. It accesses the current date and time via the **Now** property, and then uses the **ToString** method to convert it into a string representation of time. Finally, it places the information into the appropriate status bar panel.

```
Private Sub timClock_Tick(ByVal sender As System.Object, _
  ByVal e As System.EventArgs) Handles timClock.Tick

    statusBar.Panels(1).Text = Date.Now.ToString("t")

End Sub
```

At this point, the **Calculator** program is complete. If you execute it, your dialog should resemble that shown earlier in Figure 8–6.

Calendar Controls

VB.NET supports two types of calendar controls: the **MonthCalendar** and the **DateTimePicker**. Each allows the user to select a date or time from a graphical control. They should be used instead of textboxes whenever possible because they reduce the chance of data entry errors for dates (such as entering February 31).

DateTimePicker

The **DateTimePicker** control allows the user to select a date and/or time from a graphical control. The format of the date/time displayed can be controlled using the **Format** property. The properties **MinDate** and **MaxDate** can be used to specify a limit for the dates shown. The **Value** property contains the selected date/time. Additional properties control the appearance of the control.

Code Example

In the directory for this chapter, we have several versions of our case study. Each version will use specific controls to improve upon the appearance and/or ease of use of the application. **BetterAcmeGui** uses a **DateTimePicker** to select the check-in date for customer reservations.

We began by replacing the textbox for the check-in date with a **DateTimePicker** named **dtCheckinDate**. In the new reservation form's **Load** event, we placed the following code so that the check-in date defaults to the current date, reservations cannot be made for past dates and are only allowable up to one year in advance. We use the **DateAdd** function to calculate the date one year from **Now**.

```
Private Sub NewReservationForm_Load(ByVal sender As _
  System.Object, ByVal e As System.EventArgs) _
  Handles MyBase.Load

    dtCheckinDate.Value = Date.Now
    dtCheckinDate.MinDate = Date.Now
    dtCheckinDate.MaxDate = _
       DateAdd(DateInterval.Year, 1, Date.Now)

End Sub
```

The **CheckInDate** property of the **NewReservationForm** was modified to reference to the **DateTimePicker** control.

```
Public Property CheckInDate() As Date
   Get
       Return Convert.ToDateTime(dtCheckinDate.Value)
   End Get
   Set(ByVal Value As Date)
       dtCheckinDate.Value = Value.ToString()
   End Set
End Property
```

Figure 8–11 shows the reservation dialog before and after the dropdown box was selected. The advantage of using this control is that the user *must* enter a valid date; we do not have to perform any validation on the check-in date.

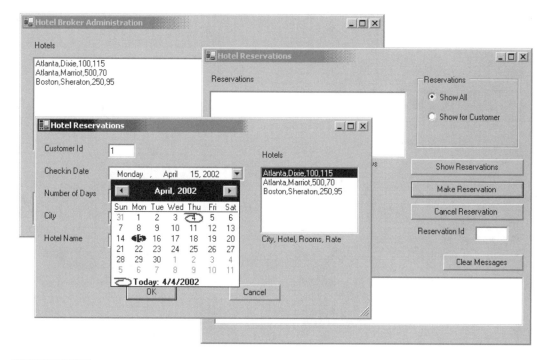

FIGURE 8–11   *Using the DateTimePicker control.*

MonthCalendar

The **MonthCalendar** control allows a user to select a date, or range of dates, from a graphical calendar. You should examine the MSDN to see some of the neat features it offers. These include the following properties:

- **FirstDayOfWeek** indicates the first day of the week that is displayed.
- **ShowTodayCircle** indicates whether the current day is circled.

- **ShowWeekNumbers** indicates whether the week number is shown next to each week.
- **AnnuallyBoldedDates** is an array of **Date** objects that represents the dates that are bolded every year.
- **MonthlyBoldedDates** is an array of **Date** objects that represents the dates that are bolded every month.
- **BoldedDates** is an array of **Date** objects that represents specific dates that are bolded.

Code
Example

The following simple program, found in **BirthdayGreetings**, displays a birthday greeting to Mary when March 6th is clicked. The program also bolds January 9th each year. Figure 8–12 shows two snapshots of the program. In the top left version, March 6th was clicked. In the bottom right version, you can see that January 1 was clicked and January 9 is bolded.

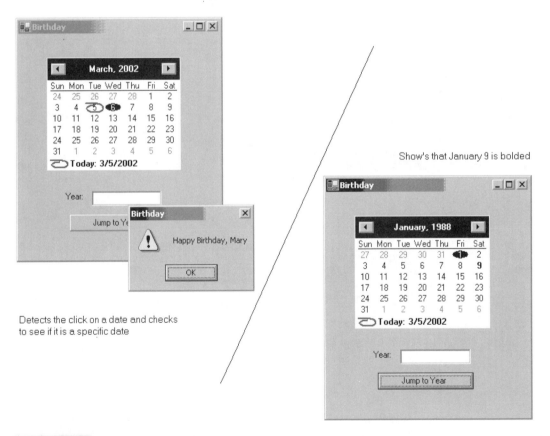

Show's that January 9 is bolded

Detects the click on a date and checks
to see if it is a specific date

FIGURE 8–12   *Using the MonthCalendar control.*

Step 1: Setting up Annually Bolded Dates

When we set annually bolded dates, we must provide valid dates. This means that the date(s) provided must include a year. However, the year is ignored when bolding *annual* dates.

```
Private Sub BirthdayGreetings_Load(ByVal sender As _
  System.Object, ByVal e As System.EventArgs) _
  Handles MyBase.Load

    calBirthday.AddAnnuallyBoldedDate(#1/9/1988#)

End Sub
```

Step 2: Programmatically Setting the Date

Our **btnJump's Click** event handler must adjust the calendar date to January 1 of the year entered. We do this using the calendar's **SetDate** method. The **DateSerial** method is used to build a date from integer values representing year, month, and day.

```
Private Sub btnJump_Click(ByVal sender As Object, _
  ByVal e As System.EventArgs) Handles btnJump.Click

    calBirthday.SetDate(DateSerial(txtYear.Text, 1, 1))
    txtYear.Text = ""

End Sub
```

Step 3: Determining the Selected Date

The calendar's **DateSelected** event is generated whenever a date on the calendar is selected (by the user or programmatically). We will handle this event in order to determine whether we should wish Mary a "happy birthday."

```
Private Sub calBirthday_DateSelected( _
  ByVal sender As Object, _
  ByVal e As System.Windows.Forms.DateRangeEventArgs) _
  Handles calBirthday.DateSelected

    If calBirthday.SelectionStart.Month = 3 And _
        calBirthday.SelectionStart.Day = 6 Then

      MessageBox.Show("Happy Birthday, Mary", "Birthday", _
          MessageBoxButtons.OK, _
          MessageBoxIcon.Exclamation)
    End If

End Sub
```

Range Controls

There are several types of range controls in VB.NET. These controls allow the user to pick some value (or display some value) within a specified range. The numeric range controls include the **ProgressBar**, **ScrollBar**, **TrackBar**, and **NumericUpDown** controls. All of the numeric range controls have certain properties in common, including the following:

- **Minimum** represents the minimum value in the range of numbers.
- **Maximum** represents the maximum value in the range of numbers.
- **Value** represents the control's current value (between minimum and maximum).

This section examines each of the range controls and the properties, methods, and events that make them unique.

ProgressBar

The **ProgressBar** is a control that allows you to display the progress of an operation towards completion. It is an output-only control—that is, the user does not directly interact with it. It displays a value by filling in a specified percentage of its client area. The **Step** property determines the amount of increase in the progress bar's position when the **PerformStep** method is called.

The following program, found in **SimpleProgress\Version 1**, displays a progress bar as it moves toward completion of a task. See Figure 8–13.

Code
Example

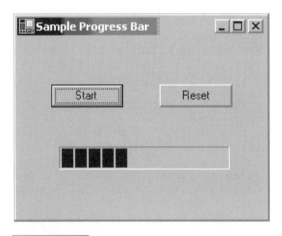

FIGURE 8–13   *Using the ProgressBar control.*

In this simple example, we have a **For** loop that executes 32,000 times. It writes the square root of 1 to 32,000 to a file. The progress bar illustrates completion in steps of 10 percent. In other words, the progress control moves after every 3,200 iterations. Table 8–4 defines the properties of the progress control.

TABLE 8–4	Property Values for the ProgressBar
Property	**Value**
Minimum	0
Maximum	100
Step	10
Value	0

This program uses file I/O so that the progress bar moves slowly enough that it can be seen moving. The code for the **Click** event of the Start and Reset buttons is shown below.

In the Click handler, we have used native VB file I/O instead of the .NET file I/O classes. The **FreeFile** function returns a file number that can be used to interact with a file. The **FileOpen** procedure opens a file so that we can write to it. The **Print** procedure writes to the file. And, finally, the **File-Close** procedure closes the file and releases the file number for reuse on other files.

```
Private Sub btnStart_Click(ByVal sender As System.Object, _
  ByVal e As System.EventArgs) Handles btnStart.Click

   ' Write square roots to a file (file i/o is slow!)

   Dim fileNum As Integer = FreeFile()   ' Get a file number
   FileOpen(fileNum, "sqrt.txt", OpenMode.Output)

   Dim s As Single
   Dim outLine As String

   Dim index As Integer
   For index = 1 To 32000
      s = Math.Sqrt(index)
      outLine = index.ToString() & " - Sqrt = " _
              & s.ToString()
      Print(fileNum, outLine)  ' Write to the file

      ' Update the progress bar  (% completion)
      prgFor.Value = (index / 32000) * 100
   Next
```

```
    FileClose(fileNum)

End Sub

Private Sub btnReset_Click(ByVal sender As Object, _
 ByVal e As System.EventArgs) Handles btnReset.Click

    prgFor.Value = 0

End Sub
```

ScrollBar

The **ScrollBar** base class represents a scrollable control that is used to input numeric data within a range. The **HScrollBar** control is displayed horizontally, and the **VScrollBar** control is displayed vertically. Useful properties of this control include **Minimum**, **Maximum**, and **Value** that were previously mentioned, as well as these additional properties:

- **LargeChange** is the increment or decrement to the value when the user clicks to either side of the scroll bar.
- **SmallChange** is the increment or decrement to the value when the user moves the scroll box a small distance.

Events generated by the **ScrollBar** control include the following:

- **Scroll** indicates that the scroll bar was moved via mouse or keyboard activity.
- **ValueChanged** indicates whether the value was changed either through mouse or keyboard activity, or by programmatically changing the **Value** property.

The following program, found in **SimpleProgress\Version 2,** uses a horizontal scroll bar to set the number of square root values written to a file (see Figure 8–14). The scroll bar, named **hsbRange**, was configured with the following properties described in Table 8–5.

TABLE 8–5	Property Values for the Horizontal ScrollBar
Property	**Value**
LargeChange	1000
Minimum	16000
Maximum	64000
SmallChange	100
Value	32000

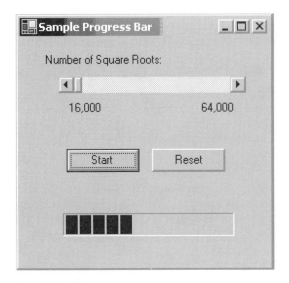

Figure 8-14 *Using the ScrollBar control.*

The only change to the code for the program from Version 1 to Version 2 is to use the current value of the scroll bar as the upper limit for the loop test.

```
Private Sub btnStart_Click(ByVal sender As System.Object, _
 ByVal e As System.EventArgs) Handles btnStart.Click

    Dim fileNum As Integer = FreeFile()
    FileOpen(fileNum, "sqrt.txt", OpenMode.Output)

    Dim s As Single
    Dim outLine As String
    Dim limits As Integer = hsbRange.Value

    Dim index As Integer
    For index = 1 To limits
        s = Math.Sqrt(index)
        outLine = index.ToString() & " - Sqrt = " _
                & s.ToString()
        Print(fileNum, outLine)

        prgFor.Value = (index / limits) * 100
    Next

    FileClose(fileNum)
End Sub
```

TrackBar

The **TrackBar** control is similar to the **ScrollBar** control. It is used to input numeric data within a range and may be displayed vertically or horizontally. In addition to **SmallChange** and **LargeChange** previously discussed, the **TrackBar** control has the following properties:

- **Orientation** indicates whether the control is displayed horizontally or vertically.
- **TickFrequency** indicates the frequency of ticks.
- **TickStyle** indicates whether tick marks are displayed on the bottom or top of the control.

The following program, found in **SimpleProgress\Version 3,** uses a **TrackBar** named **trkRange** to set the number of square root values written to a file (see Figure 8–15). Table 8–6 details its property values.

TABLE 8–6	*Property Values for the TrackBar*
Property	**Value**
LargeChange	1000
Minimum	16000
Maximum	64000
Orientation	Horizontal
SmallChange	100
TickFrequency	4000
TickStyle	Bottom Right
Value	32000

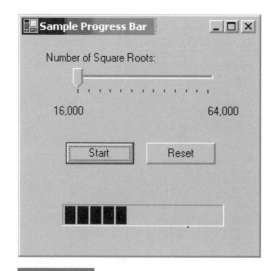

FIGURE 8–15   *Using the TrackBar control.*

Again, this version of the program uses the current value of the track bar as the upper limit for the loop test.

```
Private Sub btnStart_Click(ByVal sender As System.Object, _
 ByVal e As System.EventArgs) Handles btnStart.Click

    Dim fileNum As Integer = FreeFile()
    FileOpen(fileNum, "sqrt.txt", OpenMode.Output)

    Dim s As Single
    Dim outLine As String
    Dim limits As Integer = trkRange.Value

    Dim index As Integer
    For index = 1 To limits
       s = Math.Sqrt(index)
       outLine = index.ToString() & " - Sqrt = " _
                & s.ToString()
       Print(fileNum, outLine)

       prgFor.Value = (index / limits) * 100
    Next

    FileClose(fileNum)
End Sub
```

NumericUpDown

The **NumericUpDown** control is a scrollable control that allows a user to select a value by clicking the up and down buttons of the control. The user can also enter text in the control, unless the **ReadOnly** property is set to **True**. Properties of this control include:

- **Increment** indicates the amount by which the value is changed when scrolling through the range.
- **DecimalPlaces** indicates the number of decimal points shown.
- **ThousandsSeparator** indicates whether a thousands separator is used.
- **Hexadecimal** indicates whether the value is shown in hexadecimal.

The following program, found in **SimpleProgress\Version 4,** uses a **NumericUpDown** control named **nudRange** to set the number of square root values written to a file (see Figure 8–16). Table 8–7 details its property values.

TABLE 8–7	*Property Values for the Numeric Up/Down Control in Simple Progress (Version 4)*

Property	Value
DecimalPlaces	0
Hexadecimal	False
Increment	2000
Minimum	16000
Maximum	64000
ReadOnly	True
ThousandsSeparator	True
Value	32000

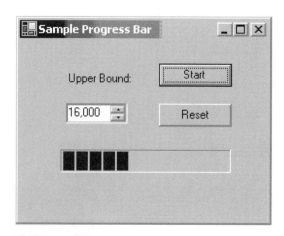

FIGURE 8–16	*Using the NumericUpDown control.*

The only change to the code for the program was to use the current value of the **NumericUpDown** control as the upper limit for the loop test.

```
Private Sub btnStart_Click(ByVal sender As System.Object, _
  ByVal e As System.EventArgs) Handles btnStart.Click

    Dim fileNum As Integer = FreeFile()
    FileOpen(fileNum, "sqrt.txt", OpenMode.Output)

    Dim s As Single
    Dim outLine As String
    Dim limits As Integer = nudRange.Value

    Dim index As Integer
    For index = 1 To limits
```

```
        s = Math.Sqrt(index)
        outLine = index.ToString() & " - Sqrt = " _
                & s.ToString()
        Print(fileNum, outLine)

        prgFor.Value = (index / limits) * 100
    Next

    FileClose(fileNum)
End Sub
```

List Controls

Several controls in VB.NET can be used to manage lists of information. These controls include the **ListBox**, **ComboBox**, **DomainUpDown**, **CheckedList-Box**, and **ListView**. These controls display lists and allow the user to select items from the lists.

Each list control shares the concept of an **Items** property that represents the collection of items in the control's list. This property is a *collection* that has its own properties (for example, **Count**) and methods (for example, **Add**, **AddRange**, **Clear**, **Remove**, and **RemoveAt**).

Domain UpDown

The **DomainUpDown** control is a scrollable control that displays a string value from a list. The user can also enter text in the control if the **ReadOnly** property is set to **False**, but the text entered must match an item in the collection. Interesting properties of the **DomainUpDown** include the following:

- **SelectedIndex** indicates the index of the item in the list that is selected. If nothing is selected, the value is -1.
- **Text** represents the text that is displayed in the control next to the up/down buttons.

USING THE DOMAINUPDOWN

Code Example

The following program, found in **Contacts**, uses a **DomainUpDown** control to select a value for data entry from a finite set of possibilities. See Figure 8–17.

The form contains two labels, one textbox, one **DomainUpDown** control, one listbox, and one button. Properties for this form are highlighted in Table 8–8.

FIGURE 8–17   *Using the DomainUpDown control.*

TABLE 8–8   *Property Values for the Contacts Form*

Control Type	Name	Text
Label	lblName	Name:
Textbox	txtName	(blank)
Label	lblAssociation	Association:
DomainUpDown	domAssociation	(blank)
Button	btnAdd	Add
ListBox	lstContacts	(blank)
Form	ContactsForm	Contacts

Code to initialize the **DomainUpDown** control has been placed in the form's **Load** event handler. The **AddRange** method is used to add an array containing a set of values to the control's list. The **Add** method could have been used to add the values one at a time.

```
Private Sub ContactsForm_Load(ByVal sender As _
    System.Object, ByVal e As System.EventArgs) _
    Handles MyBase.Load
```

```
Dim assocTypes() As String = _
    {"Colleague", "Friend", "Family", "Doctor", _
    "Dentist"}
domAssociation.Items.AddRange(assocTypes)

End Sub
```

The **Click** event handler for the Add button references the **Text** property of the **DomainUpDown** control to retrieve the selected value.

```
Private Sub btnAdd_Click(ByVal sender As System.Object, _
 ByVal e As System.EventArgs) Handles btnAdd.Click

    Dim s As String
    s = txtName.Text & " (" & domAssociation.Text & ")"
    lstContacts.Items.Add(s)

    txtName.Text = ""
    domAssociation.Text = ""

End Sub
```

CheckedListBox

The **CheckedListBox** control lists items that are selected by checking the check box next to the item(s) desired. It has the four properties that represent the checked item(s) in the control:

- **CheckedItems** represents the items checked in the control.
- **CheckedIndices** represents the indices of the items checked in the control.

The **CheckedListBox** also has other interesting properties, including:

- **CheckOnClick** indicates whether the check box is toggled when the item is selected.
- **Sorted** indicates whether items in the control are sorted.
- **MultiColumn** indicates whether the control supports multiple columns.

Typically, items in the list are checked or unchecked via user action, but they may also be programmatically manipulated using **SetItemChecked**.

We will examine the behavior of the **CheckedListBox** control in the example **TravelChoices**. This program maintains a list of vacation destinations. It allows the user to select any number of vacation requirements from a list, and then uses that list to find suitable destinations. Only those destinations that match at least 50% of your criteria will be shown. See Figure 8–18.

Table 8–9 summarizes the important properties that were specified for this application.

Code
Example

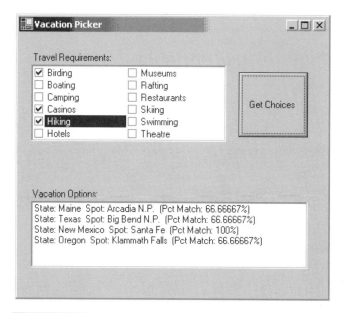

FIGURE 8–18   *Using the CheckedListBox control.*

TABLE 8–9   *Property Values for the TravelChoice Form*

Control Type	Name	Properties
Label	lblRequirements	Text: Vacation Requirements:
CheckedListBox	chkRequirements	CheckOnClick: True MultiColumn: True Sorted: True
Button	btnGetChoices	Text: Get Choices
Label	lblOptions	Text: Vacation Options:
ListBox	lstOptions	
Form	TravelChoicesForm	Text: Vacation Picker

This application required the development of a supporting class. **VacationSpot** manages a destination, the state that it is in, and a list of features available at that destination. It also features the method **GetMatchPercentage** that accepts a list of requirements and determines the percentage of those that are matched by features at the destination. Code for **VacationSpot** follows:

```
Public Class VacationSpot
    Public ReadOnly Description As String
    Public ReadOnly State As String
    Private m_features As New ArrayList()
```

```
Public Sub New(ByVal description As String, ByVal _
  state As String, ByVal ParamArray features() As String)
    Me.Description = description
    Me.State = state
    Dim s As String
    For Each s In features
        m_features.Add(s)
    Next
End Sub

Public Function GetMatchPercentage(ByVal _
  desiredfeatures As ArrayList) As Single
    Dim numMatches As Integer
    Dim o As Object
    ' Look for each feature
    For Each o In desiredFeatures
        If m_features.Contains(o) Then numMatches += 1
    Next
    If desiredfeatures.Count > 0 Then
        Return numMatches / desiredfeatures.Count
    Else
        Return 1
    End If
End Function
End Class
```

Step 1: Initializing the ArrayList

Before we begin coding the form, we must establish our list of vacation spots. We will use an **ArrayList** to hold an array of **VacationSpot** objects. We will initialize the array in the constructor,

```
Public Class TravelChoiceForm
    Inherits System.Windows.Forms.Form

    Dim choices As New ArrayList()

    Public Sub New()
        MyBase.New()
          InitializeComponent()

        choices.Add( _
          New VacationSpot("Arcadia N.P.", "Maine", _
            "Birding", "Hiking", "Camping", "Boating"))
        choices.Add( _
          New VacationSpot("Manhattan", "New York", _
            "Hotels", "Restaurants", "Theatre", "Museums"))
        ...
        choices.Add( _
          New VacationSpot("Big Bend N.P.", "Texas", _
            "Birding", "Hiking", "Camping"))
      End Sub
```

```
    ...
End Class
```

Step 2: Adding Items to the CheckedListBox Control

Items may be added to the **CheckedListBox** control (and almost any other list control) at design time or run time. To add them programmatically, you must use the **Add** or **AddRange** method of the **Items** collection.

```
chkRequirements.Items.Add("Camping")
...
Dim cityStyle As String() = _
    {"Hotels", "Restaurants", "Museums"}
chkRequirements.Items.AddRange(cityStyle)
```

In this application, we added the items at design time. To do this, we choose the **Items** property from the Property Window and launched the String Collection Editor in order to enter the strings that initialize the items in the list. Figure 8–19 shows the editor and the values for **Items** that we entered at design time.

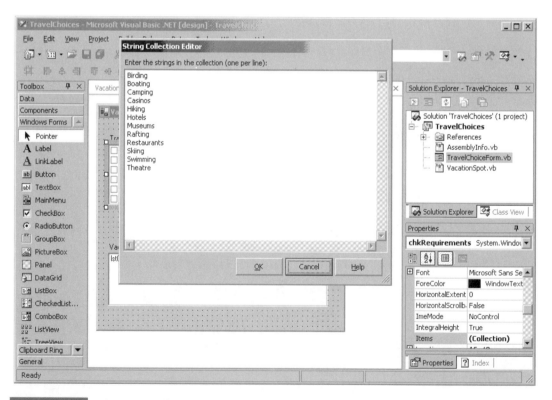

FIGURE 8–19   *The String Collection Editor.*

Step 3: Accessing Items in the Control

You can use the **Contains** method of either the **Items** or **CheckedItems** property to determine whether a specific string is found in the control:

```
If chkRequirements.CheckedItems.Contains("Camping") Then
    ' do something
End If
```

You can also access the individual elements in the **Items** collection by specifying the index of the desired item. To determine if the item is checked, you must call **GetItemChecked**.

```
For index = 0 To chkRequirements.Items.Count - 1
    If chkRequirements.GetItemChecked(i) Then
        MessageBox.Show( _
            chkRequirements.Items(index).ToString())
    End If
Next
```

You can access the individual elements in the **CheckedItems** collection by specifying the index of the desired item:

```
For index = 0 To chkRequirements.CheckedItems.Count - 1
    MessageBox.Show( _
        chkRequirements.CheckedItems(index).ToString())
Next
```

You can also access the individual elements selected by using the **CheckedIndices** collection:

```
Dim n As Integer
For index = 0 To chkRequirements.CheckedIndices.Count - 1
    n = chkRequirements.CheckedIndices(index)
    MessageBox.Show(chkRequirements.Items(n).ToString())
Next
```

In our **TravelChoices** example, maintain our list of vacation spots in the array **choices**. It is initialized in the form's **Load** event handler. The **Click** event handler for **btnGetChoices** builds an array containing the strings from the checked items and calls the **GetMatchPercentage** method in **Vacation-Spot**.

```
Public Class TravelChoiceForm
    Inherits System.Windows.Forms.Form

    ...

    Private Sub btnGetChoices_Click(ByVal sender As _
    System.Object, ByVal e As System.EventArgs) _
    Handles btnGetChoices.Click
```

```
lstOptions.Items.Clear()

Dim requirements As New ArrayList()
Dim i As Integer
For i = 0 To chkRequirements.CheckedItems.Count - 1
    requirements.Add( _
        chkRequirements.Items(i).ToString())
Next

Dim o As Object
For Each o In choices
    Dim oneOption As VacationSpot
    Dim pctmatch As Single
    oneOption = CType(o, VacationSpot)
    pctmatch = _
        oneOption.GetMatchPercentage(requirements)
    If pctmatch >= 0.5 Then
        Dim s As String
        s = "State: " & oneOption.State & "  Spot: " _
        & oneOption.Description & "  (Pct Match: " & _
        pctmatch * 100 & "%)"
        lstOptions.Items.Add(s)
    End If
Next

End Sub

End Class
```

ListView

The **ListView** control is a more flexible version of the **ListBox** control. It contains items, and optionally subitems, and can display its list in four different ways according to the style specified in the **View** property:

- **LargeIcons** specifies that the items appear as large icons with labels underneath them.
- **SmallIcons** specifies that the items appear as small icons with labels underneath them.
- **List** specifies that the items appear as small icons with a label to the right. Items are arranged in columns with no column headers.
- **Details** specifies that each item in the list appears on a separate line. Subitem information is arranged in columns and displayed beside the item. The user can resize each column at runtime.

The **ListView** control can be associated with one or more **ImageList** controls using the **LargeImageList** and **SmallImageList** properties to indicate the icons when icons they are displayed. Other properties include:

- **Sorting** indicates how items in the control are sorted.
- **MultiSelect** indicates whether the control supports multiple selection.
- **Columns** provides access to the collection of columns.
- **GridLines** indicates whether gridlines are drawn in the control.
- **FocusedItem** indicates the item with focus.
- **FullRowSelect** indicates whether clicking an item selects the item or the whole row.

Code Example

The following example, found in the project **HotelAdmin3**, uses a **ListView** control to display the list of hotels. See Figure 8–20.

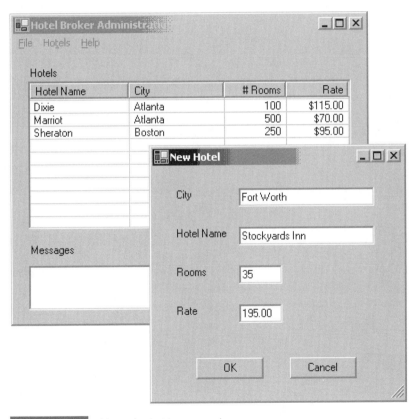

FIGURE 8–20   *Using the ListView control.*

Step 1: Adding the ListView Control

We began by replacing the listbox with a **ListView** control named **lvHotels**.
Then we set its **View** property to **Details**. Finally, we added columns to the
ListView control at design time by selecting the **Columns** property in the
Properties window. The ColumnHeader Collection Editor (see Figure 8–21)
provides an easy-to-use graphical way to add columns when they are known
at design time. (Note: It is easy to adjust the column width using the mouse
by dragging and resizing the columns after they are initially added.)

If the columns aren't known at design time, you can also programmatically add columns. You must specify the column heading, width (in pixels)
and text alignment using the **Columns.Add** method.

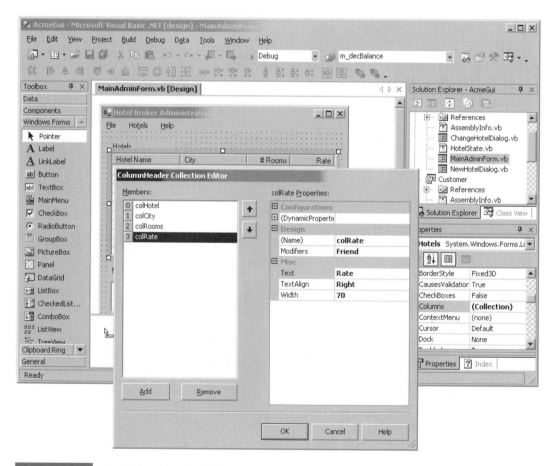

FIGURE 8–21   *The ColumnHeader Collection Editor.*

```
lvHotels.Columns.Add( _
   "Hotel", 60, HorizontalAlignment.Left)
...
lvHotels.Columns.Add( _
   "Rate", 60, HorizontalAlignment.Right)
```

Our example does not associate an image with the items in the **List-View**, so we leave the properties for **LargeImageList** and **SmallImageList** as "(none)".

Step 2: Adding Items to the Control

The items that are added to the **ListView** control are similar to items added to the **ListBox** control. They are shown when the **ListView** displays icons or a list. However, the **ListView** items may have *subitems*, which represent additional data displayed when the style indicates details are shown.

To add an item, you will use the **Items.Add** method, specifying the following:

- The item text
- Optionally, an index from the associated **ImageLists**
- Optionally, the subitems associated with the item

In **HotelAdmin3**, we replace the code that was used to populate the listbox with the following code:

```
Private Sub ShowHotelList(ByRef array As ArrayList)
   lvHotels.Items.Clear()
   If array Is Nothing Then
      Return
   End If

   Dim hotel As HotelListItem
   For Each hotel In array
      Dim li As New ListViewItem()
      Dim city As String = hotel.City.Trim()
      Dim name As String = hotel.HotelName.Trim()
      Dim rooms As String = hotel.NumberRooms.ToString()
      Dim rate As String = _
         String.Format("{0:c}", hotel.Rate)

      li.ImageIndex = -1     ' No icon image
      li.Text = name         ' The hotel name is the item
      li.SubItems.Add(city)  ' City, # rooms & rate are
      li.SubItems.Add(rooms) ' subitems
      li.SubItems.Add(rate)
      lvHotels.Items.Add(li)
   Next
End Sub
```

Step 3: Accessing the Selected Item

We used the **FocusedItem** property to determine which hotel is selected for use with editing and deleting hotels. We have replaced the member variable **currHotel** that existed in **HotelAdmin2** with the function **GetHotelSelection** that can be called anytime the currently selected hotel must be known.

```
Private Function GetHotelSelection() As HotelListItem

    Dim currHotel As New HotelListItem()
    currHotel.HotelName = ""
    currHotel.City = ""
    currHotel.NumberRooms = 0
    currHotel.Rate = 0

    Dim li As ListViewItem
    li = lvHotels.FocusedItem()
    If Not (li Is Nothing) Then
        currHotel.HotelName = li.Text()
        currHotel.City = li.SubItems(1).Text
        currHotel.NumberRooms = _
            Convert.ToInt32(li.SubItems(2).Text)
        Dim s As String = li.SubItems(3).Text
        currHotel.Rate = _
            Convert.ToDecimal(s.Substring(1, s.Length() - 1))
    End If
    Return currHotel

End Function

Private Sub mnuEdit_Click(ByVal sender As Object, ByVal _
  e As System.EventArgs) Handles mnuEdit.Click

    Dim currHotel As HotelListItem = GetHotelSelection()
    ...

End Sub

Private Sub mnuDelete_Click(ByVal sender As Object, ByVal _
  e As System.EventArgs) Handles mnuDelete.Click
    Dim currHotel As HotelListItem = GetHotelSelection()
    ...

    End Sub

Private Sub mnuContext_Popup(ByVal sender As Object, _
  ByVal e As System.EventArgs) Handles mnuContext.Popup
    Dim currHotel As HotelListItem = GetHotelSelection()
    ...
```

```
End Sub

Private Sub mnuHotels_Popup(ByVal sender As Object, ByVal _
  e As System.EventArgs) Handles mnuHotels.Popup
    Dim currHotel As HotelListItem = GetHotelSelection()
    ...

End Sub
```

At this point, **HotelAdmin3** is functional and is quite a bit more elegant than our original solution.

DataGrid Control

The **DataGrid** control is a data-bound control that automatically displays a list of information in a series of rows and columns, as in a spreadsheet. A data-bound control is self-populating; that is, it fills itself with data when told the source of the data.

A **DataGrid** control must be bound to a data source using the **Data-Source** and **DataMember** properties at design time or the **SetDataBinding** method at run time. Typically, a **DataGrid** control is bound to a **DataTable**, **DataView** or **DataSet** class (discussed in Chapter 13). However, you can also bind a **DataGrid** control to any class that implements the **IList** interface.

The **ArrayList** class, which we discussed in Chapter 6, implements the **IList** interface. In the **GridDemo** example, we will build an array of **Item** objects. These are the elements that will be displayed in our data grid. Our **Item** class, which represents a barcoded object in a store, is shown below:

```
Public Class Item
    Private m_barCode As String
    Private m_description As String
    Private m_price As Decimal

    Public Sub New()
    End Sub

    Public Sub New(ByVal barCode As String, _
     ByVal description As String, _
     ByVal price As Decimal)
        m_barCode = barCode
        m_description = description
        m_price = price
    End Sub

    Public Property BarCode() As String
        ' code not shown
    End Property
```

```
Public Property Description() As String
   ' code not shown
End Property

Public Property Price() As Decimal
   ' code not shown
End Property

Public Overrides Function ToString() As String
   Dim s As String
   s = String.Format( _
      "{0} (Barcode: {1}) priced at {2:c2}", _
      m_description, m barCode, m_price)
   Return s
End Function
End Class
```

When a **DataGrid** control is bound to a **Dataset** or **DataTable**, the columns of the underlying table are displayed in the grid. When the grid is bound to an object that implements the **IList** interface, the public properties of the elements in the underlying structure or class will be displayed. For example, in **GridDemo** the grid will display all the public properties of the **Item** objects.

Figure 8–22 illustrates the **GridDemo** application.

To achieve the effects shown in Figure 8–22, the **DataGrid** control was placed on the form and named **dgItems**. The form class then created an **ArrayList** containing Item objects. Finally, the **DataSource** property of the **DataGrid** was set to the **ArrayList**.

```
Public Class MainForm
   Inherits System.Windows.Forms.Form

   Public itemList As New ArrayList()

   Public Sub New()
      ...

      itemList.Add(New Item( _
               "1010101", "Grape Jelly", 2.49))
      itemList.Add(New Item( _
               "2010102", "Peanut Butter", 3.89))
      itemList.Add(New Item( _
               "3030303", "White Bread", 1.49))

      dgItems.DataSource = itemList
      dgItems.ColumnHeadersVisible = True
   End Sub


   ...
End Class
```

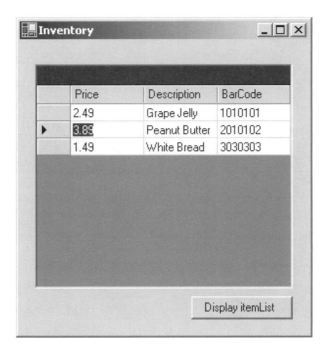

FIGURE 8–22 *Using the DataGrid control.*

Any changes made to the data in the data grid are immediately reflected back in the underlying objects found in the **ArrayList**. To illustrate this, we changed the price of peanut butter and then pressed the "Display itemList" button. Code in the **Click** event handler for this button is shown below:

```
Private Sub btnDisplay_Click(ByVal sender As _
 System.Object, ByVal e As System.EventArgs) _
 Handles btnDisplay.Click

  Dim s As String
  Dim it As Item
  For Each it In itemList
     s = s & it.ToString() & _
        Microsoft.VisualBasic.ControlChars.CrLf
  Next
  MessageBox.Show(s, "Current Items", _
     MessageBoxButtons.OK, MessageBoxIcon.Information)

End Sub
```

The result of pressing this button is shown in Figure 8–23. You can see that the data in the underlying **ArrayList** has been modified.

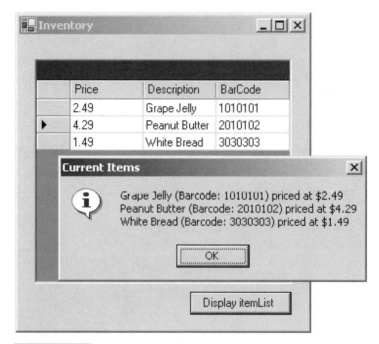

FIGURE 8–23   *Changes to data in the DataGrid are reflected in the underlying ArrayList.*

TreeView Control

The **TreeView** control displays a list of information in a hierarchical manner. Rather than use an **Items** collection like all other list-based controls, the **TreeView** uses a **Nodes** collection to manage the data in the tree. Each item in the tree is a **TreeNode**. Each **TreeNode** can, in turn, consist of a collection of other **TreeNodes**.

The **TreeView** class has properties such as **ShowLines, ShowLinesAtRoot**, and **ShowPlusMinus** that control its appearance. The control may also be associated with an image list in order to display icons. Other interesting properties and methods include:

- **SelectedNode** indicates which node is currently selected.
- **Sorted** indicates whether the nodes are sorted.
- **FullRowSelect** indicates whether the selection highlighted is as wide as the tree control.
- **GetNodeCount** returns the number of nodes in the tree.
- **GetNodeAt** retrieves a node at a specified (x, y) coordinate.

Interacting with TreeNodes

Because the **TreeView** control displays nodes in a hierarchical manner, you must indicate the parent node when adding any other node. To add a root node and obtain a reference to it, you must use the **Add** method of the **Nodes** collection:

```
Dim root As TreeNode
root = someTree.Nodes.Add("Leslye & Randy")
```

To add child nodes to the root node above, you could write this:

```
root.Add(New TreeNode("Mollye")
root.Add(New TreeNode("Ranse")
```

To add a node as a child of the currently selected node, you must write this:

```
someTree.SelectedNode.Nodes.Add(New TreeNode("Freddy"))
```

To remove the currently selected node, you must use the **Remove** method and pass it a reference to the node to remove. In the following example, we remove the current selection from the **TreeView:**

```
someTree.Nodes.Remove(someTree.SelectedNode)
```

In addition, all nodes in the **TreeView** control can be removed using the **Clear** method:

```
someTree.Nodes.Clear()
```

Iteration becomes a bit tricky. The easiest way to iterate through each node in a **TreeView** is to use a recursive procedure. To begin with, you would examine each node at the root level.

```
Dim node As TreeNode
For Each node In someTree.Nodes
    ExamineNode(node)
Next
```

Each node, however, can itself have child nodes. So you must examine each child node in that node. This recursive process continues until the node being examined has no child nodes of its own.

```
Sub ExamineNode(ByVal node As TreeNode)
   ' Process node
   ...

   ' Examine child nodes
   Dim childNode As TreeNode
   For Each childNode In node.Nodes
      ExamineNode (childNode)
   Next
End Sub
```

Example: Using the TreeView Control

This section uses the **TreeView** application to illustrate the use of the **TreeView** control. The program displays a list of departments and employees in a tree. A context menu allows employees to be added or removed from the departments. See Figure 8–24.

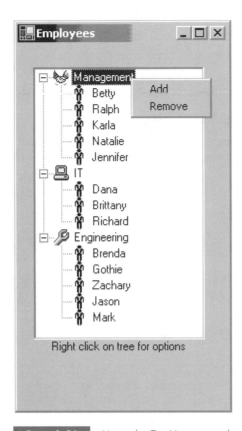

FIGURE 8–24   *Using the TreeView control.*

To completely understand the following code, you must know that we performed the following setup steps:

- Added a **TreeView** control to the form named **trePeople**.
- Added an **ImageList** to the control named **imgDepts**.
- Added four images to the image list (one for each of the three departments we will add and one to represent employees).
- Set the **ImageList** property of **trePeople** to **imgDepts**.
- Added a **ContextMenu** control to the form named **mnuContext**.

Step 1: Initializing the Control

We must define three variables to manage the three root nodes (**mgmtRoot** for the management, **ITRoot** for the IT department and **engRoot** for the Engineering department). We must also define a variable that represents the node under the context menu.

In the form's load event, we will build the context menu with Add and Remove options. We will also use the three root **TreeNode** variables to create the three departments. The **TreeNode** constructor requires three parameters that represent the 1) text in the node, 2) the image index from the **ImageList** associated with the entry, and 3) the image index from the **ImageList** used when the entry is selected. Finally, we will add two employees to the tree.

```
Public Class TreeViewForm
    Inherits System.Windows.Forms.Form

    Dim mgmtRoot, ITRoot, engRoot As TreeNode
    Dim contextMenuNode As TreeNode

    ...

    Private Sub TreeViewForm_Load(ByVal sender _
      As System.Object, ByVal e As System.EventArgs) _
      Handles MyBase.Load

        ' Define the context menu
        mnuContext.MenuItems.Add("Add", AddressOf AddOne)
        mnuContext.MenuItems.Add("Remove", _
           AddressOf RemoveOne)

        ' Add the three departments
        Dim n As Integer
        n = trePeople.Nodes.Add( _
           New TreeNode("Management", 2, 2))
        mgmtRoot = trePeople.Nodes(n)

        n = trePeople.Nodes.Add(New TreeNode("IT", 1, 1))
        ITRoot = trePeople.Nodes(n)

        n = trePeople.Nodes.Add( _
           New TreeNode("Engineering", 0, 0))
        engRoot = trePeople.Nodes(n)

        ' Add the two employees
        ITRoot.Nodes.Add(New TreeNode("Dana"))
        EngRoot.Nodes.Add(New TreeNode("Brenda"))
    End Sub

    ...

End Class
```

Step 2: Handling the Context Menu

To determine whether the context menu should be displayed when the user right-clicks on the tree, we must determine where the right-click occurred. If it occurred on a node, we can display the context menu. Otherwise, no context menu is displayed. In the **MouseDown** event handler for the tree control, we will use the **GetNodeAt** method to determine the node that the user right-clicked on. The node is saved in the variable **contextMenuNode**.

```
Private Sub trePeople_MouseDown(ByVal sender As Object, _
 ByVal e As System.Windows.Forms.MouseEventArgs) _
 Handles trePeople.MouseDown

  ' If the right button is down
  If e.Button = MouseButtons.Right Then

    ' Find the item that was clicked on
    contextMenuNode = trePeople.GetNodeAt(e.X, e.Y)

    ' If found, display the context menu
    If Not IsNothing(contextMenuNode) Then
      mnuContext.Show(trePeople, e.X, e.Y)
    End If
  End If

End Sub
```

Step 3: Adding a Node

If the user selects Add from the context menu, we will collect a new employee name using the **InputBox** function. The **InputBox** function is a part of VB.NET and collects one textual piece of data from the user (see Figure 8–25). If the user clicks Cancel when interacting with the **InputBox**, a zero-length string is returned.

We must then determine the department of the node that is selected. (Note: the user may have right-clicked on a person or a department!) We can determine if the selected node is a department by referencing the node's **Parent**.

```
Private Sub AddOne(ByVal sender As System.Object, _
 ByVal e As System.EventArgs)

  Dim parent As TreeNode = contextMenuNode.Parent()

  ' Prompt for a name using the InputBox function (it is
  ' a simple dialog similar to the MessageBox dialog)
  Dim name As String
  name = InputBox("Enter new name:", "Name", "")

  If name = "" Then Return
```

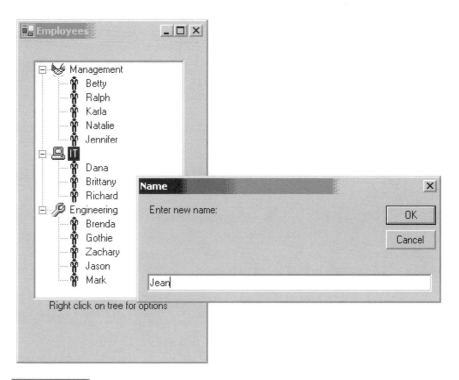

FIGURE 8–25   *Using the TreeView control.*

```
      ' If the user clicked on a person, add under department
      If Not IsNothing(parent) Then
         parent.Nodes.Add(New TreeNode(name))
      Else    ' ... clicked on a department, add here
         contextMenuNode.Nodes.Add(New TreeNode(name))
      End If

End Sub
```

Step 4: Removing a Node

If the user selects Remove from the context menu, we must determine whether the node they selected was a department or an employee. If it was an employee, we can use the **Remove** method to remove the **TreeNode** representing the employee.

```
Private Sub RemoveOne(ByVal sender As System.Object, _
 ByVal e As System.EventArgs)

   Dim parent As TreeNode = contextMenuNode.Parent()
```

```
' If the user clicked on a person, remove them
If Not IsNothing(parent) Then
   trePeople.Nodes.Remove(contextMenuNode)
Else ' ... clicked on a department, display error
   MessageBox.Show("Cannot delete entire department!")
End If

End Sub
```

Common Dialog Controls

VB.NET supports the Windows Common Dialogs. These dialogs are part of the Windows operating systems and are available for all applications to use. In VB.NET, they are provided as controls and include the following:

- OpenFileDialog
- SaveFileDialog
- ColorDialog
- FontDialog
- PrintDialog
- PrintPreviewDialog
- PageSetupDialog

These dialogs provide part of the consistency that you find in the look and feel of all Windows applications.

Each of these controls has different properties that can be used to interact with the data they collect. For example, the **ColorDialog** has a **Color** property to access the color the user selected and the **FontDialog** has a **Font** property to access the font the user selected. In addition, the **ShowDialog** method, which returns a **DialogResult**, is used to display each dialog.

USING THE COMMON DIALOG CONTROLS

Code
Example

To use any of the common dialog controls, you must place them on your form. However, they are invisible controls and are drawn in a separate area of the form by the Windows Form Designer. The program **CommonDialogEx- ample** is shown in Figure 8–26.

It uses the color and font dialogs to allow the user to change characteristics about the "sample text" label. The code that supports these features is found in the **Click** event handlers for the two buttons:

```
Private Sub btnFont_Click(ByVal sender As System.Object, _
 ByVal e As System.EventArgs) Handles btnFont.Click

   Dim answer As DialogResult
   answer = dlgFont.ShowDialog
```

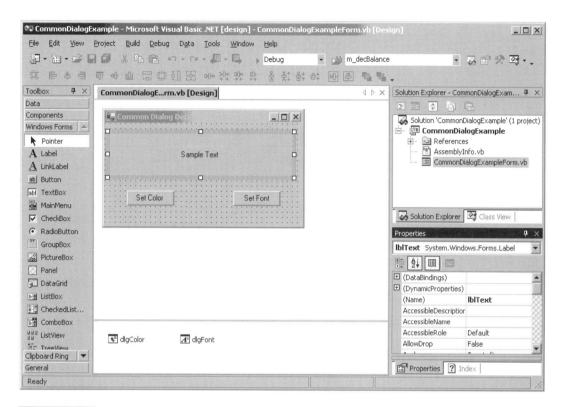

Using the Common Dialogs.

```
    If answer = DialogResult.OK Then
        lblText.Font = dlgFont.Font
    End If

End Sub

Private Sub btnColor_Click(ByVal sender As System.Object, _
    ByVal e As System.EventArgs) Handles btnColor.Click

    Dim answer As DialogResult
    answer = dlgColor.ShowDialog()
    If answer = DialogResult.OK Then
        lblText.BackColor = dlgColor.Color
    End If

End Sub
```

As you can see from Figure 8–27, the Set Font button displays the **Font-Dialog**. It displays the fonts available on the machine using a familiar dialog. When the dialog's OK button is clicked, the label's **Font** property is set to the font that was selected in the dialog.

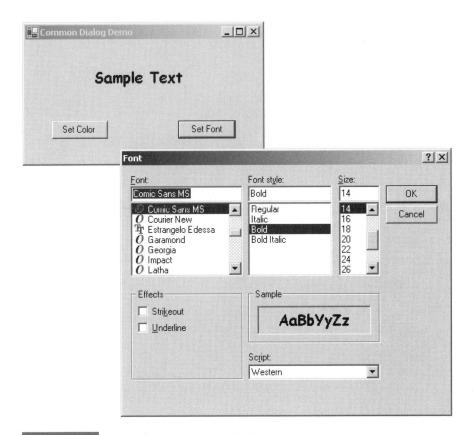

FIGURE 8–27 *Using the Common Font Dialog.*

Figure 8–28 illustrates the **ColorDialog** that is displayed when the Set Color button is clicked. It displays the color palette using another familiar dialog. When the dialog's OK button is clicked, the label's **BackColor** property is set to the color that was selected in the dialog.

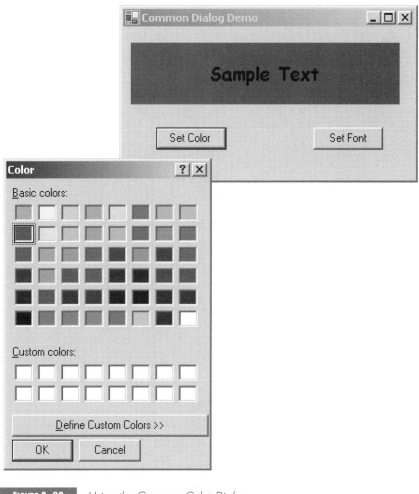

FIGURE 8–28   *Using the Common Color Dialog.*

Summary

In this chapter, we examined a variety of controls that can be used to build interesting, usable graphical user interfaces. Event handlers can be designed to trap interaction with these controls. In VB.NET, menus are built using either the **MainMenu** control or the **ContextMenu** control. Toolbars are built using both an **ImageList** control and the **Toolbar** control. And status bars are built using the **StatusBar** control. We examined a variety of calendar controls, range controls, and list controls that allow the user to interact with predefined sets of data, thus reducing the amount of validation code the programmer must write. Finally, we concluded with an examination of the common dialog controls that allow us to use the Windows dialogs (such as font, color, and printer selection) that are familiar to all Windows users.

FUNDAMENTALS OF THE .NET FRAMEWORK

FUNDAMENTALS OF THE
.NET FRAMEWORK

Part 4, consisting of Chapters 9 and 10, introduces important fundamental topics in the .NET Framework. Chapter 9 discusses assemblies and deployment, which constitute a major advance in the simplicity and robustness of deploying Windows applications, ending the notorious situation known as "DLL hell." Chapter 10 introduces important .NET Framework classes and covers the topics of metadata, serialization, threading, attributes, asynchronous programming, remoting, and memory management.

Assemblies and Deployment

*D*eployment makes the programmer's hard work available to the customer. .NET assemblies make deployment much simpler and much more reliable than traditional Windows deployment. Private assembly deployment is as simple as copying the component assembly into the same directory as the client program. Alternatively, shared assembly deployment places the component with a unique name (known as a strong name) in the Global Assembly Cache (GAC), making it available for general use.

This chapter begins with a discussion of components and how to work with them in .NET. We then cover assemblies, which are the fundamental unit of deployment in .NET. Private assembly deployment and shared assembly deployment are described next. Versioning and digital signing of assemblies are discussed in the context of shared deployment. Finally, the Visual Studio .NET deployment and setup wizards are introduced. Throughout our discussion we illustrate a number of useful tools that are part of the .NET Framework SDK.

Components

The term *component* is widely used in discussions about software, although there is no consensus about exactly what the term means. The basic concept of component is a black box piece of software that can be reused. By this loose definition, a DLL would be a component. Usually, somewhat more is meant, such as some kind of "object orientation." Examples of such object-oriented components are COM objects, JavaBeans, and CORBA objects.

It would be useful to compare objects from an object-oriented programming language with COM components. An object encapsulates data and behavior, and it facilitates reuse—*at the source code level.* If you are working entirely in one programming language, such as C++ or Java, you can gain great benefit by using a class library that provides reusable code in the form of a hierarchy of classes. An example of such a class library in C++ is Microsoft Foundation Classes (MFC). But you cannot use MFC classes in a Visual Basic program. By contrast, a COM component is a *binary* piece of software that can be reused in many different programming languages. For example, you can use COM components and ActiveX controls (a particularly rich type of COM component, typically with a graphical user interface) in Visual Basic programs. The component could be implemented in some other language, such as C++. The Visual Basic programmer does not care.

A limitation of COM components is lack of support for implementation inheritance. You cannot start with a base component and inherit its methods. (You can achieve similar reuse by other techniques, such as containment and aggregation, but such reuse is not as easy or convenient as inheritance.) Another drawback of COM components is the requirement that the component implement "plumbing" code that allows it to be called in a black box fashion from another piece of software. Visual Basic 6 hid the plumbing code, but it was there, and VB6 programs could only use a subset of the capabilities of COM. In C++ you could fully utilize COM, but there was a lot of work to be done in implementing the plumbing code. Specialized libraries like the Active Template Library (ATL) could do a lot of the work for you, but that required you to learn yet another piece of technology, and it applied only to C++.

Components in .NET

The .NET Framework provides an exceptionally attractive environment for creating and using software components. By simply setting an appropriate compiler switch or choosing a specific project type in Visual Studio, you can build a *class library,* which is the .NET version of a component and is a DLL that packages the code for a set of classes. There is no special plumbing code that must be provided. These class library DLLs can easily be used by other .NET programs, and you can mix .NET languages freely. Also, you can inherit from a class implemented in a class library, and this inheritance mechanism extends across languages, since a class library is a binary component.

CLASS LIBRARIES AT THE COMMAND LINE

To create a .NET class library from the command line, you must compile using the switch **/target:library**. You can abbreviate the **/target** switch as simply **/t**. The following command compiles the file **Customer.vb** as a class library, creating the file **Customer.dll**.

```
vbc /t:library Customer.vb
```

To use the class library from another program, you must obtain a *reference* to the class library. Compiling at the command line, you can use the **/reference** or **/r** switch. The following command compiles the test program **TestCustomer.vb** using the class library **Customer.dll**. It creates the executable **TestCustomer.exe**.

```
vbc /r:Customer.dll TestCustomer.vb
```

If you would like to try out building and using a class library at the command line, go to the directory **CustomerCL**. This directory contains both the files **Customer.vb** and the test program **TestCustomer.vb**. There is also a batch file **build.bat** that builds the class library and the console application that exercises it. The application **TestCustomer.exe** has the following output:

```
    1  Rocket        Squirrel      rocky@frosbitefalls.com
    2  Bullwinkle    Moose         moose@wossamotta.edu
New customer Christopher Robin id = 3
    1  Rocket        Squirrel      rocky@frosbitefalls.com
    2  Bullwinkle    Moose         moose@wossamotta.edu
    3  Christopher   Robin         chris@pooh.com
```

Class Libraries Using Visual Studio

Visual Studio makes it very easy to work with .NET class libraries. You can create a class library by using the Class Library project type. You can use Solution Explorer to add references. It is all quite painless. There is one nuance involved when using Visual Studio that you need to be aware of. Visual Studio by default creates a root namespace based on the name of the project. You must include this root namespace in your Imports statements. It is sometimes simpler to make this default namespace blank, which you can do in the Properties for the project.

In this section we illustrate the complete process of creating a class library in one project and creating a client application that uses the class library in another project. This exercise will not involve creating any new code. We provide all the code needed in a monolithic application. Rather, you will work on creating a component version of the application, consisting of a class library and a Windows application.

A MONOLITHIC APPLICATION

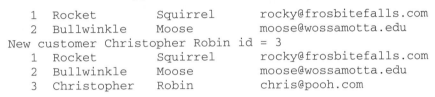

The folder **ConsoleMonolithic** contains a solution with both the **Customers** class and a GUI test program for exercising it. Figure 9–1 shows the main window of the application. The currently registered customers are shown in a list box, and buttons are provided to register a customer, unregister a customer, and change the email address. (For convenience, the **Customers** class provides two preregistered customers.) A customer is selected by clicking in the list box, and this ID can then be used for unregistering or changing an email address.

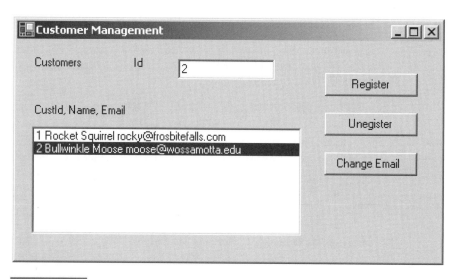

FIGURE 9–1   *Main window of program for exercising Customers class.*

CREATING A CLASS LIBRARY

Our first task will be to use Visual Studio to create a class library containing the **Customers** class. If you would like to follow along on the computer, you can do your work in the **Demos** directory for this chapter. The final project is available in the folder **CustomerLib**.

1. Bring up the New Project dialog from the menu File | New | Project. For Project Types choose Visual Basic Projects, and for Templates choose Class Library. Navigate to the desired Location, and type **CustomerLib** for the Name. See Figure 9–2. Click OK.
2. Delete **Class1.vb** from the new solution.
3. Copy the file **Customer.vb** from the **CustomerMonolithic** folder to the folder for this new solution, and add this file to the solution.
4. Bring up the Properties for the **CustomerLib** project (right-click in Solution Explorer and choose Properties from the context menu). Change the Assembly name to Customer, and the Root namespace to blank. See Figure 9–3. Click OK.
5. You should now be able to build the class library. The new DLL **Customer.dll** will be in the **bin** subdirectory.

If you would like to perform an immediate test of your new DLL, you could copy the test program **TestCustomer.exe** from **CustomerCL** into the **bin** folder. You should now be able to run the test program from the command line, and it will be using the new DLL that you just created.

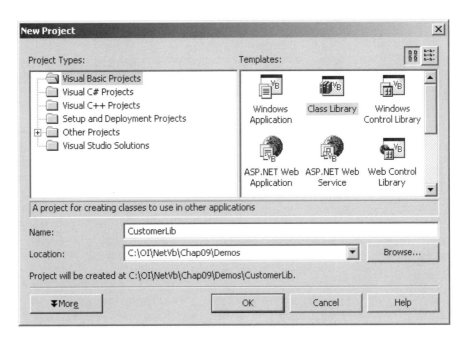

FIGURE 9-2 *Creating a new Class Library project using Visual Studio.*

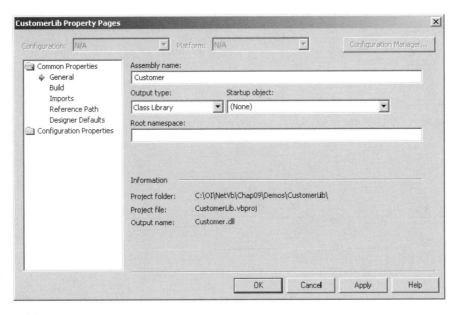

FIGURE 9-3 *Changing the assembly name and root namespace.*

WORKING WITH REFERENCES IN VISUAL STUDIO

Next we would like to use Visual Studio to create a Windows application that obtains a reference to our **Customer.dll**. Again, if you would like to follow along on the computer, you can do your work in the **Demos** directory for this project. The final project is available in the folder **CustomerGui**.

1. Bring up the New Project dialog from the menu File | New | Project. This time, create a Windows application with name **CustomerGui**.
2. Delete the file **Form1.vb** from the new solution.
3. Copy the files **CustomerForm.vb**, **RegisterDialog.vb**, and **EmailDialog.vb** from the **CustomerMonolithic** folder. Add these files to the new solution.
4. Copy the file **Customer.dll** from the **CustomerLib\bin** folder into the source file folder of the **CustomerGui** solution.
5. In Solution Explorer, right-click over References and choose Add Reference from the context menu, bringing up the Add References dialog. Click the Browse button, bringing up the Select Component dialog. If necessary, you can then navigate to find the component you want to add. In this case, because of our previous copying of the **Customer.dll**, you should find the DLL immediately. Double-click on it. You should then see the DLL in the Selected Components list box, as illustrated in Figure 9–4. Click OK.

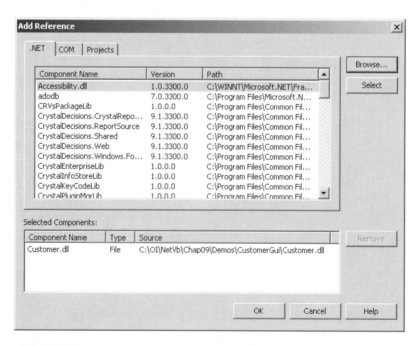

FIGURE 9–4   *Adding a reference using Visual Studio.*

6. You can now try building the application. You will get an error message, stemming from having previously deleted **Form1.vb**.

```
'Sub Main' was not found in 'CustomerGui.Form1'
```

7. You will need to make **CustomerForm** your Startup object. You can do this by right-clicking on **CustomerGui** in Solution Explorer to bring up the properties for the project. You can then choose the Startup object form the dropdown list, as illustrated in Figure 9–5. Click OK.

8. You should now be able to build and run the Windows application. It should behave identically to the monolithic application we looked at earlier.

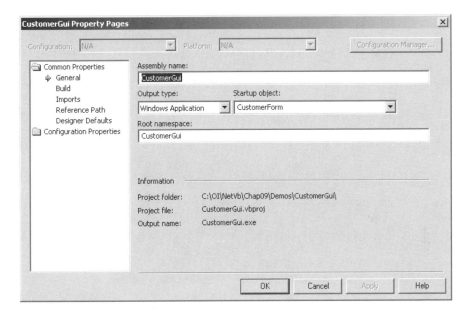

FIGURE 9–5   *Specifying the Startup object.*

REFERENCES AT COMPILE TIME AND RUN TIME

The assembly **Customer.dll** is used both at compile time and at runtime. At compile time the metadata in the assembly is used, and at runtime the code is called. When you add a reference to a DLL using Solution Explorer, Visual Studio will copy the DLL into the **bin** folder, so it will reside in the proper place at runtime. In this case we are using "private" deployment in which all assemblies reside in the same directory. With .NET it is also possible to have "shared" deployment, using the Global Assembly Cache. We will discuss these issues in detail in the rest of this chapter.

Assemblies

In .NET, assemblies are components. Assemblies, which may be composed of one or more DLL or EXE files, are the unit of deployment, not individual DLLs or EXEs. Security evidence and versioning are based on the assembly. Assemblies contain Microsoft Intermediate Language (MSIL) instructions, resource data, and metadata. Since metadata describes the content of the assembly, they do not require any external descriptions, such as in the system registry. .NET components are much simpler and less error prone to install and uninstall, than traditional COM components, which had extensive registry entries.

A digital signature is required before an assembly can be deployed in the GAC. Digitally signed assemblies provide cryptographically generated verification information that can be used by the CLR to enforce crucial dependency rules when locating and loading assemblies. This is distinct from the security verification that is done to make sure that code is type safe.

The identity of an unsigned assembly is defined simply as a human readable name, along with a version number. The identity of a digitally signed assembly also includes its originator, uniquely associated with a cryptographic key pair. Optionally, an assembly's identity may also include a culture code for supporting culturally specific character sets and string formats.

An assembly's version can be checked so that the CLR can insure that the same assembly version with which the client was built and tested is loaded. This eliminates the infamous DLL Hell problem, where Windows applications could easily break when an older version was replaced with a newer version (or vice versa). A digitally signed assembly can be used to verify that the assembly contents were not altered since the time when it was digitally signed. Not only will you not accidentally use the wrong version, but also you will not be tricked into using a malicious tampered component that could do serious harm.

Although there is often a one-to-one correspondence between namespace and assembly, an assembly may contain multiple namespaces, and one namespace may be distributed among multiple assemblies. While there is often a one-to-one correspondence between assembly and binary code file (i.e., DLL or EXE) one assembly can span multiple binary code files. While an assembly is the unit of deployment, an application is the unit of configuration.

Componentized Version of Case Study

For our next step of the case study, we split our Hotel Administrator's program into three assemblies. The **CaseStudy** directory for this chapter has an **AcmeGui** application program (EXE), and two component (DLL) assemblies: **Customer** and **Hotel**. The code associated with the customer and hotel classes have been moved to separate assemblies. When we discuss configuration later in the chapter, it is the **AcmeGui** application that will be configured.

Code
Example

We will use the **Customer** and **Hotel** assemblies to understand the issues associated with deployment. All **public** members of the **Customer** and **Hotel** assembly will be visible to code outside of their respective assemblies. Members marked as **Friend** scope can only be used within the assembly.

If you look at Figure 9–6, you will see that the Solution Explorer window shows that the **AcmeGui** project has references to the **Customer** and **Hotel** dynamic link libraries. These references enable the compiler to find the **Hotel** and **Customer** types used by **AcmeGui**, and then build the application. They do not dictate where the DLLs have to be when the project is deployed; we will explain how this works when we discuss deployment. You will also notice references made to system assemblies such as **System.dll**. Looking at the properties for the reference will show you where the assembly is located.[1]

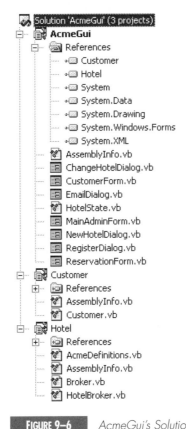

FIGURE 9–6   *AcmeGui's Solution Explorer showing References.*

---

1. Select the assembly in the Solution Explorer, right-mouse-click, and select Properties in the context menu.

Creating a DLL is simple, as we saw in the previous section. The **AcmeGui** solution illustrates a somewhat different approach than we used previously. Rather than having separate solutions for the class libraries and the application that uses them, we have one solution with several projects. To make the DLLs easy to find during compilation, we set the Output path to be up one directory, as illustrated in Figure 9–7.

We also set the project dependencies to indicate that the AcmeGui project depends on the Customer and Hotel projects. (Use the Project Dependencies dialog, as illustrated in Figure 9–8. This dialog is brought up from the menu Project | Project Dependencies.) The result is that the DLLs will be built first. The advantage of having all the projects in one solution is that you can be assured that the class libraries are kept up to date.

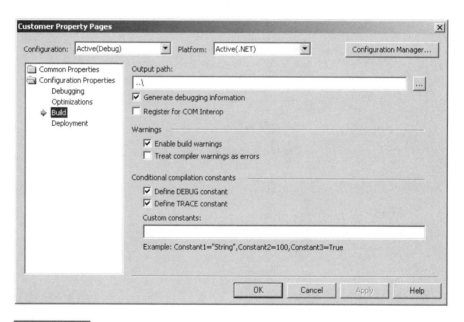

FIGURE 9–7   *Setting the Output path for the Customer class library project.*

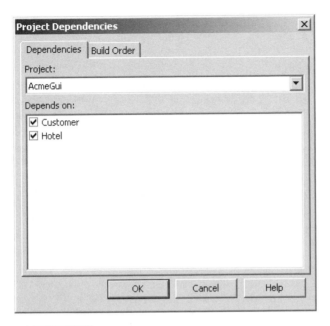

FIGURE 9–8   *Setting the project dependencies to ensure proper build order.*

Contents of an Assembly

Every Assembly has a Manifest that describes the metadata information associated with the Assembly. A manifest provides the following information about an assembly.

- Assembly identity based on name, version, culture, and, optionally, a digital signature.
- Lists files that contribute to the assembly contents.
- Lists other assemblies on which the assembly is dependent.
- Lists permissions required by the assembly to carry out its duties.

The VB.NET assembly created by Visual Studio has a file, **Assembly-Info.vb**, that contains the following attributes that can be used to set the information associated with an assembly.

```
<Assembly: AssemblyTitle("")>
<Assembly: AssemblyDescription("")>
<Assembly: AssemblyCompany("")>
<Assembly: AssemblyProduct("")>
<Assembly: AssemblyCopyright("")>
<Assembly: AssemblyTrademark("")>
<Assembly: CLSCompliant(True)>
...
<Assembly: AssemblyVersion("1.0.*")>
```

To explore how versioning, digital signing, and deployment work, we use the ILDASM tool introduced in Chapter 2 to view the appropriate metadata. If you have not already done so, you may wish to add ILDASM to your Tools menu in Visual Studio. Bring up the External Tools dialog from the Tools | External Tools menu. Click the Add button and type ILDASM for the Title. Click the ▢ button and navigate to the directory where **ildasm.exe** is located (the **bin** folder under **FrameworkSDK** under **Microsoft Visual Studio .NET** under **Program Files**). Figure 9–9 illustrates adding ILDASM as an external tool in this manner. Note that we have also specified the solution directory as the initial directory for ILDASM.

Figure 9–10 shows the top level that you will see when you open the **Customer.dll** assembly in ILDASM. You see an entry for the MANIFEST, and under the **OI.NetVB.Acme** namespace, you see entries for the **Customer** and **Customers** classes, the **ICustomer** interface, and the **CustomerListItem** value type. Clicking on a plus (+) button will expand an entry.

To view the manifest, double-click the MANIFEST node, shown in Figure 9–10, and the resulting manifest information is displayed in Figure 9–11. Some of the information will vary if you have rebuilt any of the samples or you have a later version of .NET.

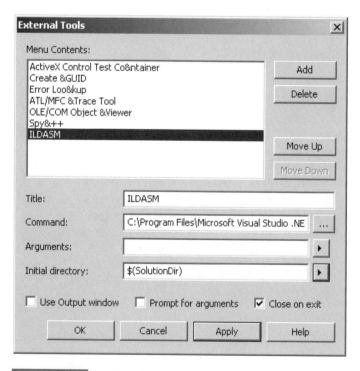

FIGURE 9–9   *Adding ildasm.exe as an external tool.*

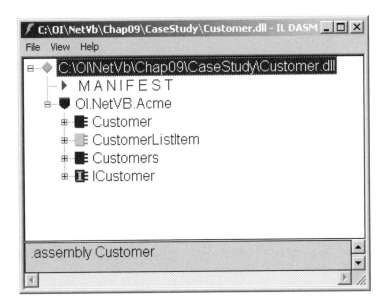

FIGURE 9–10   Top-level ILDASM view of Customer component.

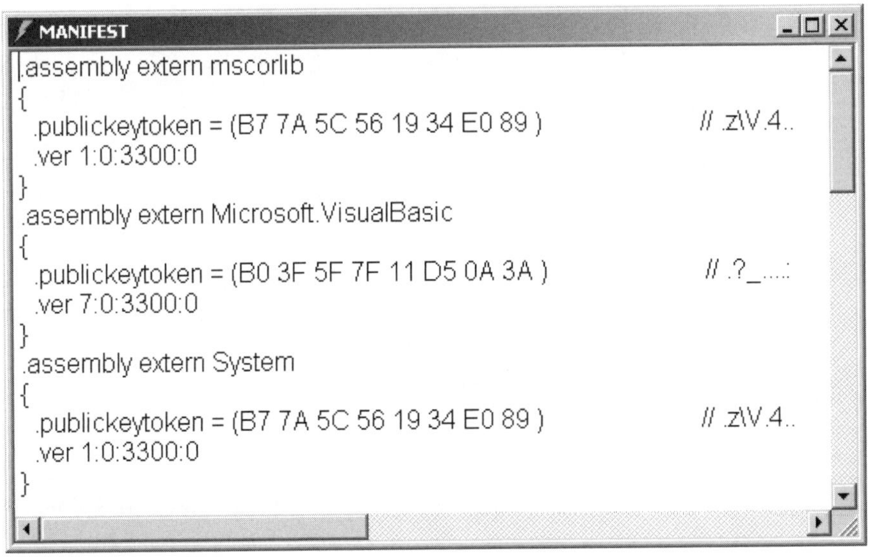

```
MANIFEST                                                          _ □ ×
.assembly extern mscorlib
{
  .publickeytoken = (B7 7A 5C 56 19 34 E0 89 )              // .z\V.4..
  .ver 1:0:3300:0
}
.assembly extern Microsoft.VisualBasic
{
  .publickeytoken = (B0 3F 5F 7F 11 D5 0A 3A )              // .?_....:
  .ver 7:0:3300:0
}
.assembly extern System
{
  .publickeytoken = (B7 7A 5C 56 19 34 E0 89 )              // .z\V.4..
  .ver 1:0:3300:0
}
```

FIGURE 9–11   ILDASM showing manifest of Customer.dll.

The manifest contains information about the dependencies and contents of the assembly. You can see that the manifest for **Customer** contains, among others, the following external dependency.

```
.assembly extern mscorlib
{
  .publickeytoken = (B7 7A 5C 56 19 34 E0 89 )
  .ver 1:0:3300:0
}
```

The **.assembly extern mscorlib** metadata statement indicates that the **Customer** assembly makes use of, and is therefore dependent on, the standard assembly **mccorlib.dll**, which is required by all managed code. When an assembly makes a reference to another assembly, you will see an **.assembly extern** metadata statement. If you open **AcmeGui** in ILDASM and look at the manifest you will see several dependencies, including the **Customer** and **Hotel** assemblies as well as the **System.Windows.Forms** assembly.

```
...
.assembly extern Hotel
{
  .ver 1:0:797:24817
}
...
.assembly extern System.Windows.Forms
{
  .publickeytoken = (B7 7A 5C 56 19 34 E0 89 )
  .ver 1:0:3300:0
}
...
.assembly extern Customer
{
  .ver 1:0:797:24817
...
```

The **System.Windows.Forms** assembly is a shared assembly, which can be seen in the **\WINNT\Assembly** directory using Windows Explorer, as illustrated in Figure 9–12.

In the **System.Windows.Forms** shared assembly, the **.publickeytoken** = (B7 7A 5C 56 19 34 E0 89) metadata statement provides a public key token, which is the lowest 8 bytes of a hash of the public key that matches the corresponding private key owned by the **System.Windows.Forms** assembly's author. This public key token cannot actually be used directly to authenticate the identity of the author of the **System.Windows.Forms**. However, the original public key specified in the **System.Windows.Forms** manifest can be used to mathematically verify that the matching private key was actually used to digitally sign the **System.Windows.Forms** assembly. Since Microsoft authored **System.Windows.Forms.dll**, the public key token seen

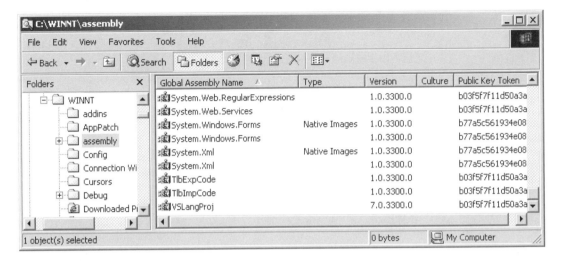

FIGURE 9-12   *Viewing shared assembly information in Windows Explorer.*

above is Microsoft-specific. Of course, the matching private key is a closely guarded corporate secret, and it is believed by most security experts that such a private key is, in practice, virtually impossible to determine from the public key. However, there is no guarantee that some mathematical genius will not find a back door someday!

The .publickeytoken declaration

The .publickeytoken declaration provides only the least significant 8 bytes of the SHA1 hash of the producer's public key (which is 128 bytes), which saves some space, but can still be used to verify at runtime that the assembly being loaded comes from the same publisher as the one you compiled against. Alternatively, the .publickey declaration could have been used, which provides the full public key. This would take up more space, but it makes it harder for villains to find a private key that matches the full public key.

mscorlib, which is also a shared assembly, is not deployed in the GAC. Microsoft made a single exception here because **mscorlib** is so closely tied with the CLR engine (**mscorwks**); it is installed in the appropriate install directory (**\WINNT\Microsoft.NET\Framework\ v1.0.3705**), where the version number reflects the current .NET version.

As we shall see shortly, the **.publickeytoken** statement is only present in the client assembly's manifest if the referenced assembly has been digitally signed, and all assemblies intended for shared deployment must be digitally signed. Microsoft has digitally signed the standard .NET assemblies, such as

mscorlib.dll and **System.Windows.Forms.dll**, with private keys belonging to them. This is why the public key token for many of those shared assemblies, seen in the **\WINNT\Assembly** directory using Windows Explorer, have the same value repeated. Assemblies authored and digitally signed by other vendors are signed with their own distinct private keys, and they will therefore result in a different public key token in their client assembly's manifests. Later, we will look at how you can create your own private and public key pair and digitally sign your own assemblies for deployment into the GAC.

Nonetheless, while unique, none of these digital keys can identify who the author of a particular module is. A developer of assemblies can use the **signcode** utility to add a digital certificate that will identify the publisher of the assembly.

The **.ver 1:0:3300:0** metadata statement indicates the version of the **System.Windows.Forms** assembly. While these numbers have no intrinsic meaning, the Microsoft suggested format of this version specification is Major:Minor:Build:Revision. Over time, as new versions of this assembly are released, existing clients that were built to use this version will continue using this version, assuming the conventional meaning of major and minor values. Newer client programs will of course be able to access newer versions of this assembly as they become available. The old and new versions can be deployed side by side via the GAC and be simultaneously available to old and new client programs.

Now let us shift our focus to the information about the component itself in its manifest. ILDASM shows the assembly metadata in the **Customer** manifest:

```
.assembly Customer
{
  ...
  .hash algorithm 0x00008004
  .ver 1:0:756:15183
}
```

The .assembly Directive

The .assembly directive declares the manifest and specifies to which assembly the current module belongs. In this example, the .assembly directive specifies the name of the assembly to be Customer. It is this name (combined with the version number and optionally a public key) rather than the name of the DLL or EXE file that is used at runtime to resolve the identity of the assembly. Also note that if the assembly is signed, you will see the .publickey defined within the .assembly directive. It also indicates what custom attributes have been added to the metadata.

The **.assembly Customer** metadata statement indicates that the assembly name is **Customer**. Note that this is not the name of a component class within the assembly, but rather the assembly itself. Note that this assembly is not digitally signed, and therefore it does not contain a public key.

In multifile assemblies (see a later section), the manifest stores a hash of each file in the assembly. The **.hash algorithm 0x00008004** metadata statement indicates that SHA1 is the hash algorithm that is to produce this hash code value. There are many hash code algorithms in existence. However, initially, only MD5 (0x000803) and SHA1 (0x000804) are supported by .NET.

Hash Algorithms

A hash algorithm is a mathematical function that takes the original data of arbitrary size as input and generates a hash code, also known as a message digest, which is a fixed-sized binary output. An effective hash function is a one-way function that is highly collision-free, with a result that is relatively small and fixed in size. Ideally, a hash function is efficient to calculate as well. A one-way function is a function that has no inverse, so that you cannot effectively reproduce the original data from the hash code value.[*] The phrase "highly collision free" means that the probability that two distinct original input data samples generate the same hash code is very small, and it is unlikely to calculate two distinct input data samples that result in the same hash code value. The well known MD5 and SHA1 hash algorithms are considered to be excellent choices for use in digital signing, and they are both supported by .NET.

[*] One way encryption codes are used to store passwords is in a passwords database. When you log in, the password you enter is encrypted and compared with what is stored in the database. If they match, you can log in. The password cannot be reconstructed from the encrypted value stored in the passwords database.

Versioning an Assembly

An assembly manifest contains the version of the assembly as well as the version of each of the assemblies that the assembly depends on. The version number of an assembly is composed of four numerical fields: Major, Minor, Build, and Revision. There are no semantics assigned to any of these fields by the CLR. Microsoft does suggest the following convention:

- Major—a change to this field indicates major incompatible changes.
- Minor—a change to this field indicates minor, but incompatible changes.
- Build—a change to this field indicates a new backward compatible release.
- Revision—a change to this field indicates a backward compatible emergency bug fix.

None of this is enforced by the CLR. You enforce this convention, or any other convention you choose, by testing assemblies for compatibility and specifying the version policy in a configuration file that we will discuss.

In the metadata for the Customer assembly, the **.ver 1:0:756:15183** gives us the assembly's version: Major Version 1, Minor Version 0, Build Number 756, Revision 15183.

The version information for the manifest can be defined in the source code using the assembly attribute **AssemblyVersion**. This attribute (as with other global attributes) must appear in a source file after the Imports statements but before any namespace or class definitions. The **AssemblyVersion-Attribute** class is defined in the **System::Reflection** namespace. If this attribute is not used, a default version number of 0.0.0.0 is listed in the assembly manifest, which is generally not desirable.

In a project created with the VisualStudio.NET project wizard, the source file named **AssemblyInfo.vb** is automatically generated, with a version of **1.0.***, producing a major version of 1, and a minor version of 0 and automatically generated build and revision values. If you change the **AssemblyVersion** to, for example, **"1.1.0.0"**, as shown below, the version number displayed in the manifest will be modified accordingly to **1:1:0:0**.

```
<Assembly: AssemblyVersion("1.1.0.0")>
```

If you specify any version number at all, you must at a minimum, specify the major number. If you only specify the major number, the remaining values will default to zero. If you also specify the minor value, you can omit the remaining fields, which will then default to zero, or you can specify an asterisk, which will provide automatically generated values. The asterisk will cause the build value to equal the number of days since January 1, 2000, and the revision value will be set to the number of seconds since midnight, divided by 2. If you specify major, minor, and build values, and specify an asterisk for the revision value, then only the revision is defaulted to the number of seconds since midnight, divided by 2. If all four fields are explicitly specified, then all four values will be reflected in the manifest. Table 9–1 shows a few valid **AssemblyVersion** specifications along with the resulting version number in the manifest.

TABLE 9–1   *Examples of Version Specifications*

Specified in Source	Result in Manifest
none	0:0:0:0
1	1:0:0:0
1.1	1:1:0:0
1.1.*	1:1:464:27461
1.1.43	1:1:43:0
1.1.43.*	1:1:43:29832
1.1.43.52	1:1:43:52

If you use the asterisk, then the revision and/or the build number will automatically change every time you rebuild the component. You must make an explicit change to the major and minor numbers if you wish to have their values changed.

Strong Names

Before we can discuss version policy, we have to introduce the idea of a strong name. A strong name is guaranteed to be globally unique for any version of any assembly. Strong names are generated by digitally signing the assembly. This ensures that the strong name is not only unique, but it is a name that can only be generated by an individual that owns a secret private key.

A strong name is made up of a simple text name, a public key, and a hash code that has been encrypted with the matching private key. The hash code is known as a message digest, and the encrypted hash code is known as a digital signature. The digital signature effectively identifies the assembly's author and ensures that the assembly has not been altered. Two assemblies that have the same strong name and versions are considered to be identical assemblies. Two assemblies with different strong names are considered to be different. A strong name is also known as a cryptographically strong name, since, unlike a simple text name, a strong name is guaranteed to uniquely identify the assembly based on its contents and its author's private key. A strong name has the following useful properties:

- A strong name guarantees uniqueness based on encryption technology.
- A strong name establishes a unique namespace based on the use of a private key.[2]
- A strong name prevents unauthorized individuals from modifying the assembly.
- A strong name prevents unauthorized individuals from versioning the assembly.
- A strong name allows the CLR to find the right version of a shared assembly.

Digital Signatures

Digital signatures are based on public key cryptographic techniques. In the world of cryptography, the two main cryptographic techniques are symmetric ciphers (shared key) and asymmetric ciphers (public key). Symmetric ciphers use one shared secret key for encryption as well as decryption. DES, Triple

---

2. Do not confuse this namespace with the namespace used by the compiler to disambiguate class names.

DES, and RC2 are examples of symmetric cipher algorithms. Symmetric ciphers can be very efficient and powerful for message privacy between two trusted cooperating individuals, but they are generally unsuitable for digital signatures. Digital signatures are not used for privacy, but are used for identification and authentication. If you share your symmetric key with everyone who would potentially want to identify or authenticate you, you would inevitably share it with people who would want to impersonate you.

Asymmetric ciphers are used in digital signatures.[3] Asymmetric ciphers, also known as public key ciphers, make use of a public/private key pair. The paired keys are mathematically related and they are generated together. It is, however, exceedingly difficult to calculate one key from the other. The public key is typically exposed to everyone who would like to authenticate its owner. On the other hand, the owner keeps the matching private signing key secret so that no one can impersonate him or her. RSA and DSA are examples of public key cipher systems.

Public key cryptography is based on a very interesting mathematical scheme that allows plain text to be encrypted with one key and decrypted only with the matching key. For example, if a public key is used to encrypt the original data (known as plain text), then only the matching private key is capable of decrypting it. Not even the encrypting key can decrypt it! This scenario is useful for sending secret messages to only the individual who knows the private key.

The opposite scenario is where the individual who owns the private key uses that private key to encrypt the plain text. The resulting cipher text is by no means a secret, since everyone who is interested can obtain the public key to decrypt it. This scenario is useless for secrecy, but very effective for authentication purposes. To improve performance, instead of encrypting the original data, a highly characteristic hash code is encrypted instead.

If you use the matching public key to decrypt the encrypted hash code, you can recalculate the hash code on the original data, and compare the two values. If the two values match, you can be certain that the owner of the private key was the digital signer. Of course, the owner of the private key has to make sure to keep the private key secret. Otherwise, you cannot prove that the data has not been tampered with from the time when it was digitally signed. Figure 9–13 shows how a digital signature works.

Digital Signing with SHA1 and RSA

To sign the assembly, the producer calculates a SHA1 hash of the assembly (with the bytes reserved for the signature preset to zero), and then encrypts the hash value with a public key using RSA encryption. The public key and the encrypted hash are then stored in the assembly's metadata.

---

3. Asymmetric ciphers are also used in shared key management, which is not discussed here.

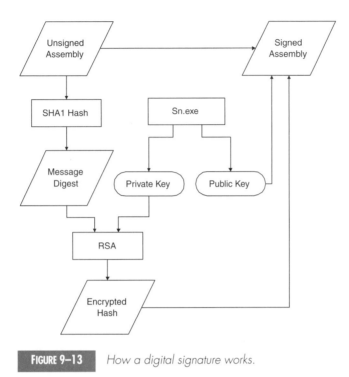

FIGURE 9–13   *How a digital signature works.*

Digitally Signing an Assembly

The process of digitally signing an assembly involves generating a public/private key pair, calculating a hash code on the assembly, encrypting the hash code with the private key, and writing the encrypted hash code along with the public key into the assembly for all to see. The encrypted hash code and public key together comprise the entire digital signature. The digital signature is written into a reserved area within the assembly that is not included in the hash code calculation. All these steps are performed with two simple tools named the Strong Name utility (**Sn.exe)** and the Assembly Linker (**Al.exe**). To build and digitally sign an assembly, the following steps are performed.

1. Develop and build the component.
2. Generate a public/private key pair.
3. Calculate a hash code on the contents of the assembly.
4. Encrypt the hash code using the private key.
5. Place the encrypted hash code into the manifest.
6. Place the public key into the manifest.

Step 1 is, of course, usually performed using Visual Studio .NET. Steps 2 through 6 are known as digital signing. Step 2 is accomplished using the

Code
Example

Strong Name utility **Sn.exe**. Steps 3 through 6 are accomplished using either Visual Studio .NET or the Assembly Linker utility **Al.exe** (that's *A-el,* not *A-one*).

To illustrate this process, we will develop a version of our **Customer** and **Hotel** assemblies that have strong names. They are located in the **SignedCaseStudy** directory. We generate key pairs for the assemblies using **Sn.exe**. This tool generates a cryptographically strong name for the assembly. You generate a public-private key pair and place them into a file named **KeyPair.snk** as shown in the following command. You can run **Sn.exe** in the **Hotel** and **Customer** source directories to generate the key files together with the source code for each assembly. In the example provided, a distinct key file is created for each of the **Hotel** and **Customer** assemblies. You could just as easily create one key file and use it in both assemblies.

```
sn -k KeyPair.snk
```

The resulting **KeyPair.snk** file is a binary file and is not intended to be human readable. If you are curious, you can write these keys into a comma-delimited text file with the following command, and then view it using **Notepad.exe**. This is not a required step.

```
sn -o KeyPair.snk KeyPair.txt
```

In the example you will find these files in the **SignedCaseStudy\Hotel** and **SignedCaseStudy\Customer** subdirectories.

The next step is to apply the private key to each assembly. For developing and testing, it is convenient to do this at compilation time. When you release the assembly, however, you have to use the official private key of the company. For security reasons, this key is probably only known to the corporate digital signing authority. The process of creating the strong name cannot be postponed until after the assembly is built because the public key is part of the assembly's identity. Users of the assembly have to compile against the full identity of the assembly. Delay signing, which splits the process of assigning the strong name into two steps, is designed to solve this problem.

If you just want to apply the digital signature automatically at compile time without delay signing, you simply use the **AssemblyKeyFileAttribute**, which in the example is in the **AssemblyInfo.vb** files of the **Customer** and **Hotel** projects. The **KeyPair.snk** files generated previously with the **Sn.exe** tool is specified in the attribute. The file path can be absolute, or it can be relative to the project output directory. Once the appropriate **KeyPair.snk** file has been added to the **AssemblyKeyFile** attribute in each assembly project, the code must be recompiled.

```
<Assembly: AssemblyKeyFile( _
  "C:\OI\NetVb\Chap09\SignedCaseStudy\Hotel\KeyPair.snk")>

<Assembly: AssemblyKeyFile( _
  "C:\OI\NetVb\Chap09\SignedCaseStudy\Customer\KeyPair.snk")>
```

Delayed signing requires a more complex procedure. When you build the assembly, the public key is supplied to the compiler so that it can be put in to the PublicKey field in the assembly's manifest. Space is reserved in the file for the signature, but the signature is not generated. When the actual signature is generated, it is placed in the file with the –R option to the Strong Name utility (**Sn.exe**).

To indicate to the compiler that you want to use delay signing, you include **AssemblyDelaySign** attribute in your source code. You also have to include the public key, using the **AssemblyKeyFile** attribute.

Assuming you have generated the public/private key pair as described previously, you then use the –p option of the Strong Name utility to obtain just the public key without giving out the still secret private key.

```
sn -p KeyPair.snk PublicKey.snk
```

You then add the following two attributes to **AssemblyInfo.vb**:

```
<Assembly: AssemblyDelaySign(true)>
<Assembly: AssemblyKeyFile("C:\...\PublicKey.snk")>
```

The assembly still does not have a valid signature. You will not be able to install it into the GAC or load it from an application directory. You can disable signature verification of a particular assembly by using the –Vr option on the Strong Name utility.

```
sn -Vr Customer.dll
```

Before you ship the assembly, you must supply the valid signature. You use the –R option on the Strong Name utility and supply the public/private key pair.

```
sn - R customer.dll KeyPair.snk
```

Regardless of whether or not you choose to delay signing, once you have actually digitally signed an assembly, if you look at the manifest in ILDASM, you will see that the **.publickey** entry has been added to the assembly's metadata.

The **.publickey** attribute represents the originator's public key that resides in the corresponding **KeyPair.snk** file. This is the public key that can be used to decrypt the message digest to retrieve the original hash code. When the assembly is deployed into the GAC, this decrypted hash code is compared with a fresh recalculation of the hash code from the actual assembly contents. This comparison is made to determine if the assembly is legitimate (i.e., identical to the original) or illegitimate (i.e., corrupt or tampered). Of course, when you use **Sn.exe**, it will produce a different key pair, and the public key shown below will be different in your case accordingly.

If you use ILDASM to examine the manifest of the **AcmeGui** client program, you will see the following:

```
.assembly extern Customer
{
  .publickeytoken = (EE FE D1 EB 3C AD 9E 15 )
  .ver 1:0:756:20269
}
...
.assembly extern Hotel
{
  .publickeytoken = (37 6E 80 FB 8D 30 1E B2 )
  .ver 1:0:756:20146
}
```

Now that **Customer** and **Hotel** have strong names, references to them have a public key token, which is a hash of the public key that matches the corresponding private key for the assembly. Note that we generated different keys for each assembly. Usually, each company will use the same key pair for all its public components.

Now that we have discussed strong names, we can discuss the two methods of deploying assemblies in .NET and their associated default version policies. After this discussion, we will show how the default policy can be overridden in a configuration file.

Private Assembly Deployment

For private assembly deployment, the assembly is copied to the same directory as the client program that references it. No registration is needed, and no fancy installation program is required. When the component is removed, no registry cleanup is needed, and no uninstall program is required. Just delete it from the hard drive.[4]

Of course, no self-respecting programmer would ever provide a commercial component that required the end user to manually copy or delete any files in this way, even if it is remarkably simple to do. Users have become accustomed to using a formal installation program, so it should be provided, even if its work is trivial. However, manually copying and deleting an assembly is an ideal way to quickly and painlessly manage deployment issues for developing, debugging, or testing purposes. Recall that the deployment of COM components was never this simple, requiring at a minimum a registry script file. Gone are the days when you have to configure the registry on installation, and then later carefully clean out the registry information when you want to discard the component.

---

4. Of course, this process does not put any icons on the desktop or entries on the Start menu.

To privately deploy our componentized Hotel Administrator Case Study, create a directory on your hard drive. Copy to that directory the **AcmeGui.exe** file in the **CaseStudy\bin** directory and the files **Customer.dll** and **Hotel.dll** in the **CaseStudy** directory. Note that we are shifting our focus back to the unsigned CaseStudy example now. Then run **AcmeGui.exe**. It will run. It is really just that simple!

If you view the **AcmeGui** manifest in ILDASM, you will see the following dependency entries:

```
.assembly extern Customer
{
  .ver 1:0:756:21093
}
...
.assembly extern Hotel
{
  .ver 1:0:756:21094
}
```

Here are the corresponding assembly definitions in the components:

```
.assembly Customer
{
  .hash algorithm 0x00008004
  .ver 1:0:756:21093
}

.assembly Hotel
{
  ...
  .hash algorithm 0x00008004
  .ver 1:0:756:21094
}
```

From this you can see that the client program was built with **Customer** assembly version 1:0:756:21093 and **Hotel** assembly version 1:0:756:21094. Since neither assembly has a strong name, however, the versions are not checked. If you were to build a **Customer** assembly with a different version and replace the one that **AcmeGui** was built with, **AcmeGui** would still run. It does not matter whether you change the major build number or the revision number.

If you were to use an incorrect version of the **Customer** component with a strong name, you will get a runtime exception (System.IO.FileLoadException) because the located assembly's manifest definition does not match the assembly reference. If the **AcmeGui** client program was built with an assembly that had a strong name, the CLR will only bind to an assembly that matches exactly with the strong name and version. Even a different revision number will cause the load to fail.

The details on binding failures can be seen in the Assembly Binding Log Viewer (**FUSLOGVW.exe**). Figure 9–14 has a sample log that resulted from an attempt to resolve **AcmeGui's** reference to a **Customer** assembly that had a strong name when it was built with a version of the assembly that did not have a strong name:

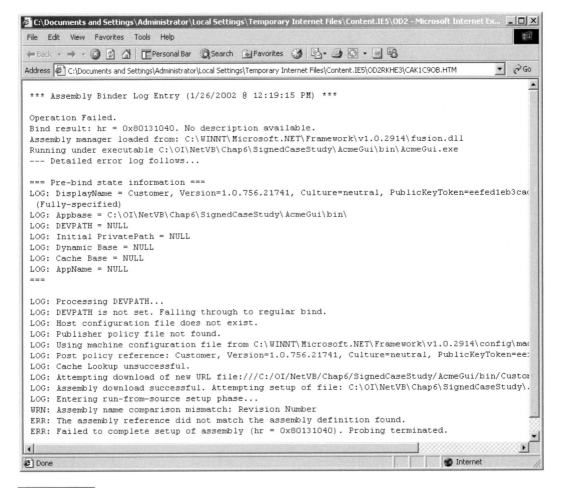

FIGURE 9–14   *Assembly Binding Log for Customer Load Failure.*

Shared Assembly Deployment

The Assembly Cache is a directory where the CLR looks for shared, side-by-side assemblies. The term "side-by-side" means that multiple versions of the same component may reside within the assembly cache along side one another. The GAC contains shared assemblies that are globally accessible to all .NET applications on the machine. There is also a download assembly cache that is accessible to applications such as Internet Explorer that automatically download assemblies over the network.

Deploying a Shared Assembly

Before an assembly can be deployed into the GAC, you must first digitally sign the assembly as discussed in a previous section. Developers can then place the assembly into the GAC by using either the Global Assembly Cache Utility **Gacutil.exe** command-line utility, the Windows Explorer with the assembly cache viewer Windows shell extension, or the .NET Admin Tool. Deploying shared assemblies on an end user's machine should be done with an installation program.

To illustrate this process, we will deploy in the GAC the version of our **Customer** and **Hotel** assemblies that are in the **SignedCaseStudy** directory. To deploy the components into the GAC, you can use the command-line utility **Gacutil.exe**.

```
Gacutil -i Customer.dll
```

You should then see the console message `Assembly successfully added to the cache`. The effect of this command is that a new GAC node named **Customer** is created in the **\WINNT\Assembly** directory. As can be seen in Figure 9–15, the version number and originator (i.e., public key token) are displayed for the assembly in Windows Explorer.

You can also can drag and drop a component into the **Assembly** directory to install it in the GAC. Alternatively, you can use the .**NET Admin Tool** to install an assembly into the GAC. The .**NET Admin Tool** is an MMC snap-in located at **\WINNT\Microsoft.NET\Framework\v1.0.2914\mscorcfg.msc**.[5] The directory version number will be different in a later release of the .NET Framework. While it may seem overkill to introduce a third tool, this MMC snap-in is a very useful utility that simplifies many tasks. Figure 9–16 shows the top-level window

---

5. To run a snap-in, you can just double-click on the .**msc** file in Windows Explorer. Since we are going to use the .NET Admin Tool extensively, you may wish to add the tool to the Visual Studio Tools menu, which you can do through Tools | External Tools... For the command enter **mmc.exe**, and for the argument, enter the complete path to **mscorcfg.msc**.

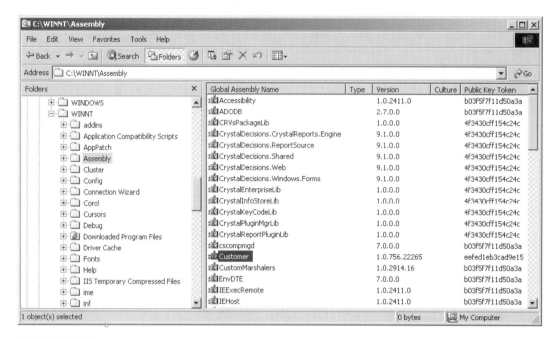

Global Assembly Name	Type	Version	Culture	Public Key Token
Accessibility		1.0.2411.0		b03f5f7f11d50a3a
ADODB		2.7.0.0		b03f5f7f11d50a3a
CRVsPackageLib		1.0.0.0		4f3430cff154c24c
CrystalDecisions.CrystalReports.Engine		9.1.0.0		4f3430cff154c24c
CrystalDecisions.ReportSource		9.1.0.0		4f3430cff154c24c
CrystalDecisions.Shared		9.1.0.0		4f3430cff154c24c
CrystalDecisions.Web		9.1.0.0		4f3430cff154c24c
CrystalDecisions.Windows.Forms		9.1.0.0		4f3430cff154c24c
CrystalEnterpriseLib		1.0.0.0		4f3430cff154c24c
CrystalInfoStoreLib		1.0.0.0		4f3430cff154c24c
CrystalKeyCodeLib		1.0.0.0		4f3430cff154c24c
CrystalPluginMgrLib		1.0.0.0		4f3430cff154c24c
CrystalReportPluginLib		1.0.0.0		4f3430cff154c24c
cscompmgd		7.0.0.0		b03f5f7f11d50a3a
Customer		1.0.756.22265		eefed1eb3cad9e15
CustomMarshalers		1.0.2914.16		b03f5f7f11d50a3a
EnvDTE		7.0.0.0		b03f5f7f11d50a3a
IEExecRemote		1.0.2411.0		b03f5f7f11d50a3a
IEHost		1.0.2411.0		b03f5f7f11d50a3a

FIGURE 9–15   *Windows Explorer showing the Global Assembly Cache.*

of this tool. To add an assembly to the GAC using this tool, just select Assembly Cache in the left pane, right-mouse-click, and select Add. Using the dialog box that pops up to navigate to the file, select the assembly you want to add, and click the Open button.

After you have installed the assemblies in the GAC, copy just the **AcmeGui** client program in the **SignedCaseStudy** directory to another directory. You can now run it without any assemblies in the same directory.

What happens if we remove the version of Customer we installed in the GAC and place in the GAC a Customer assembly signed with the same key, but a different version? A **FileNotfoundException** is thrown by the CLR. We would get the same result if we replaced it with a Customer assembly that had the same version, but was signed with a different key. The default binding policy for shared assemblies is an exact and full name match.

Versioning Shared Components

What happens if you install two versions of the same assembly in the GAC that were signed with the same key? You can place two **Customer** assemblies with different version numbers in the GAC. Figure 9–17 displays two versions of the **Customer** assembly installed in the GAC with their distinct version numbers and identical public key tokens.

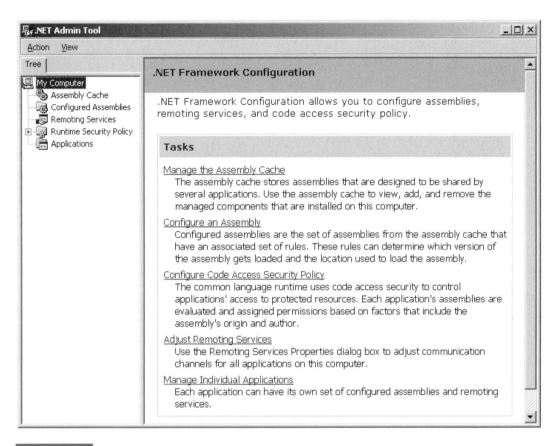

FIGURE 9–16 .NET Admin Tool supports many .NET administrative functions.

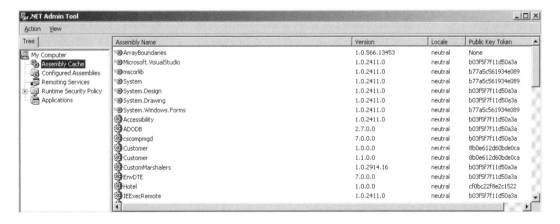

FIGURE 9–17 .NET Admin Tool with side-by-side components in the Global Assembly Cache.

This is called by-side deployment. Both assemblies are available to client programs that require them. Programs can bind to either of them without fear of getting the wrong version.

Assembly Configuration

The CLR binds to an assembly when either a static or dynamic reference is made to it at runtime. A static reference is defined permanently in the client assembly manifest when it is compiled. A dynamic reference is produced programmatically at runtime, for example, by calling the method **System.Reflection.Assembly.Load**.

You can use a strongly named assembly to force a client to bind to a specific version of an assembly whether you have private or shared deployment. Suppose you want to allow several backward compatible assemblies to match. You can use an XML configuration file to specify some rules for the CLR to use when it tries to find an assembly that matches. The .NET Admin Tool can be used to create and maintain these files through a graphical interface.

The name of the configuration file is the client program's name appended with a **.config** extension. For our **AcmeGui** client, the configuration file would be named **AcmeGui.exe.config**. It is placed in the same directory as the client executable.

In addition to an application configuration file, there is an administration configuration file called **Machine.config**. It is found in the **Config** subdirectory under the directory where the .NET runtime is installed (**\WINNT\Microsoft.NET\Framework\v1.0.3705\CONFIG**, where the version number reflects the current build of .NET). An administration version policy is defined with the same XML tags an application configuration file uses. However, the administrator configuration file overrides any settings in the application configuration file.

Resolving an Assembly Reference at Runtime

If the reference has a strong name, the configuration files are examined first to determine the correct assembly version(s) required. If the reference does not have a strong name, any version will satisfy the reference.[6] If the assembly reference has been previously resolved, that previously loaded assembly is used. The assembly cache is checked, and if the assembly is found there, that

---

6. There is also a publisher's configuration file that we do not discuss. If you are using Internet Explorer, the configuration files might have to be downloaded from another computer.

assembly is loaded. If the assembly is not found in the assembly cache, the CLR *probes* for the assembly. We will discuss probing after we discuss specifying version policy in the configuration files.

Specifying the Version Policy in a Configuration File

The **<configuration>** is the top-level tag for .NET configuration files. Assembly binding information is found in the **<runtime>** section. A sample **AcmeGui.exe.config** file might look like this:

```
<?xml version="1.0"?>
<configuration>
  <runtime>
    <assemblyBinding xmlns=
        "urn:schemas-microsoft-com:asm.v1">
      <dependentAssembly>
        <assemblyIdentity name="Customer"
          publicKeyToken="8b0e612d60bde0ca" />
        <bindingRedirect oldVersion="1.0.0.0-1.1.0.0"
          newVersion="1.1.0.0" />
      </dependentAssembly>
    </assemblyBinding>
  </runtime>
</configuration>
```

Rules defining version policy are found in the **<assemblyBinding>** section. The XML namespace specification is required. Each assembly whose version policy we want to set is placed in its own **<dependentAssembly>** section. The **assemblyIdentity** element has attributes that define the assembly this section refers to. The **name** attribute is required, but the **publicKey-Token** and **culture** attributes are optional.[7] The **bindingRedirect** element's attributes define what versions can map to another version. The **oldVersion** attribute can be a range, but the **newVersion** attribute can only be set to one version. In the above example, any references to versions 1.0.0.0 to 1.1.0.0 can be resolved by using version 1.1.0.0. In other words, 1.1.0.0 is backward-compatible with all those versions. You can specify several **bindingRedirect** elements.

You can use the **.NET Admin Tool** to specify this. First, add an application to the tool by selecting Applications in the left pane. Right-mouse-click and select Add from the context menu. Navigate to the application you want to configure. Select it and click the Open button. Figure 9–18 shows the **AcmeGui** application added to the admin tool.

---

7. You may ask, Why is the publicKeyToken optional? After all, there is no version resolution without it. As we shall see shortly, there are other policies that can be defined that do not require a public key.

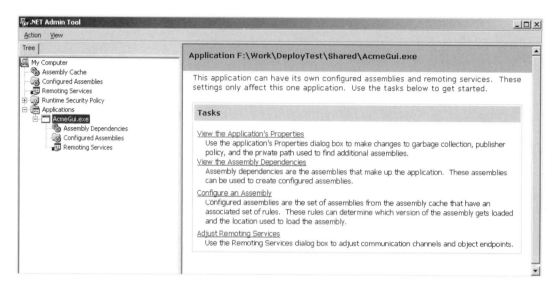

FIGURE 9–18   *AcmeGui added to the .NET Admin Tool.*

To configure the **Customer** assembly, select Configured Assemblies in the left pane, right-mouse-click and select Add from the context menu. In the dialog box that comes up, select the radio button that has the text "Choose an assembly from the list of assemblies this application uses." Then click the Choose Assembly button. Select Customer from the list that pops up, and then click the Select button. The Assembly information for the **Customer** assembly should be entered in the Configure an Assembly dialog. Click the Finish button on that dialog. Select the Binding Policy tab. Figure 9–19 shows what you should see after the binding policy that was in the sample configuration file was recorded.

After you select OK, you can navigate to the directory where the **AcmeGui** executable is and you will see a configuration file that the tool has created for you. It should resemble our previous example.

Finding the Assembly's Physical Location

At this point the CLR knows what versions of the assembly will satisfy the reference. The CLR does not yet know where the assembly resides on disk. If the assembly with the right version has been previously loaded because of another reference to that assembly earlier in the program, that assembly is used. If the assembly has a strong name, the assembly cache is checked; if the correct version is found there, that assembly is used.

There are several elements you can specify in the configuration file to tell the CLR where to try to find the assembly.

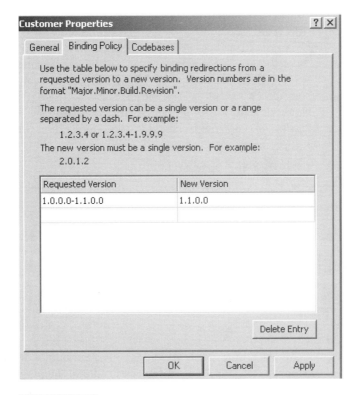

FIGURE 9-19   *Binding Policy set for the Customer assembly.*

If the assembly has not yet been found, the runtime checks to see if the codebase has been specified in the configuration file. Under the **<dependent-Assembly>** section, you can specify a **<codeBase>** element. This element has two attributes, a version and a URI, to check for the assembly. The Codebases tab on the .NET Admin Tool's assembly properties dialog can be used to set them in the configuration file. Examples of this element are:

```
<codeBase version="1.1.1.1"
 href="http://www.abc.com/Customer.dll" />
<codeBase version="1.1.1.2"
 href="file:///c:\AcmeGui\Customer.dll" />
```

To use a codeBase element outside of the application's directory or sub-directories, a strong name is required. At this point, whether or not the required assembly is found, the binding process stops. If the assembly is not found, an exception is generated at this point.

If a codeBase element was not found in the configuration file, the runtime continues to probe for the assembly. At this point all searching is relative to the directory in which the application runs, which is referred to as the **application base**.

The runtime first looks in the application base. It then looks in any subdirectories of the application base that have the same name as the assembly. If a culture is specified in the request, the runtime only looks for the assembly subdirectory under a subdirectory with the name of the culture requested.

Finally, you can specify in the **assemblyBinding** section of the configuration file a privatePath that is a semicolon-delimited list of subdirectories of the application base to look in.

```
<probing privatePath="\bin;\assemb" />
```

You can also set the privatePath on the Properties tab for the application in the .NET Admin Tool.

Multi-Module Assemblies

An assembly can be made up of multiple modules. A module is a DLL (or EXE) that contains managed code plus metadata, but not necessarily a manifest. However, an assembly must have one, and only one, manifest. Hence, an assembly can contain multiple modules, but only one of those modules can have a manifest that provides information on the contents of all the modules in the assembly. The module with the manifest may have just the manifest, or it can contain other code or resources.

The main advantage of breaking an assembly into multiple modules is that each module is contained in a separate DLL file. This allows Web downloads to be performed on demand, on a per-module basis. This can improve performance and memory consumption. Even in a local scenario, the CLR loads classes on the local machine with module granularity, which can improve efficiency. Another reason for constructing an assembly with multiple modules is that you may have written each part of an assembly in a different .NET language. To build an assembly that contains multiple modules, you need to build each module separately and then combine them with the **Al.exe** utility.

There are two ways to go about creating a multi-module assembly. One way is to create all the modules without any manifest, and then create one additional module that contains only a manifest for the entire assembly, but no actual code. The other technique is to have just one module in the assembly that contains both code and a manifest for the entire assembly, and have all other modules in the assembly contain only code, with no manifest. We will describe the first of these two alternatives.

Code Example

The **MultiModule** example illustrates the mechanics of how to create a multiple module assembly. The example directory contains the files **Add.vb** and **Sub.vb**, which will be built into separate modules and then combined together into an assembly named **Arith.dll**. **Compute.vb** uses this assembly. **Add.vb** has one class with one method, **Add**. **Sub.vb** has another class that has one method, **Subtract**.

```
'Add.vb

Imports System

Public Class MyCalcAdd
   Public Function Add( _
     a as Integer, b as Integer) as Integer
       return a + b
   End Function
End Class
```

```
'Sub.vb

Imports System

Public Class MyCalcSub
   Public Function Subtract( _
     a as Integer, b as Integer) as Integer
       return a - b
   End Function
End Class
```

We create two modules with no assembly manifest by running **build.bat**, which has two commands:

```
Rem Build.bat

vbc /target:module /out:add.dll add.vb
vbc /target:module /out:sub.dll sub.vb
```

If you look at **add.dll** in ILDASM, you will see that there is a **.module add.dll** statement, but no **.assembly** statement. We now can build an assembly with a manifest using the Assembly Linker tool **Al.exe** by running **link.bat**, which has one command:

```
Rem Link.bat

Al add.dll, sub.dll /out:arith.dll
```

The **arith.dll** assembly only contains a manifest, with no actual code. Figure 9–20 shows that the manifest is made up of two separate, distinct files (**add.dll** and **sub.dll**), and the types in those files are also listed in the manifest.

We have a simple client program, **compute.vb**, that uses the types in **arith.dll**.

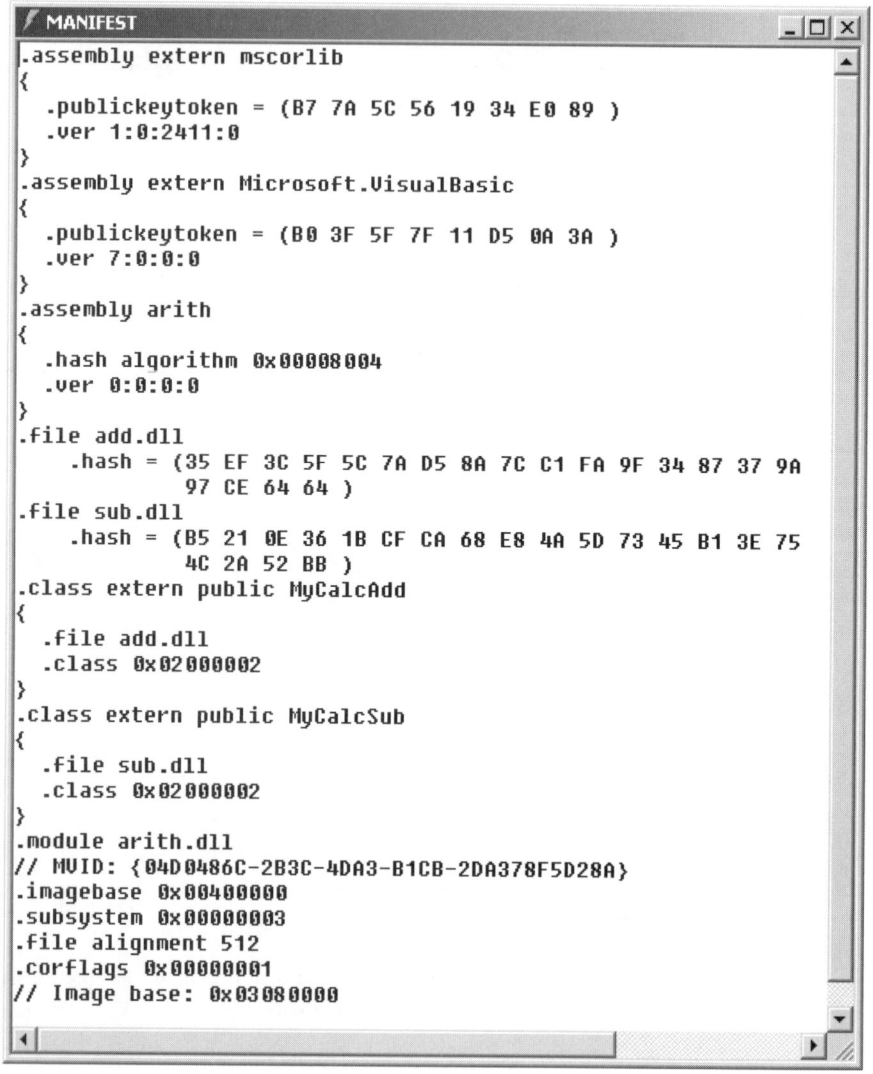

```
/ MANIFEST                                                    _ □ X
.assembly extern mscorlib
{
  .publickeytoken = (B7 7A 5C 56 19 34 E0 89 )
  .ver 1:0:2411:0
}
.assembly extern Microsoft.VisualBasic
{
  .publickeytoken = (B0 3F 5F 7F 11 D5 0A 3A )
  .ver 7:0:0:0
}
.assembly arith
{
  .hash algorithm 0x00008004
  .ver 0:0:0:0
}
.file add.dll
    .hash = (35 EF 3C 5F 5C 7A D5 8A 7C C1 FA 9F 34 87 37 9A
             97 CE 64 64 )
.file sub.dll
    .hash = (B5 21 0E 36 1B CF CA 68 E8 4A 5D 73 45 B1 3E 75
             4C 2A 52 BB )
.class extern public MyCalcAdd
{
  .file add.dll
  .class 0x02000002
}
.class extern public MyCalcSub
{
  .file sub.dll
  .class 0x02000002
}
.module arith.dll
// MVID: {04D0486C-2B3C-4DA3-B1CB-2DA378F5D28A}
.imagebase 0x00400000
.subsystem 0x00000003
.file alignment 512
.corflags 0x00000001
// Image base: 0x03080000
```

FIGURE 9–20   *Manifest for a multi-module Assembly.*

```vb
'Compute.vb

Imports System

Public Class Compute
   Public Shared Sub Main()

      Dim mca as MyCalcAdd = new MyCalcAdd()
```

```
    Dim y as Integer = mca.Add(1, 3)
    Console.WriteLine("y = " + y.ToString())

    Dim mcs as MyCalcSub = new MyCalcSub()
    y = mcs.Subtract(1, 3)
    Console.WriteLine("y = " + y.ToString())

  End Sub
End Class
```

We can build it with the command

```
vbc /r:arith.dll compute.vb
```

This will produce **compute.exe**, which we can run.

Setup and Deployment Projects

Assemblies may be deployed as regular standalone binary code files (i.e., DLL or EXE files), or they may be deployed using CAB, MSI, or MSM files. A CAB file is a cabinet file with the **.cab** file name extension. A CAB file is used to compress and combine other files into one convenient manageable file. Although CAB files can be used for general purposes, they have traditionally been used for CD-based and Web-based installation purposes. MSI and MSM files are Microsoft Windows Installer files, with the **.msi** and **.msm** file name extensions. MSI files (and indirectly, MSM files) are used with the **Msiexec.exe** Windows Installer program to deploy standalone applications and reusable components.

MSI files are Microsoft Windows Installer installation packages that have the **.msi** file name extension. MSM files are merge modules that have the **.msm** file name extension. Windows Installer supports software installation, repair, upgrade, and removal. Windows Installer packages are self-contained database files that provide installation information to the Windows Installer service. An MSM file has an internal structure that is similar to an MSI file, but it is somewhat simplified. Unfortunately, an MSM file cannot be used directly by Windows Installer, since it lacks certain important database tables. Instead, the MSM file must be merged into an MSI file to be used in an actual installation session. However, MSM files are useful for separating out shared installation information into an independent package that can then be merged into many other MSI packages.

Installation may be accomplished using the Windows Installer, Internet Explorer, or simply by manually copying assemblies and associated files. To help the programmer develop setup and deployment solutions, Visual Studio .NET provides several templates and wizards for generating starter setup projects. These tools are available by way of the New Project dialog box under the Setup and Deployment Projects node, as shown in Figure 9–21. As you can see, the following templates are provided for generating starter setup and deployment projects.

- Cab Project
- Setup Project
- Setup Wizard
- Merge Module Project
- Web Setup Project

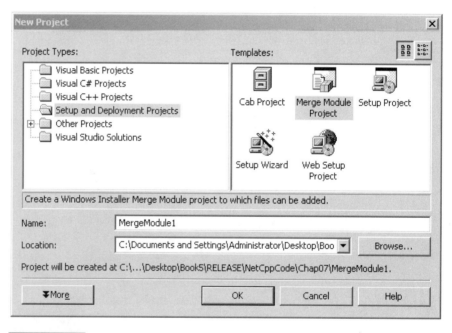

FIGURE 9–21   *Setup and deployment projects templates.*

CAB Project

A CAB project creates a cabinet file containing any number of other files that can be used for traditional deployment purposes. CAB files have been used to package legacy COM components deployed over the Internet, and they have also been used in traditional CD-based installation programs. CAB files may now also be used for packaging managed code. However, for .NET deployment, a CAB file can only contain one assembly, and the CAB file be must be assigned the same name as the contained assembly, but with the **.cab** extension. For example, an assembly named **SomeComponent.dll** would have to be contained in a cabinet file named **SomeComponent.cab**.

Setup Project

The Setup Project template creates a Windows Installer **.msi** file for a desktop or distributed application. A setup project is not intended for deployment of Web-based applications, since a specialized Web setup project is used for that purpose. A setup project produces a program that installs an application onto a target machine. You may create setup projects within the same solution that contains the other projects to be deployed. In a multitier solution, you can create one setup project for each project that is to be deployed to a particular target computer. For example, in a simple three-tier solution, you would probably have three deployment projects. Two simple deployment projects would set up the client and server. A third deployment project would then look after the more complex middle-tier business logic. Additional deployment projects may come into play if the solution is highly complex or if merge modules were incorporated into the deployment strategy.

To create a setup project, select File | New, then select Project. In the New Project dialog box, select Setup and Deployment Projects as the Project Type. Finally, select Setup Project as the Template, specify name and location, and then click OK. The result of this is shown in Figure 9–22, showing Solution Explorer and the File System Editor.

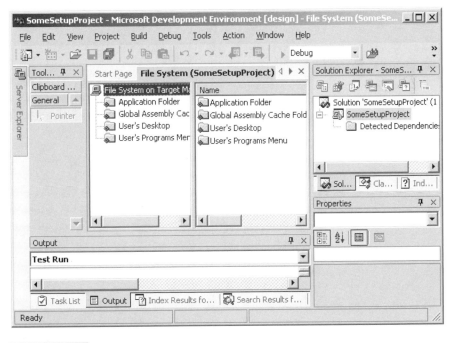

FIGURE 9–22   *Solution Explorer and the File System Editor in a setup project.*

Once the initial setup project has been created with the Setup Project template, it can be further developed using the File System Editor. The File System Editor allows you to drag and drop or copy and paste files to be deployed by the setup deployment project and control their destinations on the target machine. Initially, the File System Editor shows a list of destination folders that you can deploy into, and you can also add your own folders to this list.

Once you have an MSI file created, you can use Windows Installer, as shown in the following command line.

```
Msiexec /i SomeSetup.msi
```

The Windows Installer program then starts up and displays a series of installation dialogs. After Windows Installer has completed the deployment, you can try running the installed application to verify that the installation was successful. If you run the same command, **Msiexec /i SomeSetup.msi**, it will detect that it already exists, so it gives you the choice to either repair the installation or uninstall the application.

Merge Module Project

A merge module project packages reusable setup information that can be independently maintained and then merged as a shared installation package into other installation packages. A merge module project produces a merge module **.msm** file that can be merged into **.msi** files. This allows you to share common assemblies, associated files, registry values, and setup functionality among multiple applications.

To start the Merge Module Project Wizard, select File | New, then select Project. In the New Project dialog box, select Setup and Deployment Projects as the Project Type. Finally, select Merge Module Project Wizard as the Template, specify name and location, and then click OK.

Typically, an MSI file is intended for use by the end user for installing a complete solution in one simple deployment session. In contrast, an MSM file is typically intended for use by other developers who want to use components that you have developed in their setup projects. Those other developers can merge your MSM file into their own MSI file for deploying your components into their test and development environments, as well as for their ultimate end user. End users should not be provided any MSM files, since they are not directly installable using Windows Installer, and they are not very friendly to work with.

To add an existing merge module project to a setup project, create or open the setup project and Select File | Add Project, and then select Existing Project. In the Add Existing Project dialog box, browse to the location of the desired merge module project, select the associated **.vdp** deployment project file, and then click Open.

We just added the merge module project to the solution. We now have to add it to the setup project itself. Select the setup project and invoke Add:Project Output, then select the merge module project in the dialog that appears.

Web-Based Deployment

Web-based deployment uses Internet Explorer on the client to automatically download assemblies packaged as EXE, DLL, or CAB files on demand from a .NET Web server. HTML files can dynamically deploy assemblies as well as configuration files to control the binding process. Web-based deployment results in assemblies being downloaded into the client's assembly download cache on demand.

The XML **<object>** tag is used to download and install assemblies, using either a relative or absolute URL. The following shows a relative URL example, where the assembly is located relative to the directory of the containing HTML file on the Web server.

```
<object
  id="SomeComponent"
  classid="./SomeDirectory/MyComponent.dll#SomeClass">
</object>
```

The following shows an absolute URL example, where the assembly is located on a specified Web server.

```
<object
  id="SomeComponent"
  classid="http://www.acme.com/MyComponent.dll#SomeClass">
</object>
```

By default, IE creates a separate application domain for each Web site that it encounters. An application domain is a .NET feature that can be thought of as a scalable lightweight process. An application domain efficiently provides fault isolation without the overhead of running actual multiple processes. Each of these application domains may optionally have its own configuration file to control binding and security. Also, a configuration file may specify an isolated application domain for individual applications on the same Web server. Each HTML file that specifies the same configuration file will be placed into the same application domain.

Summary

Deployment is very important, and it constitutes one of the major phases in software development. If it is not done properly, the entire development effort becomes a waste of time and money. Fortunately, with assemblies, which are the fundamental units of .NET deployment, many of the complexities and problems relating to deployment are conveniently solved.

By simply building dynamic link libraries, you can have reusable components without all the difficulties associated with building and installing COM components.

Private assembly deployment can be simply copying the assembly to the same directory as the client application. Public assembly deployment involves the creation of a strong name for the assembly, followed by deployment into the global assembly cache. The Strong Name Utility (**Sn.exe**) can be used to create the strong name for an assembly. The Global Assembly Cache utility **Gacutil.exe** or the **.NET Admin Tool** can then be used to deploy the shared assembly into the GAC. It is also possible to combine multiple modules into a single logical assembly. To do this, you build separate modules that lack manifest information, and then a manifest module can be generated for the entire set of modules that comprise the assembly. The Visual Studio .NET CAB and setup wizards are very useful for creating starter setup and deployment projects, which can save a great deal of development time.

.NET Framework Classes

*I*t is impossible to cover in one chapter or one book all of the .NET Framework classes. Although coverage is incomplete, the .NET classes cover a large fraction of the Win32 API as well as much else. While a lot of attention has been focused on the Internet-related functionality, the development model for Windows applications has changed as well.

This chapter focuses on those classes that illustrate the key concepts and patterns that appear throughout the .NET Framework. Experienced programmers will find this approach more fruitful over the long run than our attempting to explain a little about every class that a programmer might need without giving much insight into them. Other chapters will go into more depth about other parts of the framework, such as Windows Forms, ASP.NET, ADO.NET security, and Web services.

We start out by exploring the concept of reflection and metadata. Metadata appears everywhere in .NET and is critical to understanding how the CLR can provide services for your applications. Next we explore file input/output for several reasons. First, it introduces the important topic of serialization. Second, the **Path** class provides an example of how some .NET Framework classes provide some or all of their functionality through shared methods. Third, the formatter classes are used in several places in .NET.

Understanding serialization will give you a concrete idea of how the framework can handle objects transparently for you. It also appears in a supporting role any place where objects have to be moved or transported. Our discussion of the **ISerializable** interface demonstrates how much easier it is to implement an interface in .NET than with COM.

To develop an understanding of the .NET model for applications, we introduce programming with threads under .NET and several .NET synchronization techniques to handle multithreading conflicts. The various synchronization techniques illustrate the tradeoffs of using attributes supplied by the .NET Framework versus doing it yourself.

To further your understanding of the .NET programming model, we introduce *context* and the use of proxies and stubs to implement system services. *Application domains* are much more effective than Win32 processes in achieving application isolation.

The asynchronous design pattern appears throughout .NET and is discussed in some detail. We give some examples of remoting because it is a key technology and it summarizes many of the concepts developed in this chapter. The chapter uses several attributes provided by the .NET Framework, and we show how to implement and use custom attributes. We discuss garbage collection, finalization, and the dispose pattern so that you can understand how to make sure resources are properly freed in your applications.

Metadata and Reflection

The **Serialization** example in Chapter 2 demonstrates how metadata makes many of the services of the Common Language Runtime possible. Many of the technologies we cover in the rest of the book rely on metadata, although we will not always stop and point this out.

Metadata is information about the assemblies, modules, and types that constitute .NET programs. If you have ever had to create IDL to generate a type library so that your C++ COM objects could be called by Visual Basic, or to create proxies and stubs, you will appreciate how useful metadata is and will be grateful that it comes "for free."

.NET compilers emit metadata, and the CLR, the .NET Framework, or your own programs can use this metadata. Since we want to give you an understanding of how metadata works we will focus our discussion on the use, not the creation, of metadata. Metadata is read using classes in the **System.Reflection** namespace.[1]

When you load an assembly and its associated modules and types, the metadata is loaded along with it. You can then query the assembly to get those associated types. You can also call **GetType** on any CLR type and get its metadata. **GetType** is a method on **System.Object**, which every CLR type inherits from. After you get the **Type** associated with an object, you can use the reflection methods to get the related metadata.

---

1. There is a lower level set of unmanaged COM interfaces for accessing metadata, but we will not discuss them here. See "Metadata in .NET" by Matt Pietrek in the October 2000 *MSDN Magazine*.

Code
Example

The **Reflection** example program takes the case study's **Customer** assembly and prints out some of the metadata available. You should examine the output and source code as you read the next sections. You should especially compare the output of the program with the source code in the file **customer.vb**.

The program clearly shows that it is possible to retrieve all of the types in an assembly and reconstruct the structures, interfaces, properties, events, and methods associated with those types.

First we load the assembly into memory and write out its name.

```
Dim a As System.Reflection.Assembly = _
    System.Reflection.Assembly.Load(assemblyName)
Console.WriteLine("Assembly {0} found.", a.FullName)
```

The output for this statement is appropriate for an unsigned assembly:

```
Assembly Customer, Version=1.0.765.27723, Culture=neutral,
PublicKeyToken=null found.
```

One of the properties of the **Assembly** class is the **CodeBase**, discussed in Chapter 9. The security Evidence associated with this assembly is another property. Evidence is discussed in Chapter 16.

The following code tries to get the entry point for the assembly:

```
Dim entryMethodInfo As MethodInfo = a.EntryPoint
```

Since this is a component assembly, there is no program entry point (i.e., a DLL has no Main). If this was an executable program, we could use the **Invoke** method on the **MethodInfo** class to run the startup code in the assembly.[2]

The sample uses the **Assembly.GetModules** method to find associated modules with this assembly. In this case we have only one, **customer.dll**. We could then find the types associated with the module. Instead, we use the **Assembly.GetTypes** method to return an array of the assembly's types.

Type

The abstract class **Type** in the **System** namespace defines .NET types. Since there are no functions outside of classes or global variables in .NET, getting all the types in an assembly will allow us to get all the metadata about the code in that assembly. **Type** represents all the types present in .NET: classes, interfaces, value types, arrays, and enumerations.

The **Type** class is also returned by the **GetType** method on the **System.Object** class and the shared **GetType** method on the **Type** class itself.

---

2. You can also load and execute the assembly from the AppDomain, as we discuss later in this chapter.

The latter method can only be used with types that can be resolved statically (i.e., at compile time).

One of **Type's** properties is the assembly to which it belongs. You can get all the types in the containing assembly once you have the **Type** of one object. **Type** is an abstract class. At runtime, an instance of **System.Runtime-Type** is returned.

If you examine the program's output, you will see that each type in the assembly, **CustomerListItem**, **ICustomer**, **Customer**, and **Customers**, is found, and its metadata is printed out. We can find out the standard attributes and the type from which the class derives for each type through the **Attributes** and **BaseType** properties.

The methods associated with the **Type** class enable you to get the associated fields, properties, interfaces, events, and methods. For example, the **Customer** type has no interfaces, properties, or events; four fields; three constructors; and the methods inherited from its base type **System.Object**:

```
Type Customer found.
    BaseType: Object
    Attributes: AutoLayout, AnsiClass, NotPublic, Public,
        BeforeFieldInit
    GUID: 954e6037-f861-358c-aa1b-2aef8a0044b9
    Interfaces:
    Fields:
        CustomerId
        FirstName
        LastName
        EmailAddress
    Properties:
    Events:
    Constructors:
        Public .ctor(System.String first,
                     System.String last,
            System.String email)
        Public .ctor()
        Public .ctor(System.Int32 id)
    Methods:
        Public Int32 GetHashCode()
        Public Boolean Equals(System.Object obj)
        Public String ToString()
        Public Boolean Equals(System.Object obj)
        Public Int32 GetHashCode()
        Public String ToString()
        Public Type GetType()
```

The type **Customers** inherits from one interface and has one constructor and four of its own methods in addition to the four it inherited from its base type **System.Object**:

```
Type Customers found.
   BaseType: Object
   Attributes: AutoLayout, AnsiClass, NotPublic, Public
   GUID: cd4071bc-aa3f-34c6-8e37-167925ad7ed3
   Interfaces:
      ICustomer
   Fields:
   Properties:
   Events:
   Constructors:
      Public .ctor()
   Methods:
      Public Void ChangeEmailAddress(System.Int32 id,
         System.String emailAddress)
      Public ArrayList GetCustomer(System.Int32 id)
      Public Void UnregisterCustomer(System.Int32 id)
      Public Int32 RegisterCustomer(System.String
         firstName, System.String lastName,
         System.String emailAddress)
      Public Int32 GetHashCode()
      Public Boolean Equals(System.Object obj)
      Public String ToString()
      Public Type GetType()
```

These were obtained with the **GetInterfaces**, **GetFields**, **GetProperties**, **GetEvents**, **GetConstructors**, and **GetMethods** methods on the **Type** class. Since an interface is a type, **GetInterfaces** returns an array of **Types** representing the interfaces inherited or implemented by the **Type** queried. Since fields, properties, events, and methods are not types, their accessor methods do not return **Types**. Each of their accessor methods returns an appropriate class: **FieldInfo**, **PropertyInfo**, **EventInfo**, **ConstructorInfo**, and **MethodInfo**. All these classes, as well as the **Type** class, inherit from the **MemberInfo** class that is the abstract base class for member metadata.

Let us examine some of the metadata associated with a class method. Using the reflection methods, we were able to reconstruct the signatures for all the classes and interfaces in the **Customer** assembly. Here is the output for the methods of the **Customers** class:

```
Public Void ChangeEmailAddress(System.Int32 id,
   System.String emailAddress)
Public ArrayList GetCustomer(System.Int32 id)
Public Void UnregisterCustomer(System.Int32 id)
Public Int32 RegisterCustomer(System.String firstName,
   System.String lastName, System.String emailAddress)
Public Int32 GetHashCode()
Public Boolean Equals(System.Object obj)
Public String ToString()
Public Type GetType()
```

Here is the code from the example that produced the output:

```
Dim methodInfo() As MethodInfo = t.GetMethods()
For j = 0 To methodInfo.Length - 1
   If methodInfo(j).IsStatic Then
      Console.Write("          Shared ")
   End If
   If methodInfo(j).IsPublic Then
      Console.Write("          public ")
   End If
   If methodInfo(j).IsFamily Then
      Console.Write("          Protected ")
   End If
   If methodInfo(j).IsAssembly Then
      Console.Write("          Internal ")
   End If
   If methodInfo(j).IsPrivate Then
      Console.Write("          Private ")
   End If
   Console.Write("{0} ", _
    methodInfo(j).ReturnType.Name)
   Console.Write("{0}(", methodInfo(j).Name)
   Dim paramInfo() As ParameterInfo = _
      methodInfo(j).GetParameters()
   Dim last As Long = paramInfo.Length - 1
   Dim k As Integer
   For k = 0 To paramInfo.Length - 1
      Console.Write( _
         "{0} {1}", _
         paramInfo(k).ParameterType, _
         paramInfo(k).Name)
      If k <> last Then
         Console.Write(", ")
      End If
   Next
   Console.WriteLine(")")
Next
```

Except for the fact that a constructor does not have a return type, the exact same code reconstitutes the calling sequences for the class's constructors.

The **MethodInfo** class has properties that help us determine if the method is **Shared**, **Public**, **Protected**, **Internal**, or **Private** as well as determine the return type and method name. The method parameters are stored in property array of type **ParameterInfo** class.

This example should also make clear that types are assembly relative. The same type name and layout in two different assemblies are treated by the runtime as two separate types. When versioning assemblies, you have to be careful when mixing versioned types or the same types in two different assemblies.

All this metadata allows the Common Language Runtime and the .NET Framework to provide services to your applications, because they can understand the structure of your types.

Late Binding

Code
Example

Reflection can also be used to implement late binding. Late binding is where the method to be called is determined during execution rather than compilation. It is one example of how metadata can be used to provide functionality. As the previous example demonstrates, you can extract the signature of a method associated with a type. The **MethodInfo** object has all the needed metadata for a class method. The **DynamicInvocation** sample demonstrates a very simple example of late binding.

We dynamically load an assembly and get the metadata for a method of a particular type:

```
' Load Customer assembly
Dim a As System.Reflection.Assembly = _
   System.Reflection.Assembly.Load("Customer")

' Get metadata for Customers class and one method
Dim t As Type = _
   a.GetType("Customer.OI.NetVB.Acme.Customers")
Dim mi As MethodInfo = t.GetMethod("GetCustomer")
```

Using the reflection classes, we could have made this completely dynamic by arbitrarily picking types, methods, and constructors from the **Customer** assembly using the techniques of the last example, but we wanted to keep the **DynamicInvocation** example simple.

The **System** namespace has an **Activator** class that has overloaded **CreateInstance** methods to create an instance of any .NET type using the appropriate constructor. The **Activator** class is discussed in this chapter's section on remoting. We invoke a constructor with no arguments to create an instance of the **Customers** object.

```
' Create Customers object, constructor takes no arguments
Dim customerInstance As Object = _
   Activator.CreateInstance(t)
```

We then build an argument list and use the **Invoke** method of the **MethodInfo** instance to call the **GetCustomer** method.

```
' invoke the method
Dim arguments() As Object = New Object(0) {}
Dim customerId As Integer = -1
arguments(0) = customerId
Dim returnType As Object = mi.Invoke( _
   customerInstance, arguments)
```

Using the reflection methods, we get the type information for each field in a return structure. Note the **GetValue** method that gets the data for a particular field in a structure. This is necessary because we cannot do pointer arithmetic to access an offset into a structure.

```
If returnType.GetType() Is _
 Type.GetType("System.Collections.ArrayList") Then
   Dim arrayList As ArrayList = returnType
   Dim i As Integer
   For i = 0 To arrayList.Count - 1
      Dim itemType As Type = arrayList(i).GetType()
      Dim fi() As FieldInfo = itemType.GetFields()
      Dim j As Integer
      For j = 0 To fi.Length - 1
         Dim fieldValue As Object = _
          fi(j).GetValue(arrayList(i))
         Console.Write( _
          "{0, -10} = {1, -15}", fi(j).Name, fieldValue)
      Next
      Console.WriteLine()
   Next
End If
```

This code did not use any specific objects or types from the **Customer** assembly. We did use some knowledge about the assembly to keep the code simple to illustrate the main points. It should be clear, however, how to make this completely general.

You can take this one step further and use the classes that emit metadata (in **System.Reflection.Emit**). In this way, you can dynamically create an assembly, and then load and run it.

Input and Output in .NET

Programming languages have undergone an evolution in how they deal with the important topic of input/output (I/O). Early languages, such as FORTRAN, COBOL, and the original BASIC, had I/O statements built into the language. Later languages have tended not to have I/O built into the language, but instead rely on a standard library for performing I/O, such as the **<stdio.h>** library in C. The library in languages like C works directly with files.

Still later languages, such as C++ and Java, introduced a further abstraction called a *stream*. A stream serves as an intermediary between the program and the file. Read and write operations are done to the stream, which is tied to a file. This architecture is very flexible, because the same kind of read and write operations can apply not only to a file, but to other kinds of I/O, such as network sockets. This added flexibility introduces a slight additional complexity in writing programs, because you have to deal not only with files but also with streams, and there exists a considerable variety of stream classes. But the added complexity is well worth the effort, and C# strikes a nice balance, with classes that make performing common operations quite simple.

Data can be treated as a stream of bytes or characters. We can read 500 bytes from a file to a memory buffer. Data can also be treated as a set of objects. Writing and reading the objects is referred to as serializing and deserializing the objects. We can serialize (write) the list of **Customer** objects to disk. We can then deserialize (read) the list of **Customer** objects back into memory.

The **System.IO** namespace has several classes for reading and writing to various types of storage while treating the data as bytes or characters. Serialization functionality can be found in various places in the .NET Framework. The **System.Runtime.Serialization** namespace handles serialization of the Common Type System. The **System.Xml.Serialization** namespace handles XML serialization.

Streams

Stream is an abstract class that is the basis for reading from and writing bytes to some storage such as a file. It supports both synchronous and asynchronous reading and writing. Asynchronous methods are discussed later in this chapter. The **Stream** class has the typical methods that you would expect: **Read**, **Write**, **Seek**, **Flush**, and **Close**.

The **FileStream** class is derived from **Stream** to represent the reading and writing of files as a series of bytes. The **FileStream** constructor builds the actual stream instance. The overridden **Stream** methods implement the reading and writing to the file.

Other classes derived from **Stream** include **MemoryStream**, **BufferedStream**, and **NetworkStream** (in **System.Net.Sockets**).

Code
Example

The **FileStream** example (in the **FileIO** directory, as are all the I/O examples) illustrates how to use the **Stream** classes. If the file does not exist, then a new file is created and the numbers from 0 to 9 are written to the file. If the file already exists, the code starts reading 5 bytes from the end of the file and then writes them out. (You should run the example twice, the first time to write the data and the second time to read it.)

```
Dim data() As Byte = New Byte(9) {}
Dim fs As System.IO.FileStream = _
    New System.IO.FileStream( _
    "FileStreamTest.txt", FileMode.OpenOrCreate)
If fs.Length = 0 Then
    Console.WriteLine("Writing Data...")
    Dim i As Short
```

```vbnet
    For i = 0 To 9
        data(i) = i
    Next
    fs.Write(data, 0, 10)
Else
    fs.Seek(-5, SeekOrigin.End)
    Dim count As Integer = fs.Read(data, 0, 10)
    Dim i As Integer
    For i = 0 To count - 1
        Console.WriteLine(data(i))
    Next
End If
fs.Close()
```

Primitive Datatypes and Streams

Code
Example

The stream-derived classes work well if you are reading and writing bytes of data as a block. If you need to read and write the primitive common types, such as **Boolean**, **String**, **Int32**, and so on, in and out of a stream, use the **BinaryReader** and the **BinaryWriter** classes. The **Binary** example in the **FileIO** directory shows how to use these classes. You create the appropriate stream (**FileStream** in the example) and pass it to the **BinaryReader** or **BinaryWriter** constructor. You can then use one of the overloaded **Read** or **Write** methods to read or write a datatype to or from the stream. (Again, you should run the example twice. The first time creates and writes the file, and the second time reads the file.)

```vbnet
Dim fs As FileStream = New FileStream( _
    "BinaryTest.bin", FileMode.OpenOrCreate)
If fs.Length = 0 Then
    Console.WriteLine("Writing Data...")
    Dim w As BinaryWriter = New BinaryWriter(fs)
    Dim i As Int16
    For i = 0 To 9
        w.Write(i)
    Next
    w.Close()
Else
    Dim r As BinaryReader = New BinaryReader(fs)
    Dim i As Integer
    For i = 0 To 9
        Console.WriteLine(r.ReadInt16())
    Next
    r.Close()
End If
fs.Close()
```

TextReader and TextWriter

The **TextReader** and **TextWriter** abstract classes treat the data as a sequential stream of characters (i.e., as text). **TextReader** has methods such as **Close**, **Peek**, **Read**, **ReadBlock**, **ReadLine**, and **ReadToEnd**. **TextWriter** has methods such as **Close**, **Flush**, **Write**, and **WriteLine**. The overloaded **Read** methods read characters from the stream. The overloaded **Write** and **WriteLine** methods write various types to the stream. If an object is written to the stream, the object's **ToString** method is used.

StringReader and **StringWriter** are derived from **TextReader** and **TextWriter**. These classes read and write characters from a string. The **StringWriter's** constructor uses a **StringBuilder** object. The **StringBuilder** class was discussed in Chapter 4. **StreamReader** and **StreamWriter** are also derived from **TextReader** and **TextWriter**. They read and write text to and from a **Stream** object. As with the **BinaryReader** and **BinaryWriter** class, you create a stream and pass it to the constructor. Hence, these classes can use any **Stream**-derived class data storage. The **Text** example in the **FileIO** directory uses the **StreamWriter** and **StreamReader** classes.

Code Example

```
Dim fs As FileStream = New FileStream( _
    "TextTest.txt", FileMode.OpenOrCreate)
If fs.Length = 0 Then
    Console.WriteLine("Writing Data...")
    Dim sw As StreamWriter = New StreamWriter(fs)
    sw.Write(100)
    sw.WriteLine(" One Hundred")
    sw.WriteLine("End of File")
    sw.Close()
Else
    Dim text As String
    Dim sr As StreamReader = New StreamReader(fs)
    text = sr.ReadLine()
    While text <> Nothing
        Console.WriteLine(text)
        text = sr.ReadLine()
    End While
    sr.Close()
End If
fs.Close()
```

File Manipulation

The .NET Framework has two classes that are very useful for working with files:

- File
- FileInfo

If you need to manipulate the file in addition to reading and writing to it, the **File** class provides the basic functionality. Since the **File** class just has shared members, you have to provide the name of the file as an argument. The **FileInfo** class has a constructor that creates an object that represents a file. You then use the methods to manipulate that particular file.

The **File** class methods always perform a security check. If you are going to continually access a particular file, you may want to use the **FileInfo** class, because the security check is made only once in the constructor. Security is discussed in more detail in Chapter 16.

FILE CLASS

The **File** class has methods for creating and opening files that return **FileStream**, **StreamWriter**, or **StreamReader** objects that do the actual reading and writing. The overloaded **Create** methods return a **FileStream** object. The **CreateText** method returns a **StreamWriter**. The overloaded **Open** method can either create a new file or open an existing one for reading or writing, depending on the method parameters. The object returned is a **FileStream** object. The **OpenText** method returns a **StreamReader**. The **OpenRead** method returns a **FileStream** object. The **OpenWrite** method returns a **FileStream**.

The **File** class also has methods for copying, deleting, and moving files. You can test for the existence of a file. File attributes such as the following can be read or modified:

- creation time
- last access time
- last write time
- archive, hidden, normal, system, or temporary
- compressed, encrypted
- read-only
- is the file a directory?

PATH CLASS

Many of the filenames needed for input arguments have to be full paths. Or you might only want to manipulate parts of the path. The **Path** class has shared methods that make this easier. The **Path** class has shared fields that indicate various platform-specific aspects of pathnames, such as the separator characters for directories, paths, and volumes, and the illegal characters for pathnames.

Its shared methods let you change the extension of a file or find the directory where temporary files reside. The **GetFullPath** method is particularly useful. You can pass it a relative path such as `".\foo.txt"` and it will return the full path of the file. This is very useful for the **File** or security classes that require the full file path.

FILEINFO CLASS

The **FileInfo** constructor creates an object that represents a disk file. The constructor takes one argument, a string representing the name of the file. The class has properties that represent file properties such as the creation time, full pathname, and size of the file. It has creation and open methods that are analogous to the **File** class methods, but operate on this file instance and therefore do not need a filename parameter. The **FileInfo** class also has methods to move and copy the file.

FILE EXAMPLE

The **File** example in the **FileIO** directory illustrates the use of the **File** and **FileInfo** classes. The shared **Delete** method of the **File** class is used to remove a previous version of a file if it is present. The shared **CreateText** method creates a new file and returns a **StreamWriter** instance that is used to write some text to the file. The stream is then closed. The static **Move** method then renames the file.

    A **FileInfo** instance is constructed to represent this renamed file. The complete file name, size, and creation date for the file is written to the console. The file is opened as text and a **StreamReader** instance is used to read and write out the contents of the file.

```
System.IO.File.Delete("file2.txt")

Dim sw As StreamWriter = _
    System.IO.File.CreateText("file.txt")

sw.Write("The time has come the Walrus said, ")
sw.WriteLine("to talk of many things")
sw.Write("Of shoes, and ships, and sealing wax, ")
sw.WriteLine("of cabbages and kings")
sw.Write("And why the sea is boiling hot, ")
sw.WriteLine("and whether pigs have wings.")
sw.Close()

System.IO.File.Move("file.txt", "file2.txt")

Dim fileInfo As FileInfo = New FileInfo("file2.txt")

Console.WriteLine( _
    "File {0} is {1} bytes in length, created on {2}", _
    fileInfo.FullName, _
    fileInfo.Length, _
    fileInfo.CreationTime)
Console.WriteLine("")

Dim sr As StreamReader = fileInfo.OpenText()
Dim s As String = sr.ReadLine()
```

```
While s <> Nothing
   Console.WriteLine(s)
   s = sr.ReadLine()
End While
sr.Close()
Console.WriteLine("")
```

Serialization

Using the **File** and **Stream** classes can be quite cumbersome if you have to save a complicated data structure with linked objects. You have to save the individual fields to disk, remembering which field belongs to which object and which object instance was linked to another object instance. When restoring the data structure, you have to reconstitute that arrangement of fields and object references.

The serialization technology provided by the .NET Framework does this for you. Serialization converts data structures to a byte stream. Deserialization converts the byte stream back to the data structures. Serializing and deserializing can be done on different machines so long as they both host the CLR.

Objects can be serialized without writing special code because, as we have seen, the runtime can query the object's metadata to allow it to understand the memory layout of the object. To inform the framework that a class can be serialized, mark the class with the **System.Serializable** attribute. Any field or property that should not be serialized can be marked with the **System.NonSerialized** attribute. For example, fields that represent cached values need not be serialized. All you have to do is mark the class with the attribute, and then you do not have to write any other code to be able to serialize the class' fields.

Code Example

The **Serialization** example shows how to apply serialization to the case study's **HotelBroker** class in the **Hotel** assembly. The **Serializable** attribute has been applied to the **HotelBroker** class definition. The **Serializable** attribute has also been applied to all classes that are used by or derived from **HotelBroker** (**Broker**, **Hotel**, **HotelReservation**, **Reservable**, and **Reservation**), because in order for **HotelBroker** to be serializable, those classes have to be serializable as well. If any of those classes were not marked as serializable, a runtime exception would be thrown when the framework tries to serialize an object of that type.

```
<Serializable()> Public Class Hotel
   Inherits Reservable
...
<Serializable()> Public Class HotelReservation
   Inherits Reservation
<Serializable()> Public Class HotelBroker
```

```
    Inherits Broker
    Implements IHotelInfo, IHotelAdmin, IHotelReservation
    Private Const MAXDAY As Integer = 366
    Private Const MAXUNIT As Integer = 10
    <NonSerialized()> Private cities As ArrayList
...
<Serializable()> Public MustInherit Class Reservable
...
<Serializable()> Public MustInherit Class Reservation
...
<Serializable()> Public MustInherit Class Broker
...
```

The **cities** field of **HotelBroker** has been marked as **NonSerialized**, since the hotel's city is saved with the serialized hotels and therefore can be restored, as the modified **AddCity** method demonstrates. The **cities** field would be **Nothing** if the **HotelBroker** class had been deserialized, because the cities field was not saved.[3]

```
Private Sub AddCity(ByVal city As String)
    ' check if city already on list, add if not
    If cities Is Nothing Then
       cities = New ArrayList()
       Dim h As Hotel
       For Each h In units
          AddCity(h.City)
       Next
    End If

    If Not cities.Contains(city) Then
       cities.Add(city)
    End If
End Sub
```

Serialization Objects

Although the framework knows how to save an object marked with the **Serializable** attribute, you still have to specify the format in which the object is saved and the storage medium. To specify the format in which an object is saved, you use an instance of an object that supports the **IFormatter** interface.[4]

---

3. Of course, we could have serialized the **cities** field and not have to deal with the case where **cities** could be **Nothing**, but we wanted to demonstrate the **NonSerialized** attribute.

4. How does the runtime know if a class supports the **IFormatter** interface? Query the metadata!

The Framework ships with two such classes, **System.Runtime.Serialization.Formatters.Binary.BinaryFormatter** and **System.Runtime.Serialization.Formatters.Soap.SoapFormatter**. The **BinaryFormatter** uses a binary, compact format for serializing and deserializing on platforms that support the CLR. The **SoapFormatter** uses the industry-standard SOAP protocol that is discussed in Chapter 15, "Web Services." Since it is an XML-based, and therefore a text-based, protocol, it can be used to communicate with a non-CLR-based platform. The binary format is faster when serializing and deserializing data.

You can, of course, implement your own formatter classes. You might do this if you have to talk to a system with its own legacy byte format.

The **Serialization** example has code to demonstrate saving and restoring both binary and SOAP formats using a **FileStream**. Of course you could use any **Stream** based class representing some data medium.

```
Private Sub Save(ByVal broker As HotelBroker, _
 ByVal formatter As String)
   Dim s As FileStream
   If formatter = "b" Then
      s = New FileStream("hotels.bin", FileMode.Create)
      Dim b As BinaryFormatter = New BinaryFormatter()
      b.Serialize(s, broker)
   Else
      s = New FileStream("hotels.txt", FileMode.Create)
      Dim sf As SoapFormatter = New SoapFormatter()
      sf.Serialize(s, broker)
   End If
   s.Close()
End Sub

Private Sub Load(ByRef broker As HotelBroker, _
 ByVal formatter As String)
   Dim s As FileStream
   If formatter = "b" Then
      s = New FileStream("hotels.bin", FileMode.Open)
      Dim b As BinaryFormatter = New BinaryFormatter()
      broker = b.Deserialize(s)
   Else
      s = New FileStream("hotels.txt", FileMode.Open)
      Dim sf As SoapFormatter = New SoapFormatter()
      broker = sf.Deserialize(s)
   End If
   s.Close()
   ShowHotelList(broker.GetHotels())
End Sub
```

Here is some sample output from the **Serialization** example: First we add a hotel and save it with the SOAP formatter. We then exit the program.

```
Enter command: cities
Atlanta
Boston
Commands: quit, cities, list, add, fetch, save

Enter command: list
City            Name                    Rooms       Rate
Atlanta         Dixie                   100         115
Atlanta         Marriott                500         70
Boston          Sheraton                250         95
Commands: quit, cities, list, add, fetch, save

Enter command: add
Hotel City: Philadelphia
Hotel Name: Franklin
Number Rooms: 100
Room Rate: 200
Commands: quit, cities, list, add, fetch, save

Enter command: save
Formatter: b(inary), s(oap)s
Commands: quit, cities, list, add, fetch, save

Enter command: cities
Atlanta
Boston
Philadelphia
Commands: quit, cities, list, add, fetch, save

Enter command: list
City            Name                    Rooms       Rate
Atlanta         Dixie                   100         115
Atlanta         Marriott                500         70
Boston          Sheraton                250         95
Philadelphia    Franklin                100         200
Commands: quit, cities, list, add, fetch, save

Enter command: quit
```

We then run the program again and restore what we saved[5] in the first run.

```
Enter command: cities
Atlanta
Boston
```

---

5. If you look at the **hotels.txt** file, you will see a huge file with a lot of "empty" entries. This stems from the simplistic array data structure we used for reservations, which is a very sparse matrix.

```
Commands: quit, cities, list, add, fetch, save

Enter command: list
City              Name                  Rooms       Rate
Atlanta           Dixie                 100         115
Atlanta           Marriott              500          70
Boston            Sheraton              250          95
Commands: quit, cities, list, add, fetch, save

Enter command: fetch
Formatter: b(inary), s(oap)s
City              Name                  Rooms       Rate
Atlanta           Dixie                 100         115
Atlanta           Marriott              500          70
Boston            Sheraton              250          95
Philadelphia      Franklin              100         200
Commands: quit, cities, list, add, fetch, save

Enter command: cities
Atlanta
Boston
Philadelphia
```

ISerializable

Sometimes the serialization provided by the framework is not satisfactory. You can provide custom serialization for a class by implementing the **ISerializable** interface and adding a constructor to the class. The **ISerializable** interface has one member: **GetObjectData**. This method is used when data is serialized.

Code
Example

The **ISerializable** example demonstrates how this is done. As before, the class has to be marked as **Serializable**.

```
<Serializable()> Public Class HotelBroker
    Inherits Broker
    Implements IHotelInfo, IHotelAdmin, _
    IHotelReservation, ISerializable
    ...
```

The **SerializationInfo** class is used to store all the data that needs to be saved. The **AddValue** method is overloaded to handle the saving of various types, including **object**.[6] When you save the type, you provide a name so that

---

6. Some of the **AddValue** overloads are not CLS-compliant when the types being saved are not CLS-compliant types, such as unsigned integers. Be careful not to use those types where .NET language interoperability is required. You have to watch for this in other places in the .NET Framework, such as the **Convert** class or the **Parse** methods of the various CTS types or any other place where data is formatted, converted or read, or written out (such as the **TextWriter** classes).

it can be restored later. The **StreamingContext** class gives you information about the stream being used in the serialization. For example, you can find out if the stream being used is a file or is being remoted to another computer.

```
Public Sub GetObjectData( _
 ByVal info As SerializationInfo, _
 ByVal context As StreamingContext) _
 Implements ISerializable.GetObjectData
   Dim numberHotels As Long = units.Count
   info.AddValue("NumberHotels", numberHotels)
   info.AddValue("Hotels", units)
 End Sub
```

You also have to implement a special constructor that is used by the framework when the object is deserialized. It has the same arguments as **GetObjectData** does. Here you use the various **Get** methods on **SerializationInfo** to restore the data. Note that since we did not save the cities field—we had to manually restore it. The constructor is private because it is only used by the .NET Framework. If you forget to add the constructor, you will get a **SerializationException** when you try to restore the object.

```
Private Sub New( _
 ByVal info As SerializationInfo, _
 ByVal context As StreamingContext)
   MyBase.New(MAXDAY, MAXUNIT)
   Dim numberHotels As Long = info.GetInt32("NumberHotels")
   units = info.GetValue( _
      "Hotels", Type.GetType("ArrayList"))
   If numberHotels = units.Count Then
      Console.WriteLine("All hotels deserialized.")
   Else
      Console.WriteLine("Error in deserialization.")
   End If
   cities = New ArrayList()
   Dim h As Hotel
   For Each h In units
      AddCity(h.City)
   Next
End Sub
```

In this example we did custom serialization only for the **HotelBroker** object. For all the other objects, we still relied on the framework's serialization. This example works the same way that the **Serialization** example did. The sample output would look the same.

.NET Application Model

Serialization gave you a concrete example of the flexible environment the .NET Framework provides for writing code. Now let us take a look at the model in which .NET applications run. The Win32 environment in which a program runs is called its process. This environment consists of

- the address space in which the code and data of the program resides.
- a set of environmental variables that is associated with the program.
- a current drive and directory.
- one or more threads.

Threads

A thread is the actual execution path of a program's code. One or more threads run inside of a process to allow for multiple execution paths inside of a process. For example, with multiple threads a program can update the user interface with partial results on one thread as a calculation proceeds on another thread. All threads in the same process share the process environment, and therefore all those threads can access the same process memory.

Threads are scheduled by the operating system. Processes and application domains[7] are not scheduled. Threads are given a limited timeslice in which to run so that they can share the processor with other threads. Higher priority threads will get to run more often than lower priority threads. After some time elapses, a thread will get another chance to run. When a thread is swapped back in, it resumes running from where it was swapped out.

Threads maintain a context that has to be saved and restored when the operating system's scheduler switches from one thread to another. A thread's context includes the machine registers and stack that contain the state of the executing code.

The **System.Threading.Thread** class models an executing thread. The **Thread** object that represents the current executing thread can be found from the shared property **Thread.CurrentThread**.

Unless your code runs on a multiprocessor machine or you are trying to use time while a single processor machine waits for some event such as an I/O event, multiple threads do not result in any time saved on your computing tasks. It can, however, allow the system to seem more responsive to tasks requiring user interaction. Using too many threads can decrease performance as contention between the threads for the CPU increases.

---

7. Application domains are discussed later in this chapter.

To help you understand threads, we have a four-part **Threading** example that uses the **Customer** and **Hotel** assemblies from the case study to make reservations. Let us look first at Step 0.

.NET threads run as delegates defined by the **ThreadStart** class. The delegate returns void and takes no parameters.

```
Public Delegate Sub ThreadStart()
```

The **NewReservation** class has a public member function, **MakeReservation**, that will define the thread function. Since the thread function takes no parameters, any data that this function uses is assigned to fields in the **NewReservation** instance.

The thread delegate is created and passed as a parameter to the constructor that creates the **Thread** object. The **Start** method on the **Thread** object is invoked to begin the thread's execution. When we discuss the asynchronous programming model, we will show you how to pass parameters to a thread delegate. The program now has two threads, the original one that executed the code to start the thread and now the thread we just created that attempts to make a hotel reservation.

```
Public Class NewReservation
   ...
   Public Sub MakeReservation()
      Console.WriteLine( _
         "Thread {0} starting.", _
         Thread.CurrentThread.GetHashCode())
      ...
      Dim result As ReservationResult = _
         hotelBroker.MakeReservation( _
         customerId, city, hotel, ResDate, numberDays)
      ...
   End Sub
End Class

Public Module TestThreading
   ...
   Public Sub Main()
      Try
         ...
         Dim reserve1 As NewReservation = _
            New NewReservation(Customers, HotelBroker)
         reserve1.customerId = 1
         reserve1.city = "Boston"
         reserve1.hotel = "Presidential"
         reserve1.sdate = "12/12/2001"
         reserve1.numberDays = 3

         ' create delegate for threads
         Dim threadStart1 As ThreadStart = _
```

```
            New ThreadStart( _
            AddressOf reserve1.MakeReservation)
        Dim thread1 As Thread = New Thread(threadStart1)

        Console.WriteLine( _
            "Thread {0} starting a new thread.", _
            Thread.CurrentThread.GetHashCode())
        thread1.Start()
        ...
    End Sub
End Class
```

To cause the original thread to wait until the second thread is done, the **Join** method on the **Thread** object is called. The original thread now blocks (waits) until the reservation thread is complete. The results of the reservation request are written to the console by the reservation thread.

```
thread1.Join()
Console.WriteLine("Done!")
```

THREAD SYNCHRONIZATION

Code
Example

An application can create multiple threads. Look at the code in Step 1 of the **Threading** example. Now multiple reservation requests are being made simultaneously.

```
Dim reserve1 As NewReservation = _
    New NewReservation(customers, hotelBroker)
...
Dim reserve2 As NewReservation = _
    New NewReservation(customers, hotelBroker)
...
Dim threadStart1 As ThreadStart = _
    New ThreadStart(AddressOf reserve1.MakeReservation)
Dim threadStart2 As ThreadStart = _
    New ThreadStart(AddressOf reserve2.MakeReservation)

Dim thread1 As Thread = New Thread(threadStart1)
Dim thread2 As Thread = New Thread(threadStart2)
...
thread1.Start()
thread2.Start()

thread1.Join()
thread2.Join()
```

The problem with our reservation system is that there is no guarantee that one thread will not interfere with the work being done with the other thread. Since threads only run for a small period before they give up the processor to another thread, they may not be finished with whatever operation they were working on when their timeslice expires.

For example, they might be in the middle of updating a data structure. If another thread tries to use the information in that data structure or to update the data structure, the results of operations will be inconsistent and incorrect, at the minimum, or a program crash (i.e., exception) will occur, at the worst (e.g., if references to obsolete structures were not yet updated).

Let us look at one of several places in the customer and reservation code where we could have a problem. Examine the code in **Broker.Reserve**. First a check is made of the existing bookings for a given hotel for a given date to see if there are rooms available. If the rooms are available, the booking is made.

```
...
' Check if rooms are available for all dates
Dim i As Integer
For i = Day To Day + numDays - 1
    If numCust(i, unitid) >= unit.capacity Then
        result.ReservationId = -1
        result.Comment = "Room not available"
        Return result
    End If
Next

' Reserve a room for requested dates
For i = Day To Day + numDays - 1
    numCust(i, unitid) += 1
Next
...
```

This code can produce inconsistent results! One of the threads could be swapped out after it finds that the last room is available, but before it gets a chance to make the booking. The other thread could run, find the same available room, and make the booking. When the second thread runs again, starting from where it left off, it will also book the last room at the hotel.

To simulate this occurrence, this step of the threading example puts a **Thread.Sleep** call between the code that checks for room availability and the code that makes the room booking. Of course, this could happen without calling **Sleep**, but as is often the case with threading problems, it is not necessarily very consistent. Adding the call to **Sleep** just ensures that we see the bad thing happening consistently each time we run the program. The **Sleep** call will cause the thread to stop executing and give up the remainder of its timeslice. We then set up our program so that the two threads try to reserve the only room at a hotel for the same time. Examine the code in the **Main** routine that sets this up:

```
hotelBroker.AddHotel( _
   "Boston", "Presidential", 1, 10000D)
...
Dim reserve1 As NewReservation = _
   New NewReservation(customers, hotelBroker)

reserve1.customerId = 1
reserve1.city = "Boston"
reserve1.hotel = "Presidential"
reserve1.sdate = "12/12/2001"
reserve1.numberDays = 3

Dim reserve2 As NewReservation = _
   New NewReservation(customers, hotelBroker)

reserve2.customerId = 2
reserve2.city = "Boston"
reserve2.hotel = "Presidential"
reserve2.sdate = "12/13/2001"
reserve2.numberDays = 1
```

Running the program will give results that look something like this:

```
Added Boston Presidential Hotel with one room.
Thread 110 starting  new threads.
Thread 111 starting.
Thread 112 starting.
Reserving for Customer 1 ... on 12/12/2001 ... for 3 days
Reserving for Customer 2 ... on 12/13/2001 ... for 1 days
Thread 112 entered Broker::Reserve
Thread 112 sleeping in Broker::Reserve
Thread 111 entered Broker::Reserve
Thread 111 sleeping in Broker::Reserve
Thread 112 left Broker::Reserve
Reservation for Customer 2 has been booked
ReservationId = 1
ReservationRate = 10000
Thread 111 left Broker::Reserve
Reservation for Customer 1 has been booked
ReservationId = 2
ReservationRate = 10000
ReservationCost = 30000
Comment = OK
ReservationCost = 10000
Comment = OK
Done!
```

Both customers get to reserve the last room on December 13! Note how Thread 112 enters the Reserve method and finds the room is available before it gets swapped out. Then Thread 111 enters Reserve and also finds the room is available before it gets swapped out. Thread 112 then books the room, and then Thread 111 does as well.

Operating systems provide means for synchronizing the operation of multiple threads or multiple processes accessing shared resources. The .NET Framework provides several mechanisms to prevent threading conflicts.

Every object in the .NET Framework can be used to provide a synchronized section of code (critical section). Only one thread at a time can execute within such a section. If one thread is already executing inside that synchronized code section, any threads that attempt to access that section will block (wait) until the executing thread leaves that code section.

SYNCHRONIZATION WITH MONITORS

Code
Example

The **System.Threading.Monitor** class allows threads to synchronize on an object to avoid race conditions. Step 2 of the **Threading** example demonstrates the use of the **Monitor** class with the **Me** reference of the **HotelBroker** instance.

```
Public Function Reserve(ByVal res As Reservation) _
 As ReservationResult
    ...
    Monitor.Enter(Me)
    ...
    Monitor.Exit(Me)
    Return result
End Function
```

The thread that first calls the **Monitor.Enter** method will be allowed to execute the code of the **Reserve** method because it will acquire the **Monitor** lock based on the **Me** reference. Subsequent threads that try to execute this block of code will have to wait until the first thread releases the lock with **Monitor.Exit**. At that point they will be able to return from their call to **Monitor.Enter** and acquire the lock and then proceed.

A thread can call **Monitor.Enter** several times, but each call must be balanced by a call to **Monitor.Exit**. If a thread wants to try to acquire a lock, but does not want to block, it can use the **Monitor.TryEnter** method.

In the VB.NET language, you can use the **SyncLock** keyword in place of **Monitor.Enter/Exit**. With the **SyncLock** keyword, the above fragment would be

```
Public Function Reserve(ByVal res as Reservation) _
 As ReservationResult
    ...
    SyncLock Me
       ...
    End SyncLock
    Return result
End Function
```

Now that we have provided synchronization, the identical case tried in Step 1 does not result in one reservation too many for the hotel. Notice how the second thread cannot enter the **Reserve** method until the first thread that entered has left.

```
Added Boston Presidential Hotel with one room.
Thread 108 starting  new threads.
Thread 109 starting.
Reserving for Customer 1 ... on 12/12/2001 ... for 3 days
Thread 110 starting.
Reserving for Customer 2 ... on 12/13/2001 ... for 1 days
Thread 109 trying to enter Broker::Reserve
Thread 109 entered Broker::Reserve
Thread 109 sleeping in Broker::Reserve
Thread 110 trying to enter Broker::Reserve
Thread 109 left Broker::Reserve
Reservation for Customer 1 has been booked
ReservationId = 1
ReservationRate = 10000
ReservationCost = 30000
Comment = OK
Thread 110 entered Broker::Reserve
Thread 110 left Broker::Reserve
Reservation for Customer 2 could not be booked
Room not available
Done!
```

NOTIFICATION WITH MONITORS

A thread that has acquired a **Monitor** lock can wait for a signal from another thread that is synchronizing on that same object without leaving the synchronization block. The thread invokes the **Monitor.Wait** method and relinquishes the lock. When notified by another thread, it reacquires the synchronization lock.

A thread that has acquired a **Monitor** lock can send notification to another thread waiting on the same object with the **Pulse** or the **PulseAll** methods. It is important that the thread be waiting when the pulse is sent; otherwise, if the pulse is sent before the wait, the other thread will wait forever and will never see the notification. This is unlike the reset events discussed later in this chapter. If multiple threads are waiting, the **Pulse** method will only put one thread on the ready queue to run. The **PulseAll** will put all of them on the ready queue.

The pulsing thread no longer has the **Monitor** lock, but is not blocked from running. Since it is no longer blocked but does not have the lock, to avoid a deadlock or race condition, this thread should try to reacquire the lock (through a **Monitor.Enter** or **Wait**) before doing any potentially damaging work.

Code
Example

The **Pulse** example illustrates the **Pulse** and **PulseAll** methods. Running the example produces the following output:

```
First thread: 72 started.
Thread: 74 started.
Thread: 75 started.
Thread: 75 waiting.
Thread: 74 waiting.
Thread 75 sleeping.
Done.
Thread 75 awake.
Thread: 75 exited.
Thread 74 sleeping.
Thread 74 awake.
Thread: 74 exited.
```

The class **X** has a field **o** of type **Object** that will be used for a synchronization lock. The class also has a method **Test** that will be used as a thread delegate. The method acquires the synchronization lock and then waits for a notification. When it gets the notification, it sleeps for half a second and then relinquishes the lock.

The main method creates two threads that use the **X.Test** as their thread delegate and share the same object to use for synchronization. It then sleeps for 2 seconds to allow the threads to issue their wait requests and relinquish their locks. It then calls **PulseAll** to notify both waiting threads and relinquishes its hold on the locks. Eventually, each thread will reacquire the lock, write a message to the console, and relinquish the lock for the last time.

```
Class X
   Public o As Object

   Public Sub New(ByVal o As Object)
      Me.o = o
   End Sub
   Public Sub Test()
      Try
         Dim threadId As Long = _
            Thread.CurrentThread.GetHashCode()
         Console.WriteLine( _
            "Thread: {0} started.", threadId)
         Monitor.Enter(o)
         Console.WriteLine( _
            "Thread: {0} waiting.", threadId)
         Monitor.Wait(o)
         Console.WriteLine( _
            "Thread {0} sleeping.", threadId)
         Thread.Sleep(500)
         Console.WriteLine( _
            "Thread {0} awake.", threadId)
```

```
            Monitor.Exit(o)
            Console.WriteLine( _
                "Thread: {0} exited.", threadId)
        Catch e As Exception
            Dim threadId As Long = _
                Thread.CurrentThread.GetHashCode()
            Console.WriteLine( _
                "Thread: {0} Exception: {1}", _
                threadId, e.Message)
            Monitor.Exit(o)
        End Try
    End Sub
End Class

Module Pulse
    Public o As Object = New Object()

    Sub Main()
        Console.WriteLine( _
            "First thread: {0} started.", _
            Thread.CurrentThread.GetHashCode())

        Dim a As X = New X(o)
        Dim b As X = New X(o)

        Dim ats As ThreadStart = _
            New ThreadStart(AddressOf a.Test)
        Dim bts As ThreadStart = _
            New ThreadStart(AddressOf b.Test)

        Dim at As Thread = New Thread(ats)
        Dim bt As Thread = New Thread(bts)

        at.Start()
        bt.Start()

        ' Sleep allows other threads to wait before Pulse
        Thread.Sleep(2000)
        Monitor.Enter(o)

        Monitor.PulseAll(o)
        'Monitor.Pulse(o);

        Monitor.Exit(o)

        Console.WriteLine("Done.")
    End Sub
End Module
```

Comment out the **PulseAll** call and uncomment the **Pulse** call, and only one thread completes because the other thread is never put on the ready queue. Remove the **Sleep(2000)** from the main routine, and the other threads block forever because the pulse occurs before the threads get a change to call the **Wait** method, and hence they will never be notified.

These methods can be used to coordinate several threads' use of synchronization locks. The **Thread.Sleep** method causes the current thread to stop execution (block) for a given time period. Calling **Thread.Suspend** will cause the thread to block until **Thread.Resume** is called on that same thread. Threads can also block because they are waiting for another thread to finish (**Thread.Join**). This method was used in the **Threading** examples so that the main thread could wait until the reservation requests were completed. Threads can also block because they are waiting on a synchronization lock (critical section).

A blocked thread can be awakened by calling **Thread.Interrupt** on the blocked thread. The thread will receive a **ThreadInterruptedException**. If the thread does not catch this exception, the runtime will catch the exception and kill the thread.

If, as a last resort, you have to kill a thread outright, call the **Thread.Abort** method on the thread. **Thread.Abort** causes the **ThreadAbortException** to be thrown. This exception cannot be caught, but it will cause all the **Finally** blocks to be executed. In addition, **Thread.Abort** does not cause the thread to wake up from a wait.

Since **Finally** blocks may take a while to execute, or the thread might be waiting, aborted threads may not terminate immediately. If you need to be sure that the thread has finished, you should wait on the thread's termination using **Thread.Join**.

SYNCHRONIZATION CLASSES

The .NET Framework has classes that represent the standard Win32 synchronization objects. These classes all derive from the abstract **WaitHandle** class. This class has shared methods, **WaitAll** and **WaitAny**, that allow you to wait on a set of synchronization objects being signaled or to wait on just one of a set of synchronization objects being signaled. It also has an instance method, **WaitOne**, that allows you to wait for this instance to be signaled. How the object gets signaled depends on the particular type of synchronization object that is derived from **WaitHandle**.

A **Mutex** object is used for interprocess synchronization. **Monitors** and synchronized code sections work only within one process. An **AutoResetEvent** and **ManualResetEvent** are used to signal whether an event has occurred. An **AutoResetEvent** remains signaled until a waiting thread is released. A **ManualResetEvent** remains signaled until its state is set to unsignaled with the **Reset** method. Hence, many threads could be signaled by this event. Unlike **Monitors**, code does not have to be waiting for the signal before the pulse is set for the reset events to signal a thread.

The .NET Framework has provided classes to solve some standard threading problems. The **Interlocked** class methods allow atomic operations on shared values, such as increment, decrement, comparison, and exchange. **ReaderWriterLock** is used to allow single writer, multiple reader access to data structures. The **ThreadPool** class can be used to manage a pool of worker threads.

AUTOMATIC SYNCHRONIZATION

You can use attributes to synchronize access to instance methods and fields of a class. However, access to shared fields and methods is not synchronized in this manner. To do this, you derive the class from the class **ContextBound-Object** and apply the **Synchronization** attribute to the class. The attribute is found in the **System.Runtime.Remoting.Contexts** namespace.

Code
Example

This attribute cannot be applied to an individual method or field. **ContextBoundObject** and contexts are discussed in the section on contexts. The **Threading** example Step 3 illustrates how to do this.

```
<Synchronization(SynchronizationAttribute.REQUIRED)> _
 Public MustInherit Class Broker
...
End Class
```

You can pass one of four values that are shared fields of the **SynchronizationAttribute** class to the **SynchronizationAttribute** constructor: NOT_SUPPORTED, SUPPORTED, REQUIRED, and REQUIRES_NEW. Fully understanding how these attributes work requires the discussion in our upcoming section on contexts.

NOT_SUPPORTED means that the class cannot support synchronization of its instance methods and fields, and therefore must not be created in a synchronized context. REQUIRED means that the class requires synchronization of access to its instance methods and fields. However, if a thread is already being synchronized, it can use the same synchronization lock and can live in an existing synchronization context. REQUIRES_NEW means that not only is synchronization required, but access to its instance methods and fields must be with a unique synchronization lock and context. SUPPORTED means that the class does not require synchronization of access to its instance methods and fields, and a new context does not have to be created for it.

You can also pass a **Boolean** flag to the constructor to indicate if reentrancy is required. If required, callouts from methods are synchronized. Otherwise, only calls into methods are synchronized.

With this attribute, there is no need for **Monitor.Enter** and **Monitor.Exit** in the **Broker::Reserve** method.

Just as in Step 2, this example attempts to make two reservations for the last room in a hotel. In addition, a third thread attempts to cancel a reservation. Here is the output from running this example:

```
Added Boston Presidential Hotel with one room.
Thread 111 launching 3 threads.
CancelReservation: Thread 128 starting.
Cancelling Reservation 10
Thread 128 entered CancelReservation.
Thread 128 left CancelReservation.
Thread 126 starting.
Thread 127 starting.
Reserving for Customer 2 ... on 12/13/2001 ... for 1 days
Reserving for Customer 1 ... on 12/12/2001 ... for 3 days
Thread 127 entered Broker::Reserve
Thread 127 sleeping in Broker::Reserve
Thread 127 left Broker::Reserve
Thread 126 entered Broker::Reserve
Thread 126 left Broker::Reserve
Reservation for Customer 1 could not be booked
Room not available
Reservation for Customer 2 has been booked
ReservationId = 1
ReservationRate = 10000
ReservationCost = 10000
Comment = OK
Done!
```

As in the previous case, the second thread could not enter the **Reserve** method until the thread that entered first finished. Only one reservation is made.

What is different about using this automatic approach is that you get the synchronization in *all* the methods of the class, whether you need it or not. Accessing other data in the class via other methods also causes mutually exclusive blocking. This behavior may or may not be what is desired, depending on the circumstances.

Note how only one thread can be in any method of the class at a time. For example, a thread calling **CancelReservation** blocks other threads from calling **MakeReservation**. With a reservation system, this is the behavior you would want, since you do not want the **MakeReservation** attempt to use a data structure that might be in the middle of being modified. In some situations, however, this is not desirable and can reduce performance. This is because this approach can increase contention, which can interfere with scalability, since you are not just locking around the specific areas that need synchronizing.

The attribute approach is simpler than using critical sections. You do not have to worry about the details of getting the synchronization implemented correctly at a detailed level. On the other hand, you can get behavior that reduces interactivity and scalability. Different applications or different parts of the same application will choose the approach that makes the most sense.

Thread Isolation

Code Example

An exception generated by one thread will not cause another thread to fail. The **ThreadIsolation** example demonstrates this.

```
Class tm
    Public Sub m()
        Console.WriteLine( _
            "Thread {0} started", _
            Thread.CurrentThread.GetHashCode())
        Thread.Sleep(1000)
        Dim i As Integer
        For i = 0 To 9
            Console.WriteLine(i)
        Next
        Console.WriteLine( _
            "Thread {0} done", _
            Thread.CurrentThread.GetHashCode())
    End Sub
End Class

Class te
    Public Sub tue()
        Console.WriteLine( _
            "Thread {0} started", _
            Thread.CurrentThread.GetHashCode())
        Dim e As Exception = _
            New Exception("Thread Exception")
        Throw e
    End Sub
End Class

Module ThreadIsolation
    Sub Main()
        Dim tt As tm = New tm()
        Dim tex As te = New te()

        ' create delegate for threads
        Dim ts1 As ThreadStart = _
            New ThreadStart(AddressOf tt.m)
        Dim ts2 As ThreadStart = _
            New ThreadStart(AddressOf tex.tue)

        Dim thread1 As Thread = New Thread(ts1)
        Dim thread2 As Thread = New Thread(ts2)

        Console.WriteLine( _
```

```
        "Thread {0} starting new threads.", _
        Thread.CurrentThread.GetHashCode())
      thread1.Start()
      thread2.Start()

      Console.WriteLine( _
        "Thread {0} done.", _
        Thread.CurrentThread.GetHashCode())
    End Sub
End Module
```

The following output is generated. Note how the second thread can continue to write out the numbers even though the first thread has aborted from the unhandled exception. Note also how the "main" thread that spawned the other two threads can finish without causing the other threads to terminate.

```
Thread 72 starting new threads.
Thread 72 done.
Thread 75 started
Thread 74 started

Unhandled Exception: System.Exception: Thread Exception
   at ThreadIsolation.te.tue() in
   C:\...\ThreadIsolation.vb:line 29
0
1
2
3
4
5
6
7
8
9
Thread 74 done
```

The **AppDomain** class (discussed later in the chapter) allows you to set up a handler to catch an **UnhandledException** event.

Synchronization of Collections

Some lists, such as **TraceListeners**, are thread safe. When this collection is modified, a copy is modified and the reference is set to the copy. Most collections, like **ArrayList**, are not thread safe by default. Making them automatically thread safe would decrease the performance of the collection even when thread safety is not an issue.

An **ArrayList** has a shared **Synchronized** method to return a thread-safe version of the **ArrayList**. The **IsSynchronized** property allows you to test if the **ArrayList** you are using is the thread-safe version. The **SyncRoot** property can return an object that can be used to synchronize access to a collection. This allows other threads that might be using the **ArrayList** to be synchronized with the same object.

Context

Code
Example

In order for us to understand how the runtime is able to enforce a threading requirement based on an attribute, we have to introduce the concept of context. Step 4 of the **Threading** example is the same code as Step 3, but with some additional output:

```
Is the customer object a proxy? False
Is the bookings object a proxy? True
Added Boston Presidential Hotel with one room.
Thread 111 ContextId 0 launching 3 threads.
MakeReservation: Thread 126 ContextId 0 starting.
MakeReservation: Thread 127 ContextId 0 starting.
CancelReservation: Thread 128 ContextId 0 starting.
Cancelling Reservation 10
Thread 128 ContextId 1 entered CancelReservation.
Thread 128 ContextId 1 left CancelReservation.
Reserving for Customer 2 ... on 12/13/2001 ... for 1 days
Reserving for Customer 1 ... on 12/12/2001 ... for 3 days
Thread 127 ContextId 1 entered Reserve.
Thread 127 sleeping in Broker::Reserve
Thread 127 ContextId 1 left Reserve.
Thread 126 ContextId 1 entered Reserve.
Thread 126 ContextId 1 left Reserve.
Reservation for Customer 1 could not be booked
Room not available
Reservation for Customer 2 has been booked
ReservationId = 1
ReservationRate = 10000
ReservationCost = 10000
Comment = OK
Done!
```

In this last step of the **Threading** example, we see that when a thread enters a method of the Broker class, it has a different **ContextId** than when it runs outside of the Broker class. It runs in a different context.

```
MakeReservation: Thread 127 ContextId 0 starting.
...
Thread 127 ContextId 1 entered Reserve.
```

Broker objects have different runtime requirements than the other objects in the program, since access to **Broker** objects must be synchronized and access to other objects should not be synchronized. The environment that represents the runtime requirements of an object is called a *context*. There are two contexts in the **Threading** Step 3 example: Context 1 where the **Broker** object lives and Context 0 where all other objects live. Every thread in the program runs in Context 1 when executing inside a **Broker** object and in Context 0 everywhere else. Contexts are independent of threads.

A context is a collection of one or more objects that have identical runtime requirements. The .NET concept of a context is very similar to a COM apartment or to the COM+ concept of a context.[8] In general, you cannot say what the runtime must do in a given context because it depends on exactly what the runtime requirements are. A context that has transactional requirements requires different action than one that does not. A context that has to maintain a REQUIRED synchronization requirement is different than one that has to maintain a REQUIRES_NEW synchronization requirement.

You can get the **Context** class instance that represents the current context from the shared property **Thread.CurrentContext**. **ContextId** is a property of that class.

Proxies and Stubs

How does the runtime enforce the different requirements of different contexts? When an object resides in another context (such as the **HotelBroker** object in the **NewReservation** instance), a reference to a proxy object is returned instead of a reference to the object itself. The actual object resides in its original, or home, context. The proxy is an object that represents the original object in a different context. The shared method **RemotingServices.IsTransparentProxy** determines if an object reference points to a real object instance or to a proxy. Look at the code in the **Threading** Step 4 example main routine:

```
hotelBroker = New HotelBroker()
customers = New Customers()

Dim bTrans As Boolean
bTrans = RemotingServices.IsTransparentProxy(customers)
Console.WriteLine( _
  "Is the customer object a proxy? {0}", bTrans)
```

---

8. However, at this point in time COM+ contexts and .NET contexts are different. For a discussion of contexts in COM+, see *Understanding and Programming COM+* by Robert J. Oberg.

```
bTrans = RemotingServices.IsTransparentProxy(hotelBroker)
Console.WriteLine( _
 "Is the bookings object a proxy? {0}", bTrans)
```

Which causes the following output:

```
Is the customer object a proxy? False
Is the bookings object a proxy? True
```

When a program starts up, it is given a default context.[9] All objects, like the **Customers** object, that do not have any special requirements are created inside of that context (context 0). An object, such as the **HotelBroker** object, that has a different set of requirements (synchronization) is created in a different context (context 1), and a proxy is returned to the creating context (context 0).

Now, when you access the **MakeReservation** method in the **HotelBroker** object, you are actually accessing a method on the proxy. The proxy method can then apply the synchronization lock and then delegate to the actual **HotelBroker** object's method. When the actual object's method returns, it returns to the proxy. The proxy can then remove the synchronization lock and return to the caller. This technique, where the runtime uses a proxy to intercept method calls to the actual object, is called *interception*.

ContextBoundObject

The **Broker** class has to derive from the class **ContextBoundObject** so that the runtime knows to set up a different context if one is required. If you remove the derivation of **Broker** from **ContextBoundObject**, you will once again get the threading conflict, and both customers will be able to reserve the last room at the hotel, even though the class is still marked with the **Synchronization** attribute. Objects that do not derive from **ContextBoundObject** can run in any context (agile objects).

Since other contexts work with a proxy or a reference to the actual object, the runtime must translate (marshal) the call from one context to another. Hence, **ContextBoundObject** inherits from **MarshalByRefObject**. **MarshalByRefObject** is the base class for objects that want to be able to be marshaled by reference.

One advantage of using synchronization techniques such as a **Monitor** is that a **Monitor** can be called from any context. Another potential disadvan-

---

9. As will be clear in the next section, the sentence should really read, "When a new application domain starts up, it is given a new default context." Contexts are application domain-relative. Two different application domains will have two separate default contexts, each with id 0.

tage of using automatic synchronization is the performance hit from marshaling and using proxies rather than the actual object.

As will be clear when we discuss application domains, since the customer object has no dependency on context, it is the actual object, not a proxy. It can be copied to any context within the same application domain.

Application Isolation

When writing applications, it is often necessary to isolate parts of the applications so that a failure of one part does not cause a failure in another part of the application. In Windows, application isolation has been at the process level. In other words, if a process is stopped or crashes, other processes will be unaffected. One process cannot directly address memory in another process' address space.

For an application to use separate processes to achieve isolation is expensive. To switch from one process to another, the information must be saved and restored. This includes a thread and process switch. A thread switch requires saving call stack registers, such as the instruction pointer, and loading the information for a new thread, as well as updating the scheduling information for the threads. A process switch includes I/O buffers, accounting information, and processor rights that have to be saved for the old process and restored for the new one.

Application Domain

The .NET *application domain* is a more lightweight unit for application isolation, fault tolerance, and security. Multiple application domains can run in one process. Since the .NET code can be checked for type safety and security, the CLR can guarantee that one application domain can run independently of another application domain in the same process. No process switch is required to achieve application isolation.

Application domains can have multiple contexts, but a context exists in only one application domain. Although a thread runs in one context of one application domain at a time, the **Threading** example Step 3 demonstrates that a thread can execute in more than one context. One or more threads can run in an application domain at the same time. An object lives in only one context.

Each application domain starts with a single thread and one context. Additional threads and contexts are added as needed.

There is no relationship between the number of application domains and threads. A Web server might require an application domain for each hosted application that runs in its process. The number of threads in that process would be far fewer depending on how much actual concurrency the process can support.

To enforce application isolation, code in one application domain cannot make direct calls into the code (or even reference resources) in another application domain. They must use proxies.

Application Domains and Assemblies

Applications are built from one or more assemblies, but each assembly is loaded into an application domain. Each application domain can be unloaded independently of the others, but you cannot unload an individual assembly from an application domain. The assembly will be unloaded when the application domain is unloaded. Unloading an application domain also frees all resources associated with that application domain.

Each process has a default application domain that is created when the process is started. This default domain can only be unloaded when the process shuts down.

Hosts of the CLR, such as ASP.NET and Internet Explorer, critically depend on preventing the various applications that run under them from interfering with each other. By never loading application code into the default domain, they can ensure that a crashing program will not bring down a host.

While you may never use application domains in your programs, understanding them is critical to understanding how .NET programs execute.

AppDomain Class

Code
Example

Application domains are abstracted by the **AppDomain** class. The **AppDomainTest** sample illustrates the use of application domains.

This class has shared methods for creating and unloading application domains:

```
Dim domain As AppDomain = _
    AppDomain.CreateDomain( _
    "CreatedDomain2", Nothing, Nothing)
...
AppDomain.Unload(domain)
```

While the **CreateDomain** method is overloaded, one signature illustrates application domain isolation:

```
Overloads Public Shared Function CreateDomain( _
 ByVal friendlyName As String, _
 ByVal securityInfo As Evidence, _
 ByVal info As AppDomainSetup _
) As AppDomain
```

The **Evidence** parameter is a collection of the security constraints on the application domain. While we will discuss this in greater detail in Chapter 16, the domain's creator can modify this collection to control the permissions that the executing application domain can have. The **AppDomainSetup** parameter specifies setup information about the domain. Among the information specified is the location of the application domain's configuration file and where private assemblies are loaded. Hence, each application domain can be configured independently of each other. Code isolation, setup isolation, and control over security combine to ensure that application domains are independent of each other.

Application Domain Events

To help in maintaining application isolation, the **AppDomain** class allows you to set up event handlers for

- when a domain unloads.
- when the process exits.
- when an unhandled exception occurs.
- when attempts to resolve assemblies, types, and resources fail.

AppDomainTest Example

If you run the **AppDomainTest** example, you will get the following output, shown in Figure 10–1.

First, the name, thread, and context of the default domain are written out.

```
Dim currentDomain As AppDomain = AppDomain.CurrentDomain
Console.WriteLine("At startup, Default AppDomain" _
    & " is {0} ThreadId: {1} ContextId {2}", _
    currentDomain.FriendlyName, _
    Thread.CurrentThread.GetHashCode(), _
    Thread.CurrentContext.ContextID)
```

We then load and execute an assembly. This code in this assembly just prints out a string and its domain's name, thread, and context. Notice that it executes in the default domain.

```
Dim val As Integer = _
    currentDomain.ExecuteAssembly( _
    "..\TestApp\bin\TestApp.exe")
```

We then create an instance of the **Customers** type from the **Customer** assembly in the default domain. The **CreateInstance** method of the **AppDomain** class returns an **ObjectHandle** instance. You can pass this **ObjectHandle** between application domains without loading the metadata associated

```
"c:\OI\NetCpp\Chap8\AppDomain\Debug\AppDomain.exe"                        _ □ ×
At startup, Default AppDomain is AppDomain.exe ThreadId: 3 ContextId 0
        ExecuteAssembly of TestApp.exe with no arguments in default domain.
        In TestApp Main, AppDomain AppDomain.exe ThreadId 3 ContextId 0
        Hello, Application Domain.
Execute Assembly returned: 50 AppDomain: AppDomain.exe ThreadId: 3 ContextId 0

Creating instance of serializable Customer object in default domain.
        Customers Constructor: AppDomain AppDomain.exe ThreadId 3 ContextId 0
Is handle to new customer object a proxy? : False
Is unwrapped customer object a proxy? : False
Registering a new customer object.
List customer objects.
GetCustomer: AppDomain AppDomain.exe ThreadId 3 ContextId 0
1    Rocket          Squirrel        rocky@frosbitefalls.com
2    Bullwinkle      Moose           moose@wossamotta.edu
3    John            Adams           jadams@presidents.org

Creating a new App Domain.
New AppDomain CreatedDomain1 created.
Creating instance of serializable Customer object in new domain.
        Customers Constructor: AppDomain CreatedDomain1 ThreadId 3 ContextId 0
Is handle to new customer object a proxy? : True
Is unwrapped customer object a proxy? : False
List customer objects.
GetCustomer: AppDomain AppDomain.exe ThreadId 3 ContextId 0
1    Rocket          Squirrel        rocky@frosbitefalls.com
2    Bullwinkle      Moose           moose@wossamotta.edu

Starting new thread in default AppDomain.
        Created new AppDomain CreatedDomain2 in new Thread Executing ThreadId: 7
7 ContextId 0
        ExecuteAssembly TestApp.exe with one argument in domain CreatedDomain2
        In TestApp Main, AppDomain CreatedDomain2 ThreadId 77 ContextId 0
        HotelBroker Constructor: AppDomain CreatedDomain2 ThreadId 77 ContextId
0
        HotelBroker MakeReservation: AppDomain CreatedDomain2 ThreadId 77 Contex
tId 0
        Reservation Id: 1
        Execute Assembly returned: 100 AppDomain: AppDomain.exe ThreadId: 77 Con
textId 0

Press any key to continue
```

FIGURE 10-1   *Output of AppDomainTest example.*

with the wrapped type. When you want to use the create object instance, you must unwrap it by calling the **Unwrap** method on the **ObjectHandle** instance.

```
Dim oh As ObjectHandle = currentDomain.CreateInstance( _
   "Customer", "Customer.OI.NetVB.Acme.Customers")
...
Dim custs As Customers = oh.Unwrap()
```

We then add a new customer, and then list all the existing customers. Notice that both the constructor of this type and the methods execute in the same thread and context that the default domain does.

We then create a new domain and create an instance of the same type as before in that new domain.

```
Dim domain As AppDomain = AppDomain.CreateDomain( _
   "CreatedDomain1", Nothing, Nothing)
...
oh = domain.CreateInstance( _
```

```
"Customer", "Customer.OI.NetVB.Acme.Customers")
...
Dim custs2 As Customers = oh.Unwrap()
```

Note that the constructor call that results from the **CreateInstance** method executes in the new domain and is therefore in a different context from where the **CreateInstance** call was made, but is executing on the same thread that made the **CreateInstance** call.

When we list the customers in this new object, we get a different list of customers. This is not surprising, since it is a different **Customers** object. Nonetheless, the customer list method executes in the default domain!

Using **RemotingServices.IsTransparentProxy**, we see that the **ObjectHandle** is a proxy to the **Customers** object that lives in the newly created **AppDomain**. However, when you unwrap the object to get an instance handle, you do not get a proxy, but you get an actual object reference. By default, objects are marshaled by value (copied) from one application domain to another.

If the **Customers** object is not serializable, you will get an exception when you try to copy it. This exception would be thrown when you call **Unwrap**, not when you call **CreateInstance**. The latter returns a reference, and the copy is only made when the **ObjectHandle** is unwrapped. If the object cannot be serialized, it cannot be copied from one application domain to another.

Next, we create a new thread, and that thread creates a new application domain and then loads and executes an assembly. The assembly starts executing at its entry point, the **Main** routine of the **AppDomainTest** class.

```
Dim domain As AppDomain = _
   AppDomain.CreateDomain( _
   "CreatedDomain2", Nothing, Nothing)
...
Dim args() As String = New String(0) {}
args(0) = "MakeReservation"
...
Dim val As Integer = domain.ExecuteAssembly( _
   "..\TestApp\bin\TestApp.exe", Nothing, args)
...
AppDomain.Unload(domain)
```

The **Main** routine loads the **Hotel** assembly into the newly created application domain. It then queries the metadata of the assembly for the **HotelBroker** type information. It uses that type information to create a **HotelBroker** object. The **HotelBroker** class is marked with the synchronization attribute. As a result, the **HotelBroker** constructor and the **MakeReservation** method run in a different context than the default context.

```
Dim a As System.Reflection.Assembly = _
   AppDomain.CurrentDomain.Load("Hotel")
Dim typeHotelBroker As Type = _
   a.GetType("Hotel.OI.NetVB.Acme.HotelBroker")
Dim hotelBroker As HotelBroker = _
   Activator.CreateInstance(typeHotelBroker)
Dim ResDate As DateTime = _
   DateTime.Parse("12/2/2001")
Dim rr As ReservationResult = _
   hotelBroker.MakeReservation( _
   1, "Boston", "Sheraton", ResDate, 3)
Console.WriteLine( _
   "   Reservation Id: {0}", rr.ReservationId)
```

Marshaling, Application Domains, and Contexts

By default, objects are copied from one application domain to another (marshal by value). The section "Remoting" in this chapter shows how to marshal by reference between application domains. This ensures that code in one application domain is isolated from another.

Objects are marshaled by reference between contexts. This allows the CLR to enforce the requirements (such as synchronization or transactions) of different objects. This is true whether the client of the object is in the same application domain or not.

Since most objects do not derive from **ContextBoundObject**, they can reside or move from one context to another as required. Threads can cross application domain and context boundaries within the same Win32 process.

Asynchronous Programming

.NET supports a design pattern for asynchronous programming. This pattern is present in many places in .NET (including I/O operations, as noted earlier and as we will see in Chapter 15). Asynchronous programming provides a way for you to provide a method call without blocking the method caller. Within your own code, the asynchronous model may provide an easier approach than threading, but offers much less control over the synchronization than using synchronization objects.

The Asynchronous Design Pattern

This design pattern is composed of two special methods exposed by a delegate object and the interface **IAsyncResult**. The two special methods, **Begin-Invoke** and **EndInvoke**, are emitted directly by the compiler, and not implemented in the class source code, and not inherited from a super class. The compiler emits the equivalent to these two functions for the delegate, as shown in the following code snippet. Note that **parameters...** represents the arbitrary number of parameters defined in the corresponding delegate definition, and **ReturnType** represents the return type of the corresponding delegate definition.

```
Function BeginInvoke( _
 parameters..., _
 ByVal cb As AsyncCallback, _
 ByVal AsyncObject As Object) As IAsyncResult
  ...
End Function
Function EndInvoke( _
 parameters..., _
 ByVal ar As IAsyncResult) As ReturnType
  ...
End Function
```

For general discussion purposes, "XXX" is sometimes used in referring to the actual method being called asynchronously (i.e., **BeginRead**/**EndRead** for the **System.IO.FileStream** class). The BeginXXX method should pass all input parameters of the synchronous version as well as the **AsyncCallback** and **Object** parameters. The EndXXX should have all the output parameters of the synchronous version parameters in its signature. It should return whatever object or value that the synchronous version of the method would return. It should also have an **IAsyncResult** parameter. A CancelXXX can also be provided if it makes sense.

AsyncCallback is a delegate that represents a callback function.

```
Public Delegate Sub AsyncCallback(ByVal ar As IAsyncResult)
```

AsyncObject is available from **IAsyncResult**. It is provided so that in the callback function you can distinguish which asynchronous read the callback was generated by.

The .NET Framework uses this pattern so that the **FileStream**-synchronous **Read** method

```
Overrides Public Function Read( _
   ByVal array() As Byte, _
   ByVal offset As Integer, _
   ByVal count As Integer _
) As Integer
```

becomes in the asynchronous version

```
Overrides Public Function BeginRead( _
   ByVal array() As Byte, _
   ByVal offset As Integer, _
   ByVal numBytes As Integer, _
```

```
    ByVal userCallback As AsyncCallback, _
    ByVal stateObject As Object _
) As IAsyncResult

Overrides Public Function EndRead( _
    ByVal asyncResult As IAsyncResult _
) As Integer
```

Any exception thrown from BeginXXX should be thrown before the asynchronous operation starts. Any exceptions from the asynchronous operation should be thrown from the EndXXX method.

IAsyncResult

This interface has four elements:

```
Public Interface IAsyncResult
    ReadOnly Property AsyncState() As Object
    ReadOnly Property AsyncWaitHandle() As WaitHandle
    ReadOnly Property CompletedSynchronously() As Boolean
    ReadOnly Property IsCompleted() As Boolean
End Interface
```

IsCompleted is set to true after the server has processed the call. The client can destroy all resources after **IsCompleted** is set to true. If BeginXXX completed synchronously, **CompletedSynchronously** is set to true. Most of the time this will be ignored and set to the default value of false. In general, a client never knows whether the BeginXXX method executed synchronously or asynchronously. If the asynchronous operation is not finished, the EndXXX method will block until the operation is finished.

The **AsyncWaitHandle** returns a **WaitHandle** that can be used for synchronization. As we discussed previously, this handle can be signaled so that the client can wait on it. Since you can specify a wait time period, you do not have to block forever if the operation is not yet complete.

The **AsyncState** is the object provided as the last argument in the BeginXXX call. It allows you to differentiate asynchronous reads in the callback.

Using Delegates for Asynchronous Programming

Any developer of .NET objects who wants to provide an asynchronous interface should follow this pattern. Nonetheless, there is no need for most developers to develop a custom asynchronous solution for their objects. Delegates provide a very easy way to support asynchronous operations on any method without any action on the class developer's part. Of course, this has to be done with care because the object was written with certain assumptions about which thread it is running on and its synchronization requirements.

Code Example

The two **Asynch** examples use the **Customers** object from our case study **Customer** assembly. The first example registers new customers asynchronously and does some processing while waiting for each registration to finish. The second example uses a callback function with the asynchronous processing. In addition to allowing the program to do processing while waiting for the registrations to finish, the callback allows the system to take some asynchronous action for each individual registration.

In the examples, we just print out to the console to show where work could be done. To increase the waiting time to simulate longer processing times, we have put calls to **Thread.Sleep()** in **Customers.RegisterCustomer** as well as in the sample programs. Now let us look at the code within the examples.

Suppose the client wants to call the **RegisterCustomer** method asynchronously. The caller simply declares a delegate with the same signature as the method.

```
Public Delegate Function RegisterCustomerCbk( _
  ByVal firstName As String, _
  ByVal LastName As String, _
  ByVal EmailAddress As String) As Integer
```

You then make the actual method the callback function:

```
Dim rcc As RegisterCustomerCbk = _
   New RegisterCustomerCbk( _
   AddressOf customers.RegisterCustomer)
```

BEGIN/END INVOKE

When you declare a delegate, the compiler generates a class with three methods, **BeginInvoke**, **EndInvoke**, and **Invoke.** The **BeginInvoke** and **EndInvoke** are type-safe methods that correspond to the BeginXXX and EndXXX methods and allow you to call the delegate asynchronously. The **Invoke** method is what the compiler uses when you call a delegate. To call **RegisterCustomer** asynchronously, just use the **BeginInvoke** and **EndInvoke** methods.

```
Dim rcc As RegisterCustomerCbk = _
   New RegisterCustomerCbk( _
   AddressOf customers.RegisterCustomer)

Dim i As Integer
For i = 1 To 4
   firstName = "FirstName" + i.ToString()
   lastName = "SecondName" + (i * 2).ToString()
   emailAddress = i.ToString() + ".biz"

   Dim ar As IAsyncResult = rcc.BeginInvoke( _
```

```
        firstName, lastName, emailAddress, Nothing, Nothing)
    While (Not ar.IsCompleted)
        Console.WriteLine( _
            "Could do some work here while waiting " & _
            "to complete.")
        ar.AsyncWaitHandle.WaitOne(1, False)
    End While
    customerId = rcc.EndInvoke(Nothing, Nothing, Nothing,
ar)
    Console.WriteLine("    Added CustomerId: " + _
      customerId.ToString())
Next
```

The program waits on the **AsyncWaitHandle** periodically to see if the registration has finished. If the registration is not completed yet, some work could be done in the interim. If **EndInvoke** is called before **RegisterCustomer** is complete, **EndInvoke** will block until **RegisterCustomer** is finished.

ASYNCHRONOUS CALLBACK

Instead of waiting on a handle, you could pass a callback function to **BeginInvoke** (or a BeginXXX method).

```
Dim rcc As RegisterCustomerCbk = _
 New RegisterCustomerCbk( _
  AddressOf customers.RegisterCustomer)
Dim cb As AsyncCallback = New AsyncCallback( _
 AddressOf CustomerCallback)
Dim objectState As Object
Dim ar As IAsyncResult

Dim i As Integer
For i = 5 To 9
    firstName = "FirstName" + i.ToString()
    lastName = "SecondName" + (i * 2).ToString()
    emailAddress = i.ToString() + ".biz"
    objectState = i

    ar = rcc.BeginInvoke( _
      firstName, lastName, emailAddress, cb, objectState)
Next

Console.WriteLine(
    "Finished registrations...could do some work here.")
Thread.Sleep(25)
Console.WriteLine(
    "Finished work...waiting to let registrations
complete.")
Thread.Sleep(1000)
```

You then get the results in the callback function with **EndInvoke**:

```
Public Sub CustomerCallback(ByVal ar As IAsyncResult)
    Dim customerId As Integer
    Dim asyncResult As AsyncResult = ar
    Dim rcc As RegisterCustomerCbk = _
     asyncResult.AsyncDelegate
    customerId = rcc.EndInvoke(Nothing, Nothing, Nothing, ar)
    Console.WriteLine( _
    "    AsyncState: {0} CustomerId {1} added.", _
     ar.AsyncState, _
     customerId)
    Console.WriteLine( _
     Could do processing here.")
    Return
End Sub
```

You could do some work when each customer registration was finished.

Threading with Parameters

The asynchronous callback runs on a different thread than the one on which **BeginInvoke** was called. If your threading needs are simple and you want to pass parameters to your thread functions, you can use asynchronous delegates to do this. You do not need any reference to the **Threading** namespace. The reference to the **Threading** namespace in the asynchronous threading example is just for the **Thread.Sleep** method needed for the purposes of demonstrating asynchronous callback.

Code Example

The **PrintNumbers** class in the **AsynchThreading** example sums the numbers from a starting integer passed to it as an argument to 10 greater than the starting integer. It returns the sum to the caller. **PrintNumbers** can be used for the delegate defined by Print.

```
Public Delegate Function Print( _
 ByVal i As Integer) As Integer

Class Numbers
    Public Function PrintNumbers( _
     ByVal start As Integer) As Integer
        Dim threadId As Integer = _
         Thread.CurrentThread.GetHashCode()
        Console.WriteLine( _
         "PrintNumbers Id: " + threadId.ToString())

        Dim sum As Integer = 0
        Dim i As Integer
        For i = start To start + 9
            Console.WriteLine(i.ToString())
            Thread.Sleep(500)
```

```
        sum += i
    Next

    Return sum
  End Function
  ...
End Class
```

The **Main** routine then defines two callbacks and invokes them explicitly with different starting integers. It waits until the both of the synchronization handles are signaled. **EndInvoke** is called on both, and the results are written to the console.

```
<MTAThread()> _
Public Shared Sub Main()
  Dim threadId As Integer = _
    Thread.CurrentThread.GetHashCode()
  Console.WriteLine( _
    "MainThread Id: " + threadId.ToString())

  Dim n As Numbers = New Numbers()

  Dim pfn1 As Print = _
    New Print(AddressOf n.PrintNumbers)
  Dim pfn2 As Print = _
    New Print(AddressOf n.PrintNumbers)

  Dim ar1 As IAsyncResult = _
    pfn1.BeginInvoke(0, Nothing, Nothing)
  Dim ar2 As IAsyncResult = _
    pfn2.BeginInvoke(100, Nothing, Nothing)

  Dim wh() As WaitHandle = New WaitHandle(1) {}
  wh(0) = ar1.AsyncWaitHandle
  wh(1) = ar2.AsyncWaitHandle

  ' make sure everything is done before ending
  WaitHandle.WaitAll(wh)

  Dim sum1 As Integer = pfn1.EndInvoke(ar1)
  Dim sum2 As Integer = pfn2.EndInvoke(ar2)

  Console.WriteLine( _
    "Sum1 = " + sum1.ToString() + _
    " Sum2 = " + sum2.ToString())
  Return
End Sub
```

Here is the program's output:

```
MainThread Id: 72
PrintNumbers Id: 77
0
1
2
3
4
5
6
7
8
9
PrintNumbers Id: 77
100
101
102
103
104
105
106
107
108
109
Sum1 = 45  Sum2 = 1045
```

Remoting

Remoting technology provides a summary of the key concepts in the .NET Application Model. While a complete discussion of remoting is beyond the scope of this book, a brief introduction provides a powerful example of how metadata and marshal by reference (MBR) work. Remoting also provides a mechanism to have executable servers.

Unlike remoting in Microsoft's COM technology, there is a minimal amount of infrastructure programming required. What infrastructure program is required allows the programmer either a degree of flexibility or the ability to customize remoting for their particular applications.

The .NET Framework provides two ways to provide connections between two applications on different computers. Web services, discussed in Chapter 15, enable computers that do not host the CLR to communicate with computers that do. The remoting technology discussed here builds distributed applications between computers that host the CLR.

Remoting Overview

The key parts of remoting are

- **Interception**, which allows for message generation for communication over the channels.
- **Formatters** to put the messages into a byte stream that is sent over the channel. These are the same formatters that were discussed in the section on serialization.
- Communication **channel** for transport of messages.

INTERCEPTION

Proxies and stubs (referred to in .NET as dispatchers) transform the function calls on the client or server side into messages that are sent over the network. This is called interception, because the proxies and dispatchers intercept a method call to send it to its remote destination. Unlike COM, metadata provides the information so the CLR can generate the proxies and stubs for you.

A *proxy* takes the function call off the stack frame of the caller and transforms it into a message. The message is then sent to its destination. A *dispatcher* takes the message and transforms it into a stack frame so that a call can be made to the object.

For example, assume the **UnregisterCustomer** method from the **Customer** assembly runs in one application domain and is called from another. It makes no difference if the application domains are in the same process or on the same machine.

The proxy would take the integer **id** argument on the stack frame of the client making the call and put it in a message that encoded the call and its argument. On the server side, the dispatcher would take that message and create a function call on the server's stack for the call **UnregisterCustomer(int id)** and make that call into the object. The client and server code do not know that they are being remoted.

CHANNELS AND FORMATTERS

The formatter converts the message into a byte stream. The .NET Framework comes with two formatters, binary and SOAP (text-based XML, discussed in Chapter 15). The byte stream is then sent over a communication channel.

The .NET Framework comes with two channels, although you can write your own. The HTTP channel uses the HTTP protocol and is good for communicating over the Internet or through firewalls. The TCP channel uses the TCP (sockets) protocol and is designed for high-speed communication. You have four permutations of formatters and transport: binary over TCP, binary over HTTP, SOAP over HTTP, and SOAP over TCP.

Remote Objects

Clients obtain a proxy by *activating* a remote object. Remote objects must derive from **MarshalByRefObject** because you work with a proxy to the object reference, not with the object reference itself. This is the same concept discussed in the section on contexts, where marshal by reference is also used to access context bound objects.

Local objects passed as method parameters from one application domain to another can be passed by value (copied) or by reference.

To be passed by value, they must be serializable. The object is serialized, sent across the transport layer, and recreated on the other side. We have already seen an example of this in the application domain example.

To be passed by reference, the class must derive from **MarshalByRef-Object**. The **Remoting** example illustrates pass by reference.

Remote objects can either be server-activated or client-activated. Server-activated objects are not created until the first method call on the object. Server-activated objects come in two flavors. **SingleCall** objects are stateless. Each method causes a new object to be created. **Singleton** objects can be used by multiple client activation requests. **Singleton** objects can maintain state. **SingleCall** objects will scale better than **Singleton** objects because they do not retain state and can be load balanced.

Client-activated objects are activated when the client requests them. While they can last for multiple calls and hold state, they cannot store information from different client activations. This is similar to calling **CoCreateIn-stanceEx** in DCOM.

Activation

Objects are activated on the client side in one of three ways by using the **Activator** class.

- **Activator.GetObject** is used to get a reference to a server-activated object.
- **Activator.CreateInstance** is used to create a client-activated object. You can pass parameters to the object's constructor using one of the overloaded **CreateInstance** methods that takes an array of objects to be passed to the constructor.
- The VB.NET **New** syntax can be used to create a server- or a client-activated object. A configuration file is used to describe how **New** should be used.

Sample Remotable Object

Code
Example

For our **Remoting** example, we remote our **Customers** object from the **Customer** assembly. In the **Remoting** example directory there are two solutions. One represents the client program, the other the server program. Each can be built independently of the other. Start the server program first. Notice that it waits for a client request. You can then run the client program, which will run against objects that live inside of the server. We will discuss the details of the client and server code and output in the next few sections.

Notice that we only had to make two simple changes to our object. The **Customers** class in the server project had to be made remotable by inheriting from **MarshalByRefObject**.

```
Public Class Customers
    Inherits MarshalByRefObject
    Implements ICustomer
...
End Class
```

The **CustomerListItem** that will be to be transferred by value had to be made serializable.

```
<Serializable()> Public Structure CustomerListItem
    Public CustomerId As Integer
    Public FirstName As String
    Public LastName As String
    Public EmailAddress As String
End Structure
```

SAMPLE REMOTING PROGRAM

In the **Remoting** example the client accesses a server-activated object. The server is the **TcpServerChannel** class that uses a binary format with the TCP protocol. The channel will use port 8085. The server registers the type being remoted, the endpoint name to refer to this object, and the type of activation. The server then waits for client requests.

```
Dim chan As TcpServerChannel = _
    New TcpServerChannel(8085)
ChannelServices.RegisterChannel(chan)
Dim assem As System.Reflection.Assembly = _
    System.Reflection.Assembly.Load("Customer")
Dim type As Type = assem.GetType("Customer.Customers")
RemotingConfiguration.RegisterWellKnownServiceType( _
    type, _
    "AcmeCustomer", _
    WellKnownObjectMode.Singleton)
...
```

The server has to be started before the client program can access the object.

The client sets up a **TcpClientChannel** object and then connects to the object. It specifies the type of the object it wants and the endpoint where the server is listening for object requests. If you want to run the client and server on separate machines, substitute the server machine name for **localhost** in the endpoint. Unlike COM location transparency, the client has to specify a specific endpoint; there is no redirection through an opaque registry entry.

```
Dim chan As TcpClientChannel = New TcpClientChannel()
ChannelServices.RegisterChannel(chan)
...
Dim assem As System.Reflection.Assembly = _
   System.Reflection.Assembly.Load("Customer")
Dim type As Type = assem.GetType("Customer.Customers")
Dim obj As Customers = _
   Activator.GetObject( _
   type, _
   "tcp://localhost:8085/AcmeCustomer")
If obj Is Nothing Then
   System.Console.WriteLine("Could not locate server")
Else
   ...
```

The client then uses the proxy to make calls on the object as if it were a local instance.

```
Dim bRet As Boolean = _
   RemotingServices.IsTransparentProxy(obj)
...
Dim ar As ArrayList
ar = obj.GetCustomer(-1)
ShowCustomerArray(ar)

obj.RegisterCustomer( _
   "Boris", "Badenough", "boris@no-goodnicks.com")
Console.WriteLine()

ar = obj.GetCustomer(-1)
ShowCustomerArray(ar)
```

To run the program, start the server program in one console window and then start the client program in another console window.

The output depends on what kind of server-activated object is being activated. If the server activation type is **Singleton**, which supports the maintenance of state, you get the behavior you would expect from the nonremoted case. A new customer is added, and you find that new customer in the list when you ask for all the existing customers. As you would expect, the initial activate call results in the **Customers** constructor being called once for each server invocation, no matter how many times the client program is run.

```
Customers Constructor: AppDomain Client.exe Thread 111
Context 0
RegisterCustomer: AppDomain Client.exe Thread 111 Context 0
RegisterCustomer: AppDomain Client.exe Thread 111 Context 0
Object reference a proxy?: True
```

```
Client: AppDomain Client.exe Thread 111 Context 0
1    Rocket          Squirrel        rocky@frosbitefalls.com
2    Bullwinkle      Moose           moose@wossamotta.edu

1    Rocket          Squirrel        rocky@frosbitefalls.com
2    Bullwinkle      Moose           moose@wossamotta.edu
3    Boris           Badenough       boris@no-goodnicks.com
```

If the activation type is **SingleCall**, which creates a new object instance for every method call, the results are quite different. Four different objects are created. The first object is created by the initial activate request. The second is created by the initial call to **GetCustomer**. The third object is created by the **RegisterCustomer** call. The fourth object is created by the second call to **GetCustomer**. The last object created never sees the new customer because no state is saved. Note that the shared **nextCustId** member of the **Customer** class is treated as a shared member with respect to the new object instances of the **Customer** class, just as you would expect. Same client code, different results! Since the object is already activated, if you run the client program a second time for the same server invocation, the **Customers** constructor will be called only three times.

```
Customers Constructor: AppDomain Client.exe Thread 111
Context 0
RegisterCustomer: AppDomain Client.exe Thread 111 Context 0
RegisterCustomer: AppDomain Client.exe Thread 111 Context 0
Object reference a proxy?: True
Client: AppDomain Client.exe Thread 111 Context 0
3    Rocket          Squirrel        rocky@frosbitefalls.com
4    Bullwinkle      Moose           moose@wossamotta.edu

8    Rocket          Squirrel        rocky@frosbitefalls.com
9    Bullwinkle      Moose           moose@wossamotta.edu
```

Since the client uses a proxy, the object executes inside the server's application domain, but on a different thread than the main server thread. The object's constructor is not called until the first method call on the object. Notice how in both cases we have remoted an **ArrayList** of types without any special work aside from making the type serializable. The presence of metadata makes the programmer's work much easier.

Metadata and Remoting

In order for the client to request an object of a specific type, metadata about the type has to be available to the client. For some applications, a reference can be made to the actual assembly where the object is stored.

For many applications, however, you do not want to give the client access to your source code. For the metadata that the client needs, a reference needs to be made only to an object that has none of the implementation details.

One way to do this is to build a version of the object that has methods with no implementation. This interface class can then be built into an assembly that can be given to the client. You can throw the **System.NotSupported-Exception** in the methods if you wish to make sure it is never used by mistake for the real object.

```
<Serializable()> Public Structure CustomerListItem
    Public CustomerId As Integer
    Public FirstName As String
    Public LastName As String
    Public EmailAddress As String
End Structure
...
Public Class Customers
    Inherits MarshalByRefObject
    Implements Icustomer

    Public Function RegisterCustomer( _
     ByVal firstName As String, _
     ByVal lastName As String, _
     ByVal emailAddress As String) As Integer _
      Implements ICustomer.RegisterCustomer
        Throw New NotSupportedException()
    End Function

    Public Sub UnregisterCustomer(ByVal id As Integer) _
    Implements ICustomer.UnregisterCustomer
        Throw New NotSupportedException()
    End Sub

    Public Sub ChangeEmailAddress( _
     ByVal id As Integer, ByVal emailAddress As String) _
    Implements ICustomer.ChangeEmailAddress
        Throw New NotSupportedException()
    End Sub

    Public Function GetCustomer(ByVal id As Integer) _
     As ArrayList Implements ICustomer.GetCustomer
        Throw New NotSupportedException()
    End Function
End Class
```

For Web services, you use the SOAPSUDS tool to extract the metadata from the service, and then generate an assembly that has the required metadata. You can then build a proxy DLL and have the client program refer to it. This is conceptually equivalent to the first approach. The server, of course, has to reference the real object's assembly.

Unlike the COM model, there is no reference counting, interface negotiation, building and registering separate proxies and stubs, worrying about global identifiers, or use of the registry. Because of metadata, all you have to do is inherit from **MarshalByRefObject** to make an object remotable.

Remoting Configuration Files

You use configuration files to define where the object is activated. The client can then use the **New** operator to create the object. The big advantage in doing this is that as the object location changes (such as a URL or TCP channel), or the formatter you want to use changes, the client does not have to be modified or rebuilt.

Multiple classes can be configured on the client. Configuration files are loaded into the client using the **RemotingConfiguration.Configure** method.

Custom Attributes

Chapter 6 introduced the concept of attributes, which have already appeared in several examples. In this chapter we used the **Serializable** and **Synchronization** attributes, which are provided by .NET Framework classes. The .NET Framework makes the attribute mechanism entirely extensible, allowing you to define custom attributes, which can be added to a class's metadata. This custom metadata is available through reflection and can be used at runtime. To simplify the use of custom attributes, you may declare a base class to do the work of invoking the reflection API to obtain the metadata information.

Code
Example

The example **CustomAttribute** illustrates the custom attribute **InitialDirectory**. **InitialDirectory** controls the initial current directory where the program runs. By default, the current directory is the directory containing the program's executable. In the case of a Visual Studio .NET project built in Debug mode, this directory is **bin**, relative to the project source code directory.

Using a Custom Attribute

Before we discuss implementing the custom attribute, let us look at how the **InitialDirectory** attribute is used. To be able to control the initial directory for a class, we derive the class from the base class **DirectoryContext**. We may then apply to a class the attribute **InitialDirectory**, which takes a **String** parameter giving a path to what the initial directory should be. The property **DirectoryPath** extracts the path from the metadata. If our class does not have the attribute applied, this path will be the default. Here is the code for our test program.

When you run this sample on your system, you can change the directory in the attribute to any directory that exists on your machine.

```vb
' CustomAttribute.vb

Imports System
Imports System.IO

Class Normal
    Inherits DirectoryContext
End Class

<InitialDirectory("c:\")> Class Special
    Inherits DirectoryContext
End Class

Public Module AttributeDemo
    Public Sub Main()
        Dim objNormal As Normal = New Normal()
        Console.WriteLine( _
            "path = {0}", objNormal.DirectoryPath)
        ShowDirectoryContents(objNormal.DirectoryPath)
        Dim objSpecial As Special = New Special()
        Console.WriteLine( _
            "path = {0}", objSpecial.DirectoryPath)
        ShowDirectoryContents(objSpecial.DirectoryPath)
    End Sub
    Private Sub ShowDirectoryContents(ByVal path As String)
        Dim dir As DirectoryInfo = New DirectoryInfo(path)
        Dim files() As FileInfo = dir.GetFiles()
        Console.WriteLine("Files:")
        Dim f As FileInfo
        For Each f In files
            Console.WriteLine("   {0}", f.Name)
        Next
        Dim dirs() As DirectoryInfo = dir.GetDirectories()
        Console.WriteLine("Directories:")
        Dim d As DirectoryInfo
        For Each d In dirs
            Console.WriteLine("   {0}", d.Name)
        Next
    End Sub
End Module
```

Here is the output:

```
path = C:\OI\NetVB\Chap10\CustomAttribute\bin
Files:
   CustomAttribute.exe
   CustomAttribute.pdb
Directories:
path = c:\
Files:
   BOOTLOG.TXT
   MSDOS.SYS
   DETLOG.TXT
   BOOTLOG.PRV
   OAKCDROM.SYS
   AUTOEXEC.BAT
   SETUPLOG.TXT
   VIDEOROM.BIN
   LOGO.SYS
   command.com
   SUHDLOG.DAT
   NETLOG.TXT
   CONFIG.BAK
```

Defining an Attribute Class

To create a custom attribute, you must define an attribute class derived from the base class **Attribute**. By convention, you give your class a name ending in "Attribute." The name of your class without the "Attribute" suffix will be the name of the custom attribute. In our example the class name is **InitialDirectoryAttribute**, so the attribute's name is **InitialDirectory**.

You may provide one or more constructors for your attribute class. The constructors define how to pass positional parameters to the attribute (provide a parameter list, separated by commas). It is also possible to provide "named parameters" for a custom attribute, where the parameter information will be passed using the syntax name = value.

You may also provide properties to read the parameter information. In our example, we have a property **Path**, which is initialized in the constructor.

```
<AttributeUsage(AttributeTargets.Class)> _
      Public Class InitialDirectoryAttribute
   Inherits Attribute
   Private m_Path As String
   Public Sub New(ByVal path As String)
      Me.m_Path = path
   End Sub
   Public ReadOnly Property Path() As String
      Get
            Return m_Path
      End Get
   End Property
End Class
```

Defining a Base Class

The last step in working with a custom attribute is to provide a means to extract the custom attribute information from the metadata, using the reflection classes. You can obtain the **Type** of any object by calling the method **GetType**, which is provided in the root class **Object**. Using the class's method **GetCustomAttributes**, you can read the custom attribute information.

To make the coding of the client program as simple as possible, it is often useful to provide a base class that does the work of reading the custom attribute information.[10] We provide a base class **DirectoryContext**, which is used by a class wishing to take advantage of the **InitialDirectory** attribute. This base class provides the property **DirectoryPath** to return the path information stored in the metadata. Here is the code for the base class:

```
' DirectoryContext.cs

Imports System
Imports System.Reflection
Imports System.IO

Public Class DirectoryContext
    Public Overridable ReadOnly Property DirectoryPath() _
    As String
      Get
          Dim t As Type = Me.GetType()
          Dim a As Attribute
          For Each a In t.GetCustomAttributes(True)
              Dim da As InitialDirectoryAttribute = a
              If Not da Is Nothing Then
                  Return da.Path
              End If
          Next
          Return Directory.GetCurrentDirectory()
      End Get
    End Property
End Class
```

We must import the **System.Reflection** namespace. **GetType** returns the current **Type** object, and we can then use the **GetCustomAttributes** method can obtain a collection of **Attribute** objects from the metadata. Since this collection is heterogeneous, consisting of different types, the result of the VB.NET assignment operator is tested against **Nothing** in an If statement. This is used to test if a given collection element is of the type **InitialDirecto-**

---

10. With single implementation inheritance, there is a cost to providing a base class. If you need to derive from another class, such as **ContextBoundObject**, the base class has to derive from that class.

ryAttribute. If we find such an element, we return the **Path** property. Otherwise, we return the default current directory, obtained from **GetCurrentDirectory**.

Garbage Collection and Finalization

Memory management is a critical aspect of programming and can be the source of many errors. Whenever a resource is created, memory must be provided for it. And when the resource is no longer needed, the memory should be reclaimed. If the memory is not reclaimed, the amount of memory available for other resources is reduced. If such "memory leaks" recur often enough (which can happen in long-running server programs), the program can crash. Another potential bug is to reclaim memory while it is still required by another part of the program.

.NET greatly simplifies the programming of memory management through an automatic *garbage collection* facility. The CLR tracks the use of memory that is allocated on the managed heap, and any memory that is no longer referenced is marked as "garbage." When memory is low, the CLR traverses its data structure of tracked memory and reclaims all the memory marked as garbage. Thus the programmer is relieved of this responsibility.

Although a good foundation for resource management, garbage collection by itself does not address all issues. Memory allocated from the managed heap is not the only kind of resource needed in programs. Other resources, such as file handles and database connections, are not automatically deallocated, and the programmer may need to write explicit code to perform cleanup. The .NET Framework provides a **Finalize** method in the **Object** base class for this purpose. The CLR calls **Finalize** when the memory allocated for an object is reclaimed.

Another concern with garbage collection is performance. Is there a big penalty from the automated garbage collection? The CLR provides a very efficient multigenerational garbage collection algorithm. In this section we examine garbage collection and finalization in the .NET Framework, and we provide several code examples.

Finalize

System.Object has a protected method **Finalize**, which is automatically called by the CLR after an object becomes inaccessible. (As we shall see, finalization for an object may be suppressed by a call to the method **SuppressFinalize** of the **System.GC** class.) Since **Finalize** is protected, it can only be called through the class or a derived class. The default implementation of **Finalize** does nothing. For any cleanup to be performed, a class must override **Finalize**. Also, a class's **Finalize** implementation should call the **Finalize** of its base class.

LIMITATIONS OF FINALIZATION

Finalization is non-deterministic. **Finalize** for a particular object may run at any time during the garbage collection process, and the order of running finalizers for different objects cannot be predicted. Moreover, under exceptional circumstances, a finalizer may not run at all (for example, one finalizer goes into an infinite loop or a process aborts without giving the runtime a chance to clean up). Also, the thread on which a finalizer runs is not specified.

Another issue with finalization is its effect on performance. There is significantly more overhead associated with managing memory for objects with finalizers, both on the allocation side and on the deallocation side.[11]

Thus, you should not implement a finalizer for a class unless you have very good reason for doing so. And if you do provide a finalizer, you should probably provide an alternate, deterministic mechanism for a class to perform necessary cleanup. The .NET Framework provides a **Dispose** design pattern for deterministic cleanup.

Unmanaged Resources and Dispose

The classic case for a finalizer is a class that contains some unmanaged resource, such as a file handle or a database connection. If they are not released when no longer needed, the scalability of your application can be affected. As a simple illustration, consider a class that wraps a file object. We want to make sure that a file that is opened will eventually be closed. The object itself will be destroyed by garbage collection, but the unmanaged file will remain open unless explicitly closed. Hence, we provide a finalizer to close the wrapped file.

But as we discussed, finalization is non-deterministic, so a file for a deleted object might hang around open for a long time. We would like to have a deterministic mechanism for a client program to clean up the wrapper object when it is done with it. The .NET Framework provides the generic **IDisposable** interface for this purpose.

```
Public Interface IDisposable
    Sub Dispose()
End Interface
```

---

11. Finalization internals and other details of garbage collection are discussed in depth in the two-part article "Garbage Collection" by Jeffrey Richter, *MSDN Magazine*, November and December, 2000.

The design pattern specifies that a client program should call **Dispose** on the object when it is done with it. In the **Dispose** method implementation, the class does the appropriate cleanup. As backup assurance, the class should also implement a finalizer in case **Dispose** never gets called, perhaps due to an exception being thrown.[12] Since both **Dispose** and **Finalize** perform the cleanup, cleanup code can be placed in **Dispose**, and **Finalize** can be implemented by calling **Dispose**. One detail is that once **Dispose** has been called, the object should not be finalized, because that would involve cleanup being performed twice. The object can be removed from the finalization queue by calling **GC.SuppressFinalize**. Also, it is a good idea for the class to maintain a Boolean flag, such as **disposeCalled**, so that if **Dispose** is called twice, cleanup will not be performed a second time.

Code Example

The example program **DisposeDemo** provides an illustration of finalization and the dispose pattern. The class **SimpleLog** implements logging to a file, making use of the **StreamWriter** class (discussed earlier in this chapter).

```vb
' SimpleLog.vb

Imports System.IO

Public Class SimpleLog
   Implements IDisposable
   Private writer As StreamWriter
   Private name As String
   Private disposeCalled As Boolean = False
   Public Sub New(ByVal fileName As String)
      name = fileName
      writer = New StreamWriter(fileName, False)
      writer.AutoFlush = True
      Console.WriteLine("logfile " & name & " created")
   End Sub

   Public Sub WriteLine(ByVal str As String)
      writer.WriteLine(str)
      Console.WriteLine(str)
   End Sub

   Public Sub Dispose() Implements IDisposable.Dispose
      If disposeCalled Then
         Return
      End If
      writer.Close()
      GC.SuppressFinalize(Me)
```

---

12. One of the virtues of the exception-handling mechanism is that as the call stack is unwound in handling the exception, local objects go out of scope and so can get marked for finalization. We provide a small demo later in this section.

```
      Console.WriteLine("logfile " & name & " disposed")
      disposeCalled = True
   End Sub

   Protected Overrides Sub Finalize()
      Console.WriteLine("logfile " & name & " finalized")
      Dispose()
      MyBase.Finalize()
   End Sub
End Class
```

The class **SimpleLog** supports the **IDisposable** interface, and thus
implements **Dispose**. The cleanup code simply closes the **StreamWriter**
object. To make sure that a disposed object will not also be finalized,
GC.SuppressFinalize is called. The finalizer simply delegates to **Dispose**. To
help monitor object lifetime, a message is written to the console in the constructor, in **Dispose**, and in the finalizer.[13]

Here is the code for the test program:

```
' DisposeDemo.vb

Module DisposeDemo
   Sub Main()
      Dim log As New SimpleLog("log1.txt")
      log.WriteLine("First line")
      Pause()
      log.Dispose()
      log.Dispose()
      log = New SimpleLog("log2.txt")
      log.WriteLine("Second line")
      Pause()
      log = New SimpleLog("log3.txt")
      log.WriteLine("Third line")
      Pause()
   End Sub

   Private Sub Pause()
      Console.Write("Press enter to continue")
      Dim str As String = Console.ReadLine()
   End Sub
End Module
```

The **SimpleLog** object reference **log** is assigned in turn to three different object instances. The first time, it is properly disposed. The second time,
log is reassigned to refer to a third object before the second object is disposed, resulting in the second object becoming garbage. The **Pause** method

---

13. The **Console.WriteLine** in the finalizer is provided purely for didactic purposes
    and should not be done in production code, for reasons we shall discuss shortly.

provides an easy way to pause the execution of this console application, allowing us to investigate the condition of the files **log1.txt**, **log2.txt**, and **log3.txt** at various points in the execution of the program.

Running the program results in the following output:

```
logfile log1.txt created
First line
Press enter to continue
logfile log1.txt disposed
logfile log2.txt created
Second line
Press enter to continue
logfile log3.txt created
Third line
Press enter to continue
logfile log3.txt finalized
logfile log3.txt disposed
logfile log2.txt finalized
logfile log2.txt disposed
```

After the first pause, the file **log1.txt** has been created, and you can examine its contents in Notepad. If you try to delete the file, you will get a sharing violation, as illustrated in Figure 10–2.

At the second pause point, **log1.txt** has been disposed, and you will be allowed to delete it. **log2.txt** has been created (and is open). At the third pause point, **log3.txt** has been created. But the object reference to **log2.txt** has been reassigned, and so there is now no way for the client program to dispose of the second object.[14] If **Dispose** were the only mechanism to clean up the second object, we would be out of luck. Fortunately, the **SimpleLog**

FIGURE 10–2   *Trying to delete an open file results in a sharing violation.*

14. This example illustrates that it is the client's responsibility to help the scalability of the server by cleaning up objects (using **Dispose**) before reassigning them. Once an object has been reassigned, there is no way to call **Dispose**, and the object will hang around for an indeterminate period of time until garbage is collected. Effective memory management involves both the server and client.

class has implemented a finalizer, so the next time garbage is collected, the second object will be disposed of properly. We can see the effect of finalization by running the program through to completion. The second object is indeed finalized, and thence disposed. In fact, as the application domain shuts down, **Finalize** is called on all objects not exempt from finalization, even on objects that are still accessible.

In our code we explicitly make the third object inaccessible by the assignment **log = nothing**, and we then force a garbage collection by a call to **GC.Collect**. Finally, we sleep briefly to give the garbage collector a chance to run through to completion before the application domain shuts down. Coding our test program in this way is a workaround for the fact that the order of finalization is non-deterministic. The garbage collector will be called automatically when the program exits and the application domain is shut down. However, at that point, system objects, such as **Console**, are also being closed. Since you cannot rely on the order of finalizations, you may get an exception from the **WriteLine** statement within the finalizer. The explicit call to **GC.Collect** forces a garbage collection while the system objects are still open. If we omitted the last three lines of the **Main** method, we might well get identical output, but we might also take an exception.

We provide similar code at the end of the **Main** methods of our other test programs so that our print statements in finalizers work properly without randomly throwing exceptions.

ALTERNATE NAME FOR DISPOSE

The standard name for the method that performs cleanup is **Dispose**. The convention is that once an object is disposed, it is finished. In some cases, the same object instance may be reused, as in the case of a file. A file may be opened, closed, and then opened again. In such a case the standard naming convention is that the cleanup method should be called **Close**. In other cases some other natural name may be used.

Our **SimpleLog** class could plausibly have provided an **Open** method, and then it would have made sense to name our cleanup method **Close**. For simplicity, we did not provide an **Open** method, and so we stuck to the name **Dispose**.

Garbage Collection and Generations

Using the dispose pattern, we can mitigate the issue of non-deterministic finalization, but what about the performance of the garbage collector? It turns out that the overall memory management efficiency of .NET is quite good, thanks to two main points:

- Allocation is *very* fast. Space on the managed heap is always contiguous, so allocating a new object is equivalent to incrementing a pointer. (By contrast, an allocation on an unmanaged heap is relatively slow, because a list of data structures must be walked to find a block that is large enough.)

● The CLR uses *generations* during garbage collecting, reducing the number of objects that are typically checked for being garbage.

GENERATIONS

As an optimization, every object on the managed heap is assigned to a generation. A new object is in generation 0 and is considered a prime candidate for garbage collection. Older objects are in generation 1. Since such an older object has survived for a while, the odds favor its having a longer lifetime than a generation 0 object. Still older objects are assigned to generation 2 and are considered even more likely to survive a garbage collection. The maximum generation number in the current implementation of .NET is 2, as can be confirmed from the **GC.MaxGeneration** property.

In a normal sweep of the garbage collector, only generation 0 will be examined. It is here that the most likely candidates are for memory to be reclaimed. All surviving generation 0 objects are promoted to generation 1. If not enough memory is reclaimed, a sweep will next be performed on generation 1 objects, and the survivors will be promoted. Then, if necessary, a sweep of generation 2 will be performed, and so on up until **MaxGeneration**.

Finalization and Stack Unwinding

Code
Example

As mentioned earlier, one of the virtues of the exception-handling mechanism is that as the call stack is unwound in handling the exception, local objects go out of scope and so can get marked for finalization. The program **FinalizeStackUnwind** provides a simple illustration. It uses the **SimpleLog** class discussed previously, which implements finalization.

```
' FinalizeStackUnwind.vb

Module FinalizeStackUnwind
   Sub Main()
      Try
         SomeMethod()
      Catch e As Exception
         Console.WriteLine(e.Message)
      End Try
      GC.Collect()
   End Sub

   Private Sub SomeMethod()
      ' local variable
      Dim alpha As SimpleLog = New SimpleLog("alpha.txt")
      Throw New Exception("error!!")
```

```
    End Sub
End Module
```

A local variable **alpha** of type **SimpleLog** is allocated in **SomeMethod**. Before the method exits normally, an exception is thrown. The stack unwinding mechanism of exception handling detects that **alpha** is no longer accessible, and so is marked for garbage collection. The call to **GC.Collect** forces a garbage collection, and we see from the output of the program that **Finalize** is indeed called.

```
logfile alpha.txt created
error!!
logfile alpha.txt finalized
logfile alpha.txt disposed
```

Controlling Garbage Collection with the GC Class

Normally, it is the best practice simply to let the garbage collector perform its work behind the scenes. Sometimes, however, it may be advantageous for the program to intervene. The **System** namespace contains the class **GC**, which enables a program to affect the behavior of the garbage collector. We summarize a few of the important methods of the class.

SUPPRESSFINALIZE

This method requests the system to not call **Finalize** for the specified object. As we saw previously, you should call this method in your implementation of **Dispose** to prevent a disposed object from also being finalized.[15]

COLLECT

You can force a garbage collection by calling the **Collect** method. An optional parameter lets you specify which generations should be collected. Use this method sparingly, since normally the CLR has better information on the current state of memory. A possible use would be a case when your program has just released a number of large objects, and you would like to see all this memory reclaimed right away. Another example was provided in the previous section, where a call to **Collect** forced a collection while system objects were still valid.

---

15. You should be careful in the case of an object that might be "closed" (like a file) and later reopened again. In such a case it might be better not to suppress finalization. Once finalization is suppressed, it can be made eligible for finalization again by calling **GC.ReRegisterForFinalize**. For a discussion of advanced issues in garbage collection and finalization, refer to the article by Jeffrey Richter cited in footnote 11.

MAXGENERATION

This property returns the maximum number of generations that are supported.

GETGENERATION

This method returns the current generation number of an object.

GETTOTALMEMORY

This method returns the number of bytes currently allocated. A parameter lets you specify whether the system should perform a garbage collection before returning. If no garbage collection is done, the indicated number of bytes is probably larger than the actual number of bytes being used by live objects.

Sample Program

Code
Example

The program **GarbageCollection** illustrates using these methods of the **GC** class. The example is artificial, simply illustrating object lifetime and the effect of the various **GC** methods. The class of objects that are allocated is called **Member**. This class has a **String** property called **Name**. Write statements are provided in the constructor **Dispose** and in the finalizer. A **Committee** class maintains an array list of **Member** instances. The **RemoveMember** method simply removes the member from the array list. The **DisposeMember** method also calls **Dispose** on the member being expunged from the committee. The **ShowGenerations** method displays the generation number of each **Member** object. **GarbageCollection.vb** is a test program to exercise these classes, showing the results of various allocations and deallocations and the use of methods of the **GC** class. The code and output should be quite easy to understand.

All the memory is allocated locally in a method **DemonstrateGenerations**. After this method returns and its local memory has become inaccessible, we make an explicit call to **GC.Collect**. This forces the finalizers to be called before the application domain shuts down, and so we avoid a possible random exception of a stream being closed when a **WriteLine** method is called in a finalizer. This is the same point mentioned previously for the earlier examples.

Summary

This chapter introduced the .NET application model. Through metadata, the framework can understand enough about your application to provide many services that you do not have to implement. On the other hand, we have seen how the framework is structured so that you can substitute your own objects and implementations where needed.

Type safety enables application domains to provide a robust, yet cheap, form of application isolation. Contexts, proxies, and interception allow the runtime to transparently provide services to parts of applications that require them.

Another aspect of the .NET application model is the pervasive use of attributes, which can be easily added to source code and is stored with the metadata. We saw examples of the use of attributes for serialization and for synchronization, and we demonstrated how to implement and use custom attributes.

.NET simplifies the programming of memory management through an efficient generational automatic garbage collection facility. Finalization is non-deterministic, but you can support deterministic cleanup by implementing the dispose pattern.

ADVANCED UI PROGRAMMING USING VB.NET

ADVANCED UI PROGRAMMING
USING VB.NET

Part 5, consisting of Chapters 11 and 12, covers additional advanced topics in UI programming with VB.NET. Chapter 11 introduces GDI+, which provides a graphics programming model that is both more powerful and easier to use than the classic GDI model of traditional Windows. GDI+ is also completely accessible through Visual Basic. Chapter 12 introduces some important additional advanced topics, such as Visual Inheritance, MDI, and the use of ActiveX controls in .NET applications.

Introduction to GDI+

GDI+ is a class-based application programming interface for performing two-dimensional graphics in a device-independent manner. There are both managed .NET classes and unmanaged C++ classes that implement the API. GDI+ is the successor to the older GDI (graphics device interface) that was supplied with earlier versions of Windows. In this chapter we introduce graphics programming in VB.NET using GDI+ and the .NET classes.

Earlier versions of Visual Basic provided a simple set of graphics functions, but for full-blown graphics programming, it was necessary to program at a lower level, using C or C++. Now with GDI+ Visual Basic, programmers enjoy the complete power of graphics programming. And C/C++ programmers will find that graphics programming using GDI+ is much easier than using the GDI. In this chapter we outline the architecture of GDI+ and discuss programming vector graphics, text, fonts, bitmaps, and metafiles. We also see how memory is managed in GDI+, and we learn how to implement scrolling.

The subject of GDI+ is large, and a whole book could be written about it. The purpose of this chapter is to provide you with an orientation to this important topic.

Device-Independent Graphics and Abstraction

Because of the wide variety of graphics output devices, from video displays to laser printers and plotters, the most important characteristic of any graphics API is device-independence. Without device-independence, the application programmer would be faced with great complexity and the chore of implementing many versions of the same graphics programs.

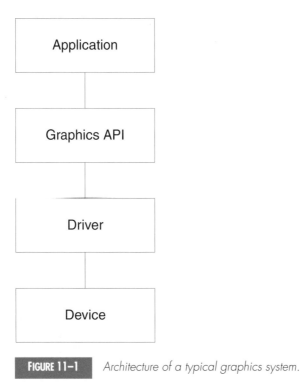

FIGURE 11–1   *Architecture of a typical graphics system.*

Figure 11–1 illustrates the basic architecture of a graphics system. An application calls functions that are provided by a graphics API. Each supported graphics device comes with a suitable driver. The graphics system takes care of translating device-independent calls into device-specific calls through the driver.

The original GDI does indeed provide such device-independence, but in a manner that is specific to Windows, and the API reflects this Windows orientation. The API is quite difficult to use, and there are a number of pitfalls. The interface to the GDI is defined in C, and programming to it requires the use of numerous complex structures. Some encapsulation was achieved for C++ programmers by a set of classes, which were part of the Microsoft Foundation Classes (MFC), but these classes are a rather thin wrapper around the GDI, and are only useful for C++ programmers.

The .NET Framework provides a higher level of abstraction, making the API easier to use. And, like other classes in the .NET Framework, the GDI+ classes are equally accessible from any .NET language. Thus, in particular, Visual Basic programmers now have a powerful graphics API that is also easy to use and can be called natively from VB.NET applications.

GDI+ Architecture

To program with GDI+, you need to understand a few basic concepts, and you must be familiar with how the key classes are organized into certain .NET namespaces. This section outlines the logical structure of GDI+ and the organization of the most important GDI+ classes. We begin with the basic concept of painting.

Windows Forms Painting

Although not directly part of GDI+, an important part of the story of drawing in Windows is the painting architecture of Windows Forms. The relevant classes and structures are in the **Windows.Forms** namespace.

The base class for objects with a visual representation is **Control**, which implements basic functionality needed for displaying information to the user. This class handles user input via the keyboard and mouse, and it routes messages by raising events. It also provides many overridable methods. Most Windows applications make use of the **Form** derived class.

PAINT EVENTS

The **OnPaint** method is an overridable method of the **Control** class, which is called whenever the control needs repainting. The base class's implementation raises the **Paint** event, which can be handled by any delegate attached to the event. A derived class may perform needed painting either by handling the **Paint** event or by overriding the **OnPaint** method. The latter is preferred. When overriding **OnPaint**, it is important to call the base class's **OnPaint** method so that **Paint** events will be raised and registered delegates can receive the event.

Code
Example

The program **PaintDemo\Version 1** illustrates painting both by overriding **OnPaint** and handling the **Paint** event. Build and run the program. You will see that one message is displayed in response to the override of **OnPaint**, and a second message is displayed by handling the **Paint** event.

Here is the code. Note that we have also overridden **OnLoad** for the purpose of setting the background color to white (which we could also have accomplished by setting the **BackColor** property in the Property window for the Form). We will discuss the drawing code and the use of the **Graphics** class a little later in the chapter. (For convenience, we use the Windows Forms designer throughout this chapter, and so all our code examples contain Forms designer support.)

```
Public Class Form1
   Inherits System.Windows.Forms.Form

#Region " Windows Form Designer generated code "
...
   Protected Overrides Sub OnPaint( _
    ByVal e As System.Windows.Forms.PaintEventArgs)
      Dim g As Graphics = e.Graphics
      g.DrawString("Overriding On Paint", Font, _
        Brushes.Black, 25, 25)
      MyBase.OnPaint(e)
   End Sub

   Private Sub Form1_Paint(ByVal sender As Object, _
    ByVal e As System.Windows.Forms.PaintEventArgs) _
    Handles MyBase.Paint
      Dim g As Graphics = e.Graphics
      g.DrawString("Handling Paint Event", Font, _
        Brushes.Black, 50, 50)
   End Sub

   Protected Overrides Sub OnLoad( _
    ByVal e As System.EventArgs)
      Me.BackColor = Color.White
      MyBase.OnLoad(e)
   End Sub
End Class
```

The **DrawString** method of the **Graphics** class is used for drawing a text string and has several overloaded versions. The version used in this code takes a string as the first parameter, a font as the second parameter, and a brush as the third parameter. The remaining parameters are coordinates that specify the location of the upper-left corner of the drawn text.

The call to **MyBase.OnPaint** at the bottom of the **OnPaint** code is important, enabling the **Paint** event to be raised. As an experiment, you can try commenting out this call. You will see that only the message from **OnPaint** is displayed. For similar reasons, you should call the base class's **OnLoad** at the bottom of your derived class's override of **OnLoad**, enabling the **Load** event to be raised.

PAINTEVENTARGS

Both the overridden **OnPaint** method and the **Paint** event handler take an argument that is an object of the **PaintEventArgs** class. This class has two read-only properties:

- **Graphics**, which specifies the **Graphics** object on which to paint.
- **ClipRectangle**, which specifies the rectangle in which to paint. Any drawing done outside this rectangle will be "clipped" and will not be shown on the drawing surface.

The clipping rectangle can make painting more efficient. We will return to this topic later in the chapter.

ON-DEMAND PAINTING

The way painting works in Windows (and in all other graphical user interface systems) is "on demand." Thus, if a window is covered up and then uncovered, a **Paint** event will be raised as a signal that the window must be repainted.

It is perfectly possible to perform drawing commands at other points in your program, and we will see some examples later in the chapter. **Paint-Demo\Version 2** illustrates drawing a third message when the mouse button is clicked. All we do is provide a handler for the **MouseDown** event. The third message is displayed at the location where the mouse was clicked. If you repeatedly click the mouse, you will see messages displayed at each point where the mouse was clicked, as illustrated in Figure 11–2.

But if you cover up the mouse event messages, they will disappear, unlike the paint messages, which will be always redisplayed.

FIGURE 11–2   *Main window shows overriding **OnPaint** and handling **Paint** and **MouseDown** events.*

Here is the code of the mouse event handler:

```
Private Sub Form1_MouseDown(ByVal sender As Object, _
  ByVal e As System.Windows.Forms.MouseEventArgs) _
  Handles MyBase.MouseDown
    Dim g As Graphics = Me.CreateGraphics
    g.DrawString("Handling Mouse Event", Font, _
         Brushes.Black, e.X, e.Y)
End Sub
```

The drawing code involving the **DrawString** method is the same as we used elsewhere in the program. What is different is how we obtain the **Graphics** object, using the **CreateGraphics** method, inherited from the **Control** class.

Now it is time to begin our study of the **Graphics** class.

Graphics Class

The heart of GDI+ is the **Graphics** class in the **System.Drawing** namespace. It is the class that has methods to draw text, lines, rectangles, and other shapes. A **Graphics** object is associated with a particular display device. Thus, the actual target of a drawing operation depends on the particular **Graphics** object used; the drawing code itself is the same.

An example of drawing with the **Graphics** class was provided in the **PaintDemo** program, where we displayed a text string using the **DrawString** method.

```
Dim g As Graphics = e.Graphics
g.DrawString("Overriding On Paint", Font, _
   Brushes.Black, 25, 25)
```

The **DrawString** method is typical of the drawing methods of the **Graphics** class. The method call contains information about *what* is to be drawn (a string, in this case), *how* it is to be displayed (a font and a brush), and *where* the output is to be located (*x* and *y* coordinates). These calls are *stateless* and do not rely on information that is stored in the **Graphics** object and is remembered from call to call. This model is different from the older GDI, in which the *device context*, which is the analog of the GDI+ **Graphics** object, preserved state such as the font and brush to be used in a drawing operation. The new model is more straightforward and easier to program.

DRAWING METHODS

Table 11–1 shows some of the common drawing methods of the **Graphics** class. This list is not exhaustive, and you should consult the .NET Framework class library reference documentation for a complete list and for details.

TABLE 11–1	*Common Drawing Methods of the Graphics Class*

Drawing Method	Description
DrawArc	Draws an arc representing a portion of an ellipse
DrawBezier	Draws a Bézier spline
DrawEllipse	Draws an ellipse defined by a bounding rectangle
DrawImage	Draws an image
DrawImageUnscaled	Draws an image with no scaling
DrawLine	Draws a line connecting two points
DrawPie	Draws a pie shape
DrawPolygon	Draws a polygon defined by an array of points
DrawRectangle	Draws a rectangle
DrawString	Draws a text string
FillEllipse	Fills the interior of an ellipse
FillPolygon	Fills the interior of a polygon
FillRectangle	Fills the interior of a rectangle

OTHER FUNCTIONALITY

The **Graphics** class supports a number of additional functions besides a wide selection of drawing methods. There are properties to give read-only access to characteristics of the associated device, such as the horizontal and vertical resolution. Coordinate transformations of various sorts are supported. A clipping region is used to more efficiently control where output is allowed to go on a drawing surface.

Pens and Brushes

The **Graphics** class represents the drawing surface and provides drawing methods. When you draw, you need to make use of drawing tools, such as pens and brushes, which are defined by their own classes in the .NET Framework. Most of these classes are in the **System.Drawing** namespace, but some classes are in the **System.Drawing.Drawing2D** namespace.

The **Pen** class defines objects that are used to draw lines and curves. A pen has a width and a color (or in fact can have an associated brush).

There are several brush classes, which are used for drawing the interior of a shape. A brush has a color and may have a pattern.

- The **SolidBrush** class defines brushes of a single color.
- The **HatchBrush** class defines brushes that have a hatch style, a foreground color, and a background color.

- The **LinearGradientBrush** and **PathGradientBrush** classes define gradient brushes that can change color gradually as you move across the shape.
- The **TextureBrush** class defines brushes that can be used to fill a shape based on a pattern stored in a bitmap.

The hatch and gradient brush classes are in the **System.Drawing.Drawing2D** namespace.

Text and Fonts

In a graphical user interface system, text data is treated as another kind of graphic, of a particularly complex sort. A *font* is used to render text data to a drawing surface. The **Font** class defines how text is to be formatted when rendered, including a font face, a size, and a style. The **Graphics** class has methods to measure a string so that you can properly position strings when you draw.

Images, Bitmaps, and Metafiles

The **Bitmap** class can be used for working with raster images, where a picture is stored as an array of pixels. The **Metafile** class can be used for storing drawing commands, which can be used to define vector images. Both **Bitmap** and **Metafile** inherit from the **Image** class. Methods are provided that make it easy to save and restore bitmaps and metafiles. Images can be manipulated by a number of methods, and they can be displayed.

Coordinates

GDI+ defines three kinds of coordinates:

- *World* coordinates are logical coordinates that are used in drawing operations.
- *Page* coordinates are relative to the upper left corner of a client area.
- *Device* coordinates are page coordinates specified in a particular unit of measurement. If the unit is pixels, device and page coordinates are the same.

The **Graphics** class has properties and methods that support coordinate transformations. A *world transform* converts world coordinates to page coordinates through methods such as **RotateTransform**, **ScaleTransform**, and **TranslateTransform**. A *page transform* converts page coordinates to device coordinates, using the **PageUnit** and **PageScale** properties of the **Graphics** object.

Coordinates are important in scrolling, which changes the world coordinates with respect to the page coordinates. The **Form** class has properties (inherited from the **ScrollableControl** class) that support "automatic" handling of scrolling.

GDI+ Structures

In order to program using GDI+, you need to use a number of simple structures that define points, rectangles, sizes, and colors. These are quite straightforward, but their use involves a few details, such as the existence of both integer and floating-point versions, converting among the structures, and so forth. In this section we summarize key features of these structures.

Coordinates and sizes can be expressed as either integer or floating-point numbers. Some methods use one type, and other methods use the other type, so you need to be familiar with both. Integer structures are **Point**, **Size**, and **Rectangle**. Floating-point structures have the same names with an "F" suffix, so they are **PointF**, **SizeF**, and **RectangleF**. Operators are overloaded in a natural way so that you can test for equality by using the equality operator and so forth.

Point and PointF

The **Point** structure represents an ordered pair of integers that defines a point in a two-dimensional plane. There are properties **X** and **Y** representing the x-coordinate and y-coordinate respectively. A constructor can create a point from two integers.

```
Dim p as Point = new Point(5, 15)
```

The **PointF** structure is the same, except it represents a pair of floating-point numbers. Since an **Integer** can be implicitly converted to a **Single**, you could convert a **Point** to a **PointF** by constructing a new **PointF** out of the **X** and **Y** members of the **PointF**.

```
Dim p As New Point(5, 16)
Dim pf = New PointF(p.X, p.Y)
```

For converting in the opposite direction, you can use the static methods **Round**, **Truncate**, or **Ceiling** of the **Point** class.

```
Dim pf As New PointF(5.3, 16.7)
Dim p As Point = Point.Round(pf)
```

Size and SizeF

A **Size** is also an ordered pair of integers, but it is used to represent the size of a rectangular region rather than a location. It has properties **Width** and

Height. The **SizeF** structure is similar, with an ordered pair of floating-point numbers. Conversion issues are handled in the same manner as with **Point** and **PointF**.

Rectangle and RectangleF

A **Rectangle** is a combination of a **Point** and a **Size**. Alternatively, it can be defined as four integers. The first two represent the location of the top-left corner, and the other two represent the width and height. There is a constructor corresponding to each definition. Thus, the following code creates identical rectangles **r1** and **r2**.

```
Dim p As New Point(5, 5)
Dim s As New Size(40, 20)
Dim r1 As New Rectangle(p, s)
Dim r2 As New Rectangle(5, 5, 40, 20)
```

A **RectangleF** is a combination of a **PointF** and a **SizeF**. The properties and methods of **RectangleF** are entirely parallel to those of **Rectangle**, and we will focus on **Rectangle** in the rest of this section.

There are numerous properties that you can use in working with rectangles. Table 11–2 shows read/write properties.

TABLE 11–2	*Read/Write Properties of Rectangle*	
Type	**Property**	**Description**
Point	Location	Location of top-left point of rectangle
Size	Size	Size of rectangle
Integer	X	x-coordinate of top-left point
Integer	Y	y-coordinate of top-left point
Integer	Width	Width of rectangle
Integer	Height	Height of rectangle

Table 11–3 shows read-only properties.

TABLE 11–3	*Read-Only Properties of Rectangle*	
Type	**Property**	**Description**
Integer	Left	Same as X
Integer	Top	Same as Y
Integer	Right	X + Width
Integer	Bottom	Y + Height

There are a number of methods you can use in working with rectangles. Many of these methods have several overloaded versions. For example, you can offset a rectangle by either a point or a pair of integers. Table 11–4 shows several of the common methods of the **Rectangle** class.

TABLE 11–4	*Common Methods of Rectangle*

Method	Description
Offset	Shift a rectangle to another location
Inflate	Make rectangle larger (or smaller with negative argument)
Union	Form the union of two rectangles
Intersect	Take the intersection of two rectangles
Contains	Check if a point is contained within a rectangle

USING RECTANGLES IN DRAWING

It is legal for the **Width** and **Height** properties of a **Rectangle** to be negative, but when you use a rectangle for drawing, these values should be positive. The "top-left" point of a rectangle that you draw should really be in that location. If you have two arbitrary points **p** and **q**, you can use the helper function **MakeRectangle** to create a rectangle with top-left and bottom-right properly oriented for drawing. (This function was created for this book and is not part of the Framework.)

```
Private Function MakeRectangle(ByVal p As Point, _
 ByVal q As Point) As Rectangle
   Dim top, left, bottom, right As Integer
   top = IIf(p.Y < q.Y, p.Y, q.Y)
   left = IIf(p.X < q.X, p.X, q.X)
   bottom = IIf(p.Y > q.Y, p.Y, q.Y)
   right = IIf(p.X > q.X, p.X, q.X)
   Return New Rectangle(left, top, right - left, _
      bottom - top)
End Function
```

Code
Example

The program **RectangleDemo\Version 1** illustrates drawing a rectangle from the point (20, 10) to the point (x, y), where the mouse is clicked. The drawing code is directly in the mouse event handler method.

```
Private Sub Form1_MouseDown(ByVal sender As Object, _
 ByVal e As MouseEventArgs) Handles MyBase.MouseDown
   Dim g As Graphics = CreateGraphics()
   Dim p1 As New Point(20, 10)
   Dim p2 As New Point(e.X, e.Y)
   Dim rect As Rectangle = MakeRectangle(p1, p2)
   g.DrawRectangle(Pens.Black, rect)
End Sub
```

Color Structure

Colors in Windows Forms are defined by the three primary colors, red, green, and blue. The **Color** structure has corresponding read-only **Byte** properties **R**, **G**, and **B**. By varying the intensity of each component from 0 to 255, different colors can be created. Table 11–5 shows the RGB values of the three primary colors, the colors made up of exactly two primaries, white, a middle shade of gray, and black.

TABLE 11–5	*RGB Values of Common Colors*
Color	**RGB Value**
Black	0, 0, 0
Red	255, 0, 0
Green	0, 255, 0
Blue	0, 0, 255
Yellow	255, 255, 0
Magenta	255, 0, 255
Cyan	0, 255, 255
Gray	127, 127, 127
White	255, 255, 255

There is also an *alpha* value, which specifies the transparency of the color. The corresponding read-only property is **A**, which is also of type **Byte**. A value of 0 means completely transparent, and a value of 255 means completely opaque.

A **Color** object can be created from the shared method **FromArgb**, which has several overloaded forms. For example, the following line of code creates a **Color** object **m_color** from the **Integer** variables **a**, **r**, **g**, and **b**.

```
m_color = Color.FromArgb(a, r, g, b)
```

STANDARD COLORS

The **Color** structure has 141 shared read-only properties that define a set of colors originally created for the Web. Thus, you can use names like **Color.Black**, **Color.Red**, and so on. There is also **Color.Transparent**.

DEMONSTRATION PROGRAM

Code
Example

The program **ColorDemo\Version 1** displays the R, G, B, and alpha values of a color, which is initialized to green. The color can be changed by using the Color Common Dialog. The chosen color is shown in a label control. You can also assign numerical values for the R, G, B, and alpha values and click

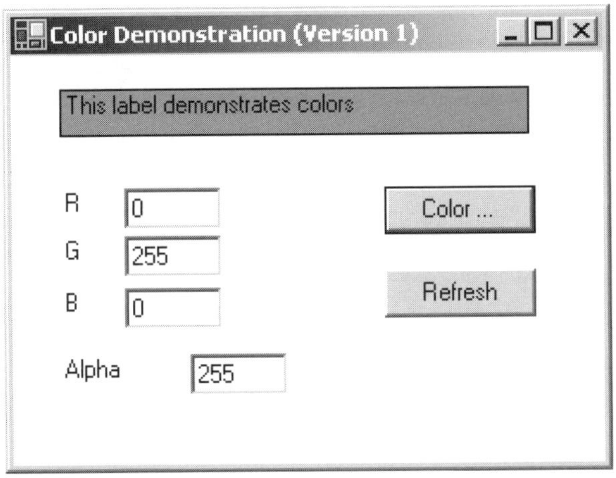

FIGURE 11-3   *Demonstration program shows R, G, B, and Alpha values.*

the Refresh button to display the chosen color. The background color of the form and the label control is set to white so that the color will be better displayed and not mix with the normal gray color of controls. Figure 11–3 shows a screen capture of the running program with the starting value of green.

If you experiment with the alpha value, you will see how the color fades out with lower alpha values. However, the opaque quality is not demonstrated very well, because the text in the label control is in the foreground and is always shown. Version 2 of the program, discussed a little later, will use a brush to paint the label control, and we will then see that an opaque alpha value indeed covers up the text, and a transparent value lets the text show through.

Here is the code of the program.

```
Public Class Form1
    Inherits System.Windows.Forms.Form

#Region " Windows Form Designer generated code "

    Private m_color As Color

    Private Sub Form1_Load(ByVal sender As Object, _
     ByVal e As System.EventArgs) Handles MyBase.Load
        m_color = Color.FromArgb(255, 0, 255, 0)
        ShowColor()
    End Sub

    Private Sub btnRefresh_Click(ByVal sender As Object, _
     ByVal e As EventArgs) Handles btnRefresh.Click
        Dim r As Integer = Convert.ToInt32(txtRed.Text)
```

```
        Dim g As Integer = Convert.ToInt32(txtGreen.Text)
        Dim b As Integer = Convert.ToInt32(txtBlue.Text)
        Dim a As Integer = Convert.ToInt32(txtAlpha.Text)
        m_color = Color.FromArgb(a, r, g, b)
        lblColor.BackColor = m_color
    End Sub

    Private Sub btnColor_Click(ByVal sender As Object, _
      ByVal e As System.EventArgs) Handles btnColor.Click
        Dim dlg As New ColorDialog()
        Dim status As DialogResult
        dlg.Color = m_color
        status = dlg.ShowDialog
        If status = DialogResult.OK Then
            m_color = dlg.Color
            ShowColor()
        End If
    End Sub

    Private Sub ShowColor()
        txtRed.Text = m_color.R
        txtGreen.Text = m_color.G
        txtBlue.Text = m_color.B
        txtAlpha.Text = m_color.A
        lblColor.BackColor = m_color
    End Sub
End Class
```

Pens and Brushes

As we mentioned earlier in our survey of GDI+ architecture, when you draw, you need to make use of drawing tools, such as pens and brushes, which are defined by their own classes in the .NET Framework. The **Pen** class defines objects that are used to draw lines and curves. A pen has a width, dash style, and a color (or in fact can have an associated brush). There are several brush classes, which are used for drawing the interior of a shape. In this section we will examine some of the details of working with pens and brushes. We begin with pens, which are simpler.

Pens

Pens are used to draw lines and curves. Compared to brushes, pens are quite simple objects. There is a single class, **Pen**, in the **System.Drawing** namespace that is used for creating custom pens. As is usual in GDI+, there are several overloaded constructors. The two most important ones take a color or a brush as the first parameter and a width as the second parameter. The width is a **Single** number. Here are two ways of specifying a red pen of width 3:

```
Dim pen1 as New Pen(Color.Red, 3)
Dim pen2 as New Pen(Brushes.Red, 3)
```

Being able to specify a brush allows great variety to the custom pens that you can create, since you can create a brush from any of the various brush classes that we will examine in the next section.

DASHSTYLE

Although you cannot specify it in a constructor, pens can have a *dash style,* which is specified by a read/write property **DashStyle**. The type of this property is the **DashStyle** enumeration, which has the following possible values:

- Custom
- Dash
- DashDot
- DashDotDot
- Dot
- Solid

The sample program at the end of this section allows you to create pens with the various dash styles.

STANDARD PENS

Besides all the various kinds of custom pens you can create, there are a number of standard pens that correspond to the standard colors. The **Pens** class has a read-only property for each of the standard colors: **Pens.Black**, **Pens.Red**, **Pens.Blue**, and so forth. Each standard pen has width 1.

DRAWING WITH PENS

Code Example

Once you have created a pen, you can draw with it using various drawing methods such as **DrawLine**, **DrawArc**, **DrawBezier**, and so on. The program **PenDemo** illustrates drawing a line with various pens, where you can specify the color, width, and dash style of the pen. Figure 11–4 shows a screen capture of the running program with a red pen of width 5 and a Dash-DotDot dash style. A horizontal line is drawn in a label control, using the specified pen.

This program illustrates painting directly on a control. Normally, in Windows Forms you can simply use a control as is, and you don't have to be concerned with painting. But if you do need to do painting yourself, it is easy to accomplish by adding a handler for the **Paint** event for the control. In code such as this you have to be careful about what happens in response

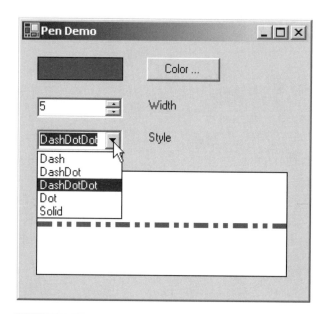

FIGURE 11–4   *Demonstration program illustrates different pens.*

to the initial **Paint** event, when things may not have been fully initialized yet. In this program, we check that the pen has been created before we attempt to use it. We use this style of program extensively in this chapter so that we can compactly illustrate drawing using various GDI+ classes, with suitable controls to allow the user to choose options. We could draw on any kind of control; we use a label control. To show the drawing surface, we set the background color to white and the **BorderStyle** to **FixedSingle**. Here is the code for the **Paint** event handler.

```
Private Sub lblRect_Paint(ByVal sender As Object, _
 ByVal e As PaintEventArgs) Handles lblRect.Paint
   Dim g As Graphics = e.Graphics
   Dim p1 As New Point(0, lblRect.Height / 2)
   Dim p2 As New Point(lblRect.Width, lblRect.Height / 2)
   If Not m_pen Is Nothing Then
      g.DrawLine(m_pen, p1, p2)
   End If
End Sub
```

There are member variables to hold the current color and pen.

```
Private m_color As Color = Color.Red
Private m_pen As Pen
```

There is a **NumericUpDown** control, **nudWidth**, to specify the width and a combo box, **cmbStyle**, to specify the style. The handler for the **Load** event performs initializations.

```
Private Sub Form1_Load(ByVal sender As Object, _
 ByVal e As EventArgs) Handles MyBase.Load
    Label1.BackColor = m_color
    nudWidth.Value = 5
    cmbStyle.Text = "Dash"
    m_pen = MakePen()
    lblRect.Invalidate()
End Sub
```

The helper method **MakePen** creates a pen having the specified characteristics.

```
Function MakePen() As Pen
    Dim width As Integer = nudWidth.Value
    Dim pen As New Pen(m_color, width)
    pen.DashStyle = Style
    Return pen
End Function
```

The read-only property **Style** is used to obtain the **DashStyle** of the pen as selected in the combo box.

```
Private ReadOnly Property Style() As DashStyle
    Get
        Select Case cmbStyle.Text
            Case "Dash"
                Return DashStyle.Dash
            Case "DashDot"
                Return DashStyle.DashDot
            Case "DashDotDot"
                Return DashStyle.DashDotDot
            Case "Dot"
                Return DashStyle.Dot
            Case "Solid"
                Return DashStyle.Solid
        End Select
    End Get
End Property
```

The handler for clicking the Color button updates the color through the helper method **UpdateColor**. It shows this color on an adjacent label control, and then creates a new pen with this color. Finally, it invalidates the label control where the line is drawn, forcing a repaint.

```
Private Sub btnColor_Click(ByVal sender As Object, _
 ByVal e As EventArgs) Handles btnColor.Click
    UpdateColor(m_color)
```

```
    Label1.BackColor = m_color
    m_pen = MakePen()
    lblRect.Invalidate()
End Sub
```

The **UpdateColor** helper method takes a color as a reference argument. It brings up a color common dialog to let the user specify a color.

```
Private Sub UpdateColor(ByRef col As Color)
    Dim dlg As New ColorDialog()
    Dim status As DialogResult
    dlg.Color = col
    status = dlg.ShowDialog
    If status = DialogResult.OK Then
        col = dlg.Color
    End If
End Sub
```

Finally, there are event handlers for changing the **NumericUpDown** control and the combo box. These handlers create a new pen having the specified characteristics and then invalidate the label control to force a repaint. The simple form of **Invalidate** shown here invalidates the entire label control. You can also invalidate a region to optimize the performance of painting. We will say more about invalidation later in the chapter when we discuss clipping.

```
Private Sub nudWidth_ValueChanged(ByVal sender As Object, _
 ByVal e As EventArgs) Handles nudWidth.ValueChanged
    m_pen = MakePen()
    lblRect.Invalidate()
End Sub
```

```
Private Sub cmbStyle_SelectedIndexChanged( _
 ByVal sender As Object, ByVal e As EventArgs) _
 Handles cmbStyle.SelectedIndexChanged
    m_pen = MakePen()
    lblRect.Invalidate()
End Sub
```

Brushes

The **Brush** class in the **System.Drawing** namespace is an abstract class. To create a brush object, you need to instantiate one of the derived classes. The derived classes such as **SolidBrush**, **HatchBrush**, and so forth cannot be inherited.

SOLIDBRUSH

The simplest kind of brush is a **SolidBrush**. This class is in the **System.Drawing** namespace. A solid brush is completely described by a **Color**, which is passed as an argument to the constructor.

```
m_brush = New SolidBrush(m_color)
```

Code
Example

The program **ColorDemo\Version 2** illustrates use of a solid brush. Version 2 uses a brush to paint the label control **lblColor**, which will paint over the text in the control. The result is that an opaque color will completely obscure the text, and a transparent color will let the text show through. Here is the code for Version 2. We show in bold the lines that are changed from Version 1. Routines that are unchanged are left out.

```
    Private m_color As Color
    Private m_brush As Brush
...

    Private Sub btnRefresh_Click(ByVal sender As Object, _
    ByVal e As EventArgs) Handles btnRefresh.Click
        Dim r As Integer = Convert.ToInt32(txtRed.Text)
        Dim g As Integer = Convert.ToInt32(txtGreen.Text)
        Dim b As Integer = Convert.ToInt32(txtBlue.Text)
        Dim a As Integer = Convert.ToInt32(txtAlpha.Text)
        m_color = Color.FromArgb(a, r, g, b)
        m_brush = New SolidBrush(m_color)
        lblColor.Invalidate()
    End Sub
...

    Private Sub ShowColor()
        txtRed.Text = m_color.R
        txtGreen.Text = m_color.G
        txtBlue.Text = m_color.B
        txtAlpha.Text = m_color.A
        m_brush = New SolidBrush(m_color)
        lblColor.Invalidate()
    End Sub
    Private Sub lblColor_Paint(ByVal sender As Object, _
    ByVal e As PaintEventArgs) Handles lblColor.Paint
        Dim g As Graphics = e.Graphics
        Dim rect = New Rectangle(0, 0, Me.Width, Me.Height)
        If Not m_brush Is Nothing Then
            g.FillRectangle(m_brush, rect)
        End If
    End Sub
End Class
```

The use of the brush is very easy. Whenever a color is assigned, a solid brush of that color is created. The **Invalidate** method is called to force the label control to be repainted. An event handler is added for the **Paint** event for this control. A rectangle is constructed, which is the size of the control, and the rectangle is painted by calling **FillRectangle**.

HATCHBRUSH

Another kind of brush is a **HatchBrush**. This class is in the **System.Drawing.Drawing2D** namespace. A hatch brush is completely described by a hatch style, a foreground color, and a background color, which are passed as arguments to the constructor. The hatch style belongs to the **HatchStyle** enumeration, and the colors are of type **Color**.

```
m_brush = New HatchBrush(HatchStyle.DiagonalCross, _
                         m_ForeColor, m_BackColor)
```

Code
Example

The program **HatchBrushDemo** illustrates use of a hatch brush. The general logic of the program is similar to Version 2 of **ColorDemo**. You can experiment by selecting colors and a hatch style. The combo box lets you pick a few of the many possible hatch styles. Figure 11–5 shows a screen capture of the running program with white foreground, black background, and a diagonal cross-hatch style.

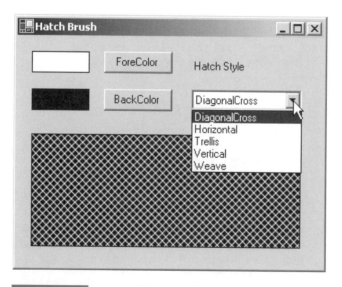

FIGURE 11–5   *Demonstration program illustrates different hatch brushes.*

GRADIENT BRUSHES

Another kind of brush are gradient brushes, which can change color gradually as you move across the shape. There are two classes of gradient brush, both in the **System.Drawing.Drawing2D** namespace:

- **LinearGradientBrush** enables a smooth shading of colors along a line.
- **PathGradientBrush** enables a smooth shading of colors from the center point of a path to the outside boundary edge of the path.

You can consult the SDK documentation for details about the **PathGradientBrush** class. There are several overloaded constructors for **LinearGradientBrush**. For example, you can construct a linear gradient brush from two points and two colors, representing starting and ending points and colors.

```
lgbrush = New LinearGradientBrush(pt1, pt2, color1, color2)
```

The program **GradientBrush** illustrates use of a linear gradient brush. The general logic of the program is similar to **HatchBrushDemo**. You can experiment by selecting starting and ending colors. Figure 11–6 shows a screen capture of the running program with a gradient that shades from white to black.

TEXTUREBRUSH

The **TextureBrush** class defines brushes that can be used to fill a shape based on a pattern stored in a bitmap. We will discuss bitmaps later in the chapter, and then you should be able to create your own texture brushes based on the SDK documentation.

FIGURE 11–6   *Demonstration program illustrates different linear gradient brushes.*

STANDARD BRUSHES

Besides all the various kinds of custom brushes you can create, there are a number of standard solid brushes that correspond to the standard colors. The **Brushes** class has a read-only property for each of the standard colors, such as **Brushes.Black**, **Brushes.Red**, and **Brushes.Blue**.

A Drawing Program

Vector graphics deals with drawing geometric shapes such as lines, curves, and polygons. In this section we illustrate vector graphics in GDI+ with an interactive drawing program. Later in the chapter we will introduce raster graphics and bitmaps.

Our sample program, **DrawDemo**, allows you to draw a picture consisting of rectangles and ellipses of various sizes, colors, and patterns. The program illustrates both standard painting (implemented by an override of **OnPaint**) and "rubber-band" drawing, in which a shape is temporarily outlined as the mouse is moved. We also illustrate use of a clipping rectangle, which can make for more efficient drawing.

Rubber-Band Drawing

Code
Example

Version 1 of **DrawDemo** illustrates drawing a single rectangle. When the program is started, a small square is shown in the top-left area of the client window. Pressing a mouse button erases the current rectangle (by redrawing the rectangle with the background color of the container) and begins a new drawing. As the mouse is moved, with the button still pressed, a rectangle is outlined. When the mouse button is released, the current rectangle is "locked" and will be always displayed via **OnPaint**. Here is the code:

```
Public Class Form1
    Inherits System.Windows.Forms.Form

#Region " Windows Form Designer generated code "

    Private m_start As Point
    Private m_end As Point
    Private m_track As Boolean

    Private Function MakeRectangle(ByVal p As Point, _
      ByVal q As Point) As Rectangle
        Dim top, left, bottom, right As Integer
        top = IIf(p.Y < q.Y, p.Y, q.Y)
        left = IIf(p.X < q.X, p.X, q.X)
```

```
      bottom = IIf(p.Y > q.Y, p.Y, q.Y)
      right = IIf(p.X > q.X, p.X, q.X)
      Return New Rectangle(left, top, right - left, _
         bottom - top)
End Function

Protected Overrides Sub OnPaint( _
 ByVal e As System.Windows.Forms.PaintEventArgs)
      Dim rect As Rectangle
      rect = MakeRectangle(m_start, m_end)
      Dim g As Graphics = e.Graphics
      g.DrawRectangle(Pens.Black, rect)
      MyBase.OnPaint(e)
End Sub

Protected Overrides Sub OnMouseDown( _
 ByVal e As System.Windows.Forms.MouseEventArgs)
      m_start = New Point(e.X, e.Y)
      m_end = m_start
      m_track = True
      Invalidate()
End Sub

Protected Overrides Sub OnMouseUp( _
 ByVal e As System.Windows.Forms.MouseEventArgs)
      m_track = False
      Invalidate()
End Sub

Protected Overrides Sub OnMouseMove( _
 ByVal e As System.Windows.Forms.MouseEventArgs)
      If m_track Then
         Dim p As New Point(e.X, e.Y)
         If Not p.Equals(m_start) Then
            Dim g As Graphics = Me.CreateGraphics()
            Dim rect As Rectangle
            ' erase previous rectangle
            rect = MakeRectangle(m_start, m_end)
            g.DrawRectangle(Pens.White, rect)
            ' draw new rectangle
            m_end = p
            rect = MakeRectangle(m_start, m_end)
            g.DrawRectangle(Pens.Black, rect)
         End If
      End If
End Sub

Private Sub Form1_Load(ByVal sender As Object, _
 ByVal e As System.EventArgs) Handles MyBase.Load
      m_start = New Point(5, 5)
```

```
        m_end = New Point(50, 50)
    End Sub
End Class
```

Multiple Shapes

Code
Example

Version 2 of **DrawDemo** is a more full-blown program, allowing the user to choose among different shapes and to specify a color and a brush. With a toolbar, the user can choose between a rectangle and an ellipse (these choices are also available from the Draw menu). The menu Draw | Brush... brings up a modeless dialog box,[1] which allows the user to specify the style of the brush. By clicking Color..., the user can pick a color. The chosen color and a text string for the shape are shown in an edit control.

Note that the settings chosen from the Brush Properties dialog apply to the *next* shape that is drawn. Each shape that is drawn is stored in a list of shapes. Figure 11–7 shows a simple drawing created using this program, consisting of a rectangle and two ellipses, with different colors and hatch styles.

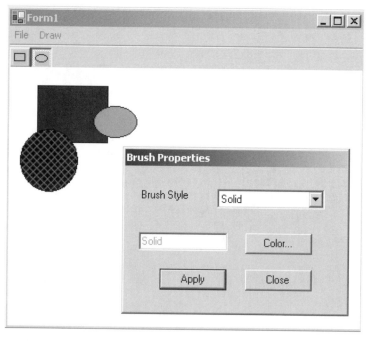

FIGURE 11–7   *With drawing program, you can draw various shapes.*

1. See Chapter 12 for a discussion of how you can create your own modeless dialog boxes using Windows Forms.

SHAPE HIERARCHY

This kind of program can be implemented by using a hierarchy of shapes. For simplicity, our hierarchy only includes rectangles and ellipses. The file **Shape.vb** provides the code for this hierarchy. The key feature is that the base class **CShape** is an abstract class with a **MustOverride** method **DrawShape**. The **DrawShape** method of the derived class draws the shape corresponding to the class. Hence **DrawShape** can be used polymorphically.

```
' Shape.vb

Imports System.Drawing

Public MustInherit Class CShape
    Protected m_p1 As Point
    Protected m_p2 As Point
    Protected m_pen As Pen
    Protected m_brush As Brush

    Public Sub New(ByVal p1 As Point, ByVal p2 As Point, _
    ByVal pn As Pen, ByVal br As Brush)
        Dim rect As Rectangle
        rect = MakeRectangle(p1, p2)
        m_p1 = rect.Location
        m_p2 = New Point(rect.Right, rect.Bottom)
        m_pen = pn
        m_brush = br
    End Sub

    Public Sub New(ByVal p1 As Point, ByVal p2 As Point)
        m_pen = Pens.Black
        m_brush = Brushes.Transparent
        Dim rect As Rectangle
        rect = MakeRectangle(p1, p2)
        m_p1 = rect.Location
        m_p2 = New Point(rect.Right, rect.Bottom)
    End Sub

    Public MustOverride Sub DrawShape(ByVal g As Graphics)

    Private Function MakeRectangle(ByVal p As Point, _
    ByVal q As Point) As Rectangle
        Dim top, left, bottom, right As Integer
        top = IIf(p.Y < q.Y, p.Y, q.Y)
        left = IIf(p.X < q.X, p.X, q.X)
        bottom = IIf(p.Y > q.Y, p.Y, q.Y)
        right = IIf(p.X > q.X, p.X, q.X)
        Return New Rectangle(left, top, right - left, _
            bottom - top)
    End Function
```

```
End Class

Public Class CRectangle
    Inherits CShape

    Public Sub New(ByVal p1 As Point, ByVal p2 As Point, _
     ByVal pn As Pen, ByVal br As Brush)
        MyBase.New(p1, p2, pn, br)
    End Sub

    Public Sub New(ByVal p1 As Point, ByVal p2 As Point)
        MyBase.New(p1, p2)
    End Sub

    Public Overrides Sub DrawShape(ByVal g As Graphics)
        Dim rect As New Rectangle(m_p1.X, m_p1.Y, _
          m_p2.X - m_p1.X, m_p2.Y - m_p1.Y)
        g.FillRectangle(m_brush, rect)
        g.DrawRectangle(m_pen, rect)
    End Sub
End Class
```

AN ARRAYLIST OF SHAPES

The main form can store the shape objects in an array list. The handler for the MouseUp event adds a shape to the list.

```
. . .
Private m_list As New ArrayList()

. . .
Private Function MakeShape(ByVal p As Point, _
 ByVal q As Point, ByVal stype As ShapeType) As CShape
    Select Case stype
        Case ShapeType.Ellipse
            Return New CEllipse(p, q, m_pen, m_brush)
        Case ShapeType.Rectangle
            Return New CRectangle(p, q, m_pen, m_brush)
    End Select
End Function

. . .
Protected Overrides Sub OnMouseUp( _
 ByVal e As MouseEventArgs)
    m_track = False
    m_shape = MakeShape(m_start, m_end, m_type)
    m_list.Add(m_shape)
    Invalidate()
End Sub
```

DISPLAYING THE SHAPES

The shapes are displayed in the override of **OnPaint** by looping through the array list. Notice how polymorphism makes this code very concise.

```
Protected Overrides Sub OnPaint(ByVal e As PaintEventArgs)
    Dim g As Graphics = e.Graphics
    Dim objShape As CShape
    For Each objShape In m_list
       objShape.DrawShape(g)
    Next
    MyBase.OnPaint(e)
End Sub
```

Clipping Rectangle

Our drawing code up until now has been straightforward, but it is not as efficient as it could be. In **OnPaint** we always redraw the entire client rectangle, whether it is necessary or not. The **PaintEventArg** argument that is passed to **OnPaint** and to paint event handlers contains a property **ClipRectangle**, which indicates the rectangle in which to paint. By paying attention to this *clipping rectangle,* you can make your painting code more efficient.

There are two ways in which the clipping rectangle can be set. The first is by the system—for example, when part of a window is obscured by another window and then uncovered. The second is by the program through a call to the **Invalidate** method of the **Control** class. This method has several overloaded versions. Either a **Rectangle** or a **Region**[2] can be passed as a parameter to **Invalidate**. As part of a window gets covered up and calls to **Invalidate** are made, an *invalid region* is built up that represents what must be repainted. The clipping rectangle is the smallest rectangle that contains the invalid region.

The program **InvalidateDemo** illustrates various scenarios in which portions of a window can become invalidated and repainted. To illustrate what is being painted on any given call to **OnPaint**, an array of brushes of different colors is created, and each time **OnPaint** is called, a different brush is used, cycling through all the brushes. Version 1 of this program just paints the entire client area with the current brush.

Code
Example

```
Public Class Form1
    Inherits System.Windows.Forms.Form
```

2. The **Region** class is used to describe the interior of a graphics shape that consists of rectangles and paths.

```
#Region " Windows Form Designer generated code "

...

   Private m_back As Brush() = {Brushes.Beige, _
     Brushes.Blue, Brushes.Coral, Brushes.Cyan, _
     Brushes.Gold, Brushes.Green, Brushes.Ivory, _
     Brushes.Magenta, Brushes.Red, Brushes.Yellow}

   Private Function NextBrush() As Brush
      Static Dim nexti As Integer = -1
      nexti += 1
      If nexti >= m_back.Length Then
         nexti - 0
      End If
      Return m_back(nexti)
   End Function

   Protected Overrides Sub OnPaint( _
     ByVal e As System.Windows.Forms.PaintEventArgs)
      Dim g As Graphics = e.Graphics
      Dim crect As Rectangle = New Rectangle( _
         New Point(0, 0), Me.ClientSize)
      g.FillRectangle(NextBrush(), crect)
      MyBase.OnPaint(e)
   End Sub

End Class
```

As an experiment, build and run this program. Minimize the window and restore it. Do this several times. Each time, you will see a different color displayed, as the entire client area has become invalidated when the window was minimized. As a second experiment, create several instances of another Windows program (e.g., Notepad). Then cover different portions of the **InvalidateDemo** main window with the other windows, and then minimize these other windows. You should see rectangular areas that are uncovered painted with a different color. (As you drag a window over the **InvalidateDemo** window, you may also see a pattern of changing colors, reflecting numerous Paint events.)

Spy++ and Windows Messages

Visual Studio .NET comes with a useful tool for investigating the underlying Windows platform. You can start Spy++ from the Tools menu. You can then "spy" on a window, observing all the Windows messages that are sent to the window, by the following procedure (which we also introduced in Chapter 7):

1. Use the menu Spy | Find Window to bring up the Find Window dialog.
2. Select the Messages radio button from the Show group.
3. Drag the Finder tool ⊕ over the window you want to spy on and release the mouse button.
4. Click OK in the Find Window dialog. Now as you interact with the window you are spying on, you will see Windows messages displayed in the spy window, as illustrated in Figure 11-8.

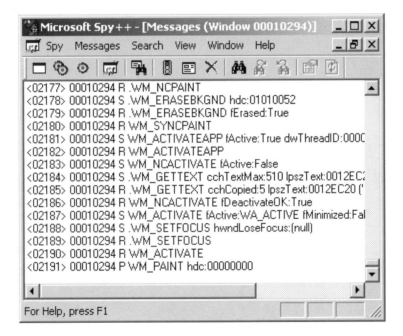

FIGURE 11-8   *Spy++ displays Windows messages for window you are spying on.*

The Windows messages you are seeing represent a low-level view of the Windows operating system, and with the .NET Framework, you are working at a much higher, more abstract level. With the Spy++ tool, you can observe WM_PAINT messages, which correspond to Paint events.

Invalidating a Window Programmatically

The changing colors we observed in our demonstration program represent the effect of the window being covered by another window, resulting in a portion of the window becoming invalid. Another scenario for a portion of a window to become invalid is for the method **Invalidate** to be called. As discussed previously, this method has several overloaded versions, and either a **Rectangle** or a **Region** can be passed as a parameter to **Invalidate**. Version 2 of the **InvalidateDemo** program illustrates drawing a square at the point where the mouse is clicked. Code is added to store a starting point and a size. The **Load** event is handled to initialize the square, and the **MouseDown** event is handled to change the starting point to the location where the mouse was clicked. **Invalidate** is called with no parameters, which results in the entire client area being invalidated.

```
Public Class Form1
    Inherits System.Windows.Forms.Form

#Region " Windows Form Designer generated code "
...
    Private m_start As Point
    Private m_size As Size
...

    Protected Overrides Sub OnPaint( _
      ByVal e As System.Windows.Forms.PaintEventArgs)
        Dim rect As Rectangle = _
            New Rectangle(m_start, m_size)
        Dim g As Graphics = e.Graphics
        Dim crect As Rectangle = New Rectangle( _
            New Point(0, 0), Me.ClientSize)
        g.FillRectangle(NextBrush(), crect)
        g.DrawRectangle(Pens.Black, rect)
        MyBase.OnPaint(e)
    End Sub

    Private Sub Form1_Load(ByVal sender As Object, _
      ByVal e As System.EventArgs) Handles MyBase.Load
        m_start = New Point(5, 5)
        m_size = New Size(50, 50)
    End Sub

    Private Sub Form1_MouseDown(ByVal sender As Object, _
      ByVal e As System.Windows.Forms.MouseEventArgs) _
      Handles MyBase.MouseDown
        m_start = New Point(e.X, e.Y)
        Invalidate()
    End Sub

End Class
```

Build and run the program. Try clicking the mouse at different locations. You should see the square drawn at the new location, and the background color of the entire client area is changed.

Invalidating a Specific Rectangle

Code Example

Invalidating the entire client area is normally not the best thing to do, because the clipping region is not optimized, and the entire client area is always repainted. Version 3 of **InvalidateDemo** illustrates a better approach, where only the new square is added to the invalid region.

```
Private Sub Form1_MouseDown(ByVal sender As Object, _
 ByVal e As System.Windows.Forms.MouseEventArgs) _
 Handles MyBase.MouseDown
    m_start = New Point(e.X, e.Y)
    Dim rect As Rectangle = New Rectangle(m_start, m_size)
    Invalidate(rect)
End Sub
```

Build and run this program. Now the entire client area is not repainted. Although the Paint event code still fills the client rectangle, it is clipped to the invalid region. Figure 11–9 illustrates several squares drawn with different colors in response to a number of mouse clicks.

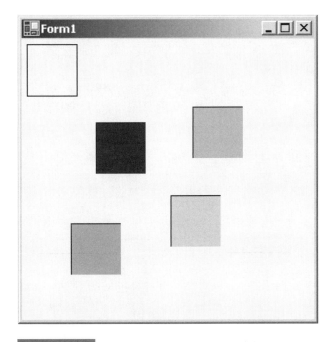

FIGURE 11–9   *Output is clipped to the invalid region.*

Who Does the Clipping?

There are two aspects to optimizing drawing code. The first is to be careful when you call **Invalidate** to pass the proper clipping rectangle (or region). The second is to make use of this information in **OnPaint** to restrict your drawing code to the clipping rectangle. Our example program illustrates the first optimization but not the second. This optimization is done for you automatically by GDI+, as long as you help by passing the proper clipping rectangle or region to your **Invalidate** calls. Your **OnPaint** code blasts out pixels everywhere, but GDI+ clips for you.

In the second optimization, you are more smart in your **OnPaint** code. For example, suppose you are looping over a list of shapes. If one of your shapes lies totally outside of the invalid rectangle, there is no need to draw it.

Is this second optimization worth the effort? It depends on how long drawing the element takes as opposed how long the logic takes to test whether the element should be drawn. A reasonable approach is to not implement the second optimization right away. If the drawing code appears sluggish, you may then wish to investigate whether you can gain an improvement by performing the second optimization.

Bitmaps and Metafile

The .NET Framework makes it very easy to work with images of various sorts. The **System.Drawing** namespace has the abstract class **Image** that provides functionality for derived classes such as **Bitmap** and **Metafile**. A bitmap stores an image as an array of pixels. A metafile stores an image as a set of drawing commands.

Drawing an Image

The shared method **FromFile** in the **Image** class creates an image from a file whose file name is specified by a string. The **DrawImage** and **DrawImage-Unscaled** methods of the **Graphics** class can be used to draw an image onto a drawing surface specified by a **Graphics** object.

The program **BitmapDemo** illustrates drawing an image that is loaded from a file. You can relocate the image by clicking the mouse, and you can change the image by using the File | Open menu command. The standard file open dialog lets you navigate to a folder where the desired image file is stored. The **FromFile** method supports a number of standard image file formats, including GIF, TIFF, BMP, and JPEG. The **Images** directory of this chapter contains a few sample images in a number of different formats.

Code
Example

```
Public Class Form1
    Inherits System.Windows.Forms.Form

#Region " Windows Form Designer generated code "
...

    Private m_loc As Point
    Private m_image As Image
    Private m_file As String

    Protected Overrides Sub OnMouseDown( _
     ByVal e As System.Windows.Forms.MouseEventArgs)
        m_loc = New Point(e.X, e.Y)
        Invalidate()
        MyBase.OnPaint(e)
    End Sub

    Private Sub Form1_Load(ByVal sender As System.Object, _
     ByVal e As System.EventArgs) Handles MyBase.Load
        m_file = "..\NET Logo.gif"
        m_image = Image.FromFile(m_file)
        m_loc = New Point(10, 10)
        BackColor = Color.White
    End Sub

    Protected Overrides Sub OnPaint( _
     ByVal e As System.Windows.Forms.PaintEventArgs)
        Dim g As Graphics = e.Graphics
        g.DrawImageUnscaled(m_image, m_loc)
    End Sub

    Private Sub mnuFileExit_Click( _
     ByVal sender As System.Object, _
     ByVal e As System.EventArgs) Handles mnuFileExit.Click
        Close()
    End Sub

    Private Sub mnuFileOpen_Click( _
     ByVal sender As System.Object, _
     ByVal e As System.EventArgs) Handles mnuFileOpen.Click
        Dim dlg As New OpenFileDialog()
        dlg.InitialDirectory = "\OI\NetVb"
        Dim status As DialogResult
        status = dlg.ShowDialog()
        If status = DialogResult.OK Then
            m_file = dlg.FileName
            m_image = Image.FromFile(m_file)
            Invalidate()
        End If
    End Sub

End Class
```

Saving a Bitmapped Image

Something else you might want to do with images is to *create* an image file. That is also easy to do with the .NET Framework. You can use drawing commands to create a bitmap by obtaining a **Graphics** object that is associated with a bitmap. You can then draw to this **Graphics** object using ordinary drawing commands, and you can then save the bitmap. The following steps outline the general procedure to be followed. A detailed code example is provided in the next section.

1. Instantiate a **Bitmap** object.
2. Obtain a **Graphics** object using the **FromImage** shared method of the **Graphics** class.
3. Perform drawing commands on the **Graphics** object.
4. Call the **Save** method of the **Bitmap** class to save the bitmap using a specified image file format.

DRAWING PROGRAM, VERSION 3

Code
Example

We illustrate with Version 3 of our drawing program **DrawDemo**. We can draw rectangles and ellipses as before. We show the bounding rectangle of our drawing with dotted lines. A menu command File | Save As Bitmap will save the image as both a BMP and a GIF file. Build and run the program. Figure 11–10 illustrates a drawing consisting of one rectangle and one ellipse.

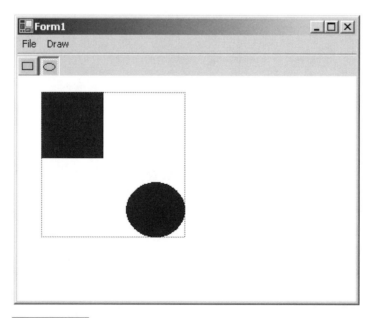

FIGURE 11–10   *Creating a bitmap using our drawing program.*

When you save, files **drawing.bmp** and **drawing.gif** will be created in the same directory as the program executable. You can then examine these files using standard graphics programs. If you have the standard file extension associations, you can double-click on these files in Windows Explorer. You will see the **.bmp** file displayed in Paint and the **.gif** file displayed in Internet Explorer.

The program imports the **System.Drawing.Imaging** namespace and declares member variables to hold a bounding region, a dotted pen, and a bounding rectangle.

```
Imports System.Drawing.Drawing2D
Imports System.Drawing.Imaging

. . .

Public Class Form1
   Inherits System.Windows.Forms.Form

. . .

   Private m_region As New Region()
   Private m_dotpen As Pen
   Private m_bounds As Rectangle
. . .
```

The load event handler initializes the region to be empty and the pen to be green with a dot style.

```
Private Sub Form1_Load(ByVal sender As Object, _
 ByVal e As System.EventArgs) Handles MyBase.Load
   . . .
   m_region.MakeEmpty()
   m_dotpen = New Pen(Color.Green)
   m_dotpen.DashStyle = DashStyle.Dot
End Sub
```

A helper method **UpdateRegion** adds a rectangle determined by two points to the region with the **Union** method. A bounding rectangle is determined by the **GetBounds** method, which returns a **RectangleF**. The **Round** method is called to obtain the bounding rectangle as a **Rectangle**.

```
Private Sub UpdateRegion(ByVal p As Point, _
 ByVal q As Point)
   m_region.Union(MakeRectangle(p, q))
   Dim g As Graphics = Me.CreateGraphics()
   Dim rectf As RectangleF
   rectf = m_region.GetBounds(g)
   m_bounds = Rectangle.Round(rectf)
End Sub
```

The **OnMouseUp** override updates the region using this helper method.

```
Protected Overrides Sub OnMouseUp( _
 ByVal e As System.Windows.Forms.MouseEventArgs)
    m_track = False
    m_shape = MakeShape(m_start, m_end, m_type)
    UpdateRegion(m_start, m_end)
    m_list.Add(m_shape)
    Invalidate()
    MyBase.OnMouseUp(e)
End Sub
```

OnPaint draws the bounding rectangle using the green dotted pen.

```
Protected Overrides Sub OnPaint(ByVal e As PaintEventArgs)
    Dim g As Graphics = e.Graphics
    Dim objShape As CShape
    For Each objShape In m_list
        objShape.DrawShape(g)
    Next
    g.DrawRectangle(m_dotpen, m_bounds)
    MyBase.OnPaint(e)
End Sub
```

Finally, the handler for the menu File | Save as Bitmap saves the drawing to a bitmap the size and location of the bounding rectangle, using the steps outlined in the previous section.

```
Private Sub mnuFileSaveBitmap_Click( _
 ByVal sender As System.Object, _
 ByVal e As System.EventArgs) _
 Handles mnuFileSaveBitmap.Click
    Dim bits As New Bitmap(m_bounds.Right, _
        m_bounds.Bottom)
    Dim g As Graphics = Graphics.FromImage(bits)
    Dim rect As New Rectangle(0, 0, _
        m_bounds.Right, m_bounds.Bottom)
    g.FillRectangle(Brushes.White, rect)
    Dim objShape As CShape
    For Each objShape In m_list
        objShape.DrawShape(g)
    Next
    bits.Save("drawing.bmp", ImageFormat.Bmp)
    bits.Save("drawing.gif", ImageFormat.Gif)
End Sub
```

Saving to a Metafile (Version 4)

There is somewhat of a mismatch between the kind of drawing we are creating and the bitmap file formats used for saving the drawing. The drawing itself illustrates vector graphics, and the bitmaps use raster graphics. Another format provided by Windows, called a *metafile,* allows us to save drawing commands into a file in place of pixels. The resulting file will in general be much smaller than a BMP file. (The GIF file is also small, but it attains its small size through compression, which loses some fidelity. The metafile is an exact representation of the drawing.)

Code
Example

The file format used is *enhanced metafile* with **.emf** extension. Like BMP, this file is Windows-specific. Version 4 of our **DrawDemo** program adds a menu command File | Save as Metafile, which will save the drawing as the file **drawing.emf** in the same folder as the program executable. Here is the code for the menu handler.

```
Private Sub mnuFileSaveMetafile_Click( _
 ByVal sender As System.Object, _
 ByVal e As System.EventArgs) _
 Handles mnuFileSaveMetafile.Click
    'Set up the metafile
    Dim gVideo As Graphics = CreateGraphics()
    Dim dc As IntPtr = gVideo.GetHdc()
    Dim meta As New Metafile("drawing.emf", dc)
    gVideo.ReleaseHdc(dc)
    gVideo.Dispose()
    'Draw to the metafile
    Dim g As Graphics = Graphics.FromImage(meta)
    Dim rect As New Rectangle(0, 0, _
        m_bounds.Right, m_bounds.Bottom)
    g.FillRectangle(Brushes.White, rect)
    Dim objShape As CShape
    For Each objShape In m_list
        objShape.DrawShape(g)
    Next
    g.Dispose()
End Sub
```

This code is a little more complex than previous examples of GDI+, because working with Windows metafiles requires you to obtain a Windows *device context,* which up until now has been completely wrapped by the **Graphics** class. The **GetHdc** method obtains a handle to a device context (of the .NET data type **IntPtr**), and this device context is used as a parameter to the **Metafile** constructor. A device context is an *unmanaged* resource, and so we must be careful to explicitly release it by a call to **ReleaseHdc**. The code also illustrates calling **Dispose** on our **Graphics** objects. We have not been careful with using **Dispose** in our GDI+ programs, but to make them robust, we should do so. We discuss memory management in GDI+ later in the chapter.

The rest of the code is similar to drawing to a bitmap. We use another overloaded version of the **Graphics** method **FromImage**, this time passing a metafile rather than a bitmap. We can then use ordinary drawing commands.

One difference from the bitmap case is that we have already made the association with the file, and so there is no save step.

Viewing the Metafile

We could write code to view the metafile using additional methods of the **Metafile** class. But we can view the metafile we've created very simply by using our previous **BitmapDemo** program. The **Image** class's shared method **FromFile** encapsulates many different kinds of file format, including enhanced metafile. Hence you can just run the **BitmapDemo** program and open the file **drawing.emf**, and you should see your drawing displayed.

GDI+ Memory Management

An important benefit in programming with the .NET Framework is memory management facilities provided by the Common Language Runtime, including automatic garbage collection. Normally, you do not have to be concerned with explicitly freeing memory, like you do in some languages, such as C++. There is an important exception to this simplification, however. Whenever you create an object that allocates *unmanaged* memory, there is the potential for running out of resources that will not be taken care of by the system garbage collector.

Objects in GDI+ provide an example of resources with unmanaged memory. Device contexts, as encapsulated by **Graphics** objects, pens, brushes, and fonts, all encapsulate GDI resources, which are not managed by .NET. Thus, even if there is plenty of free memory in the system and the garbage collector is not invoked, it is still possible for a program to fail because the system has run out of some other kind of resource. This issue is quite real for GDI resources on Windows 9x systems. It may also become an issue on new systems targeted towards mobile devices with a relatively small amount of memory.

.NET provides a design pattern for dealing with resource deallocation in such situations, as we discussed in Chapter 10. A class that wraps an unmanaged resource should implement the **IDisposable** interface, and a client of that class should call the **Dispose** method when it is finished using an object instance of that class.

Version 2 of the **RectangleDemo** program illustrates use of **Dispose**. In the Version 1 program we keep on creating **Graphics** objects in the mouse event handler. Eventually, the garbage collector would deallocate these objects, and in turn the underlying device context would be freed. However, if other memory in the system is not low, the garbage collector may not be called, and the system might run out of device context resources. To avoid

Code
Example

this possible problem, the program should call **Dispose** before exiting the mouse handler.

```
Public Class Form1
    Inherits System.Windows.Forms.Form

#Region " Windows Form Designer generated code "
...

    Private Function MakeRectangle(ByVal p As Point, _
     ByVal q As Point) As Rectangle
       Dim top, left, bottom, right As Integer
       top = IIf(p.Y < q.Y, p.Y, q.Y)
       left = IIf(p.X < q.X, p.X, q.X)
       bottom = IIf(p.Y > q.Y, p.Y, q.Y)
       right = IIf(p.X > q.X, p.X, q.X)
       Return New Rectangle(left, top, right - left, _
          bottom - top)
    End Function

    Private Sub Form1_MouseDown(ByVal sender As Object, _
     ByVal e As MouseEventArgs) Handles MyBase.MouseDown
       Dim g As Graphics = CreateGraphics()
       Dim p1 As New Point(20, 10)
       Dim p2 As New Point(e.X, e.Y)
       Dim rect As Rectangle = MakeRectangle(p1, p2)
       g.DrawRectangle(Pens.Black, rect)
       g.Dispose()
    End Sub
End Class
```

Code Examples Are Simplified

It is important to remember that code examples in this book are simplified to focus on the point at hand. Thus, the main body of GDI+ example code illustrates the various classes and programming techniques used with GDI+. We have usually not added the code to handle resource deallocation issues. This simplification is similar to our policy regarding exception handling. We try to keep our example programs simple. But in production code it is important for you to worry about resource deallocation, exception handling, and similar issues.

Text and Fonts

In a GUI environment such as Windows, displaying text is just another kind of graphical operation. In place of using pens and brushes as our drawing tool, we use *fonts*. Fonts are quite complicated and beyond the scope of this chapter to discuss in any detail. In fact, drawing with text using GDI+ is quite complicated, and normally you won't need to do that unless you are writing a rather specialized application such as a word processor. Normally, you will work with text data using the rich array of Windows controls.

We illustrate the fundamentals of working with text and fonts with the **TextDemo** program, which also demonstrates handling a **KeyPress** event for entering a character. The program allows you to type text, which is displayed in the main window as you type. A toolbar button brings up the font common dialog, which allows the user to change the font that is displayed. Figure 11–11 illustrates the string "hello text" typed in and displayed with a Times New Roman 24-point font. Note that our program also changes the font of the toolbar button!

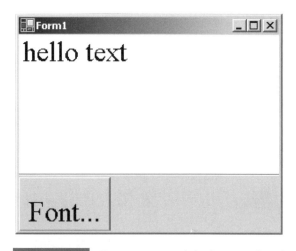

FIGURE 11–11   *Typing in text and displaying with a desired font.*

```vb
Imports System.Text

Public Class Form1
    Inherits System.Windows.Forms.Form

#Region " Windows Form Designer generated code "

...
    Private m_text As New StringBuilder()

    Protected Overrides Sub OnPaint( _
      ByVal e As System.Windows.Forms.PaintEventArgs)
        Dim str As String = m_text.ToString
        Dim g As Graphics = e.Graphics
        g.DrawString(str, Font, Brushes.Black, 0, 0)
        MyBase.OnPaint(e)
```

```
      End Sub

      Private Sub Form1_KeyPress(ByVal sender As Object, _
       ByVal e As KeyPressEventArgs) Handles MyBase.KeyPress
         m_text.Append(e.KeyChar)
         Invalidate()
      End Sub

      Private Sub ToolBar1_ButtonClick( _
       ByVal sender As System.Object, ByVal e As _
       System.Windows.Forms.ToolBarButtonClickEventArgs) _
       Handles ToolBar1.ButtonClick
         Dim dlg As New FontDialog()
         dlg.Font = Font
         Dim status As DialogResult = dlg.ShowDialog
         If status = DialogResult.OK Then
            Font = dlg.Font
         End If
         Invalidate()
      End Sub

End Class
```

Measuring Text

Another issue that arises in drawing text is the necessity to obtain suitable text metrics so that you can position text appropriately on the output surface. As an example, consider the problem of displaying multiple lines of text in a window. You can position the first line at the top-left of the window at coordinates (0,0). But where should you position the second line? You need to compute a suitable offset of the y-axis, which can be based on the height of the font used in drawing.

The program **ScrollDemo\Version 1** provides an illustration.

```
Public Class Form1
    Inherits System.Windows.Forms.Form

#Region " Windows Form Designer generated code "
...

    Private m_strings() As String = {"This is", _
       "an example", "of text", "distributed", _
       "over several", "lines"}
    Private m_deltaY As Integer

    Private Sub Form1_Load(ByVal sender As Object, _
     ByVal e As System.EventArgs) Handles MyBase.Load
       m_deltaY = Font.Height
       Me.BackColor = Color.White
```

```
        End Sub

        Private Sub Form1_Paint(ByVal sender As Object, _
          ByVal e As System.Windows.Forms.PaintEventArgs) _
          Handles MyBase.Paint
            Dim g As Graphics = e.Graphics
            Dim i As Integer
            Dim y As Integer = 0
            For i = 0 To m_strings.Length - 1
                g.DrawString(m_strings(i), Font, _
                Brushes.Black, 0, y)
                y += m_deltaY
            Next
        End Sub
End Class
```

Scrolling

Code
Example

Often a window may not be large enough to display all the information available. For example, in Version 1 of **ScrollDemo** in the previous section, if the window is made small, you will not be able to see all the lines of text displayed at the same time. In such a situation it is useful for the user to be able to *scroll* the output to view additional information. The standard way Windows handles this situation is to provide horizontal and vertical scrollbars. Version 2 of **ScrollDemo** adds scrolling capability to our program, as illustrated in Figure 11–12.

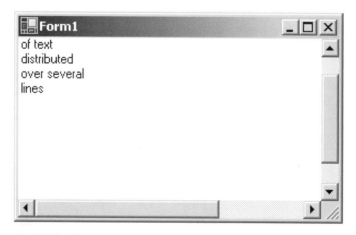

FIGURE 11–12   *Scrollbars enable user to view multiple lines of text.*

The .NET Framework makes it easy to implement scrolling in your programs through an *autoscroll* capability. You set the **AutoScroll** property of the form to **True**, and you specify a minimum scroll size through the **AutoScrollMinSize** property. You then adjust the coordinates in your output by **AutoScrollPosition**.

```
Public Class Form1
    Inherits System.Windows.Forms.Form

#Region " Windows Form Designer generated code "
...

    Private m_strings() As String = {"This is", _
        "an example", "of text", "distributed", _
        "over several", "lines"}
    Private m_deltaY As Integer

    Private Sub Form1_Load(ByVal sender As Object, _
     ByVal e As System.EventArgs) Handles MyBase.Load
        m_deltaY = Font.Height
        Me.BackColor = Color.White
        Me.AutoScroll = True
        Me.AutoScrollMinSize = New Size(400, 200)
    End Sub

    Private Sub Form1_Paint(ByVal sender As Object, _
     ByVal e As System.Windows.Forms.PaintEventArgs) _
     Handles MyBase.Paint
        Dim g As Graphics = e.Graphics
        Dim i As Integer
        Dim y As Integer = 0
        Dim pt As Point = Me.AutoScrollPosition
        For i = 0 To m_strings.Length - 1
            g.DrawString(m_strings(i), Font, _
                Brushes.Black, pt.X, pt.Y + y)
            y += m_deltaY
        Next
    End Sub

End Class
```

Summary

GDI+ is a set of .NET classes that provide an API for performing two-dimensional graphics in a device-independent manner. In this chapter we surveyed the main features of GDI+. We looked at the painting architecture of Windows

Forms, including the role of a clipping region. We studied various tools for drawing, including pens, brushes, and fonts. We examined important data structures used in GDI+, including points, sizes, rectangles, and colors. A drawing program illustrated rubber-band drawing, allowing us to create a drawing of rectangles and ellipses of various shapes, colors, and types of brush. We saw how to work with bitmaps and metafiles. We examined use of **Dispose** to properly clean up GDI+ resources in our programs, and we concluded the chapter with a discussion of scrolling.

Advanced Windows Forms

*T*he **System.Windows.Forms** namespace is a collection of classes that can be used to build sophisticated Windows applications. We've already seen that it contains a collection of control classes such as **Textbox**, **ListBox**, **DateTimePicker**, **MainMenu**, and **ToolBar**. This chapter focuses less on the controls and more on the interesting uses of the Windows Forms classes. We have already discussed how to use modal dialogs; in this chapter we discuss modeless dialogs. These dialogs can remain visible while the user interacts with other windows. We will also look at MDI applications. These applications allow us to display child forms within the context of a parent form. The parent form can manage the display of these child forms. We will also examine an interesting new feature of the .NET Windows Forms architecture: visual inheritance. Using visual inheritance, we can build new forms from existing ones. We conclude this chapter by discussing how ActiveX controls can be used within VB.NET applications.

Modeless Dialogs

VB.NET supports modeless dialogs as well as modal dialogs. You can typically identify modeless dialogs from their design: modal dialogs have OK and Cancel buttons, while modeless dialogs have Apply and Close buttons. A few programming differences must be noted:

- The **Show** method is used to display the modeless dialog (instead of the **ShowDialog** method).
- A **DialogResult** is not returned from the **Show** method; programmers must implement their own strategy for providing behavior for the Apply and Close buttons in the modeless dialog.

In the program **ModelessDialogExample**, we use a modeless dialog to add items to a list box. Figure 12–1 illustrates the program as it is executed.

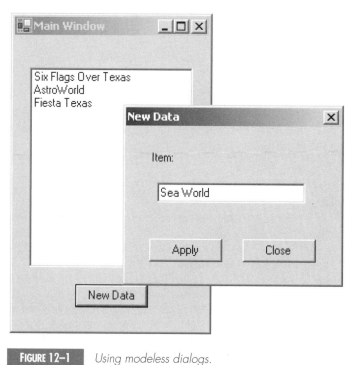

FIGURE 12–1 *Using modeless dialogs.*

Step 1: Designing the GUI

To build this application, we have added two forms to our project. The startup form's properties are summarized in Table 12–1, while the modeless dialog's properties are summarized in Table 12–2.

TABLE 12–1 *Property Values for MainWindow*

Control Type	Name	Other Properties
Listbox	lstItems	
Button	btnNew	Text: New Data
Form	MainWindow	Text: Main Window

TABLE 12–2	Property Values for NewDataForm	
Control Type	**Name**	**Other Properties**
Label	lblItem	Text: Item:
Textbox	txtItem	Text: (blank)
Button	btnApply	Enabled: False Text: Apply
Button	btnClose	Text: Close
Form	NewDataForm	MaximizeBox: False MinimizeBox: False ShowInTaskbar: False Text: New Data

Step 2: Managing the Relationship between Forms

A modeless dialog must know about the form that displayed it so the code in the **Click** event of its Apply button can copy data back to its parent form. We must add a variable to the modeless dialog to manage this relationship. We must also modify the form's constructor to accept a value for this variable.

```
Class NewDataForm
    Inherits System.Windows.Forms.Form

    Private m_myParent As MainWindow
    Public Sub New(ByVal parent As MainWindow)
        MyBase.New()
        m_myparent = parent
        . . .
    End Sub
    . . .
End Class
```

The **Click** event handler for **MainWindow's btnShowData** will pass a reference to itself when it instantiates the **NewDataForm**.

```
Private Sub btnNew_Click(ByVal sender As System.Object, _
  ByVal e As System.EventArgs) Handles btnNew.Click

    Dim newData As New NewDataForm(Me)
    newData.Show()

End Sub
```

Step 3: Programming the Apply and Close Buttons

Now that the modeless dialog can be displayed, we must provide code for the Apply and Close buttons. The Apply button must copy the data in its controls back to controls on the parent form. The Apply button's **Click** event handler is coded as follows:

```
Private Sub btnApply_Click(ByVal sender As Object, _
 ByVal e As System.EventArgs) Handles btnApply.Click

   If Trim(txtItem.Text) <> "" Then
     m_myParent.lstItems.Items.Add(txtItem.Text)
     txtItem.Text = ""
   End If

End Sub
```

The Close button's **Click** event handler should call the form's **Close** method to close the form.

```
Private Sub btnClose_Click(ByVal sender As System.Object, _
 ByVal e As System.EventArgs) Handles btnClose.Click

   Me.Close()

End Sub
```

Step 4: Enabling and Disabling the Apply Button

Many modeless dialogs enable and disable the Apply button as a user interacts with them. Only when the Apply button is enabled is the user able to move data back to the parent form.

We set **btnApply's Enabled** property to False at design time. When the user changes the data in **txtItem**, we will monitor it to determine whether the Apply button should be enabled or disabled. This can be done in the **Change** event of the textbox.

```
Private Sub txtItem_TextChanged(ByVal sender As _
 System.Object, ByVal e As System.EventArgs) _
 Handles txtItem.TextChanged

   If Trim(txtItem.Text) <> "" Then
     btnApply.Enabled = True
   Else
     btnApply.Enabled = False
   End If

End Sub
```

MDI Applications

MDI (multiple document interface) applications allow you to display multiple documents at the same time. Each document, which is actually just a set of data, is displayed in its own window within the confines of a parent window. Older versions of Word and Excel are examples of MDI applications.

In this section, we will build a small word processor. It will be an MDI version of Notepad. The program can be found in **MDIDemo**.

Step 1: Create an MDI Parent Form

The first step in building an MDI application is to define the parent form for the application. The easiest way to do this is to configure the startup form that was provided when the application was generated. We named the form **MyNotepadForm** and set the **Text** property to MyNotepad. By setting the form's **IsMDIContainer** property to True, the form becomes our MDI parent form. A side effect of setting this property to True is that the background of the form changes to a dark gray. (See Figure 12–2.)

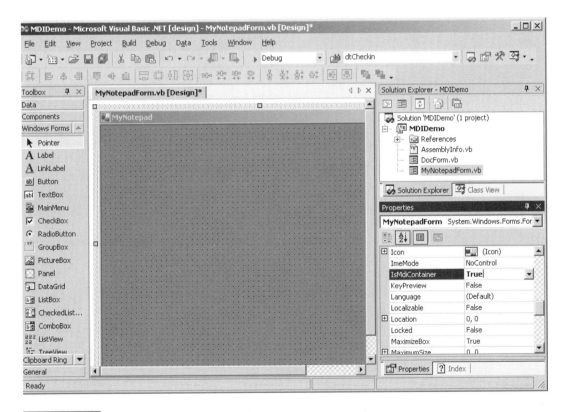

FIGURE 12–2   *Designating an MDI parent form.*

Our next step will be to add the main menu, as designed below. Table 12–3 summarizes the interesting properties.

```
File        Window    Help
  New            Tile              About MyNotepad...
  Open...    Cascade
  Save As...
  Close
  -----------
  Exit
```

TABLE 12–3   *Property Values for the MainMenu Control in MyNotepadFormDemo*

Text	Name	Other Properties
&File	mnuFile	
&New	mnuNew	
&Open...	mnuOpen	
&Save As...	mnuSaveAs	Enabled: False
&Close	mnuClose	Enabled: False
-	mnuSeparator1	
E&xit	mnuExit	
&Window	mnuWindow	MDIList: True Visible: False
&Tile	mnuTile	
&Cascade	mnuCascade	
&Help	mnuHelp	
&About MyNotepad...	mnuAbout	

To build a menu separator, which is a line that separates subitems on a menu, you must set the **Text** property to a hyphen (-). The **MDIList** property, which will be discussed in an upcoming section, causes VB.NET to place a list of all MDI child windows at the bottom of the menu.

Figure 12–3 shows the application if it is executed at this point. You can see that the Save As and Close menus are disabled because no document is open.

Step 2: Create an MDI Child Form

The MDI child forms are the primary forms that users interact with in MDI applications. The example shown in this section uses a **RichTextBox** control. However, MDI applications do not have to be word processing-type applications. Often, the child forms are reports or data entry forms.

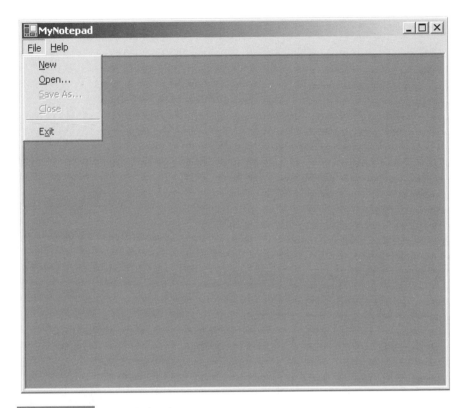

FIGURE 12–3 *An MDI form's main menu.*

In our application, we have created a child form by adding another Windows Form to our application named **DocForm**. We set the **Text** property to MyDocument, and we added a **RichTextBox** control to the form with the properties summarized in Table 12–4. A **RichTextBox** control is similar to a textbox, except that individual characters can be formatted.

TABLE 12–4 *Property Values for the RichTextBox Control in DocForm*

Property	Value
Name	rtbData
Text	(blank)
Docking	Fill

The **Docking** property is used to determine if, and how, the control docks to the window. By setting the **Docking** property to **Fill**, the **RichTextBox** consumes the entire client area of the window.

Each time the user chooses New from the menu, the application creates a new child window containing a **RichTextBox** control. At any given time, there may be zero or more of these open child windows. To achieve this behavior, we must create a new instance of the form in the **mnuNew's Click** event handler. We must also indicate that this form is a child of our parent MDI form by setting its **MdiParent** property to reference the parent form.

```
Private Sub mnuNew_Click(ByVal sender As System.Object, _
 ByVal e As System.EventArgs) Handles mnuNew.Click

    Dim myDoc As New DocForm()
    myDoc.MdiParent = Me
    myDoc.Show()

End Sub
```

Figure 12–4 illustrates the application with two child forms open.

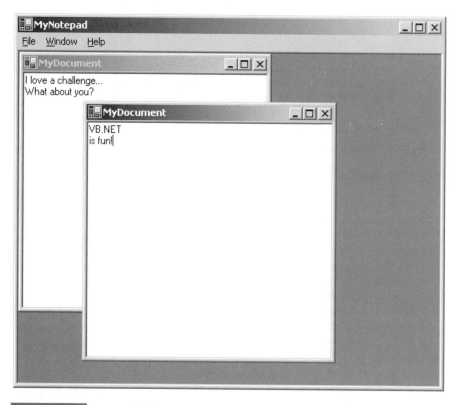

FIGURE 12–4 *MDI child forms.*

Step 3: Coding the Window Menu

MDI applications usually have a Window menu with submenus for switching between windows or documents. We saw in step 1 that our **MDIDemo** application is no exception. By setting the Window menu's **MDIList** property to True, we are telling VB.NET to automatically keep track of the open child windows and present a list of them at the bottom of this menu (see Figure 12–5).

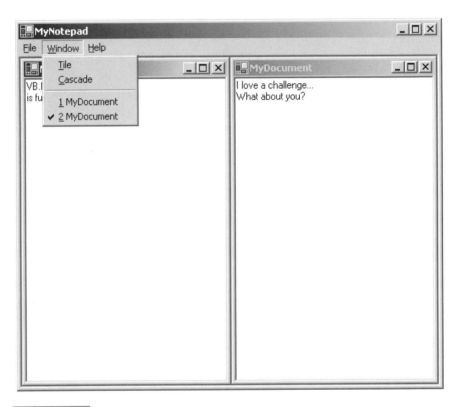

FIGURE 12–5   *A typical MDI Window menu.*

We can implement behavior to arrange the child windows using the MDI parent form's **LayoutMdi** method. It allows us to tile windows horizontally or vertically, cascade them, and arrange them as icons.

```
Private Sub mnuTile_Click(ByVal sender As System.Object, _
  ByVal e As System.EventArgs) Handles mnuTile.Click

    Me.LayoutMdi(MdiLayout.TileVertical)

End Sub
```

```
Private Sub mnuCascade_Click(ByVal sender As _
  System.Object, ByVal e As System.EventArgs) _
  Handles mnuCascade.Click

    Me.LayoutMdi(MdiLayout.Cascade)

End Sub
```

Step 4: Interacting with the Active Child Form

Within an MDI parent form, you can use the **ActiveMDIChild** property to determine which child form has focus. We will need this in the **MyNotepad-Form** so that we can implement the Close menu item. In the **Click** event handler for **mnuClose**, we close the active MDI child form.

```
Private Sub mnuClose_Click(ByVal sender As System.Object, _
  ByVal e As System.EventArgs) Handles mnuClose.Click

    Me.ActiveMdiChild.Close()

End Sub
```

When you have several controls on a form, you may also need to determine which control is active. In this case, the **ActiveControl** property is used to access the control with the focus on the active child form.

Step 5: Dealing with Menu Appearance

To begin with, we want to make sure that our menu items are only enabled (or visible, in the case of the Window menu) when their actions are allowable. We built two helper procedures for this. One is used when there are child forms, while the other is used when there are no child forms.

```
Public Sub SetMenuOpenDoc()
    mnuSaveAs.Enabled = True
    mnuClose.Enabled = True
    mnuWindow.Visible = True
End Sub

Public Sub SetMenuNoDoc()
    mnuSaveAs.Enabled = False
    mnuClose.Enabled = False
    mnuWindow.Visible = False
End Sub
```

Within an MDI application, the MDI parent form has an **MDIChildActivate** event that is triggered whenever a child form is *activated* or *closed*. In the handler for this event, we will write code to change the menu options that are available based on the status of the MDI child form that is activated.

```
Private Sub MyNotepadForm_MdiChildActivate(ByVal sender _
As Object, ByVal e As System.EventArgs) _
Handles MyBase.MdiChildActivate

    If Me.ActiveMdiChild Is Nothing Then
       SetMenuNoDoc()
    Else
       SetMenuOpenDoc()
    End If

End Sub
```

Step 6: Finishing the Application

At this point, we know enough about MDI applications to finish our application. We can begin by coding the **Click** event handlers for the Close, Exit, and About menus. They are quite simple.

```
Private Sub mnuClose_Click(ByVal sender As System.Object, _
ByVal e As System.EventArgs) Handles mnuClose.Click

    Me.ActiveMdiChild.Close()

End Sub

Private Sub mnuExit_Click(ByVal sender As System.Object, _
ByVal e As System.EventArgs) Handles mnuExit.Click

    Me.Close()

End Sub

Private Sub mnuAbout_Click(ByVal sender As Object, ByVal _
e As System.EventArgs) Handles mnuAbout.Click

    MessageBox.Show("MyNotepad v1.0", "MyNotepad", _
       MessageBoxButtons.OK, MessageBoxIcon.Information)

End Sub
```

To get the Open and Save As menus working, we will use the **File-OpenDialog** and **FileSaveDialog** respectively to prompt the user for the file name. We will then use the **RichTextEdit** box methods **LoadFile** and **Save-File** to actually read or write the file.

```
Private Sub mnuOpen_Click(ByVal sender As System.Object, _
ByVal e As System.EventArgs) Handles mnuOpen.Click

    dlgOpen.Filter = "Text Files|*.txt|All Files|*.*"
    Dim ans As DialogResult = dlgOpen.ShowDialog()
```

```
        If ans = DialogResult.OK Then
            Try
                Dim myDoc As New DocForm()
                myDoc.MdiParent = Me
                myDoc.rtbData.LoadFile(dlgOpen.FileName)
                myDoc.Show()
            Catch openErr As Exception
                MessageBox.Show(openErr.Message, "Error", _
                    MessageBoxButtons.OK, MessageBoxIcon.Error)
            End Try
        End If

End Sub

Private Sub mnuSaveAs_Click(ByVal sender As _
    System.Object, ByVal e As System.EventArgs) _
    Handles mnuSaveAs.Click

    dlgSave.Filter = "Text Files|*.txt|All Files|*.*"
    dlgSave.FileName = "Untitled.txt"
    Dim ans As DialogResult = dlgSave.ShowDialog()

    If ans = DialogResult.OK Then
        Try
            Dim myDoc As DocForm = _
                CType(Me.ActiveMdiChild, DocForm)
            myDoc.rtbData.SaveFile(dlgSave.FileName)
        Catch saveErr As Exception
            MessageBox.Show(saveErr.Message, "Error", _
                MessageBoxButtons.OK, MessageBoxIcon.Error)
        End Try
    End If

End Sub
```

Each of the above examples used the **Filter** property to specify the filters that appear in the file open and file save dialogs. A filter is defined by specifying the filter text strings and the filter's search criteria separated by the pipe (|) character. If the search criterion includes several file extensions, they are separated by semicolons. For example:

```
dlgOpen.Filter = _
    "Text Files (*.txt)|*.txt|" & _
    "Image Files (*.bmp; *.ico)|*.bmp;*.ico|" & _
    "All Files (*.*)|*.*"
```

shows three text strings in the dropdown filter list:

```
Text Files (*.txt)
Image Files (*.bmp;*.ico)
All Files (*.*)
```

The search string (ex: *.txt) does not have to appear in the text version of the filter (ex: Text Files (*.txt)). It is simply a matter of preference.

Visual Inheritance

Microsoft's .NET Framework supports an interesting new feature called Visual Inheritance. As you will recall from Chapter 5, inheritance allows you to build new classes that extend the functionality of their base class. In Windows Forms, Visual Inheritance allows you to create new forms by inheriting the appearance and functionality of existing forms. In the derived form, you can see the controls on the base form as well as add new controls. This is all accomplished using the **Inherits** keyword. For example, **SomeNewForm** can inherit the appearance, controls, events handling, etc. from **SomeBaseForm** by coding:

```
Public Class SomeNewForm
    Inherits SomeBaseForm

    . . .

End Class
```

In the following two subsections, we will discuss the development of a base form and a form that inherits the appearance and behavior of the base form.

Characteristics of the Base Form

The form that will serve as the base class for visual inheritance can be in the same project as the derived form or can be imported from another project. It can even be written in a different .NET language.

In this section, we will examine the **Messages** program. It is a VB.NET Class Library project and contains a form that will serve as our base class. **Messages**, shown in Figure 12–6, displays a list of status messages in a list box.

Code
Example

Step 1: Create a Project with the Base Form

Because the form we are building has no practical use on its own (it displays status information of something else), we have decided to place it in a VB.NET Class Library project. However, we could also have chosen a Windows Application as the project type.

We must now design both the appearance and functionality of the form. Table 12–5 summarized the form's properties.

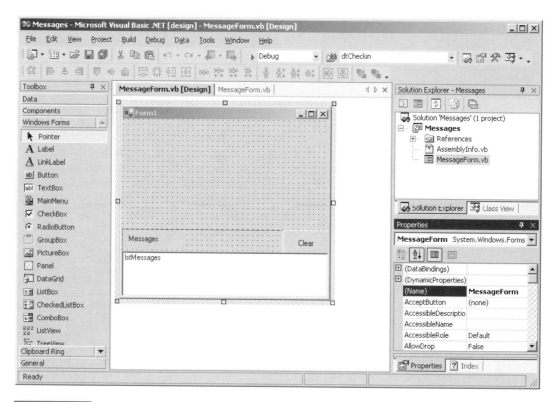

FIGURE 12–6   *Designing a base class form for visual inheritance.*

TABLE 12–5   *Property Values for Visual Inheritance Demo*

Control Type	Name	Other Properties
Panel	panMessages	
Label	lblMessages	Text: Messages
Button	btnClear	Text: Clear
Listbox	lstMessages	
Form	MessageForm	Text: Form1

Step 2: Determine the Controls Customizable by the Derived Class

As with all other applications involving inheritance, the access modifier that we specify greatly impacts which class members are accessible to the derived form. The Windows Forms Designer adds variables and code to a form when you drag a control from the toolbox, place it on the form, and configure its properties. The variables that represent the instances of the control are automatically defined using the **Friend** access modifier. In the **Messages** program, the following variables were defined at the end of step 1:

```
Friend WithEvents panMessages As System.Windows.Forms.Panel
Friend WithEvents lblMessages As System.Windows.Forms.Label
Friend WithEvents lstMessages As _
                            System.Windows.Forms.ListBox
Friend WithEvents btnClear As System.Windows.Forms.Button
```

As you recall from Chapter 5, VB.NET defines several access modifiers for class members that impact the member's accessibility from derived classes. These modifiers include:

- **Public** members are always accessible.
- **Protected** members are accessible only to a derived class's implementation.
- **Friend** members are accessible only from within the assembly that contains the class.
- **Private** members are not accessible outside the class definition.

In order for a derived form to be able to interact with controls in a base form, the controls must be defined using an access modifier that makes them accessible:

- If the base class form is in a different assembly, controls must be defined as **Public**.
- If the base class form is in the same assembly as the derived form, controls may be defined using any modifier except **Private**.

In our **Messages** program, we will allow derived classes to control the label and button. Access to the list box will be provided via a publicly accessible method. Therefore, we must make the following changes to the control declarations:

```
Private WithEvents panMessages As _
                            System.Windows.Forms.Panel
Protected WithEvents lblMessages As _
                            System.Windows.Forms.Label
Private WithEvents lstMessages As _
                            System.Windows.Forms.ListBox
Protected WithEvents btnClear As _
                            System.Windows.Forms.Button
```

Step 3: Implement the Base Form's Behavior

We must now add basic behavior to our form. In our case, we will add two methods, **ClearMessages** and **AddToMessages**, that allow access to the list box. We will also implement the **Click** event handler for **btnClear**.

```
Public Sub ClearMessages()
  lstMessages.Items.Clear()
```

```
End Sub

Public Sub AddToMessages(ByVal message As String)
   lstMessages.Items.Add(message)
End Sub

Private Sub btnClear_Click(ByVal sender As Object, _
 ByVal e As System.EventArgs) Handles btnClear.Click

   lstMessages.Items.Clear()

End Sub
```

Step 4: Building the Project

Finally, we must build the application. Because we are implementing a class library project, we will be building a DLL. The code is not immediately executable, so we will now shift our discussion to the development of the derived form.

Characteristics of the Derived Form

Code
Example

To use visual inheritance, a form must use the **Inherits** keyword to inherit features from another form. This means that it will inherit all of the control variables as well as the form behavior that has already been developed.

In this section, we will examine the Windows application **CheckoutRegister**. It will have a form that is derived from **MessageForm** in the **Messages** class library. That is, it uses a listbox to display status information.

The **CheckoutRegister** application maintains a list of items that are available for sale. It allows users to calculate the sales total of items that are purchased. A user enters the item number and clicks the Lookup button. The application searches the list of items and, if found, displays the description and price of the item. The user can then enter the number of units that are being purchased and click the Add Item button. This places the item total in the messages listbox. This process continues until the user clicks the Total Sales button, which displays the total due for all items purchased. The Clear button will be used to start a new sale. (See Figure 12–7.)

We have built the **Items** class to represent those items that are for sale. It implements the **IComparable** interface and overrides the **Equals** method (inherited from **Object**) because we will use an **ArrayList** to manage the inventory and will be searching it to find items.

```
Public Class Items
   Implements IComparable

      Private m_ItemNo As Integer
      Private m_Description As String
```

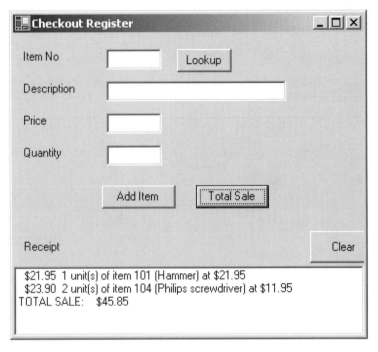

FIGURE 12–7 A form that uses visual inheritance.

```
Private m_Price As Decimal

Public Sub New(ByVal itemNo As Integer, ByVal _
  description As String, ByVal price As Decimal)
   m_ItemNo = itemNo
   m_Description = description
   m_Price = price
End Sub

Public ReadOnly Property ItemNo() As Integer
   Get
      Return m_ItemNo
   End Get
End Property

Public ReadOnly Property Description() As String
   Get
      Return m_Description
   End Get
End Property

Public ReadOnly Property Price() As Decimal
```

```
      Get
          Return m_Price
      End Get
  End Property

  Public Overloads Function CompareTo(ByVal obj As _
    Object) As Integer Implements IComparable.CompareTo

      Dim it As Items = CType(obj, Items)
      If it.ItemNo < Me.ItemNo Then
         Return -1
      ElseIf it.ItemNo = Me.ItemNo Then
         Return 0
      Else
         Return 1
      End If

  End Function

  Public Overloads Overrides Function Equals( _
    ByVal obj As Object) As Boolean

      Dim it As Items = CType(obj, Items)
      Return it.ItemNo = Me.ItemNo

  End Function
End Class
```

Step 1: Create a Project that Uses Visual Inheritance

We begin by building a Windows application named **CheckoutRegister**. When it is created, a blank form named **Form1** is generated for you. Remove **Form1** from the application by right-clicking on the form in the Solution Explorer window and choosing Delete. We will replace this form with a form that uses virtual inheritance. Now add the code for the **Items** class discussed previously.

Now we are ready to build a form that inherits from **MessageForm**. Because this form is in a different assembly, we must first add a reference to that assembly. (This would not be necessary if the base form were in this project.) To add a reference to the **Messages** project, right-click the **CheckoutRegister** project in the Solution Explorer and select Add Reference. (See Figure 12–8.)

In the References dialog box, switch to the Projects tab and click the Browse button to find **Messages.dll**. Click OK to add the reference. (See Figure 12–9.)

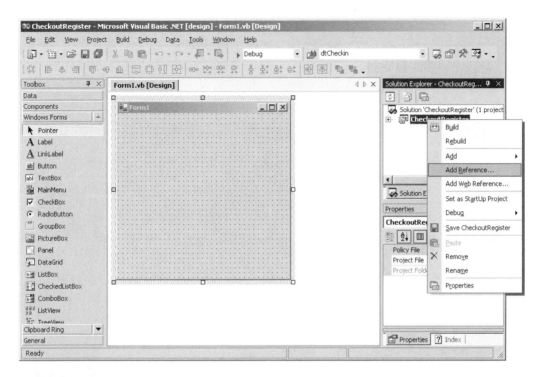

FIGURE 12–8   *Adding a reference to another .NET assembly.*

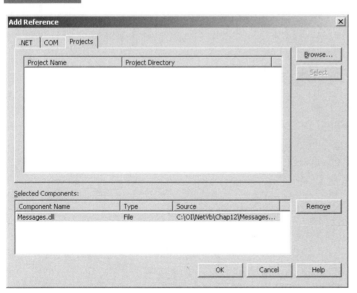

FIGURE 12–9   *Specifying the .NET assembly containing the base class.*

Step 2: Adding an Inherited Form

To add the startup form of the **CheckoutRegister** application, we must now add an Inherited Form to the project. Right-click on the **CheckoutRegister** project and select Add Inherited Form. Name the form **CheckoutRegister-Form** (see Figure 12–10).

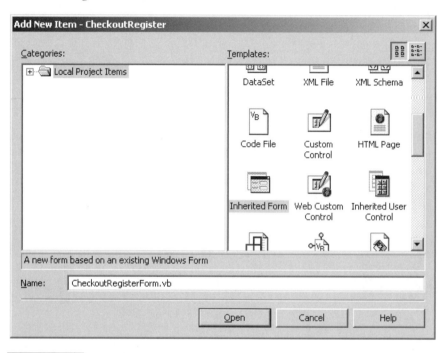

Adding an inherited form.

In the Inheritance Picker dialog, select **MessagesForm** from the **Messages** project as the form to inherit from (see Figure 12–11). This will generate the following code:

```
Public Class CheckoutRegisterForm
    Inherits Messages.MessageForm
    ...
End Class
```

You must now design the form to resemble Figure 12–12. You should notice that the new form already looks just like **MessageForm**. You may resize it and the message panel stays docked at the bottom of the form. You should notice that the inherited buttons have a special icon in their upper-left corner, indicating they are inherited. Controls that were nonprivate in the base form can be manipulated. The label and button have resize handles to indi-

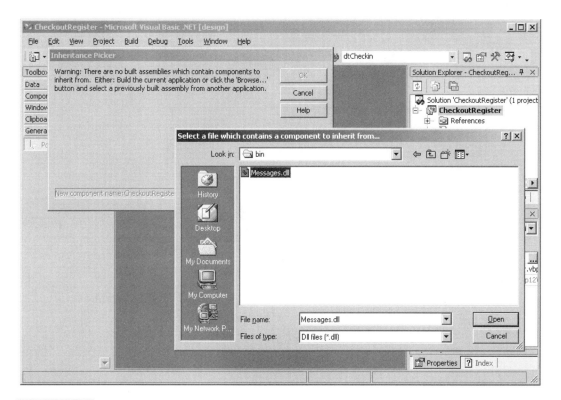

FIGURE 12-11   *Specifying the inherited form's base class.*

cate you can manipulate them, change their properties and so on; however, the private panel and listbox are grayed out.

Table 12-6 summarizes the controls you must add to the form and their properties.

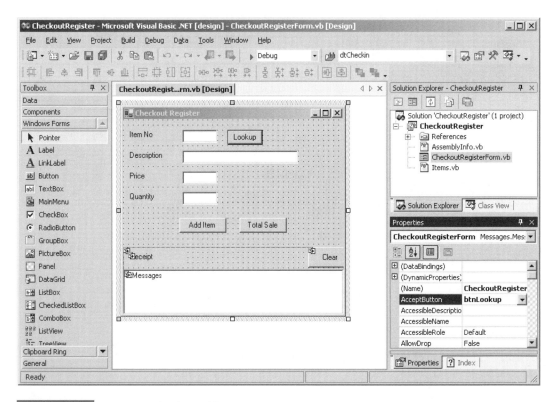

FIGURE 12–12   *Designing the derived form.*

TABLE 12–6   *Property Values for CheckoutRegisterForm*

Control Type	Name	Other Properties
Label	lblItemNo	Text: Item No
Textbox	txtItemNo	Text: (blank)
Button	btnLookup	Text: Lookup
Label	lblDescription	Text: Description
Textbox	txtDescription	Enabled: False Text: (blank)
Label	lblPrice	Text: Price
Textbox	txtPrice	Enabled: False Text: (blank)
Label	lblQuantity	Text: Quantity
Textbox	txtQuantity	Text: (blank)

TABLE 12-6	Property Values for CheckoutRegisterForm (continued)	
Control Type	**Name**	**Other Properties**
Button	btnAddItem	Text: Add Item
Button	btnTotalSale	Text: Total Sale
INHERITED LABEL	lblMessages	Text: Receipt
Form	CheckoutRegisterForm	AcceptButton: btnLookup Text: Checkout Register

STEP 3: CODING THE INHERITED FORM

To get our **CheckoutRegister** application working, we must add behavior to interact with the items that are for sale. To begin with, we will add an **Array-List** to the form and initialize it to include a small inventory. We will also add a variable to represent the running total of the current sale.

```
Public Class Register
   Inherits Messages.MessageForm

   Private inventory As New ArrayList()
   Private currentTotal As Decimal

   . . .

   Public Sub New()
      . . .

      inventory.Add(New Items(101, "Hammer", 21.95))
      inventory.Add(New Items(102, "Plyers", 14.95))
      inventory.Add( _
         New Items(103, "Flat screwdriver", 11.95))
      inventory.Add( _
         New Items(104, "Philips screwdriver", 11.95))
      inventory.Add(New Items(105, "Wrench", 15.95))
      inventory.Add(New Items(106, "Awl", 12.95))
      inventory.Add(New Items(107, "Saw", 43.95))
      inventory.Add(New Items(108, "Hacksaw", 26.95))
      inventory.Add(New Items(109, "Wire cutters", 21.95))
      inventory.Sort()
   End Sub

   . . .
End Class
```

When the user clicks on the Lookup button, we must use the item number that was entered in the textbox to locate the corresponding item in the inventory array.

```
Private Sub btnLookup_Click(ByVal sender As _
  System.Object, ByVal e As System.EventArgs) _
  Handles btnLookup.Click

    Try
        Dim itemNo As Integer = _
            Convert.ToInt32(txtItemNo.Text)
        Dim searchItem As New Items(itemNo, "", 0)
        Dim foundAt As Integer = _
            inventory.BinarySearch(searchItem)

        If foundAt >= 0 Then
            Dim foundItem As Items = _
                CType(inventory(foundAt), Items)
            txtItemNo.Text = foundItem.ItemNo
            txtDescription.Text = foundItem.Description
            txtPrice.Text = foundItem.Price
        Else
            Throw New Exception("Item not found!")
        End If
    Catch errObj As Exception
        MessageBox.Show(errObj.Message)
    End Try

End Sub
```

We must add code in the **Click** event handler of **btnAddItem** to add price information to the messages listbox. We can access the listbox via the inherited method **AddToMessages**.

```
Private Sub btnAddItem_Click(ByVal sender As _
  System.Object, ByVal e As System.EventArgs) _
  Handles btnAddItem.Click

    Try
        Dim qty As Integer = _
            Convert.ToInt32(txtQuantity.Text)
        Dim price As Decimal = _
            Convert.ToDecimal(txtPrice.Text)
        Dim lineTotal As Decimal = qty * price

        Dim s As String
        s = String.Format( _
          "{0,8:c}  {1} unit(s) of item {2}({3}) at {4:c}", _
          lineTotal, qty, txtItemNo.Text, _
          txtDescription.Text, price)
        AddToMessages(s)

        currentTotal += lineTotal

        txtItemNo.Text = ""
        txtDescription.Text = ""
        txtPrice.Text = ""
```

```
      txtQuantity.Text = ""
   Catch errObj As Exception
      MessageBox.Show(errObj.Message)
   End Try

End Sub
```

We must also add code in the **Click** event handler of **btnTotalSale** to put the current total in the messages listbox.

```
Private Sub btnTotalSale_Click(ByVal sender As _
   System.Object, ByVal e As System.EventArgs) _
   Handles btnTotalSale.Click

   Dim s As String
   s = String.Format( _
      "TOTAL SALE:   {0,8:c}   ", currentTotal)
   AddToMessages(s)

End Sub
```

As you saw, visual inheritance is based upon the widely utilized object-oriented principles of inheritance and extension. By recognizing common design elements across a set of forms, you can greatly reduce the amount of repetitive coding by designing forms that can be extended using visual inheritance.

ActiveX Controls

Microsoft's .NET Framework introduced the use of Windows Forms, which represents a consistent windowing framework across all .NET languages. The Windows Forms namespace includes a rich collection of controls that are available to use in your applications. As we saw in Chapters 7 and 8, these include textboxes, calendars, up/down controls, error providers, and more. However, occasionally you need a control that isn't found in the Windows Forms namespace. If so, you have three choices:

- Build the control you need as a .NET user control.
- Purchase the .NET control you need from a third party.
- Use an existing ActiveX control that contains the functionality you need.

This section focuses on using ActiveX controls. ActiveX controls were the preferred way of providing custom control capabilities to applications before .NET was introduced. It defines its properties, methods, and events via a type library and is based upon the COM (Component Object Model) standard.

Although Windows Forms applications are optimized to work with Windows Forms controls, you can also use ActiveX controls. However, the following issues must be taken into consideration:

● Applications that use Windows Forms can run in a fully trusted environment; when an ActiveX control is used, the application requires unmanaged code permission (see Chapter 17).

● ActiveX controls must be deployed with the application.

● Registering an ActiveX control requires writing to the registry.

In this section, we will use Microsoft's Animation ActiveX control to play .avi files. Our example is found in **ActiveXControls**.

Code
Example

Adding ActiveX Controls to the Toolbox

Before an ActiveX controls can be used on any form, it must be added to the toolbox. If you right-click on the Windows Forms tabs of the toolbox, you can choose Customize Toolbox (see Figure 12–13).

The Customize Toolbox dialog displays a list of all COM controls that are registered on your machine. To add an ActiveX control to your project, check the checkbox next to the control and choose OK. In this example, we chose the Microsoft Animation 6.0 control (see Figure 12–14).

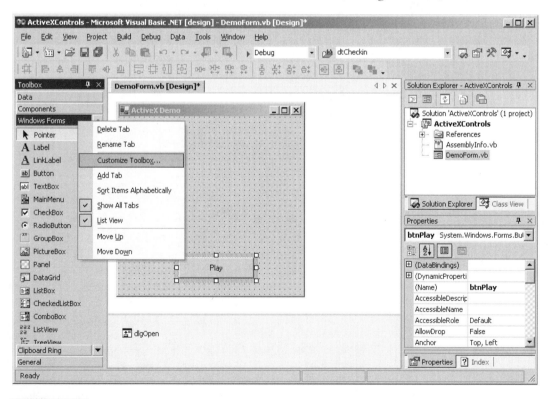

FIGURE 12–13   *Customizing the toolbox.*

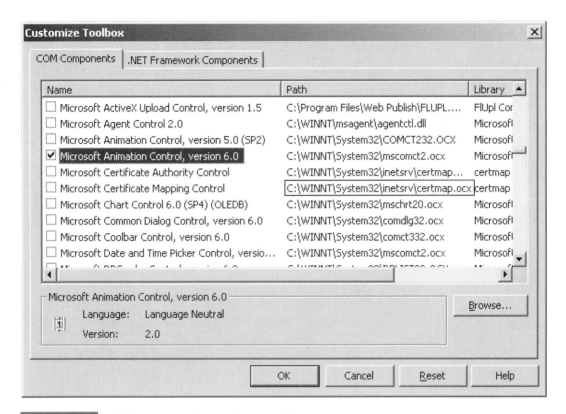

FIGURE 12-14   *Adding an ActiveX control to the toolbox.*

When we include an ActiveX control in a .NET application, it must use the Primary Interop Assembly (PIA). This wrapper class, which is added automatically, maps calls from managed code to the underlying unmanaged COM class.

Figure 12–15 shows that the animation control has been added to the toolbox and has been dropped on the form. The Solutions Explorer now references the DLL that contains the ActiveX control.

Using an ActiveX Control without Using Visual Studio

When you added the ActiveX control to your Windows Forms application by using the Visual Studio Customize Toolbar dialog, the ActiveX Control Importer converted the type definitions in the ActiveX control into a Windows Forms control. This wrapper control is derived from **System.Windows.Forms.AxHost**. The wrapper control appears as a Windows Forms control, but contains an instance of and communicates with the underlying ActiveX control.

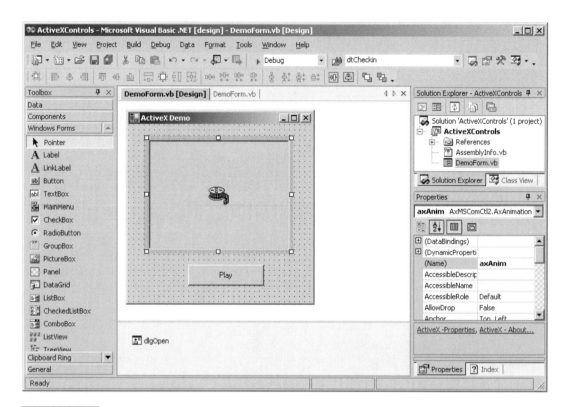

FIGURE 12–15 *Using an ActiveX control.*

If you are not working within Visual Studio, you must explicitly run the ActiveX Control Importer. It produces a set of assemblies that contain the appropriate metadata and wrapper control. The following command would also have generated MSComCtl2.dll and AxMSComCtl2.dll for the animation control:

```
aximp c:\WINNT\System32\mscomct2.dll
```

Programming with ActiveX Controls

Once the ActiveX control has been successfully added to your project, you may name it and begin working with it as you would any other control. In our **ActiveXControls** application, we have added a Play button. When it is pressed, the **FileOpenDialog** control is used to allow the user to select an .avi file. The animation control is then used to play the .avi file.

```
Private Sub btnPlay_Click(ByVal sender As System.Object, _
ByVal e As System.EventArgs) Handles btnPlay.Click
    Try
        dlgOpen.Filter = "Animations|*.avi"
        Dim ans As DialogResult = dlgOpen.ShowDialog()
        If ans = DialogResult.OK Then
            axAnim.Open(dlgOpen.FileName)
            axAnim.Play()
        End If
    Catch
        MessageBox.Show("Error playing animation!", _
            "Error", MessageBoxButtons.OK, MessageBoxIcon.Error)
    End Try
End Sub
```

Our application is now functional. Figure 12–16 illustrates the use of the **OpenFileDialog** control to select the .avi file. Figure 12–17 illustrates the ActiveX control as it plays the .avi file.

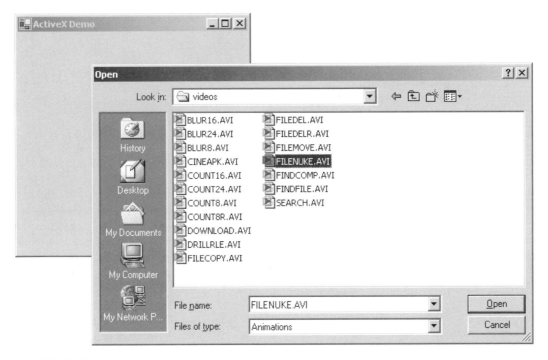

FIGURE 12–16   *Selecting the .avi file.*

FIGURE 12–17   *Playing the animation.*

Summary

In this chapter, we examined some of the additional features available to Windows Forms applications. We began by discussing modeless dialogs and how we can design forms to communicate with one another. We also saw how MDI applications can be built. The **IsMDIContainer** property is used to designate MDI parent forms and the **MDIParent** property must be set for MDI child forms. We examined how the .NET Windows Forms architecture allows visual inheritance. We saw that, because forms are implemented using classes, we can now build new forms by inheriting from existing forms. We concluded the chapter by examining how to build or use controls that are not part of the Windows Forms namespace. By this point, you have seen quite a few uses of the Windows Forms classes and should be well on your way to having the skills needed to build sophisticated, easy-to-use Windows applications.

.NET APPLICATIONS

.NET APPLICATIONS

Part 6, consisting of Chapters 13-17, covers important parts of the .NET Framework that are useful in creating a variety of different applications. Chapter 13 covers ADO.NET, which provides a consistent set of classes for accessing both relational and XML data. Chapter 14 introduces the fundamentals of ASP.NET, including the use of Web Forms, for the development of Web sites. Chapter 15 covers SOAP and Web services, which provide an easy-to-use and robust mechanism for heterogeneous systems to interoperate. Chapter 16 covers the topic of security in detail, including Code Access Security and declarative security. Chapter 17 covers interoperability of .NET with legacy COM and Win32 applications.

Programming with ADO.NET

*T*he .NET Framework database programming classes are referred to as ADO.NET. ADO.NET introduces the **DataSet** class that works with relational data in a relational manner while you are disconnected from any data source. You need not connect and update or query the database unless you have a specific reason for doing so. You can, of course, work in the traditional connected manner if you choose.

ADO.NET data providers[1] allow you to execute commands directly against the data source. Functionality is exposed directly without intermediary objects such as OLE DB, which stands between ADO and the data source. The **.NET DataAdapter** class models a data source as a set of database commands and a connection to that data source. Differences between data sources are not hidden by generic interfaces. The OLE DB data provider allows for nested transactions with data sources that support that functionality; the SQL Server data provider does not.[2]

.NET data providers supply data to a dataset or a data reader. A dataset is a memory-resident, lightweight relational database that is not connected to any database. You can also obtain a dataset from an XML document or create an XML document from a dataset. This allows you to work, if it makes sense, with your data as relational data or as hierarchical XML data.[3] Data readers model the traditional method of working with a database.

---

1. .NET data providers are what used to be called in the beta literature *managed providers*. You may still see them referred to by that term.
2. There is a **Begin** method on the **OleDbTransaction** class; the **SqlTransaction** class does not have such a method.
3. The many-to-many relations that you can have in a relational database do not automatically map to XML hierarchies. But this is no different from working with the classic object-relational model clash.

The data access classes that currently ship with the framework are found in the namespaces: **System.Data**, **System.Data.SqlClient**, **System.Data.OleDb**, **System.Data.Common**, and **System.Data.SqlTypes**. The **SqlClient** and **OleDb** namespaces reflect the SQL Server and OLE DB .NET data providers. An ODBC .NET data provider has been written, and additional ones will be written in the future.

This chapter changes the implementation of the **Customer** and **Hotel** assemblies of the case study to use SQL Server. An air travel service that the Acme Travel Agency can use to make air travel reservations is added to illustrate the use of XML. There is also a small database introduced for use by a travel agency, which offers travel services to its clients through hotel and air line brokers.

To make our examples concrete, we use SQL Server 2000 and the SQL Server data provider.[4] Nonetheless, much of the basic functionality discussed in this chapter applies to the OLE DB data provider as well, which we illustrate with an Access version of one of our databases.

This chapter assumes you have some understanding of database concepts.

Setting Up the Example Databases

This chapter assumes that SQL Server 2000 has been installed using the Local System account, with authentication mode set to Mixed Mode. The user is assumed to be sa, with a blank password.

Several examples in this chapter make use of the Northwind Traders sample database, which is installed along with SQL Server. In addition, there are other example programs that use the AcmeCustomer, HotelBroker, and AirlineBroker databases, which are supplied specifically for use with this book.

Some of the example programs make changes to these databases, and other examples assume a freshly installed database. This means that some of the examples will not always work as expected unless you reinstall them. You can reinstall each of these databases by running the SQL scripts that are provided.

Please refer to the **readme.txt** file in the sample code directory for this chapter for more information about database setup.

---

4. If you do not have a SQL Server available, you can go to the Microsoft Web site and download the MSDE, which is a scaled-down version of SQL Server. As of this writing MSDE is available for free to owners of Visual Studio. As its name suggests, MSDE is a database "engine" and does not come with any development tools, such as Enterprise Manager and Query Manager. Microsoft suggests using SQL Server Developer Edition for development. Despite the lack of developer tools, you may be able to make do with MSDE by using Visual Studio's Server Explorer. We illustrate use of Server Explorer in this chapter.

A Visual Studio .NET Database Testbed

Sample
Database

In the main part of this chapter, we write programs to access databases. We work primarily with SQL Server, but we will also illustrate an Access database, and we will see how easy it is to write programs that access different data sources in a consistent manner. An Access database is self-contained in an **.mdb** file. Our sample Access database is **AcmeCustomer.mdb** in the **Databases** folder in the chapter directory. A script, **AcmeCustomer.sql**, is provided for creating a SQL Server database **AcmeCustomer**. This script is run as part of the database setup discussed earlier in the chapter. To gain practice in working with the database tools provided with Visual Studio, let's create our own version of this database, **MyAcme**, by hand.

Sample Database

Our sample database stores ID information for customers of the Acme Travel Agency. There is only one table, **CustomerIds**, with the following columns.

- **LoginName** stores a name used by customers of Acme to identify themselves. It will be used in Chapter 14 for logging in to Acme's Web site.
- **Password** is provided for authentication, which will be used when we discuss security in Chapter 16.
- **HotelBrokerCustomerId** stores an ID that is used by the Hotel Broker.
- **AirlineBrokerCustomerId** stores an ID that is used by the Airline Broker.

The Visual Studio .NET Server Explorer

Visual Studio .NET Server Explorer is a useful tool for working with databases. Although not as powerful as the SQL Server Enterprise Manager, it can give you the basic functionality you need when writing or debugging database applications. It will be very useful when we work with the examples in this chapter.

To access the Server Explorer, use the View | Server Explorer menu item. The Server Explorer is a dockable window that can be moved around as required. Figure 13–1 illustrates the Server Explorer window after the book databases have been set up.

You can find information about all the fields in a table, or you can look at and edit the data in the tables. You can create or edit stored procedures, and you can design tables. The first thing to notice in the left-panel tree view is a list of SQL Servers installed on your system. If MMMM is the name of your machine, you may have a SQL Server named MMMM if you have SQL Server

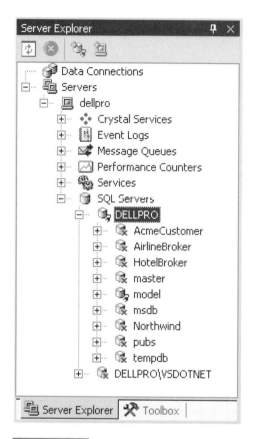

FIGURE 13–1   *The Visual Studio .NET Server Explorer window.*

itself installed. If you have installed the MSDE that comes with Visual Studio, you likely have a SQL Server named MMMM\VSDOTNET.

Below a particular SQL Server is a list of the databases on that server. Some sample databases ship with SQL Server, including the **Northwind** database. If you click the plus (+) next to a particular database, you see Database Diagrams, Tables, Views, and so on, which you can further expand by clicking the corresponding +.

We will see further features of the Server Explorer when we go through the steps of creating our sample database.

Creating a Database

It is extremely easy to create a database using SQL Server. You don't have to worry about a "database device" or initially allocating enough storage for the database, because SQL Server, beginning with version 7.0, can automatically "grow" databases as required. Follow these steps to create a database called **MyAcme**.

1. In Server Explorer, expand the tree view to show the databases on your server, as shown previously in Figure 13–1.
2. Right-click over the SQL Server Database node.
3. From the context menu that comes up, choose New Database.
4. Enter "MyAcme" as the name of your new database.
5. Select Use SQL Server Authentication, enter "sa" for the Login Name, and leave the Password blank. (Naturally, you would ***NEVER*** have such open security for a real database).
6. Click OK.

Creating Tables

You can also create tables using Server Explorer. Follow these easy steps:

1. Click the "+" to expand the node corresponding to your new database **MyAcme**.
2. Right-click over Tables and from the context menu, choose New Table.
3. Enter information as shown in Figure 13–2 to define four columns.
4. Clear the check mark from the Allow Nulls, except for the **HotelBrokerCustomerId** and **AirlineBrokerCustomerId** fields.
5. Right-click over the first column, **LoginName**, and choose Set Primary Key from the context menu.

Close the window you were using to define the new table, say "Yes" to saving the changes, and enter "CustomerIds" for the name of your new table.

Inserting Data into a Table

You can insert data into a new table using Server Explorer. We will enter data into the **CustomerIds** table. In the left pane, right-click over the table and choose Retrieve Data from Table from the context menu (or you could just double-click on the table). You can now type some sample data, like that shown in Figure 13–3. We just type in a few login names and passwords, and we leave the other two columns as <NULL>.

Performing Queries

After your database is set up, you can start to perform queries against it, making use of SQL. For example, to retrieve all the data from the **CustomerIds** table, you can perform the following query.

```
select * from CustomerIds
```

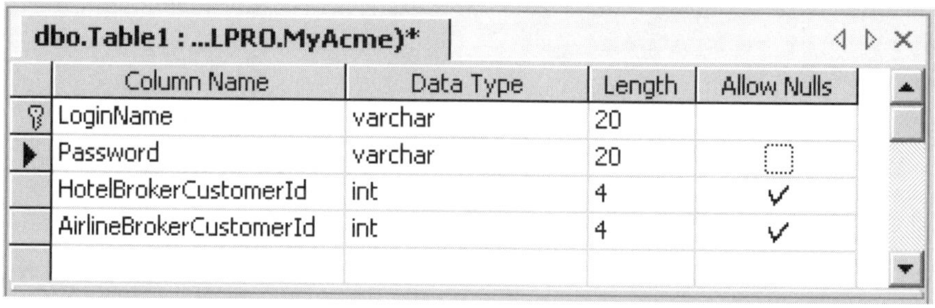

dbo.Table1 : ...LPRO.MyAcme}*				◁ ▷ ✕
Column Name	Data Type	Length	Allow Nulls	
🔑 LoginName	varchar	20		
▶ Password	varchar	20	☐	
HotelBrokerCustomerId	int	4	✓	
AirlineBrokerCustomerId	int	4	✓	

FIGURE 13–2   *Defining the schema for a table.*

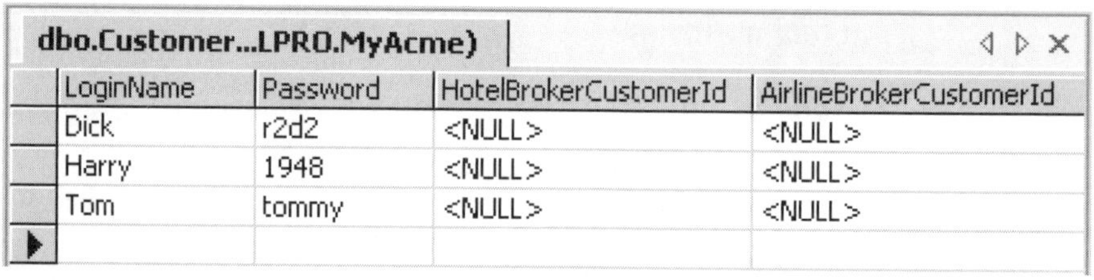

dbo.Customer...LPRO.MyAcme}			◁ ▷ ✕
LoginName	Password	HotelBrokerCustomerId	AirlineBrokerCustomerId
Dick	r2d2	<NULL>	<NULL>
Harry	1948	<NULL>	<NULL>
Tom	tommy	<NULL>	<NULL>
▶			

FIGURE 13–3   *Entering data into a table using Server Explorer.*

In this chapter our focus is on writing database *programs* using VB.NET and the ADO.NET classes. But it is useful to perform a simple query now as a quick check that your database has been set up properly. Also, as you go along in the chapter, you may want to test your SQL by using a query tool.

USING QUERY ANALYZER

If you have SQL Server installed on your system (not merely MSDE), you can make use of the Query Analyzer tool. This GUI program is easy to use. You can launch this tool by going to Start | Programs | Microsoft SQL Server | Query Analyzer. A login window appears. Select the SQL Server against which you want to perform queries, and enter the Login name and Password. Click OK.

From the database dropdown list, choose MyAcme. You can now type your query, and then click the ▶ toolbar button (or from the menu, choose Query | Execute). The results of your query are displayed in a lower pane, as illustrated in Figure 13–4.

USING OSQL COMMAND LINE TOOL

An alternative to Query Analyzer is a command-line tool, which is invoked with the command **osql**. You can enter the following at the command prompt

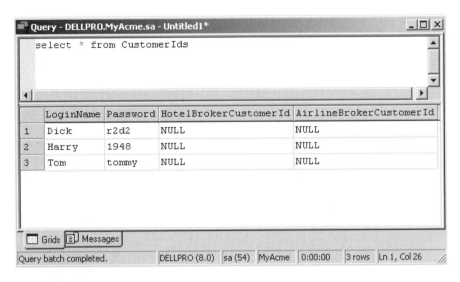

Performing a query with Query Analyzer.

to execute the same simple select (you should type it all on one line and use the name of your own server):

```
osql /Usa /P /S DELLPRO /Q "select * from
MyAcme..CustomerIds"
```

where we have used the following options:

```
/U    user name
/P    password
/S    server
/Q    query
```

In the SQL code for the query, we have prefixed the table name by the name of the database followed by two periods. Here is the result of this query (the format has been adjusted):

```
LoginName   Password   Hotel...ID   Airline...ID
---------   --------   ----------   -----------
 Dick        r2d2       NULL         NULL
 Harry       1948       NULL         NULL
 Tom         tommy      NULL         NULL

(3 rows affected)
```

ADO.NET Architecture

ADO.NET is a set of classes that provide consistent access to multiple data sources, which may be either relational data from a database or hierarchical data expressed in XML. A driving factor in ADO.NET is a provision for disconnected access to data, which is much more scalable and flexible than the connection-oriented database access that is traditional in client/server systems.

The **DataSet** class is the central component of the disconnected architecture. A dataset can be populated from either a database or an XML stream. From the perspective of the user of the dataset, the original source of the data is immaterial. A consistent programming model is used for all application interaction with the **DataSet**.

The second key component of ADO.NET architecture is the .NET data provider, which provides access to a database and can be used to populate a dataset. A data provider can also be used directly by an application to support a connected mode of database access. Figure 13–5 illustrates the overall architecture of ADO.NET.

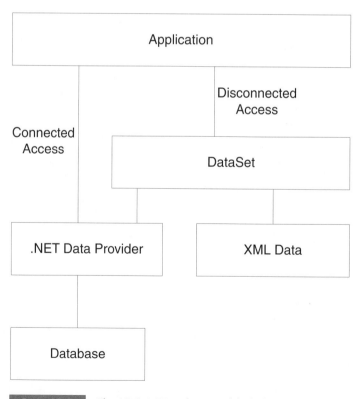

FIGURE 13–5   *The ADO.NET architecture block diagram.*

.NET Data Providers

A .NET data provider is used for connecting to a database. It provides classes that can be used to execute commands and to retrieve results. The results are either used directly by the application or they are placed in a dataset. A .NET data provider implements four key interfaces:

- **IDbConnection** is used to establish a connection to a specific data source.
- **IDbCommand** is used to execute a command at a data source.
- **IDataReader** provides an efficient way to read a stream of data from a data source. The data access provided by a data reader is forward-only and read-only.
- **IDbDataAdapter** is used to populate a dataset from a data source.

The ADO.NET architecture specifies these interfaces, and different implementations can be created to facilitate working with different data sources. A .NET data provider is analogous to an OLE DB provider, but the two should not be confused. An OLE DB provider implements COM interfaces, and a .NET data provider implements .NET interfaces.

When OLE DB first came out, it immediately supplied a provider for ODBC. This single provider offered access to an array of data sources to any data source with an ODBC driver. A native OLE DB provider was offered for SQL Server. As time passed, more OLE DB providers became available.

The situation today is similar for .NET data providers. Currently, there are two .NET data providers. The *OLE DB* data provider goes through the COM interop layer to talk to OLE DB. Thus, any data source with an OLE DB provider can be accessed through ADO.NET. The *SQL Server* data provider uses the native SQL Server wire protocol. As time passes, we can anticipate that additional native .NET data providers will be offered by different database vendors.

To make your programs more portable, you should endeavor to program with the interfaces rather than using specific classes directly. In our example programs, we illustrate using interfaces to talk to an Access database (using the OLE DB data provider) and a SQL Server database (using the SQL Server data provider).

Classes of the OLE DB provider have a prefix of OleDb, and classes of the SQL Server provider have a prefix of Sql. Table 13–1 shows a number of parallel classes between the two data providers and the corresponding interfaces.

TABLE 13–1	Comparison of Classes in the OLE DB and SQL Server Data Providers	
Interface	**OLE DB**	**SQL Server**
IDbConnection	OleDbConnection	SqlConnection
IDbCommand	OleDbCommand	SqlCommand

TABLE 13–1	Comparison of Classes in the OLE DB and SQL Server Data Providers (continued)	
Interface	**OLE DB**	**SQL Server**
IDataReader	OleDbDataReader	SqlDataReader
IDbDataAdapter	OleDbDataAdapter	SqlDataAdapter
IDbTransaction	OleDbTransaction	SqlTransaction
IDataParameter	OleDbDataParameter	SqlDataParameter

Classes such as **DataSet**, which are independent of any data provider, do not have a prefix.

.NET Namespaces

ADO.NET classes are found in the following namespaces:

- **System.Data** consists of classes that constitute most of the ADO.NET architecture.
- **System.Data.OLEDB** contains classes that provide database access using the OLE DB data provider.
- **System.Data.SQLClient** contains classes that provide database access using the SQL Server data provider.
- **System.Data.SQLTypes** contains classes that represent data types used by SQL Server.
- **System.Data.Common** contains classes that are shared by data providers.

Connected Data Access

Although much of the design of ADO.NET is geared to supporting disconnected database applications, there is also support for the connected model. Because connected applications are more familiar, we begin our detailed discussion of ADO.NET programming with the connected scenario.

Using a Connection

The connection class (**OleDbConnection** or **SqlConnection**) is used to manage the connection to the data source. It has properties for **ConnectionString**, **ConnectionTimeout**, and so forth. There are methods for **Open**, **Close**, transaction management, and so on.

A *connection string* is used to identify the information the object needs to connect to the database. You can specify the connection string when you construct the connection object, or you may specify it by setting its properties. A connection string contains a series of **argument = value** statements separated by semicolons.

To program in a manner that is independent of the data source, you should obtain an interface reference of type **IDbConnection** after creating the connection object, and you should program against this interface reference.

CONNECTING TO A SQL SERVER DATA PROVIDER

Let's begin by writing a small program to connect to the SQL Server database **MyAcme** that you created earlier in the chapter. If you would like to create this program yourself, follow the instructions. Do your work in the **Demos** directory for this chapter. If you just want to look at the finished program, examine the project in **SqlConnectAcme\Step1** (which connects to the database **AcmeCustomer** that was created by the setup for this chapter). Follow these steps to create the program yourself:

Code
Example

1. Use Visual Studio to create a new VB.NET console application called "SqlConnectAcme."
2. Type the code shown in bold. Note that we obtain an interface reference of type **IDbConnection** so that our code is more independent of the data source.

```
Imports System.Data.SqlClient

Module Module1

    Sub Main()
        Dim connStr As String = _
            "server=localhost;uid=sa;pwd=;database=MyAcme"
        Dim objConn As New SqlConnection()
        Dim conn As IDbConnection = objConn
        conn.ConnectionString = connStr
        Console.WriteLine( _
            "Using SQL Server to access MyAcme")
        Console.WriteLine("Database state: " & _
            conn.State.ToString())
        conn.Open()
        Console.WriteLine("Database state: " & _
            conn.State.ToString())
        conn.Close()
        Console.WriteLine("Database state: " & _
            conn.State.ToString())
    End Sub

End Module
```

3. Build and run the program. You should get the following output:

```
Using SQL Server to access MyAcme
Database state: Closed
Database state: Open
Database state: Closed
```

This program illustrates the correct connect string for connecting to a SQL Server database. Note the use of the database "localhost." When SQL Server is installed on your system, a SQL Server is created having the name of your computer. You could use either this name or "localhost." If you are on a network and there is a remote SQL Server running, you could connect to that SQL Server by substituting the name of the remote server. If you are running MSDE instead of SQL server, you could use "MMMM\VSDOTNET," where MMMM is the name of your machine. This assumes that you have installed the MSDE that comes with Visual Studio .NET.

The program illustrates the **ConnectionString** and **State** properties of the connection object and the **Open** and **Close** methods.

You should close your connections. If the connection is not closed explicitly, the finalizer on the **SqlConnection** object will eventually get called, and the connection will be closed. Since the garbage collector is not deterministic, there is no way to know when this will happen. So if you do not close your connections, you will use more connections than you need (even with connection pooling), and this could interfere with your applications' scalability. You could also run out of connections.

ADO.NET CLASS LIBRARIES

To run a program that uses the ADO.NET classes, you must be sure to set references to the appropriate class libraries. The following libraries should usually be included:

- **System.dll**
- **System.Data.dll**
- **System.Xml.dll**

The last one is needed when we are working with datasets; it is not required for the current examples.

References to these libraries are set up automatically when you create a console project in Visual Studio. If you create an empty project, you need to specifically add these references.

CONNECTING TO AN OLE DB DATA PROVIDER

Code Example

To connect to an OLE DB data provider instead, you need to change the namespace you are importing and instantiate an object of the **OleDbConnection** class. You must provide a connection string appropriate to your OLE DB provider. We are going to use the Jet OLE DB provider, which can be used for connecting to an Access database. The program **JetConnectAcme\Step1** illustrates connecting to the Access database **AcmeCustomer.mdb**. Note that database files for this book are installed in the directory **C:\OI\NetVb\Chap13\Databases** when you install the sample programs. The lines in bold are the only ones that are different from the corresponding SQL Server example.

```
Imports System.Data.OleDb

Module Module1

    Sub Main()
        Dim connStr As String = _
            "Provider=Microsoft.Jet.OLEDB.4.0;Data" & _
Source=C:\OI\NetVb\Chap13\Databases\AcmeCustomer.mdb"
        Dim objConn As New OleDbConnection()
        Dim conn As IDbConnection = objConn
        conn.ConnectionString = connStr
        Console.WriteLine("Using Access DB AcmeCustomer.mdb")
        Console.WriteLine("Database state: " & _
            conn.State.ToString())
        conn.Open()
        Console.WriteLine("Database state: " & _
            conn.State.ToString())
        conn.Close()
        Console.WriteLine("Database state: " & _
            conn.State.ToString())
    End Sub

End Module
```

Using Commands

After we have opened a connection to a data source, we can create a command object, which executes a query against a data source. Depending on our data source, we create either a **SqlCommand** object or an **OleDbCommand** object. In either case, we initialize an interface reference of type **IDbCommand**, which is used in the rest of our code, again promoting relative independence from the data source.

The code fragments shown below are from the **SqlConnectAcme\Step2** program, which illustrates performing various database operations on the **AcmeCustomer** database. We will look at the complete program and a sample run a little later.

Table 13–2 summarizes some of the principle properties and methods of **IDbCommand**.

Code
Example

TABLE 13–2	*Common Properties and Methods of IDbCommand*

Property or Method	Description
CommandText	Text of command to run against the data source
CommandTimeout	Wait time before terminating command attempt
CommandType	How CommandText is interpreted (e.g., Text, StoredProcedure)
Connection	The IDbConnection used by the command
Parameters	The parameters collection
Cancel	Cancels the execution of an IDbCommand
ExecuteReader	Obtains an IDataReader for retrieving data (SELECT)
ExecuteNonQuery	Executes a SQL command such as INSERT, DELETE, etc.

CREATING A COMMAND OBJECT

The following code illustrates creating a command object and returning an **IDbCommand** interface reference.

```
Private Function CreateCommand(ByVal query As String) _
  As IDbCommand
    Return New SqlCommand(query, objConn)
End Function
```

EXECUTENONQUERY

The following code illustrates executing a SQL DELETE statement using a command object. We create a query string for the command and obtain a command object for this command. The call to **ExecuteNonQuery** returns the number of rows that were updated.

```
Private Sub RemoveCustomer(ByVal login As String)
    Dim query As String = _
       "delete from CustomerIds where LoginName = " & _
       "'" & login & "'"
    Dim command As IDbCommand = CreateCommand(query)
    Dim numrow As Integer = command.ExecuteNonQuery()
    Console.WriteLine("{0} rows updated", numrow)
End Sub
```

Using a Data Reader

After we have created a command object, we can call the **ExecuteReader** method to return an **IDataReader**. With the data reader, we can obtain a read-only, forward-only stream of data. This method is suitable for reading large amounts of data, because only one row at a time is stored in memory. When you are finished with the data reader, you should explicitly close it.

Any output parameters or return values of the command object are not available until after the data reader has been closed.

Data readers have an **Item** property that can be used for accessing the current record. The **Item** property accepts either an integer (representing a column number) or a string (representing a column name). The **Item** property is the default property and can be omitted if desired.

Data readers have a method **IsDBNull**, which can be used to check if a column value is NULL. This method takes a column number as a parameter. You can obtain a column number from a column name by the **GetOrdinal** method of the data reader.

The **Read** method is used to advance the data reader to the next row. When it is created, a data reader is positioned *before* the first row. You must call **Read** before accessing any data. **Read** returns **true** if there are more rows; otherwise, it returns false.

Here is an illustration of code using a data reader to display results of a SELECT query.

```
Private Sub ShowList()
   Dim query As String = "select * from CustomerIds"
   Dim command As IDbCommand = CreateCommand(query)
   Dim reader As IDataReader = command.ExecuteReader()
   While reader.Read()
      Dim strHotelCustId As String
      Dim strAirlineCustId As String
      If reader.IsDBNull(2) Then
         strHotelCustId = "NULL"
      Else
         strHotelCustId = reader(2)
      End If
      If reader.IsDBNull(3) Then
         strAirlineCustId = "NULL"
      Else
         strAirlineCustId = reader(3)
      End If
      Console.WriteLine("{0,-20}{1,-20}{2,-8}{3,-8}", _
         reader("LoginName"), reader("Password"), _
         strHotelCustId, strAirlineCustId)
   End While
   reader.Close()
End Sub
```

Sample Database Application Using Connected Scenario

Our sample application opens a connection, which remains open during the lifetime of the application. Command objects are created to carry out typical database operations, such as retrieving rows from the database, adding rows, deleting rows, and changing rows. There are two versions of the application, one for the SQL Server version of our **AcmeCustomer** database and one for the Access version. We first look at the SQL Server version and then examine the small amount of code that must be changed for the Access version.

USING SQL SERVER DATA PROVIDER

Code Example

The first version of our program uses the SQL Server data provider. The program is provided in the folder **SqlConnectAcme\Step2**. Assuming that you have set up the **AcmeCustomer** database as described earlier in the chapter, you should be able to build and run the program. Alternatively, you can change the connect string and use the **MyAcme** database you created yourself. The Step 1 version of the program is a short program that you can use to help debug any connection problems you might have.

Here is the source code:

```
Imports System.Data.SqlClient

Module SqlConnectAcme
    Dim connStr As String = _
      "server=localhost;uid=sa;pwd=;database=AcmeCustomer"
    Dim objConn As New SqlConnection()
    Dim conn As IDbConnection = objConn

    Sub Main()
        conn.ConnectionString = connStr
        Console.WriteLine( _
          "Using SQL Server to access AcmeCustomer")
        Console.WriteLine( _
          "Database state: " & conn.State.ToString())
        conn.Open()
        Console.WriteLine("Database state: " & _
          conn.State.ToString())
        ShowList()
        ClearCustomers()
        AddCustomer("Tom", "tommy", 101, 201)
        AddCustomer("Dick", "r2d2", 102, 202)
        AddCustomer("Harry", "1948", 103, 203)
        ShowList()
        RemoveCustomer("Dick")
        ChangePassword("Harry", "1952")
        ShowList()
    End Sub
```

```
Private Function CreateCommand(ByVal query As String) _
 As IDbCommand
    Return New SqlCommand(query, objConn)
End Function

Private Sub ClearCustomers()
    Dim query As String = "delete from CustomerIds"
    Dim command As IDbCommand = CreateCommand(query)
    Dim numrow As Integer = command.ExecuteNonQuery()
    Console.WriteLine("{0} rows updated", numrow)
End Sub

Private Sub ShowList()
    Dim query As String = "select * from CustomerIds"
    Dim command As IDbCommand = CreateCommand(query)
    Dim reader As IDataReader = command.ExecuteReader()
    While reader.Read()
       Dim strHotelCustId As String
       Dim strAirlineCustId As String = "temp"
       If reader.IsDBNull(2) Then
          strHotelCustId = "NULL"
       Else
          strHotelCustId = reader(2)
       End If
       If reader.IsDBNull(3) Then
          strAirlineCustId = "NULL"
       Else
          strAirlineCustId = reader(3)
       End If
       Console.WriteLine("{0,-20}{1,-20}{2,-8}{3,-8}", _
          reader("LoginName"), reader("Password"), _
          strHotelCustId, strAirlineCustId)
    End While
    reader.Close()
End Sub

Private Sub AddCustomer(ByVal login As String, _
 ByVal pwd As String, ByVal hotelid As Integer, _
 ByVal airlineid As Integer)
    Dim query As String = _
       "insert into CustomerIds values( '" & _
       login & "', '" & pwd & "', " & hotelid & _
       ", " & airlineid & ")"
    Dim command As IDbCommand = CreateCommand(query)
    Dim numrow As Integer = command.ExecuteNonQuery()
    Console.WriteLine("{0} rows updated", numrow)
End Sub

Private Sub RemoveCustomer(ByVal login As String)
    Dim query As String = _
```

```
              "delete from CustomerIds where LoginName = " & _
              "'" & login & "'"
        Dim command As IDbCommand = CreateCommand(query)
        Dim numrow As Integer = command.ExecuteNonQuery()
        Console.WriteLine("{0} rows updated", numrow)
    End Sub

    Private Sub ChangePassword(ByVal login As String, _
      ByVal pwd As String)
        Dim query As String = _
            "update CustomerIds set Password = '" & pwd & _
            "' where LoginName = '" & login & "'"
        Dim command As IDbCommand = CreateCommand(query)
        Dim numrow As Integer = command.ExecuteNonQuery()
        Console.WriteLine("{0} rows updated", numrow)
    End Sub
End Module
```

Here is a sample run:

```
Using SQL Server to access AcmeCustomer
Database state: Closed
Database state: Open
Bullwinkle                                    1        NULL
Rocky                                         2        NULL
2 rows updated
1 rows updated
1 rows updated
1 rows updated
Dick                   r2d2                   102      202
Harry                  1948                   103      203
Tom                    tommy                  101      201
1 rows updated
1 rows updated
Harry                  1952                   103      203
Tom                    tommy                  101      201
```

USING OLE DB DATA PROVIDER

The program **JetConnectAcme\Step2** illustrates using the OLE DB data provider for the Jet database engine to talk to an Access database. This program is functionally equivalent to the program **SqlConnectAcme\Step2** that we just examined. Here is selected source code. We show in bold all the places where the program was changed:

```
Imports System.Data.OleDb

Module JetConnectAcme
    Dim connStr As String = _
        "Provider=Microsoft.Jet.OLEDB.4.0;" & _
"Data Source=C:\OI\NetVb\Chap13\Databases\AcmeCustomer.mdb"
```

```
   Dim objConn As New OleDbConnection()
   Dim conn As IDbConnection = objConn

   Sub Main()
      conn.ConnectionString - connStr
      Console.WriteLine("Using Access DB AcmeCustomer.mdb")
      ...
   End Sub

   Private Function CreateCommand( _
    ByVal query As String) As IDbCommand
      Return New OleDbCommand(query, objConn)
   End Function
End Module
```

Parameters and Stored Procedures

We have covered the basics of using ADO.NET in a connected scenario. We have seen that by using the appropriate interfaces, we can write database code that is relatively independent of the data source. We are now going to begin to examine some additional features, where there may be differences among data sources. For example, we will look at the use of stored procedures. For the rest of this chapter we will focus on the SQL Server database.

Sometimes you have to parameterize a SQL statement. You also might have to associate the input and output arguments of a stored procedure with variables in your program.

To do this you build the **SqlCommand** class's **Parameters** property, which is a collection of **SqlParameter** instances. The installation procedure added the **get_customers** stored procedure to the Northwind database to illustrate the use of a simple stored procedure, which takes one input argument that is the company name and returns the customer ID for that customer.

```
CREATE PROCEDURE get_customers
(@companyname nvarchar(40), @customerid nchar(5) OUTPUT)
AS
select @customerid = CustomerID from Customers where
  CompanyName = @companyname
RETURN

GO
```

Code Example

The **StoredProcedure** example shows how to do this.

```
cmd = New SqlCommand("get_customers", conn)
cmd.CommandType = CommandType.StoredProcedure

Dim p As New SqlParameter("@companyname",
```

```
SqlDbType.NVarChar, 40)
p.Direction = ParameterDirection.Input
p.Value = "Ernst Handel"
cmd.Parameters.Add(p)

p = New SqlParameter("@customerid", SqlDbType.NChar, 5)
p.Direction = ParameterDirection.Output
cmd.Parameters.Add(p)

cmd.ExecuteNonQuery()
Console.WriteLine("{0} CustomerId = {1}", _
   cmd.Parameters("@companyname").Value, _
   cmd.Parameters("@customerid").Value)
```

Each individual **SqlParameter** member of the **Parameters** collection represents one parameter of a SQL statement or stored procedure. As this example illustrates, the parameters need not have any relationship to any particular table or column in the database.

At a minimum, you have to specify—either through the constructor or by setting properties—the name and database type of the parameter. If the parameter is of variable length, you have to specify the size.

In this example two parameters are added to the parameters collection. The first represents the input argument to the stored procedure, the second the return value from the stored procedure.

The name of the parameter corresponds to the name of the argument in the stored procedure **get_customers**. The other values to the **SqlParameter** constructor define the data type of the parameter. The first is a variable Unicode string up to 40 characters in length. The second variable is a 5-character fixed-length Unicode string. If this were an OLE DB .NET data provider, you would bind to the parameters by position, since only the SQL Server .NET data provider binds parameters by name.

The **Value** property is used to set or get the value of the parameter. It is used to initialize the @companyname parameter for input to the stored procedure. It is also used to obtain the value that the stored procedure set for the @customerid parameter.

Output parameters must be specified as such with the **Direction** property. In this example the @companyname parameter is set as an input parameter with the value **ParameterDirection.Input**. The @customerid parameter is set as an output parameter with the value **ParameterDirection.Output**. Output parameters must be specified, since input parameters are the default. To bind to the return value of a stored procedure, use **ParameterDirection.ReturnValue**. For bidirectional parameters, use **ParameterDirection.InputOutput**.

You can use the parameter names to access individual parameters in the **SqlCommand** parameters collection.

Parameterized commands work with both **SqlDataReader** and **Data-Adapter** classes. When the **DataSet** class is discussed, you will see how to specify the **Source** property of the parameter, which indicates which column in the **DataSet** the parameter represents.

SqlDataAdapter and the DataSet Class

The **DataSet** class is a memory-resident, lightweight relational database class. It has properties that reflect the tables (**Tables**) and relationships between tables (**Relations**) within the dataset. You can control whether corresponding constraints are enforced with the **EnforceConstraints** property. You can name the dataset with the **DataSetName** property. You can also set the name of the dataset in the **DataSet** constructor.

Code
Example

The **SqlDataAdapter** class is used to get data from the database into the **DataSet**. The constructor of the **HotelBroker** class shows how to use a data adapter class to populate a dataset. The code is found in the **Hotel** subdirectory of the **CaseStudy** directory for this chapter.

```
conn = New SqlConnection(connString)
citiesAdapter = New SqlDataAdapter()
citiesAdapter.SelectCommand = New SqlCommand( _
   "select distinct City from Hotels", conn)
citiesDataset = New DataSet()
citiesAdapter.Fill(citiesDataset, "Cities")
```

The **SqlDataAdapter** class has properties associated with it for selecting, inserting, updating, and deleting data from a data source. Here the **Sql-Command** instance is associated with the **SelectCommand** property of the **SqlDataAdapter** instead of being executed independently through one of its own execute methods.

The **Fill** method of the **SqlDataAdapter** is then used to execute the select command and fill the **DataSet** with information to be put in a table, whose name is supplied as an argument. If the database connection was closed when the **Fill** method was executed, it will be opened. When finished, the **Fill** method will leave the connection in the same state as it was when it was first called.

At this point the connection to the database could be closed. You now can work with the **DataSet** and its contained data independently of the connection to the database.

SqlDataAdapter is implemented with the **SqlDataReader** class, so you can expect better performance with the latter. The **SqlDataReader** might also be more memory efficient, depending on how your application is structured. If you do not need the features of the **DataSet**, there is no point incurring the overhead. If you are doing expensive processing, you can free up the data-base connection by using a **DataSet**. You may get better scalability by loading the data into the **DataSet**, freeing the associated database resources, and doing the processing against the **DataSet**.

Disconnected Mode

This scenario of working with a database is referred to as disconnected. Con-nected mode represents a tightly coupled, connected environment where state and connections can be maintained. Client/server environments are examples where this is true. ADO and OLE DB were designed for this world. In a connected-mode environment data readers can be used. If necessary, ADO can be used through the COM interop facility. In fact, ADO was pur-posely not rewritten for .NET so that absolute backward compatibility could be maintained, bugs and all.

Connections, however, are expensive to maintain in environments where you want to be able to scale to a large number of users. In this envi-ronment there is often no need to hold locks on database tables. This aids scalability because it reduces contention on database tables. The **DataTable** objects in the **DataSet's Tables** collection with their associated constraints can mimic the tables and relationships in the original database. For applica-tions that are implemented completely with .NET, **DataSet** instances can be passed around or remoted to the various parts of an application. For applica-tions that can make optimistic assumptions about concurrency, this can pro-duce large gains in scalability and performance. This is true of many types of Internet- or intranet-based applications.

In the disconnected mode, a connection is made in the same way as with the connected mode of operation. Data is retrieved using the data pro-vider's data adapter class. The **SelectCommand** property specifies the SQL statement used to place data into the dataset. Unlike the data reader, which is related to a particular database connection, the dataset has no relationship to any database, including the one from which the data originally came.

DataSet Collections

When data is placed into a **DataSet**, the related tables and columns are also retrieved. Each dataset has collections that represent all the tables, columns, and data rows associated with it.

Code Example

The **TestHotels** folder has a special version of the **HotelBroker** class that has a method called **PrintHotels** that illustrates how to retrieve this infor-mation and write it to a Console. A console test program that uses **Hotel.dll** is provided. The **hotelsDataset** is a dataset that has already been filled with the data from the HotelBroker database.

```
Public Sub PrintHotels()
    Console.WriteLine("Hotels")
    Dim t As DataTable = hotelsDataset.Tables("Hotels")
    If t Is Nothing Then
        Return
    End If

    Dim c As DataColumn
    For Each c In t.Columns
        Console.Write("{0, -16}", c.ColumnName)
    Next
    Console.WriteLine("")

    Dim r As DataRow
    For Each r In t.Rows
        Dim i As Integer
        For i = 0 To t.Columns.Count - 1
            Dim typ As Type = r(i).GetType()
            If typ.FullName = "System.Int32" Then
                Console.Write("{0, -16}", r(i))
            Else
                Dim s As String = r(i).ToString()
                s = s.Trim()
                Console.Write("{0, -16}", s)
            End If
        Next i
        Console.WriteLine("")
    Next r
    Console.WriteLine("")
End Sub
```

The **Tables** collection includes all the **DataTable** instances in the **DataSet**. In this particular case there is only one, so there is no need to iterate through that collection. The program then iterates through all the columns in the table and sets them up as headers for the data that will be printed out. After the headers have been set up, all the rows in the table are iterated through. For each column in the row, we ascertain its type and print out the value appropriately. The program checks only for the types that are in the Hotels database table. Checking for types instead of printing out the row values as **Object** enables us to format the data appropriately.

As we will show later, you can populate the dataset through these collections without having to obtain it from a data source. You can just add tables, columns, and rows to the appropriate collections.

DataSet Fundamentals

You can also fetch a subset of the data in the **DataSet**. The **Select** method on a **DataTable** uses the same syntax as a SQL statement **where** clause. Column names are used to access the data for a particular row. This example comes for the **HotelBroker** class, where it is used to get the hotels for a particular city.

```
Public Function GetHotels(ByVal city As String) _
 As ArrayList Implements IHotelInfo.GetHotels

   ...
   Dim t As DataTable = hotelsDataset.Tables("Hotels")
   Dim rows() As DataRow = t.Select( _
      "City = '" & city & "'")
   Dim hl As HotelListItem
   Dim hotels As New ArrayList()

   Dim i As Integer
   For i = 0 To rows.Length - 1
      hl.HotelName = rows(i)("HotelName").ToString().Trim()
      hl.City = rows(i)("City").ToString().Trim()
      hl.NumberRooms = CInt(rows(i)("NumberRooms"))
      hl.Rate = CDec(rows(i)("RoomRate"))
      hotels.Add(hl)
   Next
   Return hotels
```

The **AddHotel** method of the **HotelBroker** class demonstrates how to add a new row to a **DataSet**. A new **DataRow** instance is created, and the column names are used to add the data to the columns in the row.

To propagate your new row back to a database, you have to add it to the row collection of the table and then use the **Update** method on the **Sql-DataAdapter** class to do so. It is the data adapter that mediates between the **DataSet** and the database. We will discuss later how to do perform edits on the dataset in order to accept or reject changes before propagating them back to the database.

```
Public Function AddHotel( _
 ByVal city As String, ByVal name As String, _
 ByVal number As Integer, ByVal rate As Decimal) _
 As String Implements IHotelAdmin.AddHotel
   ...
   Dim t As DataTable = hotelsDataset.Tables("Hotels")
   Dim r As DataRow = t.NewRow()

   r("HotelName") = name
   r("City") = city
   r("NumberRooms") = number
```

```
r("RoomRate") = rate

t.Rows.Add(r)

hotelsAdapter.Update(hotelsDataset, "Hotels")
```

To delete rows from the **DataSet**, you first find the particular row or rows you want to delete and then invoke the **Delete** method on each **DataRow** instance. When the **Update** method on the data adapter is called, it will be deleted from the database.

The **Remove** method removes the **DataRow** from the collection. It is not marked as deleted, since it is no longer in the **DataSet**. When the **Update** method on the data adapter is called, it will not be deleted from the database.

The **DeleteHotel** method in the **HotelBroker** class illustrates deleting rows from a **DataSet**.

```
Public Function DeleteHotel( _
 ByVal city As String, ByVal name As String) _
 As String Implements IHotelAdmin.DeleteHotel
   ...
   t = hotelsDataset.Tables("Hotels")
   r = t.Select("City = '" & city & "' and HotelName = '" _
     & name & "'")

   If r.Length = 0 Then
      Throw (New HotelNotFoundException( _
      "Hotel " & name & " in " & city & " was not found."))
   End If

   For i = 0 To r.Length - 1
      r(i).Delete()
   Next
   ...
```

To update a row in a dataset, you just find it and modify the appropriate columns. This example comes from the **ChangeRooms** method in the **HotelBroker** class. When the **Update** method on the data adapter is called, the modification will be propagated back to the database.

```
Public Function ChangeRooms( _
 ByVal city As String, ByVal name As String, _
 ByVal numberRooms As Integer, ByVal rate As Decimal) _
 As String Implements IHotelAdmin.ChangeRooms
   ...
   t = hotelsDataset.Tables("Hotels")
   Dim r() As DataRow = t.Select( _
    "City = '" & city & "' and HotelName = '" & name & "'")

   If r.Length = 0 Then
```

```
      Throw (New HotelNotFoundException( _
      "Hotel " & name & " in " & city & " was not found."))
   End If

   Dim i As Integer
   For i = 0 To r.Length - 1
      r(i)("NumberRooms") = numberRooms
      r(i)("RoomRate") = rate
   Next
   ...
```

Updating the Data Source

How does the **SqlDataAdapter.Update** method propagate changes back to the data source? Changes to the **DataSet** are placed back based on the **Insert-Command**, **UpdateCommand**, and **DeleteCommand** properties of the **Sql-DataAdapter** class. Each of these properties takes a **SqlCommand** instance that can be parameterized to relate the variables in the program to the parts of the related SQL statement. The code fragment we use to show this comes from the **HotelBroker** constructor.

A **SqlCommand** instance is create to represent the parameterized SQL statement that will be used when the **SqlDataAdapter.Update** command is invoked to add a new row to the database. At that point, the actual values will be substituted for the parameters.

```
Dim cmd As New SqlCommand("insert Hotels(City, " & _
  "HotelName, NumberRooms, RoomRate) values(@City, " & _
  "@Name, @NumRooms, @RoomRate)", conn)
```

The parameters have to be associated with the appropriate columns in a **DataRow**. In the **AddHotel** method code fragment discussed previously, columns were referenced by the column names: HotelName, City, NumberRooms, and RoomRate. Notice how they are related to the SQL statement parameters @Name, @City, @NumRooms, and @RoomRate in the **SqlParameter** constructor. This last argument sets the **Source** property of the **SqlParameter**. The **Source** property sets the **DataSet** column to which the parameter corresponds. The **Add** method places the parameter in the **Parameters** collection associated with the **SqlCommand** instance.

```
Dim param As New SqlParameter("@City", SqlDbType.Char, _
   20, "City")
cmd.Parameters.Add(param)

cmd.Parameters.Add(New SqlParameter("@Name", _
   SqlDbType.Char, 20, "HotelName"))
cmd.Parameters.Add(New SqlParameter("@NumRooms", _
   SqlDbType.Int, 4, "NumberRooms"))
cmd.Parameters.Add(New SqlParameter("@RoomRate", _
   SqlDbType.Money, 8, "RoomRate"))
```

Finally, the **SqlDataAdapters' InsertCommand** property is set to the **SqlCommand** instance. Now this command will be used whenever the adapter has to insert a new row in the database.

```
hotelsAdapter.InsertCommand = cmd
```

Similar code appears in the **HotelBroker** constructor for the **Update-Command** and **DeleteCommand** properties to be used whenever a row has to be updated or deleted.

Whatever changes you have made to the rows in the **DataSet** will be propagated to the database when **SqlDataAdapter.Update** is executed. How to accept and reject changes made to the rows before issuing the **SqlData-Adapter.Update** command is discussed in a later section.

Auto Generated Command Properties

The **SqlCommandBuilder** class can be used to automatically generate any **InsertCommand**, **UpdateCommand**, and **DeleteCommand** properties that have not been defined. Since the **SqlCommandBuilder** needs to derive the necessary information to build those properties dynamically, it requires an extra round trip to the database and more processing at runtime. Therefore, if you know your database layout in the design phase, you should explicitly set the **InsertCommand**, **UpdateCommand**, and **DeleteCommand** properties to avoid the performance hit. If the database layout is not known in advance, and a query is specified by the user, the **SqlCommandBuilder** can be used if the user subsequently wants to update the results.

This technique works for **DataTable** instances that correspond to single tables. If the data in the **DataTable** is generated by a query that uses a join, then the autogeneration mechanism cannot generate the logic to update multiple tables. The **SqlCommandBuilder** uses the **SelectCommand** property to generate the command properties.

A primary key or unique column must exist on the table in the **DataSet**. This column must be returned by the SQL statement set in the **SelectCommand** property. The unique columns are used in a **where** clause for update and delete.

Column names cannot contain special characters such as spaces, commas, periods, quotation marks, or nonalphanumeric characters. This is true even if the name is delimited by brackets. You can specify a fully qualified table name such as **SchemaName.OwnerName.TableName**.

A simple way to use the **SqlCommandBuilder** class is to pass the **Sql-DataAdapter** instance to its constructor. The **SqlCommandBuilder** then registers itself as a listener for **RowUpdating** events. It can then generate the needed **InsertCommand**, **UpdateCommand**, or **DeleteCommand** properties before the row update occurs.

The **CommandBuilder** example demonstrates how to use the **SqlCommandBuilder** class.

Code
Example

Database Transactions and Updates

When the data adapter updates the data source, it is *not* done as a single transaction. If you want all the inserts, updates, and deletes done in one transaction, you must handle the transaction programmatically.

The **SqlConnection** object has a **BeginTransaction** method that returns a **SqlTransaction** object. When you invoke the **BeginTransaction** method, you can optionally specify the isolation level. If you know what you are doing, and understand the tradeoffs, you can improve the performance and scalability of your application by setting the appropriate isolation level. If you set the isolation level incorrectly or inappropriately, you can have inconsistent or incorrect data results.[5]

The **SqlTransaction** class has **Commit** and **Rollback** methods to commit or abort the transaction. You open the **SqlConnection**, invoke the **BeginTransaction** method, use the **SqlDataAdapter** as normal, and then call **SqlTransaction.Commit** or **SqlTransaction.Rollback** as appropriate. Then close the connection. The **Save** method on **SqlTransaction** can be used to set a savepoint in the transaction.

In order to minimize the database resources you hold, and therefore increase the scalability of your application, you want to minimize the time between calling **BeginTransaction** and the call to **Commit** or **Rollback**.

Code
Example

Here is some code from the **Transactions** example. It uses the Airline-Broker database introduced later in the chapter. Note that we only open the connection right before the **Fill**, and the transaction statements bracket the **Update**.

```
conn = New SqlConnection(ConnString)
da = New SqlDataAdapter()
ds = New DataSet()
da.SelectCommand = New SqlCommand(selectCmd, conn)
da.InsertCommand = New SqlCommand(insertCmd, conn)
...
conn.Open()
da.Fill(ds, "Airlines")
...
trans = conn.BeginTransaction()
```

---

5. Discussing isolation levels in detail would remove our focus from .NET to database programming. Any good intermediate to advanced book on database programming would discuss the concept of isolation levels and locking. For specific information about the SQL Server locking mechanism, you can read the Microsoft Press *Inside SQL Server* books, among others. Tim Ewald's book *Transactional COM+* has a good chapter on the issue of isolation and its relation to building scalable applications.

```
da.InsertCommand.Transaction = trans
da.Update(ds, "Airlines")
trans.Commit()
```

To ensure that the SQL Server data provider operates properly, you should use the **Commit** and **Rollback** methods on the **SqlTransaction** object to commit or roll back the transactions started with **SqlConnection.BeginTransaction**. Do not use the SQL Server transaction statements.

If you use stored procedures for your database work, you can certainly issue SQL Server transaction statements inside the stored procedures instead of using the **SqlTransaction** object. Stored procedures can be used to encapsulate transactional changes. The **MakeReservation** stored procedure in the HotelBroker database does just that.

Optimistic Versus Pessimistic Locking and the DataSet

Transactions help preserve database consistency. When you move money from your savings to your checking account to pay your phone bill, transaction processing ensures that the credit and withdrawal will both happen, or neither will happen. You will not wind up with a situation where the money goes into your checking account but is not withdrawn from the savings (good for you, but bad for the bank) or the reverse (bad for you, but good for the bank). Nothing about that transaction prevents your spouse from using that same money to eat out at a fancy restaurant.[6]

Under an optimistic locking strategy, you assume this will not happen, but you have to be prepared to deal with it when does.[7] A pessimistic locking strategy requires coordination among all the users of a database table so that this never happens. Of course, the fewer locks you hold on database rows to prevent use by more than one user, the more scalable your application will be.

An understanding of how this affects your application applies to both reads and actual updates. For example, suppose your spouse sees that money is available in the checking account and makes plans based on that fact. This could be as much of a problem as the actual withdrawal of money from the joint checking account.

---

6. The failure to distinguish between these two leads to the apparently common problem (as related to me by a bank vice president) of people wondering why their checks bounce when their ATM balance said they had enough money to withdraw some cash.
7. This is the database equivalent of overdraft protection.

While a discussion of how to solve these problems is beyond the scope of this chapter, it is important to realize that the issue arises because no locks are held on the database records held within a **DataSet**. Just using the **DataSet** with **SqDataAdapter.Update** assumes an optimistic locking strategy.

Why does this matter? It matters because the performance and scalability of your application depend on it. Why is it so complicated? Because there is no answer that applies to all applications in all situations. If users do not share the same set of data, optimistic concurrency is an excellent assumption. If you have to lock records for a long period of time, this increases the wait to use these resources, thus decreasing performance and scalability.

You have to understand transaction isolation levels, the database's Lock Manager, the probability of contention for particular rows, and the probability that this contention results in deadlock in your application. You have to understand how much time and resources you can spend reconciling divergent operations, and how much tolerance for inconsistent or incorrect results your application can stand, in order to decide under what circumstances you want to avoid deadlock at all costs or can deal with the consequences of conflicting operations.[8]

You might have to use the **DataSet** with additional logic to test whether the records in the **DataSet** have been changed since the last time they were fetched or modified. Or you might just decide to use the **SqlDataReader** and refetch the data. It all depends.

For example, when making a reservation in our HotelBroker case study, you cannot make an optimistic assumption about the availability of rooms. It is not acceptable to assume an infinite supply of rooms at a hotel and let the reservations clerk deal with what happens when more people show up than there are rooms for.[9] We use the **MakeReservation** stored procedure to check on the availability of a room before we make the reservation.[10]

---

8. Tim Ewald's book is worth reading to understand this topic. Philip Bernstein and Eric Newcomer's *Principles of Transaction Processing* is another good reference.
9. Of course, airlines and hotels overbook. This is a conscious strategy to deal with passengers or guests not making explicit cancellations, not a database concurrency strategy.
10. In fact, the transaction in **MakeReservation** includes the checking of the availability of the room as well as the actual making of the reservation in order to maintain consistency. It also breaks up what could be one multiple table join into several queries in order to return better error information.

Sometimes, even without concurrency issues, the **DataSet** cannot be used to add new rows in isolation from the database. Sometimes, as in our HotelBroker application, an arbitrary primary key cannot be used.[11] Many users will be making reservations at the same time. Reservation ids cannot be assigned locally; some central logic on the database has to be employed to issue them.[12] The **MakeReservation** stored procedure does this as well.

The degree of disconnected operation that your application can tolerate has to be understood before you can decide how to use **SqlDataReader** or the **DataSet** in your applications.

Why bother to use the **DataSet** at all in our **HotelBroker** application? In fact, the code for the **Customer** object does not use the **DataSet** at all. The **HotelBroker** object does—for two reasons. The first is pedagogical. We wanted to show you how a complete application might use the features of the **DataSet**, rather than just isolated sample programs. Second, in the Web version of the application, which is developed in subsequent chapters, it is convenient to cache certain pieces of information. For example, it is probably reasonable to assume that users can work with their own local copy of reservations. On the other hand, the information about a customer, such as his or her email address, can be obtained just once at log in. There is no need for an elaborate mechanism to cache customer information, so the **Customer** object uses methods on the **SqlCommand** object.

Working with DataSets

Figure 13–6 depicts the hierarchy of classes that exist within the **DataSet** class. The shaded boxes represent collection classes. It will be helpful to glance at this diagram over the next few sections that discuss these classes.

---

11. For instance, a GUID. Well, theoretically, GUIDs could be used in our case, but when was the last time you got a reservation number from a hotel or airline that was composed of 32 hex digits? Many times, a primary key has meaning to an organization—for example, a part number whose subsections indicate various categories.

12. Of course, if performance were critical, instances of the **HotelBroker** could be preassigned ranges of reservation ids to give out. But this would have to be done by some central authority as well (the database? some singleton object?). But then this raises the issue of state management in the middle tier. This just reinforces our previous point about the dependency of any solution on the specific requirements of your program. It also reinforces the maxim that any programming problem can be solved either by trading memory against time or adding another level of indirection.

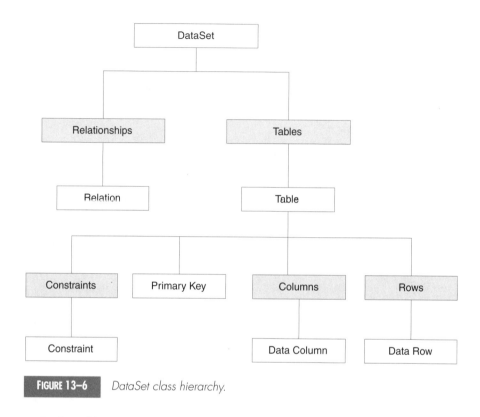

FIGURE 13–6   *DataSet class hierarchy.*

Multiple Tables in a DataSet

Each **DataSet** has a collection of one or more **DataTable** objects. Each **DataTable** object represents one table.

With a **SelectCommand** that contains a join, you can place data from multiple database tables into one **DataTable**. If you want to update the multiple tables, you will have to specify the update commands, because all relationship of the data to the original tables is lost. The **SqlDataAdapter** for the **HotelBookings** object has the following **SelectCommand** property (see the file **HotelBookings.vb** in the **CaseStudy** folder):

Code
Example

```
adapter = New SqlDataAdapter()
Dim cmd As String = "select CustomerId, HotelName, " & _
   "City, ArrivalDate, DepartureDate, ReservationId " & _
   "from Reservations, Hotels where " & _
   "Reservations.HotelId = Hotels.HotelId"
adapter.SelectCommand = New SqlCommand(cmd, conn)

ds = New DataSet()
adapter.Fill(ds, "Reservations")
```

The **DataSet** will have only one **DataTable**, called Reservations. The fact that some of the data came from the Hotels table is lost.

You can also load more than one table into a dataset. The **DataSchema** example does just this:

Code Example

```
adapter.SelectCommand = New SqlCommand("select * from " _
    & "[Order Details] where ProductId = 1", conn)
adapter.FillSchema(ds, SchemaType.Source, "Order Details")
adapter.Fill(ds, "Order Details")

adapter.SelectCommand = New SqlCommand( _
    "select * from Shippers", conn)
adapter.FillSchema(ds, SchemaType.Source, "Shippers")
adapter.Fill(ds, "Shippers")
```

There will be two tables, OrderDetails and Shippers, in the **DataSet**. The method **SqlDataAdapter.FillSchema** fills the **DataSet** with the primary key information associated with the tables. The code can now iterate through the tables and print out both the data and the primary keys of the tables. The Columns collection on the **DataTable** enables you to find the **DataColumns** for the **DataTable**.

```
Dim t As DataTable
For Each t In ds.Tables
   Console.WriteLine(t.TableName)
   Dim dc() As DataColumn = t.PrimaryKey
   Dim i As Integer
   For i = 0 To dc.Length - 1
      Console.WriteLine( _
          "    Primary Key Field {0} = {1}", _
          i, dc(i).ColumnName)
   Next i

   Console.Write("    ")
   Dim c As DataColumn
   For Each c In t.Columns
      Console.Write("{0, -15}", c.ColumnName)
   Next c
   Console.WriteLine()

   Dim r As DataRow
   For Each r In t.Rows
      Console.Write("    ")
      For Each c In t.Columns
         Console.Write("{0, -15}", r(c).ToString().Trim())
      Next c
      Console.WriteLine()
   Next r
Next t
```

The example output shows the tables, primary keys, columns, and data:

```
Order Details
        Primary Key Field 0 = OrderID
        Primary Key Field 1 = ProductID
OrderID     ProductID  UnitPrice Quantity Discount
10285       1          14.4      45       0.2
10294       1          14.4      18       0
...
Shippers
        Primary Key Field 0 = ShipperID
        ShipperID   CompanyName           Phone
        1           Speedy Express        (503) 555-9831
        2           United Package        (503) 555-3199
        3           Federal Shipping      (503) 555-9931
```

Table Creation without a Data Source

Code Example

We can use a **DataSet** as a memory-resident relational database not based on any database. In fact, we will explore various features of the **DataSet** in the **DataEditing** example by adding the data and relationships directly to the dataset without extracting them from a database.

First, we create a new **DataSet** and turn on constraint checking. We then add four **DataTables** to the **DataSet**: Books, Categories, Authors, and Book-Categories. Even though it is set in the example code for pedagogical reasons, **EnforceConstraints** by default is true.

```
Dim ds As New DataSet()
ds.EnforceConstraints = True

' Add tables to Dataset
Dim categories As DataTable = ds.Tables.Add("Categories")
Dim bookcategories As DataTable =
ds.Tables.Add("BookCategories")
Dim authors As DataTable = ds.Tables.Add("Authors")
Dim books As DataTable = ds.Tables.Add("Books")
```

Each **DataTable** object has a collection of **DataColumn** objects. Each object represents one column of the table. We then add columns to the table definition.

```
' define types for column definitions
Dim stringType As Type =
System.Type.GetType("System.String")
Dim intType As Type = System.Type.GetType("System.Int32")

' Define columns for tables

' Add column to Category table
Dim categoryname As DataColumn = _
```

```
categories.Columns.Add("Category", stringType)

' Add columns for BookCategories table
Dim cn As DataColumn = bookcategories.Columns.Add( _
    "CategoryName", stringType)
Dim loc As DataColumn = bookcategories.Columns.Add( _
    "LibraryofCongressNumber", stringType)

' Add columns for Authors table
Dim auid As DataColumn = authors.Columns.Add( _
    "AuthorId", intType)
authors.Columns.Add("AuthorLastName", stringType)
authors.Columns.Add("AuthorFirstName", stringType)

' Add columns for Books table
Dim ISBN As DataColumn = books.Columns.Add( _
    "ISBN", stringType)
Dim booksauid As DataColumn = books.Columns.Add( _
    "AuthorId", intType)
books.Columns.Add("Title", stringType)
Dim bloc As DataColumn = books.Columns.Add( _
    "LibraryofCongressNumber", stringType)
```

Constraints and Relations

Each **DataTable** object has a collection of **DataRow** objects. Each object represents one row of the table. When you add a **DataRow**, it is subject to the constraints on the **DataTable** objects (assuming the **DataSet's EnforceConstraints** property has been set to true).

PRIMARY KEYS

There are several constraints on a table. The primary key constraint is the unique identifier for the table. Other unique constraints force the values in various column(s) to which they are applied to be unique. A foreign key constraint forces the values in the column(s) to which it applies to be a primary key in another table in the **DataSet**.

The **DataTable**'s primary key is a property:

```
' Define PK for BookCategories table
Dim bookcategoriesPK() As DataColumn = New DataColumn(1) {}
bookcategoriesPK(0) = cn
bookcategoriesPK(1) = loc
bookcategories.PrimaryKey = bookcategoriesPK

' Define PK for Authors table
Dim authorsPK() As DataColumn = New DataColumn(0) {}
authorsPK(0) = auid
authors.PrimaryKey = authorsPK
```

```
' Define PK for Books table
Dim booksPK() As DataColumn = New DataColumn(0) {}
booksPK(0) = ISBN
books.PrimaryKey = booksPK
```

CONSTRAINTS

The other constraints on the **Table** are represented by the abstract base class **Constraint** and its derived classes: **UniqueConstraint** and **ForeignKey-Constraint**. The base class enables the constraints to be placed in the table's constraint collection. Primary keys also appear in the table's constraint collection as a unique constraint with a system-generated name. The **UniqueConstraint.IsPrimaryKey** property can be used to detect primary keys.

We constrain the Category column in the Categories table to be unique. Since the last argument to the **Add** method is false, this is not a primary key of the table. We do not define a primary key for this table, only a unique constraint. In fact, we do not even have to define any constraint on the table. Although that would violate the rules of relational integrity, you are not forced to use the **DataSet** in a relational manner. If you wish, you can add a name to the constraint.

```
categories.Constraints.Add( _
    "Unique CategoryName Constraint", categoryname, False)
```

Foreign keys can specify what action should be taken when the primary key on which it is based is changed. Your choices are the standard database choices: **None, Cascade, SetNull**. You can also use **SetDefault** to set the new value to the **DataColumn's DefaultValue** property. These operations can be specified for both update and delete conditions.

In this example, a foreign key constraint is set so that all author ids in the Books table have to be found in the Authors table. In other words, when a new book row is inserted, it must have an author. We give this constraint a name: Authors->Books. If the author ID is changed, the update rule forces the **DataSet** to change all the author ids in the related rows to the new author id. If the author ID is deleted, the **DataSet** will set the deleted author ids in the Book rows to null. If we had set the **DeleteRule** to **Cascade**, a cascading delete would be applied to all those rows in the Books table. The **AcceptRejectRule** applies to editing of the **DataSet**, which we will cover in a future section. This rule dictates what happens when the **AcceptChanges** method is invoked on a **DataSet**, **DataRow**, or **DataTable**. In this case all changes are cascaded. The alternative rule would be to take no action (**None**).

```
' Define FK for Books table
' (AuthorId must be in Authors table)
Dim bookauthorFK() As DataColumn = New DataColumn(0) {}
bookauthorFK(0) = booksauid
Dim fk As New ForeignKeyConstraint( _
```

```
    "Authors->Books", authorsPK, bookauthorFK)
fk.AcceptRejectRule = AcceptRejectRule.Cascade
fk.DeleteRule = Rule.SetNull
fk.UpdateRule = Rule.Cascade
books.Constraints.Add(fk)
```

DATA RELATIONS

Besides constraints, you can add a relation to the **DataSet's DataRelation** collection. A relation connects two tables so that you can navigate between the parent and the child or the child and the parent. When you add the relation, you can optionally create and add the equivalent unique and foreign key constraints to the parent and child tables' constraint collections.[13]

The Categories table is made the parent of the BookCategories table through the Categories and CategoryName columns. In a relation both columns have to be of the same type (string). You can use this relation to navigate by finding all the rows in the child table that have the same value as in the parent table or finding the row in the parent table that is the parent of a row in the child table. Similarly, the Library of Congress number associated with a book has to be found in the Library of Congress field in the BookCategory's Library of Congress field.

```
ds.Relations.Add( _
    "Category->BookCategories Relation", categoryname, cn)
ds.Relations.Add( _
    "Book Category LOC->Book LOC Relation", Loc, bloc)
```

Examining the Schema Information about a DataTable

You can examine the information about a DataTable. Here is how to examine the constraint and key information. A previous example has already shown you how to find the DataColumns for a DataTable. Note the use of the **IsPrimaryKey** property on the **UniqueConstraint** to detect a primary key.

```
Dim t As DataTable
For Each t In ds.Tables
    Console.WriteLine("  " + t.TableName)
    Console.WriteLine("  Primary Key:")
    Dim i As Integer
    For i = 0 To t.PrimaryKey.Length - 1
        Dim dc As DataColumn = t.PrimaryKey(i)
        Console.WriteLine("    {0}", dc.ColumnName)
    Next i
```

---

13. Use the optional boolean **createConstraints** argument when you add a relation to indicate whether the associated constraint should be added. If this argument is not specified, the default is to add the associated constraint.

```
        Console.WriteLine("  Constraints:")
        Dim c As Constraint
        For Each c In t.Constraints
           Dim constraintName As String
           If TypeOf c Is ForeignKeyConstraint Then
              constraintName = "Foreign Key:" & c.ConstraintName
           ElseIf (TypeOf c Is UniqueConstraint) Then
              Dim u As UniqueConstraint = _
                 CType(c, UniqueConstraint)
              If (u.IsPrimaryKey) Then
                 constraintName = "Primary Key"
              Else
                 constraintName = u.ConstraintName
              End If
           Else
              constraintName = "Unknown Name"
           End If
           Console.WriteLine("    {0, -40}", constraintName)
     Next c
Next t
```

This produces the following output. Note how the relations defined as a **DataRelation** appear in the table's constraint collection as a **ForeignKey-Constraint** instance. Primary keys appear in the constraint collection as a **UniqueConstraint** instance. Constraints defined as unique constraints or foreign keys appear as you would expect in the collection.

```
Categories
  Primary Key:
  Constraints:
    Unique CategoryName Constraint
BookCategories
  Primary Key:
    CategoryName
    LibraryofCongressNumber
  Constraints:
    Primary Key
    Foreign Key:Category->BookCategories Relation
    Constraint2
  Authors
    Primary Key:
      AuthorId
    Constraints:
      Primary Key
  Books
    Primary Key:
      ISBN
  Constraints:
    Primary Key
    Foreign Key:Authors->Books
    Foreign Key:Book Category LOC->Book LOC Relation
```

Note the BookCategories constraint with the system-generated name. If you examine the code carefully, you will see we never added this constraint. Where did it come from? If you were to look at the columns in that constraint, you would find the Library of Congress field. The system realized that since the CategoryName is a foreign key in another table, the Library of Congress field should be unique.

You can also examine the relations collection on the **DataSet**. You can examine the parent table and the columns in the parent table involved in the relationship. You can also examine the child table in the relationship and its columns.

```
Dim dr As DataRelation
For Each dr In ds.Relations
    Dim parentTable As DataTable = dr.ParentTable
    Dim childTable As DataTable = dr.ChildTable
    Console.WriteLine("    Relation: {0} ", dr.RelationName)
    Console.WriteLine("        ParentTable: {0, -10}", _
        parentTable)
    Console.Write("            Columns: ")
    Dim j As Integer
    For j = 0 To dr.ParentColumns.Length - 1
        Console.Write("                {0, -10}", _
            dr.ParentColumns(j).ColumnName)
        Console.WriteLine()
        Console.WriteLine("        ChildTable:  {0, -10}", _
            childTable)
        Console.Write("            Columns: ")
    Next j
    For j = 0 To dr.ChildColumns.Length - 1
        Console.Write("                {0, -10}", _
            dr.ChildColumns(j).ColumnName)
        Console.WriteLine()
    Next j
Next dr
```

Here is the resulting output:

```
Output Relations between tables in the DataSet...
    Relation: Category->BookCategories Relation
        ParentTable: Categories
            Columns:                 Category
        ChildTable:  BookCategories
            Columns:                 CategoryName
    Relation: Book Category LOC->Book LOC Relation
        ParentTable: BookCategories
            Columns:                 LibraryofCongressNumber
        ChildTable:  Books
            Columns:                 LibraryofCongressNumber
```

DATABASE EVENTS

Several ADO.NET classes generate events. The **SqlConnection** class generates the **StateChange** and **InfoMessage** events. The **SqlDataAdapter** generates the **RowUpdated** and **RowUpdating** events. The **DataTable** class generates the **ColumnChanging**, **ColumnChanged**, **RowChanged**, **RowChanging**, **RowDeleted**, and **RowDeleting** events.

For example, the **RowChanged** event occurs after an action has been performed on a row. Continuing with our **DataEditing** example, it defines a handler for the **RowChanged** event in the Books table. Every time a row changes in the Books table, the event handler will run. The event handler is set up by defining a handler procedure **Row_Changed** and hooking it to the **RowChanged** event by **AddHandler**.

```
Sub Row_Changed(ByVal sender As Object, _
 ByVal e As System.Data.DataRowChangeEventArgs)

    Dim table As DataTable = CType(sender, DataTable)
    Dim primaryKey() As DataColumn = table.PrimaryKey
    Dim keyName As String = primaryKey(0).ColumnName
    Console.WriteLine("Rowchanged:Table " & _
        table.TableName & " " & e.Action.ToString() & _
        "Row with Primary Key " & e.Row(keyName))
End Sub
...
AddHandler books.RowChanged, _
    New DataRowChangeEventHandler(AddressOf Row_Changed)
```

So, when the code adds some rows, including some to the Books table,

```
Dim row As DataRow
row = categories.NewRow()
row("Category") = "UnitedStates:PoliticalHistory"
categories.Rows.Add(row)
...

row = authors.NewRow()
row("AuthorId") = 1
row("AuthorLastName") = "Burns"
row("AuthorFirstName") = "James M."
authors.Rows.Add(row)
...
row = books.NewRow()
row("ISBN") = "0-201-62000-0"
row("Title") = "The Deadlock of Democracy"
row("AuthorId") = 1
row("LibraryofCongressNumber") = "E183.1"
books.Rows.Add(row)

row = books.NewRow()
```

```
row("ISBN") = "0-201-62000-3"
row("Title") = "Freedom and Order"
row("AuthorId") = 2
row("LibraryofCongressNumber") = "E183.1"
books.Rows.Add(row)
```

we get one output line for each book added, printed by the event handler:

```
Table Books AddRow with Primary Key 0-201-62000-0
Table Books AddRow with Primary Key 0-201-62000-3
```

If we were to change the ISBN numbers of the two books that were added to the same value, a **ConstraintException** would be thrown. If we changed the **DataSet.EnforceConstraints** property to false, however, no exception would be thrown.

NAVIGATING RELATIONSHIPS

Using the schema information, we can navigate from parent table to child table and print out the results. This cannot be done with relationships defined as **ForeignKeyConstraint**, only with those defined as a **DataRelation** in the relations collection of the **DataSet**.

We previously printed out the schema information associated with the relationships. Now we use this information to print out the parent and child rows in the relationships. By using relationships appropriately, you can walk through the data without using relational queries. This can be quite useful for finding all the books in a certain category or all order items in an order.

Note the use of the **DataRow** methods **GetChildRows** and **GetParentRows** to do the navigation. For a given relation, first we navigate from parent to children, then from the children to their parent. We also show how you can use different constructs to access the items in the various collections.

```
For Each dr In ds.Relations
   Console.WriteLine(dr.RelationName)
   Dim parentTable As DataTable = dr.ParentTable
   Dim childTable As DataTable = dr.ChildTable
   Dim parentRow As DataRow
   For Each parentRow In parentTable.Rows
      Console.Write("      Parent Row: ")
      Dim pc As DataColumn
      For Each pc In parentTable.Columns
         Console.Write("  {0} ", parentRow(pc))
      Next pc
      Console.WriteLine()

      Dim childRows() As DataRow = _
         parentRow.GetChildRows(dr)
      Dim k As Integer
      For k = 0 To childRows.Length - 1
```

```vb
                Console.Write("          Child Row: ")
                Dim cc As DataColumn
                For Each cc In childTable.Columns
                    Console.Write(" {0} ", childRows(k)(cc))
                Next cc
                Console.WriteLine()
            Next k
        Next parentRow
        Console.WriteLine()

        Dim childRow As DataRow
        For Each childRow In childTable.Rows
            Console.Write("        Child Row: ")
            Dim m As Integer
            For m = 0 To childTable.Columns.Count - 1
                Dim strg As String = _
childRow(childTable.Columns(m).ColumnName).ToString()
                Console.Write(" {0} ", strg.Trim())
            Next
            Console.WriteLine()

            Dim pRow As DataRow
            For Each pRow In childRow.GetParentRows(dr)
                Console.Write("           Parent Row: ")

                Dim p As Integer
                For p = 0 To parentTable.Columns.Count - 1
                    Dim strg As String = _
pRow(parentTable.Columns(p).ColumnName).ToString()
                    Console.Write(" {0} ", strg.Trim())
                Next p
                Console.WriteLine()
            Next pRow
        Next childRow
        Console.WriteLine()
Next dr
```

Next, let us look at the output that this code produces. Note how we loop through each relation. For each relation, we first loop through the parent table and output each row of the parent table with its corresponding child rows. We then loop through the child table and output each row of the child table with its corresponding parent rows.

```
...
Category->BookCategories Relation
  Parent Row:UnitedStates:PoliticalHistory
    Child Row:UnitedStates:PoliticalHistory   E183
  Parent Row:UnitedStates:PoliticalHistory:Opinion
    Child Row:UnitedStates:PoliticalHistory:Opinion E183.1
    Child Row:UnitedStates:PoliticalHistory:Opinion E183.2
```

```
Parent Row:UnitedStates:PoliticalHistory:Predictions
   Child Row:UnitedStates:PoliticalHistory:Predictions
                                         E183.3

   Child Row:UnitedStates:PoliticalHistory    E183
      Parent Row:UnitedStates:PoliticalHistory
   Child Row:UnitedStates:PoliticalHistory:Opinion  E183.1
      Parent Row:UnitedStates:PoliticalHistory:Opinion
   Child Row:UnitedStates:PoliticalHistory:Opinion E183.2
      Parent Row:UnitedStates:PoliticalHistory:Opinion
   Child Row:UnitedStates:PoliticalHistory:Predictions
                                         E183.3
      Parent Row:UnitedStates:PoliticalHistory:Predictions

Book Category LOC->Book LOC Relation
   Parent Row:UnitedStates:PoliticalHistory    E183
   Parent Row:UnitedStates:PoliticalHistory:Opinion E183.1
      Child Row:0-201-62000-0   1
                   The Deadlock of Democracy    E183.1
      Child Row:0-201-62000-3   2
                   Freedom and Order    E183.1
   Parent Row:UnitedStates:PoliticalHistory:Opinion   E183.2
   Parent Row:UnitedStates:PoliticalHistory:Predictions
                   E183.3

   Child Row:0-201-62000-0   1
                   The Deadlock of Democracy    E183.1
      Parent Row:UnitedStates:PoliticalHistory:Opinion
                                         E183.1
   Child Row:0-201-62000-3   2   Freedom and Order    E183.1
      Parent Row:UnitedStates:PoliticalHistory:Opinion
                   E183.1
```

DataRow Editing

BEGINEDIT, ENDEDIT, CANCELEDIT

If you want to make multiple edits to a **DataSet** and postpone the checking of constraints and events, you can enter a dataset editing mode. You enter this mode by invoking the **BeginEdit** method on the row. You leave it by invoking the **EndEdit** or **CancelEdit** row methods.

In the **DataEditing** example, we violate the foreign-key constraint by adding a row with a nonexistent author id. The foreign-key constraint exception will not be raised until the **EndEdit** method is called.

Since we have called **BeginEdit** in the following code fragment, there is no exception caught.

```
Dim rowToEdit As DataRow = books.Rows(0)
rowToEdit.BeginEdit()
```

```
Try
   rowToEdit("AuthorId") = 21

   Console.WriteLine( _
      "Book Author Id Field Current Value {0}", _
      rowToEdit("AuthorId", DataRowVersion.Current))
   Console.WriteLine( _
      "Book Author Id Field Proposed Value {0}", _
      rowToEdit("AuthorId", DataRowVersion.Proposed))
   Console.WriteLine( _
      "Book Author Id Field Default Value {0}", _
      rowToEdit("AuthorId", DataRowVersion.Default))
Catch e As Exception
   Console.WriteLine(vbNewLine & e.Message & _
      " while editing a row.")
   Console.WriteLine()
End Try
```

However, when we invoke the **EndEdit** method on the row, the exception is raised.

```
Try
   rowToEdit.EndEdit()
Catch e As Exception
   Console.WriteLine()
   Console.WriteLine(e.Message & " on EndEdit")
   Console.WriteLine()
End Try
```

The following message is printed out because the illegal value was still present when the editing session was finished.

```
ForeignKeyConstraint Authors->Books requires the child key
      values (21) to exist in the parent table. on EndEdit
```

DATAROW VERSIONS

Before the row changes have been accepted, both the original and the changed row data are available. The item property[14] of the row can take a **DataRowVersion** to specify which value you want. The version field can be **Original**, **Default**, **Current**, or **Proposed.**

```
Console.WriteLine("BeginEdit called for Book AuthorId.")
rowToEdit.BeginEdit()
rowToEdit("AuthorId") = 2

Console.WriteLine("Current Value {0}", _
```

---

14. The item property of the **DataRow** is the indexer for the class.

```
   rowToEdit("AuthorId", DataRowVersion.Current))
Console.WriteLine("Proposed Value {0}", _
   rowToEdit("AuthorId", DataRowVersion.Proposed))
Console.WriteLine("Default Value {0}", _
   rowToEdit("AuthorId", DataRowVersion.Default))

rowToEdit.EndEdit()
Console.WriteLine("EndEdit called.")
   ...
```

This code caused the following output to be printed out:

```
BeginEdit called for Book AuthorId.
Current Value 1
Proposed Value 2
Default Value 2
...
EndEdit called.
Current Value 2
Default Value 2
```

During editing, the **Current** and **Proposed** item values are available. After **CancelEdit**, the **Proposed** value is no longer available. After **EndEdit**, the **Proposed** value becomes the **Current** value, and the **Proposed** value is no longer available.

DATAROW ROWSTATE PROPERTY

In addition to the **Current** and **Proposed** values of a field, the **DataRow** itself has a property that indicates the state of the particular row. The values can be **Added**, **Deleted**, **Detached**, **Modfied**, or **Unchanged**.

A row is in the **Detached** state when it has been created, but has not been added to any **DataRow** collection, or it has been removed from a collection.

The **Default DataRowVersion** of a field returns the appropriate row version depending on the **RowState** property.

ACCEPTING AND REJECTING CHANGES

Calling **EndEdit** on a **DataRow** does not cause the changes to be made to the row. Calling the **AcceptChanges** or **RejectChanges** method on the **DataSet**, **DataTable**, or **DataRow** ends editing on all the contained rows of the appropriate scope. If **EndEdit** or **CancelEdit** has not been called, these methods do it implicitly for all rows within its scope.

After the **AcceptChanges** method, the **Current** value becomes the **Original** value. If **EndEdit** has not been called, the **Proposed** value becomes the new **Current and Original** values. If the **RowState** was **Added**, **Modified**, or **Deleted** it becomes **Unchanged** and the changes are accepted.

After the **RejectChanges** method, the **Proposed** value is deleted. If the **RowState** was **Deleted** or **Modified**, the values revert to their previous values and the **RowState** becomes **Unchanged**. If the **RowState** was **Added**, the row is removed from the **Rows** collection.

Since the **RowState** after **AcceptChanges** is **Unchanged**, calling the **DataAdapter's Update** method at this point will not cause any changes to be made on the data source. Therefore, you should call the **Update** method on the **DataAdapter** to update changes to the data source before calling **AcceptChanges** on any row, table, or **DataSet**.

Code
Example

Here is the code from the case study's **HotelBroker** object's **Cancel-Reservation** method. The code example is in the **HotelBookings.vb** file in the **CaseStudy** directory. Note how **AcceptChanges** on the **DataSet** is called if the **SqlDataAdapter.Update** method succeeds. If an exception is thrown or the update fails, **RejectChanges** is called.

```
Public Sub CancelReservation(ByVal id As Integer) _
  Implements IHotelReservation.CancelReservation

    Dim t As DataTable
    Try
        t = ds.Tables("Reservations")
        Dim rc() As DataRow = t.Select( _
           "ReservationId = " & id & " ")
        Dim i As Integer
        For i = 0 To rc.Length - 1
           rc(i).Delete()
           Dim NumberRows As Integer = _
            adapter.Update(ds, "Reservations")
           If (NumberRows > 0) Then
               t.AcceptChanges()
           Else
               t.RejectChanges()
           End If
        Next
    Catch e As Exception
        t.RejectChanges()
        Throw e
    End Try
End Sub
```

If you do not reject the changes on failure, the rows will still be in the **DataSet**. The next time an update is requested, the update will be rejected again, because the rows are still waiting to be updated. Since the **DataSet** is independent of a database, the fact that an update occurs on the database has nothing to do with accepting or rejecting the changed rows in the **DataSet**.

DATAROW ERRORS

If there have been any data editing errors on a row, the **HasErrors** property on the **DataSet**, **DataTable**, or **DataRow** will be set to true. To get the error, use the **DataRow's GetColumnError** or the **GetColumnsInError** methods.

Acme Travel Agency Case Study

At this point we have covered more than enough material for you to understand the database version of the **Customer** and **HotelBroker** objects in the case study. As usual, the code is in the **CaseStudy** directory for this chapter.

Since there will never be any reason for the **Customer** object to hold any state, the **Customer** object methods use **SqlDataReader** to access the database and return the results. Any state that a program might need (i.e., a list of customers) could easily be maintained in the client program and not in a middle-tier object.

The **HotelBroker** and **HotelBookings** objects are a little more complicated. As mentioned earlier, for pedagogical reasons alone, these objects would have been implemented using a **DataSet** to show you how that technology would work in an application.

Nonetheless, we will see that with Web applications there might be a reason to keep some state in the middle tier. In that scenario the **DataSet** can server as an intelligent cache.

XML Data Access

As we will discuss in Chapter 15, XML has many advantages for describing data that must move between heterogeneous systems and data sources. Since you can validate your XML against an XML schema description, you can pass it in many situations where passing a **DataSet** makes no sense.[15] Since XML is text, it can pass through firewall ports that are normally open, unlike the DCOM or RMI protocols that require special ports to be open.

---

15. When you remote a **DataSet**, it is remoted as XML; nonetheless, if you have to interact with an unmanaged program, you can convert the data in the **DataSet** to XML and send it. As discussed in the Chapter 15, the XML protocol used by remoting and Web services is not identical.

The thrust of these next sections is not to discuss XML in any great detail. We just want to demonstrate how you can move back and forth between looking at data in XML and looking at data with a **DataSet**.

XML Schema and Data

XML does not dictate how data is organized or what the meaning of XML documents are. It only describes the rules on how the documents are put together.[16] An XML schema describes the *metadata* of how the data is organized inside an XML document. XML schemas are written in XML.

For example, XML can be used to describe data in a relational database, but an XML schema can be used to describe relationships such as primary and foreign keys. Having the XML schema and the data in one document or text stream is vastly simpler than having to download each table into a dataset and then programmatically set up the relations between the tables.

XmlDataDocument

Documents can include database output within them. For example, a sales report has an explanation as well as the sales data that was pulled from a data source. The **XmlDataDocument** class can be used to represent data in the form of an XML document.

The **XmlDataDocument** class inherits from **XmlDocument**, which represents an XML document for the .NET XML Framework classes. What makes the **XmlDataDocument** particularly interesting is that you can construct an **XmlDataDocument** from a **DataSet** by passing the **DataSet** instance to the **XmlDataDocument** constructor. The **XmlDataDocument** has a read-only **DataSet** property so that you can work with the XML document as relational data if that makes sense.

DataSet and XML

The **DataSet** has methods, **WriteXml** and **WriteXmlSchema**, that can write out the data and schema associated with the dataset. The XML schema that the **DataSet** writes out is deduced from the current set of tables, columns, constraints, and relations. Unless you explicitly add the constraints to the **DataSet**, such as primary key or foreign key relationships, they will not be part of the schema.

The **DataSet** also has methods to read XML: **ReadXml** and **ReadXmlSchema**. **ReadXml** can read both the data and the schema into the

---

16. Technically speaking, XML documents in the sense that we speak of are defined by the XML Infoset and consist of documents, elements, and attributes.

dataset. If a schema is not present, it will try to infer one from the data. If it cannot infer a schema, it will throw an exception. **ReadXmlSchema** will read in a schema document.

If there is no schema in an XML document, the **DataSet** extracts elements that would be defined as tables according to a set of rules. The remaining elements, along with the attributes, are then assigned as columns to the tables.

You can use the **ColumnMapping** property of the **DataColumn** class to control whether you want columns written as XML elements or attributes. Elements that are not scalar values become tables; attributes and scalar values are columns. The exact procedure is described in the .NET documentation.

AirlineBrokers Database

Sample
Database

The AirlineBrokers database will be used to study XML data access. This database can be created using the SqlServer Enterprise Manager and the **airline-broker.sql** script found in the **Databases** directory of this chapter. The AirlineBrokers database represents another service that the Acme reservation system uses. Acme customers can make airline reservations to the places they wish to go.

The database has several tables:

- Airlines: information about the various airlines in the database.
- PlaneType: the various planes that the airlines use.
- Flights: information about the various airlines' flights.
- Customers: information about customers.
- Reservations: information about the customers' reservations.

Although in real life the Airline Broker and the Hotel Broker would not have the same Customers table, for simplicity we use the same table structure, and we use the same component to access it.

DataSet and XML

Code
Example

To illustrate the relationship between the relation model of the **DataSet** and the XML model, we will first fetch some information from the database. The **DataSetXml** example uses the same commands and techniques we have studied in this chapter to extract the data.

First, the connection, **DataSet**, and the **SqlDataAdapters** for the various tables are created.

```
Dim connectString As String = _
    "server=localhost;uid=sa;pwd=;database=AirlineBroker"
Dim conn As New SqlConnection(connectString)
```

```
Dim d As New DataSet("AirlineBroker")
Dim airlinesAdapter As New SqlDataAdapter()
Dim flightsAdapter As New SqlDataAdapter()
Dim planetypeAdapter As New SqlDataAdapter()
Dim customersAdapter As New SqlDataAdapter()
Dim reservationsAdapter As New SqlDataAdapter()
```

Then the various select commands to fetch the data are created, and the dataset is filled with the data from those tables:

```
airlinesAdapter.SelectCommand = New SqlCommand( _
   "select * from Airlines", conn)
airlinesAdapter.Fill(d, "Airlines")

flightsAdapter.SelectCommand = New SqlCommand( _
   "select * from Flights", conn)
flightsAdapter.Fill(d, "Flights")

planetypeAdapter.SelectCommand = New SqlCommand( _
   "select * from PlaneType", conn)
planetypeAdapter.Fill(d, "PlaneType")

customersAdapter.SelectCommand = New SqlCommand( _
   "select * from Customers", conn)
customersAdapter.Fill(d, "Customers")

reservationsAdapter.SelectCommand = New SqlCommand( _
   "select * from Reservations", conn)
reservationsAdapter.Fill(d, "Reservations")
```

We now have the data for the Airlines, Flights, PlaneType, Customers, and Reservations tables in the dataset.

Next, we have the **DataSet** written out as an XML schema, the schema it infers from the data. Then the **DataSet** writes out the data as XML.

```
d.WriteXmlSchema("Airlines.xsd")
d.WriteXml("Airlines.xml")
```

Here is some of the data that was written to the file **Airlines.xml**. The main element is Airline Broker, which was the name of the **DataSet**. Elements at the next lower level correspond to the various tables that were added to the database: **Airlines**, **Flights**, **PlaneType**, and **Customers**. There were no reservations in the database. There is one set for each row in the table. The elements under each of these tables correspond to the fields for that particular row.

```
<AirlineBroker>
  <Airlines>
    <Name>America West</Name>
    <Abbreviation>AW</Abbreviation>
```

```
    <WebSite>www.americawest.com</WebSite>
    <ReservationNumber>555-555-1212</ReservationNumber>
  </Airlines>
  <Airlines>
    <Name>Delta</Name>
    <Abbreviation>DL</Abbreviation>
    <WebSite>www.delta.com</WebSite>
    <ReservationNumber>800-456-7890</ReservationNumber>
  </Airlines>
...
  <Flights>
    <Airline>DL</Airline>
    <FlightNumber>987</FlightNumber>
    <StartCity>Atlanta</StartCity>
    <EndCity>New Orleans</EndCity>
    <Departure>2001-10-05T20:15:00.0000000-04:00
             </Departure>
    <Arrival>2001-10-05T22:30:00.0000000-04:00</Arrival>
    <PlaneType>737</PlaneType>
    <FirstCost>1300</FirstCost>
    <BusinessCost>0</BusinessCost>
    <EconomyCost>450</EconomyCost>
  </Flights>
...
  <Flights>
  <PlaneType>
    <PlaneType>737</PlaneType>
    <FirstClass>10</FirstClass>
    <BusinessClass>0</BusinessClass>
    <EconomyClass>200</EconomyClass>
  </PlaneType>
...
  <Customers>
    <LastName>Adams</LastName>
    <FirstName>John</FirstName>
    <EmailAddress>adams@presidents.org</EmailAddress>
    <CustomerId>1</CustomerId>
 </Customers>
</AirlineBroker>
```

From the structure of the data, the **DataSet** deduces a schema that was written to **Airlines.xsd**. We discuss here an excerpt from that file. There are no relationships or primary keys defined between any of the tables, such as **Airlines** and **Flights**, as in the database, because none were defined in the **DataSet**. If you look at the actual generated file, you will see that schema information was inferred for **Reservations** even though there was no data in the table.

The schema preamble in the first line, reproduced here, defines the name of the schema as AirlineBroker, and we are using two namespaces in this schema document. One, abbreviated **xsd**, contains the XML Schema standard definitions. The other, abbreviated **msdata**, contains Microsoft definitions.

```
. . .
<xsd:schema id="AirlineBroker" targetNamespace="" xmlns=""
    xmlns:xsd=http://www.w3.org/2001/XMLSchema
    xmlns:msdata="urn:schemas-microsoft-com:xml-msdata">
```

The next line defines an element called AirlineBroker, which has an attribute that indicates this schema came from a **DataSet**. That is a Microsoft-defined attribute, not one defined by the W3C Schema namespace. This element AirlineBroker is a complex type, which means it is a structure composed of other types. This structure can have an unlimited number of any (or even none) of the types defined in the rest of the schema.

```
<xsd:element name="AirlineBroker" msdata:IsDataSet="true">
  <xsd:complexType>
  <xsd:choice maxOccurs="unbounded">
```

The Airlines element is defined next. It, too, is a structure, or complex type, whose elements, if present, appear in the structure in the order in which they were defined. Those elements, which correspond to the columns in the database table, are all defined to be strings that are optional. No primary keys were defined, and these strings are certainly not optional in the database, but that was what the **DataSet** deduced from the set of tables, constraints, and relationships currently defined in the **DataSet**.

```
    <xsd:element name="Airlines">
      <xsd:complexType>
      <xsd:sequence>
        <xsd:element name="Name" type="xsd:string"
                                 minOccurs="0" />
        <xsd:element name="Abbreviation"
                 type="xsd:string" minOccurs="0" />
        <xsd:element name="WebSite" type="xsd:string"
                                    minOccurs="0" />
        <xsd:element name="ReservationNumber"
                   type="xsd:string" minOccurs="0" />
      </xsd:sequence>
      </xsd:complexType>
    </xsd:element>
```

The table Flights is defined similarly to Airlines. In addition to there being no primary key here, there is no foreign key defined for Airline or PlaneType.

```
    <xsd:element name="Flights">
      <xsd:complexType>
      <xsd:sequence>
```

```
            <xsd:element name="Airline" type="xsd:string"
                                minOccurs="0" />
            <xsd:element name="FlightNumber" type="xsd:int"
                                minOccurs="0" />
            <xsd:element name="StartCity" type="xsd:string"
                                minOccurs="0" />
            <xsd:element name="EndCity" type="xsd:string"
                                minOccurs="0" />
             <xsd:element name="Departure" type="xsd:dateTime"
                                 minOccurs="0" />
            <xsd:element name="Arrival" type="xsd:dateTime"
                                minOccurs="0" />
            <xsd:element name="PlaneType" type="xsd:string"
                                minOccurs="0" />
            <xsd:element name="FirstCost" type="xsd:decimal"
                                minOccurs="0" />
            <xsd:element name="BusinessCost"
                        type="xsd:decimal" minOccurs="0" />
            <xsd:element name="EconomyCost"
                        type="xsd:decimal" minOccurs="0" />
        </xsd:sequence>
        </xsd:complexType>
      </xsd:element>
...
  </xsd:choice>
  </xsd:complexType>
</xsd:element>
</xsd:schema>
```

We will come back to this schema definition, but for the moment, let us continue to work with this example.

Creating an XML Doc from a DataSet

We create a new XML document from the **DataSet**. Using an XPath query to get the top of the document, we set up an **XmlNodeReader** to read through it. We can then print out the contents of the document to the console. The **XmlNodeReader** class knows how to navigate through the document.

```
Dim xmldoc As New XmlDataDocument(d)
Dim xmlreader As XmlNodeReader

Try
   Dim node As XmlNode = xmldoc.SelectSingleNode("/")
   xmlreader = New XmlNodeReader(node)
   FormatXml(xmlreader)
Catch e As Exception
   Console.WriteLine("Exception: {0}", e.ToString())
Finally
```

```
      If Not xmlreader Is Nothing Then
          xmlreader.Close()
      End If
  End Try

  ...

  Sub FormatXml(ByVal reader As XmlReader)
     Do While reader.Read()
        Select Case reader.NodeType
           ...
           Case XmlNodeType.Element
              Format(reader, "Element")
              Do While reader.MoveToNextAttribute()
                 Format(reader, "Attribute")
              Loop
           Case XmlNodeType.Text
              Format(reader, "Text")
           Case XmlNodeType.Whitespace
              Format(reader, "Whitespace")
        End Select
     Loop
  End Sub

  Sub Format(ByVal reader As XmlReader, _
   ByVal nodeType As String)
     Static lastNodeType As String = ""
     If nodeType = "Element" Then
        If lastNodeType = "Element" Then
           Console.WriteLine()
        End If
        Dim i As Integer
        For i = 0 To reader.Depth - 1
           Console.Write("  ")
        Next
        Console.Write(reader.Name)
     ElseIf nodeType = "Text" Then
        Console.WriteLine("={0}", reader.Value)
     Else
        Console.Write(nodeType & "<" & reader.Name & _
           ">" & reader.Value)
        Console.WriteLine()
     End If
     lastNodeType = nodeType

  End Sub
```

The results resemble the XML that the **DataSet** wrote to a file.

```
AirlineBroker
  Airlines
```

```
    Name=America West
    Abbreviation=AW
    WebSite=www.americawest.com
    ReservationNumber=555-555-1212
Airlines
    Name=Delta
    Abbreviation=DL
    WebSite=www.delta.com
    ReservationNumber=800-456-7890
Airlines
    Name=Northwest
    Abbreviation=NW
    WebSite=www.northwest.com
    ReservationNumber=888-111-2222
Airlines
    Name=Piedmont
    Abbreviation=P
    WebSite=www.piedmont.com
    ReservationNumber=888-222-333
Airlines
    Name=Southwest
    Abbreviation=S
    WebSite=www.southwest.com
    ReservationNumber=1-800-111-222
Airlines
    Name=United
    Abbreviation=UAL
    WebSite=www.ual.com
    ReservationNumber=800-123-4568
Flights
    Airline=DL
    FlightNumber=987
    StartCity=Atlanta
    EndCity=New Orleans
    Departure=2001-10-05T20:15:00.0000000-04:00
    Arrival=2001-10-05T22:30:00.0000000-04:00
    PlaneType=737
    FirstCost=1300
    BusinessCost=0
    EconomyCost=450
Flights
    Airline=UAL
    FlightNumber=54
    StartCity=Boston
    EndCity=Los Angeles
    Departure=2001-10-01T10:00:00.0000000-04:00
    Arrival=2001-10-01T13:00:00.0000000-04:00
    PlaneType=767
    FirstCost=1500
    BusinessCost=1000
```

```
           EconomyCost=300
      PlaneType
        PlaneType=737
        FirstClass=10
        BusinessClass=0
        EconomyClass=200
      PlaneType
        PlaneType=767
        FirstClass=10
        BusinessClass=30
        EconomyClass=300
      Customers
        LastName=Adams
        FirstName=John
        EmailAddress=adams@presidents.org
        CustomerId=1
```

Schema with Relationships

If we add relationships to the schema we just created, we can use the schema to create a typed data class to work with our database.

We could do that programmatically by adding constraints and relationships to the dataset, as discussed earlier in the chapter, and then writing out the schema. The **DataSchemaXml** example does just that. You could also create a schema document by hand or edit the one we generated in the previous example.

The XSD Tool directory has a schema that has been revised to add the relationships between the tables in the AirlineBroker database. The first part of the file, **AirlineBroker.xsd**, looks like the previous version except that the **minOccurs=0** attribute has been removed from all the fields because we do not allow nulls in any of them.

```
. . .
  <xsd:element name="Airlines">
     <xsd:complexType>
     <xsd:sequence>
        <xsd:element name="Name" type="xsd:string" />
         <xsd:element name="Abbreviation"
                          type="xsd:string" />
        <xsd:element name="ReservationNumber"
                          type="xsd:string" />
        <xsd:element name="WebSite" type="xsd:string" />
     </xsd:sequence>
     </xsd:complexType>
  </xsd:element>
. . .
```

The last section defines the relationships. Here is the definition for the Airlines table primary key. Note the use of attributes in the **msdata** namespace. These attributes are defined by Microsoft using the W3C Schema standard to express additional semantic information about the **DataSet**. These extensions themselves are not a W3C standard. The Schema standard can express constraints with the **unique**, **key**, or **keyref** constructs. Nonetheless, they do not specify which unique key is the primary key.

XPath, which is used to specify relationships to other tables and fields, is a W3C standard for locating elements within an XML file. It is used when an XML constraint has to specify to which other element it refers.

The primary key definition states that the **Airlines_PrimaryKey** is a primary key defined for the **Airlines** element, consisting of the subelement, **Name**. Note how the **msdata:PrimaryKey** attribute is used in conjunction with the standard **unique** construct.

```
    <xsd:unique name="Airlines_PrimaryKey"
                                msdata:PrimaryKey="true">
    <xsd:selector xpath=".//Airlines" />
    <xsd:field xpath="Name" />
</xsd:unique>
```

The next section constrains the Abbreviation column in an Airlines row to be unique.

```
<xsd:unique name="Unique_Airline_Abbreviation">
  <xsd:selector xpath=".//Airlines" />
  <xsd:field xpath="Abbreviation" />
</xsd:unique>
...
```

Reservations_x0020_CustomerId is defined to be a foreign key. The CustomerId field in the Reservations table must be found in the CustomerId field of some row in the Customer table.

```
    <xsd:keyref name="Reservations_x0020_CustomerId"
                            refer="Customers_PrimaryKey"

    <xsd:selector xpath=".//Reservations" />
    <xsd:field xpath="CustomerId" />
</xsd:keyref>
```

The foreign key Flights_x0020_Abbrev has some rules defined for it.

```
<xsd:keyref name="Flights_x0020_Abbrev"
                refer="Unique_Airline_Abbreviation"

                msdata:AcceptRejectRule="Cascade"
                msdata:DeleteRule="SetNull">
  <xsd:selector xpath=".//Flights" />
  <xsd:field xpath="Airline" />
</xsd:keyref>
...
```

Typed DataSet

An XML schema can be used to generate a dataset that is "typed." Instead of using the index property of a collection to access an element of the dataset, you can use the name of a column. Here is a fragment from the **Typed-DataSet** example:

```
Dim UAL As AirlineBroker.AirlinesRow = _
    a.FindByName("United")
Console.WriteLine("{0}({1}) ReservationNumber:{2} " & _
    "WebSite:{3}", UAL.Name.Trim(), _
    UAL.Abbreviation.Trim(), _
    UAL.ReservationNumber.Trim(), UAL.WebSite.Trim())
```

You can assign a meaningful name to rows as well as use strong typing to make sure you are working with the data element you want. If you try to set the field **UAL.ReservationNumber** to an integer, the compiler will detect the mistake.

A typed **DataSet** inherits from the **DataSet** class so that everything that is available in a **DataSet** is available in a typed **DataSet**. If the schema of the database changes, however, the typed dataset class must be regenerated.

The **AirlineBroker** class that inherits from **DataSet** is defined in the file **AirlineBroker.vb**, which is automatically generated from an XML schema, as discussed in the next section. This file is created in the **XSD Tool** directory, and it is also included in the **TypedDataSet** project.

```
'------------------------------------------------------------
' <autogenerated>
'      This code was generated by a tool.
...
' </autogenerated>
'------------------------------------------------------------

...

Public Class AirlineBroker
    Inherits DataSet

    Private tableAirlines As AirlinesDataTable

    Private tableFlights As FlightsDataTable
...
```

Generating Typed DataSets

The XML Schema Definition Tool (**Xsd.exe**) is used to transform an XML schema (XSD) to a typed dataset. The syntax for doing this is

```
Xsd.exe /d /l:vb filename.xsd
```

The **/d** switch indicates that a **DataSet** should be generated. The **/l** switch indicates the language. In this case, a VB.NET class will be generated.

The **XSD Tool** directory has a batch file **xmlbuild.bat** that can be used to take the revised AirlineBroker XSD and generate a typed dataset **Airline-Broker.vb**.

Fetching Data with a Typed DataSet

The **TypedDataSet** example shows how to use a typed dataset to access the Airline Brokers database. You define your **SqlConnection** as usual and create a **SqlDataAdapter** instance for each table you want to use. You create whatever **SqlCommands** you need to work with the data. A typed **DataSet** is independent of a database, just like the untyped **DataSet**, so it needs **Sql-DataAdapter** to handle the database operations.

```
Dim connectString As String = _
    "server=localhost;uid=sa;pwd=;database=AirlineBroker"
Dim conn As New SqlConnection(connectString)

Dim airlinesAdapter As New SqlDataAdapter()
Dim flightsAdapter As New SqlDataAdapter()
Dim planetypeAdapter As New SqlDataAdapter()
Dim customersAdapter As New SqlDataAdapter()
Dim reservationsAdapter As New SqlDataAdapter()

Dim airlineBrokerDataset As New AirlineBroker()
```

Next, the select commands are defined to fetch the data, just as for use with a regular **DataSet**. For illustrative purposes, constraint checking is enabled even though it is on by default.

```
airlinesAdapter.SelectCommand = New SqlCommand( _
    "select * from Airlines", conn)
airlinesAdapter.InsertCommand = New SqlCommand( _
    "insert Airlines(Name, Abbreviation, WebSite, " & _
    "ReservationNumber) values(@Name, @Abbrev, @Web, " _
    & "@Reserve)", conn)
airlinesAdapter.InsertCommand.CommandType = _
    CommandType.Text

Dim param As New SqlParameter("@Name", SqlDbType.NChar, 40)
airlinesAdapter.InsertCommand.Parameters.Add(param)
airlinesAdapter.InsertCommand.Parameters( _
    "@Name").SourceColumn = "Name"
...
  airlineBrokerDataset.EnforceConstraints = true;
...
```

Now you can fetch the data. The order in which you do this is important. If Flights data is fetched before PlaneType data, a constraint violation
exception will occur, because the PlaneType field in the Flights table does not
exist.

```
airlinesAdapter.Fill(airlineBrokerDataset, "Airlines")
planetypeAdapter.Fill(airlineBrokerDataset, "PlaneType")
flightsAdapter.Fill(airlineBrokerDataset, "Flights")
customersAdapter.Fill(airlineBrokerDataset, "Customers")
reservationsAdapter.Fill(airlineBrokerDataset, _
   "Reservations")
```

Displaying Data with a Typed DataSet

The strong typing makes it straightforward to display the data:

```
Dim a As AirlineBroker.AirlinesDataTable = _
   airlineBrokerDataset.Airlines
Console.WriteLine(a.TableName)
Console.WriteLine("{0, -18} {1, -20} {2, -20} {3, -15}", _
   "Name", "Abbreviation", "Web Site", _
   "Reservation Numbers")
Dim i As Integer
For i = 0 To a.Count - 1
   Console.WriteLine("{0,-18} {1,-20} {2,-20} {3,-15}", _
      a(i).Name.Trim(), a(i).Abbreviation.Trim(), _
      a(i).WebSite.Trim(), a(i).ReservationNumber.Trim())
Next
...
```

Modify Data with a Typed DataSet

You modify and update the database with a typed dataset just as you do with
a regular dataset. Make sure the correct table is specified in the **Update**
method.

```
airlineBrokerDataset.Airlines.AddAirlinesRow( _
   "Southwest", "S", "1-800-111-222", "www.southwest.com")
NumberRows = airlinesAdapter.Update( _
   airlineBrokerDataset, "Airlines")
If NumberRows = 1 Then
   Console.WriteLine("Southwest added.")
Else
   Console.WriteLine("Southwest not added")
End If
```

Summary

ADO.NET provides classes that enable you to design and build a distributed data architecture. You can access databases in a connected or disconnected mode depending on your concurrency requirements. The **DataSet** enables you to work with data in a relational manner without being connected to any data source. XML can be used to model relational data inside an XML document that contains nonrelational information. A typed **DataSet** gives you the ability to work in a much easier, type-safe fashion with a **DataSet**, provided you have an XML Schema that defines your data.

ASP.NET and Web Forms

*A*n important part of .NET is its use in creating Web applications through a technology known as ASP.NET. Far more than an incremental enhancement to Active Server Pages (ASP), the new technology is a unified Web development platform that greatly simplifies the implementation of sophisticated Web applications. In this chapter we introduce the fundamentals of ASP.NET and cover Web Forms, which make it easy to develop interactive Web sites. In Chapter 15 we cover Web services, which enable the development of collaborative Web applications that span heterogeneous systems.

What Is ASP.NET?

We begin our exploration of ASP.NET by looking at a very simple Web application. Along the way we will establish a testbed for ASP.NET programming, and we will review some of the fundamentals of Web processing. Our little example will reveal some of the challenges in developing Web applications, and we can then appreciate the features and benefits of ASP.NET, which we will elaborate in the rest of the chapter.

Web Application Fundamentals

A Web application consists of document and code pages in various formats. The simplest kind of document is a static HTML page, which contains information that will be formatted and displayed by a Web browser. An HTML page may also contain hyperlinks to other HTML pages. A hyperlink (or just *link*) contains an address, or a Uniform Resource Locator (URL), specifying where the target document is located. The resulting combination of content and links is sometimes called *hypertext* and provides easy navigation to a vast amount of information on the World Wide Web.

SETTING UP THE WEB EXAMPLES

As usual, all the example programs for this chapter are in the chapter folder. To run the examples, you will need to have Internet Information Services (IIS) installed on your system. IIS is installed by default with Windows 2000 Server. You will have to explicitly install it with Windows 2000 Workstation. Once installed, you can access the documentation on IIS through Internet Explorer via the URL **http://localhost**, which will redirect you to the starting IIS documentation page, as illustrated in Figure 14–1.

The management tool for IIS is a Microsoft Management Console (MMC) snap-in, the Internet Services Manager, which you can find under Administrative Tools in the Control Panel. Figure 14–2 shows the main window of the Internet Services Manager. You can start and stop the Web server and perform other tasks by right-clicking on Default Web Site. Choosing Properties from the context menu will let you perform a number of configurations on the Web server.

The default home directory for publishing Web files is **\Inet-pub\wwwroot** on the drive where Windows is installed. You can change this home directory using Internet Services Manager. You can access Web pages

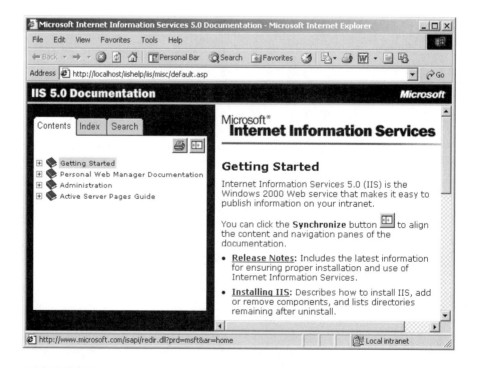

FIGURE 14–1   *Internet Information Services documentation.*

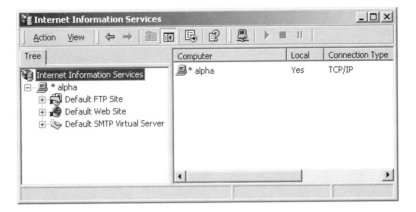

FIGURE 14–2   *Internet Services Manager.*

stored at any location on your hard drive by creating a virtual directory. The easiest way to create one is from Windows Explorer. Right-click over the desired directory, choose Sharing..., select the Web Sharing tab, click on the Add button, and enter the desired alias, which will be the name of the virtual directory. Figure 14–3 illustrates creating an alias **Chap14**, or virtual directory, for the folder **\OI\NetVb\Chap14**. You should perform this operation now on your own system in order that you may follow along as the chapter's examples are discussed.

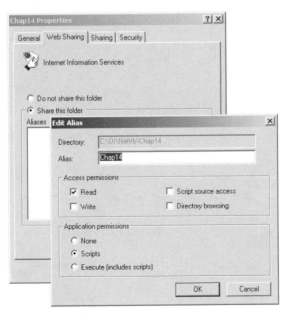

FIGURE 14–3   *Creating a virtual directory.*

Code
Example

Once a virtual directory has been created, you can access files in it by including the virtual directory in the path of the URL. In particular, you can access the file **default.htm** using the URL **http://localhost/Chap14/**. The file **default.htm** contains a home page for all the ASP.NET example programs for this chapter. See Figure 14–4.

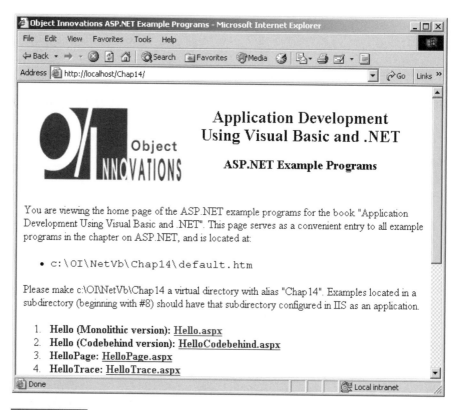

FIGURE 14–4   *Home page for ASP.NET example programs.*

An Echo Program

Code
Example

The first example program for this chapter is **Hello.aspx**, shown as a link on the home page. The example is complete in one file and contains embedded server code. Here is the source code, which consists of HTML along with some VB.NET script code. There are also some special tags for "server controls," recognized by ASP.NET.

```
<!-- Hello.aspx -->
<%@ Page Language="VB" %>
<HTML>
```

```
<HEAD>
   <SCRIPT RUNAT="SERVER">
   Sub cmdEcho_Click(Source As Object, e As EventArgs)
      lblGreeting.Text="Hello, " & txtName.Text
   End Sub
   </SCRIPT>
</HEAD>
<BODY>
<FORM RUNAT="SERVER">Your name: 
<asp:textbox id=txtName Runat="server"></asp:textbox>
<p><asp:button id=cmdEcho onclick=cmdEcho_Click Text="Echo"
runat="server" tooltip="Click to echo your name">
</asp:button></p>
<asp:label id=lblGreeting runat="server"></asp:label>
<P></P>
</FORM>
</BODY>
</HTML>
```

You can run the program using the URL **http://localhost/Chap14/Hello.aspx** or by clicking on the link **Hello.aspx** in the home page of the examples programs. The page shows a text box where you can type in your name, and there is an "Echo" button. Clicking the button will echo your name back, with a "Hello" greeting. The simple form is again displayed, so you could try out other names. If you slide the browser's mouse cursor over the button, you will see the tool tip "Click to echo your name" displayed in a yellow box. Figure 14–5 illustrates a run of this example.

This little program would not be completely trivial to implement with other Web application tools, including ASP. The key user-interface feature of such an application is its thoroughly forms-based nature. The user is presented with a form and interacts with the form. The server does some processing, and the user continues to see the same form. This UI model is second nature in desktop applications but is not so common in Web applications. Typically the Web server will send back a different page.

This kind of application could certainly be implemented using a technology like ASP, but the code would be a little ugly. The server would need to synthesize a new page that looked like the old page, creating the HTML tags for the original page, plus extra information sent back (such as the greeting shown at the bottom in our echo example). A mechanism is needed to remember the current data that is displayed in the controls in the form.

Another feature of this Web application is that it does some client-side processing too—the "tooltip" displayed in the yellow box is performed by the browser. Such rich client-side processing can be performed by some browsers, such as Internet Explorer, but not others.

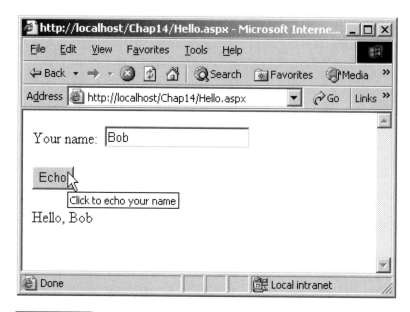

FIGURE 14–5   *Running the **Hello.aspx** echo program.*

As can be seen by the example code, with ASP.NET it is very easy to implement this kind of Web application. We will study the code in detail later. For now, just observe how easy it is!

ASP.NET Features

ASP.NET provides a programming model and infrastructure that facilitates developing new classes of Web applications. Part of this infrastructure is the .NET runtime and framework. Server-side code is written in .NET compiled languages. Two main programming models are supported by ASP.NET.

- Web Forms helps you build form-based Web pages. A WYSIWYG development environment enables you to drag controls onto Web pages. Special "server-side" controls present the programmer with an event model similar to what is provided by controls in ordinary Windows programming. This chapter discusses Web Forms in detail.
- Web services make it possible for a Web site to expose functionality via an API that can be called remotely by other applications. Data is exchanged using standard Web protocols and formats such as HTTP and XML, which will cross firewalls. We will discuss Web services in the next chapter.

Both Web Forms and Web services can take advantage of the facilities provided by .NET, such as the compiled code and .NET runtime. In addition,

ASP.NET itself provides a number of infrastructure services, including state management, security, configuration, caching, and tracing.

COMPILED CODE

Web Forms (and Web services) can be written in any .NET language that runs on top of the CLR, including C#, VB.NET, and C++ with Managed Extensions. This code is compiled, and thus offers better performance than ASP pages with code written in an interpreted scripting language such as VBScript. All of the benefits, such as a managed execution environment, are available to this code, and of course the entire .NET Framework class library is available. Legacy unmanaged code can be called through the .NET interoperability services, which are discussed in Chapter 17.

SERVER CONTROLS

ASP.NET provides a significant innovation known as *server controls*. These controls have special tags such as <asp:textbox>. Server-side code interacts with these controls, and the ASP.NET runtime generates straight HTML that is sent to the Web browser. The result is a programming model that is easy to use and yet produces standard HTML that can run in any browser.

BROWSER INDEPENDENCE

Although the World Wide Web is built on standards, the unfortunate fact of life is that browsers are not compatible and have special features. A Web page designer then has the unattractive options of either writing to a lowest common denominator of browser, or else writing special code for different browsers. Server controls help remove some of this pain. ASP.NET takes care of browser compatibility issues when it generates code for a server control. If the requesting browser is upscale, the generated HTML can take advantage of these features, otherwise the generated code will be vanilla HTML. ASP.NET takes care of detecting the type of browser.

SEPARATION OF CODE AND CONTENT

Typical ASP pages have a mixture of scripting code interspersed with HTML elements. In ASP.NET there is a clean separation between code and presentation content. The server code can be isolated within a single <SCRIPT RUNAT="SERVER"> ... /SCRIPT> block or, even better, placed within a "code-behind" page. We will discuss code-behind pages later in this chapter. If you would like to see an example right away, you can examine the second example program **HelloCodebehind.aspx**, with code in the file **HelloCodebehind.aspx.vb**. (These files are in the top-level chapter directory.)

Code
Example

STATE MANAGEMENT

HTTP is a stateless protocol. Thus, if a user enters information in various controls on a form and sends this filled-out form to the server, the information will be lost if the form is displayed again, unless the Web application provides special code to preserve this state. ASP.NET makes this kind of state preservation totally transparent. There are also convenient facilities for managing other types of session and application state.

Web Forms Architecture

A Web Form consists of two parts:

- The visual content or presentation, typically specified by HTML elements.
- Code that contains the logic for interacting with the visual elements.

A Web Form is physically expressed by a file with the extension **.aspx**. Any HTML page could be renamed to have this extension and could be accessed using the new extension with identical results to the original. Thus Web Forms are upwardly compatible with HTML pages.

The way code can be separated from the form is what makes a Web Form special. This code can be either in a separate file (having an extension corresponding to a .NET language, such as **.vb** for VB.NET) or in the **.aspx** file, within a <SCRIPT RUNAT="SERVER"> ... /SCRIPT> block. When your page is run in the Web server, the user interface code runs and dynamically generates the output for the page.

We can understand the architecture of a Web Form most clearly by looking at the code-behind version of our "Echo" example. The visual content is specified by the **.aspx** file **HelloCodebehind.aspx**.

```
<!-- HelloCodebehind.aspx -->
<%@ Page Language="VB#" Src="HelloCodebehind.aspx.vb"
Inherits= MyWebPage %>
<HTML>
  <HEAD>
  </HEAD>
<BODY>
<FORM RUNAT="SERVER">YOUR NAME: 
<asp:textbox id=txtName Runat="server"></asp:textbox>
<p><asp:button id=cmdEcho onclick=cmdEcho_Click Text="Echo"
runat="server" tooltip="Click to echo your name">
</asp:button></p>
   <asp:label id=lblGreeting runat="server"></asp:label>
<P></P>
</FORM>
</BODY>
</HTML>
```

The user interface code is in the file **HelloCodebehind.aspx.vb**,

```
' HelloCodebehind.aspx.vb

Imports System
Imports System.Web
Imports System.Web.UI
Imports System.Web.UI.WebControls

Public Class MyWebPage
   Inherits System.Web.UI.Page

   Protected txtName As TextBox
   Protected cmdEcho As Button
   Protected lblGreeting As Label

   Protected Sub cmdEcho_Click(Source As Object, _
     e As EventArgs)
      lblGreeting.Text="Hello, " & txtName.Text
   End Sub
End Class
```

Page Class

The key namespace for Web Forms and Web services is **System.Web**. Support for Web Forms is in the namespace **System.Web.UI**. Support for server controls such as textboxes and buttons is in the namespace **System.Web.UI.WebControls**. The class that dynamically generates the output for an **.aspx** page is the **Page** class, in the **System.Web.UI** namespace, and classes derived from **Page**, as illustrated in the code-behind page in this last example.

INHERITING FROM PAGE CLASS

The elements in the **.aspx** file, the code in the code-behind file (or script block), and the base **Page** class work together to generate the page output. This cooperation is achieved by ASP.NET's dynamically creating a class for the **.aspx** file, which is derived from the code-behind class, which in turn is derived from **Page**. This relationship is created by the Inherits attribute in the .aspx file. Figure 14–6 illustrates the inheritance hierarchy. Here **MyWebPage** is a class we implement, derived from **Page**.

The most derived page class, shown as *My .aspx Page* in Figure 14–6, is dynamically created by the ASP.NET runtime. This class extends the page class, shown as *MyWebPage* in the figure, to incorporate the controls and HTML text on the Web Form. This class is compiled into an executable, which is run when the page is requested from a browser. The executable code creates the HTML that is sent to the browser.

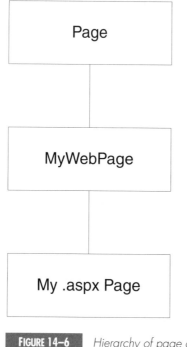

FIGURE 14–6 *Hierarchy of page classes.*

Web Forms Page Life Cycle

We can get a good high-level understanding of the Web Forms architecture by following the life cycle of our simple Echo application. We will use the code-behind version (the second example), **HelloCodebehind.aspx**.

1. User requests the **HelloCodebehind.aspx** Web page in the browser.
2. Web server compiles the page class from the **.aspx** file and its associated code-behind page. The Web server executes the code, creating HTML, which is sent to the browser. (In Internet Explorer you can see the HTML code from the menu View | Source.) Note that the server controls are replaced by straight HTML. The following code is what arrives at the browser, *not the original code on the server.*

```
<!-- HelloCodebehind.aspx -->

<HTML>
  <HEAD>
  </HEAD>
<BODY>
<form name="ctrl0" method="post"
action="HelloCodebehind.aspx" id="ctrl0">
```

```
<input type="hidden" name="__VIEWSTATE"
value="dDwxMzc4MDMwNTk1Ozs+" />
YOUR NAME:  <input name="txtName" type="text"
id="txtName" />
<p><input type="submit" name="cmdEcho" value="Echo"
id="cmdEcho" title="Click to echo your name" /></p>
   <span id="lblGreeting"></span>
<P></P>
</form>
</BODY>
</HTML>
```

3. The browser renders the HTML, displaying the simple form shown in Figure 14–7. To distinguish this example from the first one, we show "YOUR NAME" in all capitals. Since this is the first time the form is displayed, the text box is empty, and no greeting message is displayed.

4. The user types in a name (e.g., Mary Smith) and clicks the Echo button. The browser recognizes that a Submit button has been clicked. The method for the form is POST[1] and the action is HelloCodebehind.aspx. We thus have what is called a *postback* to the original **.aspx** file.

5. The server now performs processing for this page. An event was raised when the user clicked the Echo button, and an event handler in the **MyWebPage** class is invoked.

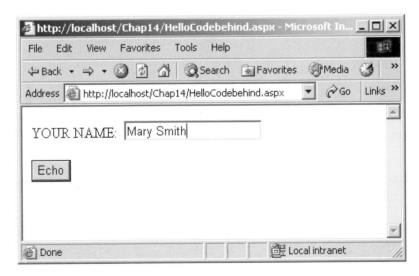

FIGURE 14–7   *The form for the Echo application is displayed for the first time.*

---

1. The HTTP POST method sends form results separately as part of the data body rather than by concatenating it onto the URL, as is done in the GET method.

```
Protected Sub cmdEcho_Click(Source As Object, _
  e As EventArgs)
    lblGreeting.Text="Hello, " & txtName.Text
End Sub
```

6. The **Text** property of the **TextBox** server control **txtName** is used to read the name submitted by the user. A greeting string is composed and assigned to the **Label** control **lblGreeting**, again using property notation.

7. The server again generates straight HTML for the server controls and sends the whole response to the browser. Here is the HTML.

```
...
<form name="ctrl0" method="post"
action="HelloCodebehind.aspx" id="ctrl0">
<input type="hidden" name="__VIEWSTATE"
value="dDwxMzc4MDMwNTk1O3Q8O2w8aTwyPjs+O2w8dDw7bDxpPDU+Oz47
bDx0PHA8cDxsPFR1eHQ7Pjtsc2PEhlbGxvLCBNYXJ5IFNtaXRoOz4+Oz47Oz4
7Pj47Pj47Pg==" />
YOUR NAME:  <input name="txtName" type="text"
value="Mary Smith" id="txtName" />
<p><input type="submit" name="cmdEcho" value="Echo"
id="cmdEcho" title="Click to echo your name" /></p>
   <span id="lblGreeting">Hello, Mary Smith</span>
...
```

8. The browser renders the page, as shown in Figure 14–8. Now a greeting message is displayed.

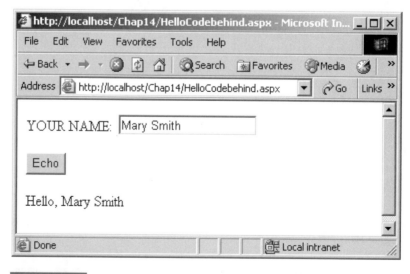

FIGURE 14-8   *After a round trip, a greeting message is displayed.*

View State

An important characteristic of Web Forms is that all information on forms is "remembered" by the Web server. Since HTTP is a stateless protocol, this preservation of state does not happen automatically but must be programmed. A nice feature of ASP.NET is that this state information, referred to as "view state," is preserved automatically by the framework, using a "hidden" control.

```
. . .
<input type="hidden" name="__VIEWSTATE"
value="dDwxMzc4MDMwNTk1O3Q8O2w8aTwyPjs+O2w8dDw7bDxpPDU+Oz47
bDx0PHA8cDxsPFRleHQ7Pjts PEhlbGxvLCBNYXJ5IFNtaXRoOz4+Oz47Oz4
7Pj47Pj47Pg==" />
. . .
```

Later in the chapter we will examine other facilities provided by ASP.NET for managing session state and application state.

Web Forms Event Model

From the standpoint of the programmer, the event model for Web Forms is very similar to the event model for Windows Forms. Indeed, this similarity is what makes programming with Web Forms so easy. What is actually happening in the case of Web Forms, though, is rather different. The big difference is that events get raised on the client and processed on the server.[2]

Our simple form with one textbox and one button is not rich enough to illustrate event processing very thoroughly. Let's imagine a more elaborate form with several textboxes, listboxes, checkboxes, buttons, and the like. Because round trips to the server are expensive, events do not automatically cause a postback to the server. Server controls have what is known as an intrinsic event set of events that automatically cause a postback to the server. The most common such intrinsic event is a button click. Other events, such as selecting an item in a list box, do not cause an immediate postback to the server. Instead, these events are cached, until a button click causes a post to the server. Then, on the server the various change events are processed, in no particular order, and the button-click event that caused the post is processed.

Page Processing

Processing a page is a cooperative endeavor between the Web server, the ASP.NET runtime, and your own code. The **Page** class provides a number of

---

2. Some controls, such as the Calendar control, raise some events on the server. Also, the Page itself raises events on the server.

events, which you can handle to hook into page processing. The **Page** class also has properties and methods that you can use. We cover some of the major ones here. For a complete description, consult the .NET Framework documentation. The example programs in this chapter will illustrate features of the **Page** class.

PAGE EVENTS

A number of events are raised on the server as part of the normal processing of a page. These events are actually defined in the **Control** base class and so are available to server controls also. The most important ones are listed below.

- **Init** is the first step in the page's life cycle and occurs when the page is initialized. There is no view-state information for any of the controls at this point.
- **Load** occurs when the controls are loaded into the page. View-state information for the controls is now available.
- **PreRender** occurs just before the controls are rendered to the output stream. Normally this event is not handled by a page but is important for implementing your own server controls.
- **Unload** occurs when the controls are unloaded from the page. At this point it is too late to write your own data to the output stream.

PAGE PROPERTIES

The **Page** class has a number of important properties. Some of the most useful are listed below.

- **EnableViewState** indicates whether the page maintains view state for itself and its controls. You can get or set this property. The default is **true**, view state is maintained.
- **ErrorPage** specifies the error page to which the browser should be redirected in case an unhandled exception occurs.
- **IsPostBack** indicates whether the page is being loaded in response to a postback from the client or is being loaded for the first time.
- **IsValid** indicates whether page validation succeeded.[3]
- **Request** gets the HTTP Request object, which allows you to access data from incoming HTTP requests.
- **Response** gets the HTTP Response object, which allows you to send response data to a browser.
- **Session** gets the current Session object, which is provided by ASP.NET for storing session state.

---

3. We discuss validation later in this chapter in the section "Server Controls."

● **Trace** gets a **TraceContext** object for the page, which you can use to write out trace information.

SAMPLE PROGRAM

Code Example

We can illustrate some of these features of page processing with a simple extension to our Echo program. The page **HelloPage.aspx** (located in the top-level chapter directory) provides handlers for a number of page events, and we write simple text to the output stream, using the **Response** property. For each event we show the current text in the **txtName** and **lblGreeting** server controls. In the handler for **Load** we also show the current value of **IsPostBack**, which should be **false** the first time the page is accessed, and subsequently **true**.

```
<!-- HelloPage.aspx -->
<%@ Page Language="VB" Debug="true" %>
<HTML>
<HEAD>
 <SCRIPT RUNAT="SERVER">
Sub cmdEcho_Click(Source As Object, e As EventArgs)
    lblGreeting.Text="Hello, " & txtName.Text
End Sub

Sub Page_Init(sender As Object, E As EventArgs)
    Response.Write("Page_Init<br>")
    Response.Write("txtName = " & txtName.Text & "<br>")
    Response.Write("lblGreeting = " & lblGreeting.Text _
        & "<br>")
End Sub

Sub Page_Load(sender As Object, E As EventArgs)
    Response.Write("Page_Load<br>")
    Response.Write("IsPostBack = " & IsPostBack & "<br>")
    Response.Write("txtName = " & txtName.Text & "<br>")
    Response.Write("lblGreeting = " & lblGreeting.Text _
        & "<br>")
End Sub

Sub Page_PreRender(sender As Object, E As EventArgs)
    Response.Write("Page_PreRender<br>")
    Response.Write("txtName = " & txtName.Text & "<br>")
    Response.Write("lblGreeting = " & lblGreeting.Text _
        & "<br>")
End Sub

</SCRIPT>
</HEAD>
<BODY>
<FORM RUNAT="SERVER">Your name: 
<asp:textbox id=txtName Runat="server"></asp:textbox>
```

```
<p><asp:button id=cmdEcho onclick=cmdEcho_Click Text="Echo"
runat="server" tooltip="Click to echo your name">
</asp:button></p>
<asp:label id=lblGreeting runat="server"></asp:label>
<P></P>
</FORM>
</BODY>
</HTML>
```

When we display the page the first time the output reflects the fact that both the text box and the label are empty, since we have entered no information. **IsPostBack** is **false**.

Now enter a name and click the Echo button. We obtain the following output from our handlers for the page events:

```
Page_Init
txtName =
lblGreeting =
Page_Load
IsPostBack = True
txtName = Robert
lblGreeting =
Page_PreRender
txtName = Robert
lblGreeting = Hello, Robert
```

In **Page_Init** there is no information for either control, since view state is not available at page initialization. In **Page_Load** the text box has data, but the label does not, since the click-event handler has not yet been invoked. **IsPostBack** is now **true**. In **Page_PreRender** both controls now have data.

Click Echo a second time. Again, the controls have no data in **Page_Init**. This time, however, in **Page_Load** the view state provides data for both controls. Figure 14–9 shows the browser output after Echo has been clicked a second time.

Page Directive

An **.aspx** file may contain a *page directive* defining various attributes that can control how ASP.NET processes the page. A page directive contains one or more attribute/value pairs of the form

```
attribute="value"
```

within the page directive syntax

```
<@ Page ... @>
```

Our example program **HelloCodebehind.aspx** illustrates an **.aspx** page that does not have any code within it. The code-behind file **HelloCode-behind.aspx.vb** that has the code is specified using the **Src** attribute.

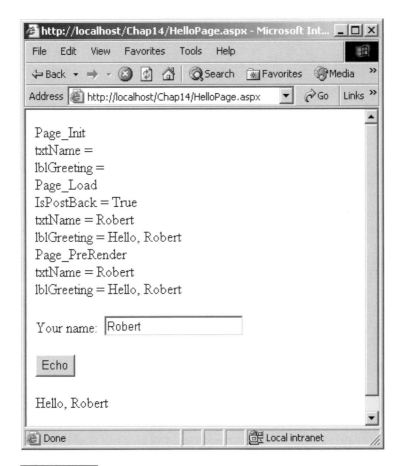

FIGURE 14–9   *Browser output after Echo has been clicked a second time.*

```
<!-- HelloCodebehind.aspx -->
<%@ Page Language="VB" Src="HelloCodebehind.aspx.vb"
Inherits=MyWebPage %>
...
```

Src

The **Src** attribute identifies the code-behind file.

Language

The **Language** attribute specifies the language used for the page. The code in this language may be in either a code-behind file or a SCRIPT block within the same file. Values can be any .NET-supported language, including C# and VB.NET.

Inherits

The **Inherits** directive specifies the page class from which the **.aspx** page class will inherit.

Debug

The **Debug** attribute indicates whether the page should be compiled with debug information. If **true**, debug information is enabled, and the browser can provide detailed information about compile errors. The default is **false**.

ErrorPage

The **ErrorPage** attribute specifies a target URL to which the browser will be redirected in the event that an unhandled exception occurs on the page.

Trace

The **Trace** attribute indicates whether tracing is enabled. A value of **true** turns tracing on. The default is **false**.

Tracing

ASP.NET provides extensive tracing capabilities. Merely setting the **Trace** attribute for a page to **true** will cause trace output generated by ASP.NET to be sent to the browser. In addition, you can output your own trace information using the **Write** method of the **TraceContext** object, which is obtained from the **Trace** property of the **Page**.

Code
Example

The page **HelloTrace.aspx** illustrates using tracing in place of writing to the **Response** object.

```
<!-- HelloTrace.aspx -->
<%@ Page Language="C#" Debug="true" Trace = "true" %>
<HTML>
<HEAD>
 <SCRIPT RUNAT="SERVER">
Sub cmdEcho_Click(Source As Object, e As EventArgs)
   lblGreeting.Text="Hello, " & txtName.Text
End Sub

Sub Page_Init(sender As Object, E As EventArgs)
   Trace.Write("Page_Init<br>")
   Trace.Write("txtName = " & txtName.Text & "<br>")
   Trace.Write("lblGreeting = " & lblGreeting.Text _
      & "<br>")
End Sub
. . .
```

Figure 14–10 shows the browser output after the initial request for the page. Notice that the trace output is shown *after* the form, along with trace information that is generated by ASP.NET itself.

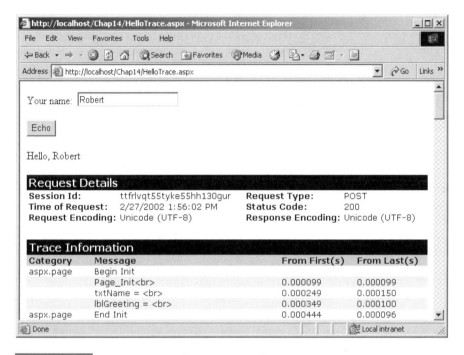

FIGURE 14–10   *Browser output showing trace information.*

Request/Response Programming

The server control architecture is built on top of a more fundamental processing architecture, which may be called *request/response*. Understanding request/response is important to solidify our overall grasp of ASP.NET. Also, in certain programming situations request/response is the natural approach.

HttpRequest Class

The **System.Web** namespace contains a useful class **HttpRequest** that can be used to read the various HTTP values sent by a client during a Web request. These HTTP values would be used by a classical CGI program in acting upon a Web request, and they are the foundation upon which higher level processing is built. Table 14–1 shows some of the public instance properties of

HttpRequest. If you are familiar with HTTP, the meaning of these various properties should be largely self-explanatory. Refer to the .NET Framework documentation of the **HttpRequest** class for full details about these and other properties.

TABLE 14–1	*Public Instance Properties of HttpRequest*
Property	**Meaning**
AcceptTypes	String array of client-supported MIME accept types
Browser	Information about client's browser capabilities
ContentLength	Length in bytes of content sent by the client
Cookies	Collection of cookies sent by the client
Form	Collection of form variables
Headers	Collection of HTTP headers
HttpMethod	HTTP transfer method used by client (e.g., GET or POST)
Params	Combined collection of QueryString, Form, ServerVariables, and Cookies items
Path	Virtual request of the current path
QueryString	Collection of HTTP query string variables
ServerVariables	Collection of Web server variables

The **Request** property of the **Page** class returns a **HttpRequest** object. You may then extract whatever information you need, using the properties of **HttpRequest**. For example, the following code determines the length in bytes of content sent by the client and writes that information to the **Response** object.

```
Dim length As Integer = Request.ContentLength
Response.Write("ContentLength = " & length & "<br>")
```

COLLECTIONS

A number of useful collections are exposed as properties of **HttpRequest**. The collections are of type **NamedValueCollection** (in **System.Collections.Specialized** namespace). You can access a value from a string key. For example, the following code extracts values for the QUERY_STRING and HTTP_USER_AGENT server variables using the **ServerVariables** collection.

```
Dim strQuery As String = _
   Request.ServerVariables("QUERY_STRING")
Dim strAgent as String = _
   Request.ServerVariables("HTTP_USER_AGENT")
```

Server variables such as these are at the heart of classical Common Gateway Interface (CGI) Web server programming. The Web server passes information to a CGI script or program by using environment variables. ASP.NET makes this low-level information available to you, in case you need it.

A common task is to extract information from controls on forms. In HTML, controls are identified by a **name** attribute, which can be used by the server to determine the corresponding value. The way in which form data is passed to the server depends on whether the form uses the HTTP GET method or the POST method.

With GET, the form data is encoded as part of the query string. The **QueryString** collection can then be used to retrieve the values. With POST, the form data is passed as content after the HTTP header. The **Forms** collection can then be used to extract the control values. You could use the value of the REQUEST_METHOD server variable (GET or POST) to determine which collection to use (the **QueryString** collection in the case of GET and the **Forms** collection in case of POST).

With ASP.NET you don't have to worry about which HTTP method was used in the request. ASP.NET provides a **Params** collection, which is a combination (union in the mathematical sense) of the **ServerVariables**, **QueryString**, **Forms**, and **Cookies** collections.

EXAMPLE PROGRAM

Code
Example

We illustrate all these ideas with a simple page **Squares.aspx** that displays a column of squares.

```
<!-- Squares.aspx -->
<%@ Page Language="VB" Trace="true"%>
<script runat="server">
Sub Page_Init(sender As Object, e As EventArgs)
   Dim strQuery As String = _
      Request.ServerVariables("QUERY_STRING")
   Response.Write("QUERY_STRING = " & strQuery & "<br>")
   Dim strAgent as String = _
      Request.ServerVariables("HTTP_USER_AGENT")
   Response.Write("HTTP_USER_AGENT = " & strAgent & "<br>")
   Dim length As Integer = Request.ContentLength
   Response.Write("ContentLength = " & length & "<br>")
   Dim strCount As String = Request.Params("txtCount")
   Dim count As Integer = Convert.ToInt32(strCount)
   Dim i As Integer
   For i = 1 To count
      Response.Write(i*i)
      Response.Write("<br>")
   Next
End Sub
</script>
```

Code
Example

How many squares to display is determined by a number submitted on a form. The page **GetSquares.aspx** submits the request using GET, and **PostSquares.aspx** submits the request using POST. These two pages have the same user interface, illustrated in Figure 14–11.

Here is the HTML for **GetSquares.aspx**. Notice that we are using straight HTML. Except for the Page directive, which turns tracing on, no features of ASP.NET are used.

```
<!-- GetSquares.aspx  -->
<%@ Page Trace = "true" %>
<html>
<head>
</head>
<body>
<P>This program will print a column of squares</P>
<form method="get" action = Squares.aspx>
How many:
<INPUT type=text size=2 value=5 name=txtCount>
<P></P>
<INPUT type=submit value=Squares name=cmdSquares>
</form>
</body>
</html>
```

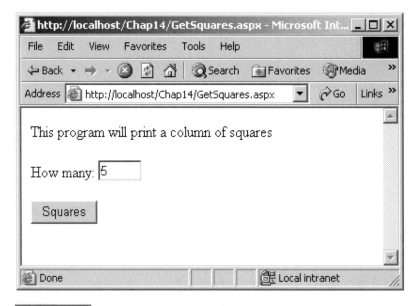

FIGURE 14–11   *Form for requesting a column of squares.*

The **form** tag has attributes specifying the method (GET or POST) and the action (target page). The controls have a **name** attribute, which will be used by server code to retrieve the value.

Run **GetSquares.aspx** and click Squares. You will see some HTTP information displayed, followed by the column of squares. Tracing is turned on, so details about the request are displayed by ASP.NET. Figure 14–12 illustrates the output from this GET request.

You can see that form data is encoded in the query string, and the content length is 0. If you scroll down on the trace output, you will see much information. For example, the **QueryString** collection is shown.

Now run **PostSquares.aspx** and click Squares. Again you will then see some HTTP information displayed, followed by the column of squares. Tracing is turned on, so details about the request are displayed by ASP.NET. Figure 14–13 illustrates the output from this POST request.

You can see that now the query string is empty, and the content length is 29. The form data is passed as part of the content, following the HTTP header information. If you scroll down on the trace output, you will see that now there is a **Form** collection, which is used by ASP.NET to provide access to the form data in the case of a POST method.

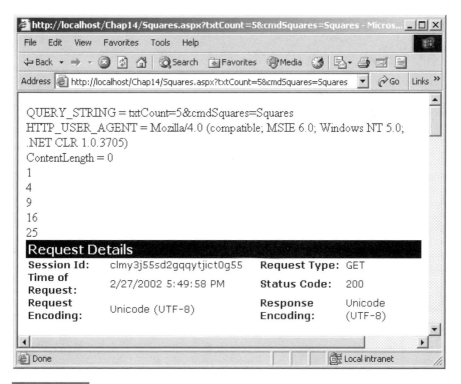

FIGURE 14–12   *Output from a GET request.*

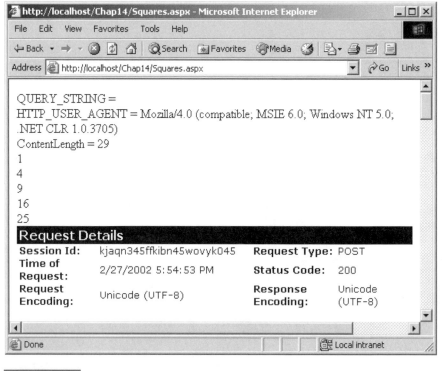

FIGURE 14-13   *Output from a POST request.*

By comparing the output of these two examples, you can clearly see the difference between GET and POST, and you can also see the data structures used by ASP.NET to make it easy for you to extract data from HTTP requests.

HttpResponse Class

The **HttpResponse** class encapsulates HTTP response information that is built as part of an ASP.NET operation. The Framework uses this class when it is creating a response that includes writing server controls back to the client. Your own server code may also use the **Write** method of the **Response** object to write data to the output stream that will be sent to the client. We have already seen many illustrations of **Response.Write**.

REDIRECT

The **HttpResponse** class has a useful method, **Redirect**, that enables server code to redirect an HTTP request to a different URL. A simple redirection without passing any data is trivial—you need only call the **Redirect** method and pass the URL. An example of such usage would be a reorganization of a

Web site, where a certain page is no longer valid and the content has been moved to a new location. You can keep the old page live by simply redirecting traffic to the new location.

It should be noted that redirection always involves an HTTP GET request, like following a simple link to a URL. (POST arises as an option when submitting form data, where the action can be specified as GET or POST.)

A more interesting case involves passing data to the new page. One way to pass data is to encode it in the query string. You must preserve standard HTTP conventions for the encoding of the query string. The class **HttpUtility** provides a method **UrlEncode**, which will properly encode an individual item of a query string. You must yourself provide code to separate the URL from the query string with a "?" and to separate items of the query string with "&".

The folder **Hotel** provides an example of a simple Web application that illustrates this method of passing data in redirection. The file **default.aspx** provides a form for collecting information to be used in making a hotel reservation. The reservation itself is made on the page **Reservation1.aspx**. You may access the starting **default.aspx** page through the URL

```
http://localhost/Chap14/Hotel/
```

As usual, we provide a link to this page in our home page of example programs. Figure 14–14 illustrates the starting page of our simple hotel reservation example.

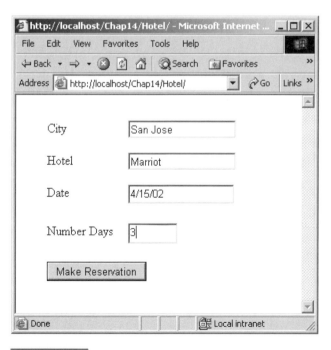

FIGURE 14–14   *Starting page for making a hotel reservation.*

Here is the script code that is executed when the Make Reservation button is clicked.

```
Sub cmdMakeReservation_Click(sender As Object, _
  e As EventArgs)
    Dim query As String = "City=" & _
        HttpUtility.UrlEncode(txtCity.Text)
    query += "&Hotel=" & _
        HttpUtility.UrlEncode(txtHotel.Text)
    query += "&Date=" & _
        HttpUtility.UrlEncode(txtDate.Text)
    query += "&NumberDays=" & _
        HttpUtility.UrlEncode(txtNumberDays.Text)
    Response.Redirect("Reservation1.aspx?" + query)
End Sub
```

We build a query string, which gets appended to the **Reservation1.aspx** URL, separated by a "?". Note the ampersand that is used as a separator of items in the query string. We use the **HttpUtility.UrlEncode** method to encode the individual items. Special encoding is required for the slashes in the date and for the space in the name San Jose. Clicking the button brings up the reservation page. You can see the query string in the address window of the browser. Figure 14–15 illustrates the output shown by the browser.

Our program does not actually make the reservation; it simply prints out the parameters passed to it.

```
<%@ Page language="VB" Debug="true" Trace="false" %>
<script runat="server">
    Sub Page_Load(sender As Object, e As EventArgs)
        Response.Write("Making reservation for ...")
```

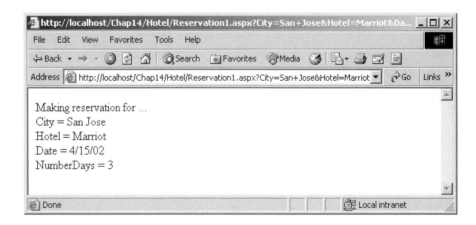

Browser output from making a hotel reservation.

```
        Response.Write("<br>")
        Dim city As String = Request.Params("City")
        Response.Write("City = " & city)
        Response.Write("<br>")
        Dim hotel As String = Request.Params("Hotel")
        Response.Write("Hotel = " & hotel)
        Response.Write("<br>")
        Dim strDate As String = Request.Params("Date")
        Response.Write("Date = " & strDate)
        Response.Write("<br>")
        Dim strDays As String = Request.Params("NumberDays")
        Response.Write("NumberDays = " & strDays)
        Response.Write("<br>")
    End Sub
</script>
<HTML>
<body>
</body>
</HTML>
```

You can turn on tracing (in the file **Reservation1.aspx**), and the trace output should serve to reinforce the ideas we have been discussing about request/response Web programming. In particular, you should examine the **QueryString** collection, as illustrated in Figure 14–16.

Querystring Collection	
Name	**Value**
City	San Jose
Hotel	Marriot
Date	4/15/02
NumberDays	3

FIGURE 14–16 *The query string is used for passing parameters in redirection.*

Web Applications Using Visual Studio .NET

We have examined the fundamentals of ASP.NET and have created some simple Web pages. To carry the story further it will be very helpful to start using Visual Studio .NET. Everything we do could also be accomplished using only the .NET Framework SDK, but our work will be much easier using the facilities of Visual Studio. A special kind of project, an "ASP.NET Web Application," creates the boilerplate code. The Forms Designer makes it very easy to create Web forms by dragging controls from a palette. We can add event handlers for controls in a manner very similar to the way event handlers are added in Windows Forms. In fact, the whole Web application development process takes on many of the rapid application development (RAD) characteristics typical of Visual Basic.

In this section we will introduce the Web application development features of Visual Studio by creating the first step of our Acme Travel Web site. We will elaborate on specific features of ASP.NET in later sections.

Form Designers for Windows and Web Applications

The basic look and feel of the Form Designers for Windows and Web applications is the same. You drag controls from a toolbox. You set properties in a Property window. You navigate between a code view and a designer view with toolbar buttons. In the following discussion we assume you have a basic familiarity with this visual paradigm. You may find it helpful to refer back to Chapter 7.

Hotel Information Web Page (Step 0)

We begin by creating a simple Web page that will display information about hotels. Dropdown listboxes are provided to show cities and hotels. Selecting a city from the first dropdown will cause the hotels in that city to be shown in the second dropdown. We obtain the hotel information from the **Hotel.dll** component, and we use data binding to populate the listboxes. As a source for the **Hotel.dll** and **Customer.dll** components used later, we provide a version of the GUI application from Chapter 7, **AcmeGui**. The **Hotel.dll** component we need in the following demonstration is in the folder **AcmeGui**.

If you would like to follow along hands-on with Visual Studio, do your work in the **Demos** folder for this chapter. The completed project is in **AcmeWeb\Step0**.

CONFIGURING WEB SERVER CONNECTION

Before getting started you may wish to check, and possibly change, your Visual Studio Web Server Connection setting. The two options are File share and FrontPage. If you are doing all your development on a local computer, you might find File share to be faster and more convenient. To access this setting, select the Visual Studio menu Tools | Options.... Choose Web Settings underneath Projects. You can then set the Preferred Access Method by using a radio button, as illustrated in Figure 14–17.

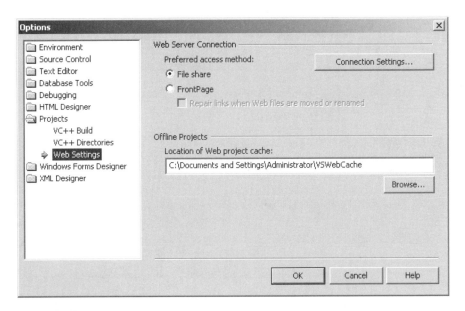

FIGURE 14–17 *Configuring Web server connection preferred access method.*

CREATING AN ASP.NET WEB APPLICATION

1. In Visual Studio select the menu File | New | Project....
2. In the New Project dialog box choose Visual Basic Projects as the Project Type and *ASP.NET Web Application* as the Template.
3. Enter **http://localhost/Chap14/Demos/AcmeWeb** as the location of your project, as illustrated in Figure 14–18. This setting assumes you have made **\OI\NetVb\Chap14** into a virtual directory with alias **Chap14**.
4. Click OK. The project files will then be created in **\OI\NetVb\Chap14\Demos\AcmeWeb**. The VS.NET solution **AcmeWeb.sln** will then be created under **MyDocuments\Visual Studio Projects\AcmeWeb**.

USING THE FORM DESIGNER

1. Bring up the Toolbox from the View menu, if not already showing. Make sure the Web Forms tab is selected.
2. Drag two Label controls and two DropDownList controls onto the form.
3. Change the Text property of the Labels to *City* and *Hotel*. Resize the DropDownList controls to look as shown in Figure 14–19.
4. Change the (ID) of the DropDownList controls to **listCities** and **listHotels**.

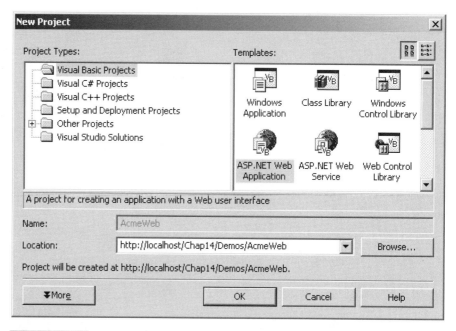

FIGURE 14–18   *Creating a Visual Studio ASP.NET Web Application project.*

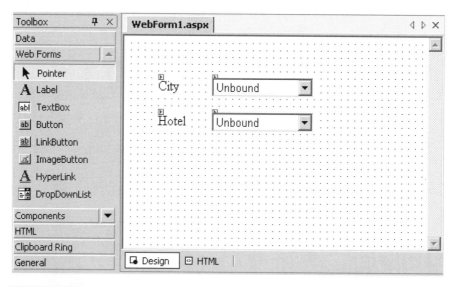

FIGURE 14–19   *Using the Form Designer to add controls to the form.*

INITIALIZING THE HOTELBROKER

1. Copy **Hotel.dll** from **AcmeGui** to **Demos\AcmeWeb\bin**.
2. In your **AcmeWeb**, project add a reference to **Hotel.dll**.
3. As shown in the following code fragment, in **Global.asax**, add the following line near the top of the file. (Use the View Code button 🗏 to show the code.)

```
Imports OI.NetVb.Acme
```

4. Add a public shared variable **broker** of type **HotelBroker**.
5. Add code to **Application_Start** to instantiate **HotelBroker**.

```
' Global.asax

Imports System.Web
Imports System.Web.SessionState
Imports OI.NetVb.Acme

Public Class Global
    Inherits System.Web.HttpApplication

#Region " Component Designer Generated Code "
    ...

    Public Shared broker As HotelBroker
    Sub Application_Start(ByVal sender As Object, _
     ByVal e As EventArgs)
       ' Fires when the application is started
      broker = New HotelBroker()
    End Sub
    ...
```

6. In **WebForm1.aspx.vb** add an **Imports OI.NetVb.Acme** statement, and declare a shared variable **broker** of type **HotelBroker**.

```
' WebForm1.aspx.vb

Imports OI.NetVb.Acme

Public Class WebForm1
    Inherits System.Web.UI.Page
    ...

    Private Shared broker As HotelBroker
    ...
```

DATA BINDING

Next we will populate the first DropDownList with the city data, which can be obtained by the **GetCities** method of **HotelBroker**. We make use of the *data* *binding* capability of the DropDownList control. You might think data binding is only used with a database. However, in .NET data binding is much more general, and can be applied to other data sources besides databases. Binding a control to a database is very useful for two-tier, client/server applications. However, we are implementing a three-tier application, in which the presentation logic, whether implemented using Windows Forms or Web Forms, talks to a business logic component and not directly to the database. So we will bind the control to an **ArrayList**.

The .NET Framework provides a number of data binding options, which can facilitate binding to data obtained through a middle-tier component. A very simple option is binding to an **ArrayList**. This option works perfectly in our example, because we need to populate the DropDownList of cities with strings, and the **GetCities** method returns an array list of strings.

The bottom line is that all we need to do to populate the **listCities** DropDownList is to add the following code to the **Page_Load** method of the **WebForm1** class.

```
Private Sub Page_Load(ByVal sender As System.Object, _
  ByVal e As System.EventArgs) Handles MyBase.Load
    'Put user code to initialize the page here
  If Not IsPostBack Then
      broker = Global.broker
      Dim cities As ArrayList = broker.GetCities()
      listCities.DataSource = cities
      DataBind()
  End If
End Sub
```

The call to **DataBind()** binds all the server controls on the form to their data source, which results in the controls being populated with data from the data source. The **DataBind** method can also be invoked on the server controls individually. **DataBind** is a method of the **Control** class, and is inherited by the **Page** class and by specific server control classes.

You can now build and run the project. Running a Web application under Visual Studio will bring up Internet Explorer to access the application over HTTP. Figure 14–20 shows the running application. When you drop down the list of cities, you will indeed see the cities returned by the **Hotel-Broker** component.

INITIALIZING THE HOTELS

We can populate the second DropDownList with hotel data using a similar procedure. It is a little bit more involved, because **GetHotels** returns an array list of **HotelListItem** structures rather than strings. We want to populate the **listHotels** DropDownList with the names of the hotels. The helper method **BindHotels** loops through the array list of hotels and creates an array list of

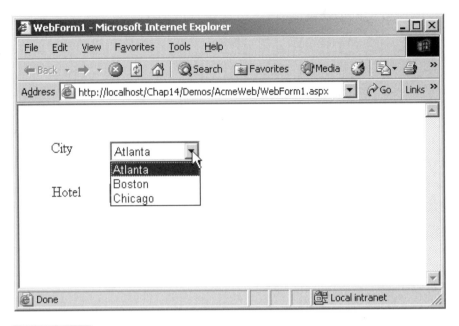

FIGURE 14–20 *Running the Web page to show information about cities.*

hotel names, which is bound to **listHotels**. Here is the complete code, which adds the logic for initializing the hotels for the first city (which has index 0).

```
Private Sub Page_Load(ByVal sender As System.Object, _
 ByVal e As System.EventArgs) Handles MyBase.Load
    'Put user code to initialize the page here
    If Not IsPostBack Then
        broker = Global.broker
        Dim cities As ArrayList = broker.GetCities()
        listCities.DataSource = cities
        Dim hotels As ArrayList = _
            broker.GetHotels(CStr(cities(0)))
        BindHotels(hotels)
        DataBind()
    End If
End Sub

Private Sub BindHotels(ByVal hotels As ArrayList)
    Dim hotelNames As ArrayList = _
        New ArrayList(hotels.Count)
    Dim hotel As HotelListItem
    For Each hotel In hotels
        hotelNames.Add(hotel.HotelName.Trim())
    Next
    listHotels.DataSource = hotelNames
End Sub
```

SELECTING A CITY

Finally, we implement the feature that selecting a city causes the hotels for the selected city to be displayed. We can add an event handler for selecting a city by double-clicking on the **listCities** DropDownList control. This is a shortcut for adding a handler for the primary event for the control. Another method for adding an event handler for this control is to select **listCities** from the first dropdown in the **WebForm1.aspx.vb** code window. You can then choose an event from the second dropdown, as illustrated in Figure 14–21. The second method allows you to add a handler for *any* event of the control. Here is the code for the **SelectedIndexChanged** event:

```
Private Sub listCities_SelectedIndexChanged( _
 ByVal sender As System.Object, _
 ByVal e As System.EventArgs) _
 Handles listCities.SelectedIndexChanged
   Dim city As String = listCities.SelectedItem.Text
   Dim hotels As ArrayList = broker.GetHotels(city)
   BindHotels(hotels)
   DataBind()
End Sub
```

Build and run the project. Unfortunately, the event does not seem to be recognized by the server. What do you suppose the problem is?

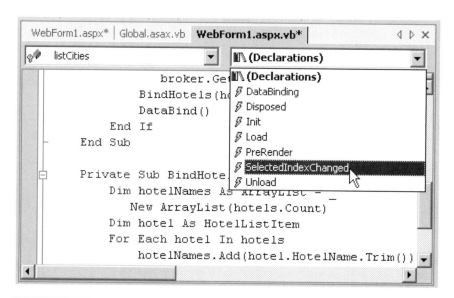

FIGURE 14–21   *Adding an event handler for a control.*

AUTOPOSTBACK

For an event to be recognized by the server, you must have a postback to the server. Such a postback happens automatically for a button click, but not for other events. Once this problem is recognized, the remedy is simple. In the Properties window for the cities DropDownList control, change the **AutoPost-Back** property to **true**. Figure 14–22 illustrates setting the **AutoPostBack** property. The program should now work properly. The project is saved in the folder **AcmeWeb\Step0**.

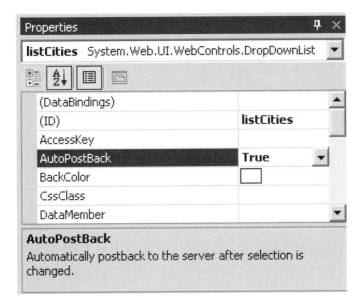

FIGURE 14–22   *Setting the AutoPostBack property of a DropDownList control.*

DEBUGGING

One advantage of using Visual Studio for developing your ASP.NET applications is the ease of debugging. You can set breakpoints, single-step, examine the values of variables, and so forth, in your code-behind files just as you would with any other Visual Studio program. All you have to do is build your project in Debug mode (the default) and start the program from within Visual Studio using Debug | Start (or F5 at the keyboard or the toolbar button ▶).

As an example, set a breakpoint on the first line of the **SelectedIndex-Changed** event handler for **listCities**. Assuming you have set the **AutoPost-Back** property to **True**, as we have discussed, you should hit the breakpoint.

Deploying a Web Application Created Using Visual Studio

Developing a Web application using Visual Studio is quite straightforward. You can do all your work within Visual Studio, including testing your application. When you start a Web application within Visual Studio, Internet Explorer will be brought up automatically. And it is easy to debug, as we have just seen.

Deploying a Web application created using Visual Studio is also easy, but you need to be aware of a few things.

1. The Project | Copy Project... menu can be used to deploy a Web project from Visual Studio.
2. Visual Studio precompiles Web pages, storing the executable in the **bin** folder.
3. The **Src** attribute in the Page directive is not used. Instead, the **Inherits** attribute is used to specify the Page class.
4. The directory containing the Web pages must be marked as a Web application. This marking is performed automatically by Visual Studio when you deploy the application. If you copy the files to another directory, possibly on another system, you must perform the marking as an application yourself, which you can do using Internet Services Manager. (We will discuss this procedure later in the chapter.)

USING PROJECT | COPY PROJECT...

To illustrate using Visual Studio to deploy a Web project, let's deploy the Acme Hotel Information page we have created. We will deploy it to a new directory **AcmeWeb** in the **Deploy** directory for Chapter 14.

1. Bring up the Copy Project dialog from the menu Project | Copy Project....
2. Enter the following information (see Figure 14–23).
   - **http://localhost/Chap14/Deploy/AcmeWeb** for Destination project folder
   - File share for Web access method
   - **\OI\NetVb\Chap14\Deploy\AcmeWeb** for Path
   - "Only files needed to run this application" for Copy
3. You can test the deployment by using Internet Explorer. Enter the following URL: **http://localhost/Chap14/Deploy/AcmeWeb/WebForm1.aspx**. You should then see the hotel information Web page displayed, and you should be able to select a city from the City dropdown and see the corresponding hotels displayed in the Hotel dropdown.

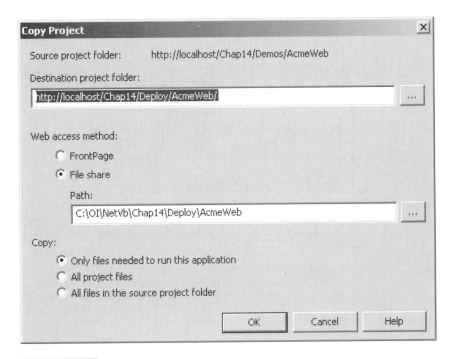

FIGURE 14–23 *Copying Web project files using Visual Studio.*

PRECOMPILED WEB PAGE

Examining the files in the folder **Deploy\AcmeWeb**, you will see no code-behind file **WebForm1.aspx.vb**. Instead, in the **bin** folder you will see the DLL **AcmeWeb.dll**.

INHERITS ATTRIBUTE IN PAGE DIRECTIVE

Examining the file **WebForm1.aspx**, we see there is no **Src** attribute. Instead, the **Inherits** attribute specifies the Page class **WebForm1**, which is implemented in the assembly **AcmeWeb.dll**.

```
<%@ Page Language="vb" AutoEventWireup="false"
Codebehind="WebForm1.aspx.vb"
Inherits="AcmeWeb.WebForm1"%>
```

CONFIGURING A VIRTUAL DIRECTORY AS AN APPLICATION

Code Example

The identical files you copied to **Deploy\AcmeWeb** are also provided in the directory **AcmeRun**. Try the URL **http://localhost/Chap14/AcmeRun/WebForm1.aspx** in Internet Explorer. You will obtain a configuration error, as illustrated in Figure 14–24.

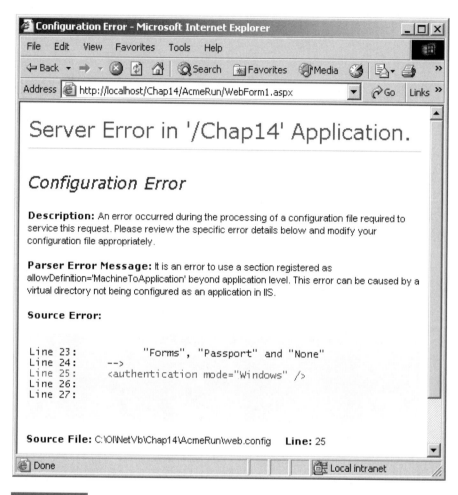

FIGURE 14–24   *Error message when virtual directory is not configured as an application.*

The key sentence in the error message is "This error can be caused by a virtual directory not being configured as an application in IIS." The remedy is simple. Use Internet Services Manager to perform the following steps.

1. Find the folder **AcmeRun** in the virtual directory **Chap14**.
2. Right-click and choose properties. See Figure 14–25. Click Create.
3. Accept all the suggested settings and click OK.
4. Now again try **http://localhost/Chap14/AcmeRun/WebForm1.aspx** in Internet Explorer. You should be successful in bringing up the application.

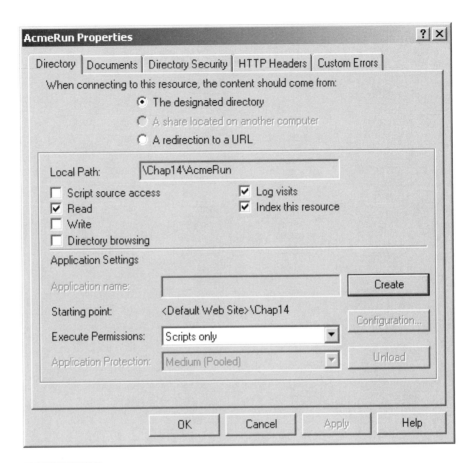

FIGURE 14–25   *Configuring a virtual directory as an application in IIS.*

MOVING A VISUAL STUDIO ASP.NET WEB APPLICATION PROJECT

Sometimes you will need to move an entire ASP.NET Web Application project so that you can continue development under Visual Studio. The simplest way to do this is to use the Visual Studio menu command Project | Copy Project. In the Copy Project dialog, select "All project files" for the Copy option. You will then enter the Destination project folder and the Path, as you did in deploying a Web application project. You will also need to edit the **.vbproj.webinfo** file to specify a correct URL path.

As an example, let's copy the **AcmeWeb** project we have been working on in the **Demos** directory, saving our current work in a new folder, **AcmeWeb0** in the **Demos** directory.

1. Perform Copy | Copy Project, as described above. For Destination project folder enter **http://localhost/Chap14/Demos/AcmeWeb0**. Use

File share as the Web access method. Enter **C:\OI\NetVb\Chap14\ Demos\AcmeWeb0** for the Path.

2. Edit the file **AcmeWeb.vbproj.webinfo** to rename **Web URLPath** to:

```
"http://localhost/Chap14/Demos/AcmeWeb0/AcmeWeb.vbproj"
```

3. Double-click on the file **AcmeWeb.vbproj**. This should bring up Visual Studio and create a new solution with a project **AcmeWeb**.

4. Build the solution. When presented with a Save As dialog, save the solution by the suggested name **AcmeWeb.sln**. You should get a clean build.

5. Try to run the project. You will be asked to set a start page. Set the start page as **WebForm1.aspx**.

6. Build and run. If you get a configuration error, use Internet Services Manager to configure the virtual directory as an application in IIS, as previously discussed. You should now be able to run the application at its new location.

You can view what we have done as establishing a snapshot of Step0. You can go back to new development in the main directory **Demos\AcmeWeb**, and if you want to compare with the original version, you have **Demos\AcmeWeb0** available.

Acme Travel Agency Case Study

Code Example

Throughout this book we have been using the Acme Travel Agency as a case study to illustrate many concepts of .NET. In this section we look at a Web site for the Acme Travel Agency. The code for the Web site is in the **AcmeWeb** directory in three progressive versions: Step0, Step1, and Step2. Step0 corresponds to our Visual Studio .NET demonstration from the preceding section. (A final step, discussed later in the chapter, is a database version of the case study. We deliberately avoid the database during most of the chapter, so as not to distract focus from the core Web programming topics.)

In this section we will give an overview of the case study, and in the next we will discuss some more details about Web applications, using the case study as an illustration.

Configuring the Case Study

Links are provided to the three steps of the case study on the ASP.NET example programs "home page" for this chapter, which you can access through the URL **http://localhost/Chap14/**. To be able to run the Web applications, you must use IIS to configure the directories **AcmeWeb/Step0**, **AcmeWeb/**

Step1, **AcmeWeb/Step2** as Web applications. Follow the instructions provided in the previous section. If you want to experiment with any of the versions in Visual Studio, you can double click on the **.vbproj** file to create a Visual Studio solution.

Acme Web Site Step 1

In Step 1 we provide a simple two-page Web site. In the first page you can make reservations, and in the second you can manage your reservations. We have hard-coded the customer as "Rocket Squirrel," who has a CustomerId of 1.

HotelReservations.aspx

The start page for the application is **HotelReservations.aspx**. Figure 14–26 shows this page in Internet Explorer, after a reservation has been booked at the hotel Dixie in Atlanta.

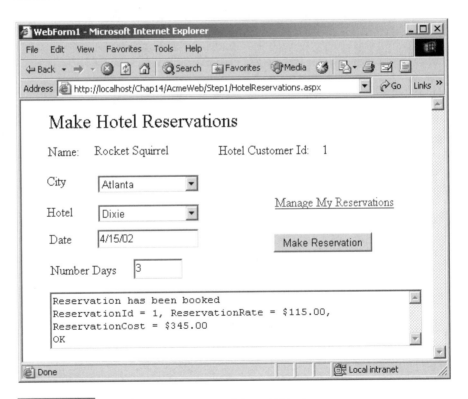

FIGURE 14–26   *Hotel reservations page of Acme Web site.*

The code for initializing the DropDownList controls is the same as for Step 0, as is the code for handling the **SelectedIndexChanged** event for the City dropdown. The key new code is making a reservation. This code should have no surprises for you. It makes use of the **HotelBroker** class, which we already have instantiated for displaying the hotels.

The design of the Web page enables a user to quickly make a number of reservations without leaving the page. We are relying on the postback mechanism of ASP.NET. When done making reservations, the user can follow the link "Manage My Reservations."

ManageReservations.aspx

The second page for the application is **ManageReservations.aspx**. Figure 14–27 shows this page in Internet Explorer, after reservations have been booked for Atlanta, Boston, and Chicago.

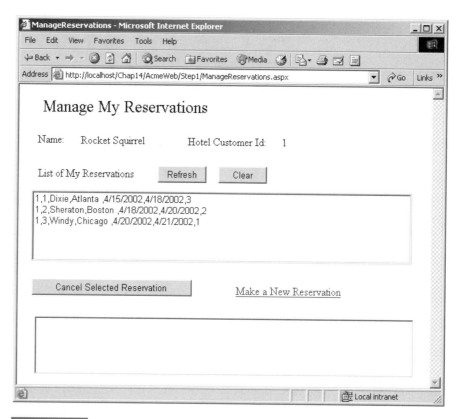

FIGURE 14–27   *Manage reservations page of Acme Web site.*

The user can cancel a reservation by selecting a reservation in the list-box and clicking the Cancel Selected Reservation button. A link is provided to the hotel reservations page. The code for this page is quite straightforward, making use of the capability to provide event handlers in a server-side control. Here is the code for a helper method to show the reservations in the list-box. This code is very similar to the Windows Forms code that we looked at in Chapter 7.

```
Private Sub ShowReservations()
    Dim id As Integer = _
        Convert.ToInt32(lblHotelCustomerId.Text)
    Dim array As ArrayList = _
        broker.FindReservationsForCustomer(id)
    If array Is Nothing Then
        Return
    End If
    ClearReservations()
    Dim item As ReservationListItem
    For Each item In array
        Dim rid As String = item.ReservationId.ToString()
        Dim hotel As String = item.HotelName
        Dim city As String = item.City
        Dim arrive As String = item.ArrivalDate.ToString("d")
        Dim depart As String = _
            item.DepartureDate.ToString("d")
        Dim number As String = item.NumberDays.ToString()
        Dim str As String = id & "," & rid & "," & hotel & _
            "," & city & " ," & arrive & "," & depart & "," _
            & number
        listReservations.Items.Add(str)
    Next
End Sub
```

Acme Web Site Step 2

Code
Example

Step 2 is the full-blown implementation of our Web site case study. Acme customers do not interact with the Hotel Broker directly. Instead, they go through Acme's Web site. In order to use the Web site, a customer must register, providing a user ID, name, and email address. Subsequently, the user can log in by just providing the user ID.

ACMELIB COMPONENT

Internally, Acme maintains a database of user IDs and corresponding Hotel Customer IDs.[4] The interface **IAcmeUser** encapsulates this database main-

---

4. The Web site is Acme's, and Acme maintains user IDs for its own customers. Acme connects to various brokers (such as hotel and airline), and each broker will have its own customer ID.

Code Example

tained by Acme. The class library project **AcmeLib** contains a collection-based implementation of such a database. The file **AcmeTravelDefs.cs** contains the definitions of interfaces and of a structure.

```
' AcmeTravelDefs.vb

Imports OI.NetVb.Acme

Public Interface IAcmeUser
    Function Login(ByVal uid As String) As Boolean
    Function Register(ByVal uid As String, _
        ByVal firstName As String, _
        ByVal lastName As String, _
        ByVal emailAddress As String) As Boolean
    Function Unregister(ByVal uid As String) As Boolean
    Function ChangeEmailAddress(ByVal uid As String, _
        ByVal emailAddress As String) As Boolean
    Function GetUserInfo(ByVal uid As String, _
        ByRef info As UserInfo) As Boolean
End Interface

Public Interface IAcmeAdmin
    Function GetUsers() As ArrayList
End Interface

Public Structure UserInfo
    Public HotelCustomerId As Integer
    Public FirstName As String
    Public LastName As String
    Public EmailAddress As String
End Structure
```

Login will return **True** if **uid** is found. **Register** will register a new user with the Hotel Broker. Methods are also provided to unregister and change email address. These methods will call the corresponding methods of the **ICustomer** interface. **GetUserInfo** will return a **UserInfo** struct as a **ByRef** parameter. This structure defines an Acme user. The method **GetUsers** of the **IAcmeAdmin** interface returns an array list of **UserInfo** structures.

The class **Acme** wraps access to the **Customers** class, whose methods get invoked indirectly through methods of **IAcmeUser**. The class **Acme** also contains a public member **broker** of type **HotelBroker**. Thus to gain complete access to the Hotel Broker system, a client program or Web page simply has to instantiate an instance of **Acme**. Here is the start of the definition of **Acme**.

```
Public Class Acme
    Implements IAcmeUser, IAcmeAdmin

    Public broker As HotelBroker
    Private custs As Customers
```

```
Private users As ArrayList
Private currUser As User

Public Sub New()
   users = New ArrayList()
   broker = New HotelBroker()
   custs = New Customers()
   InitializeUsers()
End Sub

' Initialize users with data from Customers list
Private Sub InitializeUsers()
   Dim arr As ArrayList = custs.GetCustomer(-1)
   Dim cust As CustomerListItem
   For Each cust In arr
      Dim uid As String = cust.FirstName
      Dim custid As Integer = cust.CustomerId
      Dim us As User = New User(uid, custid)
      users.Add(us)
   Next
End Sub
...
```

The class **Acme** also implements the interface **IAcmeAdmin**.

```
Public Interface IAcmeAdmin
   Function GetUsers() As ArrayList
End Interface
```

The method **GetUsers** returns an array list of **UserInfo**.

Login.aspx

To get a good feel for how this Web application works, it would be a good idea for you to register and make a few reservations. You could then try logging in as another user.[5] You can start up the application through the ASP.NET Example programs home page, link to Acme (Step 2), or else directly enter the URL:

```
http://localhost/Chap14/AcmeWeb/Step2/Main.aspx
```

The start page for the application is **Main.aspx**. If there is no currently logged-in user, the new user will be redirected to **Login.aspx**. We will examine the logic in **Main.aspx** shortly. For now, let's do the experiment of registering and logging in. Figure 14–28 shows the login page. In our implementation we offer "Rocket" as a possible user ID. Later you can quickly log in as "Rocket Squirrel" by simply clicking Login. But now click Register.

---

5. We are ignoring security considerations in this chapter. Security in ASP.NET will be discussed in Chapter 16.

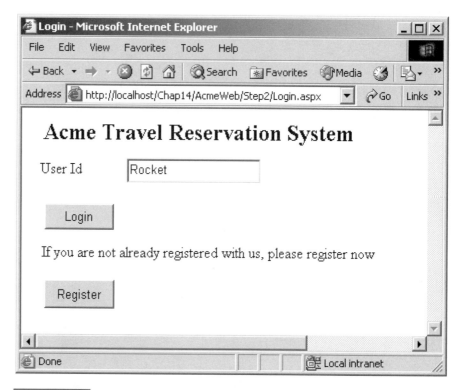

FIGURE 14–28 *Login page of Acme Web site.*

RegisterNewUser.aspx

The "Register New User" page allows the user to pick a User ID and enter some identifying information (first name, last name, and email address). Figure 14–29 shows this page after "John Smith" has entered information for himself. When done entering information, the user should click Register, which will directly bring up the Acme Travel Agency home page, bypassing a need for a separate login.

Main.aspx

The home page of the Acme Web Site is **Main.aspx**. Figure 14–30 shows this home page for the user John Smith, who has just registered. A link is provided to "Login" as a different user, if desired. There are links for "Make a Hotel Reservation" and "Manage Your Reservations." These pages are the same as shown previously for Step 1.

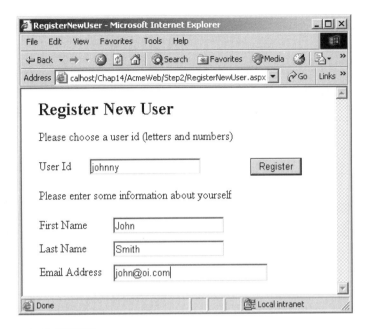

FIGURE 14-29   *Register new user page of Acme Web site.*

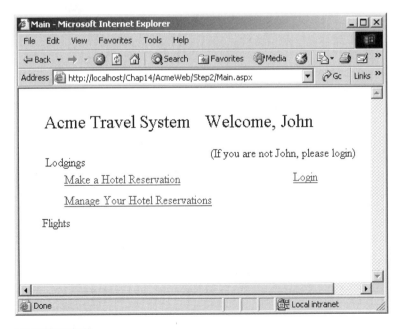

FIGURE 14-30   *Home page of the Acme Web site.*

ASP.NET Applications

An ASP.NET application consists of all the Web pages and code files that can be invoked from a virtual directory and its subdirectories on a Web server. Besides **.aspx** files and code-behind files such as those we have already examined, an application can also have a **global.asax** file and a configuration file **config.web**. In this section we examine the features of ASP.NET applications. We then investigate the mechanisms for working with application state and session state and for configuring Web applications. Our illustration will be our Acme Case Study (Step 2).

Sessions

To appreciate the Web application support provided by ASP.NET, we need to understand the concept of a Web *session*. HTTP is a stateless protocol. This means that there is no direct way for a Web browser to know whether a sequence of requests is from the same client or from different clients. A Web server such as IIS can provide a mechanism to classify requests coming from a single client into a logical session. ASP.NET makes it very easy to work with sessions.

Global.asax

An ASP.NET application can optionally contain a file **Global.asax**, which contains code for responding to application-level events raised by ASP.NET. This file resides in the root directory of the application. Visual Studio will automatically create a **Global.asax** file for you when you create an ASP.NET Web Application project. If you do not have a **Global.asax** file in your application, ASP.NET will assume you have not defined any handlers for application-level events.

Global.asax is compiled into a dynamically generated .NET Framework class derived from **HttpApplication**.

Here is the **Global.asax** file for our AcmeWeb case study, Step 2.

Code
Example

```
' Global.asax

Imports System.Web
Imports System.Web.SessionState
Imports OI.NetVb.Acme

Public Class Global
    Inherits System.Web.HttpApplication

#Region " Component Designer Generated Code "
    ...
```

```
Public Shared acmedat As Acme

Sub Application_Start(ByVal sender As Object, _
 ByVal e As EventArgs)
    ' Fires when the application is started
    acmedat = New Acme()
End Sub

Sub Session_Start(ByVal sender As Object, _
 ByVal e As EventArgs)
    ' Fires when the session is started
    Session("UserId") = ""
End Sub

Sub Application_BeginRequest(ByVal sender As Object, _
 ByVal e As EventArgs)
    ' Fires at the beginning of each request
End Sub

Sub Application_AuthenticateRequest( _
 ByVal sender As Object, ByVal e As EventArgs)
    ' Fires upon attempting to authenticate the use
End Sub

Sub Application_Error(ByVal sender As Object, _
 ByVal e As EventArgs)
    ' Fires when an error occurs
End Sub

Sub Session_End(ByVal sender As Object, _
 ByVal e As EventArgs)
    ' Fires when the session ends
End Sub

Sub Application_End(ByVal sender As Object, _
 ByVal e As EventArgs)
    ' Fires when the application ends
End Sub

End Class
```

The most common application-level events are shown in this code. The typical life cycle of a Web application would consist of these events:

- **Application_Start** is raised only once during an application's lifetime, on the first instance of **HttpApplication**. An application starts the first time it is run by IIS for the first user. In your event handler you can initialize a state that is shared by the entire application.
- **Session_Start** is raised at the start of each session. Here you can initialize session variables.

- **Application_BeginRequest** is raised at the start of an individual request. Normally you can do your request processing in the **Page** class.
- **Application_EndRequest** is raised at the end of a request.
- **Session_End** is raised at the end of each session. Normally you do not need to do cleanup of data initialized in **Session_Start**, because garbage collection will take care of normal cleanup for you. However, if you have opened an expensive resource, such as a database connection, you may wish to call the **Dispose** method here.
- **Application_End** is raised at the very end of an application's lifetime, when the last instance of **HttpApplication** is torn down.

In addition to these events, there are other events concerned with security, such as **AuthenticateRequest** and **AuthorizeRequest**. We will discuss ASP.NET security in Chapter 16.

In the case study, we instantiate a single global **Acme** object instance **acmedat** in **Application_OnStart**. This single instance is stored as a shared data member of **Global**.

In the **Session_Start** event handler we initialize the session variable **UserId** to be a blank string. We discuss session variables later in this section.

State in ASP.NET Applications

Preserving state across HTTP requests is a major problem in Web programming, and ASP.NET provides several facilities that are convenient to use. There are two main types of state to be preserved.

- **Application state** is global information that is shared across all users of a Web application.
- **Session state** is used to store data for a particular user across multiple requests to a Web application.

Shared Data Members

Shared data members of a class are shared across all instances of a class. Hence shared data members can be used to hold application state.

In our case study the class **Global** has a single shared member **acmedat** of the class **Acme**.

Thus the **broker** and **custs** objects within **Acme** will hold shared data that is the same for all users of the application. Each user will see the same list of hotels. You can view the source code for the **Acme** class in the **AcmeLib** project.

Code Example

```
Public Class Acme
    Implements IAcmeUser, IAcmeAdmin

    Public broker As HotelBroker
    Private custs As Customers
    Private users As ArrayList
    Private currUser As User
```

If you like, you may perform a small experiment at this stage. The directory **HotelAdmin** contains a special version of the Acme Web site that makes available the hotel administration interface **IHotelAdmin** to the special user with user ID of "admin". When this privileged user logins, a special home page will be displayed that provides a link to "Administer Hotels," as illustrated in Figure 14–31.

Run this Web application, either from the "Hotel Admin" link on the example programs home page or else via the URL **http://localhost/ Chap14/HotelAdmin/Main.aspx**. Log in as "admin" and follow the link to "Administer Hotels." You will be brought to a page showing a list of all the hotels. Select the first hotel (Dixie) on the list and click the Delete Selected Hotel button and then the Refresh button. You will now see an updated list of hotels, as shown in Figure 14–32.

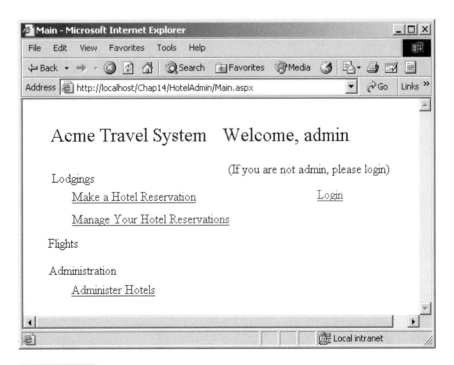

FIGURE 14-31   *Home page of the Acme Web site tailored for administrators.*

FIGURE 14-32 *Hotel administration page after deleting the hotel Dixie.*

If your Web server is on a network, you can now try running the same Web application from a different client. Use the URL

```
http://<server-name>/Chap14/HotelAdmin/Main.aspx
```

where <server-name> is the name of your server machine.[6] Again log in as "admin" and go to the "Hotel Admin" page. You should see the same list of hotels seen by the other client, with hotel Dixie not on the list.[7] You can also experiment with different browser sessions on the same machine, adding and deleting hotels, and using the Refresh button.

---

6. On a local machine you can use either the machine name or "localhost."
7. Remember that at this point we are not using a database. Thus our example illustrates application state preserved in memory.

Application Object

You can store global application information in the built-in **Application** object, an instance of the class **HttpApplicationState**. You can conveniently access this object through the **Application** property of the **Page** class. The **HttpApplicationState** class provides a key-value dictionary that you can use for storing both objects and scalar values.

For example, as an alternative to using the class **Global** with the shared member **acmedat** that we previously used, we could instead use the **Application** object. We make up a string name for the key—for example, "Hotel-State." In **Global.asax** we can then instantiate an **Acme** object and store it in the **Application** object using the following code.

```
Sub Application_Start(ByVal sender As Object, _
  ByVal e As EventArgs)
    Application("HotelState") = New Acme()
End Sub
```

You can then retrieve the **Acme** object associated with "HotelState" by using the index expression on the right-hand side and casting to **Acme**, as illustrated in the code,

```
Dim acmedat As Acme = _
    CType(Application("HotelState"), Acme)
Dim name As String = acmedat.CurrentUserInfo.FirstName
```

As a little exercise in employing this technique, you may wish to modify Step 2 of **AcmeWeb** to use the **Application** object in place of a shared data member. The solution to this exercise can be found in the directory **Applica-tionObject**.[8]

Code Example

Session Object

You can store session information for individual users in the built-in **Session** object, an instance of the class **HttpSessionState**. You can conveniently access this object through the **Session** property of the **Page** class. The **HttpSessionState** class provides a key-value dictionary that you can use for storing both objects and scalar values, in exactly the same manner employed by **HttpApplicationState**.

---

8. In our current example of a Web application that is precompiled by Visual Studio, it is quite feasible to use a static variable that can be shared across pages. But if your application is not precompiled, each page will be compiled individually at runtime, and sharing a static variable is no longer feasible. Hence you will have to use the **Application** object to share data.

Our **AcmeWeb** case study provides an example of the use of a session variable UserId for storing a string representing the user ID. The session variable is created and initialized in **Global.asax**.

```
Sub Session_Start(ByVal sender As Object, _
 ByVal e As EventArgs)
    ' Fires when the session is started
    Session("UserId") = ""
End Sub
```

We use this session variable in the **Page_Load** event of our home page **Main.aspx** to detect whether we have a returning user or a new user. A new user is redirected to the login page. (Note that "returning" means coming back to the home page during the same session.)

```
Private Sub Page_Load(ByVal sender As System.Object, _
 ByVal e As System.EventArgs) Handles MyBase.Load
    'Put user code to initialize the page here
    Dim userid As String = CStr(Session("UserId"))
    If userid = "" Then
       Response.Redirect("Login.aspx")
    End If
    If Not IsPostBack Then
       Dim name As String = _
       Global.acmedat.CurrentUserInfo.FirstName
       lblUserName.Text = "Welcome, " & name
       lblLogin.Text = "(If you are not " & name & _
         ", please login)"
    End If
End Sub
```

There are some interesting issues in the implementation of session variables.

- Typically, cookies are used to identify which requests belong to a particular session. What if the browser does not support cookies, or the user has disabled cookies?
- There is overhead in maintaining session state for many users. Will session state "expire" after a certain time period?
- A common scenario in high-performance Web sites is to use a server farm. How can your application access its data if a second request for a page is serviced on a different machine from that on which the first request was serviced?

SESSION STATE AND COOKIES

Although by default ASP.NET uses cookies to identify which requests belong to a particular session, it is easy to configure ASP.NET to run cookieless. In this mode the Session ID, normally stored within a cookie, is instead embedded within the URL. We will discuss cookieless configuration in the next section.

SESSION STATE TIMEOUT

By default session state times out after 20 minutes. This means that if a given user is idle for that period of time, the session is torn down; a request from the client will now be treated as a request from a new user, and a new session will be created. Again, it is easy to configure the timeout period, as we will discuss in the section on Configuration.

SESSION STATE STORE

ASP.NET cleanly solves the Web farm problem, and many other issues, through a session state model that separates storage from the application's use of the stored information. Thus different storage scenarios can be implemented without affecting application code. The .NET state server does not maintain "live" objects across requests. Instead, at the end of each Web request, all objects in the Session collection are serialized to the session state store. When the same client returns to the page, the session objects are deserialized.

By default, the session state store is an in-memory cache. It can be configured to be memory on a specific machine, or to be stored in an SQL Server database. In these cases the data is not tied to a specific server, and so session data can be safely used with Web farms.

ASP.NET Configuration

In our discussion of session state we have seen a number of cases where it is desirable to be able to configure ASP.NET. There are two types of configurations:

- **Server configuration** specifies default settings that apply to all ASP.NET applications.
- **Application configuration** specifies settings specific to a particular ASP.NET application.

Configuration Files

Configuration is specified in files with an XML format, which are easy to read and to modify.

SERVER CONFIGURATION FILE

The configuration file is **machine.config**. This file is located within a version-specific folder under **\WINNT\Microsoft..NET\Framework**. Because there are separate files for each version of .NET, it is perfectly possible to run different versions of ASP.NET side-by-side. Thus if you have working Web applications running under one version of .NET, you can continue to run them, while you develop new applications using a later version.

APPLICATION CONFIGURATION FILES

Optionally, you may provide a file **web.config** at the root of the virtual directory for a Web application. If the file is absent, the default configuration settings in **machine.config** will be used. If the file is present, any settings in **web.config** will override the default settings.

CONFIGURATION FILE FORMAT

Both **machine.config** and **web.config** files have the same XML-based format. There are sections that group related configuration items together, and individual items within the sections. As an easy way to get a feel both for the format of **web.config** and also for some of the important settings you may wish to adjust, just look at the **web.config** file that is created by Visual Studio when you create a new ASP.NET Web Application project.

```
<?xml version="1.0" encoding="utf-8" ?>
<configuration>

  <system.web>

    <!--   DYNAMIC DEBUG COMPILATION
           Set compilation debug="true" to insert debugging
           symbols (.pdb information) into the compiled
           page. Because this creates a larger file that
           executes more slowly, you should set this value
           to true only when debugging and to false at all
           other times. For more information, refer to the
           documentation about debugging ASP.NET files.
           ...
    -->
    <compilation
        defaultLanguage="vb"
        debug="true"
    />

    <!--   CUSTOM ERROR MESSAGES
           Set customErrors mode="On" or "RemoteOnly" to
           enable custom error messages, "Off" to disable.
           Add <error> tags for each of the errors you want
           to handle.
    -->
    <customErrors
    mode="Off"
    />
```

```
<!--   AUTHENTICATION
       This section sets the authentication policies of
       the application. Possible modes are "Windows",
       "Forms", "Passport" and "None"
-->
<authentication mode= "Windows" />

...

</system.web>
</configuration>
```

Application Tracing

Earlier in the chapter we examined page-level tracing, which can be enabled with the **Trace="true"** attribute in the Page directive. Page-level tracing is useful during development but is rather intrusive, because the page trace is sent back to the browser along with the regular response. Application tracing, which is specified in **web.config**, writes the trace information to a log file, which can be viewed via a special URL.

As a demonstration of the use of **web.config**, let's add application tracing to our original **Hello.aspx** application. The folder **HelloConfig** contains **Hello.aspx** and **web.config**. We have added a trace statement in **Hello.aspx**.

```
<!-- Hello.aspx -->
<%@ Page Language="VB" %>
<HTML>
<HEAD>
    <SCRIPT RUNAT="SERVER">
   Sub cmdEcho_Click(Source As Object, e As EventArgs)
      lblGreeting.Text="Hello, " & txtName.Text
      Trace.Write("cmdEcho_Click called")
   End Sub
    </SCRIPT>
</HEAD>
<BODY>
<FORM RUNAT="SERVER">Your name: 
<asp:textbox id=txtName Runat="server"></asp:textbox>
<p><asp:button id=cmdEcho onclick=cmdEcho_Click Text="Echo"
runat="server" tooltip="Click to echo your name">
</asp:button></p>
<asp:label id=lblGreeting runat="server"></asp:label>
<P></P>
</FORM>
</BODY>
</HTML>
```

We have provided a trace section in **web.config** to enable tracing.

```
<?xml version="1.0" encoding="utf-8" ?>
<configuration>
```

```
<system.web>
  <trace
      enabled="true"
  />
</system.web>
</configuration>
```

You can run this application from Internet Explorer by simply providing the URL **http://localhost/Chap14/HelloConfig/Hello.aspx**.[9] Enter a name and click the Echo button. The application should run normally, without any trace information included in the normal page returned to the browser.

Now enter the following URL: **http://localhost/Chap14/HelloConfig/ trace.axd** (specifying **trace.axd** in place of **hello.aspx**), and you will see top-level trace information, with a line for each trip to the server, as shown in Figure 14–33. If you click on the "View Details" link, you will see a detailed page trace, as we saw earlier in the chapter. The detailed trace corresponding to the POST will contain the trace output "cmdEcho_Click called" provided by our own code.

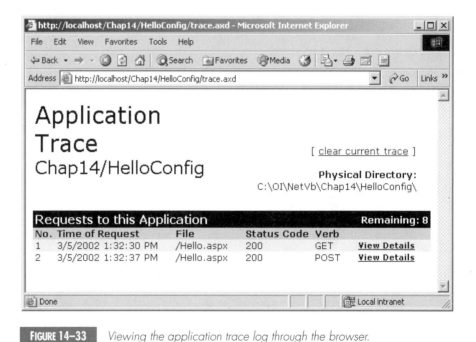

FIGURE 14–33   *Viewing the application trace log through the browser.*

---

9. If you get a configuration error, try configuring the directory in IIS as an application. See "Configuring a Virtual Directory as an Application" in the section "Deploying a Web Application Created Using Visual Studio."

Session Configuration

As another example of configuration, modify the **web.config** file for Step 2 of the case study to change the timeout value to be 1 minute.

```
<?xml version="1.0" encoding="utf-8" ?>
<configuration>
  <system.web>
...
    <!--  SESSION STATE SETTINGS
          By default ASP.NET uses cookies to identify which
          requests belong to a particular session. If
          cookies are not available, a session can be
          tracked by adding a session identifier to the
          URL. To disable cookies, set sessionState
          cookieless="true".
    -->
    <sessionState
          mode="InProc"
          stateConnectionString="tcpip=127.0.0.1:42424"
          sqlConnectionString=
            "data source=127.0.0.1;user id=sa;password="
          cookieless="false"
          timeout="1"
    />
...
  </system.web>
</configuration>
```

   Now run the application, log in, do some work, and return to the home page. You should be welcomed by your name without having to log in again. Now do some more work, wait more than a minute, and return to the home page. Now the session will have timed out, and you will be redirected to log in again.

Server Controls

An important innovation in ASP.NET is server controls. They provide an event model that is startlingly similar to Windows GUI programming, and they encapsulate browser dependencies. They integrate seamlessly into the Visual Studio development environment. The end result is an extremely powerful tool for Web development.

   We have been using server controls from the very beginning of the chapter, where we presented our "Hello" program. In this section we will look at server controls more systematically, and we will see a number of examples of interesting controls.

Web Controls

The most important kind of control in ASP.NET is the *Web Forms server control* or just *Web control*. These are new controls provided by the .NET Framework, with special tags such as <asp:textbox>. These controls run at the server, and they generate HTML code that is sent back to the browser. They are easy to work with, because they behave consistently. For example, you can determine the value returned by a control by using simple property notation.

```
Dim name As String = txtName.Text
```

All of our previous examples of server controls in this chapter have been Web controls. In this section, we will look at several additional kinds of Web controls, including validation controls, list controls, and rich controls such as the Calendar control. But first we will look at HTML server controls.

HTML Server Controls

HTML server controls provide equivalent functionality to standard HTML controls, except that they run on the server, not on the client. In fact, the only way to distinguish an HTML server control from an ordinary HTML control on a Web page is the presence of the **runat="server"** attribute.

Here are two controls. Both are INPUT controls. The first is a server control. The second is of type password and is a regular HTML control.

```
<INPUT id=txtUserId
style="WIDTH: 135px; HEIGHT: 22px" type=text size=17
runat="server"></P>
<INPUT id=""
style="WIDTH: 138px; HEIGHT: 22px" type=password size=17
name=txtPassword>
```

Working with HTML server controls is much like working with the Web Forms server controls we've used already. In server-side code you access the control through a control variable that has the same name as the **id** attribute. However, we are dealing with HTML controls, so there are some differences. You access the string value of the control not through the **Text** property but through the **Value** property. Here is some code that uses the value entered by the user for the **txtUserId** control.

```
lblMessage.Text = "Welcome, " & txtUserId.Value
```

The advantage of HTML server controls for the experienced Web programmer is that they match ordinary HTML controls exactly, so that your knowledge of the details of HTML control properties and behavior carries over to the ASP.NET world. However, this similarity means they carry over all the quirks and inconsistencies of HTML. For example, rather than having two different controls for the somewhat different behaviors of a textbox and a password control, HTML uses in both cases the INPUT control, distinguishing between the two by the **type=password** attribute. Web Forms controls, in contrast, are a fresh design and have an internal consistency. Also, as we shall soon see, there is a much greater variety to Web Forms controls.

HTML CONTROLS EXAMPLE

Let's look at an example of HTML controls. All of our server control examples in this section can be accessed from the page **ServerControls\WebForms1.aspx**. (As usual, you should use IIS to configure the folder **ServerControls** as an application.) The top-level page gives you a choice of three examples,

- HTML Controls
- Validation
- Calendar

Follow the link to HTML Controls, and you will come to a login page, as illustrated in Figure 14–34.

FIGURE 14–34 *A login page illustrating HTML server controls.*

There is a textbox for entering a user ID and a password control for entering a password. Both of these controls are HTML INPUT controls, as shown previously. The textbox runs at the server, and the password is an ordinary HTML control. Clicking the Login button (implemented as a Windows Forms Button control) results in very simple action. There is one legal password, hardcoded at "77." The button event handler checks for this password. If legal, it displays a welcome message; otherwise, an error message.

```
Private Sub btnLogin_Click(ByVal sender As Object, _
 ByVal e As EventArgs) Handles btnLogin.Click
   If Request.Params("txtPassword") = "77" Then
      lblMessage.Text = "Welcome, " & txtUserId.Value
   Else
      lblMessage.Text = "Illegal password"
   End If
End Sub
```

Since the password control is *not* a server control, no server control variable is available for accessing the value. Instead, we must rely on a more fundamental technique, such as using the **Params** collection.[10]

HTML CONTROLS IN VISUAL STUDIO

It is easy to work with HTML controls in Visual Studio.[11] The Toolbox has a palette of HTML controls, which you can access through the HTML tab. Figure 14–35 shows some of the HTML controls in the Visual Studio Toolbox.

You can drag HTML controls onto a form, just as we have done with Web Forms controls. You have the option of using FlowLayout or GridLayout. The default is GridLayout, which enables absolute positioning of controls on a form. FlowLayout is the simplest layout, resulting in elements positioned in a linear fashion. You can set the layout mode through the **pageLayout** property of the form. In our example we used FlowLayout for the two INPUT controls and their associated labels.

The default choice for HTML controls is not to run at the server. To make an HTML control into a server control, right-click on it in the Form Designer. Clicking on Run As Server Control toggles back and forth between running on the server and not running on the server. You can inspect the **runat** property in the Properties panel, but you cannot change it there.

---

10. We described the various collections earlier in the chapter in the section "Request/Response Programming." The collections are included in Table 14-1.

11. But it is also confusing, because there is only *one* palette for HTML controls, and you distinguish between classical HTML controls and server HTML controls by **runat="server"**. The Forms Designer UI for setting this attribute is described below.

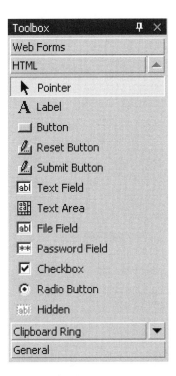

FIGURE 14–35 *HTML controls in the Visual Studio Toolbox.*

Validation Controls

The rest of our discussion of server controls will focus on Web controls. A very convenient category of control is the group of validation controls. The basic idea of a validation control is very simple. You associate a validation control with a server control whose input you want to validate. Various kinds of validations can be performed by different kinds of validation controls. The validation control can display an error message if the validation is not passed. Alternatively, you can check the **IsValid** property of the validation control. If one of the standard validation controls does not do the job for you, you can implement a custom validation control. The following validation controls are available:

- RequiredFieldValidator
- RangeValidator
- CompareValidator
- RegularExpressionValidator
- CustomValidator

There is also a **ValidationSummaryControl** that can give a summary of all the validation results in one place.

An interesting feature of validation controls is that they can run on either the client or the server, depending on the capabilities of the browser. With an upscale browser such as Internet Explorer, ASP.NET will emit HTML code containing JavaScript to do validation on the client.[12] If the browser does not support client-side validation, the validation will be done only on the server.

REQUIRED FIELD VALIDATION

A very simple and useful kind of validation is to check that the user has entered information in required fields. Our second server control demonstration page provides an illustration. Back on the top-level **ServerControls\WebForms1.aspx** page, follow the link to "Validation" (or click the Register button from the Login page). You will be brought to the page **RegisterNewUser.aspx**, as illustrated in Figure 14–36. The screenshot shows the result of clicking the Register button after entering a UserId, a Password, and a First Name, but leaving Last Name blank. You will see an error message displayed next to the Last Name textbox, because that is where the validator control is on the form.

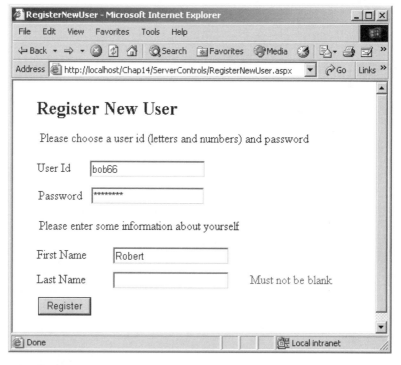

FIGURE 14–36   *Register New User page illustrates ASP.NET validation controls.*

---

12. Validation will also be done on the server, to prevent "spoofing."

The textboxes for First Name and Last Name both have an associated **RequiredFieldValidator** control. In Visual Studio you can simply drag the control to a position next to the associated control. You have to set two properties of the validator control:

- **ControlToValidate** must be set to the ID of the control that is to be validated.
- **ErrorMessage** must be specified.

Then, when you try to submit the form, the validator control will check whether information has been entered in its associated control. If there is no data in the control, the designated error message will be displayed.

Internet Explorer supports client-side validation using JavaScript. You can verify that ASP.NET generates suitable JavaScript by looking at the generated source code in the browser (View | Source).

This form also requires that the UserId field not be blank. Since the primary validation of this field is done by a regular expression validator, as discussed shortly, we will use another technique for the required field validation. Figure 14–37 shows the location of the various validator controls in the Visual Studio Form Designer.

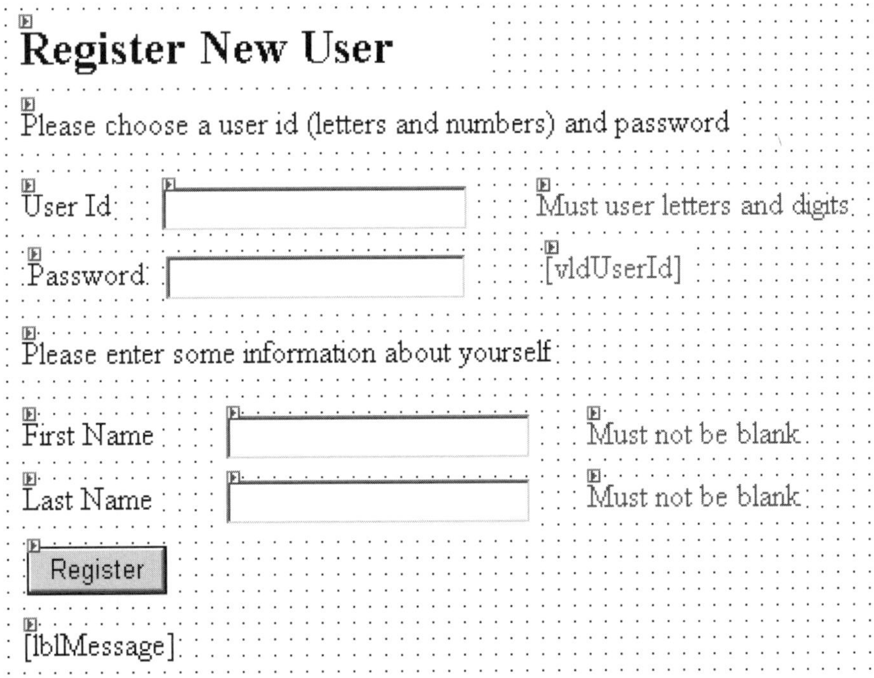

Register New User

Please choose a user id (letters and numbers) and password

User Id: [   ]   Must user letters and digits:

Password: [   ]   [vldUserId]

Please enter some information about yourself

First Name   [   ]   Must not be blank

Last Name   [   ]   Must not be blank

[Register]

[lblMessage]

FIGURE 14–37   *Layout of validation controls for Register New User page.*

We assign the ID **vldUserId** to the required field validator control associated with the UserId control, and we clear the error message. We also set the **EnableClientScript** property to **False**, to force a postback to the server for the validation. The event handler for the Register button then checks the **IsValid** property of **vldUserId**.

```
private void cmdRegister_Click(object sender,
                                    System.EventArgs e)
{
    if (vldUserId.IsValid)
        lblMessage.Text = "Welcome, " + txtFirstName.Text;
    else
        lblMessage.Text = "UserId must not be blank";
}
```

If the control is valid, we display the welcome message; otherwise, an error message. Note that we won't even reach this handler if other validation is false.

REGULAR EXPRESSION VALIDATION

The **RegularExpressionValidator** control provides a very flexible mechanism for validating string input. It checks whether the string is a legal match against a designated regular expression. Our example illustrates performing a regular expression validation of UserId. The requirement is that the ID consist only of letters and digits, which can be specified by the regular expression

```
[A-Za-z0-9]+
```

The following properties should normally be assigned for a **RegularExpressionValidator** control:

- **ValidationExpression** (the regular expression, not surrounded by quotes)
- **ControlToValidate**
- **ErrorMessage**

You can try this validation out on our Register New User page by entering a string for UserId that contains a non-alphanumeric character.

Rich Controls

Another category of Web Forms controls consists of "rich controls," which can have quite elaborate functionality. The Calendar control provides an easy-to-use mechanism for entering dates on a Web page. Our third sample server control page provides an illustration, as shown in Figure 14–38.

The user can select a date on the Calendar control. The **SelectedDate** property then contains the selected date as an instance of the **DateTime** structure. You can work with this date by handling the **SelectionChanged**

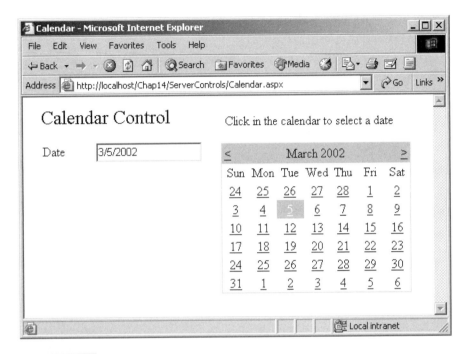

Using the Calendar control to select a date.

event. In our example page, the event handler displays the date as a string in a textbox.

```
Private Sub Calendar1_SelectionChanged( _
  ByVal sender As Object, ByVal e As EventArgs) _
  Handles Calendar1.SelectionChanged
    txtDate.Text = _
       Calendar1.SelectedDate.ToShortDateString()
End Sub
```

Database Access in ASP.NET

A great deal of practical Web application development involves accessing data in various kinds of databases. A great thing about the .NET Framework is that it is very easy to encapsulate a database, allowing the rest of the program to work with data in a very generic way, without worrying about where it came from. In this section we discuss data binding in Web Forms controls, and we then present a database version of our Acme Travel Agency Web site.

Data Binding in ASP.NET

ASP.NET makes it easy to display data from various data sources by permitting a Web Forms control to be bound to data source. The data source can be specified in a variety of ways—for example, by directly giving a connection string to a database. This form of data binding is quite convenient in a two-tier type of application, where the presentation layer talks directly to the database. In three-tier applications it is more convenient to bind to some data structure that is returned by a middle-tier component, which does the actual connection to the database. Our Acme case study illustrates this approach. The **Hotel.dll** and **Customer.dll** components encapsulate access to a SQL Server database through the **HotelBroker** and **Customers** classes. Methods such as **GetCities** return an **ArrayList**, and the array list can be bound to a Web Forms control.[13]

We will look at two examples of data binding. The first, mentioned earlier in the chapter, illustrates binding to an **ArrayList**. The second illustrates binding to a **DataTable** through a **DataView**.

BINDING TO AN ARRAYLIST

Code Example

It is extremely simple to bind to an array list. The **AcmeWeb** example, beginning with Step 0, provides an illustration. You may wish to bring up Step 0 and examine the code in **AcmeWeb\Step0\WebForm1.aspx.vb**. When the page is loaded, the **DropDownList** control **listCities** is initialized to display all the cities in the database of the hotel broker. The **GetCities** method returns the cities as strings in an array list. The following code will then cause the cities to be displayed in the dropdown.

```
broker = Global.broker
Dim cities As ArrayList = broker.GetCities()
listCities.DataSource = cities
...
DataBind()
```

The **DataBind** method of the **Page** class causes all the Web Forms controls on the page to be bound to their data sources, which will cause the controls to be populated with data from the data sources. You could also call the **DataBind** method of a particular control.

---

13. The component could be hidden behind a Web service, which will be illustrated in Chapter 15. We can still use data binding in such a scenario by binding to an array list.

BINDING TO A DATATABLE

As we saw in Chapter 13, ADO.NET defines a very useful class, the **DataTable**, which can be used to hold data from a variety of data sources. Once created, a data table can be passed around and used in a variety of contexts. One very useful thing you can do with a data table is to bind it to a Web Forms control. Since a data table is self-describing, the control can automatically display additional information, such as the names of the columns. We illustrate with the **DataGrid** control.

Code Example

To run this example, you need to have SQL Server or MSDE installed on your system, and you should also have set up the Acme database, as described in Chapter 13. The example Web page is **DataGridControl/ ShowHotels.aspx**. As usual, you should use IIS to configure the folder **Data- GridControl** as an application. This page will display all the hotels in the Acme database in a data grid, with appropriate headings, as illustrated in Figure 14–39. When you work with Web Forms controls you can easily change styles, such as fonts and colors, by setting properties appropriately.

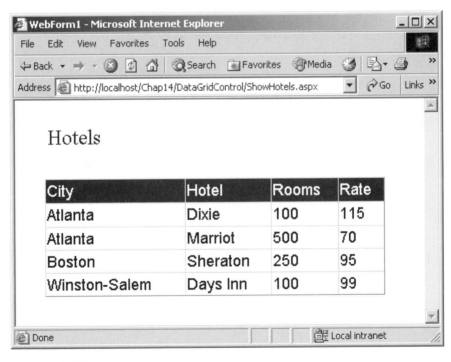

FIGURE 14–39   *Displaying hotels in the Acme database using a DataGrid control.*

The relevant VB.NET code is in the files **Global.asax.vb** and **ShowHotels.aspx.vb**. The first thing we need to do is to create an instance of the **HotelBroker** class. We create a single instance, once, when the application starts up. We save this instance as a public shared variable.

```
' Global.asax.vb

Imports System.Web
Imports System.Web.SessionState
Imports OI.NetVb.Acme

Public Class Global
    Inherits System.Web.HttpApplication

#Region " Component Designer Generated Code "
...

    Public Shared broker As HotelBroker

    Sub Application_Start(ByVal sender As Object, _
      ByVal e As EventArgs)
        broker = New HotelBroker()
    End Sub
    ...
```

In the **Page_Load** method (in file **ShowHotels.aspx.vb**) we get the hotels from the Hotel Broker, call a helper method to obtain the data source, assign the data source, and bind. We are using the **DataTable** to hold data obtained from the middle-tier component.

```
Private Sub Page_Load(ByVal sender As System.Object, _
  ByVal e As System.EventArgs) Handles MyBase.Load
    If Not IsPostBack Then
        broker = Global.broker
        Dim arr As ArrayList = broker.GetHotels()
        dgHotels.DataSource = CreateDataSource(arr)
        dgHotels.DataBind()
    End If
End Sub
```

It is in the helper method **CreateDataSource** that the interesting work is done. A data table is created and populated with hotel data obtained from the Hotel Broker.

```
Private Function CreateDataSource( _
  ByVal list As ArrayList) As ICollection
    If list Is Nothing Then
        Return Nothing
    End If
```

```
Dim dt As New DataTable()
Dim dr As DataRow

dt.Columns.Add(New DataColumn("City", GetType(String)))
dt.Columns.Add(New DataColumn("Hotel", GetType(String)))
dt.Columns.Add(New DataColumn("Rooms", _
   GetType(Integer)))
dt.Columns.Add(New DataColumn("Rate", GetType(Decimal)))

Dim hi As HotelListItem
For Each hi In list
   dr = dt.NewRow()

   dr(0) = hi.City.Trim()
   dr(1) = hi.HotelName.Trim()
   dr(2) = hi.NumberRooms
   dr(3) = hi.Rate

   dt.Rows.Add(dr)
Next

Dim dv As New DataView(dt)
Return dv
End Function
```

Acme Travel Agency Case Study (Database Version)

We have illustrated many concepts of ASP.NET with our Acme Travel Agency case study. For simplicity we used a version of the case study that stored all data as collections in memory. This way you did not have to worry about having a database set up properly on your system, so you could focus on just ASP.NET. Also, the results are always deterministic, since sample data is hardcoded.

Now, however, we would like to look at the "real" case study, based upon our HotelBroker database, and the database version of the **Hotel.dll** and **Customer.dll** components created in Chapter 13.

ACMECUSTOMER DATABASE

The Acme Travel Agency maintains its own database of customers. Customers register with Acme through the Web site. The following information is stored in Acme's database:

- LoginName
- Password
- HotelBrokerCustomerId
- AirlineBrokerCustomerId

Currently we use LoginName (corresponding to what we called "UserId" earlier in the chapter) and HotelBrokerCustomerId. The AirlineBrokerCustomerId field will facilitate Acme adding an airplane reservation system later. A Password field is also provided for possible future use.

The **AcmeCustomer** database should have been set up as part of the database setup from Chapter 13. To set up the **AcmeCustomer** database (or restore it to its original state), all you need to do is to run the script **acmedb.sql**, which is located in the **Databases** directory from Chapter 13. This script assumes you have SQL Server installed on partition **c:**. If your installation is in a different partition, edit the script accordingly.

ACME WEB SITE (CASE STUDY)

Code
Example

The Case Study version of the Acme Web site is in the **CaseStudy** folder for this chapter. As usual, you will need to use IIS to configure this directory as an application. You can start from the home page for this chapter, or directly from the URL

```
http://localhost/netcs/CaseStudy/Main.aspx
```

You should find the code very easy to understand, because it relies on the same interfaces as the implementation we used earlier based on collections. The database code for accessing the **AcmeCustomer** database is in the file **Acme.vb**.

Summary

ASP.NET is a unified Web development platform that greatly simplifies the implementation of sophisticated Web applications. In this chapter we introduced the fundamentals of ASP.NET and Web Forms, which make it easy to develop interactive Web sites. Server controls present the programmer with an event model similar to what is provided by controls in ordinary Windows programming. This high-level programming model rests on a lower-level request/ response programming model that is common to earlier approaches to Web programming and is still accessible to the ASP.NET programmer.

The Visual Studio .NET development environment includes a Form Designer, which makes it very easy to visually lay out Web forms, and with a click you can add event handlers. ASP.NET makes it very easy to handle state management. Configuration is based on XML files and is very flexible. There are a great variety of server controls, including wrappers around HTML controls, validation controls, and rich controls such as a Calendar. Data binding makes it easy to display data from a variety of data sources.

In the next chapter we cover Web Services, which enable the development of collaborative Web applications that span heterogeneous systems.

Web Services

*D*istributing functionality and data beyond the enterprise in which they were developed is the next step in component technology. Developers can integrate into their applications a much more extensive set of services than they could ever hope to develop on their own. Our Acme Reservation System case study is a simple example. The Acme Travel Agency, by using the reservation systems of the airlines and hotels, can provide a wider range of services to their clients.

One vendor will not be able to supply the necessary distributed technology infrastructure. At the very minimum, the worlds of Java, .NET, mobile computers, and legacy systems will continue. Fortunately, TCP/IP and HTTP have established themselves as industry-standard networking protocols and can be the basis for any attempt to interconnect heterogeneous systems. HTTP is a text-based protocol, so using the industry standard XML to describe the interactions of these systems makes sense. *Web services* use XML-based and HTTP-based protocols to provide an industry standard to allow diverse systems to interconnect.

Web services is the second part of the .NET distributed computing story. If all the applications and services that need to interconnect are all based on the Common Language Runtime, .NET remoting can be used. Its advantage is that you can remote any .NET data structure through the remoting serialization. Environments that do not run .NET, however, cannot handle the full range of .NET data types. Hence, Web services transmit only a much more limited set of data structures that can be expressed in the XML-based protocols that Web services use today. The versions of the SOAP protocol used by Web services and by .NET remoting have different programming models. The latter offers full CLR fidelity. The former is constrained by interoperability standards.

Besides the ability of heterogeneous systems to interconnect, Web services allow business partners to share information or integrate with legacy systems without having to write specialized interconnection applications. Even within a single enterprise, you will be able to integrate information from internal and external sources. If Web services are to be more than just distributed application development, however, the necessary financial, reliability, security, and legal infrastructure have to be developed.

Protocols

Behind the Web services technology are several protocols: XML, XML Namespaces, XML Schema, SOAP, and WSDL. Some of these are formal W3C industry standards. Some, like WSDL, are just gaining widespread use without yet being codified in a standard.

XML

XML is a W3C industry standard[1] that provides a way to structure documents to provide relationships between the basic *elements* of the document. Elements can also have descriptive information called *attributes*. Elements can be composed of other elements, so they can have complex structure. Since such documents can be represented as text,[2] XML can provide a platform-neutral way to represent data that is transmitted over a network. In particular, as text it can go safely out through a firewall because HTTP port 80 will invariably be open. Here is an example of an XML document that describes a CustomerList composed of several customers.

```
<CustomerList>
  <Customer>
      <FirstName>John</FirstName>
```

---

1. Technically, W3C final documents are called recommendations. However, we will refer to them as standards or specifications. W3C documents that have not reached recommendation status are referred to by their W3C names: proposed recommendations, candidate recommendations, last call working drafts, working drafts, and notes.
2. But they do not have to be text. You can build programs using the abstractions defined in the W3C proposed recommendation Information Set. Using these abstractions, such as *document, namespace, element, character,* and *attribute,* to represent the hierarchy of an XML document, you are independent of the particular format in which the XML is stored. Mobile solutions will probably use a more efficient binary format for XML encoding rather than text. The XML Schema Recommendation is written based on the Infoset, not the angle-bracket syntax. The Information Set assumes the existence of XML namespaces.

```
      <LastName>Smith</LastName>
      <EmailAddress>smith@smith.org</EmailAddress>
  </Customer>
  <Customer>
    <FirstName>Mary</FirstName>
    <LastName>Jones</LastName>
    <EmailAddress>mary@jones.org</EmailAddress>
  </Customer>
</CustomerList>
```

XML Namespaces

A set of elements and attributes in an XML document can be referred to as a vocabulary. This is particularly useful if this vocabulary can model information that might be reused. For example, we could have vocabularies for financial or chemical information. Namespaces not only allow these vocabularies to be uniquely named in order to prevent conflicts, but allow them to be reused.

The following example XML document uses a namespace attribute to uniquely identify the elements <FirstName>, <LastName>, and <EmailAddress> from any other definitions that might use the same tag names with a different meaning or context. The example also shows that abbreviations can be used with namespaces. This is very convenient if multiple namespaces are used in a document.

```
<Customer xmlns:c=
          "urn:uuid 28833F1C-CBE4-4042-9B35-BF641DFB35DC">

  <c:FirstName>John</c:FirstName>

  <c:LastName>Smith</c:LastName>

  <c:EmailAddress>smith@smith.org</c:EmailAddress>

</Customer>
```

A Uniform Resource Identifier (URI) is used to identify a particular XML namespace. A URI can either be a Uniform Resource Locator (URL) or a Uniform Resource Name (URN). Both represent a unique name. URLs are the familiar Web site addresses, which are unique because they are given out by a central naming authority. A URN is just a unique string. For example, you could use a URN defined by a GUID[3] such as **urn:uuid:28833F1C-CBE4-**

---

3. A GUID, or Globally Unique Identifier, is a 128-bit identifier that is guaranteed to be unique. GUIDs are widely used in COM. You can generate your own GUIDs using the tool **guidgen.exe** (Windows UI) or **uuidgen.exe** (command-line UI). These tools are in the directory ...\Microsoft Visual Studio.NET\Common7\Tools.

4042-9B35-BF641DFB35DC.[4] URIs used for namespaces do not have to resolve to any location on the Web.

XML Schema

XML with namespaces, however, does not assign any semantics to the data. The XML Schema Definition (XSD) defines a basic set of data types and the means to define new data types. In other words, an XML Schema can assign meaning to the structure of a document. The schema itself is written in XML. The CustomerList document described previously could be defined by the following schema:

```
<schema xmlns:xsd="http://www.w3.org/2001/XMLSchema"
      xmlns:c="http://www.acme.com/Customer"
      targetNamespace="http://www.acme.com/CustomerList">
  <xsd:complexType name="Customer">
    <xsd:sequence>
      <xsd:element name="FirstName" type="xsd:string" />
      <xsd:element name="LastName" type="xsd:string" />
      <xsd:element name="EmailAddress" type="xsd:string"/>
    </xsd:sequence>
  </xsd:complexType>
</schema>
```

The targetNamespace element defines the name of the schema being defined. This particular string uses the XSD-defined element **string**. Using XSD, we can restrict the range of values, specify how often particular instances occur, as well as provide attributes to the elements. The schema itself is written in XML. Both the document and its associated schema can be validated and managed as XML documents. The same document, interpreted by two different schemas, will have two different meanings.

SOAP

While XML schemas can define the types used by the data, you need a set of conventions to describe how the data and its associated type definitions are transmitted. SOAP, the Simple Object Access Protocol, uses XML as a wire protocol to do just this.

While SOAP can use XML Schema types to describe the transmitted types, it was designed before the XML Schema specification was finished, so there are some divergences between the two. The reason is that XML Schema

---

4. GUIDs are used in the examples for simplicity and to reinforce the idea that uniqueness, but not existence, is required for a namespace identifier. In real systems URL-based names are used whether or not the URLs actually exist.

describes a hierarchy or tree structure. SOAP wants to be able to represent objects, and objects can have far more complicated relationships than a hierarchy. Classes, for example, can have multiple parent classes. As we will discuss later, this has some implications for Web services. The W3C is currently working on reconciling SOAP with XML Schema.

SOAP 1.1 can be used with several transport protocols, not just HTTP.

The use of SOAP for Web services on Microsoft platforms is not unique to .NET. Microsoft has released the SOAP Toolkit that has allowed Windows-based platforms to develop Web services. The support for SOAP, however, is built into .NET. The SOAP Toolkit does contain, however, the SOAP Trace Utility, which is useful for tracking raw and formatted SOAP messages.

WSDL

Objects contain both state and behavior. Schemas define the data. WSDL, the Web Services Description Language, defines the methods and the data associated with a Web service. As the simple example we shall describe shortly demonstrates, WSDL is not necessary for writing Web services. It is important, however, if you want to be able to automatically generate classes that can call Web services or to do anything that requires automatic machine intervention with Web services.[5] Otherwise, you would have to craft and send the SOAP messages by hand.

As you will see in the following example, the SOAP that is used to describe the Web service's transport format is defined in the WSDL. WSDL is a W3C note.

Web Service Architecture

Besides handling ASP.NET, Microsoft's Internet Information Server (IIS) can handle Web services, since they come in as HTTP requests. These requests are encoded in the URL or as XML. IIS then creates the required object to fulfill the Web service request. IIS then calls the object's method that is associated with the request. Any returned values are converted to XML and returned to the client, using the HTTP protocol.

---

5. This is similar to VB 6's use of type libraries to make COM programming simpler. Of course, WSDL is a complete description of the Web service, unlike a type library's incomplete description of a COM object and interfaces.

Setting Up the Web Services Examples

Code Example

As usual, all the example programs for this chapter are in the chapter folder, **Chap15**. To run the examples, you will need to have Internet Information Services (IIS) installed on your system, as discussed in Chapter 14. Following the procedure described in Chapter 14, make **\OI\NetVb\Chap15** into a virtual directory with alias **Chap15**. Once a virtual directory has been created, you can access files in it by including the virtual directory in the path of the URL. In particular, you can access the file **default.htm** using the URL **http://localhost/Chap15/**. The file **default.htm** contains a home page for all the Web services example programs for this chapter. See Figure 15–1.

The Add Web Service Example

To illustrate how this works under Microsoft .NET, we will build a simple Web service to illustrate this architecture and how the associated protocols are used. Our Web service will simply add two numbers. To make things clear, we will build the Web service **Add** in the simplest possible way.

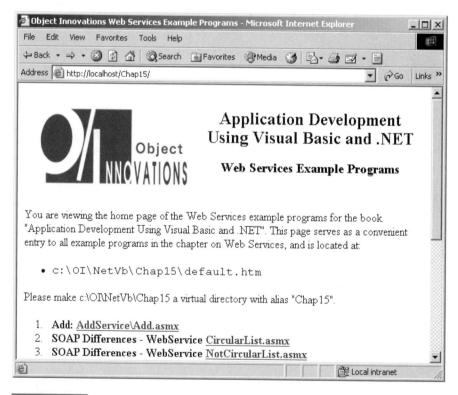

FIGURE 15–1   *Home page for Web services example programs.*

By writing code in a file with the suffix **asmx** and placing it in a subdirectory of the IIS root directory, we can have a simple Web service.[6] IIS has the concept of virtual directories so that the actual directory does not have to physically be under the IIS root directory. All our examples in this chapter will be in subdirectories of the virtual directory **Chap15** created in the previous section.

The file **add.asmx** first defines the language used to write the Web service and the class that has the definitions. That class inherits from the **WebService** class in the namespace **System.Web.Services**. Note the use of the **WebService** attribute to define a namespace for the service. This file is found in the **AddService** directory for this chapter.

A method of that class can be used as a Web service if the attribute **WebMethod** is applied to it. (Note the **:=** syntax in VB.NET for assigning a value to an attribute parameter.)

```
<%@ WebService language="VB" class="AddService" %>

Imports System
Imports System.Web
Imports System.Web.Services

<WebService(Namespace:="http://www.oi.com/netvb")> _
Public Class AddService
    Inherits System.Web.Services.WebService

    <WebMethod()> Public Function Add( _
    ByVal x As Long, ByVal y As Long) As Long
        Return x + y
    End Function

End Class
```

A Client Program for the Add Web Service

Internet Explorer can be used as a simple client program that uses the HTTP GET protocol's URL encoding of a Web service request. You can access the Add Web service from the home page for this chapter, or you may use the URL **http://localhost/Chap15/AddService/Add.asmx** as the address. Figure 15–2 shows the result.

By clicking on the Add link you will get a form enabling you to submit a request to the Add service. In addition, the form describes the various HTTP protocols that can be used for submitting the request. For our purposes, two protocols are worth mentioning: HTTP GET and SOAP.

---

6. By default this directory is \inetpub\wwwroot.

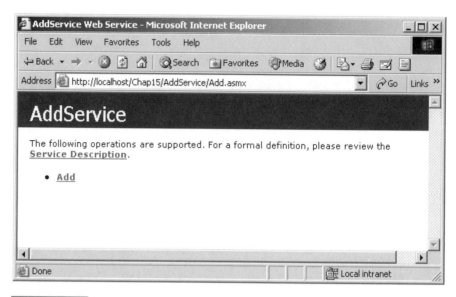

FIGURE 15–2   *Web service request in Internet Explorer.*

The HTTP GET protocol is worth exploring because the form that appears in IE uses it. The protocol has boldfaced placeholders for data that has to be entered:

```
GET Chap15/AddService/Add.asmx/Add?x=string&y=string
 HTTP/1.1
...
```

The data entered into the form is added to the URL in the standard way that any HTTP GET request is made. Data is returned as

```
<?xml version="1.0" encoding="utf-8" ?>
<long xmlns="http://www.oi.com/netvb">long</long>
```

Figure 15–3 shows values entered into the form. By pressing the Invoke button, you can call the Web service.

An IE window will appear with the part of the HTTP response data generated by the Web service that contains the actual returned value:

```
...
<long xmlns="http://www.oi.com/netvb">12</long>
```

This is exactly the format that appeared in the description of the protocol with the answer (12) substituted for the placeholder. HTTP GET, however, can handle only simple types.

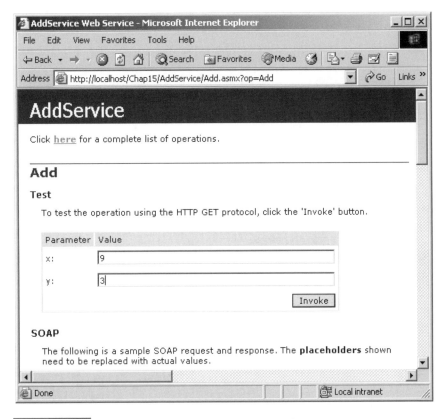

FIGURE 15–3   *Values entered on the Internet Explorer form.*

The more interesting protocol is SOAP. Both the SOAP HTTP POST request and response are described with placeholders for information that has to be provided in the actual call. Those placeholders are in boldface type.

First, let us look at the SOAP HTTP POST request. The first part is a set of HTTP headers. The XML for the SOAP protocol is in the data (entity-body) section of the HTTP request, which is always separated from the headers by a blank line. The content-length header is the length of the data, which is dependent on the size of the parameters in the data section.

The method header identifies the file to which the request is directed. It could also name an object that is to handle the request (endpoint). The SOAP-Action header indicates the name of the method, qualified by a namespace, to be invoked for the Web service.[7]

SOAP uses XML to specify the parameters of the method.[8] The SOAP body contains the parameters for the method call. In a real method call, the

long placeholders would be replaced by the actual parameters to be passed to the Web service method.

```
POST /Chap15/AddService/Add.asmx HTTP/1.1
Host: localhost
Content-Type: text/xml; charset=utf-8
Content-Length: length
SOAPAction: "http://www.oi.com/netvb/Add"

<?xml version="1.0" encoding="utf-8"?>
<soap:Envelope xmlns:xsi="http://www.w3.org/2001/XMLSchema-
instance" xmlns:xsd="http://www.w3.org/2001/XMLSchema"
xmlns:soap="http://schemas.xmlsoap.org/soap/envelope/">
  <soap:Body>
    <Add xmlns="http://www.oi.com/netvb">
      <x>long</x>
      <y>long</y>
    </Add>
  </soap:Body>
</soap:Envelope>
```

Next, the HTTP response is described. The **long** placeholder will be replaced by the actual value returned.

```
HTTP/1.1 200 OK
Content-Type: text/xml; charset=utf-8
Content-Length: length

<?xml version="1.0" encoding="utf-8"?>
<soap:Envelope xmlns:xsi="http://www.w3.org/2001/XMLSchema-
instance" xmlns:xsd="http://www.w3.org/2001/XMLSchema"
xmlns:soap="http://schemas.xmlsoap.org/soap/envelope/">
  <soap:Body>
    <AddResponse xmlns="http://www.oi.com/netvb">
      <AddResult>long</AddResult>
    </AddResponse>
  </soap:Body>
</soap:Envelope>
```

---

7. For those with a COM background, you can think of the namespace for the method as equivalent to the GUID that identifies an interface (IID).

8. The parallel to IDL is WSDL, which we will discuss shortly. SOAP is analogous to NDR, the wire format used for DCOM calls. All these parallels to COM appear in Don Box's March 2000 MSDN article "A Young Person's Guide to the Simple Object Access Protocol."

WSDL

SOAP does not describe the Web service interface. While you could encode the SOAP yourself, it would be nice to be able to generate proxy classes for the client to use. Otherwise, you would have to understand all the details of the SOAP specification and how to parse the returned XML.

WSDL provides a description of the Web service interface. You can view this description from IE by clicking on the Service Description link, as illustrated in Figure 15–2. Here is the WSDL description for our **AddService**, which has one method, **Add**. We have omitted the WSDL for invocations of the Web service that do not use SOAP. The <types> section defines the types:

- **Add** is used when SOAP invokes the Web service.
- **AddResponse** is used when the SOAP Web service invocation returns.

Add has two elements, each occurring exactly once. Both are defined with the XSD type long, and they have the names x and y. The return parameter, whose name is **AddResponse**, has one element named **AddResult**, which occurs once, defined with the XSD type long. Note how these types were used in the SOAP definitions we looked at previously.

```
...
<types>
...
  <s:element name="Add">
    <s:complexType>
      <s:sequence>
        <s:element minOccurs="1" maxOccurs="1" name="x"
                                        type="s:long" />
        <s:element minOccurs="1" maxOccurs="1" name="y"
                                        type="s:long" />
      </s:sequence>
    </s:complexType>
  </s:element>
  <s:element name="AddResponse">
    <s:complexType>
      <s:sequence>
        <s:element minOccurs="1" maxOccurs="1"
                       name="AddResult" type="s:long" />
      </s:sequence>
    </s:complexType>
  </s:element>
  ...
</types>
```

The <message> section relates the types to their use as parameters.

```
<message name="AddSoapIn">
<part name="parameters" element="s0:Add" />
```

```
</message>
<message name="AddSoapOut">
  <part name="parameters" element="s0:AddResponse" />
</message>
. . .
```

The <portType> section relates the Web service to the individual Web methods defined by the <operation> elements. If there had been more Web methods in the Web service, there would have been more operation elements associated with the portType.[9] Each method's input and output operation is associated with the appropriate message defined previously.

```
<portType name="TestSoap">
  <operation name="Add">
    <input message="s0:AddSoapIn" />
    <output message="s0:AddSoapOut" />
  </operation>
</portType>
. . .
```

The <binding> section defines the encodings and protocols to be used for each operation.

```
<binding name="TestSoap" type="s0:TestSoap">
  <soap:binding
        transport="http://schemas.xmlsoap.org/soap/http"
        style="document" />
  <operation name="Add">
    <soap:operation http://www.oi.com/netvb/Add"
        style="document" />
    <input>
      <soap:body use="literal" />
    </input>
    <output>
      <soap:body use="literal" />
    </output>
  </operation>
</binding>
. . .
```

The <service> section relates the Web service to its port and how it is invoked.

```
<service name="Test">
  <port name="TestSoap" binding="s0:TestSoap">
    <soap:address location=
          "http://localhost/AddService/Add.asmx" />
```

---

9. For those of you keeping score, this is analogous to a COM interface.

```
    </port>
    ...
    </service>
    ...
```

Proxy Classes

The **wsdl** tool can be used to read the WSDL description and generate a proxy class that will make the SOAP calls for you. The following command will generate a VB.NET proxy class file with the name **addproxy.vb**, where the **/l** parameter is used to specify the language:

```
wsdl /l:VB /out:addproxy.vb /protocol:SOAP
http://localhost/Chap15/AddService/Add.asmx?WSDL
```

The **/l** parameter is used here to specify the language (default is CS for C#), and the **/protocol** parameter is used to specify the protocol (default is SOAP).

The generated proxy defines a constructor and three methods. The constructor sets the URL that this Web service uses. One of the methods represents a synchronous, blocking call on the Web service. The other two methods correspond to the asynchronous design pattern discussed in Chapter 10. If you want to call the Web service asynchronously, you can use the BeginXXX and the EndXXX methods associated with the proxy.[10] The proxy class has the same name as the WebService class.

The **Invoke** method of the **SoapHttpClientProtocol** class will make the HTTP request and process the HTTP response associated with the transmitted and received SOAP packets. This example is found in the **AddClient** directory. Here is the code for the generated proxy class, in file **addproxy.vb**.

```
Public Class AddService
    Inherits _
    System.Web.Services.Protocols.SoapHttpClientProtocol

    Public Sub New()
      MyBase.New
      Me.Url = _
         "http://localhost/Chap15/AddService/Add.asmx"
    End Sub

    ...
    Public Function Add(ByVal x As Long, ByVal y As Long) _
      As Long
        Dim results() As Object = Me.Invoke( _
```

_____

10. Of course, in this particular case XXX=Add.

```
      "Add", New Object() {x, y})
   Return CType(results(0),Long)
End Function


...
Public Function BeginAdd(ByVal x As Long, ByVal y As _
  Long, ByVal callback As System.AsyncCallback, _
  ByVal asyncState As Object) As System.IAsyncResult
     Return Me.BeginInvoke("Add", New Object() {x, y}, _
        callback, asyncState)
End Function


...
Public Function EndAdd(ByVal asyncResult As _
  System.IAsyncResult) As Long
     Dim results() As Object = Me.EndInvoke(asyncResult)
     Return CType(results(0), Long)
End Function
End Class
```

You can then write a program to use the proxy classes to issue a Web service request.

```
' AddClient.vb

Module AddClient

   Sub Main()
      Dim adder As New AddService()
      Dim sum As Long = adder.Add(1, 2)
      Console.WriteLine(sum)
   End Sub

End Module
```

Web Service Client with Raw SOAP and HTTP

Code
Example

To show you what the **SoapHttpClientProtocol** class does, the final client program for this example uses sockets to send both the HTTP headers and the SOAP directly and to receive the response from the Web service. This example is the **RawAddClient** directory.

The main routine first sets up variables for talking to the HTTP server on port 80.

```
Dim httpServer As String = "localhost"
Dim httpPort As Integer = 80
```

It then reads in a file that has the SOAP headers for the service to be called. It returns the length of the content, which will have to be placed in one of the HTTP POST headers.

```
Dim contentLength As Long
Dim contentData As StringBuilder = _
   BuildContent("SoapAdd.txt", contentLength)
Dim requestHeader As StringBuilder = _
   BuildHeader(contentLength)
```

It then connects to the server, sends the data, and receives the response, which it writes out to the console.

```
Dim endPoint As New IPEndPoint(Dns.Resolve( _
   httpServer).AddressList(0), httpPort)
Dim sock As New Socket(AddressFamily.InterNetwork, _
   SocketType.Stream, ProtocolType.Tcp)

sock.Connect(endPoint)
If Not sock.Connected Then
   Console.WriteLine("Unable to connect to host")
   Return
End If

Console.WriteLine(requestHeader.ToString())
Console.WriteLine(contentData.ToString())

Dim ASCII As Encoding = Encoding.ASCII
Dim header() As Byte = _
   ASCII.GetBytes(requestHeader.ToString())
Dim content() As Byte = _
   ASCII.GetBytes(contentData.ToString())

' make the request
sock.Send(header, header.Length, 0)
sock.Send(content, content.Length, 0)

' Receive the response
ASCII = Encoding.ASCII
Dim bytes As Integer

Dim receivedData() As Byte = New Byte(4096) {}

' receive actual response
bytes = sock.Receive(receivedData, receivedData.Length, 0)
Console.WriteLine(ASCII.GetString(receivedData, 0, bytes))

sock.Close()
```

The routine **BuildHeader** just builds a standard HTTP POST request with the addition of the SOAPAction header.

```
Function BuildHeader(ByVal contentLength As Long) _
 As StringBuilder
   Dim sb As New StringBuilder(1024)
   Const QUOTE = ChrW(&H22)

   sb.Append("POST /SimpleWebService/Add.asmx HTTP/1.1" _
      & vbCrLf)
   sb.Append("Host: localhost" & vbCrLf)
   sb.Append("Content-Type: text/xml; charset=utf-8" _
      & vbCrLf)

   Dim line As String = "Content-Length: " & _
      contentLength.ToString() & vbCrLf
   sb.Append(line)
   sb.Append("SOAPAction: " & QUOTE & _
    "urn:uuid:10C14FCF-BF4A-477a-BFE7-41B9F2A4514E/Add" _
    & QUOTE & vbCrLf)

   sb.Append(vbCrLf)

   Return sb
End Function
```

BuildContent just reads a file to a buffer and calculates the size of the buffer in bytes.

```
Function BuildContent(ByVal filename As String, _
 ByRef contentLength As Long) As StringBuilder

   Dim sb As New StringBuilder(1024)
   Dim fs As New StreamReader(File.OpenRead(filename))
   contentLength = 0

   Dim line As String = fs.ReadLine()
   Do While line <> Nothing
      sb.Append(line)
      sb.Append(vbCrLf)
      contentLength += line.Length + 2
      line = fs.ReadLine()
   Loop

   fs.Close()
   Return sb
End Function
```

Based on our previous discussion, the SOAP file, **SoapAdd.txt**, looks as we would expect it to. The input parameters 9 and 3 appear as the WSDL would dictate.

```
<?xml version="1.0" encoding="utf-8"?>
<soap:Envelope
   xmlns:xsi="http://www.w3.org/2001/XMLSchema-instance"
   xmlns:xsd="http://www.w3.org/2001/XMLSchema"
   xmlns:soap="http://schemas.xmlsoap.org/soap/envelope/">
  <soap:Body>
    <Add xmlns=
         "urn:uuid:10C14FCF-BF4A-477a-BFE7-41B9F2A4514E">
      <x>9</x>
      <y>3</y>
    </Add>
  </soap:Body>
</soap:Envelope>
```

The program first writes out the HTTP POST request. First come the standard HTTP headers with a special SOAPAction header, then the SOAP encoding of the request.

```
POST /SimpleWebService/Add.asmx HTTP/1.1
Host: localhost
Content-Type: text/xml; charset=utf-8
Content-Length: 393
SOAPAction:
       "urn:uuid:10C14FCF-BF4A-477a-BFE7-41B9F2A4514E/Add"

<?xml version="1.0" encoding="utf-8"?>
<soap:Envelope
   xmlns:xsi="http://www.w3.org/2001/XMLSchema-instance"
   xmlns:xsd="http://www.w3.org/2001/XMLSchema"
   xmlns:soap="http://schemas.xmlsoap.org/soap/envelope/">
  <soap:Body>
    <Add xmlns=
         "urn:uuid:10C14FCF-BF4A-477a-BFE7-41B9F2A4514E">
      <x>9</x>
      <y>3</y>
    </Add>
  </soap:Body>
</soap:Envelope>
```

The program then writes out the response.[11] Again, the HTTP headers come first, then the SOAP encoding of the result, 12.

---

11. If you don't get the output result the first time you run the program, try running the program a second time.

```
...
HTTP/1.1 200 OK
Server: Microsoft-IIS/5.0
Date: Mon, 17 Sep 2001 02:11:30 GMT
Cache-Control: private, max-age=0
Content-Type: text/xml; charset=utf-8
Content-Length: 383

<?xml version="1.0" encoding="utf-8"?>
<soap:Envelope
    xmlns:soap="http://schemas.xmlsoap.org/soap/envelope/"
    xmlns:xsi="http://www.w3.org/2001/XMLSchema-instance"
    xmlns:xsd="http://www.w3.org/2001/XMLSchema">
  <soap:Body>
    <AddResponse xmlns=
        "urn:uuid:10C14FCF-BF4A-477a-BFE7-41B9F2A4514E">
      <AddResult>12</AddResult>
    </AddResponse>
  </soap:Body>
</soap:Envelope>
```

SOAP Differences

Before we finish our basic examination of SOAP and WSDL, a more detailed look at the relationship of SOAP, WSDL, and the XML Schema specification is in order. As mentioned earlier, the SOAP encodings used by .NET remoting differ from those used by Web services and the XML serializer.

To illustrate the differences between the two, we will take the same program and serialize it to disk and use it as a Web service. The program builds a circular list of two customer items. The two programs are found in the **SOAP Differences** directory.

The first program, **Formatter**, creates a circular list and then serializes it to disk using the .NET SOAP formatter.

```
' Formatter.vb

Imports System.Web.Services
Imports System.IO
Imports System.Runtime.Serialization.Formatters.Soap

<Serializable()> Public Class Customer
    Public name As String
    Public id As Long
    Public nextc As Customer
End Class
```

```
Module Formatter

    Sub Main()
        Dim list As Customer = GetList()
        Dim s As New FileStream("cust.xml", FileMode.Create)
        Dim f As New SoapFormatter()
        f.Serialize(s, list)
        s.Close()
        Console.WriteLine("File written: cust.xml")
    End Sub

    Function GetList() As Customer
        Dim cust1 As New Customer()
        cust1.name = "John Smith"
        cust1.id = 1

        Dim cust2 As New Customer()
        cust2.name = "Mary Smith"
        cust2.id = 2
        cust2.nextc = cust1

        cust1.nextc = cust2

        Return cust1
    End Function

End Module
```

This program produces the file **cust.xml** that has the following SOAP encoding. Note the use of the **id** attribute to identify objects and fields, and the **href** attribute that serves as an object reference.

```
...
<SOAP-ENV:Body>
<a1:Customer id="ref-1"
...
<name id="ref-3">John Smith</name>
<id>1</id>
<nextc href="#ref-4"/>
</a1:Customer>
<a1:Customer id="ref-4"
...
<name id="ref-5">Mary Smith</name>
<id>2</id>
<nextc href="#ref-1"/>
</a1:Customer>
</SOAP-ENV:Body>
...
```

The second program, **WebService**, as its name suggests, is a Web service. The first version **CircularList.asmx** creates a circular list, like the previous example. The second version, **NotCircularList.asmx**, comments out the line that makes the list circular.

```
<%@ WebService language="VB" class="Test" %>

Imports System.Web.Services
Imports System.IO

Public Class Customer
    Public name As String
    Public id As Long
    Public nextc As Customer
End Class

<WebService(Namespace:="http://www.oi.com/netvb")> _
Public Class Test
    Inherits WebService

    <WebMethod()> Function GetList() As Customer
        Dim cust1 As New Customer()
        cust1.name = "John Smith"
        cust1.id = 1

        Dim cust2 As New Customer()
        cust2.name = "Mary Smith"
        cust2.id = 2
        cust2.nextc = cust1

        ' Comment out next line to make not circular
        cust1.nextc = cust2

        Return cust1
    End Function
End Class
```

You may run this Web service from the home page for this chapter or with the URL **http://localhost/Chap15/SOAP%20Differences/WebService/CircularList.asmx**. Internet Explorer will indeed recognize it as a Web service. See Figure 15–4.

However, if you go on to invoke the Web service, you will get the following error:

```
...
System.InvalidOperationException: A circular reference was
detected while serializing an object of type Customer.
...
```

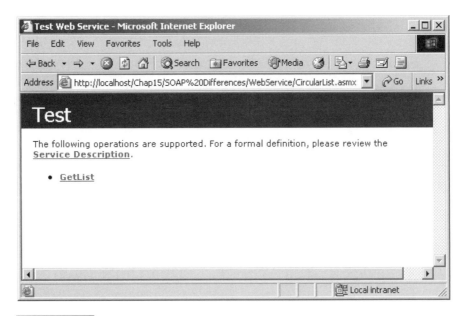

Internet Explorer recognizes CircularList.asmx as a Web service.

The XML Serializer used to produce the SOAP for Web services cannot handle the circular reference. If you comment out the line of code **cust2.nextc = cust1**, the Web service will be able to respond, as shown in Figure 15–5, although the whole circular list is not returned.

```
. . .
  <name>John Smith</name>
  <id>1</id>
  <next>
    <name>Mary Smith</name>
    <id>2</id>
    <next xsi:nil="true" />
  </next>
. . .
```

There is no notion, however, of any real relationship between the items, as there was in the remoting case. Why can the SOAP in .NET remoting handle the relationships while the SOAP in Web services cannot?

SOAP handles the complicated relationships (multiple parents, graphs, etc.) that exist in an object model. XML Schema still reflects the XML heritage of document processing where you can model a document as a tree with a single root, each node having one parent. Since SOAP was being developed before XML Schema was finished, SOAP has some extensions to handle those

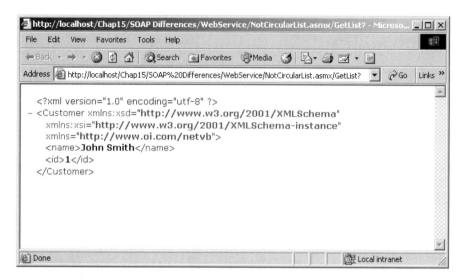

FIGURE 15-5   *NonCircularList.asmx behaves as a legal Web service.*

cases. Since they are in Section 5 of the SOAP specification, they are often referred to as the Section 5 encoding rules.

Those parts of the Section 5 encoding rules that are extensions cannot be incorporated in any XML document that has to be validated against a schema. Hence, the .NET XML serialization classes do not use them. On the other hand, the .NET remoting serializer does not care about schema validation; it cares about the ability to remote full object fidelity and hence uses all the Section 5 rules. In order to maximize interoperability, Web services implementations tend to use only XML Schema-compliant forms that can be validated against a schema.[12] The counterargument can be made that schema validation is not as important when machines are generating the XML, but the industry has not yet taken that approach.[13]

If you want applications and Web services that reside on different operating system platforms to interoperate, define your Web services with XML Schema first, then develop the associated WSDL. You can then create an abstract class that can be the basis for an **.asmx** file by using the **/server** option on the **wsdl** tool.

---

12. If you have a COM background, think of the work the proxy has to do to handle pointer aliasing if the pointer_default(unique) attribute is not used.
13. Although we will not discuss them here, there are attributes you can set on your Web service class and methods to have them use the Section 5 rules.

Starting with an object model and then modeling it with XML Schema might result in incompatible systems. Of course, if only simple types and structures are involved, you are not going to have problems. If you have existing object models, you may need a wrapper layer that translates the Web services layer and moves it into your existing object model. This is the major technological challenge of Web services—getting the object models on different platforms to work together.[14]

WebService Class and Visual Studio

As we have previously demonstrated, a Web service is nothing but an HTTP request. As such, a Web service can access the intrinsic objects associated with its HTTP request. These are the same intrinsic objects discussed in the section "State in ASP.NET Applications" in the previous chapter. The **WebService** class has properties that access these intrinsic objects. In this section we discuss the **WebService** class, and we use Visual Studio, which makes developing Web services and clients much easier.

You need not derive your Web service class from the framework **WebService** class. You can derive your Web service class from a different base class if necessary. In this case you can use the current **HttpContext** to access the intrinsic objects. The **WebService** class inherits from **MarshalByRefObject**, however, so if you want your Web service class to be remotable, and you do inherit from a different base class, make sure that class also inherits from **MarshalByRefObject**. The **HttpContext** enables you to get information about an HTTP request. By using the static **Current** property, you can get access to the current request.

We will now build a Web service inside Visual Studio .NET that will illustrate the use of these intrinsic objects inside a Web service. As Figure 15–6 demonstrates, choose ASP.NET Web service from the New Project dialog box in Visual Studio .NET. Call your project **Arithmetic**, and create it in the **Demos** directory for this chapter.

When you click the OK button, VS.NET will set up a Web service project for you. Figure 15–7 shows the resulting VS.NET project.

---

14. There is no intent here to slight the security issues associated with Web services, but if you cannot get the object models to work together in some fashion, security becomes irrelevant because there is nothing to make secure.

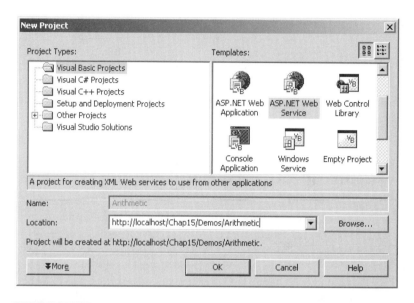

FIGURE 15–6   *Visual Studio .NET New Project dialog with ASP.NET Web service project selected.*

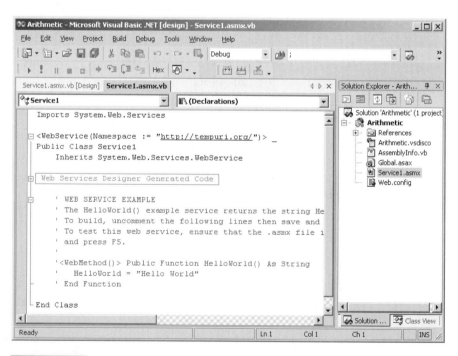

FIGURE 15–7   *Visual Studio .NET Web services project.*

Hello World Web Service

The project created by Visual Studio has commented-out code already provided for a simple "Hello World" Web service. All you have to do to implement a Web service is to uncomment this code, build, and run! Before creating our real example, let's pause and do this simple exercise. Uncomment the last three code lines of the class. You will then have the following code, which is also saved in the folder **HelloWebService** in the file **Service1.asmx**.

Code
Example

```
Imports System.Web.Services

<WebService(Namespace := "http://tempuri.org/")> _
Public Class Service1
    Inherits System.Web.Services.WebService

#Region " Web services Designer Generated Code "

...
    ' WEB SERVICE EXAMPLE
    ' The HelloWorld() example service returns the string
    ' Hello World. To build, uncomment the following lines
    ' then save and build the project. To test this web
    ' service, ensure that the .asmx file is the start
    ' page and press F5.
    '
    <WebMethod()> Public Function HelloWorld() As String
        HelloWorld = "Hello World"
    End Function

End Class
```

If you run from inside Visual Studio, you will get the familiar test page, with a recommendation to change the default namespace before the Web service is made public. See Figure 15–8. You may go ahead and test the Web service in the usual manner, and you should see that, sure enough, the string "Hello World" is returned.

Change the default namespace to the one we have been using for our other examples, **http://www.oi.com/netvb**. You may then build and run again, and this time you should just get the plain test page without any recommendation.

Arithmetic Web Service

Our Web service will have several methods that demonstrate how to use the intrinsic objects. As you will see, this is really no different from their use in

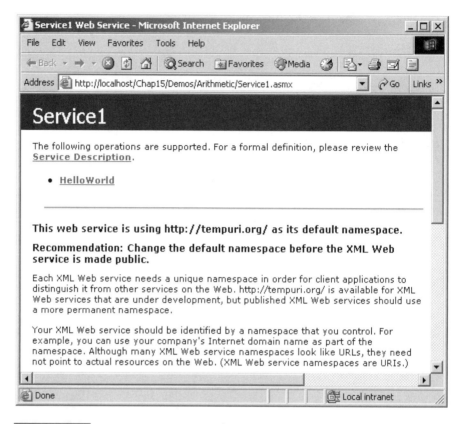

FIGURE 15–8 *Web service test page with recommendation to change default namespace.*

ASP.NET. Two of the methods will illustrate the use of application and session state by calculating a cumulative sum of numbers.

Global.asax

In the **global.asax** file we initialize our sum to zero in the appropriate event handlers. **Global.asax** has the same function in Web services as it does for ASP.NET, as discussed in the previous chapter in the section "ASP.NET Applications." Since the **Global** class inherits from **System.Web.HttpApplication**, it can access the **Application** and **Session** intrinsic objects.

```
' Global.asax

Imports System.Web
Imports System.Web.SessionState
```

```
Public Class Global
    Inherits System.Web.HttpApplication

#Region " Component Designer Generated Code "
...

    Sub Application_Start(ByVal sender As Object, _
     ByVal e As EventArgs)
        Application("TotalSum") = 0.0
    End Sub

    Sub Session_Start(ByVal sender As Object, _
     ByVal e As EventArgs)
        Session("SessionSum") = 0.0
    End Sub
...
```

Arithmetic.asmx

Renaming the **Service1.asmx** file to **arithmetic.asmx**, we define several Web methods. We have methods for the four fundamental arithmetic operations, **Add**, **Subtract**, **Multiply**, and **Divide**. To see the effect of the **<Web-Method>** attribute, we apply this attribute to all of these methods except **Add**. As usual, we specify a namespace for our **Arithmetic** class that inherits from the **WebService** class.

```
' Arithmetic.asmx

Imports System.Web
Imports System.Web.Services

<WebService(Namespace:="http://www.oi.com/netvb")> _
Public Class Arithmetic
    Inherits System.Web.Services.WebService
...
    Public Function Add(ByVal x As Double, _
     ByVal y As Double) As Double
        Return x + y
    End Function

    <WebMethod()> Public Function Subtract( _
     ByVal x As Double, ByVal y As Double) As Double
        Return x - y
    End Function

    <WebMethod()> Public Function Multiply( _
     ByVal x As Double, ByVal y As Double) As Double
        Return x * y
    End Function
```

```
<WebMethod()> Public Function Divide( _
  ByVal x As Double, ByVal y As Double) As Double
    Return x / y
End Function
```

By setting the **EnableSession** argument to the **WebMethod** attribute to **true**, we turn on session state for the **SessionSum** method. (Note the **:=** syntax in VB.NET for assigning a value to an attribute parameter.) Every time a new session is started, the sum is reset to zero.

```
<WebMethod(EnableSession:=True)> _
Public Function SessionSum(ByVal x As Double) As Double
    Dim sum As Double = CDbl(Session("SessionSum"))
    sum += x
    Session("SessionSum") = sum
    Return sum
End Function
```

On the other hand, for the **CumulativeSum** Web method, **EnableSession** is set to its default value or false, so that the sum is reset to zero only when the Web service application is restarted. The **Application** intrinsic object is used from the **HttpContext** object to show how that class is used.

```
<WebMethod()> _
Public Function CumulativeSum(ByVal x As Double) As Double
    Dim sum As Double = CDbl(Application("TotalSum"))
    sum += x
    Application("TotalSum") = sum
    Return CDbl(HttpContext.Current.Application("TotalSum"))
End Function
...
```

It should be clear from this code that **HttpApplication**, **WebService**, and **HttpContext** all reference the same intrinsic objects. If you need to save state for the application or session of a Web service, you can use the collections associated with **HttpApplicationState** and **HttpSessionState** to do so.

The **GetUserAgent** method shows how to use the **Context** object to access information about the request. We return what kind of application is accessing the Web service. The **GetServerInfo** method accesses the **Server** intrinsic object.

```
<WebMethod()> Public Function GetUserAgent() As String
    Return Context.Request.UserAgent
End Function

<WebMethod()> Public Function GetServerInfo() As String
    Dim msg As String = "Timeout for " & _
        Server.MachineName & " = " & _
        Server.ScriptTimeout & _
        "; Located at " & Server.MapPath("")
    Return msg
End Function
```

Running the program from inside Visual Studio brings up the normal test page in Internet Explorer, as illustrated in Figure 15–9. Note that there are links for testing each of our methods, except for **Add**, which did not have the **<WebMethod()>** attribute.

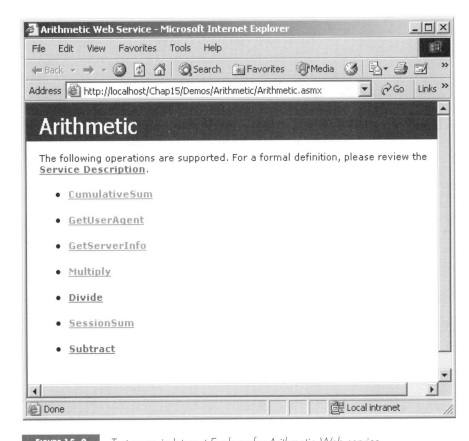

FIGURE 15–9   *Test page in Internet Explorer for Arithmetic Web service.*

Client Program for Arithmetic Web Service

Visual Studio makes it very easy to create client programs for Web services. You do not need to explicitly use the **wsdl** tool to generate a proxy. You can achieve the same effect by adding a "Web Reference" to your project. As a demonstration, we will create a client program for our **Arithmetic** Web service, saved in the directory **ArithmeticClient**. If you would like to follow along, do your work in the **Demos** directory.

Code Example

1. Use Visual Studio to create a new Visual Basic console project **ArithmeticClient** in the **Demos** directory.

2. Rename Module1 to **Arithmetic**, and make it the startup object.

3. In Solution Explorer, right-click over References and choose Add Web Reference from the context menu.

4. In the Add Web Reference dialog box that comes up, type in the HTTP address of the Web service in the Address edit box, followed by a carriage return. Information about the Arithmetic Web service will appear, as in Figure 15–10.

5. Click on the Add Reference button to add the Web reference. This will add a Web References set of subdirectories below the current project that will contain the proxy class and the **wsdl** file for the Web service. See Figure 15–11.

6. Examine the file **Reference.vb**, in the **localhost** subdirectory of the **Web References** directory in your project. You will see code for a VB.NET proxy class, in the namespace **localhost**.

7. To the client program, we will have to reference the proxy class's namespace:

```
Imports ArithmeticClient.localhost
```

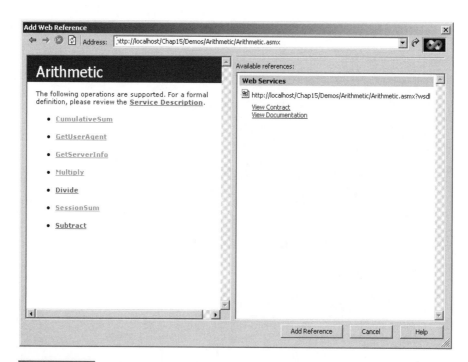

FIGURE 15–10   *Visual Studio display of Arithmetic Web service information.*

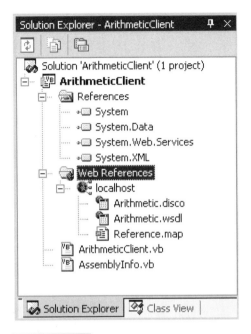

FIGURE 15-11 *Web references are displayed in Visual Studio Solution Explorer.*

8. Now add code to exercise the Web service by calling methods of the proxy.

We calculate a sum using the total held by the **Application** intrinsic object. Next, we calculate a sum for the total held by the **Session** intrinsic object.

```
Dim a As New Arithmetic()
Dim sum As Double
Dim i As Integer
For i = 0 To 4
   sum = a.CumulativeSum(i)
   Console.WriteLine( _
     "Adding {0}, Application sum is now {1}", i, sum)
Next

Dim sessionSum As Double
For i = 0 To 4
   sessionSum = a.SessionSum(i)
   Console.WriteLine( _
     "Adding {0}, Session sum is now {1}", i, sessionSum)
Next
```

This will give us the following output. The exact numbers for the application-based sum will depend on how many times you have run the application. The output shown is for the first run of the application.

```
Adding 0, Application sum is now 0
Adding 1, Application sum is now 1
Adding 2, Application sum is now 3
Adding 3, Application sum is now 6
Adding 4, Application sum is now 10
Adding 0, Session sum is now 0
Adding 1, Session sum is now 1
Adding 2, Session sum is now 2
Adding 3, Session sum is now 3
Adding 4, Session sum is now 4
```

We now create another instance of the proxy class and make the same method calls.

```
Dim a2 As New Arithmetic()
For i = 0 To 4
   sum = a2.CumulativeSum(i)
   Console.WriteLine( _
      "Adding {0}, Application sum is now {1}", i, sum)
Next

For i = 0 To 4
   sum = a2.SessionSum(i)
   Console.WriteLine( _
      "Adding {0}, Session sum is now {1}", i, sum)
Next
```

We get the following output. Notice how the application sum continues to increase, while the session bases sum starts again from zero. A new browser session is not the only way to start a new Web service session.

```
Adding 0, Application sum is now 10
Adding 1, Application sum is now 11
Adding 2, Application sum is now 13
Adding 3, Application sum is now 16
Adding 4, Application sum is now 20
Adding 0, Session sum is now 0
Adding 1, Session sum is now 1
Adding 2, Session sum is now 2
Adding 3, Session sum is now 3
Adding 4, Session sum is now 4
```

Finally, we call the **GetUserAgent** and **GetServerInfo** Web methods.

```
Console.WriteLine(a2.GetUserAgent())
Console.WriteLine(a2.GetServerInfo())
```

The output will look something like this:

```
Mozilla/4.0 (compatible; MSIE 6.0; MS Web Services Client
Protocol 1.0.3705.0)
Timeout for DELLPRO = 90; Located at
C:\OI\NetVb\Chap15\Demos\Arithmetic
```

Hotel Broker Web Services (Case Study)

The next step in the case study is to make the **Customer** and **Hotel** components of the Hotel Broker available as a Web services. For simplicity, we implement two Web services:

- **CustomerWebService.asmx**, which implements the **ICustomer** interface.
- **HotelInfoWebService.asmx**, which implements the **IHotelInfo** interface.

These Web services are found in the **WebServices** subdirectory of the **Case-Study** directory for this chapter.

At this point in your study, you have encountered many different variations of our Acme Travel Agency case study, and this chapter provides a good opportunity to investigate alternative configurations of essentially the same functionality. The **CaseStudy** folder contains a number of example programs. We highlight several programs in this section, which will illustrate a number of features of working with Web services.

We provide two versions of **Customer.dll** and **Hotel.dll**. These assemblies provide complete implementations of all the interfaces. The first version is in the folder **LibraryCollection** and provides an implementation using collections. This code was introduced in Chapter 6. The second version is in the folder **LibraryDatabase** and provides an implementation using databases, introduced in Chapter 13. Each folder contains a solution with three projects consisting of a console test program and two class libraries. If you prefer to avoid dealing with a database, you can use the collection version. You can easily switch back and forth between them in exercising Web services built upon them. The **Bin** directory for this chapter is used to hold these assemblies for use by Web services, and subdirectories are provided for saving the collection and database versions. For simplicity, the projects are arranged to build the assemblies in the top-level directories.

As mentioned, the Web services are provided by two **.asmx** files in the **WebServices** directory. You can exercise the Web services through Internet Explorer either by entering the proper HTTP addresses directly or by using the home page for this chapter.

The **WebServicesProxies** directory contains a project for building a proxy DLL for accessing the two Web services. This Visual Studio project makes use of Web References.

In the **ConsoleClient** subdirectory you will find a version of a console test program that uses the proxies assembly instead of the **Customer** and **Hotel** assemblies.

Since at this stage in the book you have a lot of experience with .NET, we do not spell out the details of building the various pieces of the case study.

Customer Web Service

Code Example

To implement the customer Web service, we created a file, **CustomerWeb-Service.asmx** (in the folder **WebServices**), that uses the **Customer** component to implement the details of the Web service:

```
<WebService(Namespace:="http://www.oi.com/netvb")> _
Class CustomerWebService
    Inherits System.Web.Services.WebService

Private custs As Customers

Public Sub New()
    custs = New Customers()
End Sub

<WebMethod()> _
Public Function RegisterCustomer( _
 firstName As String, lastName As String, _
 emailAddress As String) As Integer

    Dim customerId As Integer = _
        custs.RegisterCustomer(firstName, lastName, _
            emailAddress)
    Return customerId
End Function

<WebMethod()> _
Public Sub UnregisterCustomer(customerId As Integer)
    custs.UnregisterCustomer(customerId)
End Sub

<WebMethod(), _
XmlInclude(GetType(CustomerListItem))> _
Public Function GetCustomer(customerId As Integer) _
 As ArrayList
    Dim ar As ArrayList
    ar = custs.GetCustomer(customerId)
    Return ar
End Function
```

```
<WebMethod()> _
Public Sub ChangeEmailAddress(customerId As Integer, _
  emailAddress As String)
    custs.ChangeEmailAddress(customerId, emailAddress)
End Sub
```

The only new attribute is **XmlInclude**, which allows the XmlSerializer used to create the SOAP protocol to serialize a custom type, in this case **CustomerListItem**. (Without the attribute, you would get a runtime exception.) This attribute is found in the **System.Xml.Serialization** namespace. Nonetheless, if you examine the proxy class for this Web service, which is found in the **WebServiceProxies** directory, you will see that GetCustomer proxy (**customerproxy.cs**) returns only an array of objects.

```
Public Function GetCustomer(ByVal customerId As Integer) _
  As Object()
```

Code Example

Although the attribute instructs the serializer to save the custom type, the SOAP protocol understands only how to transmit a generic object type. So the **ConsoleClient** code using the proxy has to treat the return type as an object and then extract the custom type from it.

```
Private Sub ShowCustomerArray(ByVal array() As Object)
    Dim cli As CustomerListItem
    For Each cli In array
    ...
```

All the other array lists in the Customer and Hotel Web services are treated as arrays of objects where the appropriate type has to be extracted. Arrays that use types such as strings and integers, however, need no special treatment by the XmlSerializer.

HotelInfo Web Service

We do not provide a full-blown Web service interface to the Hotel Broker. Some features, such as adding or deleting hotels, would only be performed by administrators working for the hotel broker, and not by general people coming in over the Web. However, the **IHotelInfo** interface makes perfect sense to be exposed over the Web, and that is the interface we implement as a Web service.

Code Example

To implement this Web service we created a file, **HotelInfoWebService.asmx** (in the folder **WebServices**), that uses the **Hotel** component to implement the details of the Web service:

```
<WebService(Namespace:="http://www.oi.com/netvb")> _
Class HotelInfoWebService

    Private broker As HotelBroker
```

```
Public Sub New()
   broker = New HotelBroker()
End Sub

<WebMethod(), _
XmlInclude(GetType(HotelListItem))> _
Public Function GetHotels(city As String) As ArrayList
   Dim ar As ArrayList
   ar = broker.GetHotels(city)
   Return ar
End Function

<WebMethod(MessageName:="GetAllHotels"), _
XmlInclude(GetType(HotelListItem))> _
Public Function GetHotels() As ArrayList
   Dim ar As ArrayList
   ar = broker.GetHotels()
   Return ar
End Function

<WebMethod()> _
Public Function GetCities() As ArrayList
   Dim ar As ArrayList
   ar = broker.GetCities()
   Return ar
End Function

End Class
```

As was the case with the Customer Web service, we need XmlInclude attributes to enable the XmlSerializer to deal with custom types. Since Web service names have to be unique, we had to use the **MessageName** property of the **WebMethod** attribute to give one of the overloaded **GetHotels** methods a unique name.

Summary

Web services provide a means to extend component functionality across the network between platforms and languages from different vendors. Unlike .NET remoting, however, the types that can be used are much more limited.

Nonetheless, if you start your design from the point of view of the XML Schema specification and then build your WSDL and Web service classes, you will have a much greater chance of being able to interoperate.

Microsoft .NET provides powerful tools, making it very easy for developers to create Web services.

Security

Security prevents a user or a piece of code from doing things it should not be allowed to do. Traditionally, security has focused on restricting operations based on the identity of the user or the group to which the user belongs. Naturally, this approach to security is supported by .NET, and it is known as *user-based security* (a closely related concept is known as *role-based security,* also discussed later in this chapter). .NET also allows you to place restrictions on what a piece of code is permitted to do according to security evidence associated with that code. This new approach to security is known as *Code Access Security* (also known as *evidence-based security*). For example, you can prevent certain code from accessing certain files based on permissions relating to who digitally signed the code or based on the location from which the code originated. This is particularly useful when you have public Web sites or services where it is impractical to create user accounts, and lock-down files or other resources, for a large set of unknown users. Code Access Security is critical when you are executing code that may attempt to invoke functionality in other code created by third parties that you may or may not know or trust. Code Access Security is particularly useful for defending against malicious mobile code.

.NET security sits on top of the underlying operating system's security system. For the purposes of this chapter, the underlying operating system is assumed to be Windows 2000. While we will discuss some security issues associated with the underlying infrastructure, including Microsoft's Internet Information Server (IIS), we will only go into details on those aspects of security that are relevant to .NET security.

Code always runs under some identity, or in other words, as some user ID. For example, irrespective of the file creation .NET security permissions that may be in effect, if the underlying Win32 Access Control List (ACL) denies you the right to create a file, you will not be able to create a file.

User-based security always starts with two questions. The first is the authentication question and the second is the authorization question:

1. Authentication: *Who* are you?
2. Authorization: *Are you permitted* to do what you are attempting to do?

Code access security has to answer the same two basic questions as user-based security; however, the "you" in these questions refers to an assembly identity rather than a user identity.

In this chapter we will focus on how to implement user-based security and code access security. Other related aspects of security that will be discussed in this chapter are role-based security, IIS security, ASP.NET Web application security, administrative security policy management, and certain security utility tools.

User-Based Security

From the perspective of traditional user-based security, the authentication question is, Who is the *identity* attempting to do the action? An identity is typically a user or group name. *Credentials* are what the users present to prove who they are. Credentials are evidence presented for verification of identity. A credential might be your password, a smart card, or a biometric device. The users' credentials must be verified with some security authority. An example of this is verification of the user's password against his or her login name based on a database of user names and encrypted passwords. Systems that allow unverified access are said to allow anonymous access. In security lingo, an identity that can be authenticated is referred to as a *principal*.

The authorization question is, Can the identity perform the action it is attempting? The principal is then compared against some list of rights to determine whether access is granted or denied. For example, when you access a file, your user name is compared with an ACL for the action you want to do to determine if you can access the file. Of course, access is not always all or nothing. For example, you might have read, but not modify, rights to a file.

In a client/server or multitier architecture, the identity under which the server executes is often very powerful, and you typically want to restrict the ability of the client that makes a request on the server to some subset of privileges that the server has. In other cases, such as anonymous access, the server may not know who the client really is and must act accordingly. In these situations, the server can *impersonate* the client so that the privileges are limited to those of the client. In other words, code executes under the identity of the client instead of the server. In the case of anonymous access, the server runs under the identity of some preset user account with carefully selected privileges. Windows security and ASP.NET security are based on the concepts of user-based security.

Code Access Security

One of the challenges of the modern software world of third-party components and downloadable mobile code is that you open your system to damage from executing code from unknown sources. For example, you may want to restrict macros from accessing anything other than the document that contains them, or you may want to defend against potentially malicious scripts. You may even want to shield your system from bugs in software from known reputable vendors. You typically do not want to completely disable all this potentially useful functionality, but rather, you want to control what that functionality may attempt to do. To handle these situations, .NET security supports *Code Access Security* (CAS).

Code Access Security can be applied to verifiable code only. During JIT compilation, the verification process examines the MSIL code to verify its type safety. Type-safe code can only access memory locations that it is supposed to access. Pointer operations are not allowed in type-safe code so that methods can only be entered or left from well-defined entry points and exit points. You cannot calculate an address and enter code at an arbitrary point. Disallowing pointer operations means that random memory access is not possible, and code can only behave in a restricted manner.[1]

Security Policy

Code Access Security is based on the idea that you can assign levels of trust to assemblies and restrict the operation of the code within those assemblies to a certain set of operations. Code-based security is also referred to as evidence-based security. The name *evidence* stems from the fact that there is a set of information (i.e., evidence) that is used by the CLR to make decisions about what this code is allowed to do. A piece of evidence might be where the code was downloaded from, its digital signature, and so on. *Security policy* is the configurable set of rules that the CLR uses to make those decisions. The

---

1. Of course, bugs are still possible; it just means that bugs cannot overwrite the stack, overrun a buffer, or do anything that could be exploited to cause the program to do anything that it does not have the security rights to do. If you give your code unlimited rights, then you do have potential problems. This is especially true of the unmanaged code permission, which we will discuss later.

administrator normally establishes security policy. Security policy can be established at the enterprise, machine, user, or application domain level.

Permissions

Security policy is defined in terms of permissions. Permissions are objects that are used to describe the rights and privileges of assemblies to access other objects or undertake certain actions. Assemblies can request to be granted certain permissions, and security policy dictates what permissions will be granted to an assembly.

Examples of the classes that model permissions include the following:

- **SecurityPermission** controls access to the security system.
- **FileIOPermission** controls access to the file system.
- **ReflectionPermission** controls access to nonpublic metadata.

All the permission classes inherit from the **CodeAccessPermission** base class, so they all behave in very much the same way. Code can request permissions in one of two ways: either by using attributes or programmatically.

Attributes can be applied to the assembly to represent a request for certain permissions. The CLR will use metadata to determine what permissions are being requested. Based on the code's identity and trust level, the CLR will use the established security policy to determine whether it will grant or deny those requested permissions.

Alternatively, code can programmatically demand[2] that its callers have certain permissions before it will execute certain code paths. This can be useful in situations where you would like to know up front that you have the necessary permissions before you enter into a particular piece of code, rather than simply plow into it and hope for the best. If the demand fails, the CLR will throw a **System.Security.SecurityException**.

Whenever you demand a permission, you have to be prepared to catch the security exception and handle the case that the permission is not granted. Most code will not have to demand permissions because the .NET Framework libraries will do that for you on your behalf in most cases. However, you should still be prepared to handle the security exception in any situation where it could be thrown.

To be defensively proactive, code can even request that the permissions that it was granted be restricted or denied. This is important for code that uses third-party components or relies on third-party Web scripts. Since such code

---

2. Actually, this is more like a request than a demand, since it may be denied. However, the word demand is generally used in this context. In fact, as we will soon see, **Demand** is actually the name of the method used to programmatically request desired permissions.

may have a lower level of trust than your own code, you might want to restrict the available rights while that code is running. When it is finished running, you can restore the level of permissions back to their original levels.

Determining the identity of the code is equivalent to the authentication question of traditional security. The authorization question is based on the security permissions that are given or taken away from an assembly.

Many of the classes that support permissions are found in the **System.Security.Permissions** namespace. Some are found in the **System.Net** namespace.

Internet Security

You can use the Internet Protocol Security (IPSec) to restrict access to your computer to certain IP addresses. Of course, this will only work if you know the IP addresses of your clients. The advantage is that you do not have to change your client application, ASP.NET code, or Web service code to use it. This is impractical for public Web sites or services where you do not know who your clients are.

Internet Information Server

While the focus of this chapter is on .NET security, some knowledge of IIS security is important to have. Since both Web services and ASP.NET use IIS, your IIS settings do affect these aspects of .NET security.

In the previous chapters on ASP.NET and Web services, we have used the default settings of Anonymous access. Anonymous access does not require a user name or password to access an account. You run under some default user account. Anonymous access is useful for public Web sites and services that do their own authentication by asking for a user name or password or that use some other means. In such a scenario you could use ASP.NET forms-based authentication. You can build forms to get the user name and password, and then validate them against a configuration file or database.

IIS supports the major HTTP authentication schemes. These schemes require you to configure IIS appropriately. These schemes are listed in Table 16–1. In each of these scenarios IIS authenticates the user if the credentials match an existing user account. Secure Sockets Layer (SSL) is used whenever you need to encrypt the HTTP communication channel. SSL degrades performance, but remains a very important Internet technology where privacy is a major concern. We do not discuss SSL further, since it is not directly relevant to .NET security.

TABLE 16-1	*IIS Authentication Schemes*

Scheme	Description
Basic	User and password information is effectively sent as plain text. This is standard HTTP authentication and is not secure.
Basic over SSL	Basic authentication, but the communication channel is encoded so the user name and password are protected.
Digest	Uses hashing to transmit user name and password. This is not really a secure method because the hash codes are potentially reversible by way of an exhaustive brute force attack.[*] This was introduced in HTTP 1.1 to replace Basic authentication.
Windows Integrated Security	Traditional Windows security using NTLM or Kerberos protocols. IIS authenticates if credentials match a user account. Cannot be used across proxies and firewalls. NTLM is the legacy Windows security protocol.
Certificates over SSL	Client obtains a certificate that is mapped to a user account.

[*]   A hash code is produced by applying a hash function on some arbitrary length data. The resulting hash code is a fixed length fingerprint that is highly characteristic of the original data. A message digest is another name for the result of applying a hash function to a message. Message Digest 5 (MD5) and Secure Hash Algorithm (SHA-1) are popular hash algorithms.

You can also adjust access rights to individual files (graphics, data files, etc.) and other resources (e.g., databases) for specific user accounts. For public Web sites and Web services, this approach is not useful because Web clients will not usually have user accounts.

Microsoft has introduced the *Passport* authentication scheme as a convenience. While ASP.NET does have support for Passport (**System.Web.Security.PassportIdentity** class) on the server side, developer tools to handle the client side for Passport authentication do not yet exist as of this writing. Passport avoids the problem of requiring specific accounts on specific machines, allowing the user to be authenticated by many systems, from any client machine, all with a single password. We will not discuss Passport further, since it is not directly relevant to .NET security.

The security specification for SOAP is being worked on by the W3C. You could create your own custom authentication using SOAP messages. Since XML is transmitted as text, you may want to use SSL to encrypt the messages (especially if you use tags such as <user> and <password>). In general, secure data has to be encrypted when using SOAP.

Role-Based Security in .NET

Most people have at least an intuitive understanding of users, groups, and passwords. MTS and COM+ have provided an additional security system based on *roles*. The best place to start a more detailed look at .NET security is with user identities and roles. First, we will look at this from the point of view of a Windows application and then from the point of view of an ASP.NET application.

Principals and Identities

Each thread has associated with it a CLR principal. That principal contains an identity that represents the current user ID that is running that thread. The static property **Thread.CurrentPrincipal** will return the current principal associated with the current thread.

Principal objects implement the **IPrincipal** interface. **IPrincipal** has one method and one property. The **Identity** property returns the current identity object, and the method **IsInRole** is used to determine whether a given user is in a specific role. The **RoleBasedSecurity** example illustrates the use of principals, identities, and roles.

Code Example

Currently there are two principal classes in the .NET Framework: **WindowsPrincipal** and **GenericPrincipal**. The **GenericPrincipal** class is useful if you need to implement your own custom principal. The **WindowsPrincipal** represents a Windows user and its associated roles. Since the **RoleBasedSecurity** example is a Windows (console) application, we will have a **WindowsPrincipal** associated with the **CurrentPrincipal** property.

. . .[3]
```
Dim ip As IPrincipal
ip = Thread.CurrentPrincipal

' verify Current Principal is a Windows Principal
Dim wp As WindowsPrincipal = ip
If wp Is Nothing Then
   Console.WriteLine( _
      "Thread.CurrentPrincipal NOT a WindowsPrincipal")
Else
```

---

3. The program starts out with a demand for a **SecurityPermission** and then proceeds to set the application domain principal policy. While the reasons for this will be discussed later, the quick answer is to make sure that the example functions properly on your machine. If you get an exception, you will have to set the policy on your local machine to allow you to run the example. This should not normally happen. What to do if it does is discussed later in this chapter.

```
      Console.WriteLine( _
         "Thread.CurrentPrincipal is a WindowsPrincipal")
End If
...
```

An identity object implements the **IIdentity** interface. The **IIdentity** interface has three properties:

- **Name**, which is the string associated with the identity. This is given to the CLR by either the underlying operating system or authentication provider. ASP.NET is an example of an authentication provider.
- **IsAuthenticated**, which is a Boolean value indicating whether the user was authenticated or not.
- **AuthenticationType**, which is a string that indicates which authentication type was used by the underlying operating system or authentication provider. Examples of authentication types are Basic, NTLM, Kerberos, and Passport.

There are several types of identity objects. Since this is a Windows program, we will have a **WindowsIdentity** object associated with the **WindowsPrincipal**. The example next prints out the property information associated with the identity object.

```
Dim ii As IIdentity = ip.Identity
Console.WriteLine( _
"Thread.CurrentPrincipal Name: {0} Type: {1}
 IsAuthenticated: {2}", _
ii.Name, _
ii.AuthenticationType, _
ii.IsAuthenticated)
```

On my machine this output is displayed:

```
Thread.CurrentPrincipal Name: HPDESKTOP\Administrator Type:
 NTLM IsAuthenticated: True
```

Therefore, the operating system on this machine (HPDESKTOP) has authenticated the user (Administrator) running this program using the NTLM protocol. The example then validates that this is indeed a **WindowsIdentity** object. The **WindowsIdentity** object has additional properties and methods beyond those of the **IIdentity** interface. One of them is the Win32 account token ID associated with the currently running user.

```
Dim wi As WindowsIdentity = wp.Identity
If Not wi Is Nothing Then
   Console.WriteLine( _
      "WindowsPrincipal.Identity Name: {0} Type: {1}
       Authenticated: {2} Token: {3}", _
   wi.Name, wi.AuthenticationType, _
   wi.IsAuthenticated, wi.Token)
End If
```

You can use the name of the user to decide (i.e., authorize) in an if statement whether the user has the right to undertake certain actions by executing or refusing to execute certain code paths.

.NET Windows Roles

Instead of checking each individual user name, you can assign users to *roles*. You can then check to see if a user belongs to a certain role. The standard administrators group is an example of how a role works. You do not have to individually assign a user identity all the privileges that an administrator has and then check to see if individual users have certain privileges. Instead, you just assign the user to the administrators group. Code can then check to see if the user is in the administrator's group before attempting actions such as creating a new user. .NET roles are similar to, but distinct from, COM+ roles.

You define roles by defining groups in NT4 or Windows 2000. Each group represents one role. To do this, go to the Control Panel and select Administrative Tools. From the Administrative Tools list, select Computer Management. In the Computer Management MMC snap-in, expand the Local Users and Groups node. As Figure 16–1 shows, if you select Groups, you will see all the Groups defined on your machine.

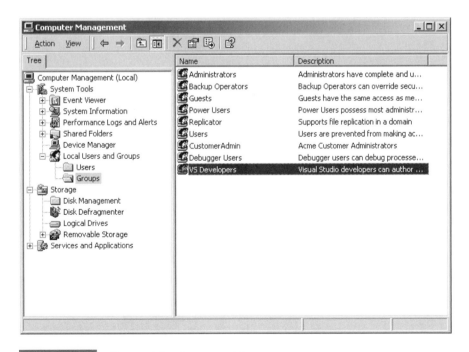

FIGURE 16–1   *Groups defined on a machine.*

Some groups, such as Administrators and Guests, are "built-in" because they are predefined for you. The CustomerAdmin group shown in Figure 16–1 is a user-defined group that represents administrators who have the right to modify the Acme Customer application information.

To add a new group to the local machine, right mouse click on the Groups node, select New Group, and a dialog box that you can fill in pops up. Figure 16–2 shows this dialog is filled in for a new group entitled Hotel-Admin, which is designed to have all users on the machine who can add or modify information about hotels in the HotelBroker application. Clicking the Create button will add the group to the system. You can use the Add and Remove buttons to add or remove users from the group.

To modify an existing group, select that group, right mouse click, and select Properties. Clicking the Add button will bring up a dialog of all users on the system. You can then select users and add them to the group. Figure 16–3 shows a user about to be added to the HotelAdmin group. The Remove button is used to remove users from the group.

Within code you can qualify the name using the domain or machine name. The CustomerAdmin role is referred to as HPDESKTOP\CustomerAdmin. For groups that are preinstalled, such as the Administrators group, you use the BUILTIN prefix—for example, BUILTIN\Administrators. To avoid translation and internationalization problems, the **System.Security.Princi-**

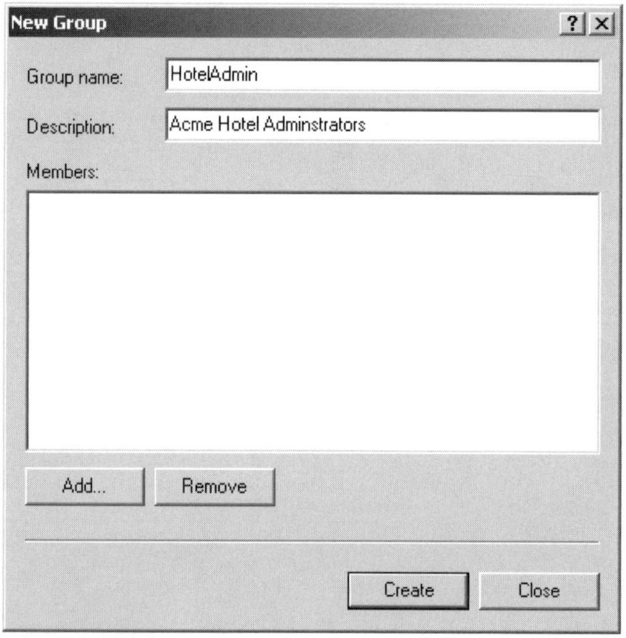

FIGURE 16–2   *Dialog to create a HotelAdmin group.*

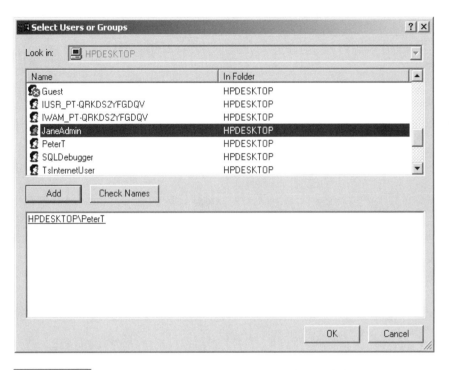

FIGURE 16–3   *User JaneAdmin about to be added to the HotelAdmin group. User PeterT has already been added.*

pal.WindowsBuiltInRole enumeration can be used to refer to built-in roles. Instead of using the BUILTIN\Administrators string, you can refer to the Administrators group as **WindowsBuiltInRole.Administrator**.

The **RoleBasedSecurity** example now checks to see if the current user is in a role. You can either pass the role as a string or use the **WindowsBuilt-InRole** enumeration. Remember to modify the program to use the name of your machine when you run the book samples on your computer.

```
Dim inRole As Boolean = _
  wp.IsInRole("HPDESKTOP\CustomerAdmin")
Console.WriteLine( _
  "In Customer Administrator role?: {0}", inRole)

' using built in roles
inRole = wp.IsInRole(WindowsBuiltInRole.Administrator)
Console.WriteLine( _
  "Is in Administrators group: {0}", inRole)
inRole = wp.IsInRole(WindowsBuiltInRole.Guest)
Console.WriteLine("Is in Guests group: {0}", inRole)
inRole = wp.IsInRole(WindowsBuiltInRole.User)
Console.WriteLine("Is in Users group: {0}", inRole)
```

The program produces the following output, assuming that you are logged in as Administrator. Note that because the Administrator user ID was added to the CustomerAdmin group in the Computer Management MMC snap-in described earlier, the call to wp.IsInRole("HPDESKTOP\Customer-erAdmin") results in the value **True**.

```
Demanding right to change AppDomin principal policy
AppDomain Principal Policy changed to WindowsPrincipal
Thread.CurrentPrincipal is a WindowsPrincipal
Thread.CurrentPrincipal Name: HPDESKTOP\Administrator Type:
NTLM IsAuthenticated
: True
WindowsPrincipal.Identity Name: HPDESKTOP\Administrator
Type: NTLM Authenticated
: True Token: 308
In Customer Administrator role?: True
Is in Administrators group: True
Is in Guests group: False
Is in Users group: True
```

Other Identity Classes

Now let us look into more detail at the other Identity classes. Currently there are four in the .NET Framework:

- **FormsIdentity** is used by the **FormsAuthenticationModule** class. We will discuss this class when we discuss ASP.NET forms authentication.
- **GenericIdentity** can represent any user. This class is used with the **GenericPrincipal** for generic or custom identities and principals.
- **PassportIdentity** is used with Passport authentication. Since we do not discuss Passport, we will not discuss this class.
- **WindowsIdentity** represents a Windows user. A **WindowsPrincipal** instance will have a **WindowsIdentity** instance as its **Identity** property. For authenticated users, the type of authentication used (NTLM, Kerberos, and so on) is available.

Note that the properties of the **IIdentity** interface are read-only and therefore cannot be modified.

Even if your users are unauthenticated, you can get the **WindowsIdentity** for any thread, using the static method **WindowsIdentity.GetCurrent** to get the **WindowsIdentity** instance of the current user. You can then use the **WindowsPrincipal** constructor to build a **WindowsPrincipal** instance from this **WindowsIdentity**. What this identity represents will be discussed in the next section.

Code Example

The AcmeGui case study program has been modified so that you cannot run it if you are not in the HotelAdmin role. See the file **MainAdminForm.vb** in the **HotelBrokerAdministrationRoles** example.

```vb
Private Sub Form1_Load( _
 ByVal sender As System.Object, _
 ByVal e As System.EventArgs) Handles MyBase.Load
    Dim sp As SecurityPermission = _
        New SecurityPermission( _
            SecurityPermissionFlag.ControlPrincipal)
    Try
        sp.Demand()
    Catch se As SecurityException
        MessageBox.Show(se.Message)
        Close()
    End Try

    Dim ap As AppDomain = AppDomain.CurrentDomain
    ap.SetPrincipalPolicy( _
        PrincipalPolicy.WindowsPrincipal)

    Dim ip As IPrincipal
    ip = Thread.CurrentPrincipal

    Dim inRole As Boolean = _
        ip.IsInRole("HPDESKTOP\HotelAdmin")

    If inRole = False Then
        MessageBox.Show( _
            "Cannot run. Must be a Hotel Administrator.", _
            "Acme Customer Management System", _
            MessageBoxButtons.OK, MessageBoxIcon.Exclamation)
        Close()
    End If
End Sub
```

ASP.NET Roles

Now that we have a fundamental understanding about principals, identities, and roles, we can apply this to our AcmeReservationSystem Web site. The Web site has been modified so that you can link to a HotelAdministration page where you can add, modify, or delete the hotels that are part of the HotelBroker system. This example is found in **AcmeWeb** under the **Step0** subdirectory of the **ASP.NET_Roles** directory. To run this example, make sure that the **Chap16** directory is a virtual directory with the name **Chap16**. Figures 16–4 and 16–5 show the new Web pages.

Code Example

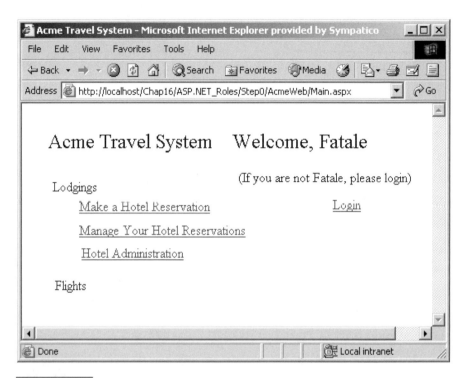

FIGURE 16–4 *The new Acme home page with the link to the administration page.*

At this point there is no security associated with these pages. Anyone who can access the Web site can also access the administration page and modify the hotel information. We have also modified the login page to print out the principal and identity information currently running the application as well as the information associated with the current Windows identity.

```
Dim ip As IPrincipal
ip = Thread.CurrentPrincipal
Dim ii As IIdentity = ip.Identity
Dim isAnonymous As Boolean
Dim wit As Type
If TypeOf ii is WindowsIdentity
    Dim wii As WindowsIdentity = ii
    isAnonymous = wii.IsAnonymous()
    wit = GetType(WindowsIdentity)
ElseIf TypeOf ii Is GenericIdentity Then
    isAnonymous = True
    wit = GetType(GenericIdentity)
End If
Dim principalText As String = _
    "Current Principal: " & wit.ToString() & Chr(10) & _
    "    IsAnonymous: " & isAnonymous & Chr(10) & _
```

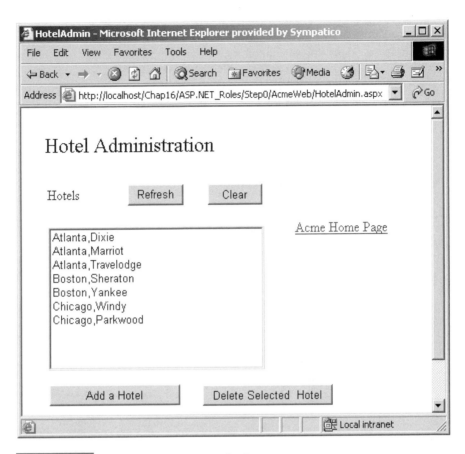

FIGURE 16–5   *The administration page for the AcmeReservation system.*

```
"    Name: " & ii.Name & Chr(10) & _
"    Is current Principal authenticated? : " & _
ii.IsAuthenticated.ToString() & Chr(10) & _
"    AuthenticationType: " & _
ii.AuthenticationType & Chr(10)
Dim wi As WindowsIdentity = WindowsIdentity.GetCurrent()
Dim identityText As String = _
  "Current Windows Identity: " & Chr(10) & _
"    IsAnonymous: " & wi.IsAnonymous & Chr(10) & _
"    Name: " & wi.Name & Chr(10) & _
"    Is current Windows Identity Authenticated?: " & _
wi.IsAuthenticated & Chr(10) & _
"    AuthenticationType: " & _
wi.AuthenticationType & Chr(10)
Dim text As String = principalText & identityText
IdentityInfo.Text = text
```

As Figure 16–6 illustrates, looking at the information on the login page, we find that we have an unauthenticated principal for the thread, yet the current Windows identity indicates that we are running as the authenticated SYSTEM account. What does this mean? In the previous examples, we used the **IsInRole** method associated with the current principal. But that user is now not authenticated, so the **IsInRole** method will always return false and is therefore now useless!

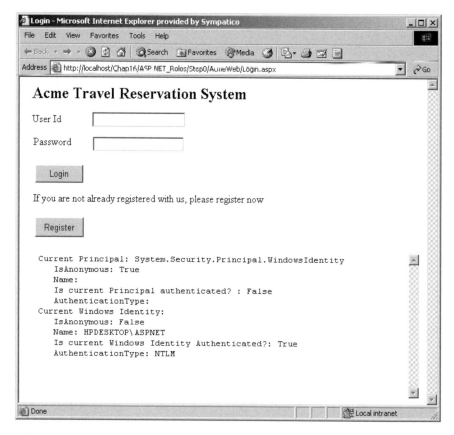

FIGURE 16–6   *Principal and Windows identity information for AcmeWebSecurity Step0.*

Operating System Identity and CLR Identity

As we mentioned at the start of the chapter, .NET security sits on top of the underlying operating system security. The identity associated with a thread by the CLR and the identity associated with that thread by the operating system are not the same identities. The identity of the thread from the operating system's perspective is indicated by the **WindowsIdentity** object returned by the static **Windows.IdentityGetCurrent** method. The CLR identity is indicated by the value of the **Thread.CurrentPrincipal** object. What values the current **WindowsIdentity** and **Thread.CurrentPrincipal** have are set in different places: IIS Settings and the ASP.NET configuration files. Recall from the start of this chapter that if you access a file from within .NET, both the managed (.NET) and unmanaged (Win32) identities must have rights to the file within their respective environments.

UNAUTHENTICATED USERS

Every machine that runs .NET has a **machine.config** file that has the default configuration for the computer. This file is found in the **\WINNT\ Microsoft.NET\Framework\v1.0.2914\CONFIG** directory, where **v1.0.2914** would be replaced by the version of Microsoft .NET that is running on your machine. A Web or Web service application may have a **web.config** file that has the configuration settings for that application. The settings for **web.config** affect all applications in the directory where it lives and all its subdirectories. **web.config** files in the subdirectories override the settings in the higher level directories.

If you look in the settings in **web.config** for the Step0 project, you will see the following setting:

```
<authentication mode="Windows" />
```

This sets the CLR-based identity returned by **Thread.CurrentPrincipal**. If you were to change this authentication mode from Windows to None, then **Thread.CurrentPrincipal** would return a **GenericPrincipal**. Leaving this authentication mode set to Windows, however, causes **Thread.CurrentPrincipal** to return a **WindowsPrincipal**, but it is still unauthenticated and has no name associated with it. Other possible values for this authentication mode are Forms and Passport. Figure 16–7 shows the result of changing the authentication mode to None.

Next, add the following code to the **web.config** file to set identity impersonate to true, and see what effect that has.

```
<identity impersonate="true" />
```

Figure 16–8 shows the results of setting the identity impersonation tag to true.

Where does the identity HPDESKTOP\IUSR_HPDESKTOP come from? This user is the identity that is set in the properties for this Web application for anonymous access. Select this Web application in the Internet Services Manager, right mouse click and select Properties. Navigate to the Directory Security tab. Click on the Edit button associated with Anonymous access and authentication control. Note that the Anonymous access checkbox is checked. Click the Edit button associated with Account used for anonymous access,

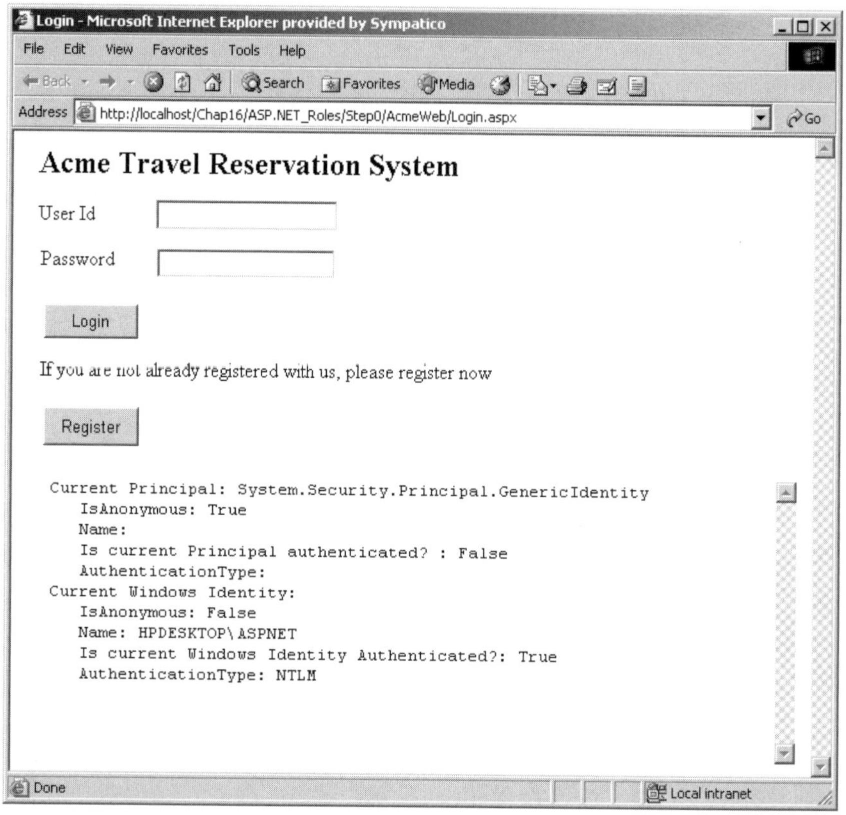

FIGURE 16-7 *Results when authentication mode is set to None.*

and you will see this user account listed. Figure 16–9 shows Internet Services Manager and the Anonymous User Account dialog box. You could change this setting to some other account, but this is the default value set when IIS was installed, according to your machine name at that time.

Actually, if you set the identity impersonate tag to true, you will see the identity HPDESKTOP\IUSR_HPDESKTOP, regardless of whether the authentication mode is set to None or Windows. Only if you set the identity impersonation tag to false or remove it altogether do you see the identity change back to the default HPDESKTOP\ASPNET.

AUTHENTICATED USERS

Now let us use the Internet Services Manager to set our Web application to use Windows Integrated Security instead of anonymous access, as shown in Figure 16–10. We uncheck the Anonymous access box and check the Integrated Windows authentication box. Running our application, still with the identity impersonate tag to true, gets the results in Figure 16–11.

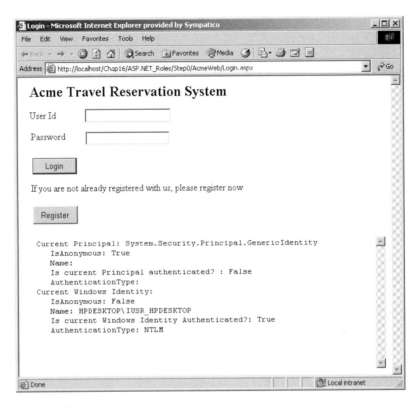

FIGURE 16-8   *Results when identity impersonate is set to true.*

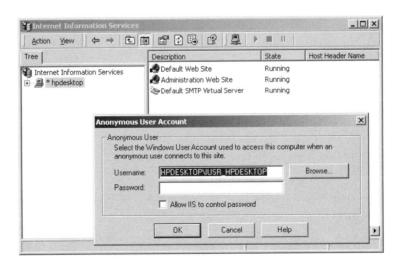

FIGURE 16-9   *Internet Services Manager settings for anonymous access.*

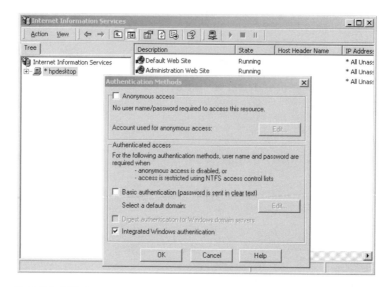

FIGURE 16–10   *Internet Services Manager settings for authenticated access.*

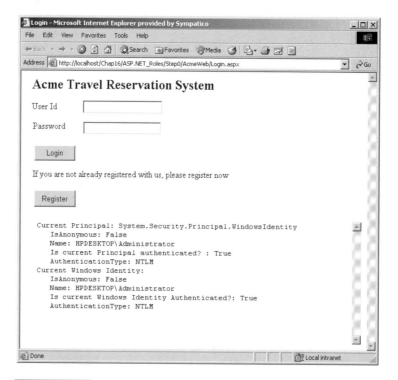

FIGURE 16–11   *Authenticated access gets us an authenticated WindowsPrincipal.*

We now have an authenticated **Thread.CurrentPrincipal** whose identity is the same as the current **WindowsIdentity**. They are associated with whatever user account is currently logged in. Both the managed and unmanaged principals are now the same, and the technique of calling **IsInRole** will now work again.

Now uncheck the Integrated Windows authentication box and check the Basic authentication box in the Internet Services Manager dialog. If you run the application, still with the identity impersonate tag to true, you see a user and password dialog appear. You now have to enter the user name and password associated with an account on the system. Again, when the login page appears, both the **Thread.CurrentPrincipal** and current **WindowsIdentity** identities are the same, but they are associated with whichever user account you entered into the dialog box, as shown in Figure 16–12.

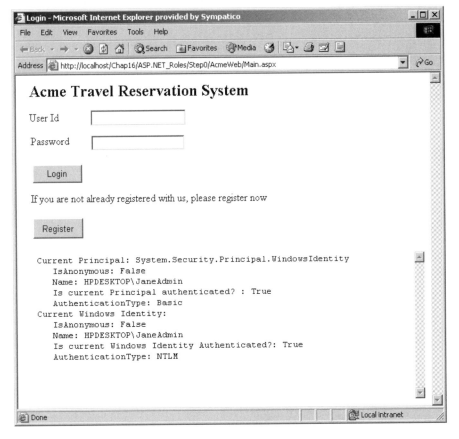

FIGURE 16–12 *Authenticated Access with principal based on Basic login dialog.*

Within ASP.NET you can access the **Thread.CurrentPrincipal** through the **User** object. Step1 of the **ASP.NET_Roles** example adds the following code to the **Page_Load** method of main.aspx.vb:

```
If (User.IsInRole("HPDESKTOP\HotelAdmin")) Then
   HotelAdminLink.Visible = True
Else
   HotelAdminLink.Visible = False
```

The effect of this is to hide the link to the Hotel Administration Web page unless you are logged into Windows as a hotel administrator. For this to work, we must ensure that the Internet Services Manager security settings are set at Windows Integrated Security, with no Anonymous access. We must also ensure that the following settings exist in the application's **web.config** file:

```
<authentication mode="Windows" />
<identity impersonate="true" />
```

Therefore, if a user who is logged into Windows is a member of the Hotel-Admin group, he or she will see the Administration link; otherwise, the user will not. Of course, what name you enter into the login page has nothing to do with what you see happening here. It is the identity of the thread that matters.

If you want to test your Web application as a different user, you do not have to log out and log in as that user. Instead, just navigate to Internet Explorer on the Start menu, and right mouse click *while holding down the shift key.* You will then see menu item Run As..., as shown in Figure 16–13. Of course, without the shift key, this menu item will not appear. Select it, and in the dialog box that comes up, log in as the user you want to use. That particular instance of Internet Explorer will then be running under that user identity.

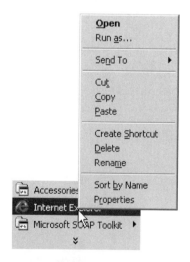

FIGURE 16-13   *RunAs Menu item to run as a different user.*

PROBLEMS WITH IMPERSONATION

It would seem that all we have to do is make sure that the user ID that the thread impersonates is a member of the HotelAdmin group that does not have any more privileges than are absolutely needed (i.e., not SYSTEM or Administrator, and with no ACL rights to any unnecessary files, and so on), and then everything would be just fine.

Unfortunately, life is not so simple. Impersonation is designed for use by a server to alter its rights by running a thread as another user. When the server is done impersonating a user, however, it can revert to its original set of rights by calling the **RevertToSelf** Win32 API. If you call out to a third-party assembly or any unmanaged DLL after it has made the call to **RevertToSelf**, it would then be running as SYSTEM. As SYSTEM, the assembly or DLL could cause havoc on your computer if it was malicious or even just buggy.

Step 2 of **ASP.NET_Roles** uses the following code to demonstrate this:[4]

```
Imports System.Runtime.InteropServices
...
<DllImport("Advapi32.dll")> _
Public Shared Function RevertToSelf() As Boolean
End Function
...
Dim text As String
text = "Windows Identity: " & _
    WindowsIdentity.GetCurrent().Name & Chr(10)
text = text & "CLR Identity: " & User.Identity.Name &
Chr(10)
text = text & "Calling RevertToSelf()..." & Chr(10)

Dim bRet As Boolean = RevertToSelf()

text = text & "Windows Identity: " & _
    WindowsIdentity.GetCurrent().Name & Chr(10)
text = text & "CLR Identity: " & _
    User.Identity.Name & Chr(10)

txtInfo.Text = text
```

On the Acme home page, calling **RevertToSelf** changes the identity of the thread from the point of view of unmanaged code. The identity from the CLR perspective is unchanged. The HotelAdmin link will be visible or not, depending on the original impersonated identity. Figure 16–14 shows the results.

---

4. You use the PInvoke interop facility to access the Win32 function. The DllImport attribute and PInvoke are discussed in Chapter 17.

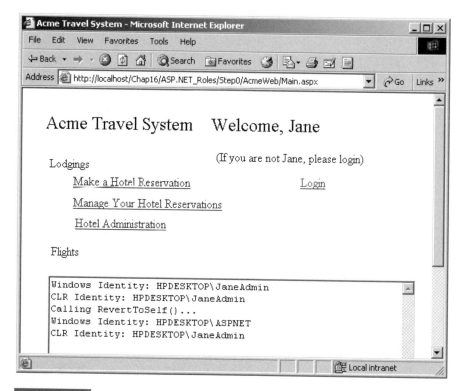

FIGURE 16–14   *Acme home page showing changes in Thread Identities.*

To avoid running as the HPDESKTOP\ASPNET account, you can set the identity of the process that your Web application runs under.[5] If you look in **machine.config** under the <ProcessModel> tag, you will find the userName and password attributes.

```
<processModel enable="true"
...
userName="machine" password="AutoGenerate"
...
/>
```

Because of this, by default, your application process runs under the HPDESKTOP\ASPNET account. You can modify this value in the

---

5. HPDESKTOP\ASPNET is the identity of the process token used by IIS. Unless impersonating, all threads in the Web application would use that token. Calling **RevertToSelf** removes the impersonation from the thread and reverts back to this original identity.

machine.config file. We can therefore change this value to be a specific user name:[6]

```
<processModel enable="true"
...
userName="JaneAdmin" password="midas"
...
/>
```

Figure 16–15 shows the results.[7] As you can see, the password for this user is written in plain text inside **machine.config**. By default, **machine.config** is readable by everyone, so if you use this approach, then rights to that file should be restricted.

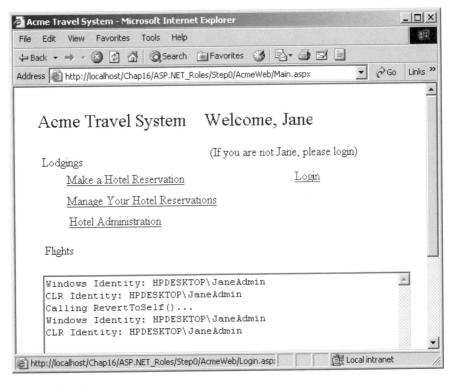

FIGURE 16–15   *Results of using RevertToSelf when a specific user is set in <process-Model>.*

---

6. You will have to stop and start the WWW service on your machine to make the changes to **machine.config** effective.
7. If you have problems running with a user ID you supply here, that ID will probably need ACL rights to various system directories on your machine, such as the ASP.NET temporary file directory.

To summarize, if impersonation is turned off, as Figure 16–16 shows, then you would run as whatever identity is specified in the process model. If you use Anonymous access, then Figure 16–17 shows the results you would expect: that the CLR thread identity is unauthenticated.

This discussion also makes clear that the ACLs on **machine.config** and **web.config** should be set so that only administrators can modify these files. Who can read the files should be restricted appropriately as well. You have to also guard against someone browsing and downloading from those files.

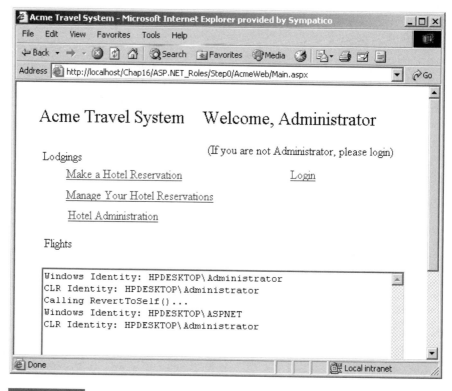

FIGURE 16–16   *Impersonation turned off, MACHINE specified in <processModel>.*

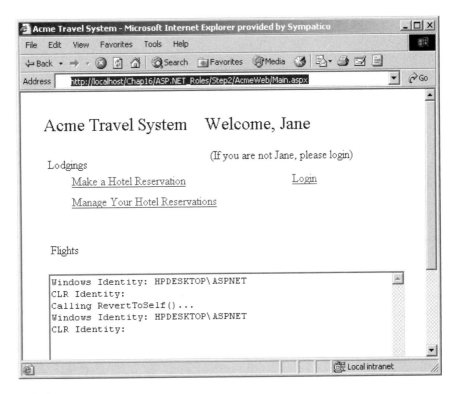

FIGURE 16-17 *Impersonation turned off, Anonymous access, MACHINE specified in <processModel>.*

Specifying Users and Groups for Access in Web.Config

ASP.NET allows you to specify groups and users who are allowed to access the Web site. Inside the <authorization> section of **web.config**, you can use the <allow> and <deny> elements with user accounts or groups. To specify groups, you use the **roles** attribute; to specify users, you use the **users** attribute. The asterisk (*) symbol used with one of those elements means all. A question mark (?) used with a user attribute means Anonymous access.

```
<allow roles=" HPDESKTOP\HotelAdmin" users="
 HPDESKTOP\Peter">
<deny users=" HPDESKTOP\John>
```

A reference to a specific user overrides that user's membership in a group or a wildcard. Deny references take precedence over allow references. These settings do not help you in assigning users to particular roles or prevent access to different areas of the Web site. Only access to the entire Web site is controlled.

Forms-Based Authentication

The previous discussion is relevant for intranets or other scenarios where users will have Windows user accounts on the servers or domains. Furthermore, Windows Integrated Security does not work across firewalls or proxies. For public Web sites, we need another approach.

The alternative approach is to bring up a login form to authenticate the user. We will look at two of the several approaches possible within .NET to login forms. The **FormsBasedAuthentication** example uses the .NET **Forms-Authentication** class and the **web.config** file.

Forms Authentication and Authorization

.NET Forms-based authentication uses the application's **web.config** file, a login form, and an optional cookie to authenticate the user. Typically, in this scenario you will set up the Web site for anonymous access so that no users will be screened out by IIS. Here is the **web.config** file section for the **FormsBasedAuthentication** example:

```
<authentication mode="Forms">
    <forms name = "HotelBrokerCookie" path="/"
                    loginUrl="Login.aspx"
                    protection="All" timeout="10">
      <credentials passwordFormat="Clear">
        <user name="Natasha" password="Natasha" />
        <user name="Adams" password="Adams" />
        <user name="peter" password="peter" />
      </credentials>
    </forms>
  </authentication>

  <authorization>
    <allow users="Natasha,peter" />
    <deny users="*" />
  </authorization>
```

The authentication mode is set to Forms. This means that the **User.Identity** object will be a **FormsIdentity** instance if the user is authenticated. The forms element has several attributes that define how the authentication is set up. The name attribute is the name of the cookie. The path attribute indicates where on the site the cookie is valid, "/" indicates the entire site. The loginUrl indicates where the login form resides. The protection attribute indicates how the cookie should be encrypted. "All" indicates that the cookie should be validated and encrypted. Other options are None, Encryption, Validation. Timeout indicates how many minutes before the cookie becomes invalid (expires).

The credential elements indicate how the password should be stored in the configuration file. For simplicity, we have used clear text. You could also specify SHA-1 or MD5 to hash the passwords. If passwords are stored in **web.config**, it should be secured against download. Passwords for the configuration file can be encrypted with the static **FormsAuthentication** method **HashPasswordForStoringInConfigFile**.

The user elements indicate the user names and passwords. The authorization section, as discussed earlier, determines which authenticated users are authorized to access the Web site.

Since this example uses redirection and cookie validation, a user should attempt to access the main page, **http://localhost/FormsBasedAuthentication/default.aspx**, instead of the **login.aspx** file. If a valid cookie does not exist on the system, the user will be sent to the login page. If a valid cookie exists, it will be used to validate the user and will go straight to the **default.aspx** page. If the user went straight to the login page, he or she would have to log in every time, even with a valid cookie.

Here is the code for handling the Login button event:

```
Private Sub btnLogin_Click(...) Handles btnLogin.Click
    If FormsAuthentication.Authenticate( _
        txtUserId.Text, txtPassword.Text) Then
      FormsAuthentication.RedirectFromLoginPage( _
        txtUserId.Text, True)
    Else
      lblErrorMessage.Text = "Could not authenticate user."
    End If
    ...
End Sub
```

For simplicity, the Password textbox does not bother to hide the password, but of course, in real life, the password should be hidden in the user interface.

The **FormsAuthentication** class's **Authenticate** method validates the user name and password from the **web.config** file. If a valid cookie is on the system, this authentication is skipped. **RedirectFromLoginPage** does several things. It checks the authorization section of **web.config** to see if the users have the rights to access the file, creates a cookie, and redirects the user to the **default.aspx** page. If the second argument is true, a persistent cookie is placed on the user's system. Using persistent cookies is a security risk, because the cookie can be stolen as it is transmitted. You could use SSL to protect the cookie. You can remove the session or persistent cookie with the **SignOut** method.

If you run the **FormsBasedAuthentication** example, only Natasha, peter, and Adams will be authenticated. However, only Natasha and Peter will be authorized to use the site. Of course, only Natasha will be found in the database of Acme customers. That test has been moved to **default.aspx** to distinguish it from the forms authentication done in **login.aspx**.

Default.aspx can refer to the name of the user through the **User** object. The type of identity object is **FormsIdentity**.

```
Dim ok As Boolean = _
    HotelState.acme.Login(User.Identity.Name)
```

If you succeed and log in as Natasha once, subsequent tries will succeed without the login page because we have created a persistent cookie. To avoid persistent cookies, set the second argument to **RedirectFromLoginPage** to **false**.

The application, however, runs under the identity of the system process or thread, not the identity of the user name that is logged in. Hence, role-based security in ASP.NET can be used only with Windows authentication, not with Forms authentication. You will have to write code to control access to the Hotel Administration page.

Code Access Permissions

Code needs permissions in order to access a resource such as a file or to perform certain operations. A security policy (discussed later in the chapter) will give certain permissions to each assembly. Code access permissions can be requested by code. The CLR will decide which permissions to grant based on the security policy for that assembly. You can even implement your own custom permissions for very specialized security situations. However, that is beyond the scope of this book. Here are some examples of predefined code access permissions:

- **DNSPermission** controls access to domain name servers on the network.
- **EnvironmentPermission** controls read or write access to environment variables.
- **FileIOPermission** controls access to files and directories.
- **FileDialogPermission** allows files selected in an Open dialog box to be read. This is useful if **FileIOPermission** has not been granted.
- **ReflectionPermission** controls the ability to access nonpublic metadata.
- **RegistryPermission** controls the ability to access and modify the registry.
- **SecurityPermission** controls the use of the security subsystem.
- **SocketPermission** controls the ability to make or accept connections on a transport address.

- **UIPPermission** controls the user of various user interface features, including the clipboard.
- **WebPermission** controls making or accepting connections on a Web address.

The use of these permissions is referred to as *Code Access Security* because this permission is based not on the identity of the user running the code, but on whether the code itself has the right to take certain actions.

Simple Permission Code Request

Code Example

The **SimplePermissionCodeRequest** example first requests permission to access a file. If the CLR does not grant that request, the CLR will throw a **SecurityException** inside the file constructor. However, this code first tests to see if it has that permission. If it does not, it just returns instead of trying to access the file.[8]

This step is generally superfluous because the CLR will do the demand inside of the constructor, but often you want to check permissions before you execute some code to ascertain if you have the rights you need.

The **FileIOPermission** class models the CLR file permissions. A full path must be supplied to its constructor, and we use the **Path** class we discussed in Chapter 10 to get the full path. We are asking for read, write, and append file access. Other possible access rights are NoAccess or PathDiscovery. The latter is required to access information about the file path itself. You might want to allow access to the file, but you may want to hide information in the path, such as directory structure or user names.

The demand request checks to see if we have the required permission. The **Demand** method checks all the callers on the stack to see if they have this permission. In other words, we want to make sure not only that the assembly that this code is running in has this permission, but that all the assemblies that this code is running on behalf of has this permission. If an exception was generated, we do not have the permission we demanded, so we then exit the program.

```
Dim filename As String = "..\read.txt"

' need full path for security check

Dim fileWithFullPath As String = _
    Path.GetFullPath(filename)
Try
```

---

8. We have not yet discussed how you set security policy, so we do not yet know how to grant or revoke this permission. By default, however, code running on the same machine that it resides on has this permission.

```
        Dim fileIOPerm As FileIOPermission = _
            New FileIOPermission( _
                FileIOPermissionAccess.AllAccess, _
                fileWithFullPath)
        fileIOPerm.Demand()
    Catch e As Exception
        Console.WriteLine(e.Message)
        Return
    End Try

    Try
        Dim file As FileInfo = New FileInfo(filename)
        Dim sr As StreamReader = File.OpenText()
        Dim text As String
        text = sr.ReadLine()

        While Not text Is Nothing
            Console.WriteLine(text)
            text = sr.ReadLine()
        End While

        sr.Close()
    Catch e As Exception
        Console.WriteLine(e.Message)
    End Try
```

Even if the code has the CLR read permission, the user must have read permission from the file system. If the user does not, the **UnauthorizedAccessException** will be thrown when the **OpenText** method is called.

You have to be careful when passing objects that have passed a security check in their constructor to code in other assemblies. Since the check was made in the constructor, no further check is made by the CLR to ascertain access rights. The assembly you pass the object to might not have the same rights as your assembly. If you were to pass this **FileInfo** object to another assembly that did not have the CLR read permission, it would not be prevented from accessing the file by the CLR, because no additional security check will be made. This is a design compromise for performance reasons to avoid making security checks for every operation. This is true for other code access permissions as well.

How a Permission Request Works

To determine whether code is authorized to access a resource or perform an operation, the CLR performs checks on all the callers on the stack frame to make sure that each assembly that has a method call on the stack can be granted the requested permission. If any caller in the stack does not have the permission that was demanded, a **SecurityException** is thrown.

Less trusted code is not permitted to use trusted code to perform an unauthorized action. The procedures on the stack could come from different assemblies that have different sets of permissions. For example, an assembly that you build might have all rights, but it might be called by a downloaded component that you would want to have restricted rights, so that it cannot open your email address book, delete files, and so on.

As discussed in the next sections, you can modify the results of the stack walk by using **Deny** or **Assert** methods on the **CodeAccessPermission** base class.

Strategy for Requesting Permissions

Code should request permissions that it needs before it uses them so that it is easier to recover if the permission request is denied. For example, if you need to access several key files, it is much easier to check to see if you have the permissions when the code starts up rather than when you are halfway through a delicate operation and then have to roll back several operations. In some situations, the user could be told up front that certain functions will not be available, so that he or she will not be surprised later when certain operations are blocked.

On the other hand, you should not request permissions that you do not need. This will minimize the chances that your code will do damaging things from bugs or malicious third-party code and components. In fact, you can restrict the permissions you have to the minimum necessary to prevent such damage. For example, if you do not want a program to read and write the files on your disk, there is no good reason to permit it, and therefore, you should explicitly deny the right to do so.

Denying Permissions

One can apply the **Deny** method to the permission. Even though security policy would permit access to the file, any attempt to access the file will fail. The **SimplePermissionCodeDenial** example demonstrates this. Instead of demanding the permission, we invoke the **Deny** method on the **FileIOPermission** object. We then try to read the file in a separate method named **ReadFile**.

```
...
Try
    fileIOPerm.Deny()
    Console.WriteLine("File Access Permission Denied")
Catch se As SecurityException
    Console.WriteLine(se.Message)
End Try

ReadFile()
...
```

The reason we attempt to read the file in the separate **ReadFile** method will be explained shortly, when we discuss the **Assert** method. For now, notice that since the permission was denied, the **FileInfo** constructor in the **ReadFile** method will throw a **SecurityException**.

```
Public Sub ReadFile()
    Try
        Dim file As FileInfo = New FileInfo(filename)
        Dim sr As StreamReader = File.OpenText()
        Dim text As String
        Text = sr.ReadLine()

        While text <> Nothing
            Console.WriteLine("      " + text)
            text = sr.ReadLine()
        End While

        sr.Close()
    Catch se As SecurityException
        Console.WriteLine( _
            "Could not read file: " + se.Message)
    End Try
End Sub
```

We then call the static **RevertDeny** method on the **FileIOPermission** class to remove the permission denial, and attempt to read the file again. This time the file can be read without throwing an exception. The call to **Deny** is good until the containing code returns to its caller or a subsequent call to **Deny**. **RevertDeny** removes all current **Deny** requests.

```
...
Try
    FileIOPermission.RevertDeny()
    Console.WriteLine( _
        "File Access Permission Restored")
Catch se As SecurityException
    Console.WriteLine(se.Message)
End Try

ReadFile()
...
```

We then invoke the **Deny** method to once again remove the permission and attempt to read the file, throwing an exception.

```
...
Try
    fileIOPerm.Deny()
    Console.WriteLine( _
        "File Access Permission Denied")
```

```
Catch se As SecurityException
  Console.WriteLine(se.Message)
End Try

ReadFile()
...
```

Asserting Permissions

The **Assert** method allows you to demand a permission even though you do not have access rights to do so due to callers higher in the stack that have not been granted the necessary permission. Of course, you can only assert permissions that your assembly itself has been granted. If this were not the case, it would be trivial to circumvent CLR security.

The **SimplePermissionCodeDenial** example now asserts the **FileIO-Permission** and then attempts to read the file by calling the **ReadFile** method, then the **ReadFileWithAssert** method, and finally the **ReadFile** method again. The **ReadFileWithAssert** method is much the same as the **ReadFile** method, but it has its own call to the **Assert** method.

```
Try
    fileIOPerm.Assert()
    Console.WriteLine( _
       "File Access Permission Asserted")
Catch se As SecurityException
    Console.WriteLine(se.Message)
End Try

ReadFile()

ReadFileWithAssert(fileIOPerm)

Console.WriteLine( _
    "Returned from read routine with assert.")

ReadFile()
```

The file-read operations in both calls to the **ReadFile** method fail, but the file-read in **ReadFileWithAssert** succeeds. The permission assertion is only good within the method that calls **Assert**, and the assertion disappears after returning from that method. The **ReadFileWithAssert** method can read the file because it asserts the permission within the method and then attempts the read. **Assert** stops the permission stack walk from checking permissions higher in the stack frame and allows the action to proceed, but it does not cause a grant of the permission. Therefore, if code further down the stack frame (like **Read-File**) tries to demand the denied permission (as the **FileInfo** constructor does), a **SecurityException** will be thrown. Similarly, **Deny** prevents callers higher in the stack frame from an action, but not on the current level.

```
Public Sub ReadFileWithAssert(ByVal f As FileIOPermission)
    Try
        f.Assert()
        Console.WriteLine( _
            "File Permission Asserted in same procedure
            as read.")

        Dim file As FileInfo = New FileInfo(filename)
        Dim sr As StreamReader = file.OpenText()
        Dim text As String
        text = sr.ReadLine()

        While text <> Nothing
            Console.WriteLine("      " + text)
            text = sr.ReadLine()
        End While

        sr.Close()
    Catch se As SecurityException
        Console.WriteLine( _
            "Could not read file: " + se.Message)
    End Try
End Sub
```

Remember that the permission assertion only applies to I/O operations done in this one method for the specific file that was passed into the **FileIO-Permission** constructor (i.e., read.txt). The call to **Assert** is good until the containing method returns. Hence, **ReadFile** fails again when it is attempted after **ReadFileWithAssert** returns. **RevertAssert** removes all current **Assert** requests.

Assert opens up security holes, because some caller in the stack frame might be able to use the routine that calls **Assert** to violate security.

Other Permission Methods

PermitOnly specifies the permissions that should succeed. You simply specify what resources you want to access. The call to **PermitOnly** is good until the containing code returns or a subsequent call to **PermitOnly**. **RevertPermitOnly** removes all current **PermitOnly** requests. **RevertAll** removes the effect of **Deny**, **PermitOnly**, and **Assert**.

SecurityPermission Class

The **SecurityPermission** class controls "meta permissions" that govern the CLR security subsystem. Let us look again at the **RoleBasedSecurity** example from earlier in the chapter. It used the **AppDomain.SetPrincipalPolicy** method to set the application domain's principal policy.

```
Dim ap As AppDomain = AppDomain.CurrentDomain
ap.SetPrincipalPolicy(PrincipalPolicy.WindowsPrincipal)
```

The type of principal returned by **Thread.CurrentPrincipal** will depend on the application domain's principal policy. An application domain can have one of three authentication policies, as defined by the **System.Security.PrincipalPolicy** enumeration:

- **WindowsPrincipal** uses the current user associated with the thread. **Thread.CurrentPrincipal** returns a **WindowsPrincipal** object.
- **UnauthenticatedPrincipal** uses an unauthenticated user. **Thread.- CurrentPrincipal** returns a **GenericPrincipal** object. This is the default.
- **NoPrincipal** returns Nothing for **Thread.CurrentPrincipal**.

You set the policy with the **SetPrincipalPolicy** method on the **AppDomain** instance for the current application domain. The static **method AppDomain.CurrentDomain** will return the current instance. This method should be called before any call to **Thread.CurrentPrincipal** because the principal object is not created until the first attempt to access that property.

In order for the **RoleBasedSecurity** example to set the principal policy, it needs to have the **ControlPrincipal** right. To ascertain if the executing code has that right, you can demand that **SecurityPermission** before you change the policy. A **SecurityException** will be thrown if you do not have that permission.

```
. . .
Dim sp As SecurityPermission = _
   New SecurityPermission( _
      SecurityPermissionFlag.ControlPrincipal)

Try
   sp.Demand()
Catch se As SecurityException
   Console.WriteLine(se.Message)
   Return
End Try
. . .
```

We first construct a new **SecurityPermission** instance, passing to the constructor the security permission we want to see if we have the right to use. **SecurityPermissionFlag** is an enumeration of permissions used by the **SecurityPermission** class. The **ControlPolicy** permission represents the right to change policy. Obviously, this should only be granted to trusted code. We then demand (i.e., request) the permission.

As mentioned earlier, you can only assert permissions that your assembly actually has, so rogue components cannot just assert permissions when running within your code. You can either set security policy or use the **Security-**

Permission class to prevent components from calling **Assert**. Construct an instance of the class with the **SecurityPermissionFlag.Assertion** value, and then **Deny** the permission. Among the other actions you can control with the **SecurityPermission** class are the ability to create and manipulate application domains, specify policy, allow or disallow execution, control whether verification is performed, and access unmanaged code.

Calling Unmanaged Code

Asserts are necessary for controlling access to unmanaged code, because in order to call unmanaged code, you need the unmanaged code permission, since the CLR performs a stack walk to check if all the callers have the unmanaged code permission. Therefore, if you did not use the **Assert** method, you would have to grant all code the unmanaged code permission. Hence, assemblies other than your own trusted assemblies could perform operations through the Win32 API calls and subvert the framework's security system.[9]

It is much better to make unmanaged code calls through wrapper classes that are contained in an assembly that has the unmanaged code permission. The code in the wrapper class would first ascertain that the caller has the proper CLR rights by demanding the minimal set of permissions necessary to accomplish the task (such as writing to a file). If the demand succeeds, then the wrapper code can assert the right to call unmanaged code.[10] No other assembly in the call chain then needs to have the unmanaged code permission.

For example, if you ask the .NET file classes to delete a file, they first demand the delete permission on the file. If that permission is granted, then the code asserts the unmanaged code permission and calls the Win32 API to perform the delete.

Attribute-Based Permissions

Code
Example

The **SimplePermissionAttributeRequest** example shows how you can use attributes to make permission requests. This example uses an attribute to put in the metadata for the assembly that you need to have the **ControlPrincipal** permission to run. This enables you to query in advance which components conflict with security policy.

---

9. The underlying operating system identity that is running the program must have the rights to perform the operating system function.
10. By demanding first and then asserting, you can ensure that a luring attack (i.e., unprivileged code calling privileged code to do evil things) is not in progress.

```
...
<Assembly: SecurityPermissionAttribute( _
   SecurityAction.RequestMinimum, _
   ControlPrincipal:=True)>
...
```

The **SecurityAction** enumeration has several values, some of which can be applied to a class or method and some that can be applied to an entire assembly, as in this example. For assemblies these are **RequestMinimum**, **RequestOptional**, and **RequestRefuse**. **RequestMinimum** indicates to the metadata those permissions the assembly requires to run. **RequestOptional** indicates to the metadata permissions that the assembly would like to have, but can run without. **RequestRefuse** indicates permissions that the assembly would like to be denied.[11]

If you change the attribute in this example to **RequestRefuse** and run it, you will find that the assembly will load, but you will get a **SecurityException** when you attempt to change the policy.

Other values apply to classes and methods. **LinkDemand** is acted upon when a link is made to some type. It requires your immediate caller to have a permission. The other values apply at runtime. **InheritanceDemand** requires a derived class to have a permission. **Assert**, **Deny**, **PermitOnly**, and **Demand** do what you would expect.

Here is an example of a **FileIOPermission** demand being applied to a class through an attribute. The named value **All** means all file access is being demanded for the specified file. A full file path is required.

```
<FileIOPermissionAttribute(SecurityAction.Demand, _
   All:="c:\foo\read.txt")> _
Public Class Simple
   ...
End Class
```

Principal Permission

Code
Example

Role-based security is controlled by the **PrincipalPermission** class. The **PrincipalPermission** example uses this class to make sure that the user identity under which the program is being run is an administrator. We do that by passing the identity name and a string representing the role to the constructor. Once again, we use the **Demand** method on the permission to check the validity of our permission request.

---

11. An assembly would do this to prevent code from another assembly executing on its behalf from having this permission.

```
Dim PrincipalPerm As PrincipalPermission = _
    New PrincipalPermission( _
        wi.Name, adminRole)
Try
   PrincipalPerm.Demand()
   Console.WriteLine( _
      "Code demand for an administrator succeeded.")
Catch e As SecurityException
   Console.WriteLine( _
      "Demand for Administrator failed.")
End Try
```

If the current user were an administrator, the demand would succeed; otherwise, it would fail with an exception being thrown. The code then checks for the user with the name JaneAdmin (not a system administrator, but part of the CustomerAdmin group).

```
Dim customerAdminRole As String = _
   "HPDESKTOP\CustomerAdmin"
Dim pp As PrincipalPermission
pp = New PrincipalPermission( _
   "HPDESKTOP\JaneAdmin", customerAdminRole)
Try
   pp.Demand()
   Console.WriteLine( _
      "Demand for Customer Administrator succeeded.")
Catch e As SecurityException
   Console.WriteLine( _
      "Demand for Customer Administrator failed.")
End Try
```

Next, the **PrincipalPermission** example tests to see if either of these two administrators is the identity of the running code. The **PrincipalPermission** class has methods for creating permissions that are the union or the intersection of other permissions. The following shows how to form a union of the permissions of the users Administrator and PeterT.

```
Dim id1 As String = "HPDESKTOP\Administrator"
Dim id2 As String = "HPDESKTOP\PeterT"

Dim pp1 As PrincipalPermission = _
   New PrincipalPermission( _
      id1, adminRole)
Dim pp2 As PrincipalPermission = _
   New PrincipalPermission( _
      id2, adminRole)

Dim ipermission As IPermission = pp2.Union(pp1)
Try
   ipermission.Demand()
```

```
    Console.WriteLine( _
        "Demand for either administrator succeeded.")
Catch e As SecurityException
    Console.WriteLine( _
        "Demand for either administrator failed.")
End Try
```

The code then sees if any administrator is the current identity of the running code.

```
Dim pp3 As PrincipalPermission = _
    New PrincipalPermission( _
        Nothing, adminRole)
Try
    pp3.Demand()
    Console.WriteLine( _
        "Demand for any administrator succeeded.")
Catch e As SecurityException
    Console.WriteLine( _
        "Demand for any administrator failed.")
End Try
```

If the users are unauthenticated, even if they do belong to the appropriate roles, the **Demand** will fail.

PermissionSet

You can deal with a set of permissions through the **PermissionSet** class. The **AddPermission** and **RemovePermission** methods allow you to add instances of a **CodeAccessPermission** derived class to the set. You can then **Deny**, **PermitOnly**, or **Assert** sets of permissions instead of individual permissions. This makes it easier to restrict what third-party components and scripts might be able to do. The **PermissionSet** example demonstrates how this is done.

We first define an interface **IUserCode** that our trusted code will use to access some third-party code. While in reality this third-party code would be in a separate assembly, to keep the example simple, we put everything in the same assembly.

```
Public Interface IUserCode
    Function PotentialRogueCode() As Integer
End Interface

Public Class ThirdParty
    Implements IUserCode
    Public Function PotentialRogueCode() As Integer _
        Implements IUserCode.PotentialRogueCode
        Try
```

```
         Dim filename As String = "..\read.txt"

         Dim file As FileInfo = New FileInfo(filename)
         Dim sr As StreamReader = file.OpenText()
         Dim text As String
         text = sr.ReadLine()

         While text <> Nothing
            Console.WriteLine(text)
            text = sr.ReadLine()
         End While

         sr.Close()
      Catch e As Exception
         Console.WriteLine(e.Message)
      End Try
      Return 0
   End Function
End Class
```

Our code will create a new instance of the third party, which would cause the code to be loaded into our assembly. We then invoke the **OurCode** method passing it the third-party code.

```
...
Public Module PSTest
    Public Sub Main()
        Dim thirdParty As ThirdParty = New ThirdParty()
        Dim ourClass As OurClass = New OurClass()
        ourClass.OurCode(thirdParty)
    End Sub
End Module
...
```

Now let us look at the **OurCode** method. It creates a permission set consisting of unrestricted user interface and file access permissions. It then denies the permissions in the permission set. The third-party code is then called. After it returns, the permission denial is revoked and the third-party code is called again.

```
Public Class OurClass
   Public Sub OurCode(ByVal code As IUserCode)
      Dim uiPerm As UIPermission = _
         New UIPermission(PermissionState.Unrestricted)
      Dim fileIOPerm As FileIOPermission = _
         New FileIOPermission(PermissionState.Unrestricted)

      Dim ps As PermissionSet = _
         New PermissionSet( _
            PermissionState.None)
```

```
    ps.AddPermission(uiPerm)
    ps.AddPermission(fileIOPerm)

    ps.Deny()

    Console.WriteLine("Permissions denied.")

    Dim v As Integer = code.PotentialRogueCode()

    CodeAccessPermission.RevertDeny()

    Console.WriteLine("Permissions allowed.")

    v = code.PotentialRogueCode()

  End Sub
End Class
```

The first time the **PotentialRogueCode** method is called, it fails, and the second time, it succeeds. Each stack frame can have only one permission set for denial of permissions. If you call **Deny** on a permission set, it overrides any other calls to **Deny** on a permission set in that stack frame.

Code Identity

The characteristics by which a particular assembly can be identified are its identity permissions. An example is a signed assembly's strong name or the Web site that originated the assembly. Based on the evidence provided to the assembly loader or trusted host, identity permissions are granted by the CLR.

Identity Permission Classes

To identify running code, there are several identity permission classes.

- **PublisherIdentityPermission** models the software publisher's digital signature.
- **SiteIdentityPermission** models the Web site where code originated.
- **StrongNameIdentityPermission** models the strong name of an assembly.
- **ZoneIdentityPermission** models the zone where the code originated.
- **URLIdentityPermission** models the URL and the protocol where the code originated.

These identity permissions represent evidence that can be used to determine security policy. It is important to recognize that identity permissions are not code access permissions.

Evidence

Security policy is based on a set of rules that administrators can establish. The .NET security system can use those rules to enforce the security policy. The evidence, represented by the identity permissions, is used to determine which security policy to apply.

The **AppDomain** class has a function **ExecuteAssembly** that causes an assembly to load and run. One of the possible arguments to this overloaded method is an **Evidence** object argument. This **Evidence** class is a collection of objects that represent the identity of the assembly, which is used in making security policy decisions.

The Evidence example illustrates this. This example gets the collection of evidence associated with a strongly named assembly and prints out the associated values.

Code
Example

```
Dim ev As System.Security.Policy.Evidence = _
    AppDomain.CurrentDomain.Evidence
Dim iEnum As IEnumerator = ev.GetEnumerator()
Dim bNext As Boolean

Console.WriteLine( _
    "Evidence Enumerator has {0} members", _
    ev.Count)
bNext = iEnum.MoveNext()
While bNext = True
    Dim x As Object = iEnum.Current
    Dim t As Type = x.GetType()
    Console.WriteLine(t.ToString())
    If t Is Type.GetType( _
        "System.Security.Policy.Zone") Then
      Dim zone As Zone = x
      Console.WriteLine("    " + _
        zone.SecurityZone.ToString())
    ElseIf t Is Type.GetType( _
        "System.Security.Policy.Url") Then
      Dim url As Url = x
      Console.WriteLine("    " + _
        url.Value.ToString())
    ElseIf t Is Type.GetType( _
        "System.Security.Policy.Hash") Then
      Dim hash As Hash = x
      Dim md5Hash() As Byte = hash.MD5
      Dim sha1Hash() As Byte = hash.SHA1
      Console.WriteLine("    MD5 Hash of Assembly:")
```

```
        Console.Write("        ")
        Dim i As Integer
        For i = 0 To md5Hash.Length - 1
            Console.Write(md5Hash(i))
        Next
        Console.WriteLine()
        Console.WriteLine("    SHA1 Hash of Assembly:")
        Console.Write("        ")
        For i = 0 To sha1Hash.Length - 1
            Console.Write(sha1Hash(i))
        Next
        Console.WriteLine()
    ElseIf t Is Type.GetType( _
            "System.Security.Policy.StrongName") Then
        Dim sn As StrongName = x
        Console.WriteLine( _
            "    StrongName of Assembly is: {0} " & _
            "version: {1}", sn.Name, sn.Version)
        Console.WriteLine("    Assembly public key:")
        Console.Write("        ")
        Console.WriteLine(sn.PublicKey.ToString())
    End If
    bNext = iEnum.MoveNext()
End While
```

The example's output would look something like this:

```
Evidence Enumerator has 4 members
System.Security.Policy.Zone
    MyComputer
System.Security.Policy.Url
    file://C:/OI/NetVB/Chap16/Evidence/bin/Evidence.exe
System.Security.Policy.StrongName
    StrongName of Assembly is: Evidence version:
1.0.808.39413
    Assembly public key:
        0024000004800000940...5EA897BA
System.Security.Policy.Hash
    MD5 Hash of Assembly:
        5934823522219523214991281651989082141 68
    SHA1 Hash of Assembly:
        159237806917498548961174251206237193181 4814718180
```

The evidence associated with the **Zone** for this assembly is MyComputer. The **Url** evidence is the location on disk of the assembly. The **Hash** evidence can give us the MD5 and SHA-1 hashes of the assembly. The **StrongName** evidence tells us information about the unique assembly name.

Some of this evidence is convertible to the associated identity permissions. For example, the **Zone** class has a **CreateIdentityPermission** method that returns an **IPermission** interface representing the **ZoneIdentityPermis-**

sion instance associated with this piece of evidence. The **Url** and **Strong-Name** classes have similar methods.

Another way of looking at the identity permissions is that they answer a series of questions:

- Who published (signed) it?
- What is the name of the assembly?
- What Web site or URL did it come from?
- What zone did the code originate from?

The creator of the application domain (host) can also provide evidence by passing in an **Evidence** collection when the **ExecuteAssembly** method is called. Of course, that code must have the **ControlEvidence** permission. The CLR is also trusted to add evidence, which is reasonable, since it enforces the security policy. Evidence is extensible. You can define evidence types and use them in your own customized security policies.

Security Policy

Now that we understand evidence and how the evidence about an assembly is gathered, we can discuss security policy. Based on the evidence for an assembly, the assembly is assigned to a code group. Associated with each code group is a set of permissions that represent what code associated with that code group can do.

Security Policy Levels

Security policy is set at several levels. The permissions allowed are defined by the intersection of the policy levels. These levels are enterprise, machine, application domain, and user. If there is a conflict between permissions assigned from a particular level, the more restrictive version overrides. So, enterprise policy can override all the machines in the enterprise, and machine policy can override all policies for an application domain or a particular user.

Code Groups

The enterprise, machine, and user policy levels are a hierarchy of code groups. Associated with each code group is a set of permissions. Code that meets a specified set of conditions belongs to a particular code group.

The root node is referred to as All_Code. Below this level is a set of child nodes, and each of these children can have children. Each node represents a code group. If code belongs to a code group, it might be a member of one of its children. If it does not belong to a given code group, it cannot belong to any of its children.

By evaluating the evidence, you assign code a group. By assignment of code to a group, you get an associated set of permissions. This set of conditions corresponds to a named permission set. Since code can belong to more than one group, the set of permissions that can be granted to code is the union of all the permission sets from the all groups that it belongs to.

Therefore, code policy is determined in two steps. For each level, the permissions for an assembly are determined by the union of all the permission sets to which it belongs. Each level, then, effectively has one permission set. Each of these permission sets is intersected so that the most restrictive of each permission setting is the final value. For example, if the machine level gives all access to an assembly, but the user level restricts the file I/O permissions to just read, the assembly will have unlimited permissions for everything but file I/O, where it will just have the read permission.

Code groups can have two attributes. The **exclusive** attribute dictates that code will never be allowed more permissions than associated with the exclusive group. Obviously, code can belong to only one group, marked exclusive. The **level final** attribute indicates that no policy levels below this one are considered when calculating code group membership. The order of levels is machine, user, and then application domain.

Named Permission Sets

A named permission set consists of one or more code access permissions that have a name. An administrator can associate a code group with this permission set using its name. More than one code group can be associated with a named permission set. Administrators can define their own named permission sets, but there are several built-in named permission sets:

- **Nothing**: no permissions (cannot run).
- **Execution**: permission only to run, but no permissions that allow use of protected resources.
- **Internet**: the default policy permission set suitable for content from unknown origin.
- **LocalIntranet**: the default policy permission set for within an enterprise.
- **Everything**: all standard (i.e., built-in) permissions except permission to skip verification.
- **FullTrust**: full access to all resources protected by permissions that can be unrestricted.

Of the built-in named permission sets, only the **Everything** set can be modified. You can also define your own custom permission sets as well.

Altering Security Policy

Security policy is stored in several XML-based configuration files. Machine security configuration is in the **security.config** file that is stored in the **\WINNT\Microsoft.NET\Framework\vx.x.xxxx\CONFIG** directory. User security configuration is in the **security.config** file that is stored in the **\Documents and Settings\UserName**[12]**\Application Data\Microsoft\CLR Security Config\vx.x.xxxx directory**.

It is not recommended that you edit these XML files directly. The Code Access Security Policy tool (**caspol.exe**) is a command-line tool that can be used to modify enterprise, machine, and user policy levels.

The .NET Admin Tool provides a friendlier, but more limited, interface to changing these policy configuration files. To use this tool, go to the Control Panel and select Administrative Tools. From the Administrative Tools list, select Microsoft .NET Framework Configuration, and then open the Runtime Security Policy node. Figure 16–18 shows the code groups and permission sets defined for the machine and the current user security policy levels as they appear in the left pane in the .NET Admin Tool.

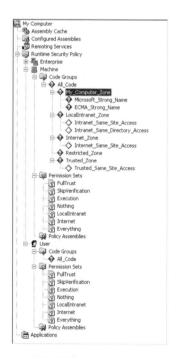

FIGURE 16–18   *Permission sets and groups for machine and user policy.*

---

12. Of course, the actual user name is to be substituted into this path at this point.

Let us use this tool to examine the current policies in the machine level. First, let us look at the named permission sets. As you can see from Figure 16–18, on the machine level, no new named permission sets have been created; only the default ones are present. If you select the Internet named permission set and in the right pane select view permissions, you can then select any permission and look at its settings. Figure 16–19 shows the settings for UserInterface permission in the Internet named permission set.

Figure 16–20 shows the properties for the Internet Zone code group on the machine policy level. You can see that Zone identity permission is chosen for this group, and the value associated with it is the Internet zone. On the permission set tab, you can view or select the named permission set associated with the Internet zone.

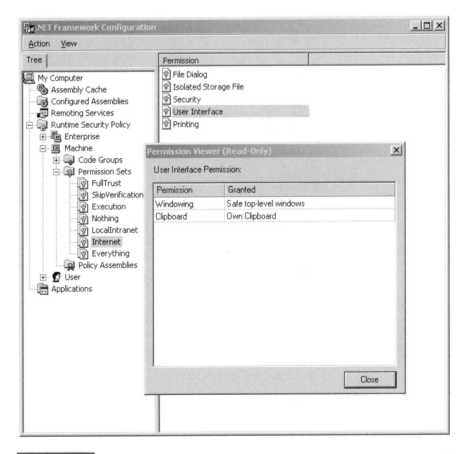

FIGURE 16–19   *Permissions for UserInterface permission in machine-level Internet named permission set.*

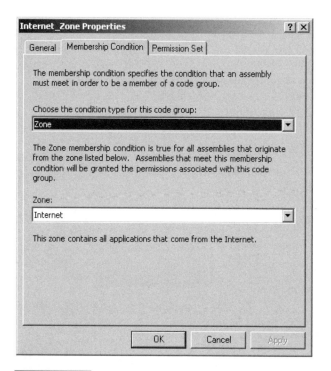

FIGURE 16–20   *Properties dialog for Internet zone, machine policy level.*

Code
Example

To illustrate how security policy affects running code, we use a slightly modified version of the **Evidence** example. Besides writing out the associated evidence, the Policy example also prints out the contents of a file.

```
Dim filename As String = "..\read.txt"
Try
   Dim fileWithFullPath As String = _
      Path.GetFullPath(filename)
   Dim File As FileInfo = New FileInfo(filename)
   Dim sr As StreamReader = File.OpenText()
   Dim text As String
   Text = sr.ReadLine()

   While text <> Nothing
      Console.WriteLine(text)
      text = sr.ReadLine()
   End While

   sr.Close()
Catch e As Exception
   Console.WriteLine(e.Message)
End Try
```

Figure 16–21 shows a permission set named TestStrongName and two new code groups named My_Computer_Zone and TestStrongNameGroup that we will be adding at the user policy level to control security policy for the **Policy** example assembly just described.

First, we create the new permission set named TestStrongName using the .NET Admin Tool. You create this new permission set by selecting the PermissionSets node below the level where you want to create it (in this case, under User). Then right-click and select New, and fill in the fields as shown in Figure 16–22.

Clicking the Next button brings up the dialog in Figure 16–23. Use the Add and Remove buttons to define the permissions that you want to be part of this permission set.

To define the permission itself, select the permission and click the Properties button and make the appropriate choices. Figure 16–24 shows the dialog that appears for the UserInterface permission. When you are finished adding permissions, you click Finish.

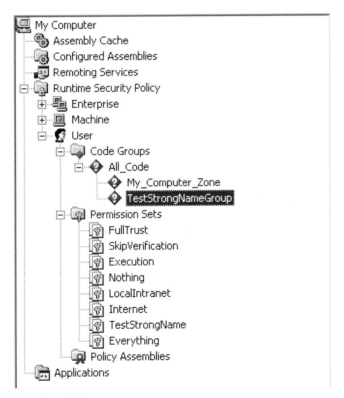

FIGURE 16–21   *Revised user policy level for the Policy assembly example.*

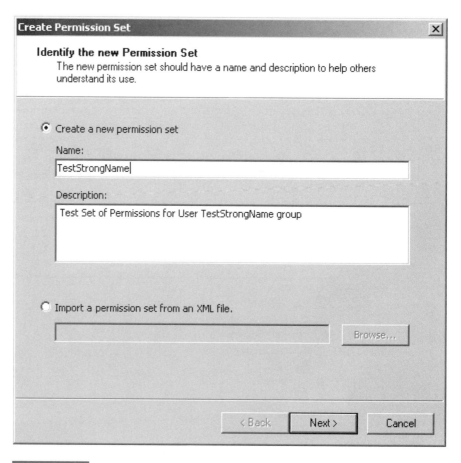

FIGURE 16–22 *Initial Create Permission Set dialog.*

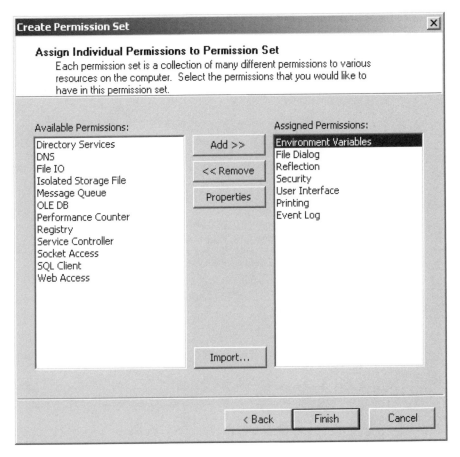

FIGURE 16–23   *TestStrongName permission set definition.*

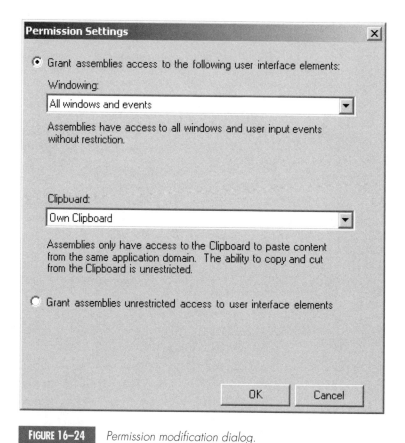

FIGURE 16–24   *Permission modification dialog.*

Now this permission has to be associated with a code group. How do assemblies get assigned to code groups? We have already seen that each code group maps to one piece of evidence. Figure 16–25 is a diagram of the User Code Level with its three groups.

Now we want to create two new code groups named My_Computer_Zone and TestStrongNameGroup before we can associate them with the desired permission sets. To do this, right click on the All_Code node under Code Groups, under User, and then select New. Figure 16–26 shows this for the TestStrongNameGroup group. After entering the fields, click Next three times. The group has now been created. You can then follow the same steps for the other group named My_Computer_Zone. The details on establishing the My_Computer_Zone group will be described shortly.

After you have added the groups, you can modify them by associating each of them with a particular permission set. For example, to modify the TestStrongNameGroup group, right-click on that node in the .NET Admin

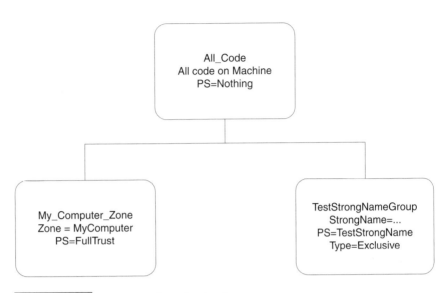

FIGURE 16–25   *Diagram of user level policy groups.*

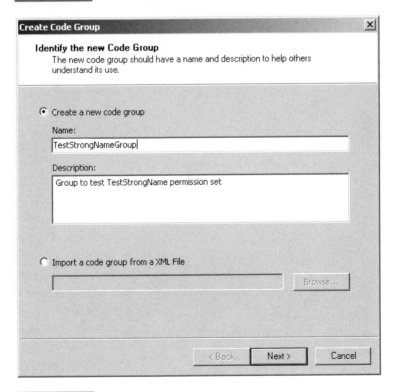

FIGURE 16–26   *Membership condition for TestStrongNameGroup.*

Tool and select Properties. You can then select the Permission Set tab and choose the TestStrongName permission set from the PermissionSet combo box. Figure 16–27 shows how it is associated with this permission set. Note that there is no FileIOPermission in this permission set. This will become important when we look at the effect of this group membership on the **Policy** example, since it does attempt to perform I/O.

Figure 16–28 shows how to make the group's membership condition depend on the assembly's strong name. The Import button can be used to browse to **Policy.exe**, and the strong name of that digitally signed assembly is automatically entered into the Public Key field.

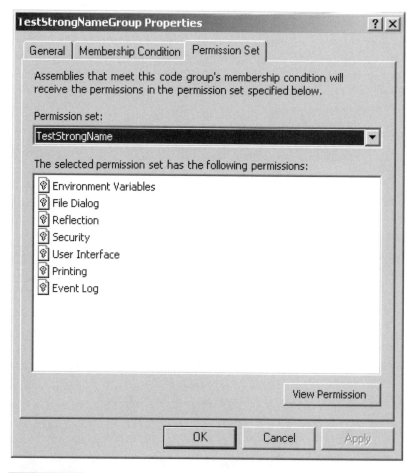

Permissions associated with TestStrongNameGroup from TestStrong- Name permission set.

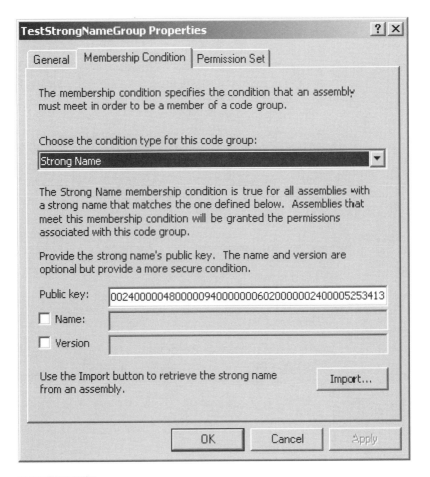

FIGURE 16–28 *Making TestStrongNameGroup.*

The My_Computer_Zone group is defined to encompass all code on this computer. It is defined in a similar fashion as the TestStrongNameGroup. The membership condition is Zone and the MyComputer zone is picked as the associated value. FullTrust is selected for its associated permission set. The All_Code group encompasses all code on the machine. It grants no rights to any code. We set its permission set to Nothing so that it grants no rights.

To find out how an assembly matches the code groups, its evidence is compared with the membership conditions for the group. All code that resides on the current machine (as opposed to another machine on the network or the Internet) matches the All_Code and My_Computer_Zone groups. Only **policy.exe** matches the membership condition for the TestStrongName-Group. The tree is walked from parent to child node; if a parent node does not match, then no further navigation down the tree is done. On a given level the rights assigned to the assembly are the union of all the groups that it matches. In this case, even though policy.exe matches a group that does not give it the FileIOPermission, it gets that permission from the My_Computer_ Zone group that grants FullTrust to code.

A similar analysis of the enterprise and machine levels reveals that they also grant code from this machine FullTrust. So, if you run **policy.exe**, it will run successfully, performing I/O.

Now, if you modify the TestStrongNameGroup on its General tab to be exclusive, as shown in Figure 16–29, by checking the indicated checkboxes, this will cause any code that belongs to this group to get its rights from only this group. Since policy is determined by the intersection of all the three levels, **policy.exe** will not have the FileIOPermission. If you try to run it, you will see that it cannot read the file successfully.

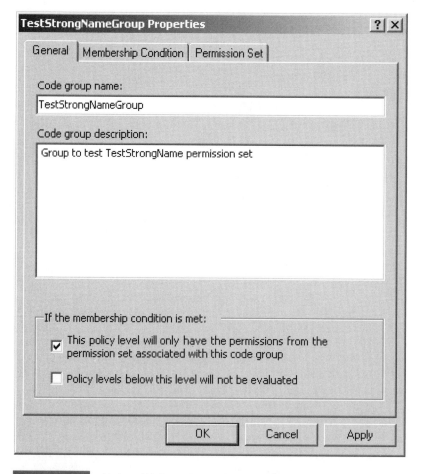

FIGURE 16–29   *Making TestStrongNameGroup exclusive.*

Summary

In this chapter we have attempted to explain the basics of .NET security. .NET security comes in two basic flavors: user-based security, and Code Access Security. The former determines which identity is executing code. The latter determines what rights the executing code itself has. Combining the two, you have the basic tools to provide robust security for all your .NET applications.

Interoperability

Microsoft .NET is a powerful platform, and there are many advantages in writing a new application within the .NET Framework. However, a typical application is not a world unto itself, but is built from legacy components as well as new components, and so issues of interoperability are very important. We discussed one kind of interoperability in Chapter 15 in connection with Web services. Using the SOAP protocol, it is possible for .NET applications to call Web services on other platforms, including Unix and mainframes. It is also possible for applications on diverse platforms, including mobile ones, to call .NET Web services running on Microsoft Windows.

In this chapter we will look at another kind of interoperability, the interfacing of managed and unmanaged code running under Windows. The dominant programming model in modern Windows systems is the Component Object Model, or COM. There exist a great many legacy COM components, and so it is desirable for a .NET program, running as managed code, to be able to call unmanaged COM components. The converse situation, in which a COM client needs to call a .NET server, can also arise. Apart from COM, we may also have need for a .NET program to call any unmanaged code that is exposed as a DLL, including the Win32 API. The .NET Framework supports all these interoperability scenarios through COM interoperability and the Platform Invocation Services, or PInvoke.

Calling COM Components from Managed Code

The first interoperability scenario we will look at is managed code calling COM components. The .NET Framework makes it easy to create a Runtime Callable Wrapper (RCW), which acts as a bridge between managed and unmanaged code. The RCW is illustrated in Figure 17–1.

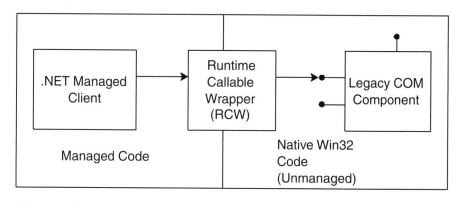

FIGURE 17–1 *A Runtime Callable Wrapper between managed and unmanaged code.*

You could implement an RCW assembly yourself, using the PInvoke facility (described in a later section) to call into the necessary APIs, such as **CoCreateInstance** and the **IUnknown** methods directly. But that is not necessary, because the **Tlbimp.exe** tool can read type library information and automatically generate the appropriate RCW for you. Visual Studio .NET makes it even easier, as you can add a reference to a COM object in Solution Explorer. We will examine both of these facilities as we look at some examples of COM components and .NET clients.

The Tlbimp.exe Utility

The **Tlbimp.exe** utility (Type Library to .NET Assembly Converter) program is provided in the **\Program Files\Microsoft.NET\FrameworkSDK\Bin** directory. It is used to generate managed classes that wrap unmanaged COM classes. The resulting RCW is a .NET component (i.e., a managed DLL assembly) that managed client code can use to access the COM interface methods that are implemented in the COM component. The **Tlbimp.exe** tool is a command-line program that reads COM type library information, generates a managed wrapper class along with the associated metadata, and places the result into the RCW assembly. You can view the resulting contents in this assembly using the **Ildasm.exe** tool. The command line syntax for **Tlbimp.exe** is shown below.

```
Tlbimp TypeLibName [options]
Where options may contain the following:
    /out:FileName              Assembly file name
    /namespace:Namespace       Assembly Namespace
    /asmversion:Version        Assembly version number
    /reference:FileName        Reference assembly
```

```
/publickey:FileName       Public key file
/keyfile:FileName         Key pair file
/keycontainer:FileName    Key pair key container
/delaysign                Delay digital signing
/unsafe                   Suppress security checks
/nologo                   Suppress displaying logo
/silent                   Suppress output except errors
/verbose                  Display extra information
/primary                  Make primary interop assembly
/sysarray                 SAFEARRAY as System.Array
/strictref                Only /reference assemblies
/? or /help               Display help information
```

When the **Tlbimp.exe** tool imports a COM type library, it creates a .NET namespace with the same name as the library defined in the type library (that is, the name of the actual library, not the name of the type library file that contains it). **Tlbimp.exe** coverts each COM coclass defined in the type library into a managed .NET wrapper class in the resulting .NET assembly that has one constructor with no parameters. **Tlbimp.exe** coverts each COM interface defined in the type library into a .NET interface in the resulting .NET assembly.

Consider the typical COM IDL file library statement shown below, which would be used to create a type library using **Midl.exe**. The TLB or DLL file produced by this IDL file would cause **Tlbimp.exe** to generate an assembly containing metadata, including the namespace **BANKDUALLib**, a managed wrapper class named **Account2**, and a managed interface named **IAccount2**.

```
library BANKDUALLib
{
    importlib("stdole32.tlb");
    importlib("stdole2.tlb");
    [
        uuid(04519632-39C5-4A7E-AA3C-3A7D814AC91C),
        helpstring("Account2 Class")
    ]
    coclass Account2
    {
        [default] interface IAccount2;
    };
};
```

Once you have used **Tlbimp.exe** to generate the wrapper assembly, you can view its contents using the **Ildasm.exe** tool, as shown in Figure 17–2. Note that the namespace shown by **Ildasm.exe** is **BANKDUALLib**, the name of the interface is **IAccount2**, and the wrapper class is named **Account2**.

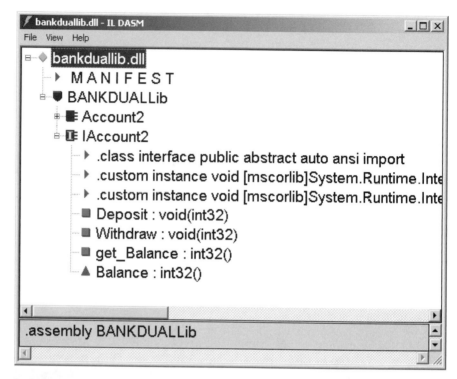

FIGURE 17–2   *Ildasm.exe showing contents of a COM wrapper assembly.*

Demonstration: Wrapping a Legacy COM Server

The best way to get a feel for how this wrapping process works is to perform the operations yourself. The .NET client program is in the directory **NetClient**. The directory **LegacyComServer** contains the following files:

```
BankDual.dll          COM server DLL
BankDual.tlb          Type library
reg_bankdual.bat      Batch file to register the server
unreg_bankdual.bat    Batch file to unregister the server
BankConsole.exe       Client executable file
```

The source code for the client and server are in the directories **Client-Source** and **ServerSource** respectively. Both programs are written in Visual C++, and project files are provided for Visual C++ 6.0. Unless you have Visual C++ 6.0 installed on your system in addition to Visual Studio .NET, you will not be able to build these projects, but that will not prevent you from creating and running the .NET client that uses the C++ COM server **BankDual.dll**.

We could also have implemented the legacy COM server and client programs using Visual Basic 6, and the code would have been much simpler. But to run the programs, you would need the Visual Basic 6 runtime installed on your computer. In this book we are only assuming that you have Visual Studio .NET installed on your computer, which includes the CLR as a runtime but not the VB6 runtime. In any event, the source code for the legacy server and client does not matter, because we are going to be coding a client program using VB.NET.

This COM server implements a simple bank account class that has **Deposit** and **Withdraw** methods and a **Balance** property. The simple code[1] is shown in **Account2.cpp** in the **ServerSource** directory.

```
STDMETHODIMP CAccount2::get_Balance(long *pVal)
{
    *pVal = m_nBalance;
    return S_OK;
}
STDMETHODIMP CAccount2::Deposit(long amount)
{
    m_nBalance += amount;
    return S_OK;
}
STDMETHODIMP CAccount2::Withdraw(long amount)
{
    m_nBalance -= amount;
    return S_OK;
}
```

REGISTER THE COM SERVER

The first step is to register the COM server. You can do that by running the batch file **reg_bankdual.bat**, which executes the command

```
regsvr32 bankdual.dll
```

You can now see the registration entries using the Registry Editor (**regedit.exe**) or the OLE/COM Object Viewer (**oleview.exe**). The latter program is provided on the Tools menu of Visual Studio .NET. It groups related registry entries together, providing a convenient display. You can also perform other operations, such as instantiating objects. Figure 17–3 shows the entries for the **Account2** class that is implemented by this server. We have clicked the little "+" in the left-hand pane, which instantiates an object and queries for the standard interfaces. You can release the object by right-clicking over the class and choosing Release Instance from the context menu.

---

1. We will not discuss the somewhat intricate infrastructure code provided by this ATL-based COM server. Such "plumbing" is much easier with .NET. Our focus is on calling COM components, not implementing them.

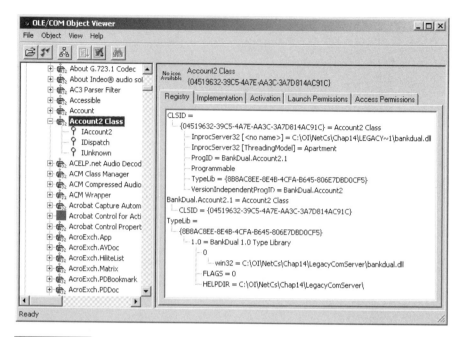

FIGURE 17–3   *OLE/COM Object Viewer showing registry entries.*

RUN THE LEGACY COM CLIENT

You can now run the legacy COM client by double-clicking on **BankConsole.exe** in Windows Explorer. The starting balance is shown, followed by a withdrawal of 25, and the balance is shown again. Here is the legacy source code, in the file **BankConsole.cpp** in **ClientSource**.

```
// BankConsole.cpp

#include <stdio.h>
#include <stdlib.h>
#include <objbase.h>
#include "bankdual.h"
#include "bankdual_i.c"

IAccount2* g_pAccount;

void ShowBalance()
{
   long balance;
   HRESULT hr = g_pAccount->get_Balance(&balance);
   printf("balance = %d\n", balance);
}
```

```
int main(int argc, char* argv[])
{
    // Initialize COM
    HRESULT hr = CoInitializeEx(NULL,
        COINIT_APARTMENTTHREADED);
    // Instantiate Account object, obtaining interface
     // pointer
    hr = CoCreateInstance(CLSID_Account2, NULL,
        CLSCTX_SERVER, IID_IAccount2, (void **) &g_pAccount);
    // First obtain and display initial balance
    ShowBalance();
    // Deposit 25 and show balance
    hr = g_pAccount->Deposit(25);
    ShowBalance();
    // Clean up
    g_pAccount->Release();
    CoUninitialize();
    printf("Press enter to quit: ");
    char buf[10];
    gets(buf);
    return 0;
}
```

For simplicity, no error checking is done. Robust code should check the HRESULT that is returned from each of the COM calls. Here is the output from running the client program:

```
balance = 150
balance = 125
Press Enter to quit:
```

IMPORT THE TYPE LIBRARY (TLBIMP.EXE)

In order to call the COM component from managed code, we must create an RCW. We can do that by running the **TlbImp.exe** utility that we have discussed. Later, we will see how to accomplish the same thing by simply setting a reference to the **BANKDUALLib** library. We will now run the **TlbImp.exe** utility from the command line, in the directory **NetClient**, where we want the RCW assembly to wind up. We provide a relative path to the type library file[2] **BankDual.tlb** in the directory **LegacyComServer**. What we have to type is shown in bold.

```
tlbimp ..\legacycomserver\bankdual.tlb
TlbImp - Type Library to .NET Assembly Converter Version
1.0.2914.16
```

---

2. The file **BankDual.dll** also contains the type library and could have been used in place of **BankDual.tlb**.

Type library imported to BANKDUALLib.dll

The RCW assembly that is created is **BANKDUALLib.dll**, taking its name from the name of the type library, as discussed earlier.

IMPLEMENT THE .NET CLIENT PROGRAM

Code
Example

It is now easy to implement the .NET client program. The code is in the file **NetClient.vb** in the **NetClient** example.

```
' NetClient.vb

Imports System
Imports BANKDUALLib

Module NetClient
    Public Sub Main()
        Dim acc As Account2
        acc = New Account2()
        Console.WriteLine("balance = {0}", acc.Balance)
        acc.Withdraw(25)
        Console.WriteLine("balance = {0}", acc.Balance)
    End Sub
End Module
```

As with the COM client program, for simplicity we do no error checking. In the .NET version we should use exception handling to check for errors. The RCW uses the namespace **BANKDUALLib**, based on the name of the type library.

You must add a reference to **BANKDUALLib.dll**. In the Visual Studio Solution Explorer you can right-click over References, choose Add Reference, and use the ordinary .NET tab of the Add Reference dialog.

Build and run the project inside of Visual Studio. You should see the following output:

```
balance = 150
balance = 125
Press any key to continue
```

Once you have added a reference to an RCW, you have all the features of the IDE available for .NET assemblies, including Intellisense and the Object Browser. You can bring up the Object Browser from View | Other Windows | Object Browser. Figure 17–4 illustrates the information shown.

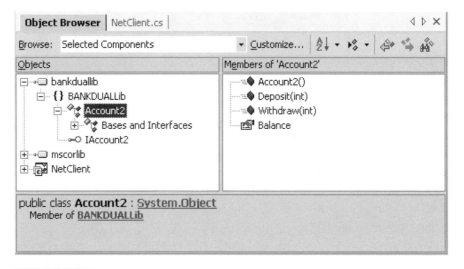

FIGURE 17-4   *Object Browser showing information about the RCW.*

IMPORT A TYPE LIBRARY USING VISUAL STUDIO

When you are using Visual Studio, you can import a COM type library directly, without first running **TlbImp.exe**. To see how to do this, use Solution Explorer to delete the reference to **BANKDUALLib.dll**. In fact, delete the file itself, and delete the **bin** and **obj** directories of **NetClient**. Now right-click over References, choose Add Reference, and this time select the COM tab from the Add Reference dialog. The listbox will show all the COM components with a registered type library. Select BankDual 1.0 Type Library, as illustrated in Figure 17–5, click Select, and then click OK.

You will see a message telling you that a primary interop assembly is not registered for this type library. You will be invited to have a wrapper generated for you, as illustrated in Figure 17–6. Click Yes. The generated RCW is the file **Interop.BANKDUALLib_1_0.dll** in the directory **bin\Debug**. You should be able to build and run the .NET client program.

The *primary interop assembly* that was created by Visual Studio is normally created by the publisher of the COM component. This can be done using the **TlbImp.exe** utility with the **/primary** option.

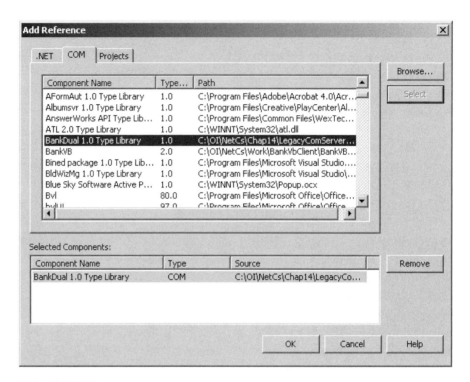

FIGURE 17–5   *Add a reference to a COM component in Visual Studio.*

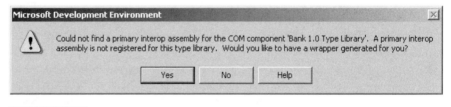

FIGURE 17–6   *Visual Studio will create a primary interop assembly.*

Wrapping a COM Component with a Pure V-Table Interface

DUAL INTERFACES

Our example legacy COM component **BankDual.dll** had a *dual* interface **IAccount2**. This means that the interface could be called by both an early-binding COM client using the v-table and also by a late-binding client using **IDispatch**. The IDL file **BankDual.idl** specifies the interface **IAccount2** as dual.

```
[
   object,
   uuid(AAA19CDE-C091-47BF-8C96-C80A00989796),
   dual,
   helpstring("IAccount2 Interface"),
   pointer_default(unique)
]
interface IAccount2 : IDispatch
{
   [propget, id(1), helpstring("property Balance")] HRESULT
Balance([out, retval] long *pVal);
   [id(2), helpstring("method Deposit")] HRESULT
Deposit([in] long amount);
   [id(3), helpstring("method Withdraw")] HRESULT
Withdraw([in] long amount);
};
```

Code
Example

An example of late binding is VB Script code for client-side scripting on a Web page. The **BankHtml** example contains the file **Bank.htm** with an HTML form and VBScript code to exercise our bank account server.

```
<!-- bank.htm -->
<HTML>
<HEAD>
<TITLE>Bank test page for Account object</TITLE>

<SCRIPT LANGUAGE="VBScript">
<!--

dim account

Sub btnCreate_OnClick
   set account = createobject("BankDual.Account2.1")
   Document.Form1.txtAmount.Value = 25
   Document.Form1.txtBalance.Value = account.Balance
End Sub

Sub btnDestroy_OnClick
   set account = Nothing
   Document.Form1.txtAmount.Value = ""
   Document.Form1.txtBalance.Value = ""
End Sub

Sub btnDeposit_OnClick
   account.Deposit(Document.Form1.txtAmount.Value)
   Document.Form1.txtBalance.Value = account.Balance
End Sub

Sub btnWithdraw_OnClick
   account.Withdraw(Document.Form1.txtAmount.Value)
```

```
    Document.Form1.txtBalance.Value = account.Balance
End Sub

-->
</SCRIPT>

<FORM NAME = "Form1" >
Amount <INPUT NAME="txtAmount" VALUE="" SIZE=8>
<P>
Balance <INPUT NAME="txtBalance" VALUE="" SIZE=8>
<P>
<INPUT NAME="btnCreate" TYPE=BUTTON VALUE="Create">
 <INPUT NAME="btnDestroy" TYPE-BUTTON VALUE="Destroy">
 <INPUT NAME="btnDeposit" TYPE=BUTTON VALUE="Deposit">
 <INPUT NAME="btnWithdraw" TYPE=BUTTON VALUE="Withdraw">
</FORM>

</BODY>
</HTML>
```

The **createobject** function instantiates a COM object using late binding, referencing a program ID rather than a CLSID. This is perfectly legitimate, because **BankDual.dll** implements a dual interface on the **Account2** object. Since this is client-side script, we can exercise it locally in Internet Explorer, simply double-clicking on **bank.htm** in Windows Explorer. This will bring up Internet Explorer and show the form. You can click the Create button and instantiate an object,[3] as shown in Figure 17–7. The starting balance of 150 is shown. You can then exercise Deposit and Withdraw, and when you are done, you can click Destroy.

PURE V-TABLE INTERFACE

Dual interfaces are very common. The default in an ATL wizard-generated COM component is dual interface. Visual Basic 6.0 also creates COM components with dual interfaces. However, if there is no occasion for a COM component to be called by a late-binding client, it is more efficient to implement only a pure v-table interface.

There is a slight issue in generating wrappers for COM components with a pure v-table interface that can depend on the threading model that you choose for your client program. To see the problem, consider the COM component the **VtableComServer** example. As with our **LegacyComServer** example, the top-level directory contains the DLL, the type library file, batch

Code
Example

---

3. Depending on your security settings, you may get a warning message about an ActiveX control on the page. Click Yes to allow the interaction. If you have trouble running the ActiveX control at all, check your security settings.

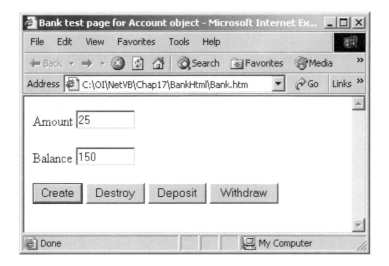

FIGURE 17–7 *Accessing a late-bound COM object in Internet Explorer.*

files to register and unregister the server, and a client test program. Source code for the COM server and client is provided in **ServerSource** and **Client-Source** respectively. We want to implement the managed client program **VtableNetClient**.

First, verify that the legacy COM client and legacy COM server work. All you have to do is run the batch file **reg_bank.bat** to register the server, and you can double-click on **BankConsole.exe** in Windows Explorer to run the client.

Next, open up the solution **VtableNetClient.sln** in Visual Studio. Add a reference to the COM type library Bank 1.0 Type Library. You should get a clean build. But when you run the program, you get an exception:

```
Unhandled Exception: System.InvalidCastException:
 QueryInterface for interface B
ANKLib.IAccount failed.
   at BANKLib.AccountClass.GetBalance(Int32& pBalance)
   at VtableNetClient.VtableNetClient.ShowBalance() in
C:\OI\NetVB\Chap17\Vtable
NetClient\Module1.vb:line 12
   at VtableNetClient.VtableNetClient.Main() in
C:\OI\NetVB\Chap17\VtableNetClie
nt\Module1.vb:line 29
```

The problem is that the .NET client is in a separate apartment due to the fact that the **<MTAThread()>** attribute is applied to the client's Main method, and it needs marshaling. You can use any of the following solutions:

1. Mark the interface as *dual.*
2. Mark the interface as *oleautomation,* and limit types used to *oleautomation* friendly types.
3. Build and register the proxy/stub DLL for the interface.
4. Mark the **Main** method in the VB.NET client with the **<STAThread()>** (or **<MTAThread()>** attribute if appropriate to the situation), to place it into the same threading model as the COM server.

Examining the source code for **VtableNetClient.vb**, we see that we commented out the attribute **<STAThread()>** in front of **Main**. Uncomment it, and comment out the **<MTAThread()>** attribute, build, and run again. This time it should work!

As an alternate solution, comment out **<STAThread()>** again. Now, in the server directory **VtableComServer** run the batch file **reg_bankps.bat** to register the proxy/stub DLL. Build and run the .NET client. Again, it should work!

Notice another feature of this .NET client program. Rather than calling methods on a class object, we go through interface references. Also note that the assignment operator is the analog in .NET of **QueryInterface** in COM.

Calling Managed Components from a COM Client

Obviously, it is much more likely that you will want to write new .NET applications that make use of legacy COM components; however, there may be times when you need to go in the opposite direction. For example, you may have an existing application that makes use of one or more COM components, and you would like to rewrite several of those COM components as .NET components to be used in future .NET solutions. However, in the meantime, you may want to make use of those new .NET components in your existing COM client applications as well.

COM client programs may use early binding (v-table interface) or late binding (**IDispatch** interface) to access managed .NET components. Early binding requires that type library information is available at compile time. Late binding does not require any type library information at compile time, since binding takes place at runtime via the **IDispatch** interface methods.

However, regardless of whether the client uses early or late binding, a bridge is required between the unmanaged native execution environment of the COM client and the managed execution environment of the .NET component. This bridge is known as the COM Callable Wrapper (CCW), which acts as a proxy for the managed object, as shown in Figure 17–8. Only one CCW object is created for any given managed object created for a COM client. The CCW manages object lifetime according to the reference counting rules of **IUnknown**, and it also manages marshaling for the method calls made on the object.

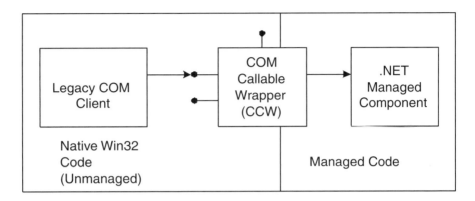

FIGURE 17–8 *A COM callable wrapper between unmanaged and managed code.*

While the RCW assembly is explicitly created as a file, the CCW is created dynamically at runtime by the Common Language Runtime. The CLR creates exactly one CCW for a managed object regardless of the number of COM clients that request its services, and both COM and .NET clients can make requests on the same .NET object simultaneously.

A Late Binding COM Client

There are many variations of a COM client calling a .NET component. We will illustrate with just one scenario, a late binding COM client calling a managed component. We will create a .NET component that can be called through VBScript on the **bank.htm** Web page.

Looking at the VBScript code used in **createobject** on **bank.htm**, we see that the ProgId of the COM object is BankDual.Account2.1. We wish to create a .NET object that can be used in place of this COM object and that has the same ProgId. To avoid confusion with the COM object, unregister it running the batch file **unreg_bankdual.bat** in the directory **LegacyComServer**. Now, if you access **bank.htm** in Internet Explorer and click the Create button, you will get an error.

VB.NET code for implementing a compatible bank account object is in the file **Account.vb** in the **NetServer** example.

Code
Example

```
' Account.vb

Imports System
Imports System.Runtime.InteropServices

<ProgId("BankDual.Account2.1")> _
Public Class Account
    Private m_balance As Integer
```

```
    Sub New()
        m_balance = 1000
    End Sub
    Public Sub Deposit(ByVal amount As Integer)
        m_balance += amount
    End Sub
    Public Sub Withdraw(ByVal amount As Integer)
        m_balance -= amount
    End Sub
    Public ReadOnly Property Balance() As Integer
        Get
            Return m_balance
        End Get
    End Property
End Class
```

The code shown in bold enables us to assign BankDual.Account2.1 as the ProgId, making it compatible with the COM object we are replacing. If we left these lines out, we would still be able to call the object through COM. The ProgId would be created from the namespace and the class name, or Net-Server.Account. Other attributes would let us assign various GUIDs, which would be useful in an early binding scenario. Note that to distinguish our .NET component from the COM component it is replacing, we have assigned the starting balance to be 1000.

We are going to deploy our component in the Global Assembly Cache, so we need to create a strong name, as discussed in Chapter 9. We generate a public-private key pair and place them in a file **keypair.snk**, using the command

```
sn -k keypair.snk
```

In our Visual Studio project we reference this key file in **Assembly-Info.vb**,

```
<Assembly: AssemblyVersion("1.0.*")>
<Assembly: AssemblyKeyFile("..\..\keypair.snk")>
```

Our project creates the target assembly **NetServer.dll** in the top-level source directory, where we also have the **keypair.snk** file. We can run all the command-line programs from the directory **C:\OI\NetVB\Chap17\Net-Server**. We can then place our assembly in the GAC using the command

```
gacutil /i netserver.dll
```

You can use the .NET Admin Tool discussed in Chapter 9 to inspect the contents of the GAC, verifying that **NetServer** has indeed been deployed there. See Figure 17–9.

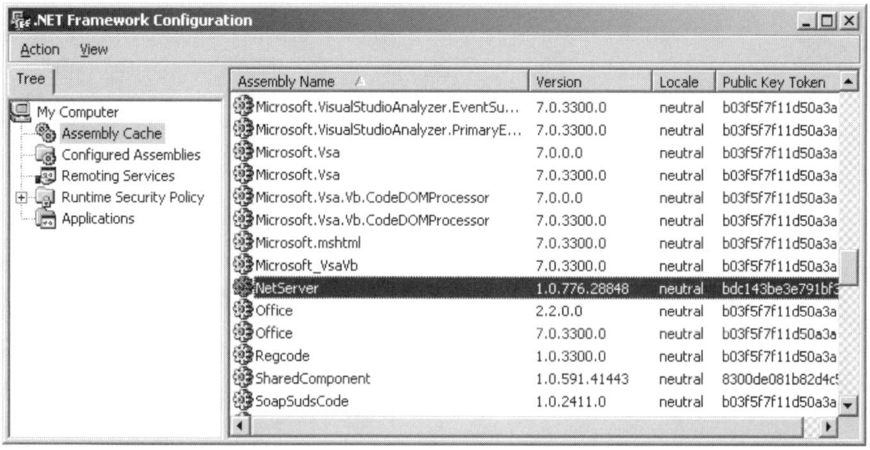

FIGURE 17–9   *Inspecting the GAC using the .NET Admin Tool.*

In order to make our .NET component available to COM clients, we must provide suitable entries in the Registry. This will enable the COM run-time to locate the appropriate server path and so on. The Assembly Registration Utility, **Regasm.exe**, reads the metadata within an assembly and adds these necessary entries to the Registry, which allows COM clients to use the .NET assembly's components as if they were just old-fashioned registered COM components (via the CCW proxy).

The syntax for using **Regasm.exe** is shown next. This allows COM client programs to create instances of managed classes defined by in the assembly.

```
Regasm AssemblyPath [options]
Where the options may be any of the following.
/unregister          Unregister types
/tlb[:FileName]      Specified typelib
/regfile[:FileName]  Specified output reg file name
/codebase            Sets the code base in the registry
/registered          Only refer to preregistered typelibs
/nologo              Prevents displaying logo
/silent              Prevents displaying of messages
/verbose             Displays extra information
/? or /help          Display usage help message
```

We run this utility on **NetServer** using the command **shown in bold**,

```
C:\OI\NetVB\Chap17\NetServer>regasm netserver.dll
RegAsm - .NET Assembly Registration Utility Version
1.0.2914.16
Copyright (C) Microsoft Corp. 2001.  All rights reserved.

Types registered successfully
```

We can use the OLE/COM Object Viewer to inspect the entries made in the Registry. Note that there is a special category of COM objects called .NET Category. Figure 17–10 shows the Registry entries for our NetServer.Account object. Note that the ProgId is BankDual.Account2.1, as specified by the attribute in our VB.NET source code. Note also that the InprocServer32 is **mscoree.dll**, which is the DLL implementing the CLR. As previously mentioned, there is no file created for the CCW. Instead, when the wrapped component is to be instantiated, the CLR creates the CCW on the fly.

A late-binding COM client can now call our .NET component. That is all there is to it! You can double click on **bank.htm**, and Internet Explorer will run the VBScript we looked at before. Only this time, the .NET component **NetServer.Account** is invoked, as you can tell by noticing that the starting balance is 1000, as shown in Figure 17–11.

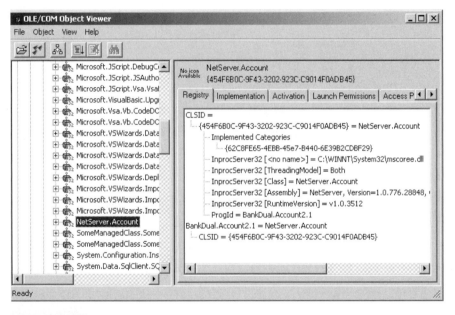

FIGURE 17–10   *OLE/COM Object Viewer shows Registry entries for a .NET object.*

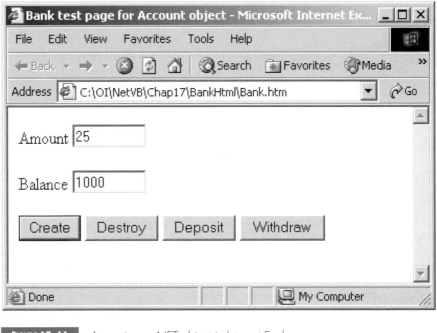

FIGURE 17-11 *Accessing a .NET object in Internet Explorer.*

Platform Invocation Services (PInvoke)

Platform Invocation Services, also known as PInvoke, makes unmanaged exported DLL functions available to managed client code. PInvoke allows this to be done from managed code written in any .NET programming language. Notice that PInvoke is not the name of a class or a method, but is just a nickname for Platform Invocation Services. PInvoke looks after marshaling between CLR data types and native data types, and bridges other differences between the managed and unmanaged runtime environments. Although PInvoke is primarily used to access the Win32 APIs, it can be used to call into your own legacy DLLs that you may find are still useful. Unfortunately, PInvoke is in most circumstances a one-way street. You can use it to call from managed code into unmanaged DLL code and of course return back into managed code; however, the converse is much more problematic. Currently, PInvoke is used to access global exported DLL functions, so even though it is possible for DLLs to export class methods, they are currently not accessible via PInvoke.

If you are an experienced Windows programmer and have a good knowledge of the Win32 API, you may be tempted, after learning about

PInvoke, to call a familiar Win32 API function to perform a task. You should resist this temptation, as calling unmanaged code defeats much of the purpose of .NET. Usually, there will be a native .NET Framework class method that can accomplish your aim, and you should endeavor to use .NET Framework classes wherever possible. Nonetheless, there are occasions when it is necessary to drop down to the underlying platform, and then PInvoke is invaluable.

A Simple Example

Code Example

Let's begin with a very simple example of the use of PInvoke, to call the Windows **MessageBox** function. Our sample program is in the **SimplePInvoke** example.

```
' SimplePInvoke.vb

Imports System
Imports System.Runtime.InteropServices

Module SimplePInvoke

    <DllImport("user32.dll")> _
    Public Function MessageBox( _
    ByVal hWnd As Integer, _
    ByVal text As String, _
    ByVal caption As String, _
    ByVal type As Integer) As Integer
    End Function

    Public Sub Main()
        MessageBox(0, "Hello, World", "From PInvoke", 0)
    End Sub

End Module
```

As an alternative to using the **DllImport** attribute syntax, you can use the traditional Declare keyword syntax to declare an external DLL function.

```
Declare Auto Function MessageBox Lib "user32.dll" ( _
ByVal hWnd As Integer, _
ByVal txt As String, _
ByVal caption As String, _
ByVal Typ As Integer) As Integer
```

The key step is to provide a **DllImport** attribute (or Declare statement) for the prototype of the function that we want to call. The function must take ordinary VB.NET data types as parameters, which match the C data types of the native function. The function will be treated as a shared method in the class where it is defined. The one required parameter to the **DllImport** attribute is the name of the DLL exporting the function. There are various named parameters that can be used with the **DllImport** attribute. For a complete list, consult the documentation of the **DllImportAttribute** class in the **System.Runtime.InteropServices** namespace. Figure 17–12 shows the output from this little program.

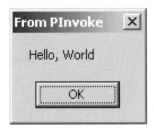

FIGURE 17–12   *Calling the Win32 MessageBox function through PInvoke.*

Marshaling ByRef Parameters

The previous PInvoke example did not demonstrate how PInvoke automatically marshals **ByRef** parameters for you. This is because the **MessageBox** takes only ingoing parameters, and **ByValue** was sufficient to get the parameter into the method call. The next example calls the **GetComputerName** and **GetLastError** APIs via PInvoke. The code for this example is in the **PInvoke** example.

Code
Example

```vb
' PInvoke.vb

Imports System
Imports System.Text
Imports System.Runtime.InteropServices

Public Module Test
    <DllImport("kernel32.dll")> _
    Public Function GetComputerName( _
    ByVal name As StringBuilder, _
    ByRef buffer As Integer) As Boolean
    End Function
    <DllImport("kernel32.dll")> _
    Public Function GetLastError() As Integer
    End Function

    Public Sub Main()
        Dim result As Boolean = True
        Dim error_code As Integer = 0
        Dim name As StringBuilder = New StringBuilder(128)
```

```
        Dim length As Integer = 128
        result = GetComputerName(name, length)

        If result Then
            Console.WriteLine(name)
        Else
            error_code = GetLastError()
            Console.WriteLine("Error: {0:x}", error_code)
        End If
        Return
    End Sub
End Module
```

TRANSLATING TYPES

Since **GetComputerName** returns a name in its first parameter, **String-Builder** was used instead of **String**. For input-only arguments, you can use **String**, but outgoing parameters must not be **String**, since **String** is immutable. The **ByRef** keyword was placed on the length attribute because the second argument to **GetComputerName** is an outgoing primitive data type parameter. The Integer type is used because DWORD is a 32-bit integer quantity. For comparison, here are the prototypes of the corresponding Win32 functions:

```
BOOL GetComputerName(
  LPTSTR lpBuffer,   // computer name
  LPDWORD lpnSize    // size of name buffer
);

DWORD GetLastError(VOID);
```

Some CLR types do not map directly into unmanaged types. For example, you have to tell the Execution Engine (**mscoree.dll**) how to translate to a BSTR. You do that by annotating the declaration with the **MarshalAs** attribute:

```
<MarshalAs(UnmanagedType.BStr)> _
Public Function Foo() As String
```

The **UnmanagedType** enumeration lists all the translatable types.

Summary

In this chapter we studied mixing managed and unmanaged code running under Windows. We saw how to call legacy COM components from within the managed .NET environment using a Runtime Callable Wrapper, or RCW. We also looked at the use of a COM Callable Wrapper (CCW) to enable a COM client to call a .NET component. Finally, we looked at using Platform Invocation Services (PInvoke), and saw how automatic marshaling is provided for both in and out parameters.

Visual Studio .NET

Although it is possible to program .NET using only the command-line compiler, it is much easier and more enjoyable to use Visual Studio .NET. In this chapter, we cover the basics of using Visual Studio to edit, compile, run, and debug programs. You will then be equipped to use Visual Studio in the rest of the book. We will introduce additional features of Visual Studio later in the book as we encounter a need. This book was developed using beta software, so you may encounter some changes to the information presented here in the final released product. Visual Studio is a highly configurable Windows application. Your installation may be configured differently than ours, in which case you would encounter variations in the exact layout of windows and other specifications shown here. As you work with Visual Studio, think of yourself as an explorer discovering a rich and varied new country.

Overview of Visual Studio .NET

Open Microsoft Visual Studio .NET, and you will see a starting window similar to what is shown in Figure A–1.

What you see on default startup is the main window with an HTML page that can help you navigate among various resources, open or create projects, and change your profile information. (If you close the start page, you can get it back anytime from the menu using Help | Show Start Page.) Clicking on **My Profile** brings up a profile page on which you can change various settings. Several profiles are available in Visual Studio, including a standard one for "typical" work (called the Visual Studio Developer profile) and special ones for various languages. Because Visual Studio .NET is the unification of many development environments, programmers used to one particular previous environment may prefer a particular keyboard scheme, window layout, and so on. For example, if you choose the profile Visual Basic Developer, you will get the Visual Basic 6 keyboard scheme. In this book, we use all the

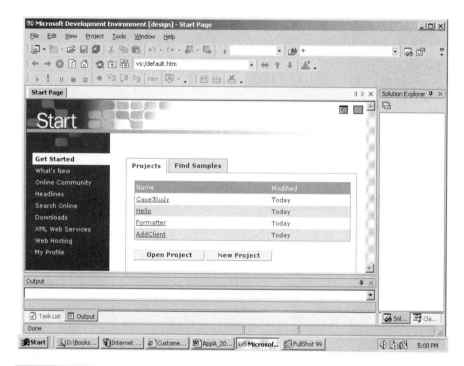

FIGURE A–1   *Visual Studio .NET main window.*

defaults, so go back to the profile Visual Studio Developer if you made any
changes. See Figure A–2.

To gain an appreciation for some of the diverse features in Visual Studio
.NET, open the **Bank** console solution in this chapter: Choose File | Open
Solution..., navigate to the **Bank** directory, and open the file **Bank.sln.** You
will see several windows. (See Figure A–3.)

Starting from the left is the Toolbox,[1] followed by the main window
area, which currently is just a gray area. Below the main window is the Output window, which shows the results of builds and so on. On the top right,
the Solution Explorer enables you to conveniently see all the files in a solution, which may consist of several projects. On the bottom right is the Properties window, which lets you conveniently edit properties on forms for
Windows applications.

From the Solution Explorer, you can navigate to files in the projects. In
turn, double-click on **Account.vb** and **Bank.vb**, the two source files in the

---

1. The Toolbox is used in Windows Forms applications, and will be discussed in
   Chapter 7. You can show or hide the Toolbox from the View menu.

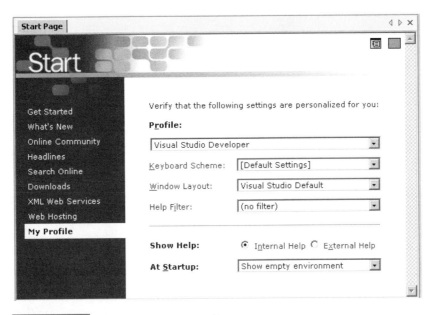

FIGURE A–2   Visual Studio .NET profile page.

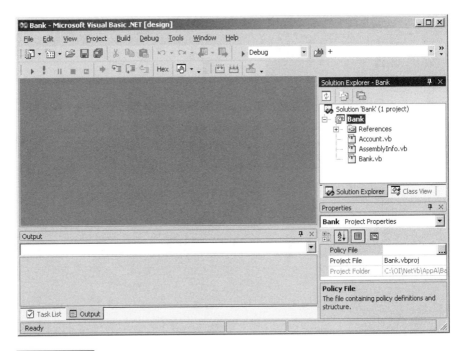

FIGURE A–3   A console project in Visual Studio .NET.

Bank project. Text editor windows appear in the main window area. Across the top of the main window are horizontal tabs that let you quickly select any of the open windows. Visual Studio .NET is a Multiple Document Interface (MDI) application, so you can also select the window to show from the Windows menu. Figure A–4 shows the open source files with the horizontal tabs.

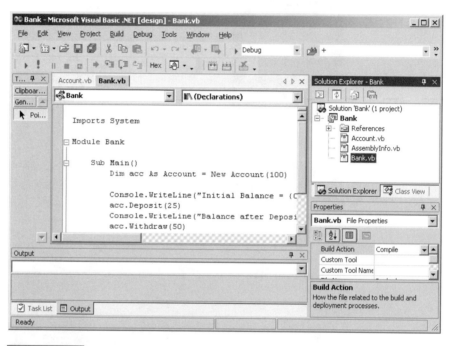

FIGURE A–4   *Horizontal tabs for open source files.*

Toolbars

Visual Studio comes with many different toolbars. You can configure the toolbars you want displayed, and you can drag toolbars to the position you find most convenient. You can also customize toolbars by adding or deleting buttons that correspond to different commands. To specify which toolbars are displayed, use the menu View | Toolbars. You can also right-click in any empty area of a toolbar. A list of toolbars appears with check marks beside the ones currently displayed. By clicking on an item on this menu, you can make the corresponding toolbar appear or disappear. For your work in this book, add these toolbars:

- Build
- Debug

CUSTOMIZING A TOOLBAR

We want to make sure that the Start Without Debugging command is available on the Debug toolbar. If this command (which looks like a red exclamation point) is not already on your Debug toolbar, you can add it using the following procedure, which can be used to add other commands to toolbars:

1. Select menu Tools | Customize... to bring up the Customize dialog.
2. Select the Commands tab.
3. In Categories, select Debug, and in Commands, select Start Without Debugging. See Figure A–5.
4. Drag the selected command onto the Debug toolbar, positioning it where you desire. For now, place it to the immediate right of the wedge-shaped Start ▸ button.
5. Close the Customize dialog.

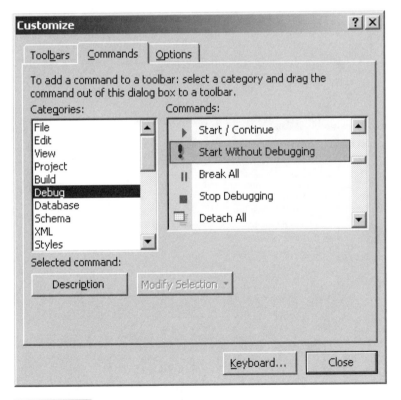

FIGURE A–5   *Adding a new command to a toolbar.*

Creating a Console Application

As our first exercise in using Visual Studio, we will create a simple console application. Our program **Bytes** will attempt to calculate how many bytes are in a kilobyte, a megabyte, a gigabyte, and a terabyte. If you want to follow along on your PC as you read, you can use the **Demos** directory for this chapter. The first version is in **Bytes\Version1**. A final version can be found in **Bytes\Version3**.

Creating a VB.NET Project

1. From the Visual Studio main menu, choose File | New | Project.... This will bring up the New Project dialog.
2. For Project Types, choose Visual Basic Projects, and for Templates, choose Empty Project.
3. Click the Browse button, navigate to **Demos,** and click Open. See Figure A–6.
4. In the Name field, type **Bytes**.
5. Click OK.

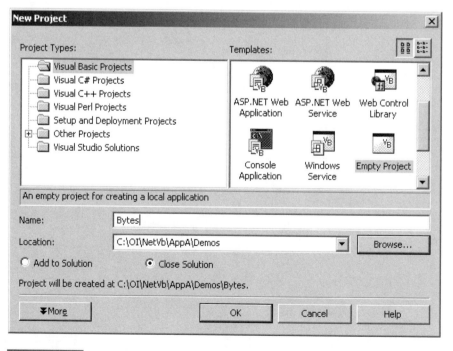

FIGURE A–6   *Creating an empty VB.NET project.*

Adding a VB.NET Module

At this point, you have an empty VB.NET project. We will now add a file called **Bytes.vb**, which will contain the source code for our program.

1. In the Solution Explorer, right-click over **Bytes**, and choose Add | Add New Item.... This will bring up the Add New Item dialog.
2. For Categories, choose Local Project Items.
3. For Templates, choose Module.
4. For Name, type **Bytes.vb**. See Figure A–7.
5. Click Open.

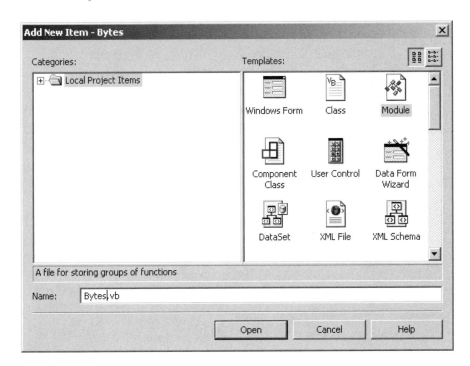

FIGURE A–7   *Adding a VB.NET module to a VB.NET project.*

Using the Visual Studio Text Editor

In the Solution Explorer, double-click on **Bytes.vb**. This will open the file in the Visual Studio text editor. Notice that a skeleton version of a module already exists because you selected Module as the template for the file. Type the following code in **Bytes.vb**. You should notice that the editor uses color-coded syntax highlighting as you type.

```
' Bytes.vb - Version 1

Imports System

Module Bytes

    Sub Main()
        Dim bytes As Integer = 1024

        Console.WriteLine("1 kilobyte = {0} bytes", bytes)
        bytes = bytes * 1024
        Console.WriteLine("1 megabyte = {0} bytes", bytes)
        bytes = bytes * 1024
        Console.WriteLine("1 gigabyte = {0} bytes", bytes)

    End Sub

End Module
```

Besides the color syntax highlighting, other features include automatic indenting and automatically adding End statements to various programming constructs. All in all, you should find the Visual Studio editor friendly and easy to use.

Building the Project

You can build the project using one of the following:

- Menu Build | Build
- Toolbar
- Keyboard shortcut Ctrl + Shift + B

Running the Program

You can run the program using one of the following:

- Menu Debug | Start Without Debugging
- Toolbar
- Keyboard shortcut Ctrl + F5

You won't see any output. This is because the default project type for an "empty project" is a Windows application. To change it, you must right-click on the project name (**Bytes**) in the Solution Explorer window and choose Properties. See Figure A–8. In the Output type dropdown, select Console Application. Using the Project Properties dialog, you can also configure the Startup Object of the applications.

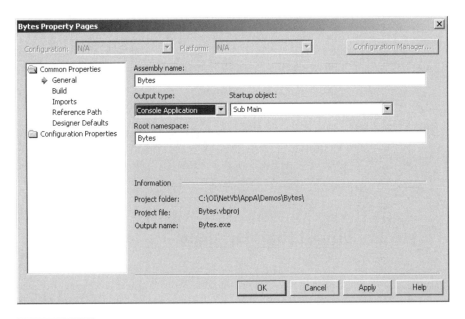

Changing project properties.

Now rebuild your application, and try to run it again. You will see the following output in a console window:

```
1 kilobyte = 1024 bytes
1 megabyte = 1048576 bytes
1 gigabyte = 1073741824 bytes
Press any key to continue
```

If you press any key, as indicated, the console window will close.

Defining the Startup Object

In VB.NET, you must define the startup object. You do this via the project Properties dialog shown in Figure A-8. Depending on how the project was built and whether you changed the name of the module after it was generated, you may need to set the startup object to **Sub Main**. The compiler will generate a syntax message if it is unable to find **Sub Main**.

Running the Program in the Debugger

You can run the program in the debugger using one of the following:

● Menu Debug | Start
● Toolbar ▶
● Keyboard shortcut F5

A console window will briefly open up and then immediately close. If you want the window to stay open, you must explicitly program for it, for example, by asking for input. Add the following two lines to your program right above the **End Sub** statement.

```
Console.WriteLine("Press enter to continue...")
Console.ReadLine()
```

When you run your program, the output will stay on the screen until you press the Enter key. You can also set a breakpoint to stop the execution before the program exits. We will outline features of the debugger later in the appendix.

Project Configurations

A project *configuration* specifies build settings for a project. You can have several different configurations, and each configuration will be built in its own directory, so you can exercise the different configurations independently. Every project in a Visual Studio solution has two default configurations, **Debug** and **Release**. As the names suggest, the **Debug** configuration will build a debug version of the project, in which you can do source-level debugging by setting breakpoints, among other things. The **obj\Debug** directory will then contain a *program database* file with a **.pdb** extension that holds debugging and project state information.

You can choose the configuration from the main toolbar ▶ Debug ▼. You can also choose the configuration using the menu Build | Configuration Manager..., which brings up the Configuration Manager dialog. From the Active Solution Configuration drop-down box, choose **Release**. See Figure A–9.

Build the project again. A second version of the IL language file **Bytes.exe** is created, this time in the **obj\Release** directory. There will be no **.pdb** file in this directory.

Debugging

Some of the most exciting features of any IDE are the debugging features. To take advantage of these features, you must make sure that you built your executable using a Debug configuration. There are two ways to enter the debugger:

- **Just-in-Time Debugging:** You run as normal, and if an exception occurs, you will be allowed to enter the debugger. The program has

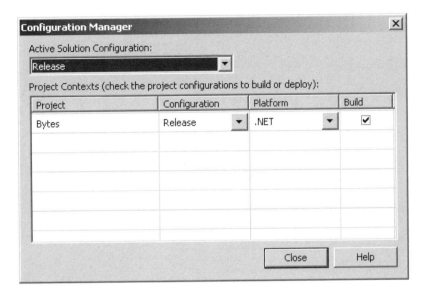

FIGURE A–9   *Choosing Release in the Configuration Manager.*

crashed, so you will not be able to run any further. But you will be able to see the value of variables, and you will see the point at which the program failed.

● **Standard Debugging:** You start the program under the debugger. You may set breakpoints, single step, and so on.

To experiment with the debugger, add the following two lines to your program after the calculation of gigabytes:

```
bytes = bytes * 1024
Console.WriteLine("1 terabyte = {0} bytes", bytes)
```

Then rebuild the application. You can find this version of the program in **Bytes\Version2**.

Just-in-Time Debugging

Build and run (without debugging) the **Bytes** program from the preceding section, making sure to use the **Debug** configuration. This time, the program will not run through smoothly to completion, because an exception will be thrown. A Just-In-Time Debugging dialog will appear (see Figure A–10). Click Yes to debug.

The Attach to Process dialog will then be displayed (see Figure A–11). Click OK to debug.

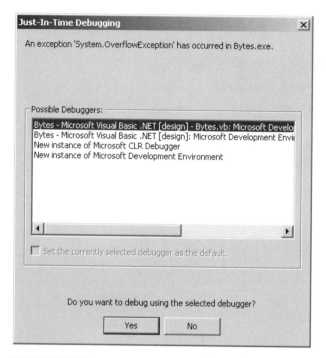

Just-In-Time Debugging dialog is displayed in response to an exception.

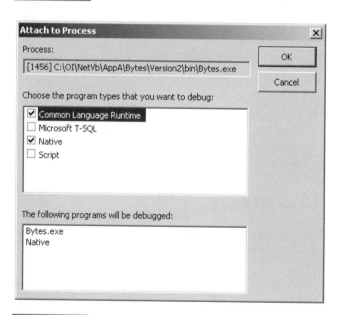

Attach to Process dialog.

Finally, the Microsoft Development Environment dialog will be displayed (see Figure A–12). Click Break to debug. If you originally executed the program using Start instead of Start Without Debugging, the dialogs in Figures A–10 and A–11 will not be displayed.

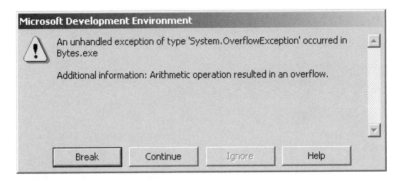

FIGURE A–12   *Microsoft Developer Environment options for responding to exceptions.*

You will now see a window showing the source code where the problem arose, with an arrow pinpointing the location (see Figure A–13).

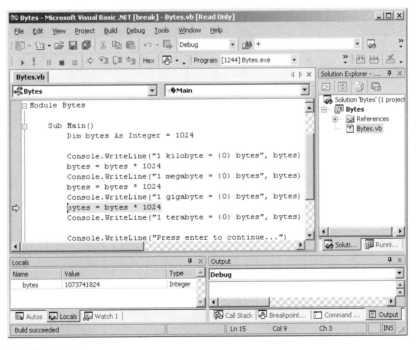

FIGURE A–13   *Breaking on a System.OverflowException.*

If you look in the Locals window, which is docked across the bottom of the Visual Studio window (click on the Locals tab at the bottom), you will see that the current value of the variable **bytes** is 1073741824. When the expression **bytes * 1024** was executed, the resulting value was larger than the largest possible integer. This is why the exception indicated that you had an *overflow*.

To stop debugging, you can use the ■ toolbar button or the menu Debug | Stop Debugging.

Standard Debugging

BREAKPOINTS

Typically, when you want to debug, you set a breakpoint at a line in the code where you want to begin to follow the execution. Then you run using the debugger. As an example, set a breakpoint at the first line:

```
bytes = bytes * 1024
```

The easiest way to set a breakpoint is to click in the gray bar to the left of the source code window. You can also set the cursor on the desired line and click the "hand" toolbar button ✋ to toggle a breakpoint. (It sets a breakpoint if one is not set, and removes the breakpoint if a one is set.)

Now you can run under the debugger. Execution begins in **Main** and pauses when the breakpoint is hit. A yellow arrow over the red dot of the breakpoint shows the next line to be executed. See Figure A–14.

When you are finished with a breakpoint, you can remove it by clicking again in the gray bar or by toggling with the hand toolbar button. If you want to remove all breakpoints, you can use the menu Debug | Clear All Breakpoints, or you can use the toolbar button 🖐.

WATCHING VARIABLES

At this point, you can inspect variables. Several options are available to accomplish this: Locals window, tool tips, Quick Watch window, and Watch window.

You have already seen in Figures A–13 and A–14 the Local window that is displayed when a breakpoint is encountered. It lists all the variables that are defined in the current procedure, as well as their current values. If you don't see the Locals window, you can use the menu Debug | Windows | Locals to bring up the window.

Another easy way to examine the value of a variable is to hover the mouse over the variable. The value of the variable will be shown as a yellow tool tip, as illustrated in Figure A–15.

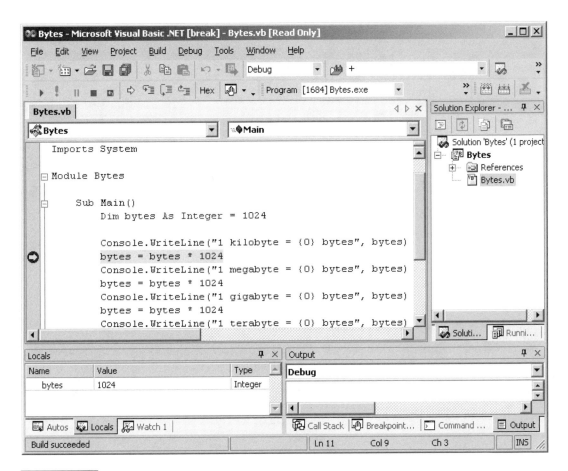

FIGURE A–14 *A breakpoint has been hit.*

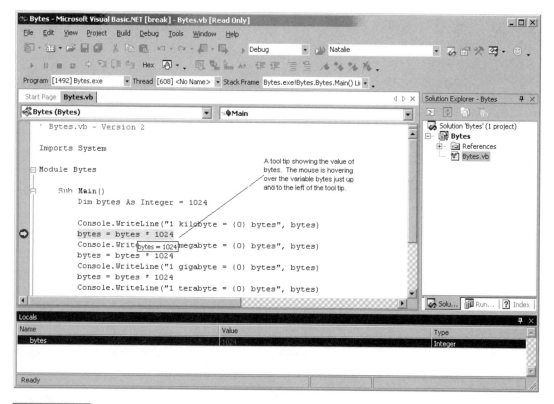

FIGURE A–15   *Using tool tips to show a variable's value.*

You can also right-click over a variable and choose Quick Watch (or use the eyeglasses toolbar button 👓). Figure A–16 shows a typical Quick Watch window. You can also change the value of a variable from this window.

Finally, you can use the Watch window to manage a custom list of variables you want to watch. To add a variable to the Watch window, right-click on it and choose Add Watch. The Watch window is similar to the Locals window, and it stays docked at the bottom of the Visual Studio window. When a variable changes value, the new value is shown in red. Figure A–17 shows the Watch window. (Note that the display has been changed to hex, as described in the next section.)

The Quick Watch window shows the variable, allowing you to change it.

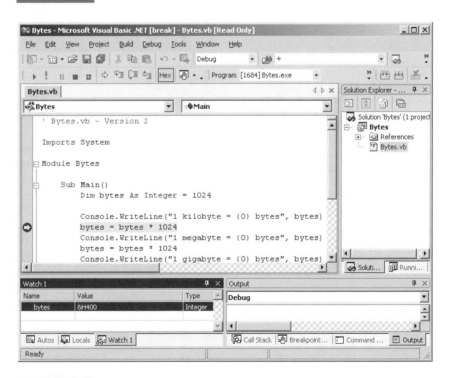

FIGURE A–17   *The Visual Studio Watch window.*

DEBUGGER OPTIONS

You can change debugger options by choosing from the menu Tools | Options and then selecting Debugging from the list. Figure A–18 illustrates setting a hexadecimal display. If you then go back to a Watch window, you will see a hex value such as **0x400** displayed.[2]

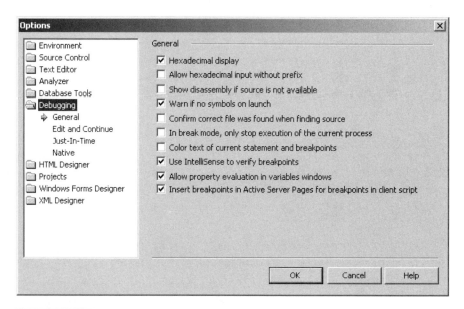

FIGURE A–18   *Setting hexadecimal display in Debugging Options.*

    Another useful debugging option to change under the Edit and Continue category allows you to edit code while your are in Break mode (see Figure A–19). This option is automatically set for C# projects, but not for VB projects.

SINGLE STEPPING

When you are stopped in the debugger, you can *single step* through the code. This means that you can execute one line at a time and examine the results of each statement. You can also begin execution by single stepping. There are a number of single step buttons: ⟦⟧ ⟦⟧ ⟦⟧. These are the most common (in the order shown on the toolbar):

●   Step Into

_____

2. You could also simply right-click over the value in the Locals or Watch window and choose Hexadecimal Display from the context menu.

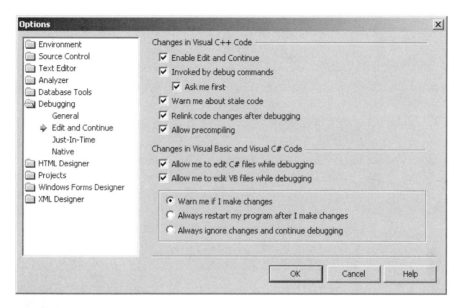

FIGURE A–19 *Setting Edit and Continue options.*

- Step Over
- Step Out

There is also a Run to Cursor button ⊒ .

With Step Into, you execute the current statement. If it is a call to a procedure, execution will step into the procedure. With Step Over, you execute current statement. If it is a call to a procedure, it will execute the entire procedure.

To illustrate Step Into, build the **Bytes\Version3** project, where the expression **bytes * 1024** has been replaced by a call to the function **Multiply-ByOneK**. Set a breakpoint at the first function call, and then select Step Into. The result is illustrated in Figure A–20. Note the red dot at the breakpoint and the yellow arrow in the function.

When debugging, Visual Studio maintains a call stack. You can display the call stack by using the menu Debug | Windows | Call Stack. In our example, the Call Stack is just two deep when you used Step Into to step into the function. See the Call Stack pane in Figure A–20. It shows that the **Main** function called **MultiplyByOneK**.

Stop debugging and start again. But instead of choosing Step Into, choose Step Over. You will see that you are immediately placed on the call to **WriteLine**.

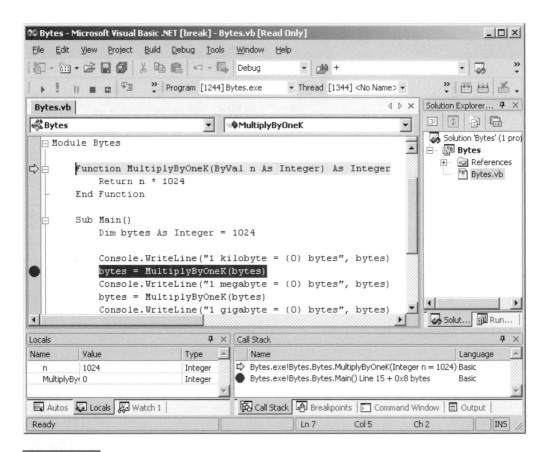

FIGURE A–20 *Stepping into a function.*

Summary

Visual Studio .NET is a very rich integrated development environment (IDE) with many features to make programming more enjoyable. In this appendix we covered the basics of using Visual Studio to edit, compile, run, and debug programs so that you will be equipped to use Visual Studio in the rest of the book. Visual Studio .NET has a vast array of features for building database applications, Web applications, components, and many other kinds of projects. It supports many different languages. A project can be built in different configurations, such as Debug and Release, and when you finish an application, you should produce a Release build and use that executable to run the program. In this book we are using only a tiny fraction of the capabilities of this powerful tool. However, the simple features we employ are very useful and will certainly make your life as a VB.NET programmer easier.

Tracing and Debugging in .NET

*C*omplicated applications cannot be put under the debugger to find out what went wrong. Duplicating or even understanding what conditions are needed to replicate the problem is often difficult. The **System.Diagnostics** namespace has several classes that help you instrument your application.[1]

Instrumenting your application for debugging and tracing will enable you to make your applications more robust. It also illustrates the common pattern of how the framework divides classes into separate tasks (writing the output, controlling the output, and the output destination) so that you can customize parts and still rely on the .NET Framework classes for the rest. The mechanics of instrumenting your application has three aspects.

The **Trace** and **Debug** classes are used to generate the debug or trace output. These classes have identical methods and properties that allow you to write diagnostic output. They do not, however, specify the destination of the output.

The **Listeners** classes are used to direct the output to various destinations, although a default destination does exist.

Finally, there are mechanisms for turning on or off the instrumentation. You can set the DEBUG and TRACE compilation flags to have different tracing for debug or release builds. You can have the output of the **Trace** and **Debug** classes depend on the conditional evaluation of expressions. Or, you can con-

---

1. The security of your Web site or Web service is enhanced by using tracing and debugging output. You do not want to give out information in an error message that could be used to compromise your system. Capturing that information in a trace or debug log allows the program to generate a generic error message for the user. You could also assign an identifier to the user message that is also recorded with the log message. If necessary, that ID could be used to help the user diagnose any problems with his or her system.

trol the verbosity of the output, depending on your need for information, using the **BooleanSwitch** and **TraceSwitch** classes.

The TraceDemo Example

The **TraceDemo** example illustrates the use of the diagnostic functionality. If you run the example, you will get the following output:

```
Trace Listeners:
   Default

Trace Listeners:
   Default
   Console.Out Listener
   Output File Listener

This was compiled with a DEBUG directive!
This was compiled with a TRACE directive!
                Debug Boolean Switch enabled at startup.
                Debug Boolean Switch enabled!
Trace Switch Startup Value = Warning
          TraceError!
          TraceWarning!
Trace Listeners:
   Console.Out Listener
   Output File Listener

File output.txt has been created
```

Refer to this output in the ensuing discussion. You will also find a file called **output.txt** on your computer in the directory where this program ran.

Enabling Debug and Trace Output

To use the **Debug** class, the DEBUG flag must be defined, or else the methods of this class will not be compiled into the executable or library. Similarly, to use the **Trace** class, the TRACE flag must be defined. This way you can have different diagnostics for release and debug builds. Bring up the project property pages from the menu Project | Properties. Choose Build under Configuration Properties. You can then check or uncheck the DEBUG and TRACE conditional compilation constants, as shown in Figure B–1.

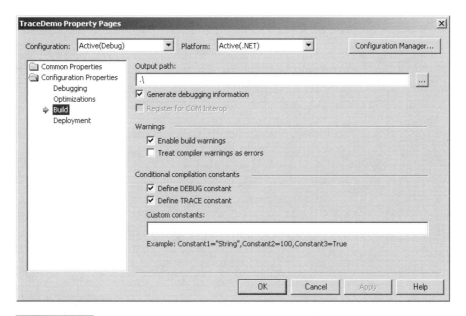

Visual Studio window for setting conditional compilation constants.

Using the Debug and Trace Classes

The useful methods and properties are shared. The overloaded **WriteLine** and **Write** are used to write debug or trace output. The overloaded **WriteLineIf** and **WriteIf** write output if the condition in their first argument is true.

```
Debug.WriteLine( _
    "This was compiled with a DEBUG directive!")
Trace.WriteLine( _
    "This was compiled with a TRACE directive!")
...
Debug.WriteLineIf(DebugBooleanSwitch.Enabled, _
    "Debug Boolean Switch enabled at startup.")
Debug.WriteLineIf(Not DebugBooleanSwitch.Enabled, _
    "Debug Boolean Switch disabled at startup.")
```

Output is indented with the **Indent** and **Unindent** methods. The indentation size is controlled with the **IndentSize** property.

```
Trace.Indent()
...
Trace.IndentSize = 10
```

You can also set the indentation size in the application configuration file.

```xml
<?xml version="1.0"?>
<configuration>
    <system.diagnostics>
        <trace indentsize="15" />
            <switches>
                <add name="DebugSwitch" value = "1" />
                <add name="TraceSwitch" value = "2" />
            </switches>
    </system.diagnostics>
</configuration>
```

The **Assert** method can check an assertion. The **AutoFlush** property and the **Flush** method control the flushing of the output buffer.

Using Switches to Enable Diagnostics

Switches give you finer grain control over the diagnostic output. You can use the **BooleanSwitch** class to turn output on or off based on the value of its **Enabled** property.

The **TraceSwitch** class gives you five hierarchical levels of control for its **Level** property: **TraceError**, **TraceWarning**, **TraceInfo**, **TraceVerbose**, and **Off**. These values are part of the **TraceLevelEnumeration**. Setting a lower Trace level means that the higher ones are set as well. For example, if the **TraceWarning** level is set, both the **TraceError** and **TraceWarning** levels are enabled.

```
DebugBooleanSwitch.Enabled = True
Debug.WriteLineIf(DebugBooleanSwitch.Enabled, _
   "Debug Boolean Switch enabled!")
...
  Trace.WriteLineIf(TraceLevelSwitch.TraceError, _
   "TraceError!")
```

The constructors for these switches take two parameters. The first is the name of the switch, the second is a text description of the switch. Both **BooleanSwitch** and **TraceSwitch** classes inherit from the abstract class **Switch**. You can write your own customized switch classes by inheriting from the **Switch** class. Note that the **Enabled** property of the **BooleanSwitch** and the **Level** and named level properties of the **TraceSwitch** are not part of the **Switch** class.

Enabling or Disabling Switches

You can use settings in your application configuration file to enable or disable a switch at startup. This can also be done programmatically.

Configuration File Switch Settings

You can set the switch's initial setting in the application's configuration file.

```
<?xml version="1.0"?>
<configuration>
    <system.diagnostics>
        <trace indentsize="15" />
            <switches>
                <add name="DebugSwitch" value = "1" />
                <add name="TraceSwitch" value = "2" />
            </switches>
    </system.diagnostics>
</configuration>
```

If no values are found, the initial value of the **DebugSwitch's Enabled** property is set to false and the **TraceSwitch's Level** property is set to off.

Programmatic Switch Settings

The **Enabled** property of the **DebugSwitch** can be set to true or false. The **Level** property of the **TraceSwitch** can be set to one of the options of the **TraceLevelEumeration**: **TraceOff, TraceError, TraceWarning, TraceInfo, TraceVerbose**. You can get the level of the **TraceSwitch's** setting by examining the **TraceError, TraceWarning, TraceInfo, TraceVerbose** properties.

Using Switches to Control Output

You can test the value of the switch before you write, debug, or trace output. You can do this with an if statement, or as an argument to one of the **Trace** or **Debug** classes' methods.

```
Trace.WriteLineIf(TraceLevelSwitch.TraceError, _
    "TraceError!")
Trace.WriteLineIf(TraceLevelSwitch.TraceWarning, _
    "TraceWarning!")
Trace.WriteLineIf(TraceLevelSwitch.TraceInfo, _
    "InfoMessage!")
Trace.WriteLineIf(TraceLevelSwitch.TraceVerbose, _
    "VerboseMessage!")
```

Since you can set these values outside of your program's code, you can select the circumstances under which you get a particular level of debug or trace output. For example, you can turn on **TraceVerbose** output if you really need a high level of diagnostics, but turn it off after you have found the problem.

TraceListener

Classes derived from the abstract class **TraceListener** represent destinations for the diagnostic output. The **TextWriterTraceListener** is designed to direct output to a **TextWriter**, **Stream**, or **FileStream**. **Console.Out** is an example of a commonly used output stream. The **EventLogTraceListener** class allows you to send output to an EventLog. You can create your own event logs with the EventLog's static method **CreateEventSource**. The **DefaultTraceListener** sends output to the debugging output window. Default Debug output can be viewed in Visual Studio .NET's Output window or with utilities (such as DBMon). You can customize where output appears by implementing your own class derived from **TraceListener**.

Listeners Collection

Both the **Debug** and **Trace** classes have a static **Listeners** collection. This collection of **TraceListeners** represents a list of **TraceListener** objects that want to receive the output from the **Debug** or **Trace** class. Listeners are added to or removed from the collection just as with any other .NET collection.

```
' Create a listener that writes to the console
Dim ConsoleOutput As New TextWriterTraceListener( _
    Console.Out, "Console.Out Listener")
Trace.Listeners.Add(ConsoleOutput)

' Create a listener that writes to a text file
Dim OutputFile As Stream = File.Create("output.txt")
Dim OutputFileListener As TextWriterTraceListener = New _
    TextWriterTraceListener(OutputFile, _
    "Output File Listener")
Trace.Listeners.Add(OutputFileListener)

' Show the listeners now
ShowListeners()
```

```
' Remove the default listener
Trace.Listeners.Remove("Default")
```

In this code extract, the **OutputFileListener** in the example will send the Trace output to a file called **output.txt**. The **DefaultTraceListener** is added automatically to the **Listener** collections. Any of the listeners, including the default listener, can be removed from the collection by invoking the collection's **Remove** method. To list all listeners in the collection:

```
Sub ShowListeners()
   Console.WriteLine("Trace Listeners:")
   Dim tr As TraceListener
   For Each tr In Trace.Listeners
      Console.WriteLine("   " & tr.Name)
   Next
   Console.WriteLine("")
End Sub
```

Summary

Instrumenting your application for degrees of debugging and diagnostic output is a common program task. The diagnostic classes exemplify the way .NET provides classes to handle standard programming tasks so you can concentrate on developing the business logic of your programming, not on building infrastructure. On the other hand, they also exemplify how the .NET classes are partitioned so that you can customize the infrastructure using as much or as little of the other classes as you require.

INDEX

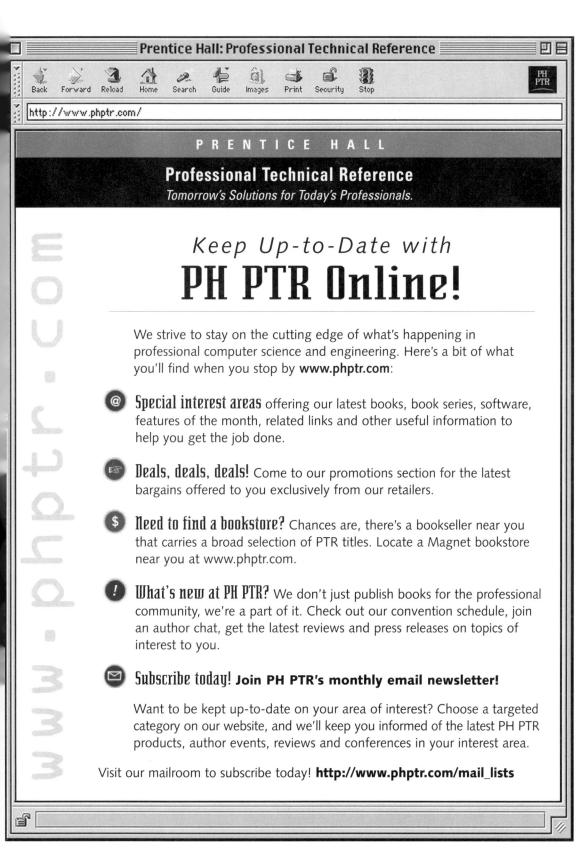

Object
INNOVATIONS

DEVELOPER TRAINING

OBJECT INNOVATIONS offers training course materials in fundamental software technologies used in developing applications in modern computing environments. We emphasize object-oriented techniques, with a focus on Microsoft® technologies, XML, Java™, and Linux™. Our courses have been used by businesses, training companies, and universities throughout North America. End clients include IBM®, HP®, Dell®, Compaq®, FedEx®, UPS®, AOL®, U.S. Bank®, Mellon Bank®, and NASA. Our courses are frequently updated to reflect feedback from classroom use. We aggressively track new technologies and endeavor to keep our courseware up-to-date.

Founded in 1993, Object Innovations has a long record of firsts in courseware. Our Visual C++ course was released before Microsoft's, we introduced one of the first courses in JavaServer Pages, and our Linux Internals 2.4 kernel course came out several months before Red Hat's course. Now we are leading the development of comprehensive developer training in Microsoft's .NET technology.

.NET DEVELOPER TRAINING

OBJECT INNOVATIONS is writing the premier book series on .NET for Prentice Hall PTR. These authoritative books are the foundation of our curriculum. Each book matches a corresponding core course between the course materials and the book, and students have comprehensive reference materials after the course. Each core course is five days in length and is very rich in content, containing well over five days worth of material. In addition, we offer many modules on .NET technology, making it easy to offer custom training. We are continually creating new modules and courses, so check our Web site for the latest information.

Modules on .NET technology include:

M411	C# Essentials (2 days)
M412	.NET Framework Using C# (3 days)
M413	ASP.NET Using C# (2 days)
M421	VB.NET Essentials (2 days)
M422	.NET Framework Using VB.NET (3 days)
M423	ASP.NET Using VB.NET (2 days)

.NET courses include:

410	Introduction to C# Using .NET (5 days)
414	Application Development Using C# and .NET (5 days)
420	Introduction to Visual Basic Using .NET (5 days)
424	Application Development Using Visual Basic and .NET (5 days)
434	.NET Architecture and Programming Using Visual C++ (5 days)
440	Programming Perl in the .NET Environment (5 days)
454	Web Applications Using C# and XML (5 days)
455	Web Applications Using VB.NET and XML (5 days)

MICROSOFT DEVELOPER TRAINING

Our Microsoft curriculum is very extensive, with introductory and advanced courses on C++, Visual C++, MFC, COM/DCOM, OLE, COM+, and advanced topics in Visual Basic™. Selected courses include:

    123   Programming COM and DCOM Using ATL (5 days)
    127   Programming COM and OLE Using MFC (5 days)
    149   Distributed COM+ Programming (5 days)
    133   Distributed COM+ Programming Using Visual Basic (5 days)
    145   MFC Windows Programming for C++ Programmers (5 days)
    146   Advanced Windows Programming Using Visual C++ (5 days)
    157   Advanced C++ Programming (5 days)

XML DEVELOPER TRAINING

Our XML curriculum covers the broad range of XML technology. We offer courses in "pure" XML – all discussion and exercises based entirely in W3C-recommended standards – as well as training in use of XML through today's dominant enterprise platforms, Java and .NET. Selected courses include:

    501   XML for the Enterprise (5 days)
    504   Powering Websites with XML (4 days)
    506   XML Transformations (3 days)
    531   XML and Java for the Enterprise (5 days)
    454   Web Applications Using C# and XML (5 days)

JAVA DEVELOPER TRAINING

Java training courses span the spectrum from beginning to advanced and provide extensive coverage of both client-side and server-side technologies. Selected courses include:

    103   Java Programming (5 days)
    105   Using and Developing JavaBeans (4 days)
    106   Advanced Java Programming (5 days)
    107   CORBA Architecture and Programming Using Java (4 days)
    109   Java Server Pages (2 days)
    110   Java Servlet Programming (2 days)
    163   Enterprise JavaBeans (5 days)
    172   Java Foundation Classes (5 days)

LINUX COURSES

Linux courses range from fundamentals and system administration to advanced courses in internals, device drivers and networking. Selected courses include:

    135   Fundamentals of Linux (4 days)
    310   Linux Internals (5 days)
    314   Linux Network Drivers Development (3 days)

See our .NET website for complete course listings: www.objectinnovations.com/dotnet.htm

OBJECT INNOVATIONS' .NET TRAINING PARTNERS

For information about .NET training using OBJECT INNOVATIONS courseware,
please check with our .NET Training Partners.

ANEW TECHNOLOGY CORPORATION   www.Anew.net

Specialized in IT consulting, training, mentoring, and development, Anew Technology has been serving many satisfied clients. Our business mission is threefold: to stay at the forefront of IT technologies, to satisfy client needs by applying these technologies, and to provide the best service in our industry. Anew Technology is a business partner with Object Innovations in operations and courseware development.

COMPUTER HORIZONS EDUCATION DIVISION   www.ComputerHorizons.com/Training

For over seventeen years Computer Horizons Education Division (CHED) has been providing on-site, instructor-led IT training and customized workshops for organizations nationwide. We have developed extensive curriculum offerings in Web Technologies, Relational Databases, Reporting Tools, Process Improvement, UNIX™ and LINUX™, Client/Server, Mainframe & Legacy Systems, Windows® 2000, and much more. CHED will design, develop and deliver a training solution tailored to each client's training requirements.

COMPUWORKS SYSTEMS, INC.   www.CompuWorks.com

CompuWorks Systems, Inc. is an IT solutions company whose aim is to provide our clients with customized training, support and development services. We are committed to building long term partnerships with our clients in an effort to meet their individual needs. Cutting-edge solutions are our specialty.

CUSTOM TRAINING INSTITUTE   www.4CustomTraining.com

Custom Training Institute is a provider of high quality High-End training since 1989. Along with our full line of "off-the-shelf" classes, we excel at providing a customized Solutions—from technical needs assessment through course development and delivery. We specialize in Legacy Skills Transformation, Oracle, UNIX, C++, Java™ and other subjects for computer professionals.

DB BASICS   www.DBBasics.com

DBBasics, founded in 1988 as a Microsoft® solution development company, has developed and delivered Microsoft technology training since its inception. DBBasics specializes in delivering database and developer technology training to corporate customers. Our vast development experience, coupled with the requirement for instructors to consistently provide hands-on consulting to our customers, enables DBBasics to provide best of breed instruction in the classroom as well as customized eLearning solutions and database technology consulting.

DEVCOM   www.dev-cominc.com

Devcom Corporation offers a full line of courses and seminars for software developers and engineers. Currently Devcom provides technical courses and seminars around the country for Hewlett® Packard, Compaq® Computer, Informix® Software, Silicon Graphics®, Quantum/Maxtor® and Gateway® Inc. Our senior .NET/C# instructor is currently working in conjunction with Microsoft to provide .NET training to their internal technical staff.

FOCAL POINT   www.FocalPoint-Inc.com

Focal Point specializes in providing optimum instructor-led Information Technology technical training for our corporate clients on either an onsite basis, or in regional public course events. All of our course curricula is either developed by our staff of "World Class Instructors" or upon careful evaluation and scrutiny is adopted and acquired from our training partners who are similarly focussed. Our course offerings pay special attention to Real World issues. Our classes are targeted toward topical areas that will ensure immediate productivity upon course completion.

I/SRG   www.isrg.com

The I/S RESOURCE GROUP helps organizations to understand, plan for and implement emerging I/S technologies and methodologies. By combining education, training, briefings and consulting, we assist our clients to effectively apply I/S technologies to achieve business benefits. Our eBusiness Application Bootcamp is an integrated set of courses that prepares learners to utilize XML, OOAD, Java™, JSP, EJB, ASP, CORBA and .NET to build eBusiness applications. Our eBusiness Briefings pinpoint emerging technologies and methodologies.

OBJECT INNOVATIONS' .NET TRAINING PARTNERS

For information about .NET training using OBJECT INNOVATIONS courseware,
please check with our .NET Training Partners.

RELIABLE SOFTWARE   www.ReliableSoftware.com

Reliable Software, Inc. uses Microsoft technology to quickly develop cost-effective software solutions for the small to mid-size business or business unit. We use state-of-the-art techniques to allow business rules, database models and the user interface to evolve as your business needs evolve. We can provide design and implementation consulting, or training.

SKILLBRIDGE TRAINING   www.SkillBridgeTraining.com

SkillBridge is a leading provider of blended technical training solutions. The company's service offerings are designed to meet a wide variety of client requirements. Offering an integration of instructor-led training, e-learning and mentoring programs, SkillBridge delivers high value solutions in a cost-effective manner. SkillBridge's technology focus includes, among others, programming languages, operating systems, databases, and internet and web technologies.

/TRAINING/ETC INC.   www.trainingetc.com

A training company dedicated to delivering quality technical training, courseware development, and consulting in a variety of subject matter areas, including Programming Languages and Design (including C, C++, OOAD/UML, Perl, and Java), a complete UNIX curriculum (from UNIX Fundamentals to System Administration), the Internet (including HTML/CGI, XML and JavaScript Programming) and RDBMS (including Oracle and Sybase).

WATERMARK LEARNING   www.WatermarkLearning.com

Watermark Learning provides a wide range of IT skill development training and mentoring services to a variety of industries, software / consulting firms and government. We provide flexible options for delivery: onsite, consortium and public classes in three major areas: project management, requirements analysis and software development, including e-Commerce. Our instructors are seasoned, knowledgeable practitioners, who use their industry experience along with our highly-rated courseware to effectively build technical skills relevant to your business need.